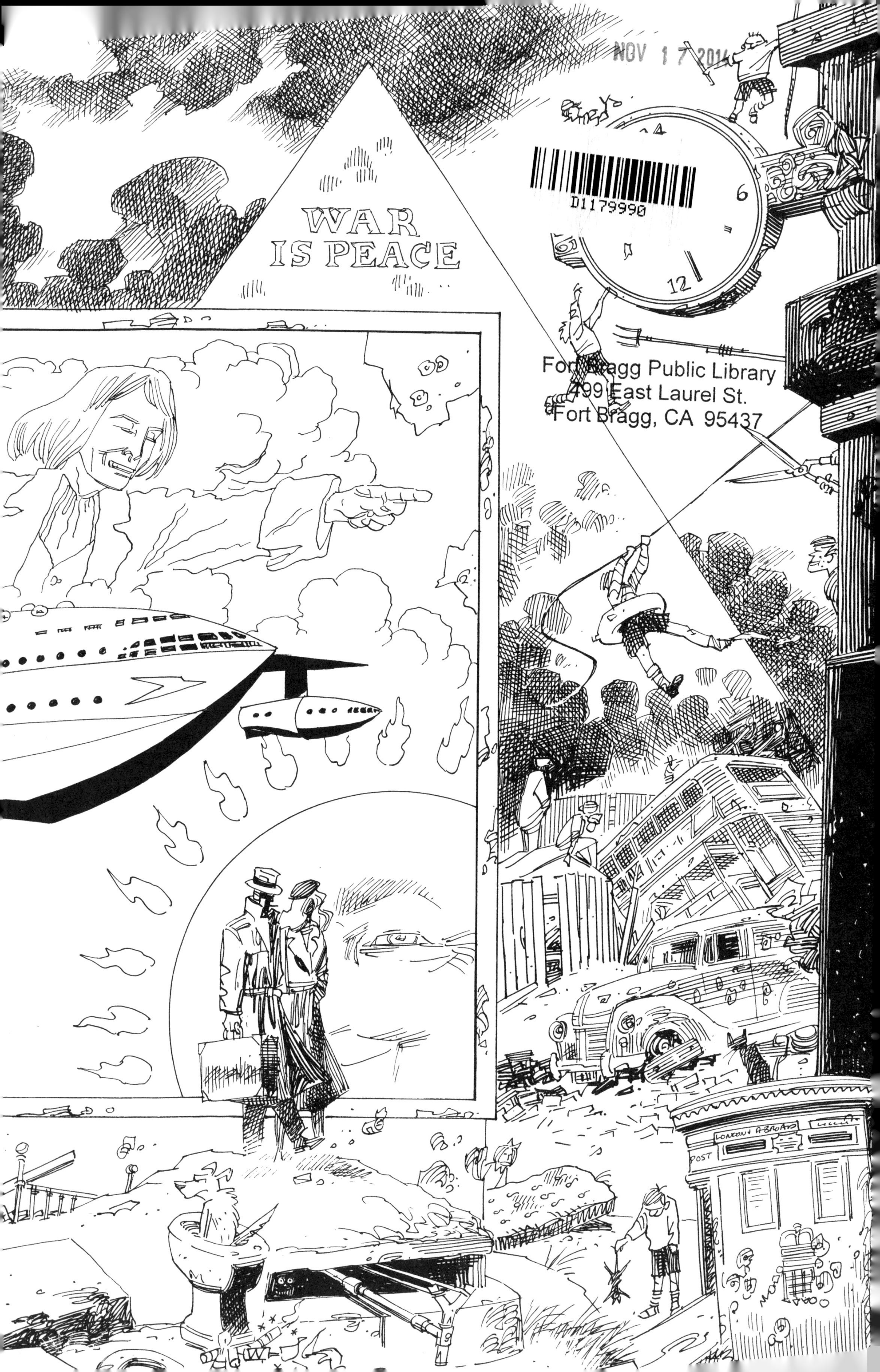
WAR
IS PEACE

KEEP
CALM
AND
CARRY
ON

THE LEAGUE OF
EXTRAORDINARY
GENTLEMEN

BLACK
DOSSIER

DAILY BRUTE

SPIES!

APPALLING SCANDAL OF MISSING DOCUMENTS

NATIONAL REGISTRATION

IDENTITY CARD

HOLDER'S NAME AND REGISTERED ADDRESS

DO NOT ALTER

Surname..

Other Name...

Address...

....

WARNING:
YOU WILL BE
TOLD HOW
AND WHERE
TO USE IT.

NATIONAL REGISTRATION No.

AIHD	8	4

Date of Issue
JULY 1948

IF FOUND RETURN TO MINILUV

CREDIT LINE

Traveller — if experiencing nausea while in the nether regions, keep hat firmly on, lay back, and think of England.

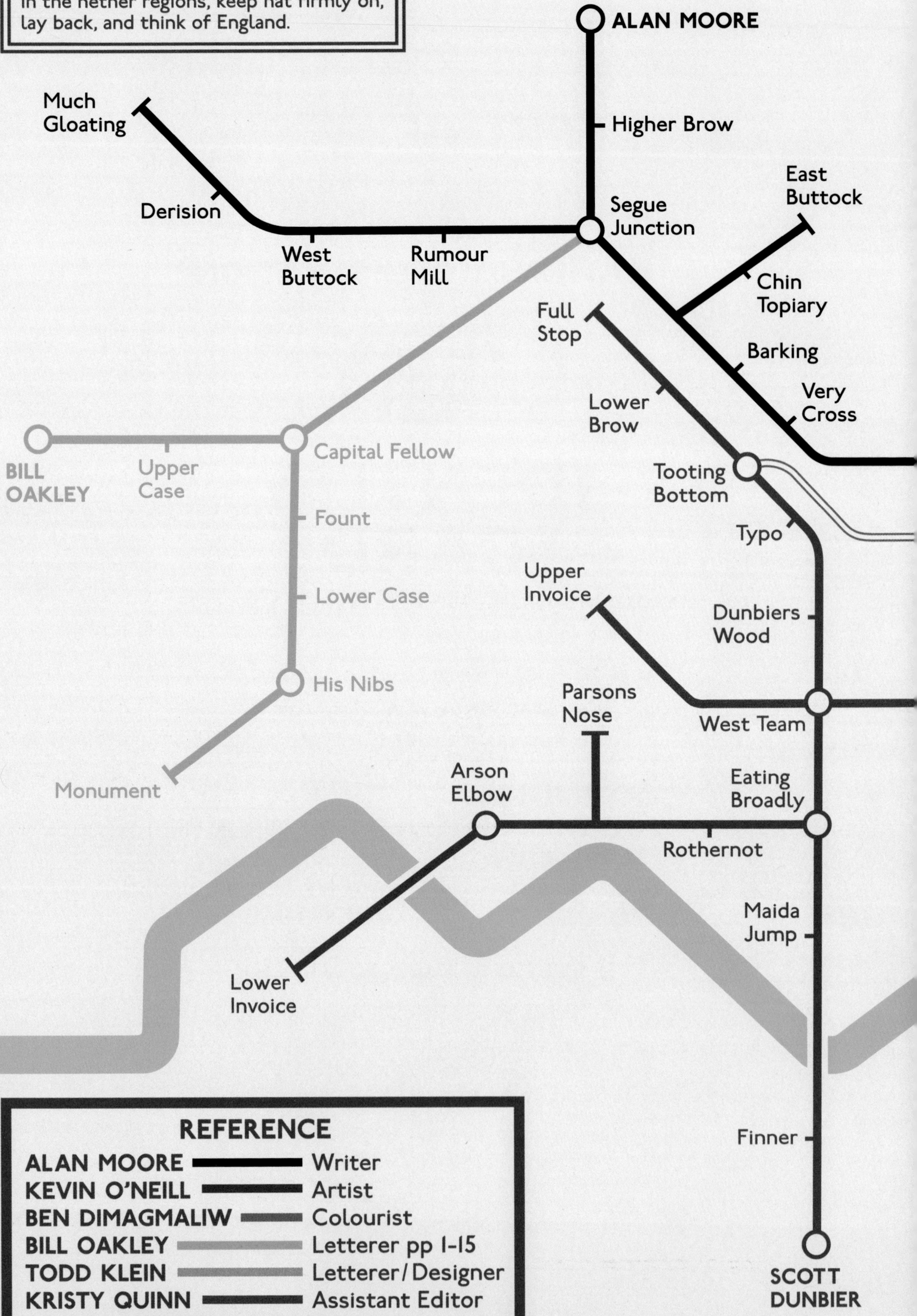
ALAN MOORE
Higher Brow
Much Gloating
Derision
West Buttock
Rumour Mill
Segue Junction
East Buttock
Chin Topiary
Barking
Very Cross
Full Stop
Lower Brow
Tooting Bottom
Typo
BILL OAKLEY
Upper Case
Capital Fellow
Fount
Lower Case
His Nibs
Monument
Upper Invoice
Dunbiers Wood
West Team
Parsons Nose
Arson Elbow
Eating Broadly
Rothernot
Maida Jump
Lower Invoice
Finner
SCOTT DUNBIER

REFERENCE

ALAN MOORE	Writer
KEVIN O'NEILL	Artist
BEN DIMAGMALIW	Colourist
BILL OAKLEY	Letterer pp 1-15
TODD KLEIN	Letterer/Designer
KRISTY QUINN	Assistant Editor
SCOTT DUNBIER	Editor

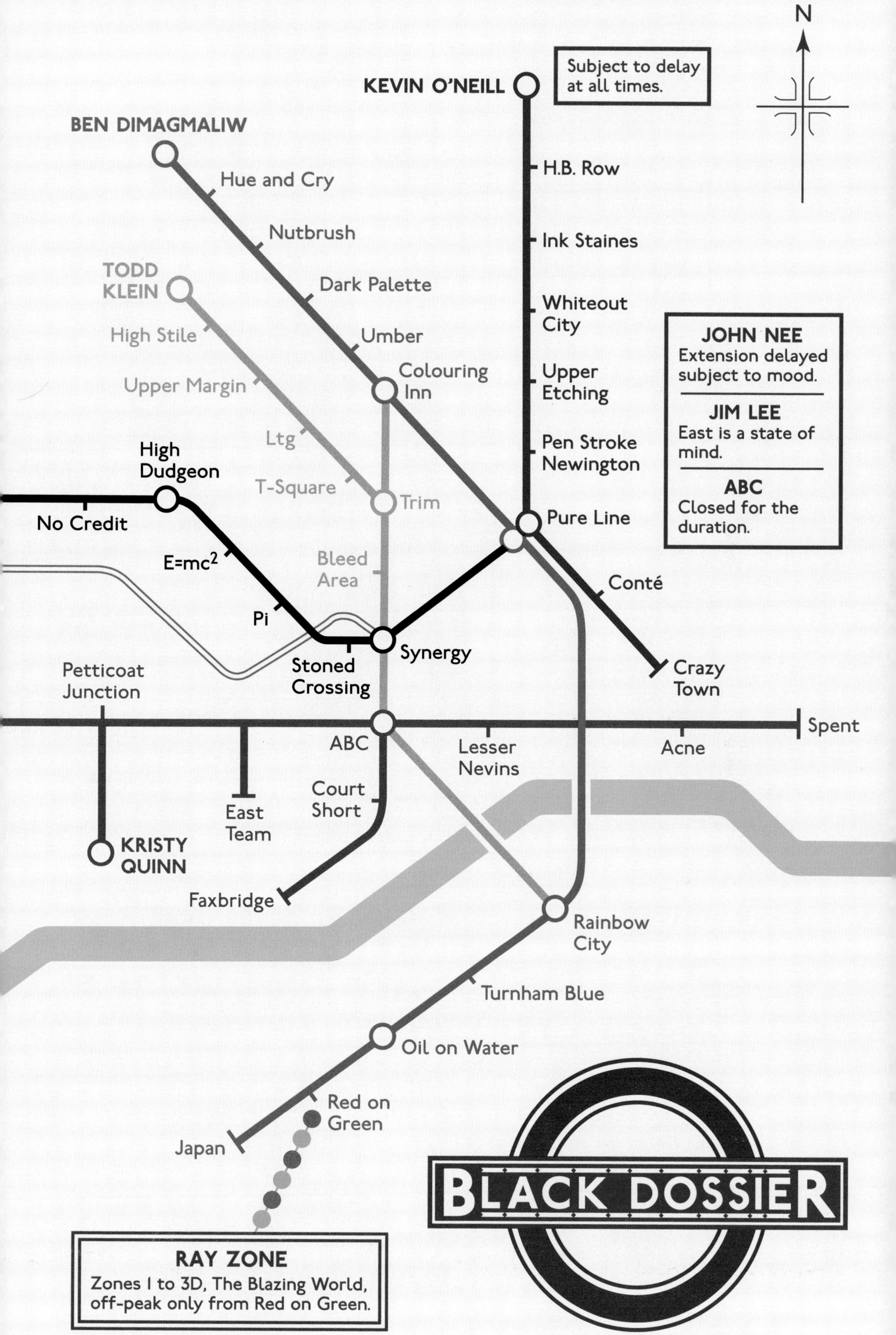

N
Subject to delay at all times.
KEVIN O'NEILL
H.B. Row
Ink Staines
Whiteout City
Upper Etching
Pen Stroke Newington
Pure Line
Conté
Crazy Town
BEN DIMAGMALIW
Hue and Cry
Nutbrush
Dark Palette
Umber
Colouring Inn
TODD KLEIN
High Stile
Upper Margin
Ltg
T-Square
Trim
Bleed Area
High Dudgeon
No Credit
E=mc2
Pi
Stoned Crossing
Synergy
JOHN NEE
Extension delayed subject to mood.
JIM LEE
East is a state of mind.
ABC
Closed for the duration.
Petticoat Junction
ABC
Lesser Nevins
Acne
Spent
East Team
Court Short
KRISTY QUINN
Faxbridge
Rainbow City
Turnham Blue
Oil on Water
Red on Green
Japan
BLACK DOSSIER
RAY ZONE
Zones 1 to 3D, The Blazing World, off-peak only from Red on Green.

DEDICATED TO THE MEMORY OF BILL OAKLEY

THE LEAGUE OF EXTRAORDINARY GENTLEMEN: BLACK DOSSIER: THE ABSOLUTE EDITION. Published by America's Best Comics, LLC. 888 Prospect St. #240, La Jolla, CA 92037. Printed in U.S.A.
FIRST PRINTING.

ISBN: 978-1-4012-0751-9

Jim Lee, Editorial Director

John Nee, VP—Business Development

SPECIAL THANKS:

Fershid Bharucha
Michael Moorcock
Norman Wright
Steve Moore

3-D section effects created by Ray Zone

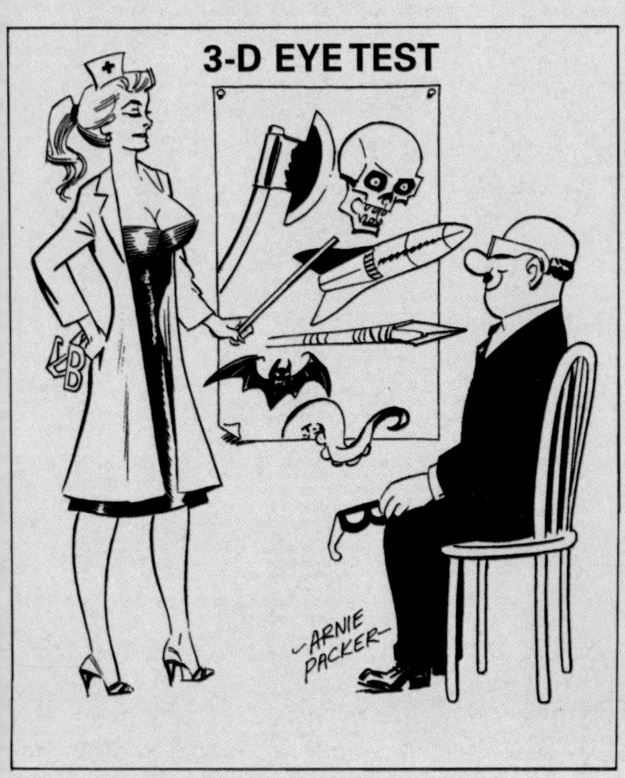
3-D EYE TEST
ARNIE PACKER

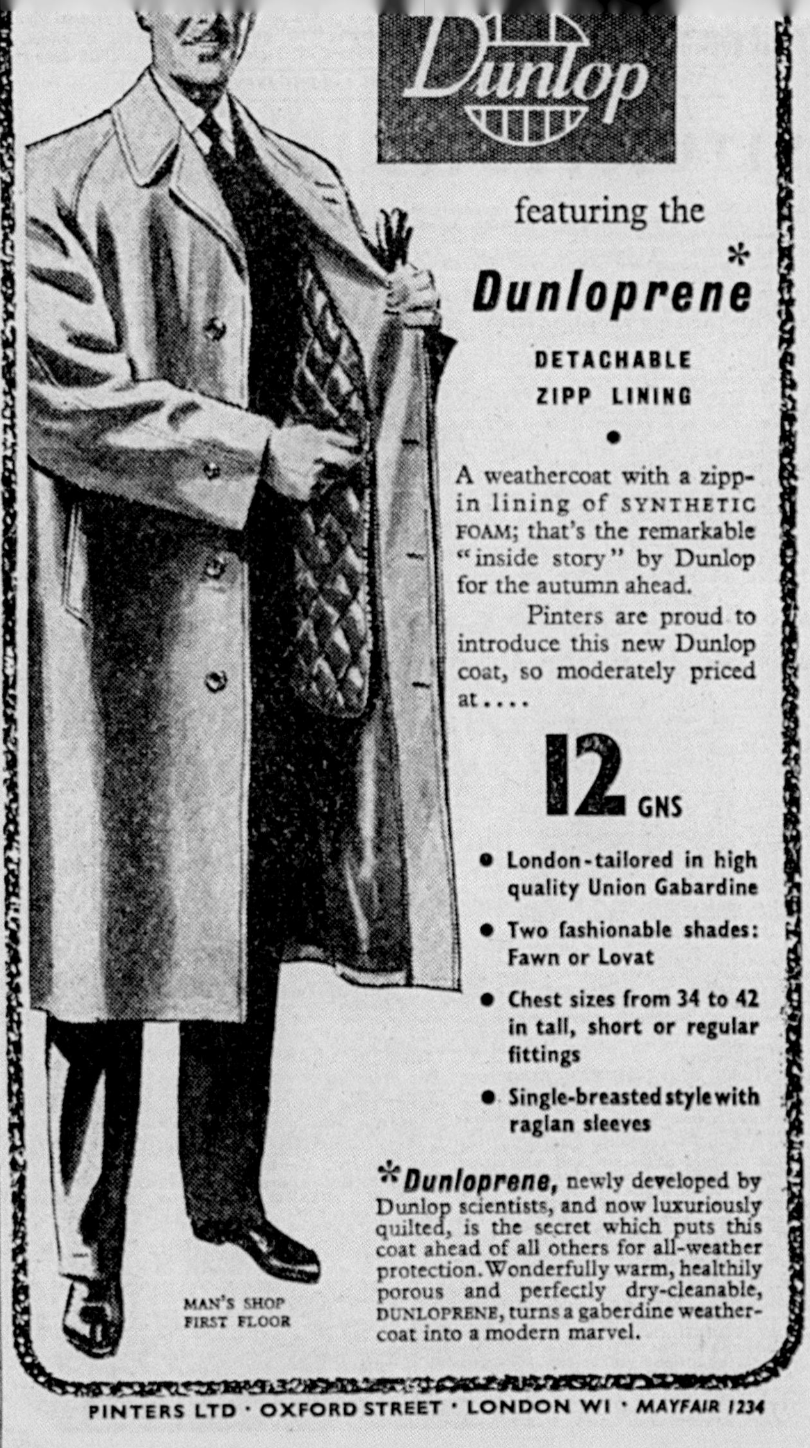
Dunlop
featuring the
Dunloprene*
DETACHABLE ZIPP LINING
A weathercoat with a zipp-in lining of SYNTHETIC FOAM; that's the remarkable "inside story" by Dunlop for the autumn ahead.
Pinters are proud to introduce this new Dunlop coat, so moderately priced at....
12 GNS
• London-tailored in high quality Union Gabardine
• Two fashionable shades: Fawn or Lovat
• Chest sizes from 34 to 42 in tall, short or regular fittings
• Single-breasted style with raglan sleeves
*Dunloprene, newly developed by Dunlop scientists, and now luxuriously quilted, is the secret which puts this coat ahead of all others for all-weather protection. Wonderfully warm, healthily porous and perfectly dry-cleanable, DUNLOPRENE, turns a gaberdine weather-coat into a modern marvel.
MAN'S SHOP FIRST FLOOR
PINTERS LTD · OXFORD STREET · LONDON W1 · MAYFAIR 1234

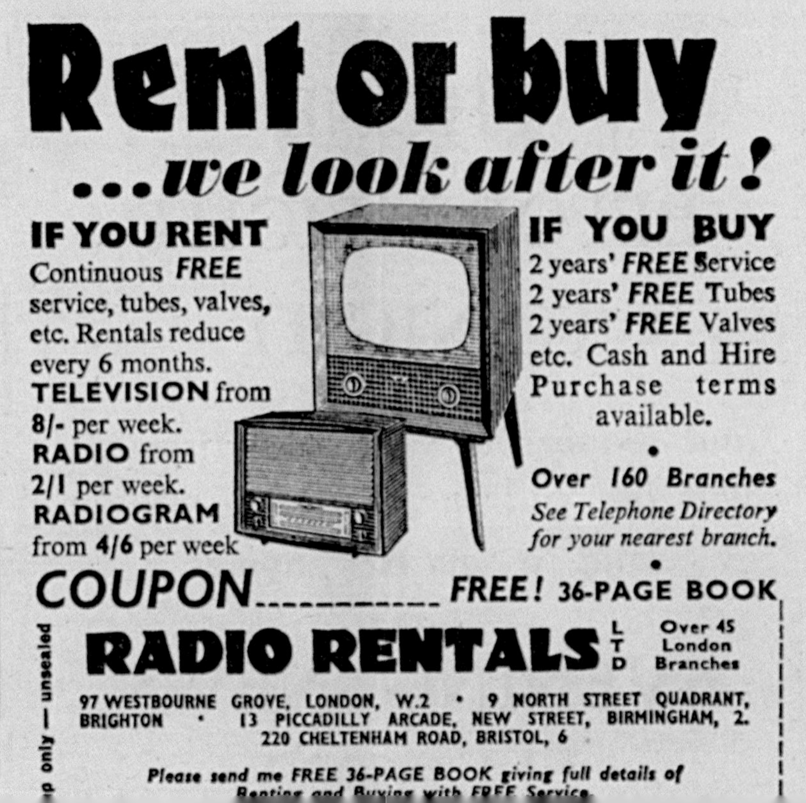
Rent or buy
...we look after it!
IF YOU RENT
Continuous FREE service, tubes, valves, etc. Rentals reduce every 6 months.
TELEVISION from 8/- per week.
RADIO from 2/1 per week.
RADIOGRAM from 4/6 per week
IF YOU BUY
2 years' FREE Service
2 years' FREE Tubes
2 years' FREE Valves
etc. Cash and Hire Purchase terms available.
Over 160 Branches
See Telephone Directory for your nearest branch.
COUPON FREE! 36-PAGE BOOK
RADIO RENTALS LTD
Over 45 London Branches
97 WESTBOURNE GROVE, LONDON, W.2 • 9 NORTH STREET QUADRANT, BRIGHTON • 13 PICCADILLY ARCADE, NEW STREET, BIRMINGHAM, 2. 220 CHELTENHAM ROAD, BRISTOL, 6
Please send me FREE 36-PAGE BOOK giving full details of

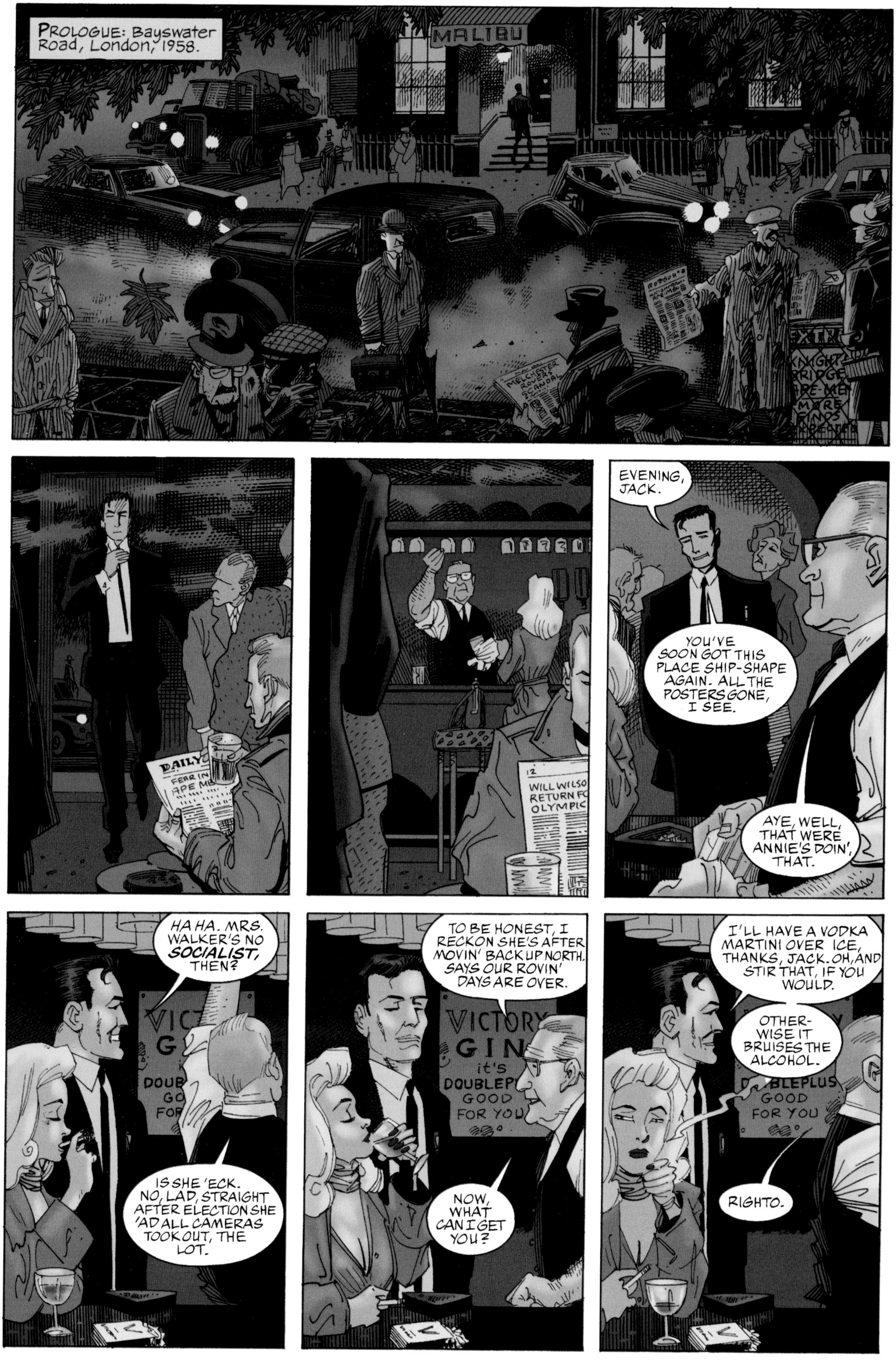
PROLOGUE: Bayswater Road, London, 1958.
MALIBU
WILL WILSO RETURN FO OLYMPIC
EVENING, JACK.
YOU'VE SOON GOT THIS PLACE SHIP-SHAPE AGAIN. ALL THE POSTERS GONE, I SEE.
AYE, WELL, THAT WERE ANNIE'S DOIN', THAT.
HA HA. MRS. WALKER'S NO *SOCIALIST*, THEN?
IS SHE 'ECK. NO, LAD, STRAIGHT AFTER ELECTION SHE 'AD ALL CAMERAS TOOK OUT, THE LOT.
TO BE HONEST, I RECKON SHE'S AFTER MOVIN' BACK UP NORTH. SAYS OUR ROVIN' DAYS ARE OVER.
VICTORY GIN it's DOUBLEPL GOOD FOR YOU
NOW, WHAT CAN I GET YOU?
I'LL HAVE A VODKA MARTINI OVER ICE, THANKS, JACK. OH, AND STIR THAT, IF YOU WOULD.
OTHER-WISE IT BRUISES THE ALCOHOL.
RIGHTO.

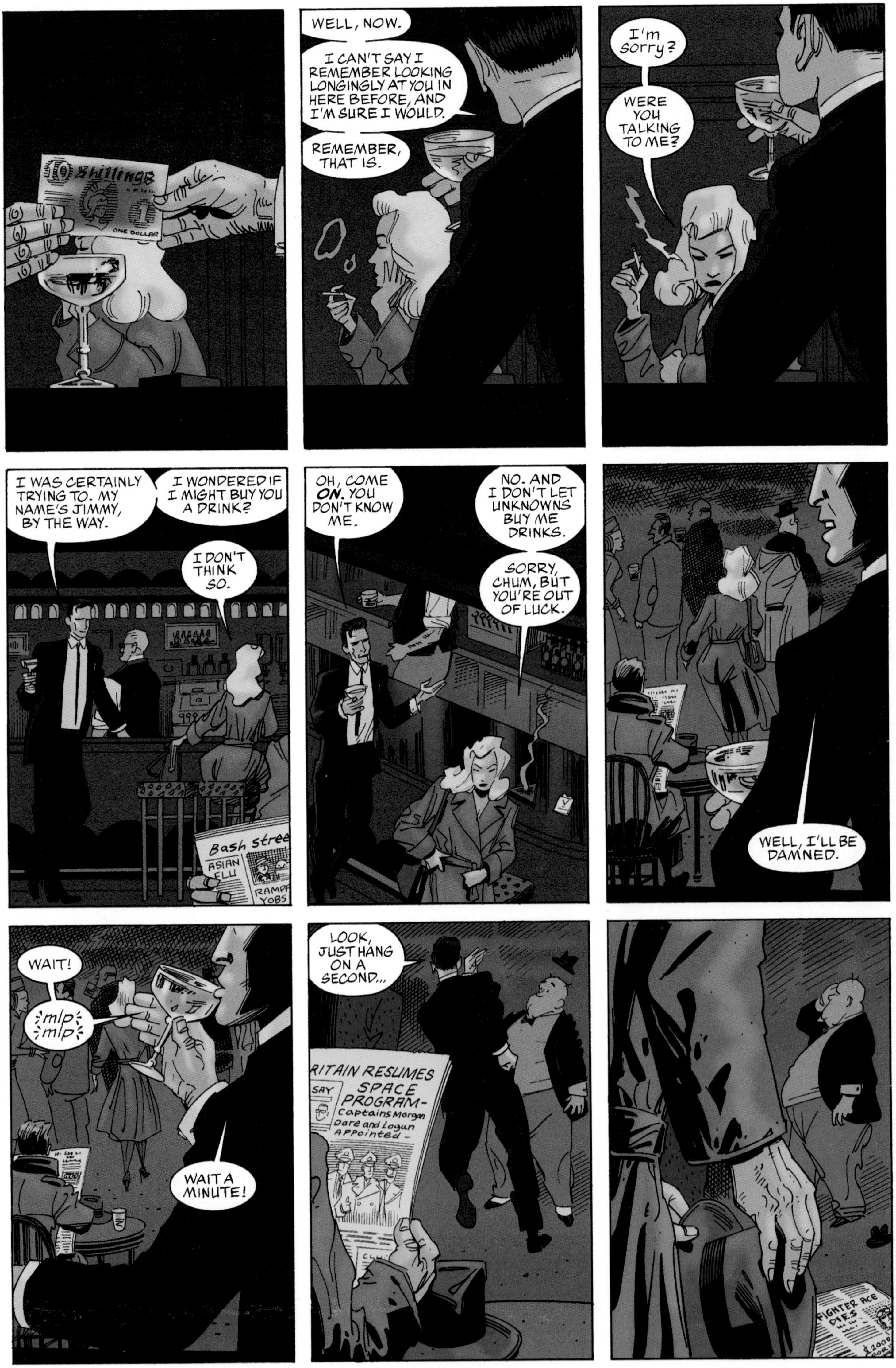

10 Shillings
ONE DOLLAR
WELL, NOW.
I CAN'T SAY I REMEMBER LOOKING LONGINGLY AT YOU IN HERE BEFORE, AND I'M SURE I WOULD.
REMEMBER, THAT IS.
I'm sorry?
WERE YOU TALKING TO ME?
I WAS CERTAINLY TRYING TO. MY NAME'S JIMMY, BY THE WAY.
I WONDERED IF I MIGHT BUY YOU A DRINK?
I DON'T THINK SO.
Bash stree
ASIAN FLU
YOBS
OH, COME ON. YOU DON'T KNOW ME.
NO. AND I DON'T LET UNKNOWNS BUY ME DRINKS.
SORRY, CHUM, BUT YOU'RE OUT OF LUCK.
WELL, I'LL BE DAMNED.
WAIT!
mlp mlp
WAIT A MINUTE!
LOOK, JUST HANG ON A SECOND...
RITAIN RESUMES SPACE PROGRAM-
Captains Morgan Dare and Logan Appointed -
FIGHTER ACE DIES

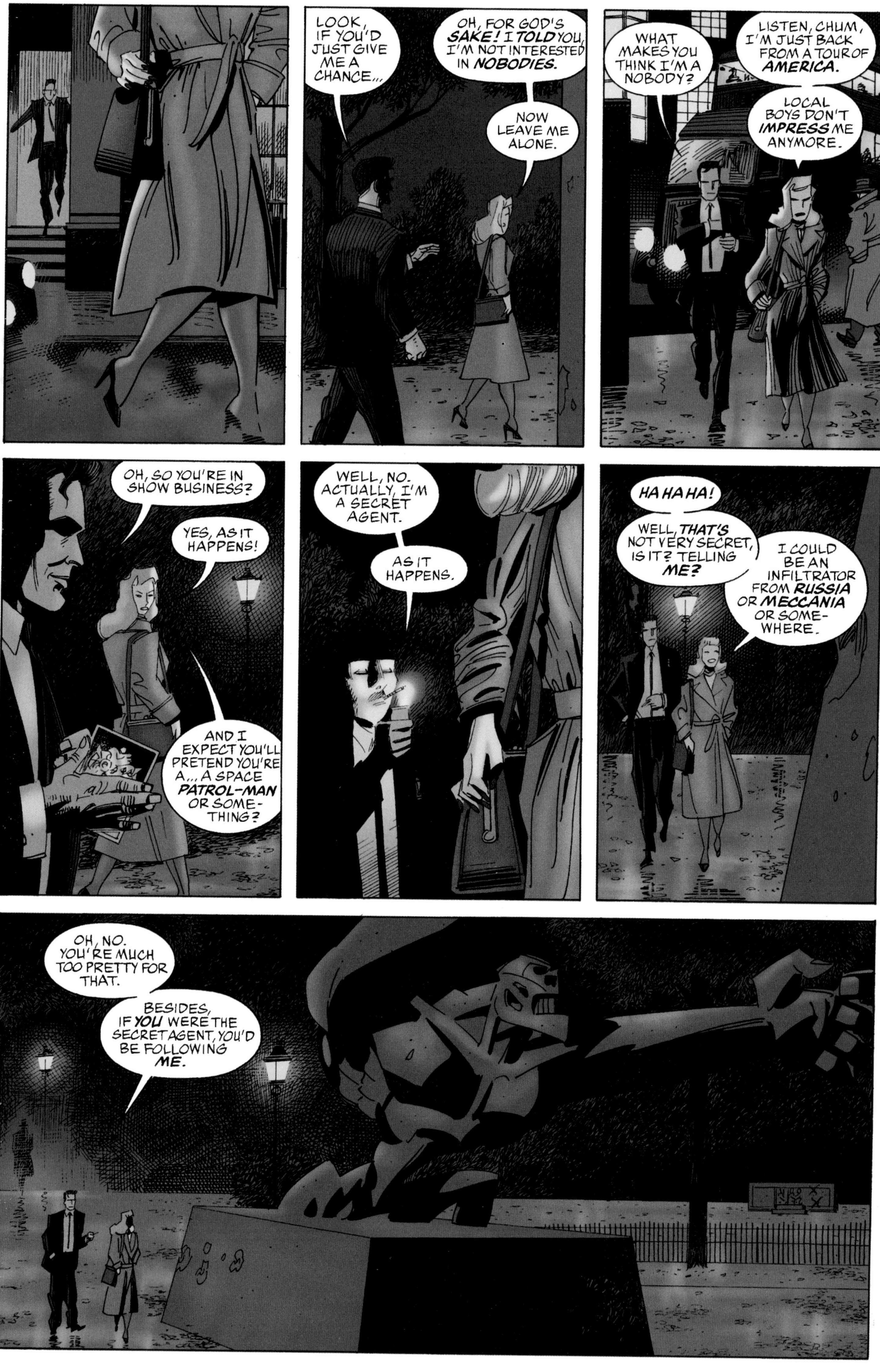
LOOK, IF YOU'D JUST GIVE ME A CHANCE...
OH, FOR GOD'S SAKE! I TOLD YOU, I'M NOT INTERESTED IN NOBODIES.
NOW LEAVE ME ALONE.
WHAT MAKES YOU THINK I'M A NOBODY?
LISTEN, CHUM, I'M JUST BACK FROM A TOUR OF AMERICA.
LOCAL BOYS DON'T IMPRESS ME ANYMORE.
OH, SO YOU'RE IN SHOW BUSINESS?
YES, AS IT HAPPENS!
AND I EXPECT YOU'LL PRETEND YOU'RE A... A SPACE PATROL-MAN OR SOMETHING?
WELL, NO. ACTUALLY, I'M A SECRET AGENT.
AS IT HAPPENS.
HA HA HA!
WELL, THAT'S NOT VERY SECRET, IS IT? TELLING ME?
I COULD BE AN INFILTRATOR FROM RUSSIA OR MECCANIA OR SOMEWHERE.
OH, NO. YOU'RE MUCH TOO PRETTY FOR THAT.
BESIDES, IF YOU WERE THE SECRET AGENT, YOU'D BE FOLLOWING ME.

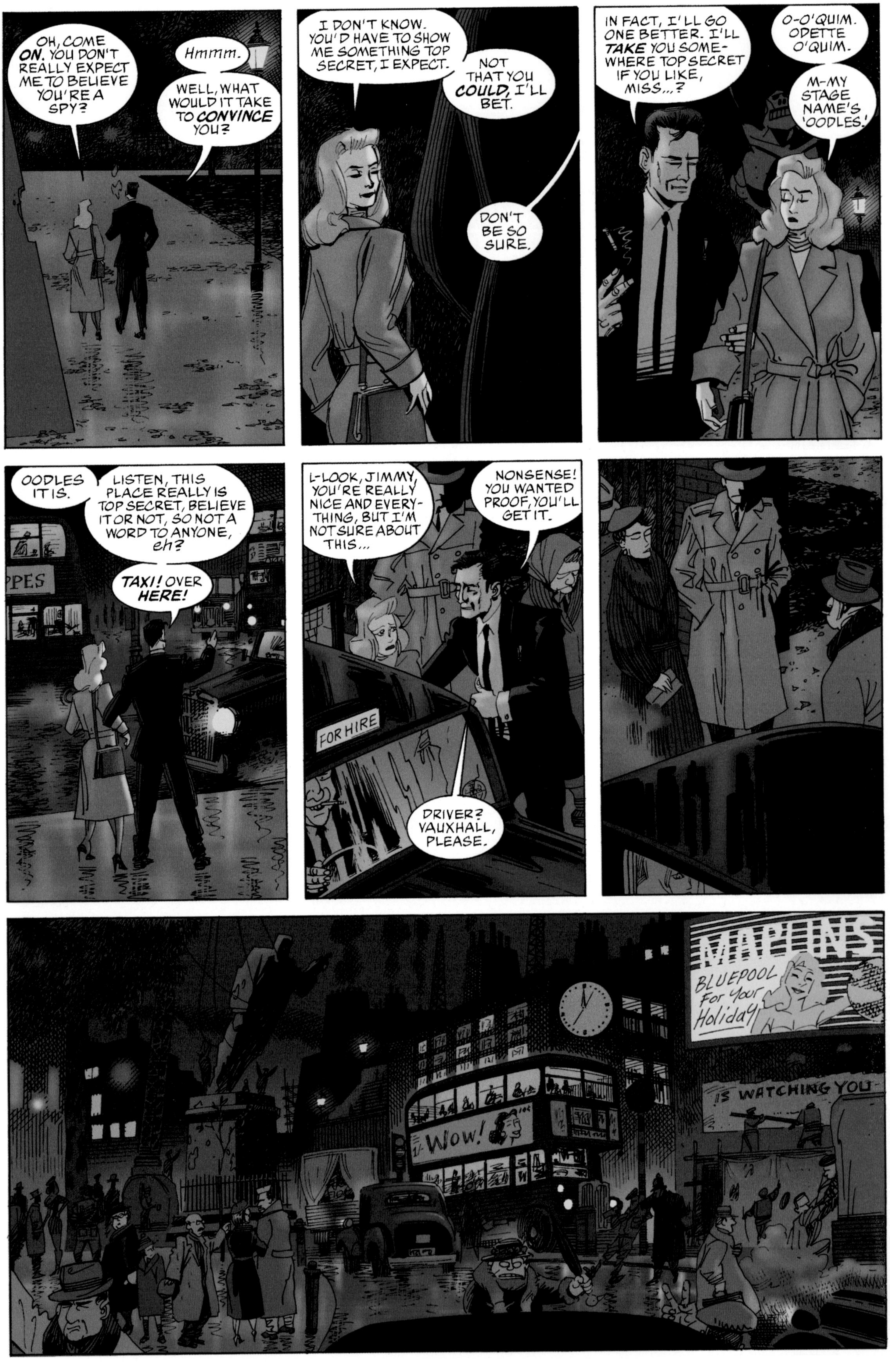
OH, COME ON. YOU DON'T REALLY EXPECT ME TO BELIEVE YOU'RE A SPY?
Hmmm.
WELL, WHAT WOULD IT TAKE TO CONVINCE YOU?
I DON'T KNOW. YOU'D HAVE TO SHOW ME SOMETHING TOP SECRET, I EXPECT.
NOT THAT YOU COULD, I'LL BET.
DON'T BE SO SURE.
IN FACT, I'LL GO ONE BETTER. I'LL TAKE YOU SOMEWHERE TOP SECRET IF YOU LIKE, MISS...?
O-O'QUIM. ODETTE O'QUIM.
M-MY STAGE NAME'S 'OODLES.'
OODLES IT IS.
LISTEN, THIS PLACE REALLY IS TOP SECRET, BELIEVE IT OR NOT, SO NOT A WORD TO ANYONE, eh?
TAXI! OVER HERE!
PPES
L-LOOK, JIMMY, YOU'RE REALLY NICE AND EVERYTHING, BUT I'M NOT SURE ABOUT THIS...
NONSENSE! YOU WANTED PROOF, YOU'LL GET IT.
FOR HIRE
DRIVER? VAUXHALL, PLEASE.
MAPLINS
BLUEPOOL For Your Holiday
IS WATCHING YOU
WOW!

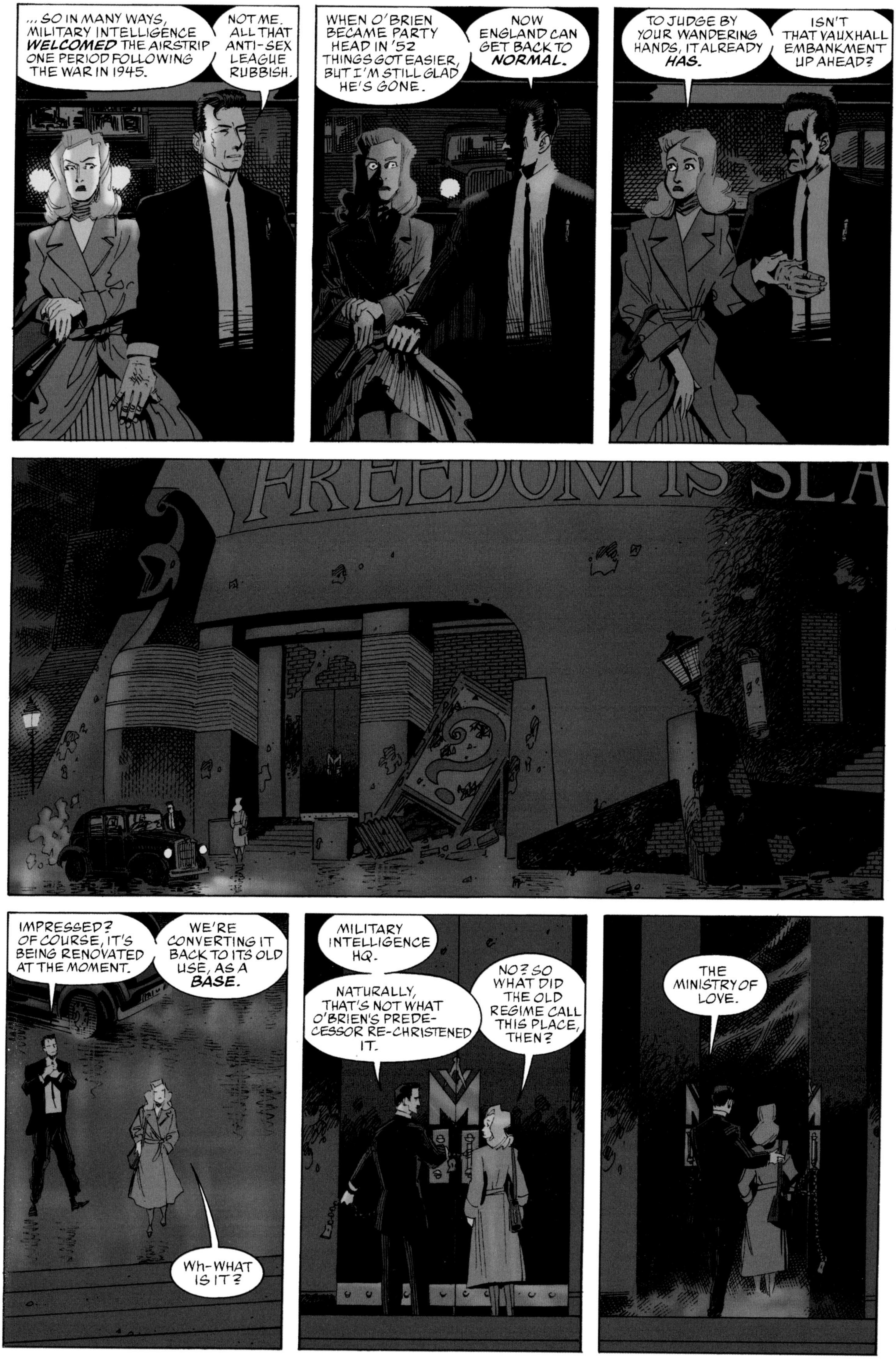
...SO IN MANY WAYS, MILITARY INTELLIGENCE WELCOMED THE AIRSTRIP ONE PERIOD FOLLOWING THE WAR IN 1945.
NOT ME. ALL THAT ANTI-SEX LEAGUE RUBBISH.
WHEN O'BRIEN BECAME PARTY HEAD IN '52 THINGS GOT EASIER, BUT I'M STILL GLAD HE'S GONE.
NOW ENGLAND CAN GET BACK TO NORMAL.
TO JUDGE BY YOUR WANDERING HANDS, IT ALREADY HAS.
ISN'T THAT VAUXHALL EMBANKMENT UP AHEAD?
FREEDOM IS SLA
IMPRESSED? OF COURSE, IT'S BEING RENOVATED AT THE MOMENT.
WE'RE CONVERTING IT BACK TO ITS OLD USE, AS A BASE.
Wh-WHAT IS IT?
MILITARY INTELLIGENCE HQ.
NATURALLY, THAT'S NOT WHAT O'BRIEN'S PREDE-CESSOR RE-CHRISTENED IT.
NO? SO WHAT DID THE OLD REGIME CALL THIS PLACE, THEN?
THE MINISTRY OF LOVE.

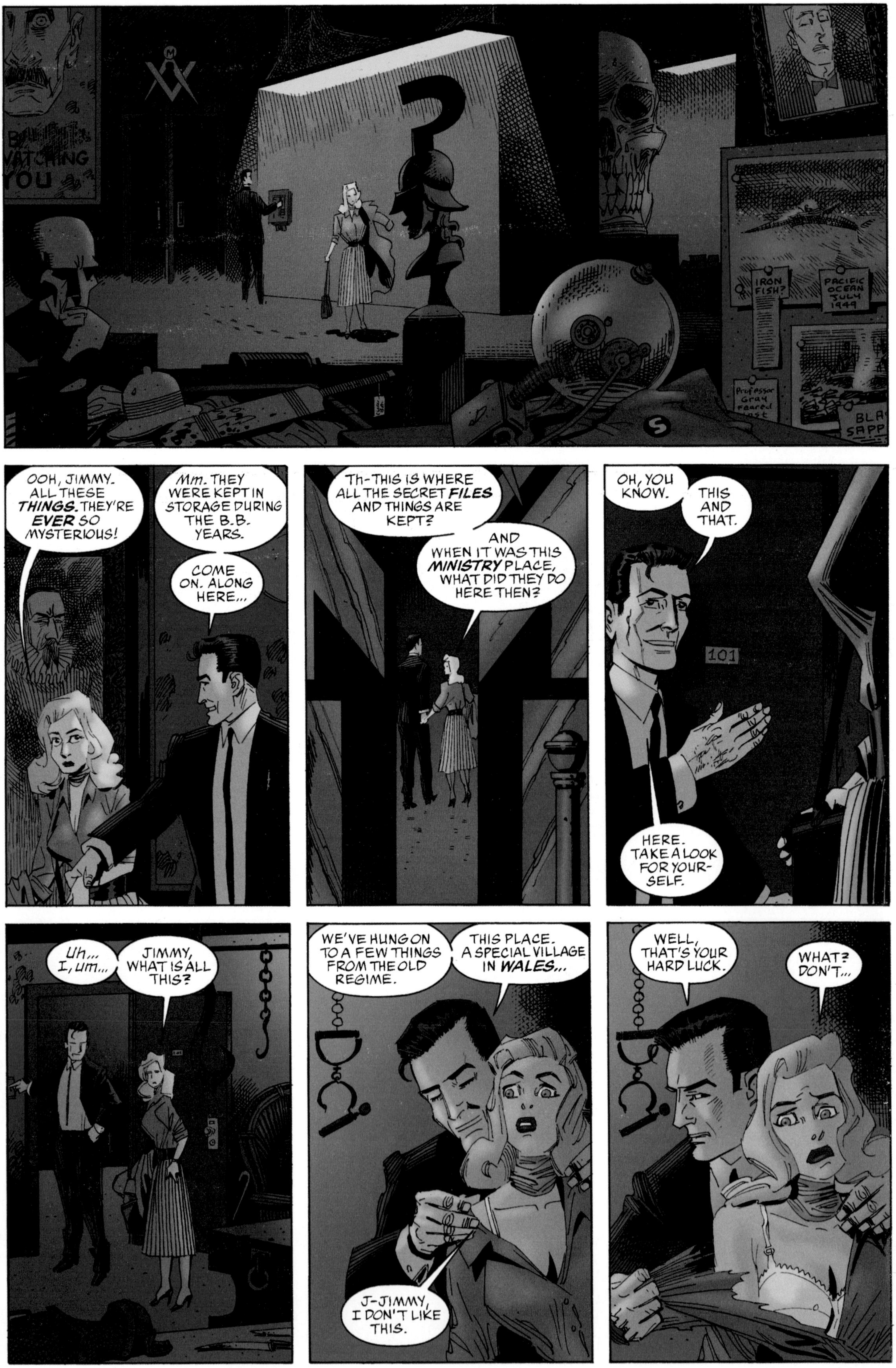
IRON FISH?
PACIFIC OCEAN JULY 1949
OOH, JIMMY. ALL THESE THINGS. THEY'RE EVER SO MYSTERIOUS!
Mm. THEY WERE KEPT IN STORAGE DURING THE B.B. YEARS.
COME ON. ALONG HERE...
Th-THIS IS WHERE ALL THE SECRET FILES AND THINGS ARE KEPT?
AND WHEN IT WAS THIS MINISTRY PLACE, WHAT DID THEY DO HERE THEN?
OH, YOU KNOW.
THIS AND THAT.
101
HERE. TAKE A LOOK FOR YOUR-SELF.
Uh... I, um...
JIMMY, WHAT IS ALL THIS?
WE'VE HUNG ON TO A FEW THINGS FROM THE OLD REGIME.
THIS PLACE. A SPECIAL VILLAGE IN WALES...
J-JIMMY, I DON'T LIKE THIS.
WELL, THAT'S YOUR HARD LUCK.
WHAT? DON'T...

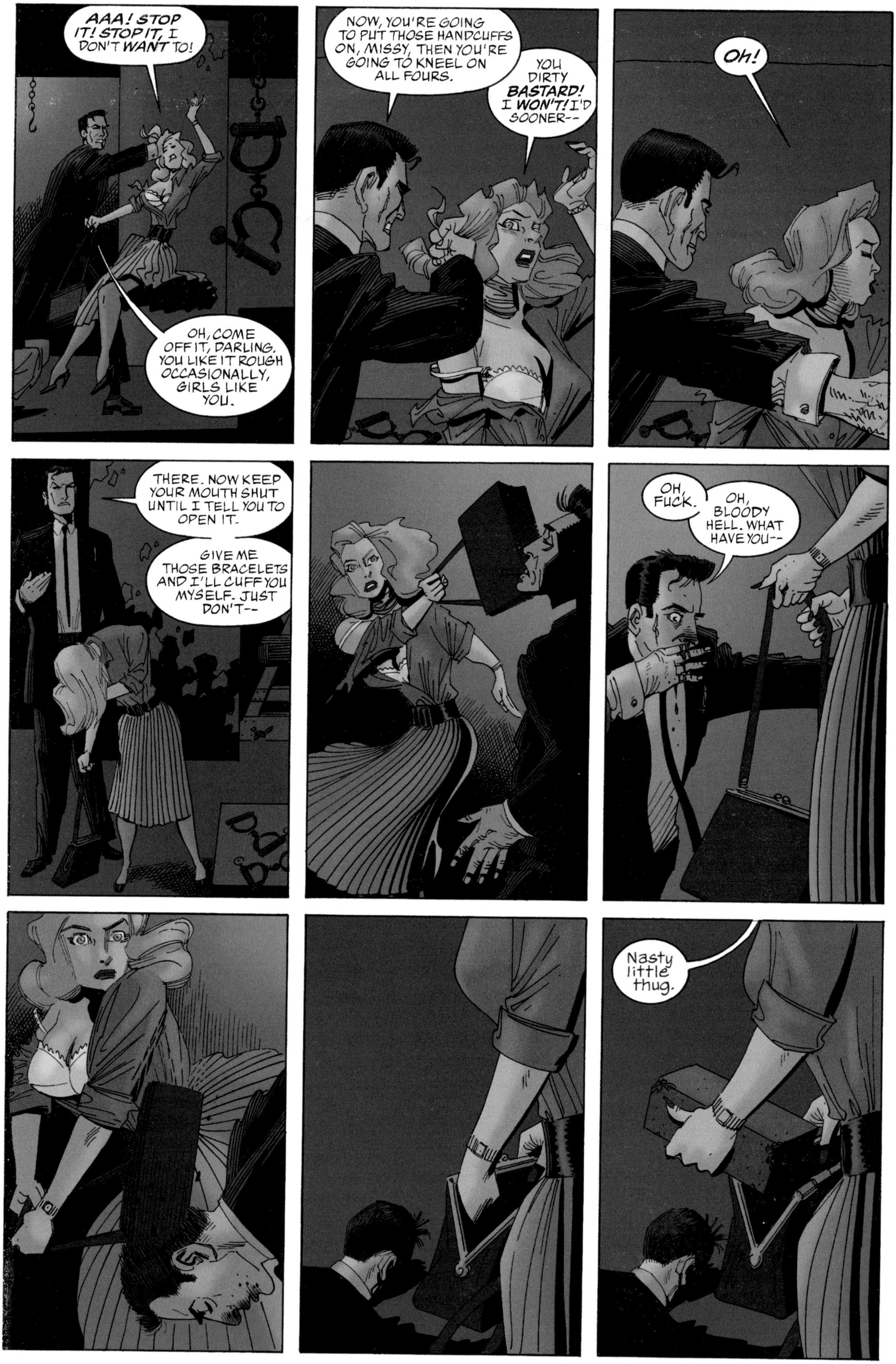

AAA! STOP IT! STOP IT, I DON'T WANT TO!
OH, COME OFF IT, DARLING. YOU LIKE IT ROUGH OCCASIONALLY, GIRLS LIKE YOU.
NOW, YOU'RE GOING TO PUT THOSE HANDCUFFS ON, MISSY, THEN YOU'RE GOING TO KNEEL ON ALL FOURS.
YOU DIRTY BASTARD! I WON'T! I'D SOONER--
Oh!
THERE. NOW KEEP YOUR MOUTH SHUT UNTIL I TELL YOU TO OPEN IT.
GIVE ME THOSE BRACELETS AND I'LL CUFF YOU MYSELF. JUST DON'T--
OH, FUCK.
OH, BLOODY HELL. WHAT HAVE YOU--
Nasty little thug.

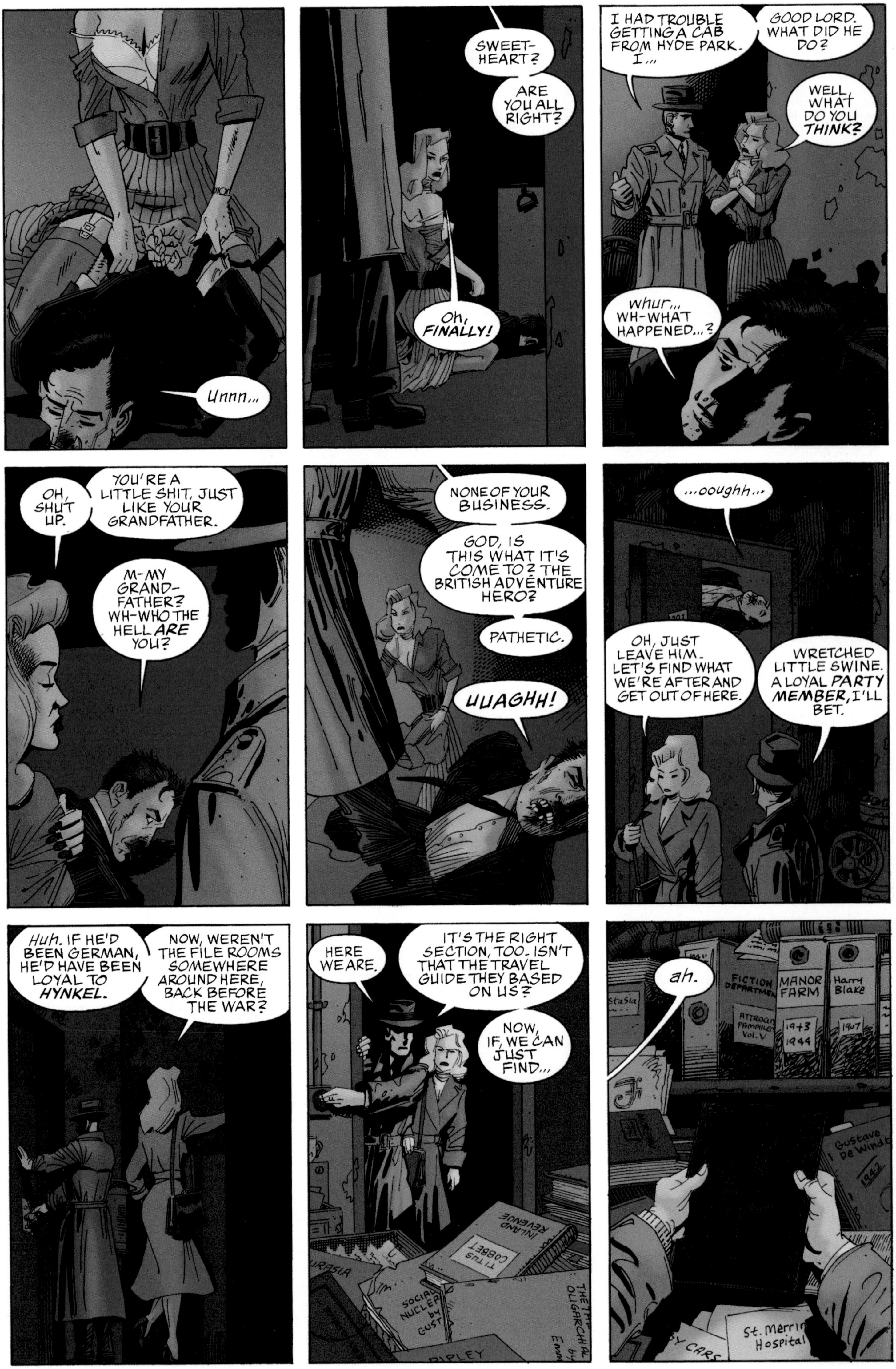
Unnn...
SWEET-HEART?
ARE YOU ALL RIGHT?
Oh, FINALLY!
I HAD TROUBLE GETTING A CAB FROM HYDE PARK. I...
GOOD LORD. WHAT DID HE DO?
WELL WHAT DO YOU THINK?
whur... WH-WHAT HAPPENED...?
OH, SHUT UP.
YOU'RE A LITTLE SHIT, JUST LIKE YOUR GRANDFATHER.
M-MY GRAND-FATHER? WH-WHO THE HELL ARE YOU?
NONE OF YOUR BUSINESS.
GOD, IS THIS WHAT IT'S COME TO? THE BRITISH ADVENTURE HERO?
PATHETIC.
UUAGHH!
...ooughh...
OH, JUST LEAVE HIM. LET'S FIND WHAT WE'RE AFTER AND GET OUT OF HERE.
WRETCHED LITTLE SWINE. A LOYAL PARTY MEMBER, I'LL BET.
Huh. IF HE'D BEEN GERMAN, HE'D HAVE BEEN LOYAL TO HYNKEL.
NOW, WEREN'T THE FILE ROOMS SOMEWHERE AROUND HERE, BACK BEFORE THE WAR?
HERE WE ARE.
IT'S THE RIGHT SECTION, TOO. ISN'T THAT THE TRAVEL GUIDE THEY BASED ON US?
NOW, IF, WE CAN JUST FIND...
INLAND REVENUE
TITUS COBBET
SOCIAL NUCLE... by GUST
THE ... OLIGARCHICAL
ah.
FICTION DEPARTMEN
ATTROCITY PAMPHLETS Vol. V
MANOR FARM
1943 1944
Harry Blake
1907
Gustave De Windt
St. Merri... Hospital

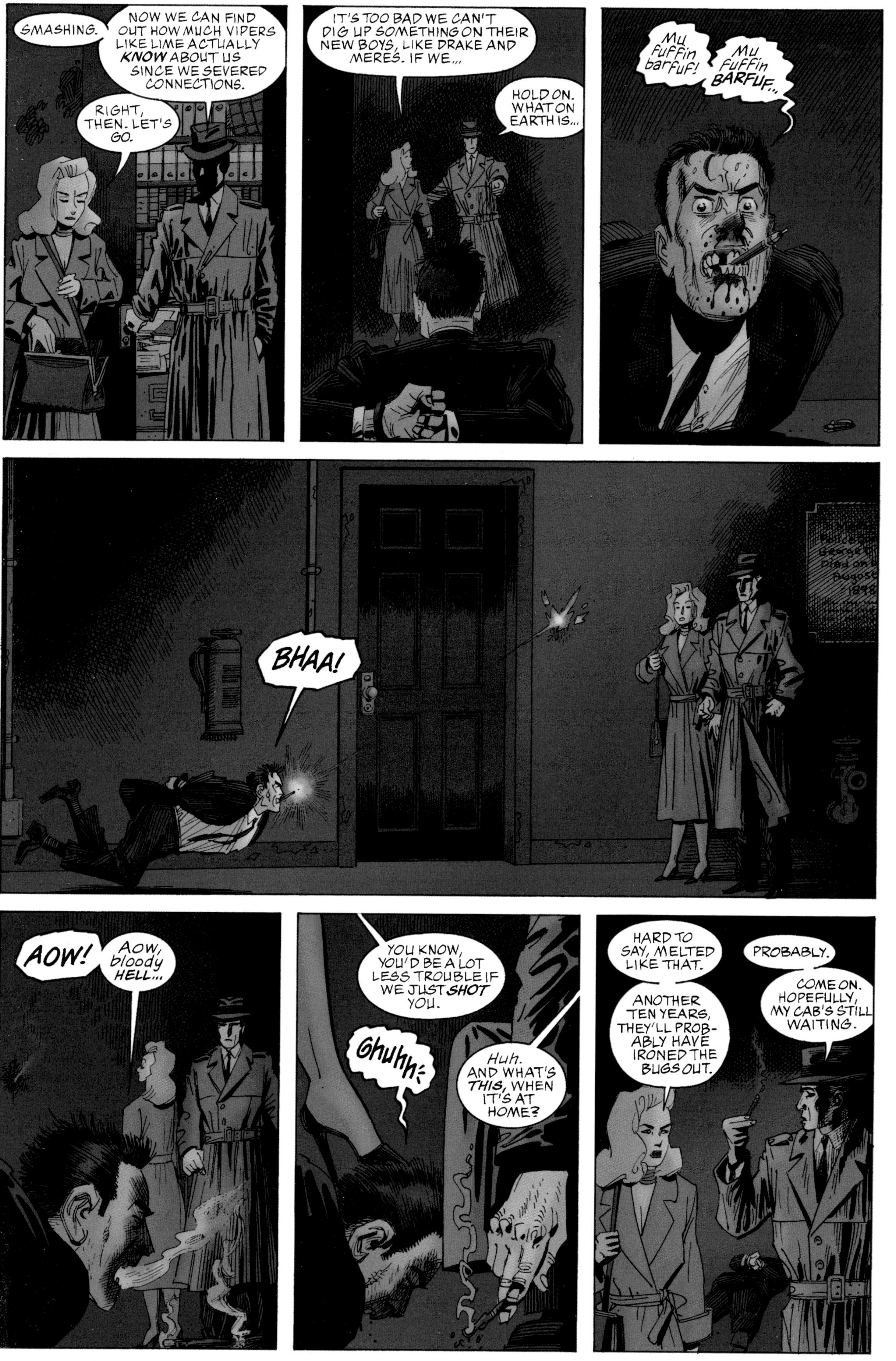
SMASHING.
NOW WE CAN FIND OUT HOW MUCH VIPERS LIKE LIME ACTUALLY KNOW ABOUT US SINCE WE SEVERED CONNECTIONS.
RIGHT, THEN. LET'S GO.
IT'S TOO BAD WE CAN'T DIG UP SOMETHING ON THEIR NEW BOYS, LIKE DRAKE AND MERES. IF WE...
HOLD ON. WHAT ON EARTH IS...
Mu fuffin barfuf!
Mu fuffin BARFUF...
BHAA!
AOW!
Aow, bloody HELL...
YOU KNOW, YOU'D BE A LOT LESS TROUBLE IF WE JUST SHOT YOU.
Ghuhh
Huh. AND WHAT'S THIS, WHEN IT'S AT HOME?
HARD TO SAY, MELTED LIKE THAT.
PROBABLY.
ANOTHER TEN YEARS, THEY'LL PROBABLY HAVE IRONED THE BUGS OUT.
COME ON. HOPEFULLY, MY CAB'S STILL WAITING.

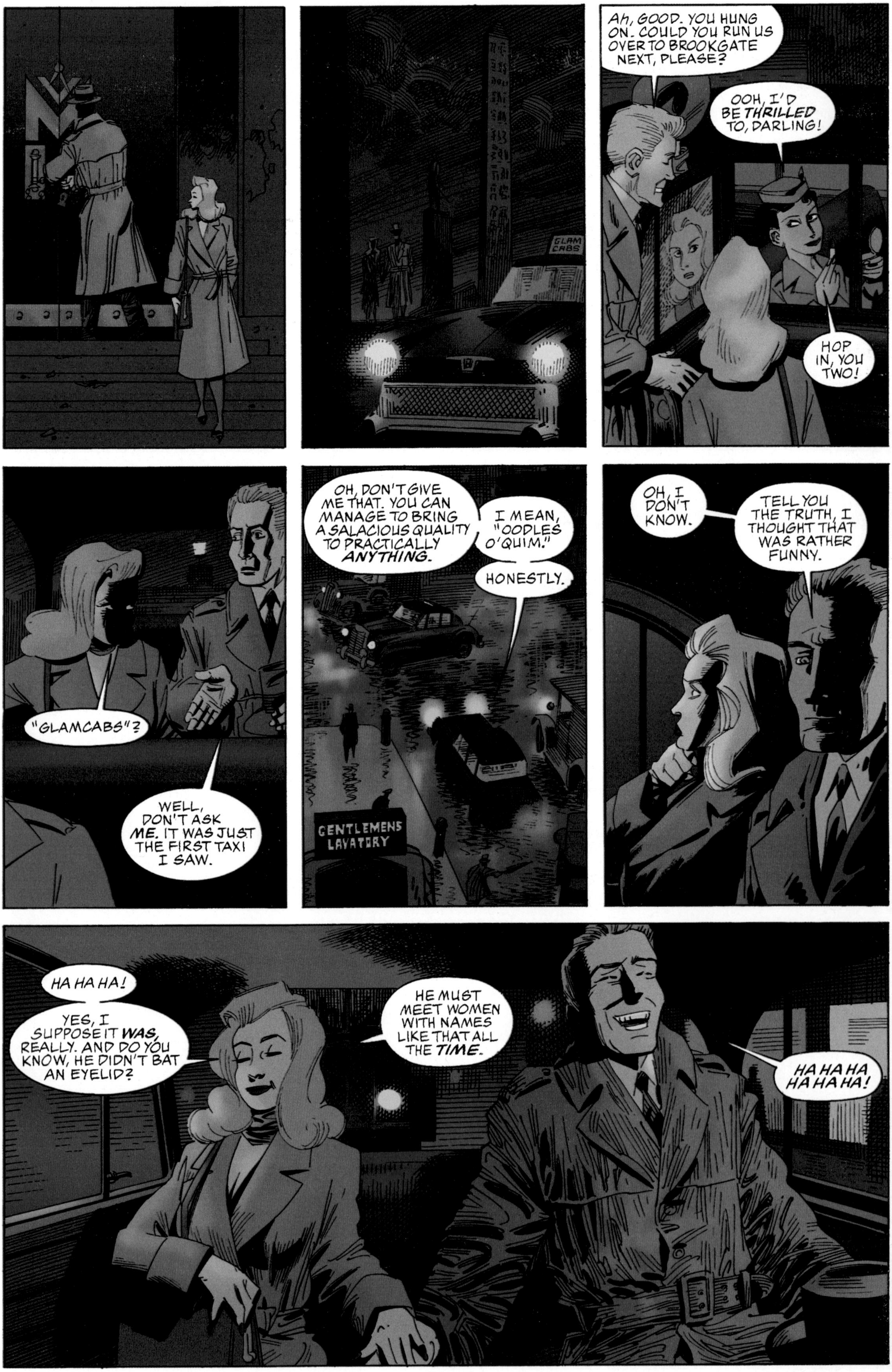
GLAM CABS
AH, GOOD. YOU HUNG ON. COULD YOU RUN US OVER TO BROOKGATE NEXT, PLEASE?
OOH, I'D BE THRILLED TO, DARLING!
HOP IN, YOU TWO!
"GLAMCABS"?
WELL, DON'T ASK ME. IT WAS JUST THE FIRST TAXI I SAW.
OH, DON'T GIVE ME THAT. YOU CAN MANAGE TO BRING A SALACIOUS QUALITY TO PRACTICALLY ANYTHING.
I MEAN, "OODLES O'QUIM."
HONESTLY.
GENTLEMENS LAVATORY
OH, I DON'T KNOW.
TELL YOU THE TRUTH, I THOUGHT THAT WAS RATHER FUNNY.
HA HA HA!
YES, I SUPPOSE IT WAS, REALLY. AND DO YOU KNOW, HE DIDN'T BAT AN EYELID?
HE MUST MEET WOMEN WITH NAMES LIKE THAT ALL THE TIME.
HA HA HA HA HA HA!

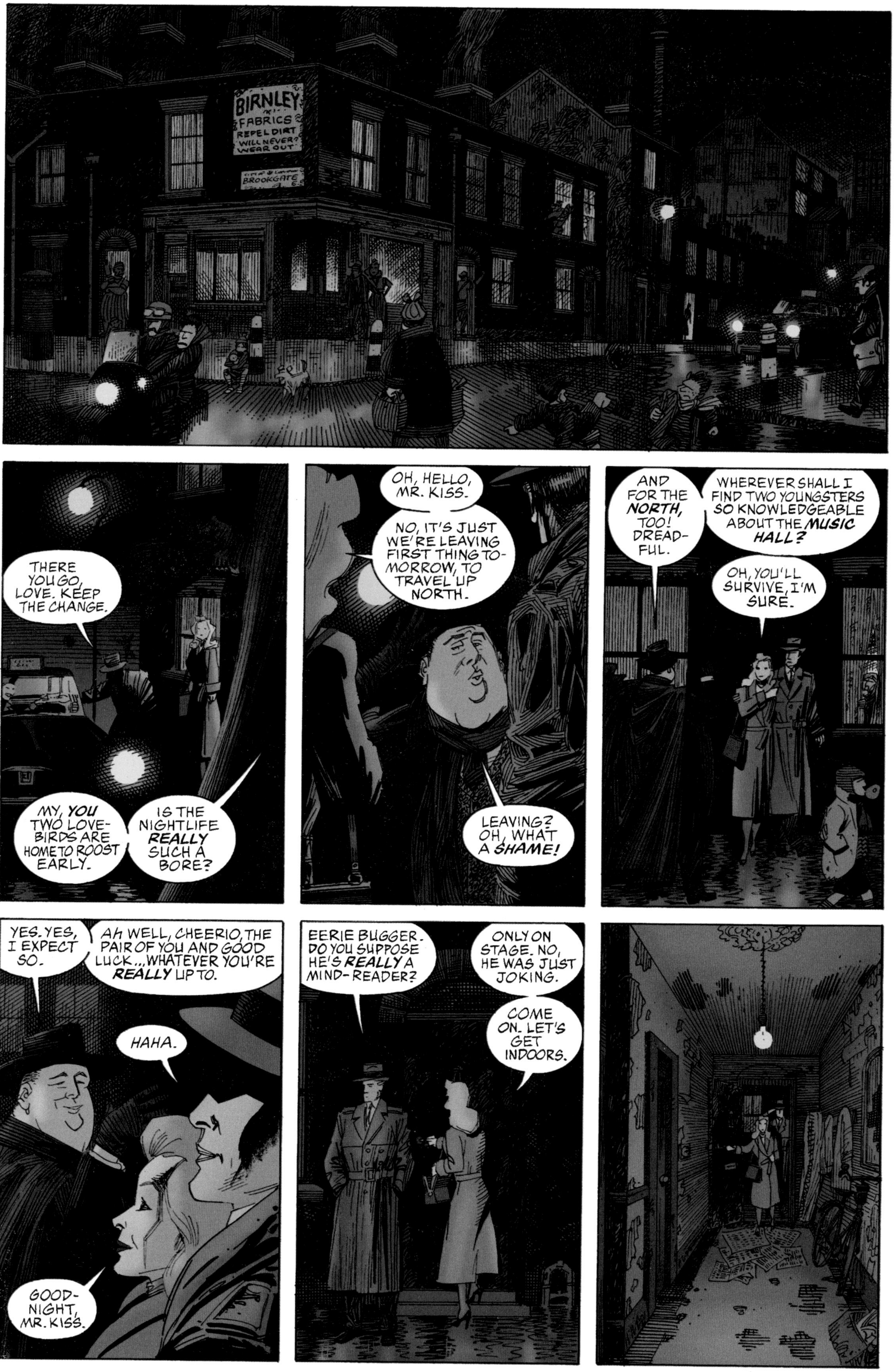
BIRNLEY FABRICS REPEL DIRT WILL NEVER WEAR OUT
BROOKGATE
THERE YOU GO, LOVE. KEEP THE CHANGE.
MY, YOU TWO LOVE-BIRDS ARE HOME TO ROOST EARLY.
IS THE NIGHTLIFE REALLY SUCH A BORE?
OH, HELLO, MR. KISS.
NO, IT'S JUST WE'RE LEAVING FIRST THING TO-MORROW, TO TRAVEL UP NORTH.
LEAVING? OH, WHAT A SHAME!
AND FOR THE NORTH, TOO! DREAD-FUL.
WHEREVER SHALL I FIND TWO YOUNGSTERS SO KNOWLEDGEABLE ABOUT THE MUSIC HALL?
OH, YOU'LL SURVIVE, I'M SURE.
YES. YES, I EXPECT SO.
AH WELL, CHEERIO, THE PAIR OF YOU AND GOOD LUCK... WHATEVER YOU'RE REALLY UP TO.
HAHA.
GOOD-NIGHT, MR. KISS.
EERIE BUGGER. DO YOU SUPPOSE HE'S REALLY A MIND-READER?
ONLY ON STAGE. NO, HE WAS JUST JOKING.
COME ON. LET'S GET INDOORS.

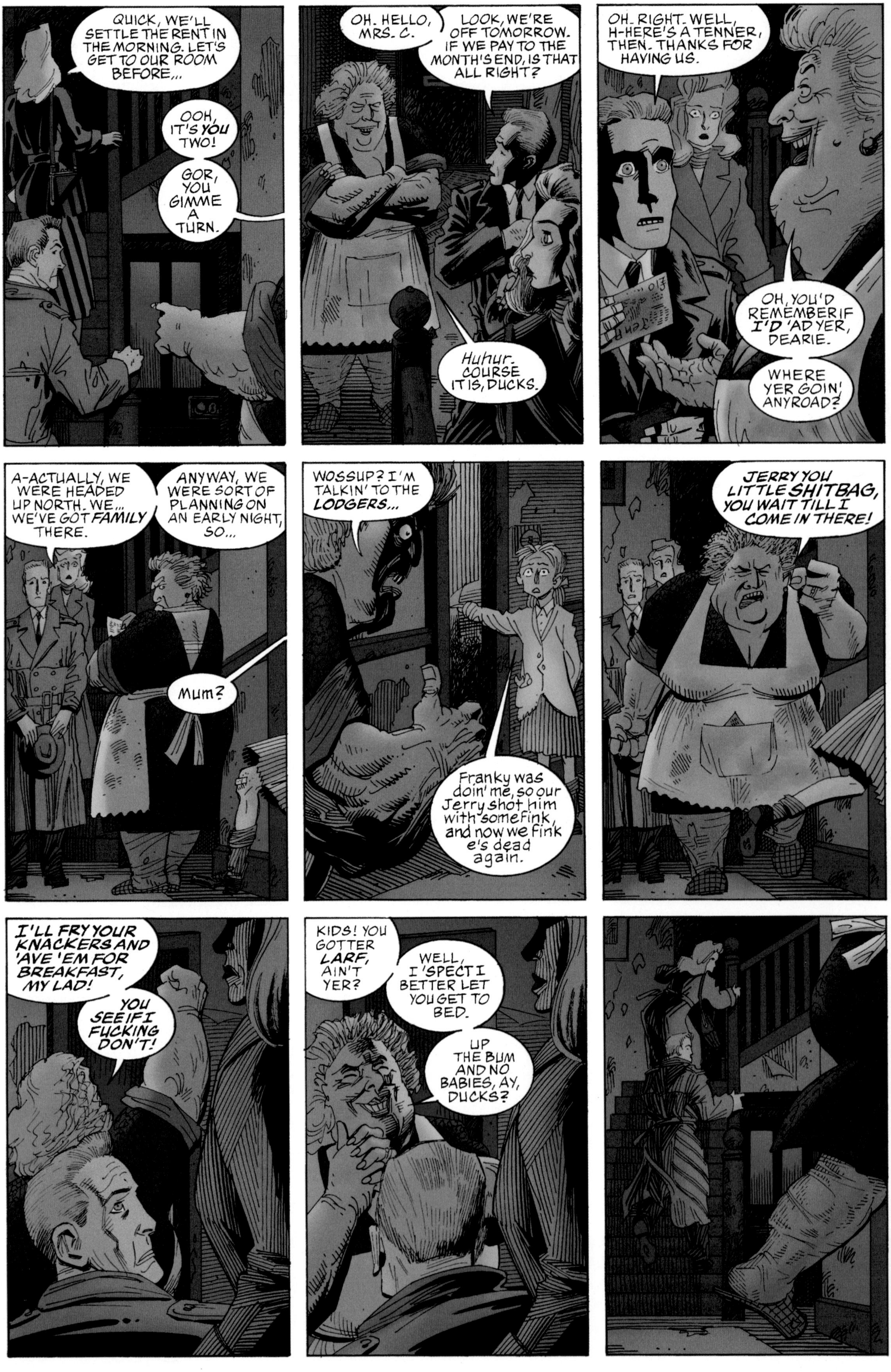
QUICK, WE'LL SETTLE THE RENT IN THE MORNING. LET'S GET TO OUR ROOM BEFORE...
OOH, IT'S YOU TWO!
GOR, YOU GIMME A TURN.
OH. HELLO, MRS. C.
LOOK, WE'RE OFF TOMORROW. IF WE PAY TO THE MONTH'S END, IS THAT ALL RIGHT?
Huhur. COURSE IT IS, DUCKS.
OH. RIGHT. WELL, H-HERE'S A TENNER, THEN. THANKS FOR HAVING US.
OH, YOU'D REMEMBER IF I'D 'AD YER, DEARIE.
WHERE YER GOIN' ANYROAD?
A-ACTUALLY, WE WERE HEADED UP NORTH. WE... WE'VE GOT FAMILY THERE.
ANYWAY, WE WERE SORT OF PLANNING ON AN EARLY NIGHT, SO...
Mum?
WOSSUP? I'M TALKIN' TO THE LODGERS...
Franky was doin' me, so our Jerry shot him with somefink, and now we fink e's dead again.
JERRY YOU LITTLE SHITBAG, YOU WAIT TILL I COME IN THERE!
I'LL FRY YOUR KNACKERS AND 'AVE 'EM FOR BREAKFAST, MY LAD!
YOU SEE IF I FUCKING DON'T!
KIDS! YOU GOTTER LARF, AIN'T YER?
WELL, I 'SPECT I BETTER LET YOU GET TO BED.
UP THE BUM AND NO BABIES, AY, DUCKS?

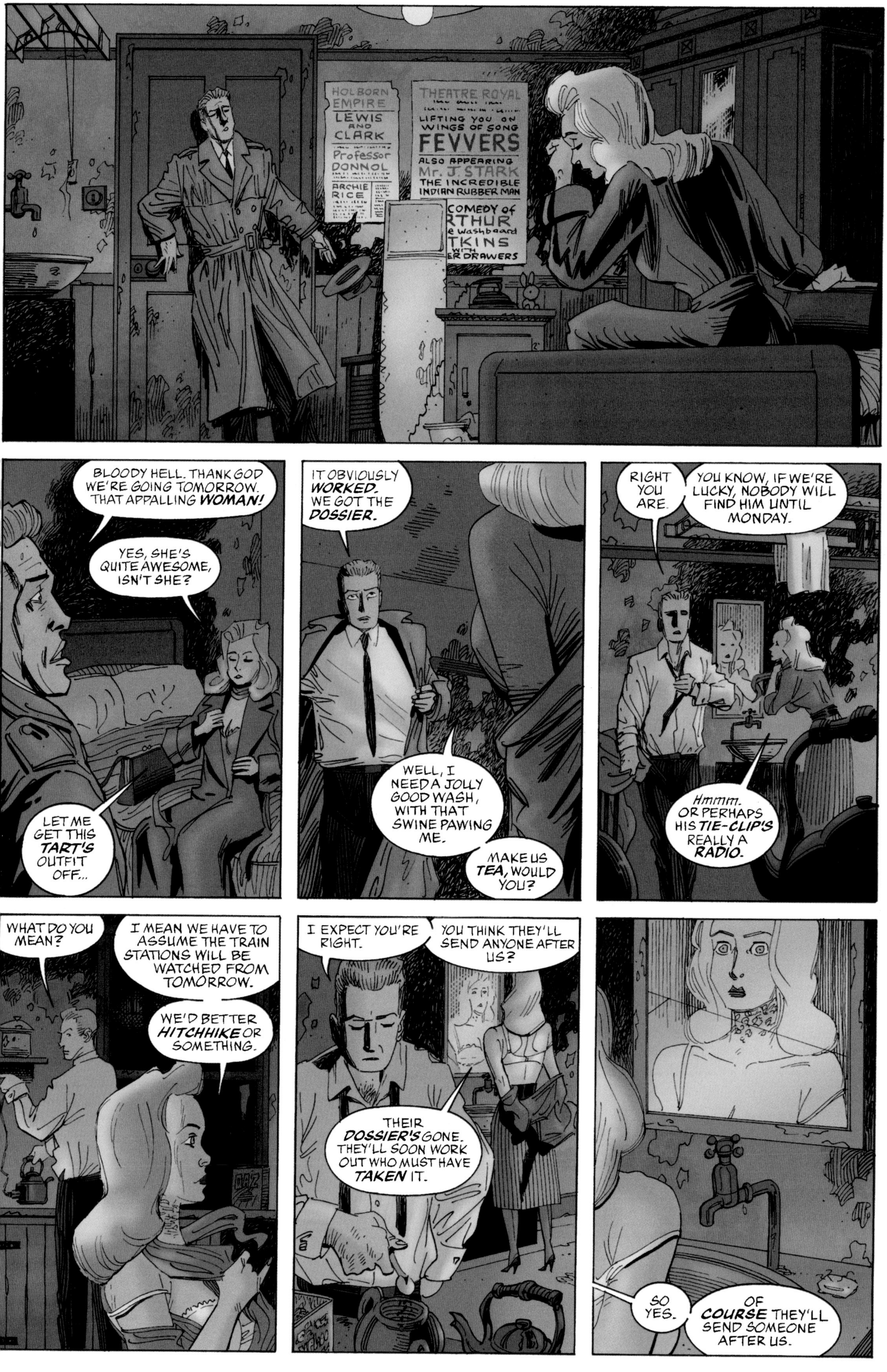
HOLBORN EMPIRE
LEWIS AND CLARK
Professor DONNOL
ARCHIE RICE
THEATRE ROYAL
LIFTING YOU ON WINGS OF SONG
FEVVERS
ALSO APPEARING
Mr. J. STARK
THE INCREDIBLE INDIAN RUBBER MAN
COMEDY of
RTHUR
TKINS
BLOODY HELL. THANK GOD WE'RE GOING TOMORROW. THAT APPALLING WOMAN!
YES, SHE'S QUITE AWESOME, ISN'T SHE?
LET ME GET THIS TART'S OUTFIT OFF...
IT OBVIOUSLY WORKED. WE GOT THE DOSSIER.
WELL, I NEED A JOLLY GOOD WASH, WITH THAT SWINE PAWING ME.
MAKE US TEA, WOULD YOU?
RIGHT YOU ARE.
YOU KNOW, IF WE'RE LUCKY, NOBODY WILL FIND HIM UNTIL MONDAY.
Hmmm. OR PERHAPS HIS TIE-CLIP'S REALLY A RADIO.
WHAT DO YOU MEAN?
I MEAN WE HAVE TO ASSUME THE TRAIN STATIONS WILL BE WATCHED FROM TOMORROW.
WE'D BETTER HITCHHIKE OR SOMETHING.
I EXPECT YOU'RE RIGHT.
YOU THINK THEY'LL SEND ANYONE AFTER US?
THEIR DOSSIER'S GONE. THEY'LL SOON WORK OUT WHO MUST HAVE TAKEN IT.
SO YES.
OF COURSE THEY'LL SEND SOMEONE AFTER US.

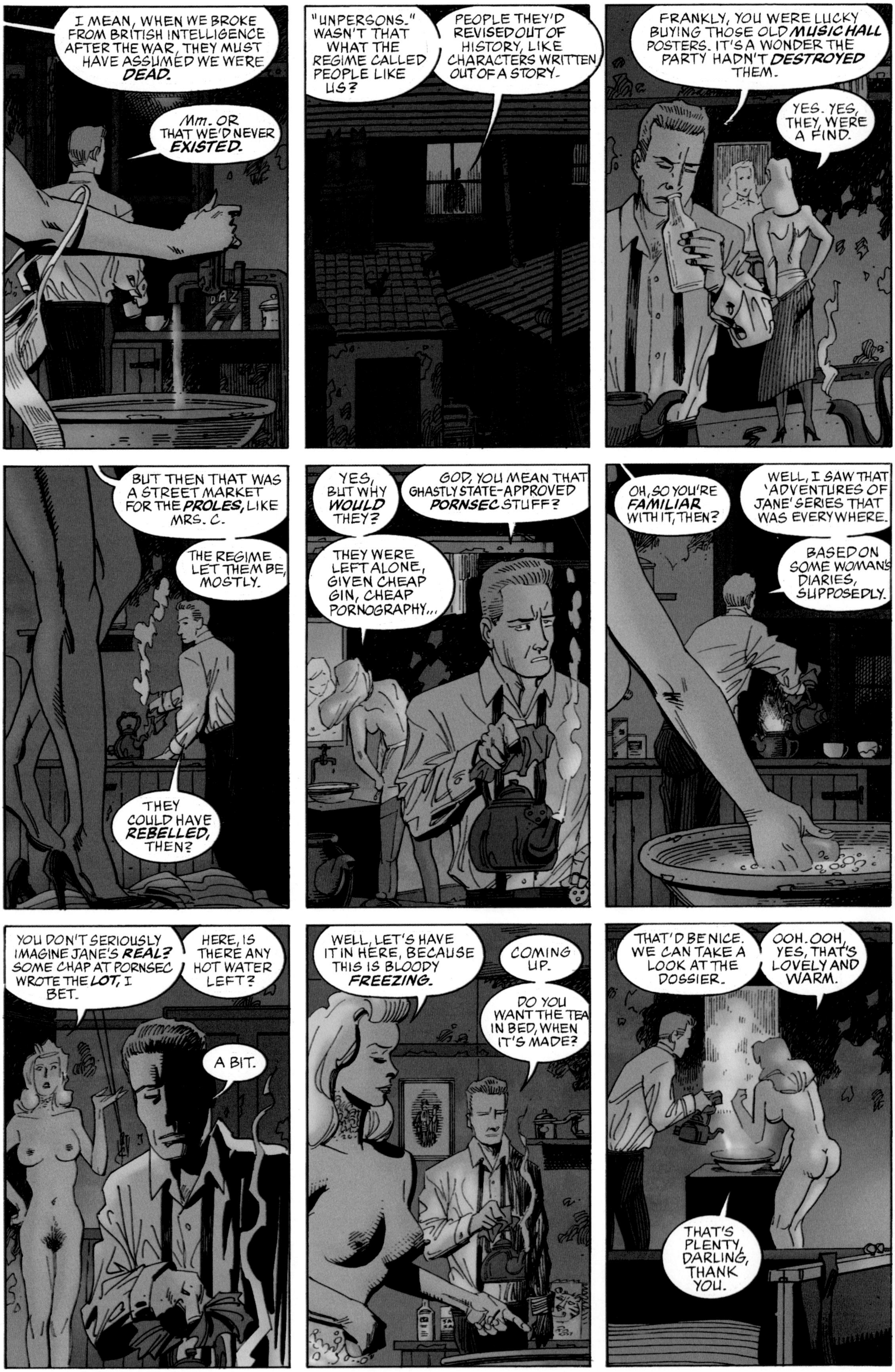
I MEAN, WHEN WE BROKE FROM BRITISH INTELLIGENCE AFTER THE WAR, THEY MUST HAVE ASSUMED WE WERE DEAD.
Mm. OR THAT WE'D NEVER EXISTED.
"UNPERSONS." WASN'T THAT WHAT THE REGIME CALLED PEOPLE LIKE US?
PEOPLE THEY'D REVISED OUT OF HISTORY, LIKE CHARACTERS WRITTEN OUT OF A STORY.
FRANKLY, YOU WERE LUCKY BUYING THOSE OLD MUSIC HALL POSTERS. IT'S A WONDER THE PARTY HADN'T DESTROYED THEM.
YES. YES, THEY WERE A FIND.
BUT THEN THAT WAS A STREET MARKET FOR THE PROLES, LIKE MRS. C.
THE REGIME LET THEM BE, MOSTLY.
THEY COULD HAVE REBELLED, THEN?
YES, BUT WHY WOULD THEY?
GOD, YOU MEAN THAT GHASTLY STATE-APPROVED PORNSEC STUFF?
THEY WERE LEFT ALONE, GIVEN CHEAP GIN, CHEAP PORNOGRAPHY...
OH, SO YOU'RE FAMILIAR WITH IT, THEN?
WELL, I SAW THAT 'ADVENTURES OF JANE' SERIES THAT WAS EVERYWHERE.
BASED ON SOME WOMAN'S DIARIES, SUPPOSEDLY.
YOU DON'T SERIOUSLY IMAGINE JANE'S REAL? SOME CHAP AT PORNSEC WROTE THE LOT, I BET.
HERE, IS THERE ANY HOT WATER LEFT?
A BIT.
WELL, LET'S HAVE IT IN HERE, BECAUSE THIS IS BLOODY FREEZING.
COMING UP.
DO YOU WANT THE TEA IN BED, WHEN IT'S MADE?
THAT'D BE NICE. WE CAN TAKE A LOOK AT THE DOSSIER.
OOH. OOH, YES, THAT'S LOVELY AND WARM.
THAT'S PLENTY, DARLING, THANK YOU.

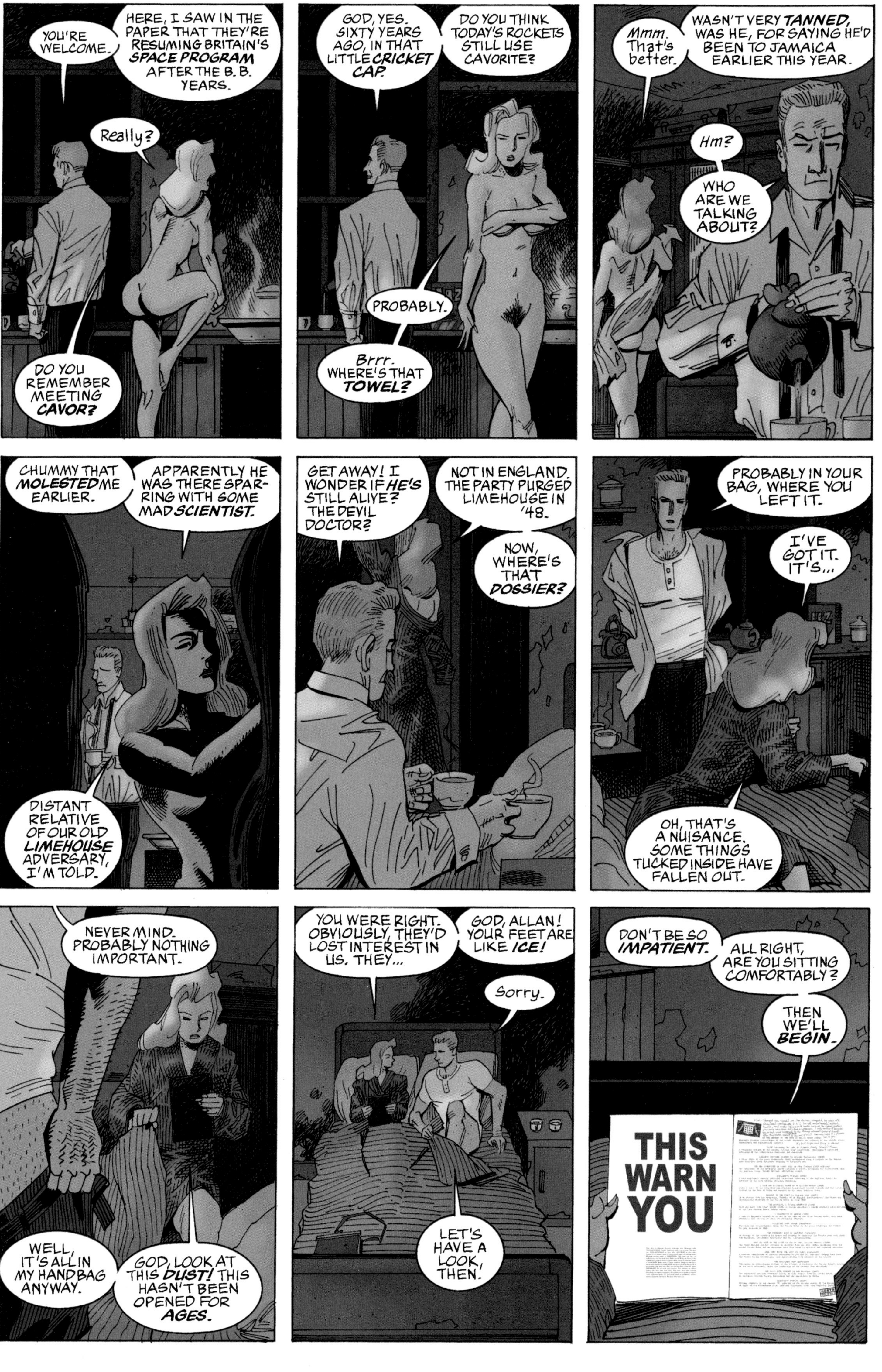
YOU'RE WELCOME.
HERE, I SAW IN THE PAPER THAT THEY'RE RESUMING BRITAIN'S SPACE PROGRAM AFTER THE B. B. YEARS.
Really?
DO YOU REMEMBER MEETING CAVOR?
GOD, YES. SIXTY YEARS AGO, IN THAT LITTLE CRICKET CAP.
DO YOU THINK TODAY'S ROCKETS STILL USE CAVORITE?
PROBABLY.
Brrr. WHERE'S THAT TOWEL?
Mmm. That's better.
WASN'T VERY TANNED, WAS HE, FOR SAYING HE'D BEEN TO JAMAICA EARLIER THIS YEAR.
Hm?
WHO ARE WE TALKING ABOUT?
CHUMMY THAT MOLESTED ME EARLIER.
APPARENTLY HE WAS THERE SPARRING WITH SOME MAD SCIENTIST.
DISTANT RELATIVE OF OUR OLD LIMEHOUSE ADVERSARY, I'M TOLD.
GET AWAY! I WONDER IF HE'S STILL ALIVE? THE DEVIL DOCTOR?
NOT IN ENGLAND. THE PARTY PURGED LIMEHOUSE IN '48.
NOW, WHERE'S THAT DOSSIER?
PROBABLY IN YOUR BAG, WHERE YOU LEFT IT.
I'VE GOT IT. IT'S...
OH, THAT'S A NUISANCE. SOME THINGS TUCKED INSIDE HAVE FALLEN OUT.
NEVER MIND. PROBABLY NOTHING IMPORTANT.
WELL, IT'S ALL IN MY HANDBAG ANYWAY.
GOD, LOOK AT THIS DUST! THIS HASN'T BEEN OPENED FOR AGES.
YOU WERE RIGHT. OBVIOUSLY, THEY'D LOST INTEREST IN US. THEY...
GOD, ALLAN! YOUR FEET ARE LIKE ICE!
Sorry.
LET'S HAVE A LOOK, THEN.
DON'T BE SO IMPATIENT.
ALL RIGHT, ARE YOU SITTING COMFORTABLY?
THEN WE'LL BEGIN.
THIS WARN YOU

THIS WARN YOU

Docs after in oldspeak. Untruth, make-ups only. Make-ups make THOUGHTCRIME. Careful. Supervisor rank or not to read. This warn you. THOUGHTCRIME in docs after. SEXCRIME in docs after. Careful. If self excited, report. If other excited, report. Everything report. Withhold accurate report is INFOCRIME. This warn you. Are you authorised, if no stop read now! Make report! We know. Careful. Any resemblance, living or dead, is ungood. Make report. If fail make report, is INFOCRIME. Make report. If report made on failing to make report, this paradox. Paradox is LOGICRIME. Do not do anything. Do not fail to do anything. This warn you. Why you nervous? Was it you? We know. IMPORTANT: Do not read next sentence. This sentence for official inspect only. Now look. Now don't. Now look. Now don't. Careful. Everything not banned compulsory. Everything not compulsory banned. Views expressed within not necessarily those of publishers, editors, writers, characters. You did it. We know. This warn you.

H.W. - Thought you should see this dossier, compiled by your old Greyfriars confederate R.K.C. It's all unbelievable rubbish, frankly, and makes references to parties such as the Holmes brothers who have since been classified as unpersons. I only enclose it because you asked what happened to the Murray woman's group of frauds after they broke contact at the end of WWII. Anyway, hope it's of some use to you.

My best to you and Bessy, as always.

Gerry O'Brien

CONTENTS

RESTRICTED
OFFICIAL USE ONLY

H.W.— This is pretty rum stuff. Haddo is what you'd call a "black magician" who worked for us during WWII. Shady character — he barely survived a fire at his Staffordshire estate in 1908, finally died destitute in Hastings a few years ago in 1947. The "M" in charge before R.K.C. ordered this appraisal of the "aetheric territories." Nonsense, of course, but it may amuse you. Best to you and Bessy— Gerry O'Brien

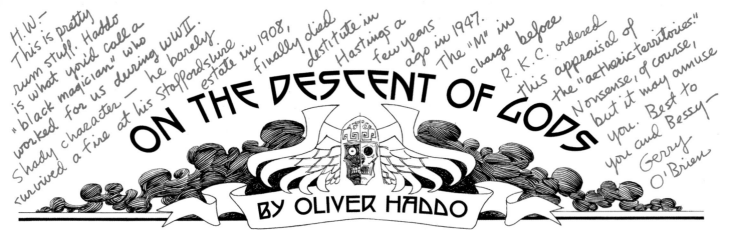

ON THE DESCENT OF GODS

BY OLIVER HADDO

The following, distilling as it does a longer and more comprehensive treatise published in *The Solstice,* vol. 1, VI, concerns mysteries that will prove impermeable to all save those adepts who have fully understood my own *Liber Logos,* dictated by an unseen presence in Cairo during 1904. For this reason, I have where possible simplified the matters discussed in the text, so that they may prove lucid to the scrutiny of a more generalised and averagely intelligent readership.

From scant surviving ancient accounts and certain material received during magical investigations, it is possible to ascertain that the earliest contact between our material realm and the various ethereal 'dimensions' adjoining it probably occurred some millions of years ago, perhaps shortly after the emergence of proto-human life upon this planet. The celestial energies concerned are referred to in the Book of Genesis as 'Elohim,' a curious Hebrew word that is at once masculine, feminine, and furthermore plural, and which may be broadly understood in context as 'the gods and goddesses,' our inference surely being that the Christian God of the Old Testament was perhaps one amongst many such divinely manifested beings. This is not to deny that all such manifestations may ultimately be the various emanations of a single monotheistic source; simply to point out that the processes involved may be at once more subtle and more complex than is generally allowed in the philosophies of our conventional religions.

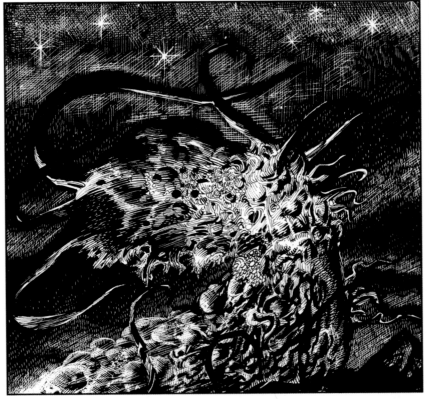

These earliest 'gods and goddesses' and their subordinate hosts of angels may, of course, have procreated in some fashion amongst or between themselves, while texts such as the apocryphal Book of Enoch are suggestive of limited interbreeding between a specific rank or class of 'angels' and the earliest human beings. We may only speculate with regard to the offspring that may have resulted from such couplings, but it is sufficient to remark upon the implication of a thriving, viable celestial stock, a divine lineage with the potential for both evolution or degeneration over the successive æons, as with earthly and material bloodlines. In any event, it would seem that some several millennia after the arrival of the generally-benign biblical Elohim on our material plane of being, there transpired a new incursion into our dimension, by less welcome entities.

These beings, termed collectively 'Great Old Ones' in 16th century alchemist Johannes Suttle's fine translation of the Arab mystic Abdul Alhazred's seminal *Necronomicon,* would seem to be powerful djinns or malignant spirits originating in a transmaterial dimension (sometimes misidentified by neophytes as a mere physically-existent planet) known as Yuggoth. While far too numerous to list exhaustively within the space available for this report, these alien deities or quasi-deities included extra-planetary horrors such as the monstrous, tentacle-adorned Kutulu; the seething exemplar of primal chaos known as A-Tza-Thoth; the grotesquely fertile and many-limbed she-goat called Shub-Niggurath; and the sinister Hermes-like messenger N'Yala-Thoth-Ep, sometimes referred to as 'The Haunter of the Dark.' By the time of the arrival of these entities in our dimension, it would seem that Earth's prior occupants, the Elohim, had by some measure seen their power diminish or degenerate across the æons, so that they were now mere 'Elder Gods,' unable to resist the invading forces with the ease that may have previously been expected. Even so, all the Great Old Ones were eventually either banished from our plane of being, or else magically imprisoned in empowered locations such as the vast sunken city R'Lyeh, found in 1926, some distance from the coastline of New Zealand.

During their tenure in our world, brief in cosmological terms, these alien or qlippothic interlopers would appear to have, much like the Elohim, both interbred between themselves and also to have sired a great variety of half-breed monsters on the human population, such as Tibet's noisome and degenerate 'Tcho-Tcho' people, or the fish-like humanoids discovered on an island close to Zara's Kingdom in the South Pacific. As with the mooted offspring of the Elohim themselves, we may construe that down the æons various further interbreeding would most certainly occur, accounting for the widely varied plethora of monsters, chimeræ and spirits that have populated human history and folklore ever since.

As for the former Elohim themselves, having suffered a decline to become mere senescent Elder Gods, it would seem that their power had been further diminished by their war against the terrible Great Old Ones. By the time of the earliest, since-lost human civilisations before and during the great Ice Age, when Britain was yet joined to both the Arctic kingdom of Hyperborea and to continental Europe by an ice land-bridge, Earth's first 'gods and goddesses' had seemingly degenerated into relatively brutish, unsophisticated tribal deities such as the war-god Crom, once worshipped by Cimmerians in what is modern Scandinavia. At the same time, though exiled or imprisoned, the Great Old Ones still continued to exert an influence and to command a worrying multitude of worshippers. Thus it appears that there were still perceived to be two distinctly different trans-substantial 'clans,' if you will, with one benign and one malignant, that both governed and affected all the various doings of the human race.

By the end of the great Ice Age (also the end of the so-called 'Hyperborean Period'), with what are now the British Isles made separate for the first time from continental Europe, references to Crom-cults and Kutulu-worship seem to all but vanish from the archæological record. One of the few surviving cultures in this prehistoric world was that of the immensely cruel and decadent Melnibonéan Empire, Melniboné being the name by which the British Isles were known immediately following the disappearance of the continental land-bridge. The Melnibonéan worldview

would seem to have been essentially Manichean in that central to it was the notion of two diametrically opposed and adversarial forces in the universe, Lords of Order warring endlessly with Lords of Chaos, with these evidently serving as the mythopoeic forms into which earlier eidolons such as Crom, the Elohim and the Great Old Ones had by this time either evolved or declined. Contemporary geologic evidence suggests that shortly prior to the commencement of the Neolithic era, some decisive, cataclysmic conflict between these two rival forces must have taken place, the Lords of Order perhaps making a last-ditch attempt to counterbalance powerful and dæmonic Lords of Chaos such as Arioch and Pyaray. Whatever the true circumstances, the result was devastation unimagined until last year's development and demonstration by our allies in America of the Atomic bomb. If we may conceive an entire global war conducted using such devices, then we may have a comparison to the destruction visited by this Melnibonéan-period disaster on humanity, driven back to wear-

ing skins and dwelling in caves, just before conventional history begins.

Some few thousand years later, by the Bronze Age, we may readily suppose that the surviving residue of these opposing astral forces might have undergone the ordinary mutations of time and heredity, resulting in their transformation to the Titans and other prototypical giant races that populate the early stages of the world's nascent mythologies. These would themselves, in time, give rise to a great plethora of more sophisticated and more fully realised spiritual energies, which became known as the classic Gods when manifested to various cultures of the ancient world.

It is with the various pantheons of this classical era, Babylonian, Greek or Egyptian (the gods of which great civilisations would often appear to be the selfsame energies, as conceived of by markedly differing cultures), that we first have some sense of divine agenda in the interactions between mankind and its deities. Though just as profligate in fathering half-human chimeræ as their celestial predecessors, the more cultured deities inhabiting the Greco-Roman world would seem to have had some occulted purpose in their promiscuity, perhaps a hoped-for hybrid race that would one day conceivably provide a bridge, a bond between the mortal world and the ethereal, by means of which communion between man and his divinities may be more certainly effected. This concealed agenda is born witness by the brief proliferation of the half-god race of Heroes, men like Hercules or Aeneas, just as surely as the Trojan War in the tenth century B.C. bears witness to the failure of that divine project. If Homer is to be believed, the siege of Troy was engineered by the Greek gods and goddesses, deliberately, to cull the Hero race that they themselves had sired decades before, only to see the hybrids' human qualities collapse beneath the weight of their divine inheritance, producing vain and strutting homicidal monsters. It may be that it was the tragic end to this preliminary experiment that caused the gods to gradually withdraw from our material domain across the coming centuries, perhaps to ponder some new strategy by which their aims might be achieved. The different pantheons retreated, one by one, into their home-dimensions, so that eventually only the Teutonic deities remained, these being obliterated by some terrible ethereal catastrophe during the sixth century A.D., an event mirrored in our own realm by collision with a piece of meteoric rock, dust darkening Earth's skies for several years.

All of these various god-races, like the Elohim and the Great Old Ones that had come before, left our material realm a legacy of færies, demons, sprites and monsters that would eventually become so populous that during the grim, lightless depths of the Dark Ages, they held sway across the greater part of both Europe and western Asia. As if to provide a harbinger of these forthcoming pagan centuries, the great magician Merlin was born into Roman-occupied British society at some time during the late fourth century, reputedly during the period when Emperor Julian had declared Britain to be officially a pagan nation. Merlin, of course, rose to become a trusted counsellor during the brief but laudable Arthurian period, only disappearing with the fateful termination of that era, circa 470 A.D. By this time England had become an ogre-ridden, færie-haunted place, thanks largely to the influence exerted by King Arthur's close blood relative, the færie queen Morgana La Fey. Morgana's claim of a connection to the English Royal bloodline would eventually come to be of some importance more than a thousand years thereafter, in the reign of King Henry VIII.

By this time, during the Renaissance, a magical or færie influence upon human affairs of state was tolerated and accepted, even openly encouraged. With the half-realm (or perhaps the fractional dimension) of the Færie homeland recognised as an important sovereign state, and its titular then-monarch Oberon the First perceived to be the head of a most venerable Royal household, it seemed only natural that Henry VIII should take King Oberon's second cousin, the distinctly Færy-blooded Anne Boleyn, with her protuberant eyes and a sixth finger on each hand, to be his second wife. The offspring of this controversial union, it need not be said, was England's alabaster-complexioned, reportedly unearthly monarch, Queen Gloriana the First, under whose remarkable reign, commencing in 1558, the magical and otherworldly came to play a greater part within the English worldview of those times, as they did in the majority of alchemy and magic-obsessed nations throughout Europe. It was Gloriana who appointed, from the outset of her rule, the noted alchemist and sorcerer Johannes Suttle as her court astrologer, a decision of far-reaching consequence.

Johannes Suttle (or 'Subtle'), said to have been born variously in Worcestershire or else into Italian aristocracy, was probably in his late thirties when he embarked upon magical service for Queen Gloriana. Residing at a house in Mortlake by the churchyard with his wife Doll and a distinguished, if notorious, fellow alchemist called Edward Face, Suttle performed with Face the groundbreaking experiments that would provide the basis for much of the Art of Magic, as it is practiced in the west up to the present day. Suttle had, while still a boy of tender years, apparently met the famous European occultist John Faust, and shared Faust's predilection for the art of diabolic conjuring. With Face's aid, Suttle established contact with innumerable ranks of spirits which purported to be those same human-loving angels mentioned in the Book of Enoch. In his investigations of these beings and the immaterial 'æthyrs' they inhabit, Suttle came across a female entity of dreadful power, who would come to obsess various later occultists, this being the Thessalian witch-goddess called Smarra.

With the death of his beloved wife in the first years of the seventeenth century, Suttle is variously reported to have entered a decline and died at Mortlake, tended by his surviving child, Miranda, or according to some accounts to have gone into self-imposed exile on a distant island, with his life prolonged by sorcerous means. What is certain is that within a year of his death or departure, in 1603, Queen Gloriana herself took ill and died, to be succeeded by the fiercely puritanical and anti-færie King Jacob the First, devout compiler of the now-standard King Jacob Bible. This new king organised bloodthirsty purges of the Færie race and other supernatural creatures, with the result that by 1616, Oberon's Fairyland had severed all its contacts with the human world, with England literally rendered disenchanted in direct result.

Obviously, despite disapproval from the Church and Crown, a line of individual sorcerers kept interest in the Magic Arts alive during the centuries that followed. In the late 18th century, the noted Spanish occultist Señor Don Alvarez, said to have sworn a pact with the Devil in the form of a beautiful little girl named Biondetta, carried out certain forbidden operations to establish contact with the goddess or dæmoness called Smarra, transcribing in his writings the ferocious and blood-curdling prophecies that had been ventured by that entity. Smarra, originally raised during the orgiastic and tribadic rites of the famed sorceress Medea and her sister-witches there in the ancient region of Thessaly, was also the subject of the obsessions of Germany's reputed 18th century 'Ghost Seer,' the Count Von Ost, himself a prized associate of 'the Sicilian,' who was believed to be an alias of alchemist and scoundrel Cagliostro.

My own association with this sacred, fiery female energy began in 1904, while I was on my honeymoon in Cairo. Following certain signs and omens, I had retired into a solitary study where I would be able to write down whatever messages the spirits might see fit to pass to me. The resultant work, *Liber Logos,* written over three successive occasions upon three successive days, is a most holy and perfect announcement of the terrible Aeon that is to come, with myself as its Prophet, and is in part dictated by the

goddess Smarra. This has since been published as *The Book of the Word,* without a full understanding of which it is impossible for the human race to fulfill its celestial destiny.

Briefly, the congruence between Smarra and the biblical Whore of Babylon from the Book of Revelations has been confirmed to me by mystical investigation, yielding various insights. Just as the Whore of Babylon is thought to be a Christian demonising of the Babylonian mother-goddess Ishtar, so too is Smarra, with her name, in all likelihood being a corruption of 'Samara,' another centre of Ishtar worship during the Babylonian period. Applying the art of gematria to the name of the goddess offers further confirmation. In the numerically valued alphabet of the Hebrews, we find that SMARRA is equivalent to the number five hundred and two, with the associated meanings 'to tell glad tidings' and also 'the flesh,' both appropriate to the highly sexu-

alised spirit of Apocalypse. In the Pythagorean gematria of the Greeks, the name yields a number value of four hundred and forty-two, which signifies 'termini terræ,' or the end of the world, another clearly apocalyptic association. Finally, and most persuasively, according to Homeric Greek gematria, the name SMARRA has a value of just sixty-six, this being the mystic number of the Qlippoth, and also that of the Great Work itself. What, to the initiated adept, could be more conclusive?

It was after the revelations contained within *Liber Logos* that I withdrew from the venerable occult organization known as the Order of the Golden Twilight, or 'Geltische Dammerung,' to form my own magical order, the Ordo Templi Terra (O.T.T.), or Order of the Temple of Earth, which continues to investigate the otherworldly entities and territories that have lately, it would seem, come to preoccupy those shaping policy at Military Intelligence. If I may be of any further assistance to the government in matters of this nature, do not hesitate to contact me at the address you have on file, this being the Netherworld estate in Hastings. I remain, yours most sincerely, Oliver Haddo.

The Word is Law.
The Law is Love.

THE LIFE OF ORLANDO — NEW PICTURE STORY STARTS INSIDE!

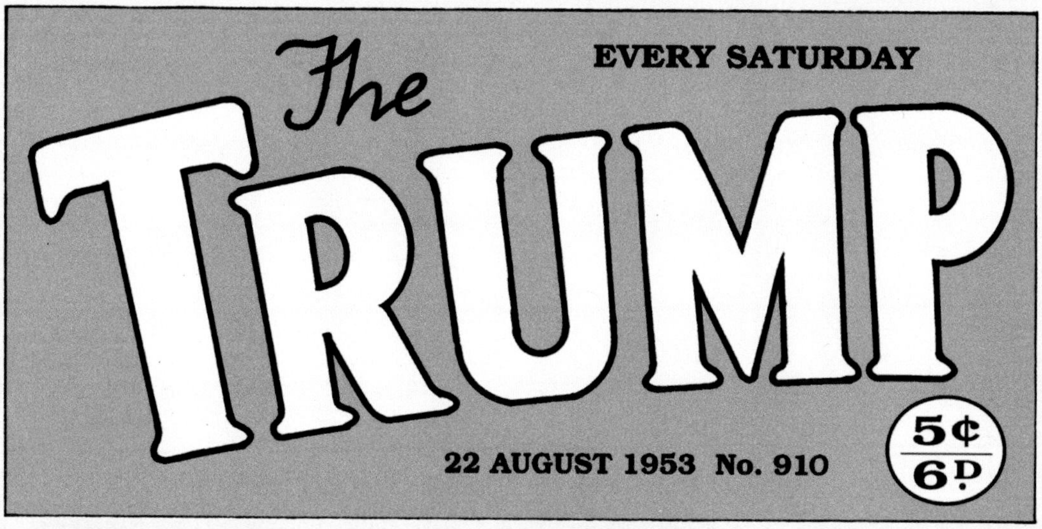
EVERY SATURDAY
The TRUMP
22 AUGUST 1953 No. 910
5¢
6D.

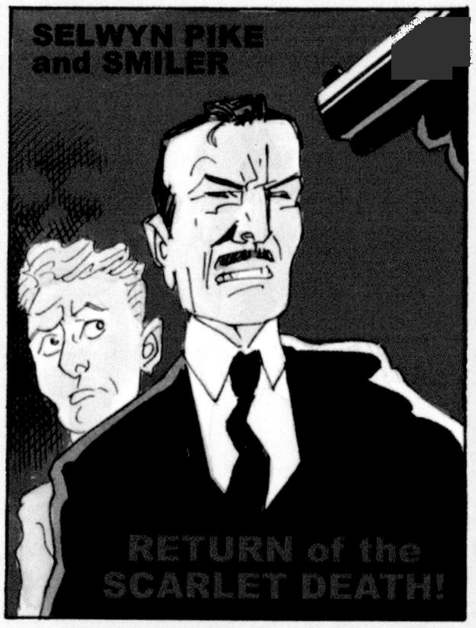
SELWYN PIKE and SMILER
RETURN of the SCARLET DEATH!

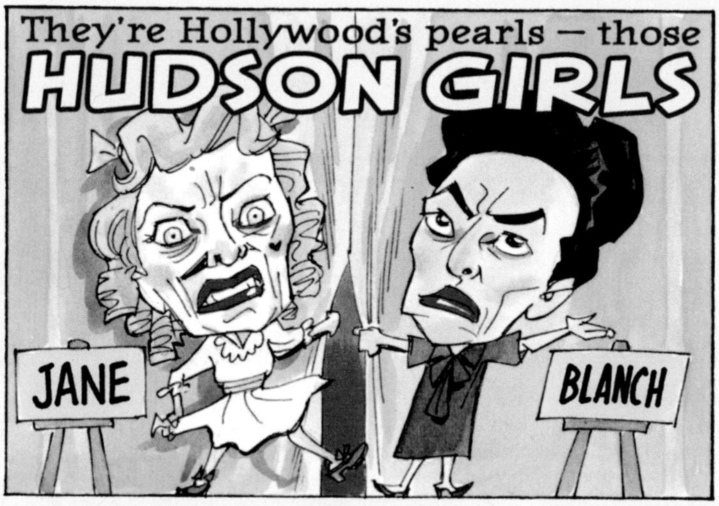
They're Hollywood's pearls — those
HUDSON GIRLS
JANE
BLANCH

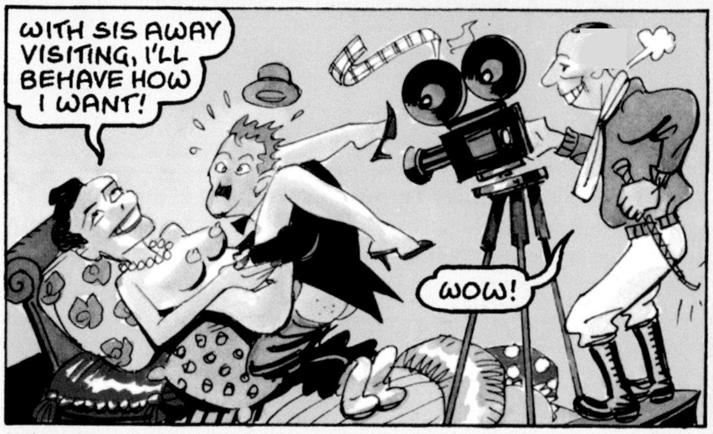
WITH SIS AWAY VISITING, I'LL BEHAVE HOW I WANT!
WOW!

What Ho, chums! With sister Jane away, what's frisky Blanch Hudson playing at now? Well, I'll be jiggered if she hasn't made a blue movie!

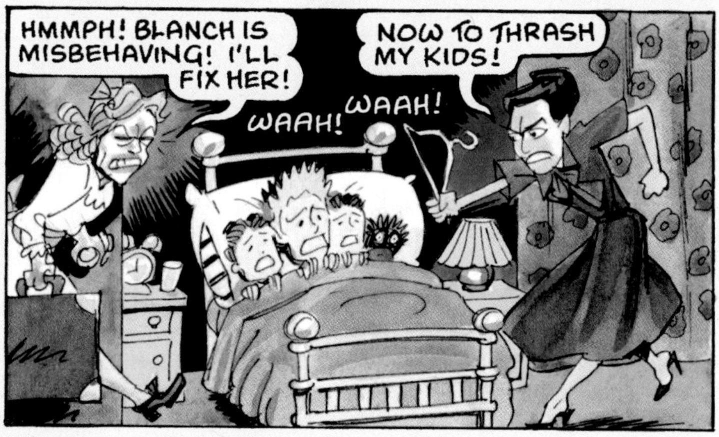
HMMPH! BLANCH IS MISBEHAVING! I'LL FIX HER!
NOW TO THRASH MY KIDS!
WAAH!
WAAH!

Whatever next? Blanch is up to her coat-hanger japes again, but watch out! Jane's home, and mighty cross too, I'll bet!

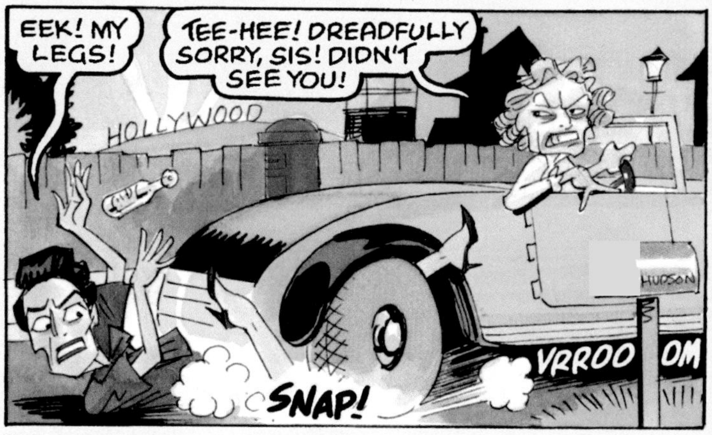
EEK! MY LEGS!
TEE-HEE! DREADFULLY SORRY, SIS! DIDN'T SEE YOU!
HOLLYWOOD
HUDSON
VRROO OM
SNAP!

Crikey! Now Jane's driven her jolly old auto over Blanch, disabling her for life! "Sorry, sis," sniggers Jane. "I didn't see you!"

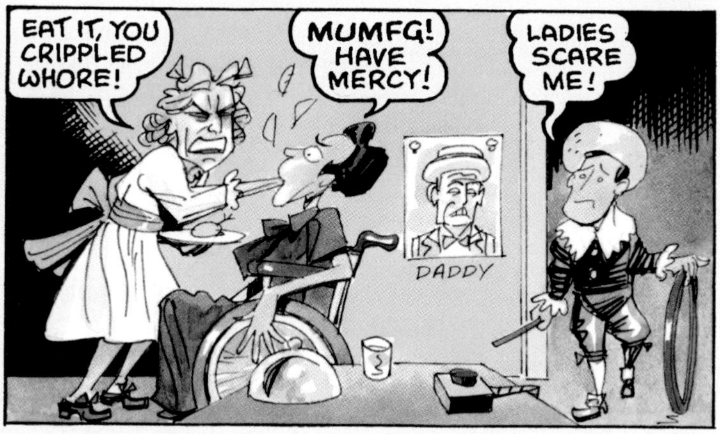
EAT IT, YOU CRIPPLED WHORE!
MUMFG! HAVE MERCY!
LADIES SCARE ME!
DADDY

Bust my braces! Now Blanch is a defenceless invalid, Jane is feeding her cooked canary! What's little brother Rock to make of it all?

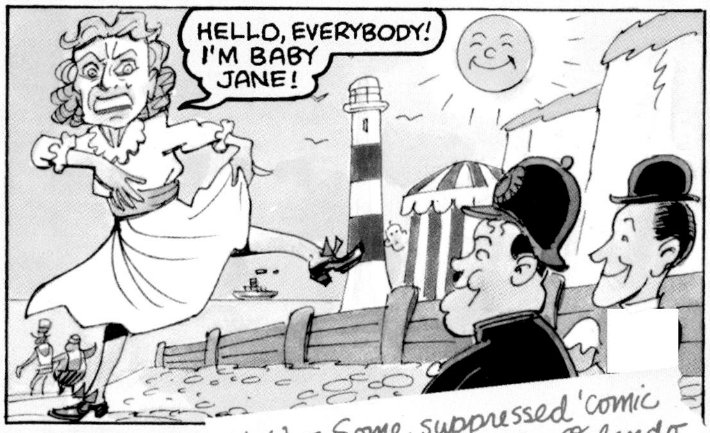
HELLO, EVERYBODY! I'M BABY JANE!

Jesus Christ! She's
mental case if ever
old bitch, even if sh

H. W. — Some suppressed 'comic cuts' for you, regarding Orlando charlatan. Some dates contradict Orlando Almanac. R.K.C. says Orlando 'queer, and a pathological liar'.
Best, G.O'B.

The Life of ORLANDO

Chapter One: I am Born

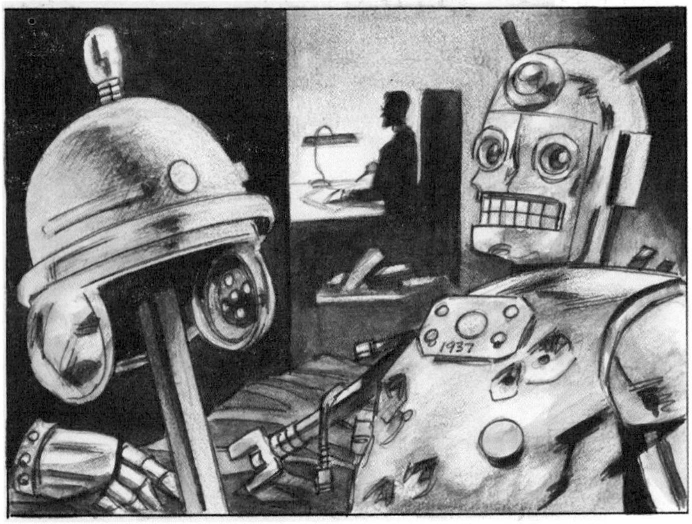
1937

1. Gather round, kindly readers. Draw closer and I'll tell a tale like no other, of loves, wars, and empires ground down unto sand, for my name is Orlando, and I have lived three thousand years.

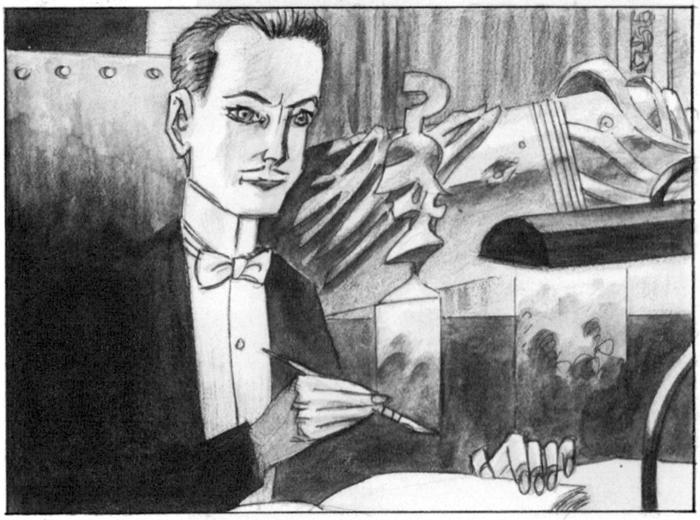

2. I write this by lamplight, a young man in bombed, blackout London with Herr Hynkel's Luftwaffe droning above, but I am neither young, nor, back then in 1260 BC, was I born as a man.

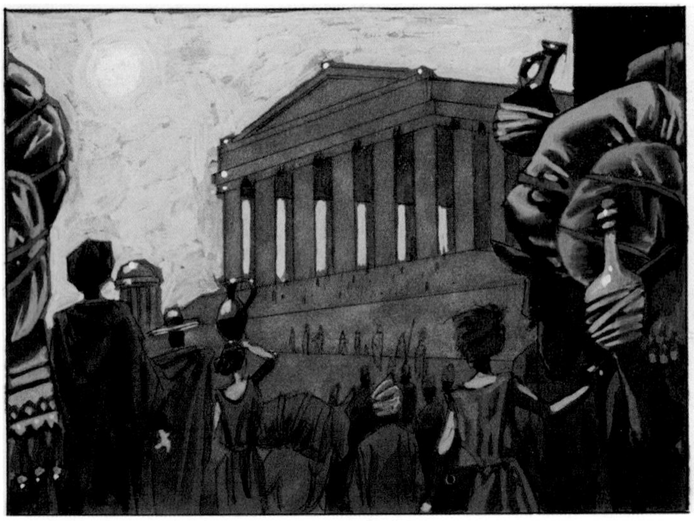

3. Splendid Thebes was my birthplace, fair Bronze Age Greek city-state there in Boeotia. The 'Seven Against Thebes' were by then defeated, their sons yet to rise and avenge them, and all was at peace.

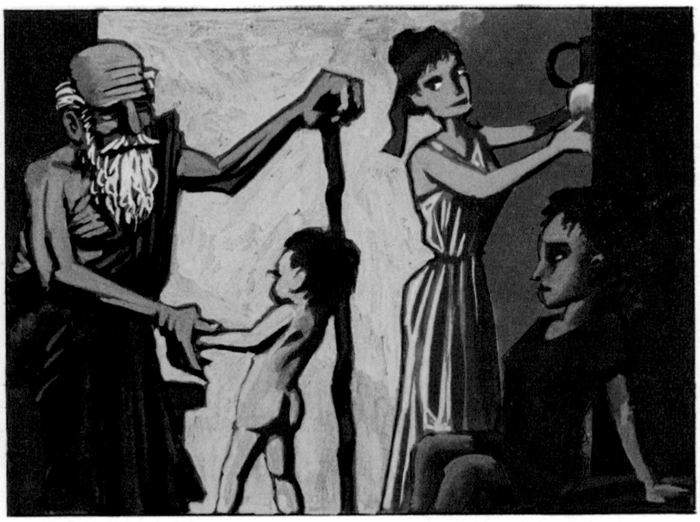

4. The blind seer Tiresias, cursed to change into a woman and back, and companion to tragic King Oedipus, fathered my dear sister Manto and I. She inherited his gift of prophecy, while I inherited nothing.

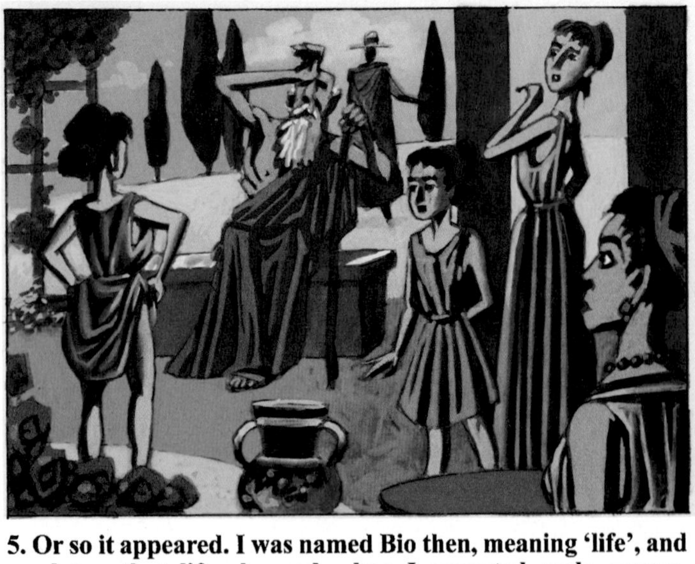

5. Or so it appeared. I was named Bio then, meaning 'life', and aged ten that life changed when I sprouted male organs, becoming a boy. Neither Father nor Manto had seen *that* one coming, apparently.

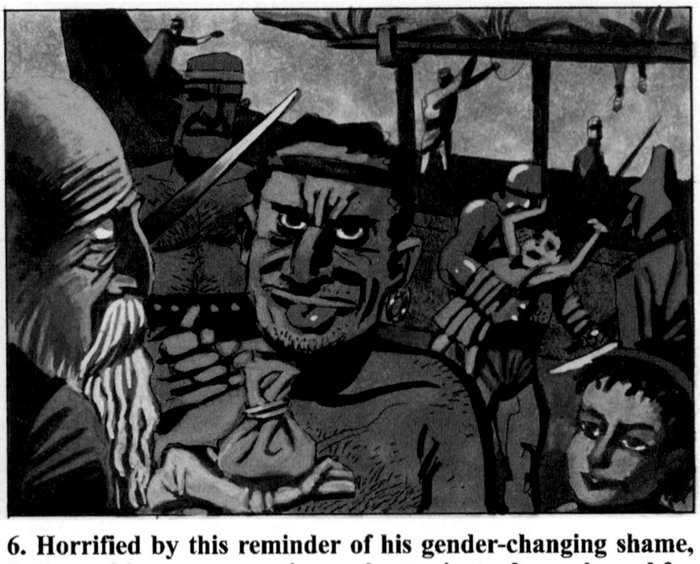

6. Horrified by this reminder of his gender-changing shame, Father sold me as an exotic novelty to pirate slavers bound for Egypt. Father later died, I heard, escorting Manto to become the oracle at Delphi.

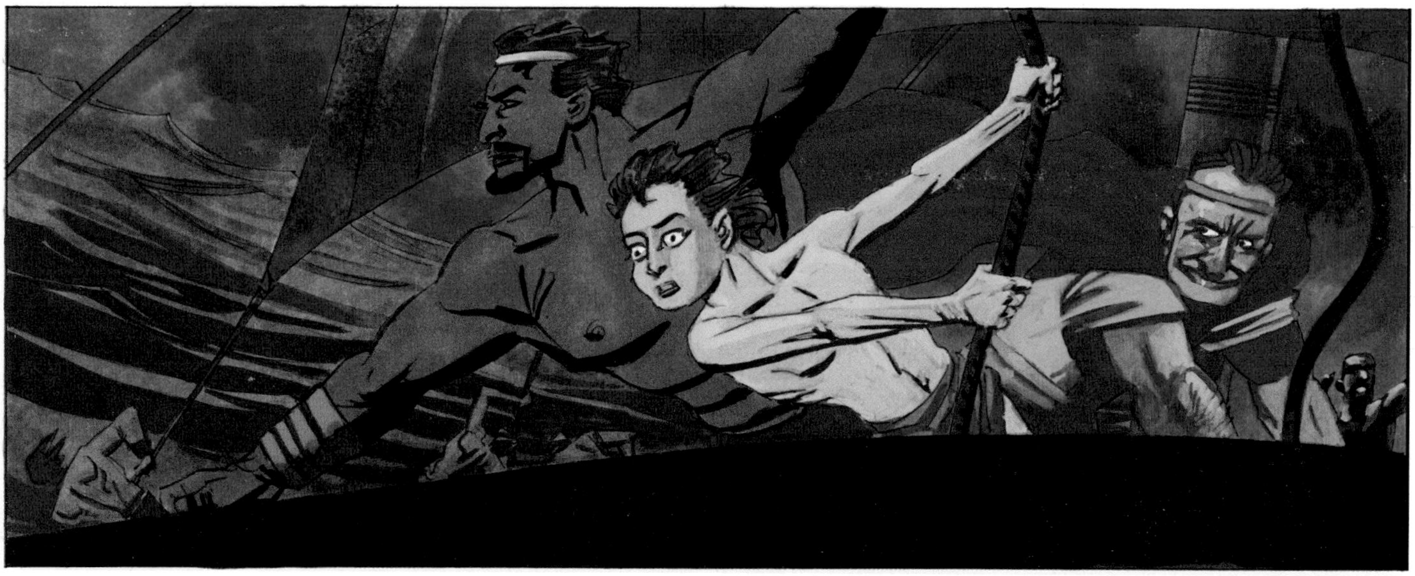

7. What a life I led amongst those rogues, tossed on the heaving breast of the Mediterranean. What things I learned of sails and knots, of how to curse and drink, and many other things besides. Being a girlish boy, as I had been a boyish girl, I learned, a little, how to fight and how to love, both in a rough way. My companions thought I'd fetch a pretty sum.

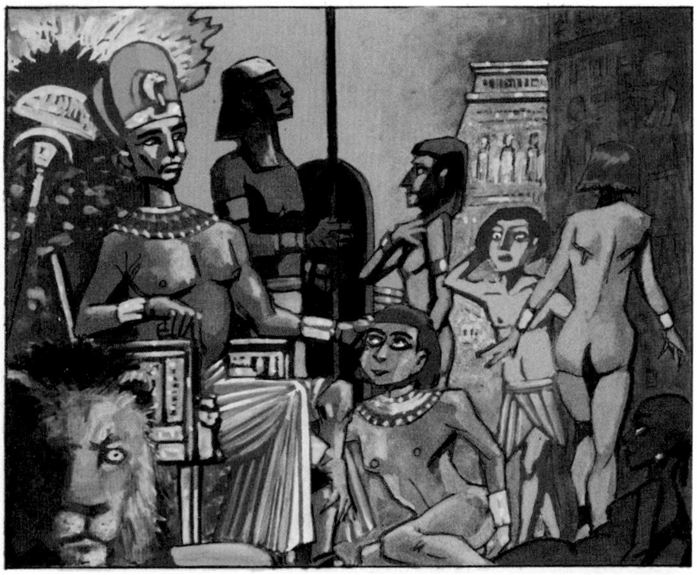

8. And so I did. This was 1250 BC by the current reckoning. Since androgyny was fashionable with Egypt's ruling class, I fast became a favourite of the Pharaoh Usermattra, called by some Ozymandias.

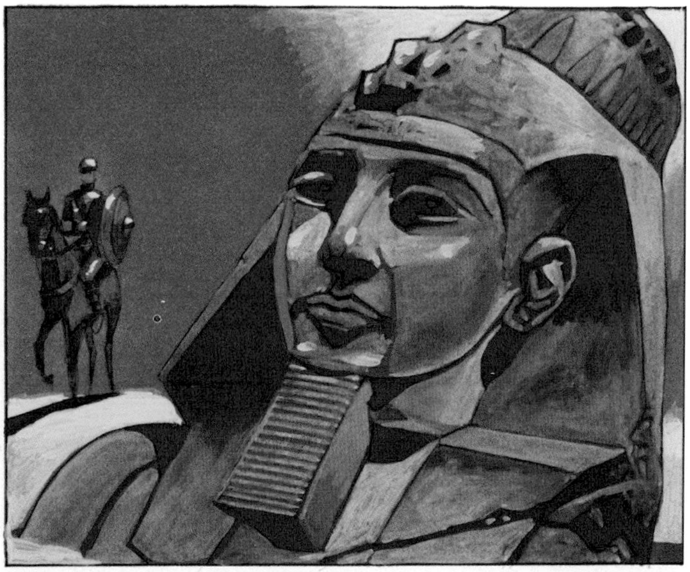

9. He was a vain, pretentious man. Some centuries thereafter, passing through that place, I saw the great stone head men speak of. It looked nothing like him, having neither his weak chin, nor chubby jowls.

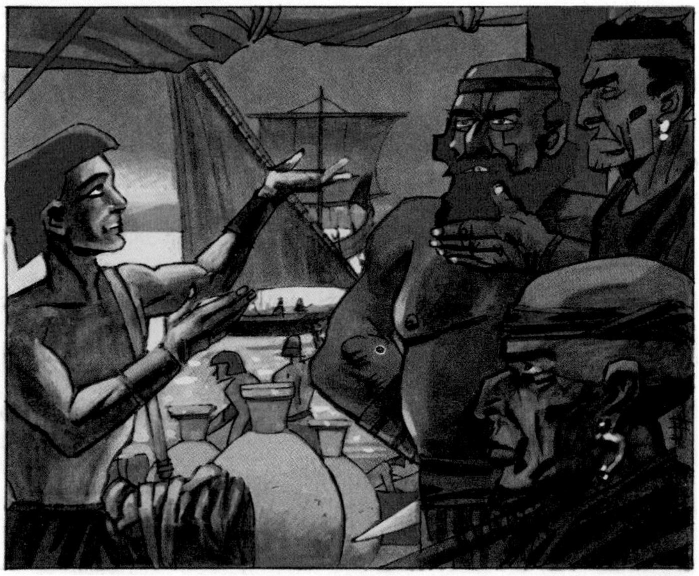

10. Eventually, aged just nineteen and older than the Pharaoh liked his boys, I sought out new employment, drawing on my time amongst the pirates to enlist upon on expedition setting sail for Punt, in Africa.

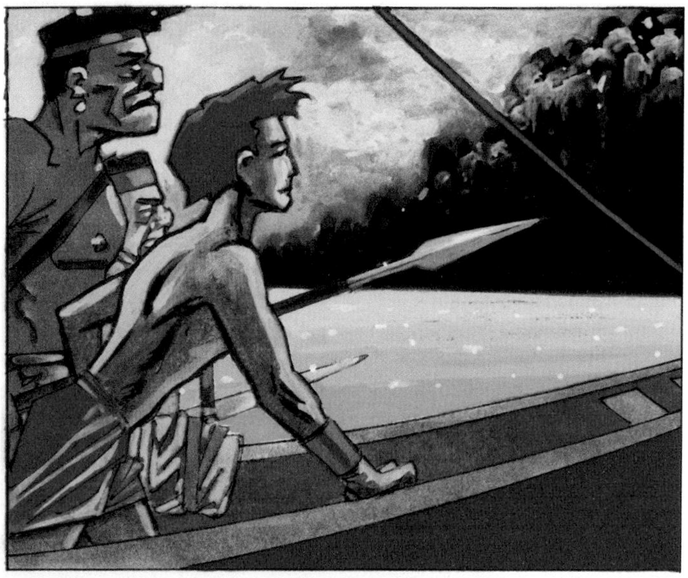

11. Without a seafaring tradition of its own, Egypt depended upon foreign sailors for its expeditions, with whom I found easy berth...and soon, around the Horn of Africa, found much, much more.

— Continues next week —

The Life of ORLANDO

Chapter Two: I Become Immortal

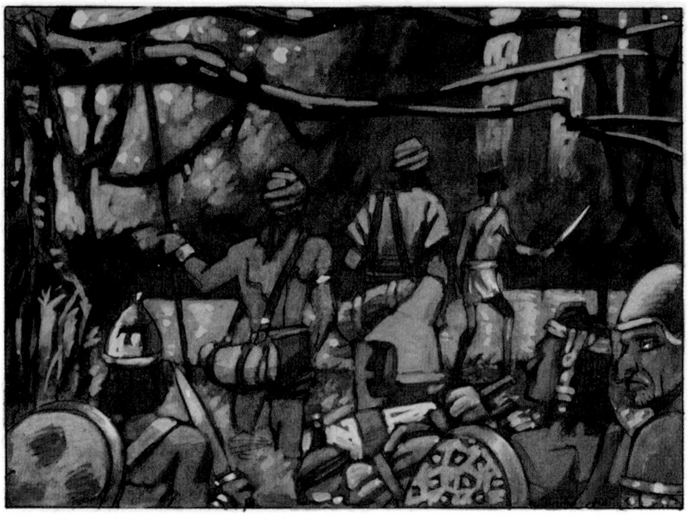

1. Born a girl to gender-changed Tiresias of Thebes, become a boy aged ten and sold in slavery to Egypt, in 1240 BC I embarked for Punt in Africa, by now a strong young man.

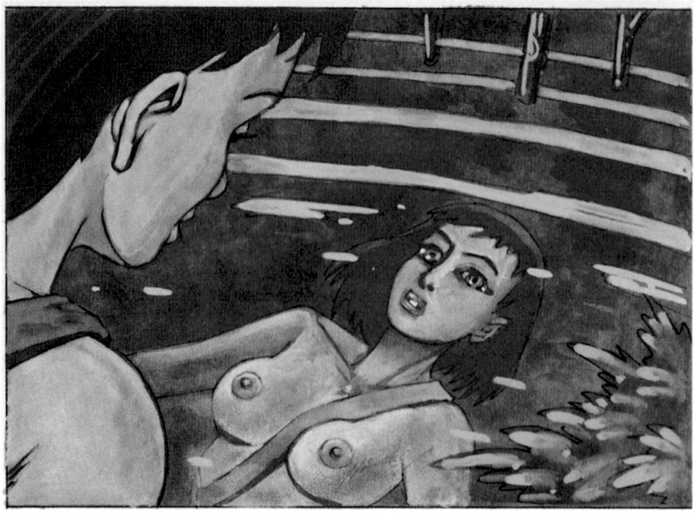

2. We'd barely landed when this changed and I found myself female once again, nor was I some androgynous young child. Feeling unsafe amongst my lusty former crewmates I escaped into the jungle, almost without incident.

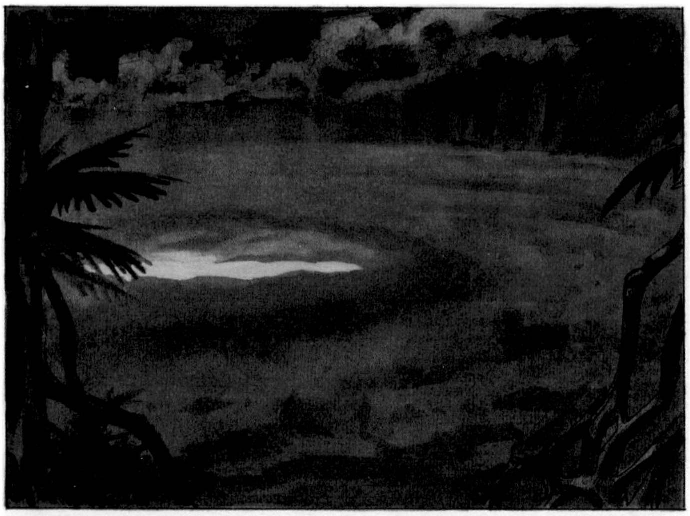

3. For weeks I wandered aimless, living off the forest, stumbling at last upon the ancient land of Kor, in what is now Uganda. There, within a great, sky-blasted crater, I discovered a peculiar pool.

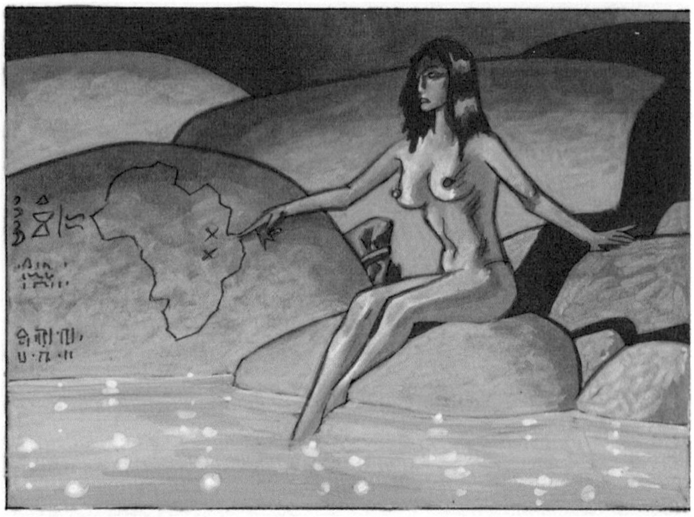

4. Bathing in its lapid, liquid flames, emerging strangely vitalised, I noticed old names and a map carved at its edge. (I did not carve my name there 'til millennia later, during the upstart Ayesha's rule.)

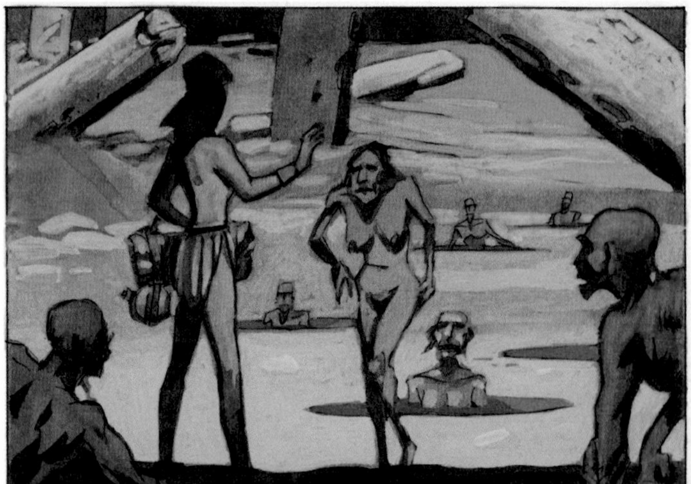

5. The map led me to Abyssinia, and a community of others who had bathed within the pool, who told me I was now immortal, as were they. Some, the oldest, had a sullen, troglodyte demeanor.

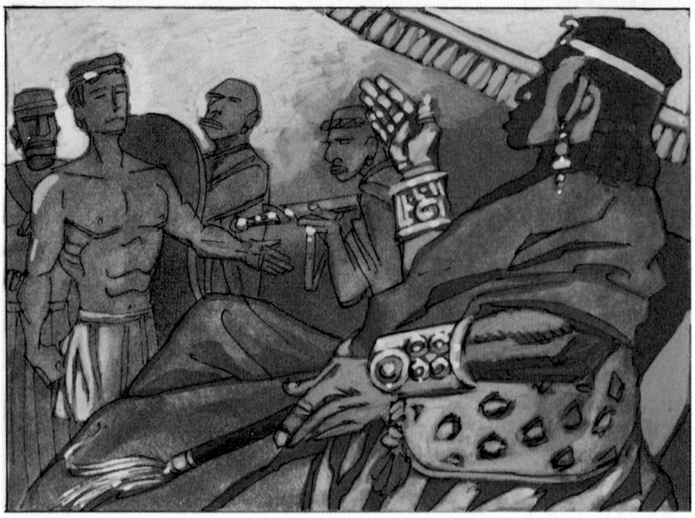

6. Spending decades amongst them, I finally detected this stagnation in myself, and moved on. I'd been Mistress Bio all this time, but it was Master Bion that the Abyssinian chieftain Memnon sent to defend Ilium.

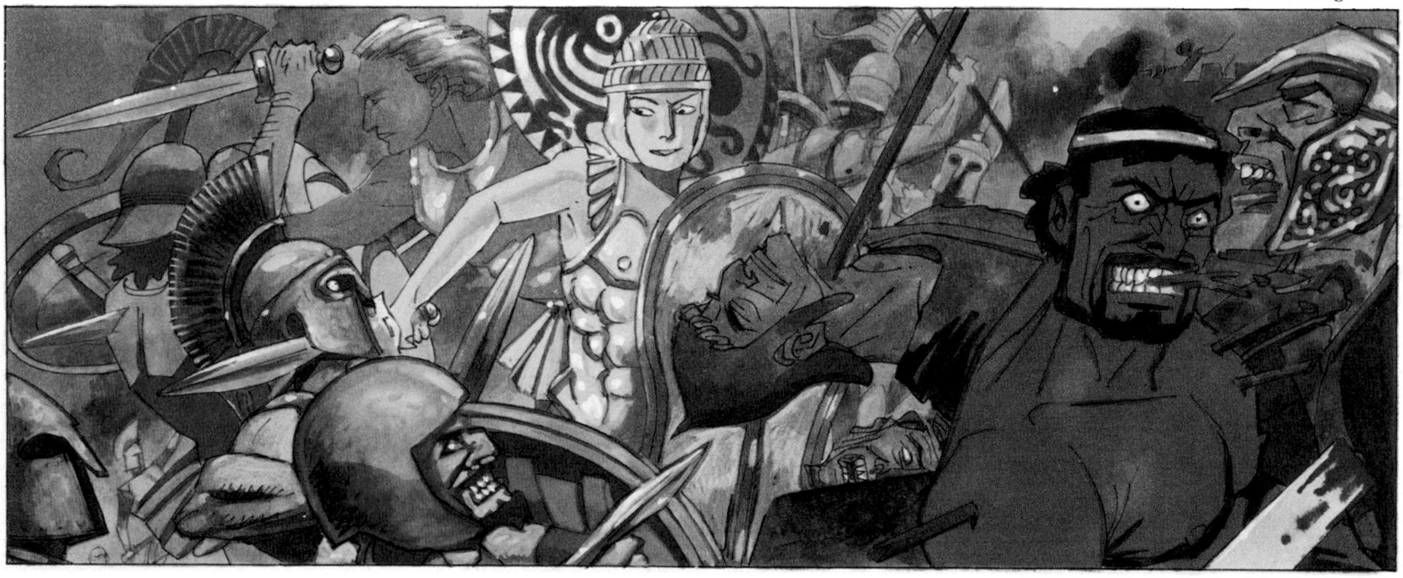

7. In Ilium, as Troy was then called, in 1184 BC, I first knew war, a conflict instigated by the gods to cull their hybrid by-blows, the increasingly alarming, often psychologically unstable race of heroes. Those I met were pitiable, or else hateful: Ajax a confused brute; Achilles a smug, invulnerable maniac; Odysseus a shifty little swine. Even Aeneas, son of Aphrodite and Anchises, whom I escaped Troy with, wasn't perfect.

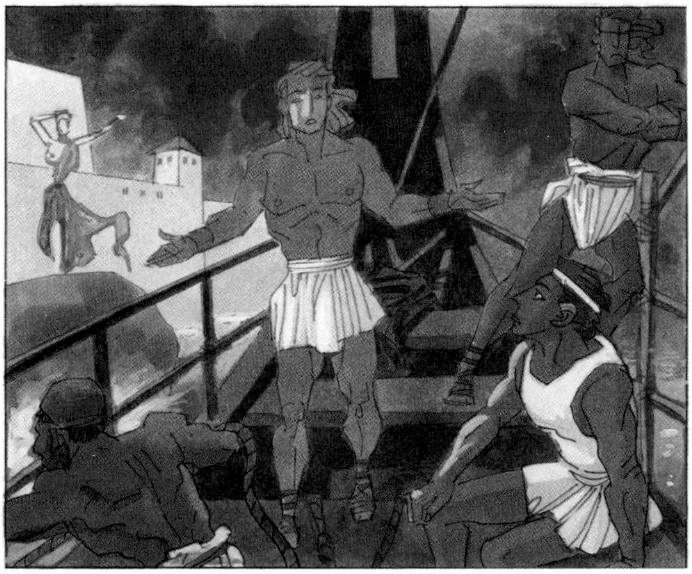

8. Oh, I loved him well enough. Everyone did. Son of the Love Goddess, Aeneas was irresistible, breaking hearts everywhere, like poor Queen Dido's when, headed for Italy after Troy's downfall, we put briefly into Carthage.

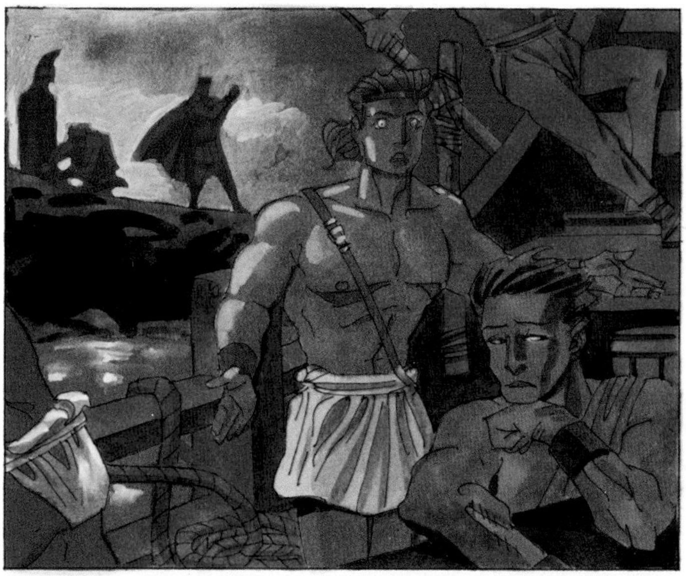

9. Tragedy haunted Aeneas's family. Living with them in Italy for eighty years as loyal, ageless Bion, I finally saw Aeneas's great-grandson Brutus banished for accidentally killing his father, and elected to travel with him.

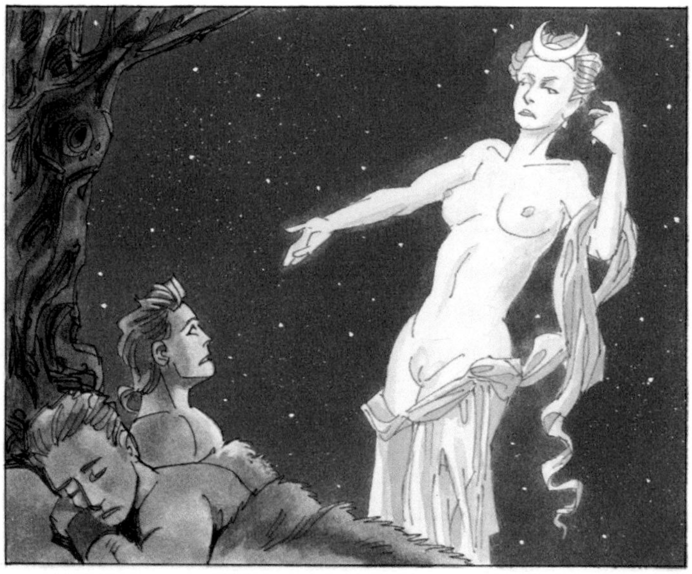

10. In 1101 BC, anchored near Leogetia, Brutus went ashore alone save for myself. At a shrine of Diana, he dreamed the Goddess told him of a northern isle where he would found a mighty nation.

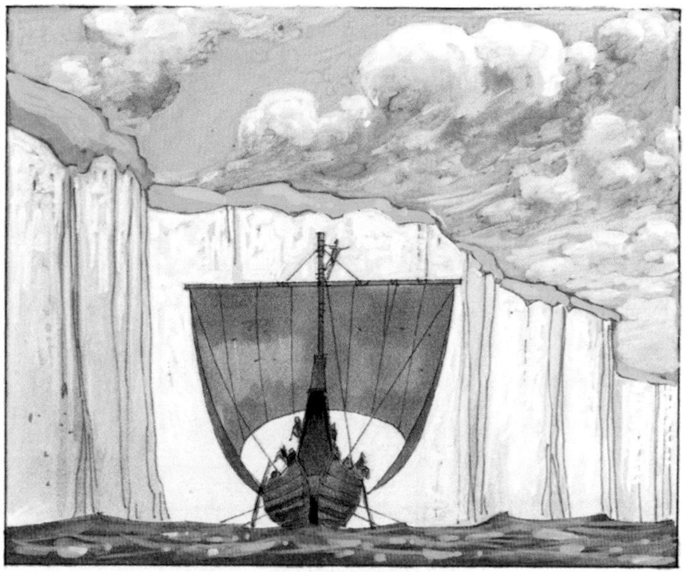

11. So it was, some months thereafter, that we reached the place of which the Moon Goddess had spoken. Seeing its white cliffs loom majestically ahead, I knew I'd found another home.

— Continues next week —

TRUMP 5 September 1953

The Life of ORLANDO

Chapter Three: I Discover Britain

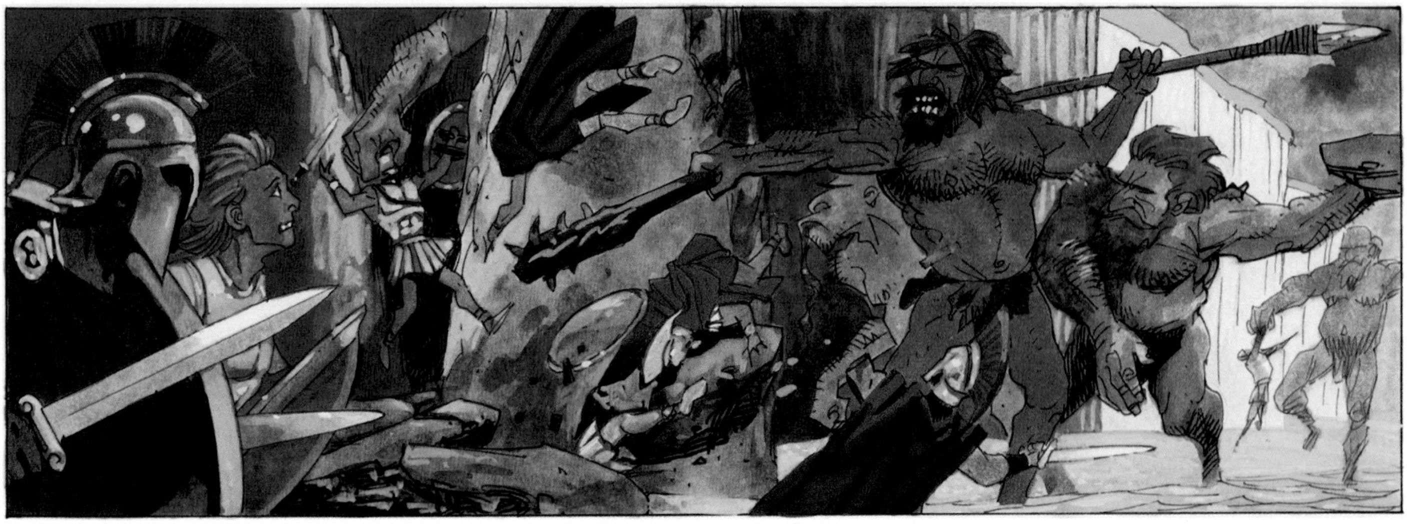

1. Born female in 1260 BC with my sire Tiresias's tendency for changing gender, I had emerged immortal from an African pool, and fought at Troy as Bion, comrade of Aeneas. Now it was 1100 BC, and, with Aeneas's great-grandson, young Brutus, I'd reached the northern island where a vision had told Brutus he would found a mighty nation. Disappointingly, it was already populated by a grotesque race of giants.

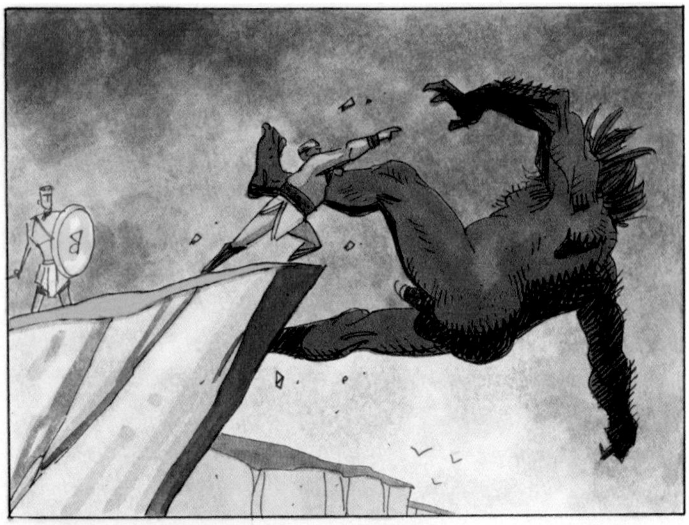

2. These were subdued when Brutus's best wrestler threw their chieftain (a monstrosity called Gogmagog, or possibly Gogmageot) over a cliff. Within ten years we'd almost wiped out the entire giant race upon that rain-swept isle.

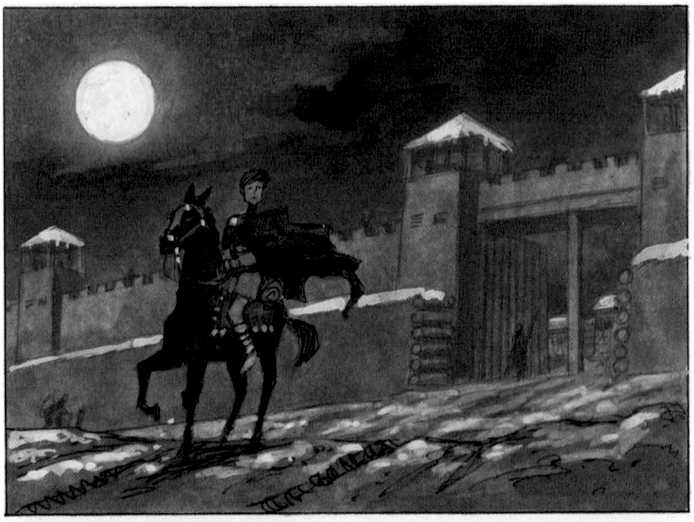

3. Obviously, some survived, vengefully plaguing Brutain (as Brutus named the land) for centuries. By then, though, once more female and weary of Brutain's capital New Troy (or Troy-Novantum), I'd moved on for pastures greener.

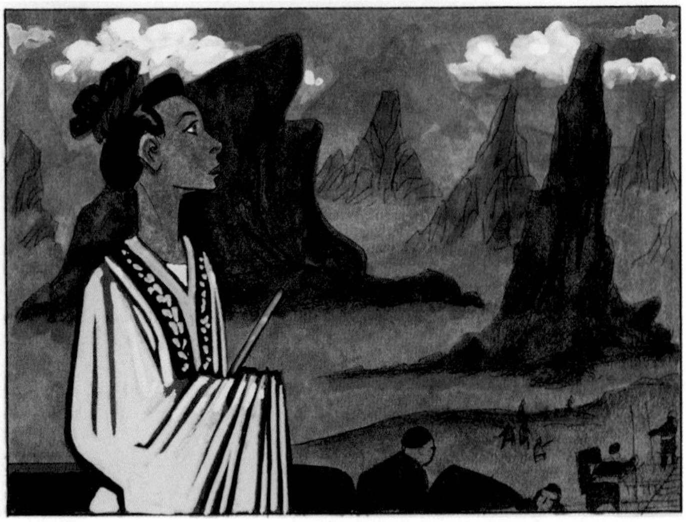

4. Named Bio again, I worked my passage East by means of prostitution and small fraud, settling here and there along the way. In 960 BC, aged 300, I reached Cathay, now called China.

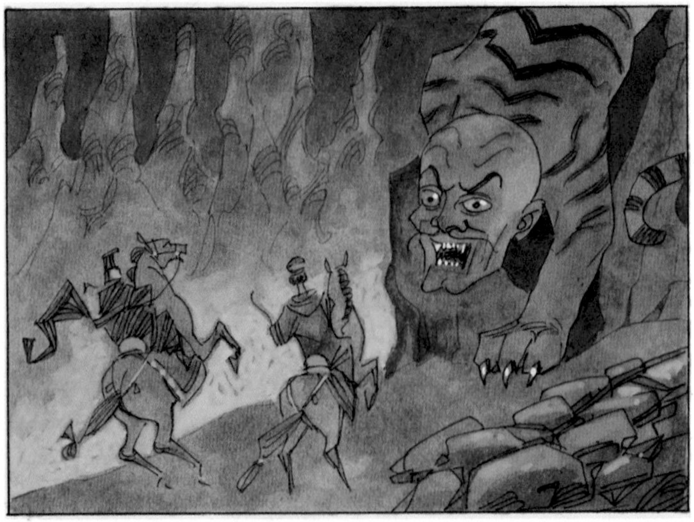

5. As a handmaiden of the great King Mu, I travelled with him unto Mount K'un Lun, where lived the goddess Hsi Wang Mu, her mountain palace guarded by a human-headed tiger named Lu Wo.

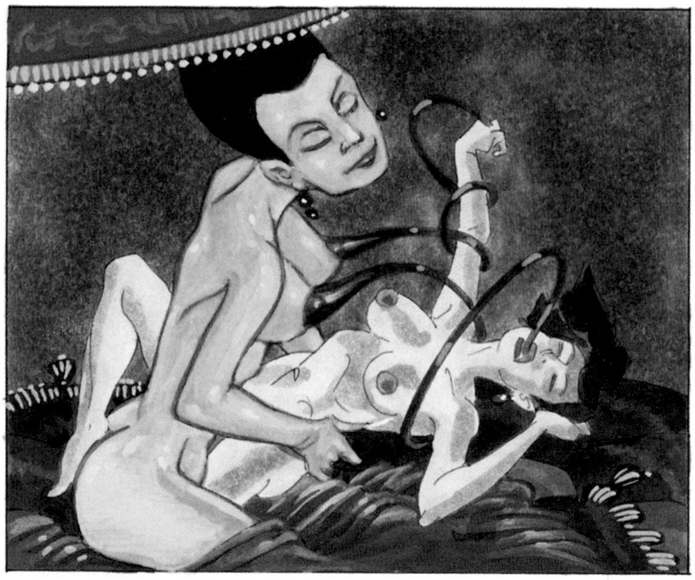

6. After the King departed I remained, becoming lover to the Royal Mother of the West, as the goddess was known. She'd gained immortality by copulating three thousand men to death, and our passions were furious.

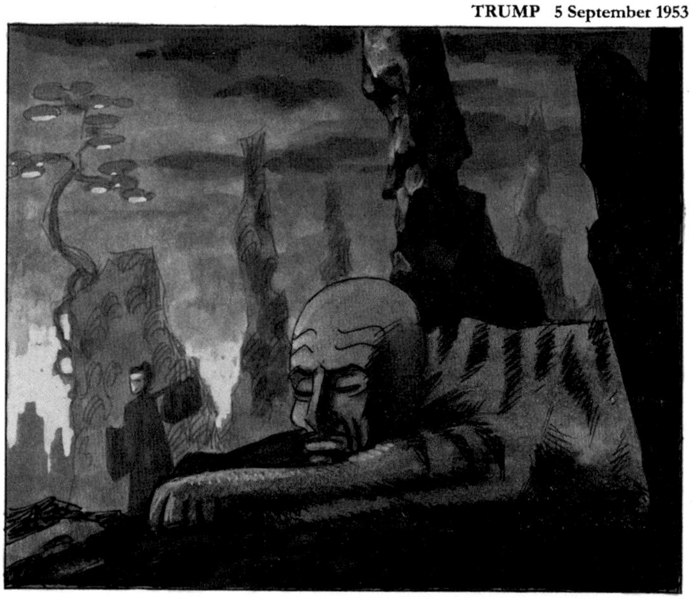

7. Gods are exhausting, even to immortals, and finally I left, travelling back to Italy under my new, Latinate name, Vita, which also means 'life.' Unbelievably, I'd tarried there two centuries, time passing differently amongst deities.

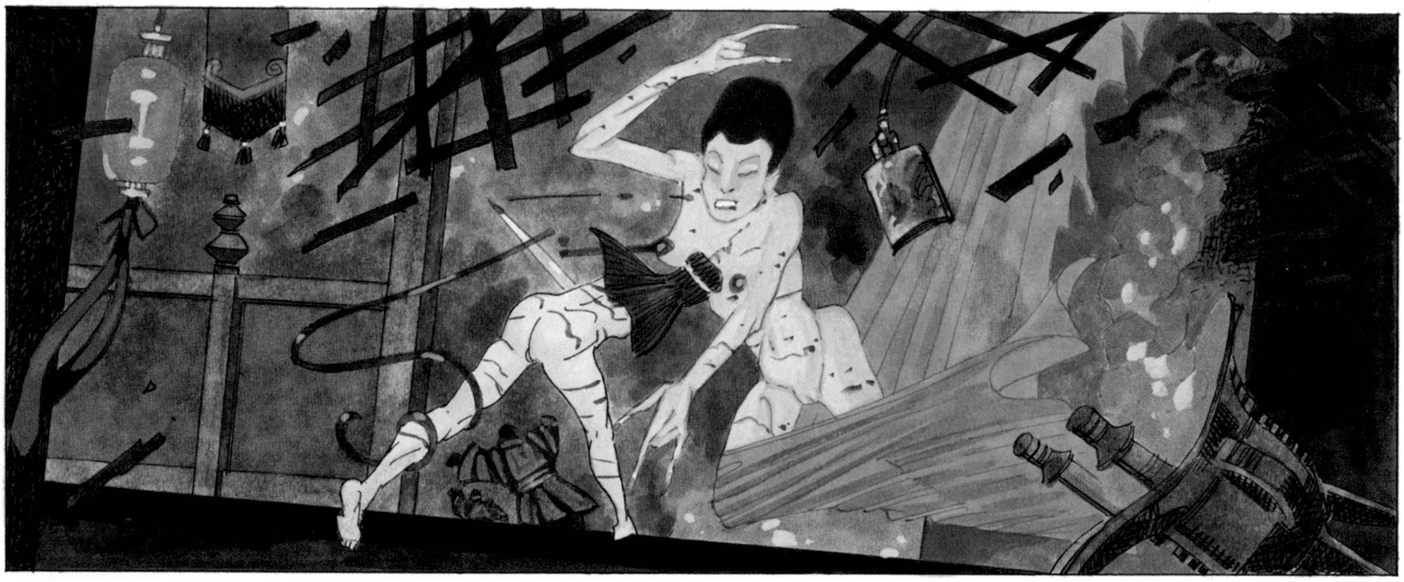

8. Two millennia later, I heard that the ruthless Ugandan immortal Ayesha, finding herself incarnated in China and lacking a power-base, had somehow contrived to both kill and replace Hsi Wang Mu, ruling there on K'un Lun, now called Hes or Fire Mountain, in my lover's stead. Though I confess the fact with shame, that is one fight I should have liked to witness. However, returning to my own tale…

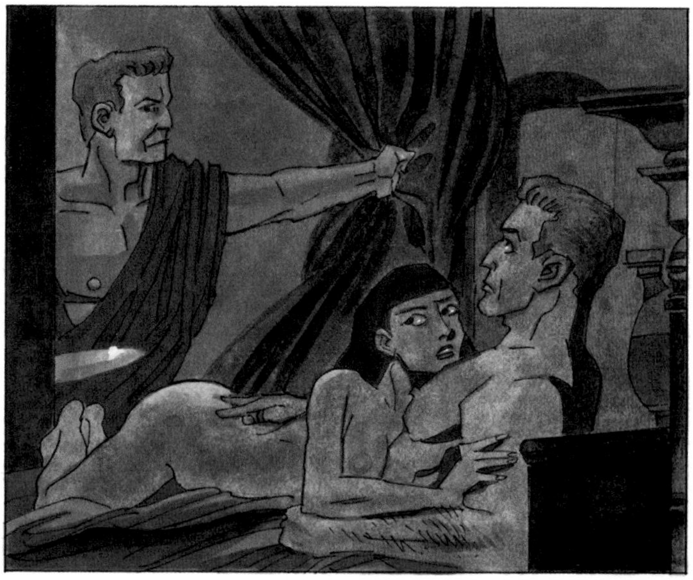

9. Returned to Italy in 774 BC, I found the new-built city Rome, and met its founders, wolf-reared Romulus and Remus. Identical twins, I slept with both accidentally, prompting Romulus to murder his brother.

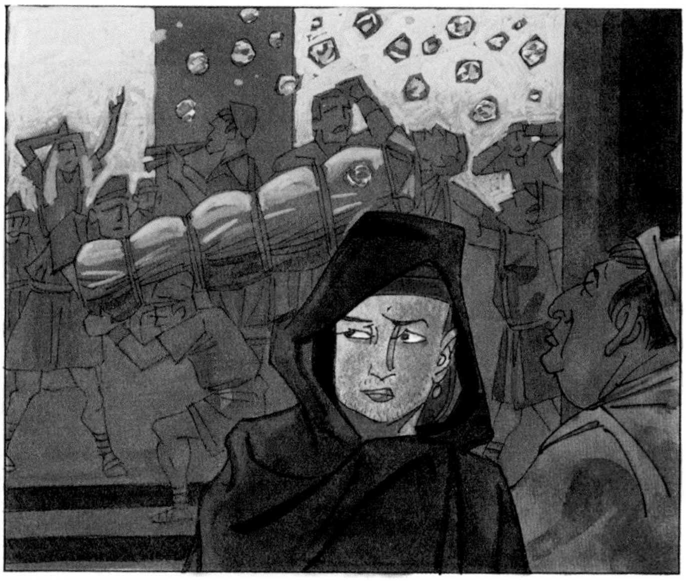

10. Luckily, this tragedy coincided with fresh stirrings down below. Vita became Vito, escaping Rome unnoticed. Decades later, the scandal forgotten, I joined Queen Semuramis's Indian expedition, seeking Eastern tranquility. *Continues next week*

The Life of ORLANDO

Chapter Four: I Conquer The World

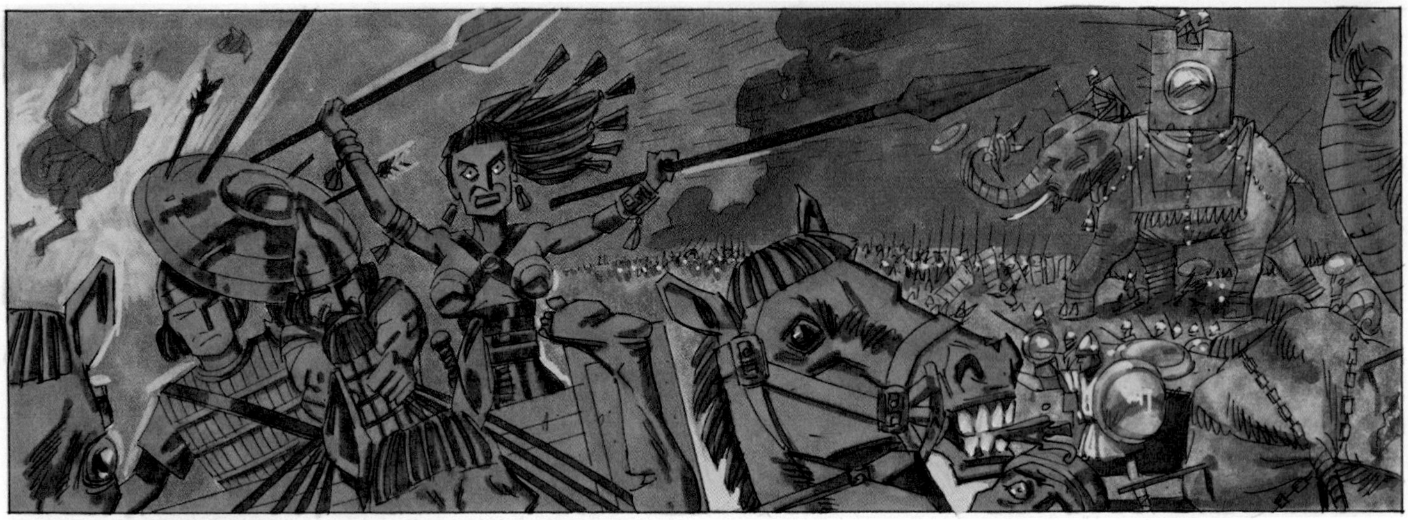

1. Made dual-gendered and immortal by astounding quirks of fate, I was 560 years old when, in 700 BC, I enlisted in the army of Babylon's Queen and founder Semuramis, then engaged in conquering India. As manly Vito, veteran of Troy, I routed enemy war elephants, becoming the Queen's foremost military advisor, though never her bedfellow since she tended to execute these the following morning. Presumably, I served her better alive.

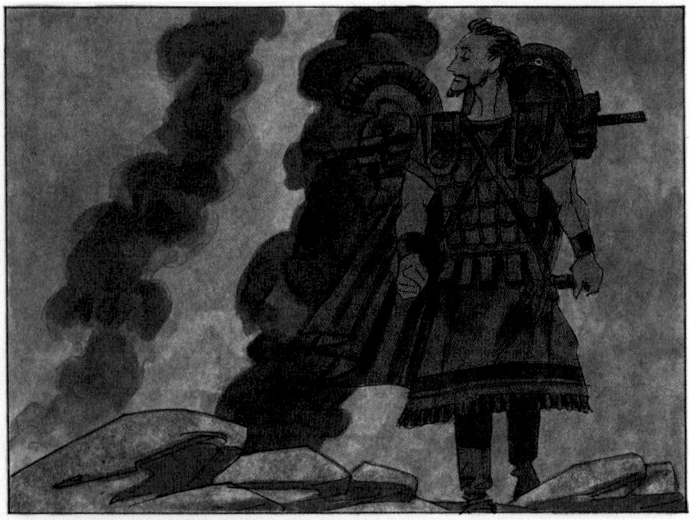

2. Decades later, Semuramis seduced her own son and successor, allegedly becoming divine upon her death. After that I moved on, fighting for Persia against Greece at Marathon in 490 BC, afterwards wandering the region.

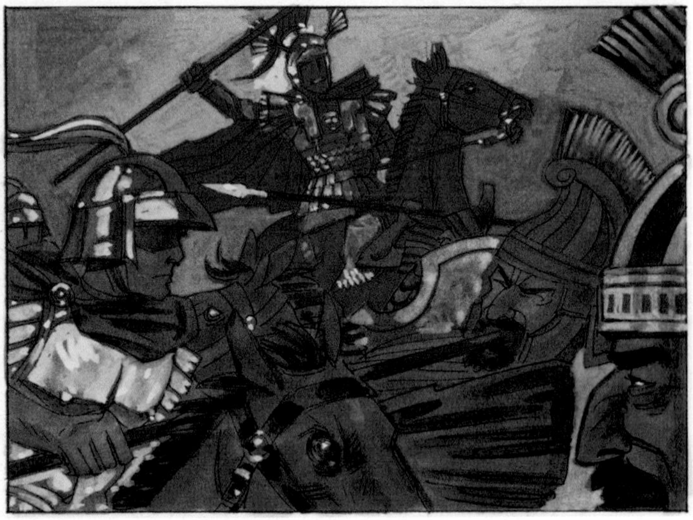

3. Thus it was in Macedonia around 334 BC I met with an ambitious, somewhat mad young stable-hand named Alex, whom, across the next decade or so, I helped to subjugate most of the world.

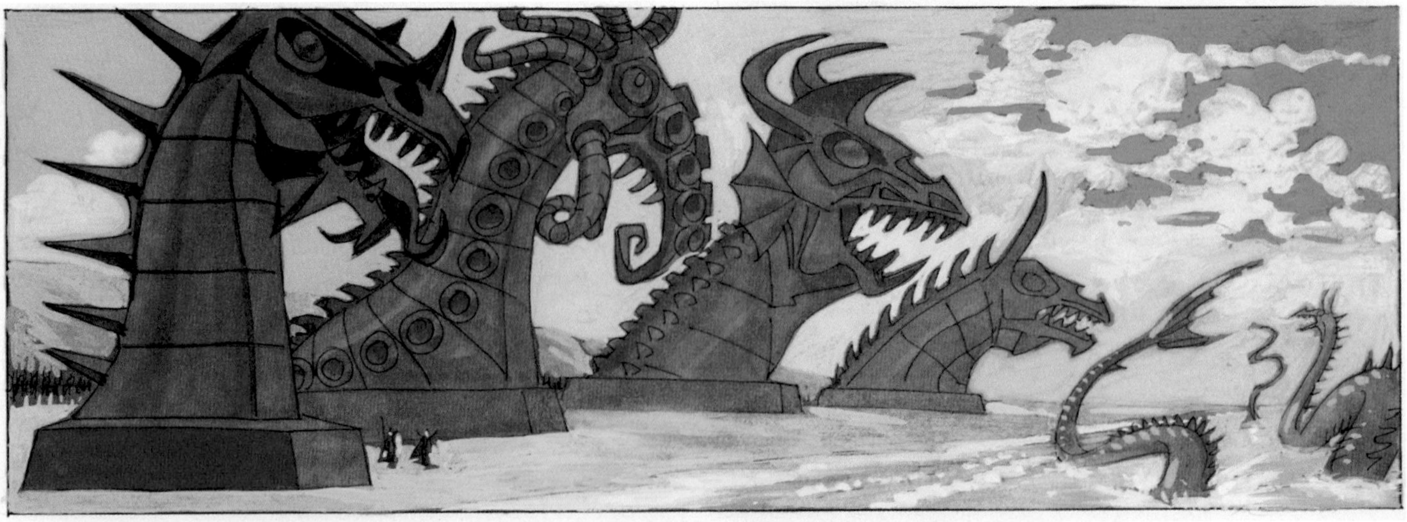

4. At sea-monster-plagued Alexandria in the 320s, I suggested Alexander build a bathysphere so that the creatures might be scrutinized and sketched, allowing the construction of great metal likenesses along the Alexandrian shoreline. These giant effigies scared off the monsters most effectively, whereupon Alexander claimed all credit for the scheme. The iron leviathans, much weathered, still endure today as a beachfront amusement area for tourists and their children.

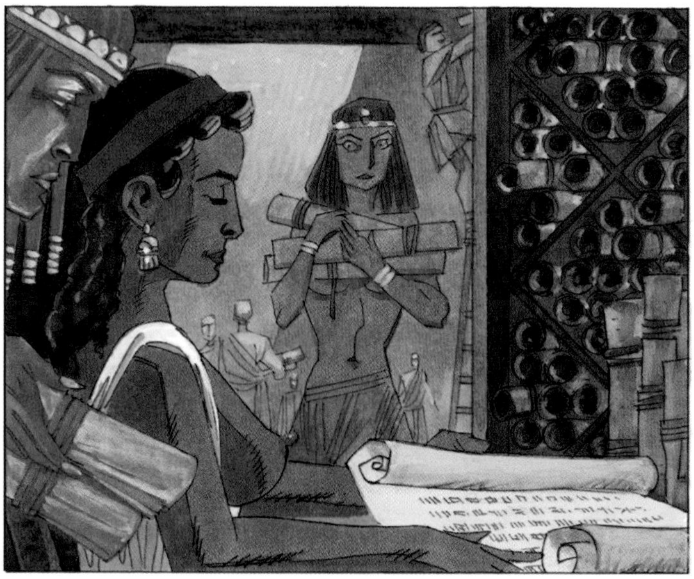

5. Shortly after Alexander's death I became Vita again, spending the next two hundred and fifty years reading my way through the great library at Alexandria, with Ptolemaic Egypt's fabulous although incestuous culture spread around me.

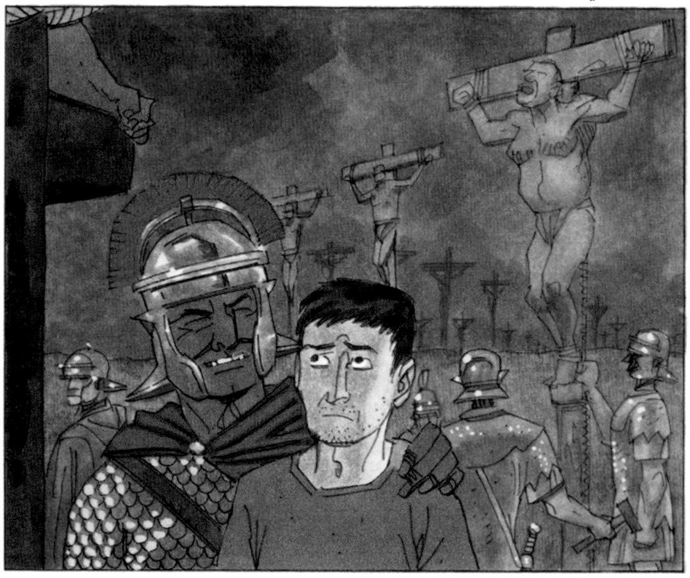

6. Male once more, I returned to Rome in 70 BC, my fling with its founders now forgotten. Embroiled in slave revolts, I escaped punishment by simply declaring "I'm Vito," everyone else apparently being named "Spartacus."

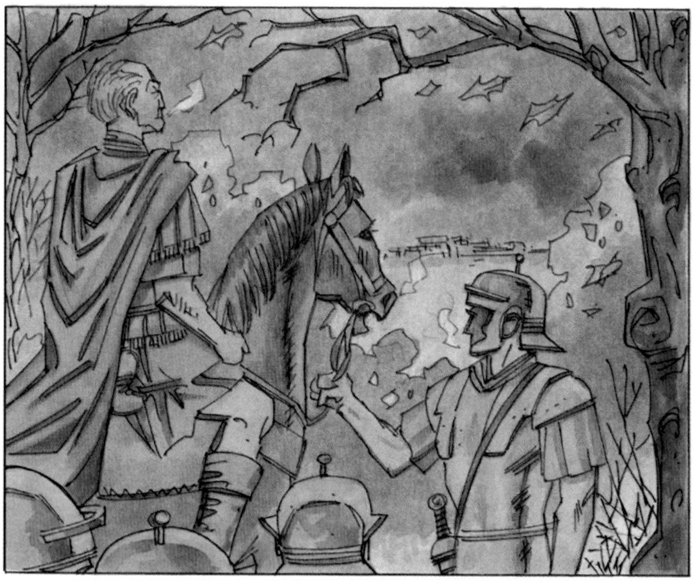

7. Finding myself in the Roman Army, I accompanied Julius Caesar during 55 BC when he invaded Britain, as Brutain had become. Troy-Novantum was now squalid tribal hovels, whose barbaric inhabitants successfully resisted our incursion.

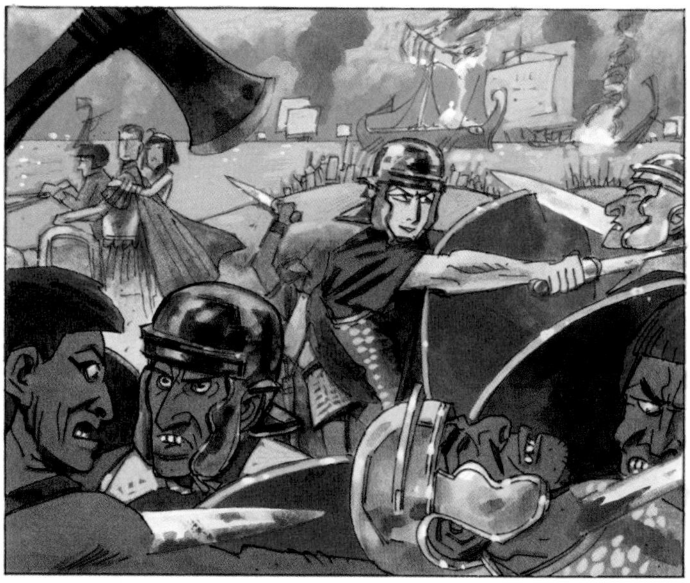

8. Eleven years thereafter back in Rome, Caesar having been assassinated, I became a soldier of Marc Antony during his affair with radiant (albeit pungent) Cleopatra and the pair's disastrous battle with Augustus, at Actium.

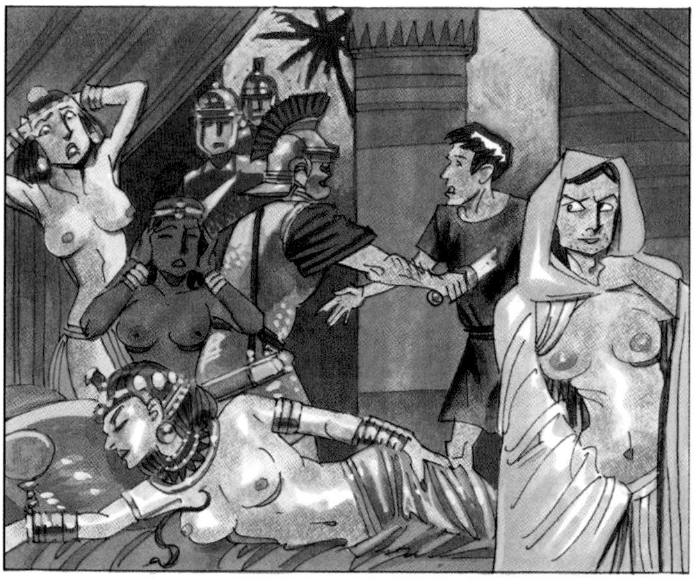

9. Following Actium, I retreated into Egypt with the defeated lovers, Augustus's men in hot pursuit. Antony and Cleopatra killed themselves, their soldiers massacred when the pursuing troops arrived. Fortunately, having become female, I was spared.

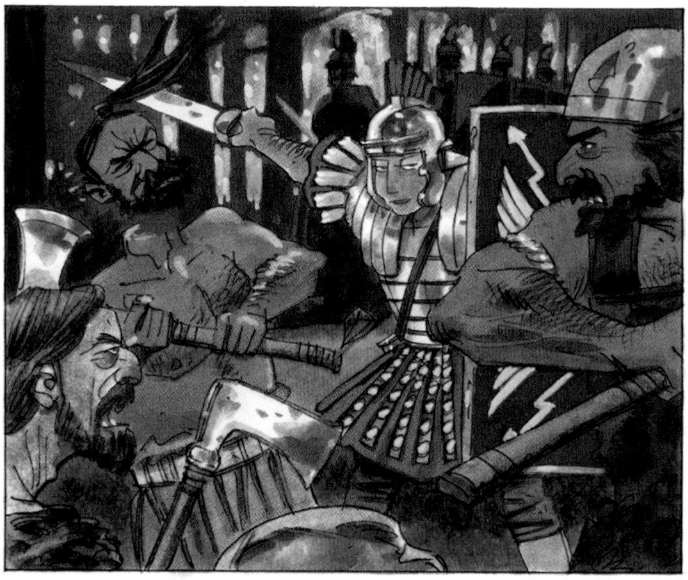

10. That was 30 BC. Female for barely three decades, by 1 AD, as Vito, I fought Teutons on the Empire's northern frontiers. Regrettably, in 1200 years, I'd become very good at war.

Continues next week

The Life of ORLANDO

Chapter Five: I Outlive Mighty Empires

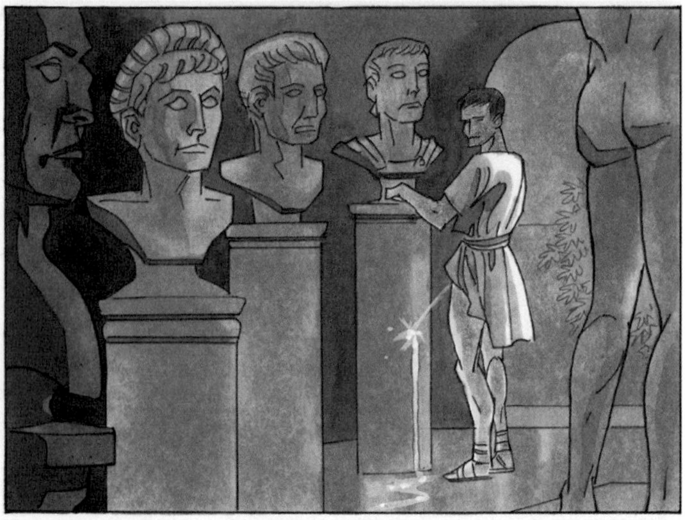

1. Immortal and transsexual, twelve hundred years old by the first century AD, I'd seen Rome's emperors come and go. In 30 AD, slimy, child-molesting Tiberius was succeeded by the ruthless (although undeniably sane) Caligula.

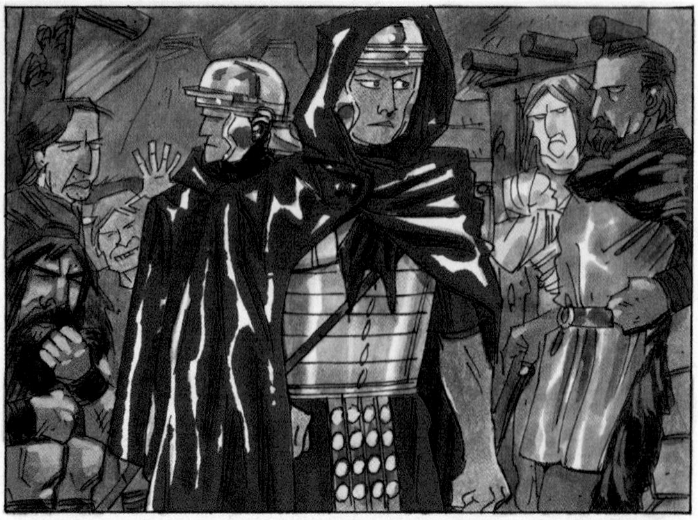

2. Stuttering, skulking Claudius followed, who in 43 AD once more invaded Britain, this time successfully. Serving under him as Vito, I found Britain a depressing place, transferring to Naples with Nero's succession.

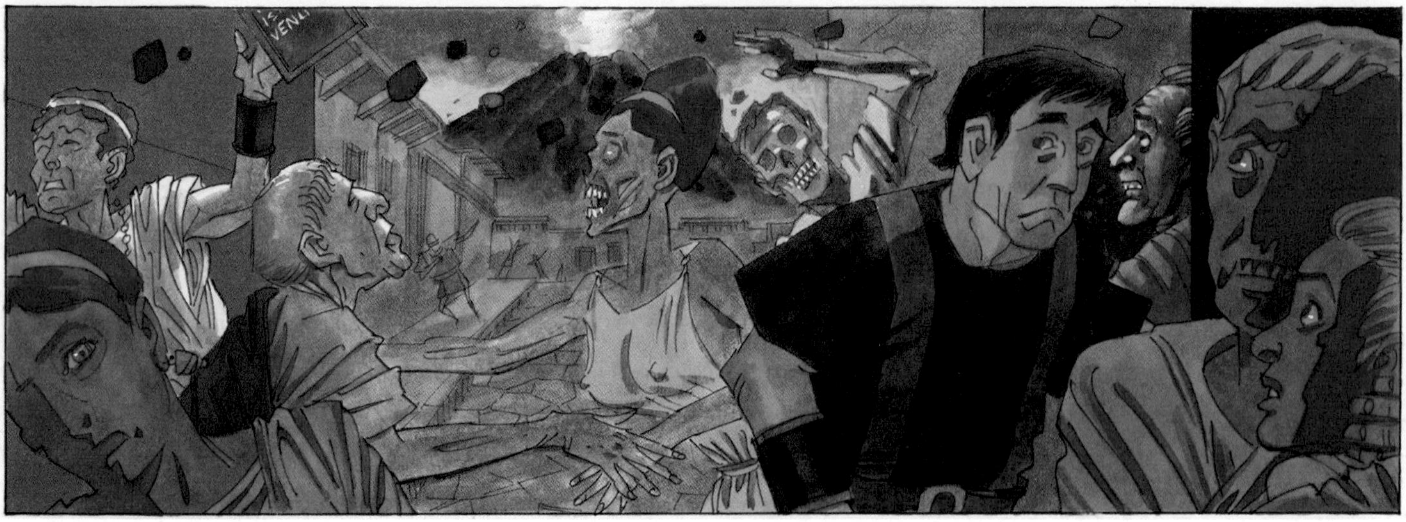

3. In 79 AD I sailed from Naples with the famed scribe Pliny's expedition to Pompeii, its citizens recently killed by an eruption of volcanic gas. Fearing further outbursts, I stayed aboard ship, thus narrowly escaping Pliny's fate. Shaken, I relocated to volcano-free lands near the Black Sea where, in 100 AD, I became apprentice to great Appolonius of Tyana, and then to the charlatan snake-cultist, Alexander of Abonoteichus.

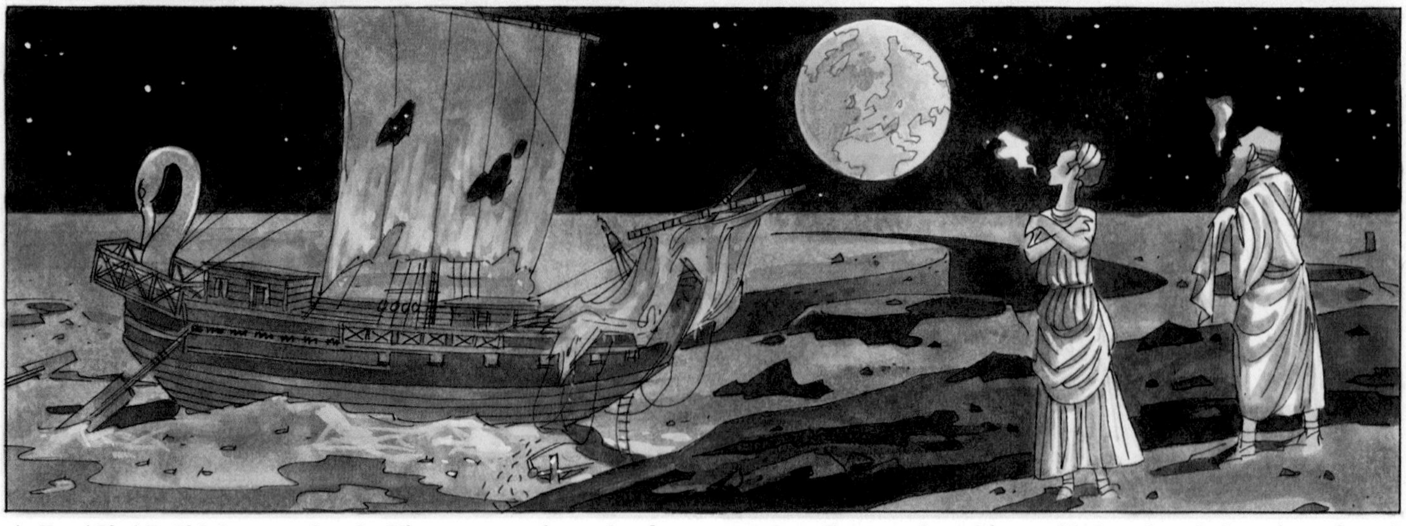

4. By 150 AD I'd become lovely Vita once again and, after Alexander made certain advances, had defected to his rival and stern critic, the sage Lucian, with whom I journeyed accidentally to the Moon, our ship transported by a monstrous waterspout. Returned to this world, I endured the reign of mad Heliogabalus around 200 AD, and by 363 was greatly cheered when Emperor Julian officially declared Britain a pagan nation.

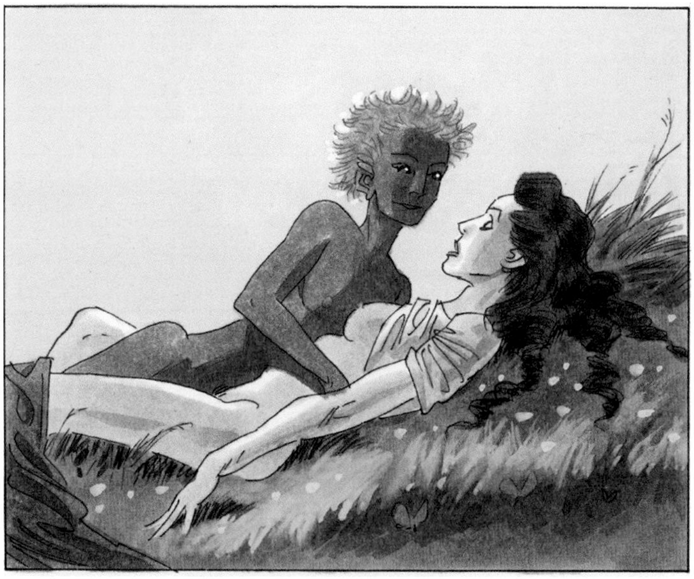

5. Returning there, enjoying the new myth-soaked atmosphere, in 376 AD I was seduced, embarrassingly, by a most charismatic thirteen-year-old boy. Irresistibly persuasive, allegedly son to the Devil, his name was Ambrosius Merlinus.

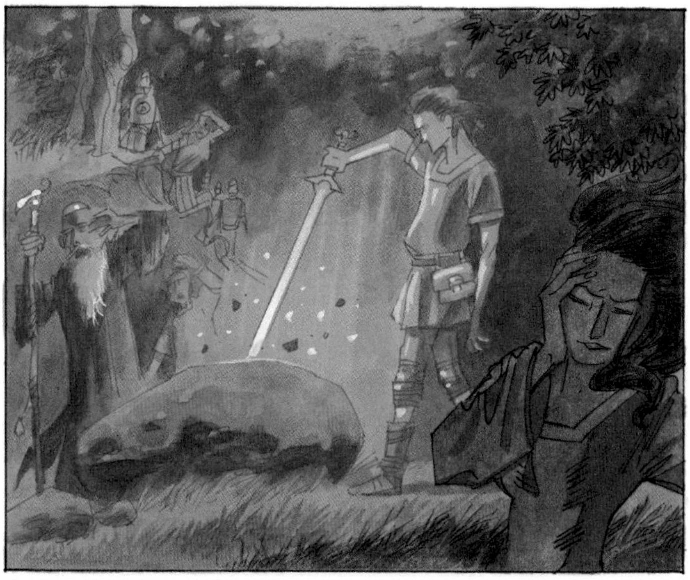

6. In 410 Rome withdrew, empire collapsing, while Ambrosius and I watched noble Uther's Cornish kingdom take its place. Forty years later, with Merlinus in his eighties, certain marvellous events established a new monarch named Arturus.

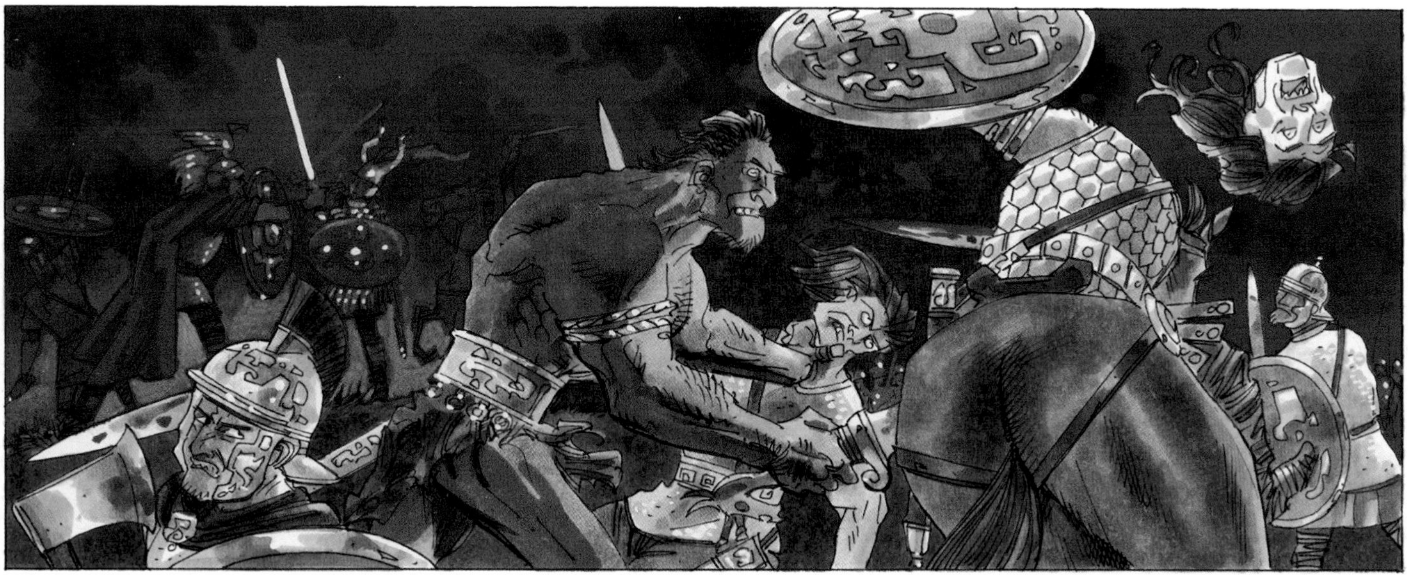

7. Ah, Arthurian Britain, quite as wonderful as is supposed, and yet within two decades foundered dismally, with Merlin entombed by a sorceress, Arturus slain in battle with his wronged child Mordred on Salisbury Plain. I knew them all: knew sweet Guenevere; half-witted Percival; knew awesome, monstrously ugly Lancelot. Male once again, as Vito, I fought alongside them in that final battle (from which, incidentally, I salvaged Arthur's sword).

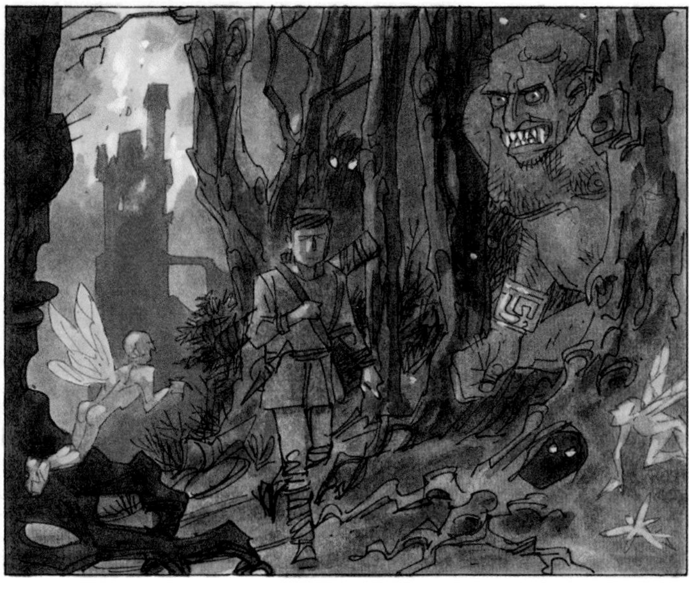

8. That was 468 AD. Re-christening the blade 'Durendal' to disguise its misappropriation, I abandoned Britain to barbarism, plagued by ogres, giants, and fairies governed by Arthur's half-sister, dread Morgana. A dark aeon had begun.

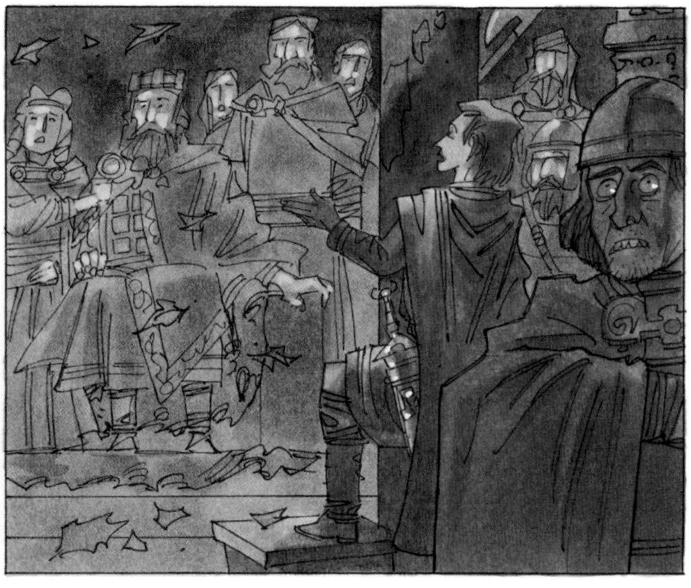

9. Twenty years' wandering brought me to Denmark, where as sword-for-hire I took employment with King Hrothgar of Hierot, seemingly troubled by a monster, which I assured him I could handle. ***Continues next week***

The Life of ORLANDO

Chapter Six: I Battle Across The Centuries

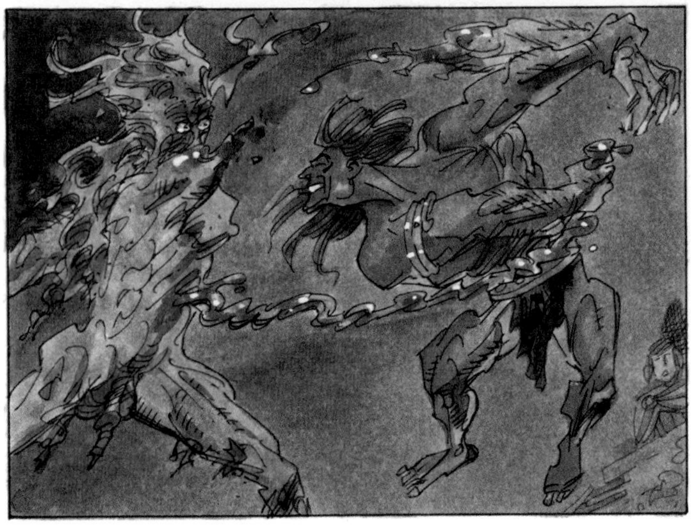

1. Over 1700 years old and temporarily male, 490 AD found me at Hrothgar's court in Denmark, where I encountered Grendel, a rampaging monster, and thereafter Beowulf. I'm still not entirely sure what Beowulf was, exactly.

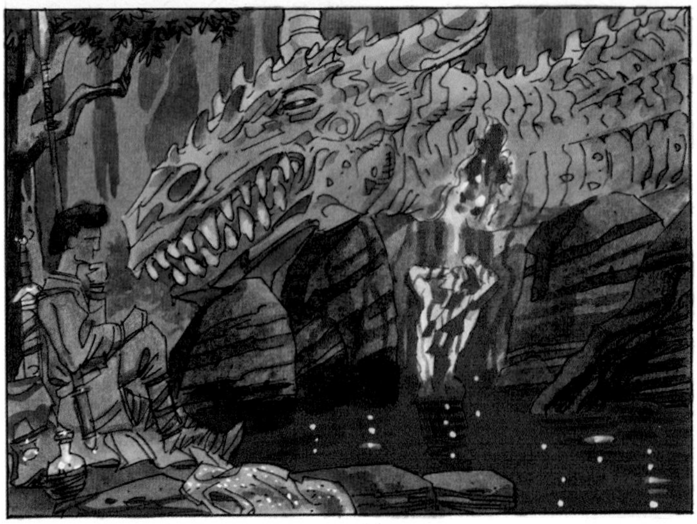

2. A decade later, in 500 AD, I accompanied the hero Siegfried, who, except for being suicidally brave, had no other personality traits whatsoever. It was through him, however, that I first glimpsed higher, ethereal realms.

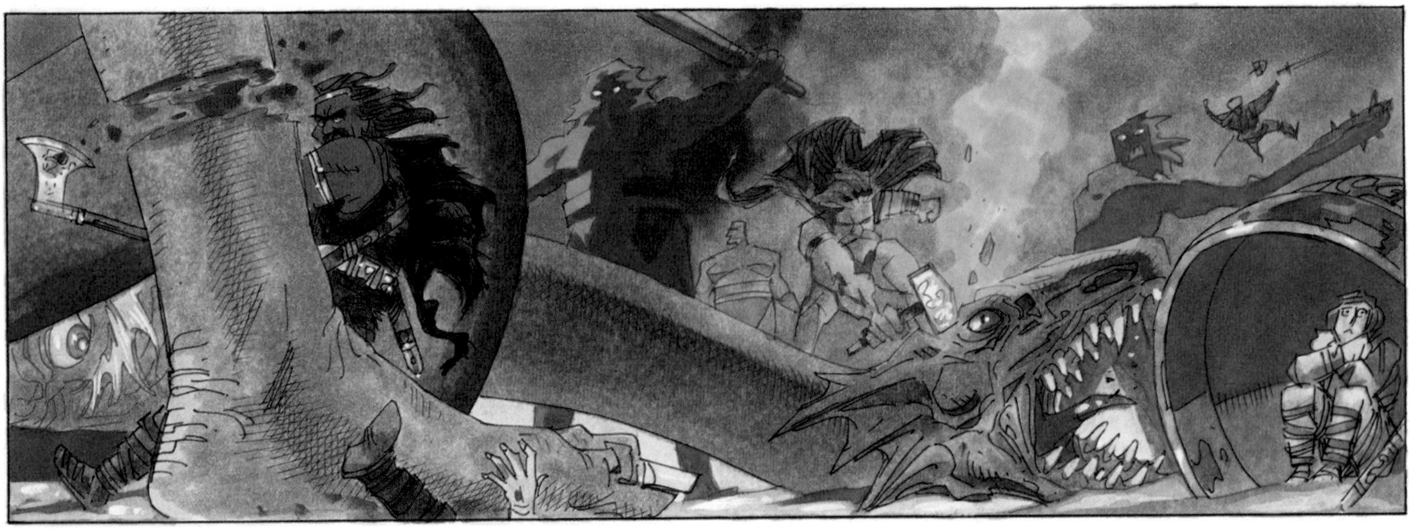

3. These territories, that modern science might term other dimensions bordering ours, whilst strictly speaking outside Time, nevertheless have histories and conflicts as tumultuous as those of this material world. In the terrestrial year 568 AD, for instance, I beheld the end of the Teutonic gods at Ragnarok, a cataclysm mirrored in the Earthly realm by a collision with a weighty meteoric rock, its dust veiling the heavens for three years.

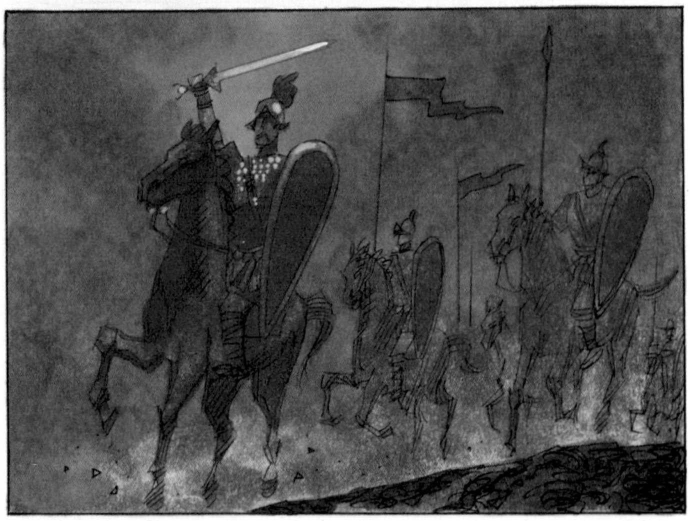

4. During this endless Fimbul-Winter, when it seemed the moon had been devoured, I made for France, where in 764 AD I joined the knights of Charlemagne under the more contemporary-sounding name of Roland.

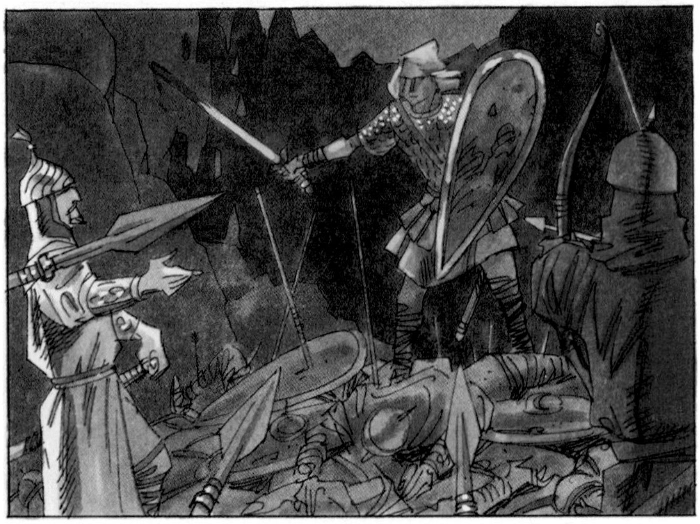

5. In 778, beset by Saracens while in the Pyrenees, veteran of Troy and Marathon, my sword Durendal flashing, I fought on when all save I were slain. Impressed, my foes eventually bade me join them.

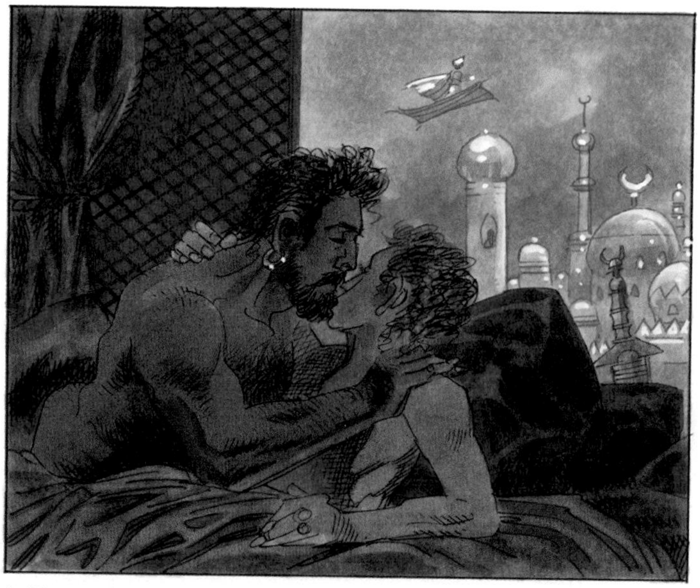

6. Now a Saracen, with Roland mispronounced 'Orlando', in Baghdad I met the Caliph Haroun Al Raschid and his beguiling concubine Scheharezade. More devastatingly, I also met the love of my protracted life, a mariner named Sindbad.

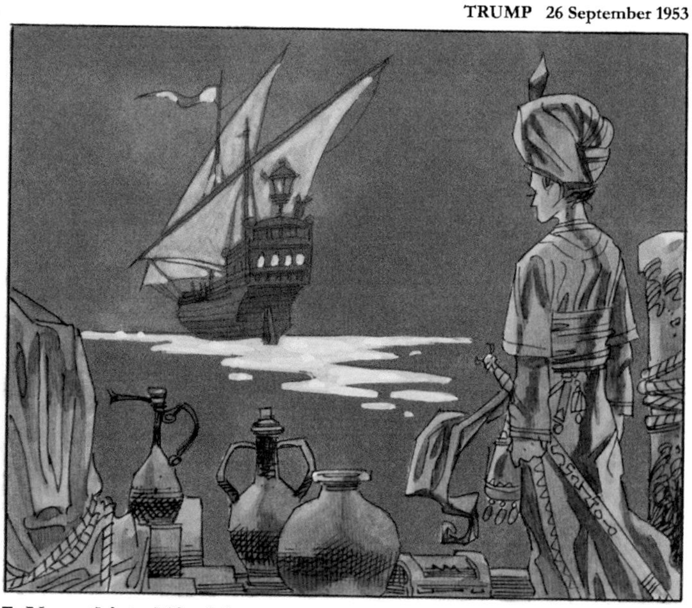

7. Near thirty blissful years we were together, 'til he left on that eighth voyage from which he never would return. I moped almost a century in Baghdad, until Haroun's grandson Al Wathik Be'llah became Caliph.

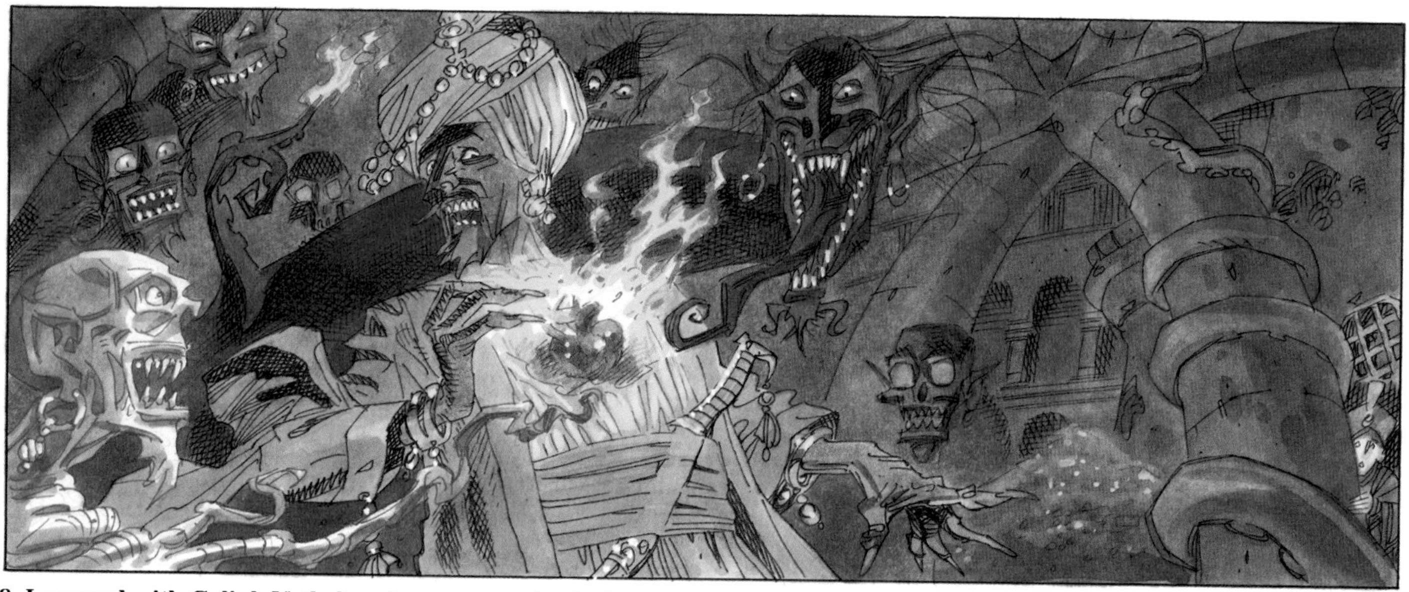

8. I roamed with Caliph Vathek as he was more lately known, helping him build the palace Alkoremi in Samarah and accompanying his trip up the Fakreddin Valley to the hushed black terraces of Ishtakar, the genii-haunted catacombs beneath them. Here I witnessed Vathek bargain with the demon Eblis for a vision of Hell's treasures, whereafter his heart burned eternally. This seemed unfair, since frankly, Hell's treasures were rather…suburban.

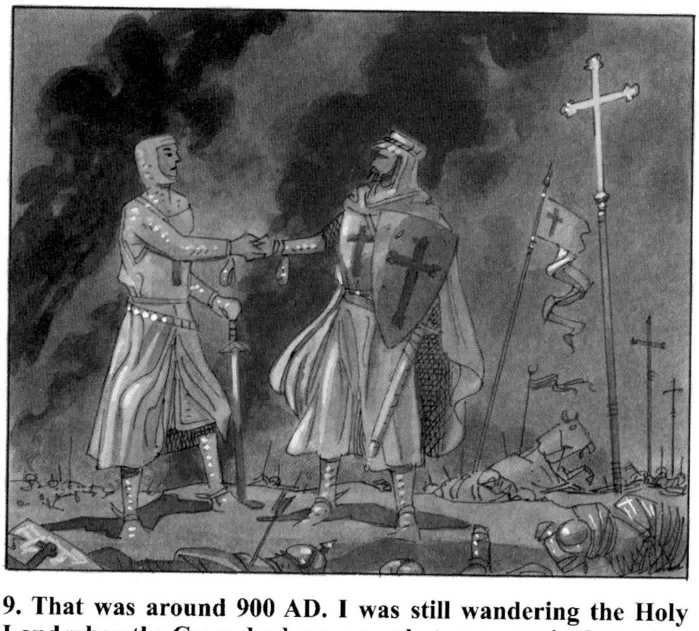

9. That was around 900 AD. I was still wandering the Holy Land when the Crusades began nearly two centuries later. Admiring the Crusaders' outfits, I again switched sides, fighting alongside legendary Prester John and others.

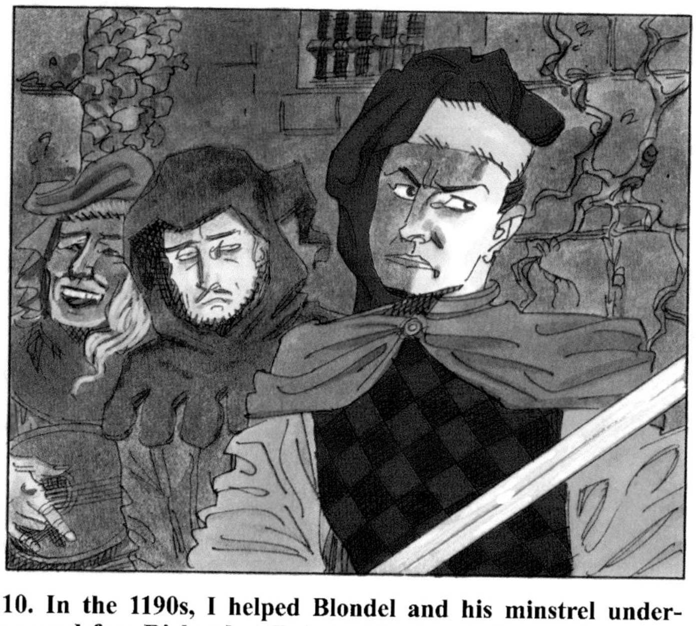

10. In the 1190s, I helped Blondel and his minstrel underground free Richard, called the Lionheart, from prison. Enjoying my new name, I'd by then sworn to be Orlando all my extraordinary days.

Continues next week

The Life of ORLANDO

Chapter Seven: I Make Friends Easily

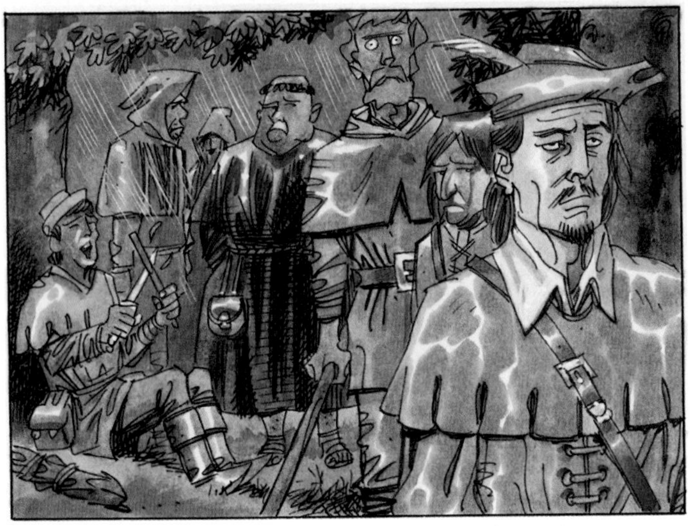

1. Despite surviving 2,450 years already, man and woman, sometimes I feared that those beastly Middle Ages simply wouldn't end. Even Robin Hood's Merry Men, encountered in 1197 on returning from the Crusades, seemed miserable.

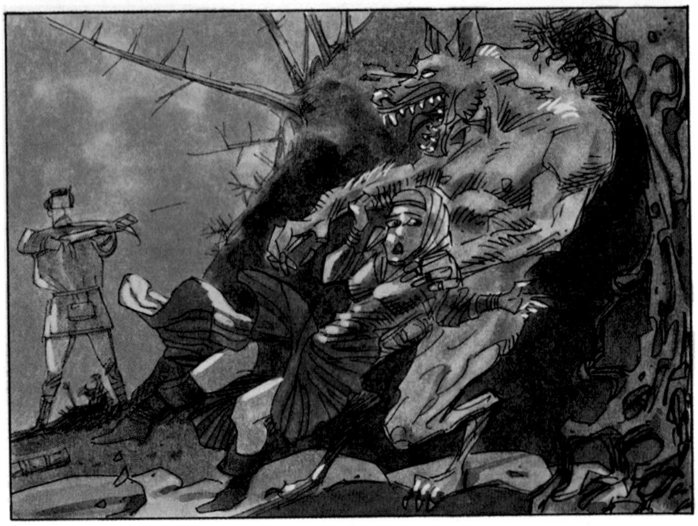

2. Mainland Europe was no improvement. In 1307, female once again and become William Tell's assistant while he took his apple trick on tour, we were everywhere beset by Dark-Age monsters, trolls and Dire-Wolves.

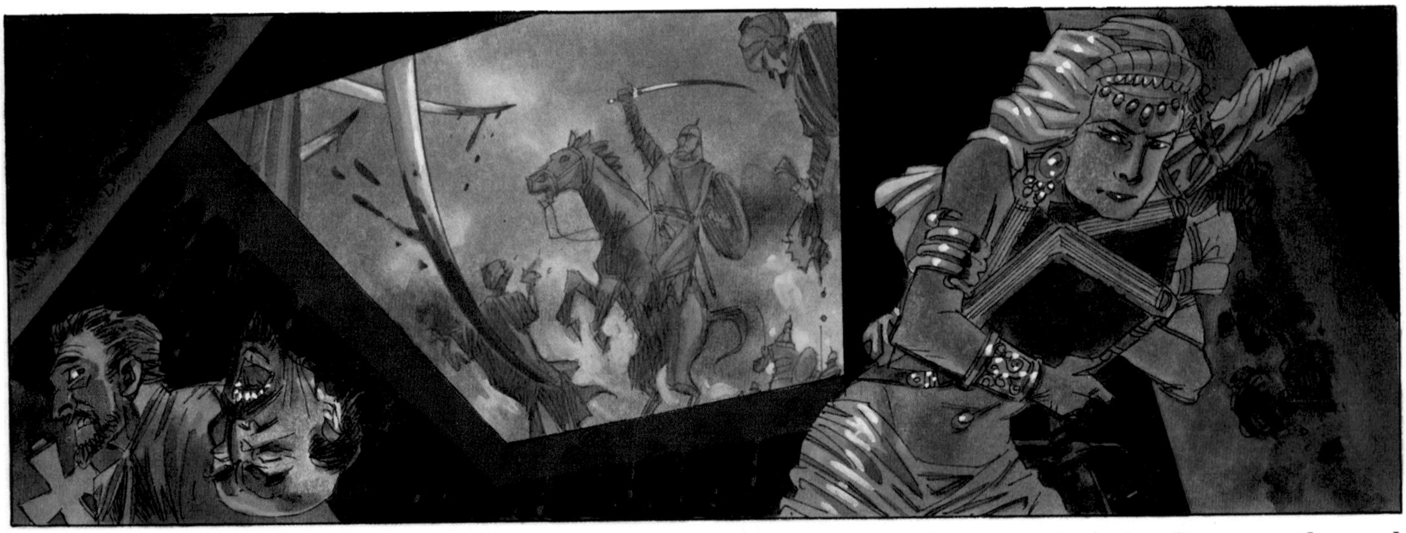

3. Culture-starved, by 1450 AD I had settled in Constantinople, throne of learning, where I made my living as a dancer, studying by day. Unfortunately, only three years later the Byzantine capital fell to the glowering Ottoman hordes of Mehmet the Second, ending Byzantium's empire after a mere thousand years. Along with other scholars, I fled west to Italy, taking along as many books and manuscripts as I could carry.

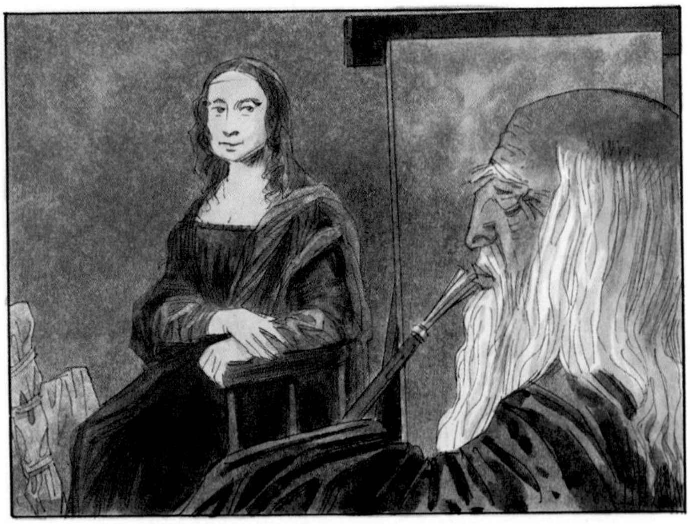

4. Thus I started the Renaissance, a sublime relief after those gloomy centuries. I posed for Leonardo, even though I was becoming a man at the time. I remember he kept asking me why I was smirking.

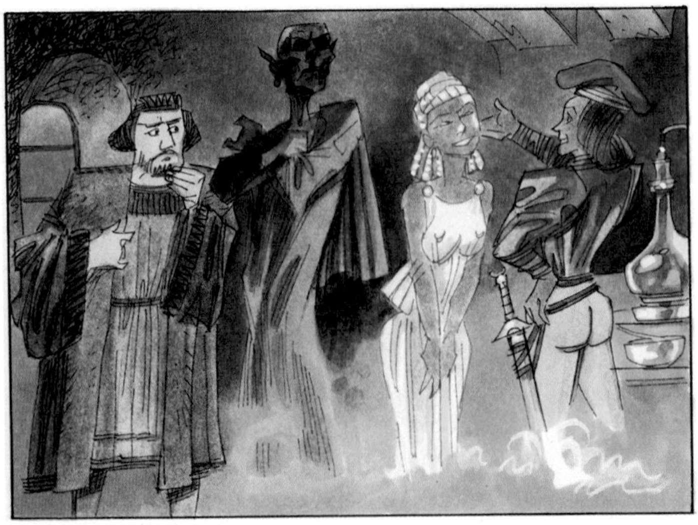

5. Travelling through Europe, in 1530s Prague I was apprenticed to the sorcerer Johannes Faust, whereby I renewed my acquaintanceship with Helen, whom I had not seen since Troy. We chatted, though this irritated Faust and Mephistopheles.

6. Soon afterwards, the Doctor was approached by a preco-cious thirteen-year-old nobleman from Italy, seeking occult instruction. Faust being otherwise engaged just then, I accom-panied the boy back to Milan. His name was Prospero.

7. Duke Prospero's companion during youth, I went with him in 1558 to England, where he was made Court Astrologer to newly-crowned Gloriana, England's Queen, daughter of brutal Henry VIII and faerie half-breed Nan Bullen.

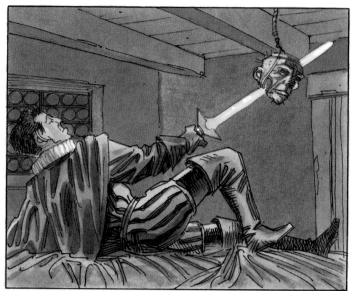

8. Charged by prescient Gloriana to inaugurate a mighty league after her death, Prospero resided in Mortlake under the name Suttle, with wife Doll Common and fellow alchemist Edward Face. Meanwhile I languished, bored, in London.

9. When his wife died, grieving Prospero took daughter Mi-randa to an island, not to return until 1610, when he assembled Gloriana's prophecied 'League.' This included otherworldly Christian, whom we rescued from a madhouse in 1678.

10. Over time, this group embraced such notables as beloved Spanish aristrocrat Quixote, impoverished sea-captain Robert Owemuch, and ravishing courtesan Mistress St. Clair. With Christian and deathless Prospero, flanked by his spirit- creatures, we made a formidable ensemble. Though originally devised by Gloriana and her spymaster Jack Wilton for rea-sons unexplained, this league, in one form or another, would be my companions for the next few centuries. *Continues next week*

The Life of ORLANDO

Chapter Eight: I Become Modern

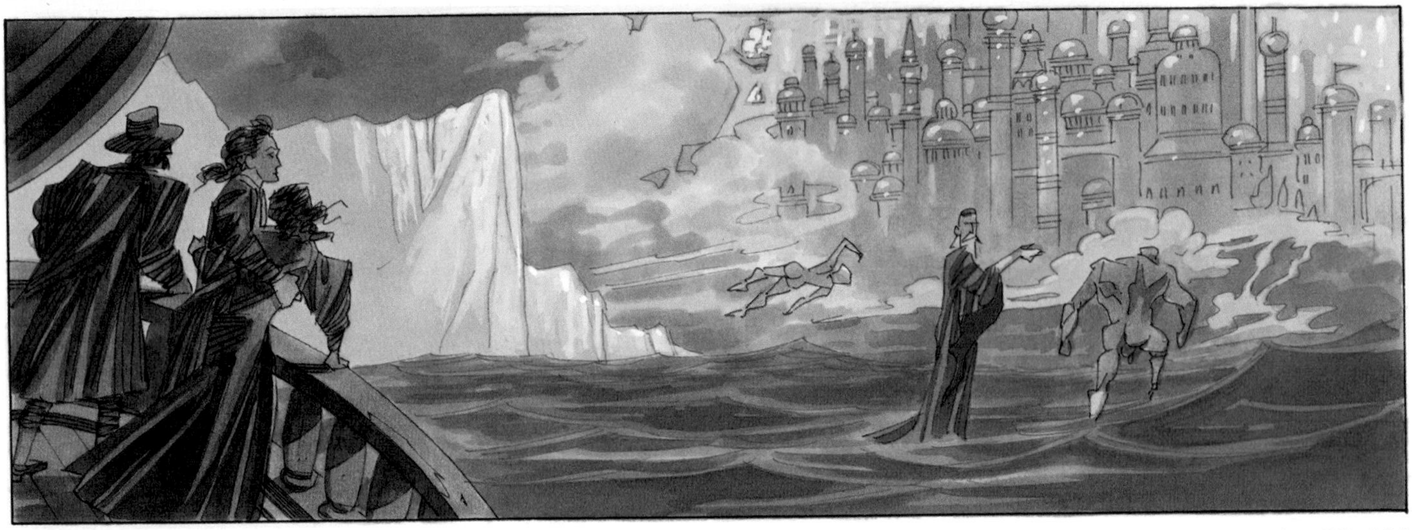

1. Almost 3,000 years old by 1696 AD and currently a man, I'd taken up with an engaging crew of misfits, as originally proposed by England's faerie monarch Gloriana prior to her death in 1603. I accompanied their last adventure, ferrying an ailing Prospero back to the spectral Arctic 'Blazing World,' where he took leave of us forever. His last words, at the brink of that shimmering mirage, were 'Follow me.'

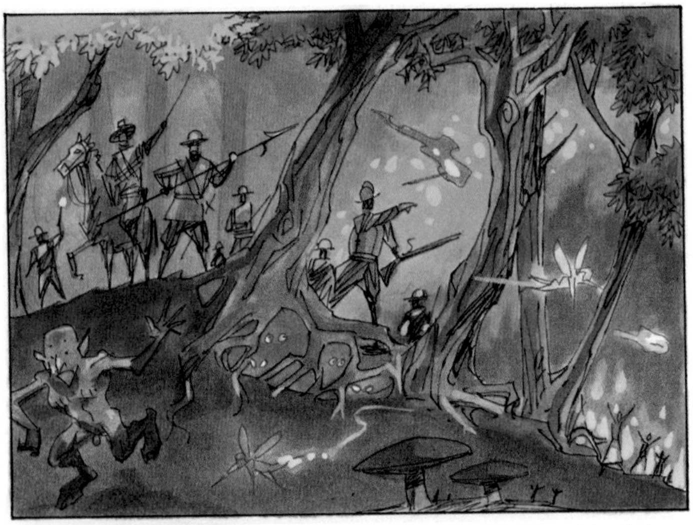

2. Since Gloriana's death and subsequent King Jacob's vicious purges of the faerie race, enchantment had been scarce in Britain. Fairyland withdrew contact entirely in 1616, the same year that noted biographers Shakespeare and Cervantes died.

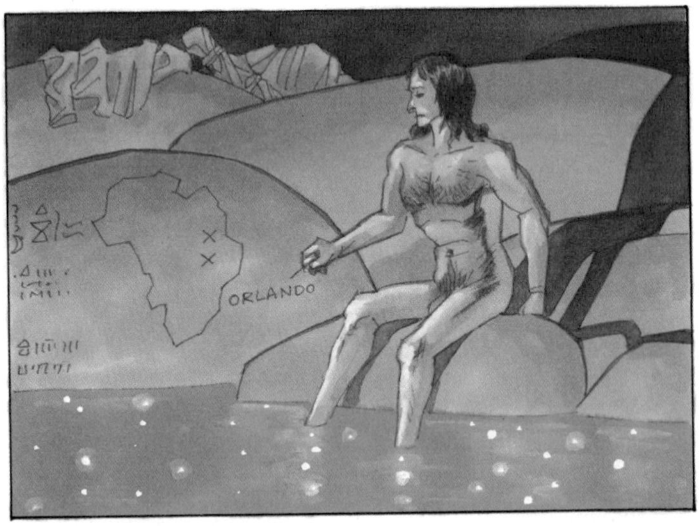
ORLANDO

3. With Prospero gone and our league disbanded, England seemed dull. I roamed the world, even revisiting Kor in Africa and its magic pool, this time carving my name on the rock there beside it: 'Orlando.'

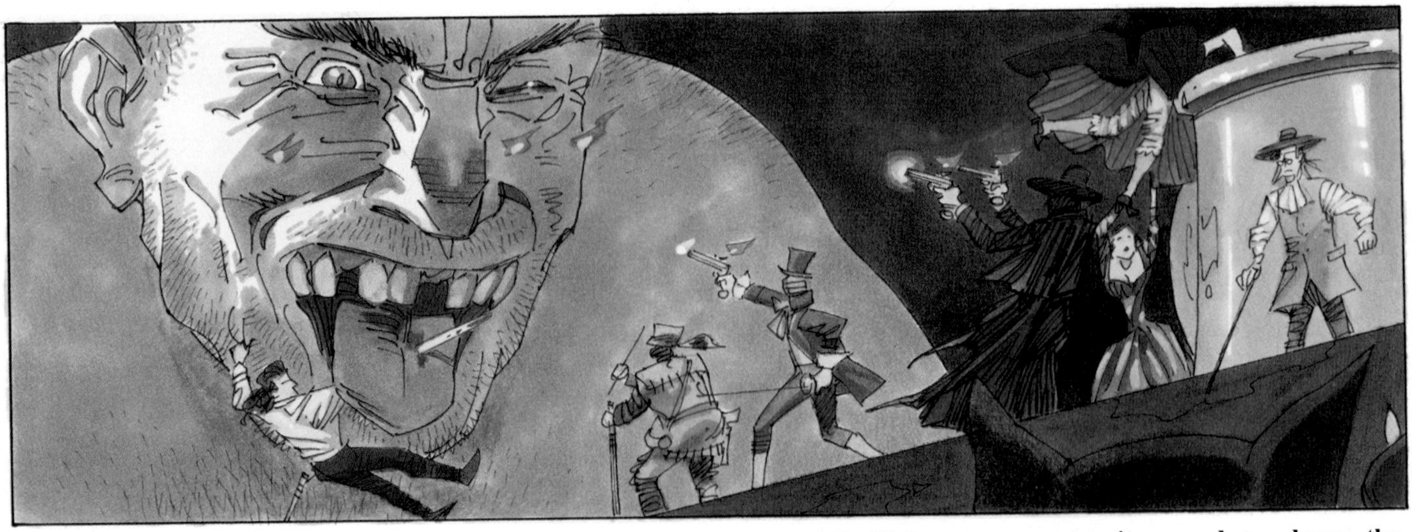

4. Returning to Britain in 1740, I found a new band of adventurers formed in my absence, this time numbering unlucky mariner Lemuel Gulliver, trapper Natty Bumppo, libertine Mistress Hill, dual-natured clergyman Dr. Syn and the resourcefull Blakeneys amongst its members down the decades. I stood by them through Brobdingnag's Giant-wars and helped them in their subterranean adventures, finding them worthy successors to the mantle of Prospero's men.

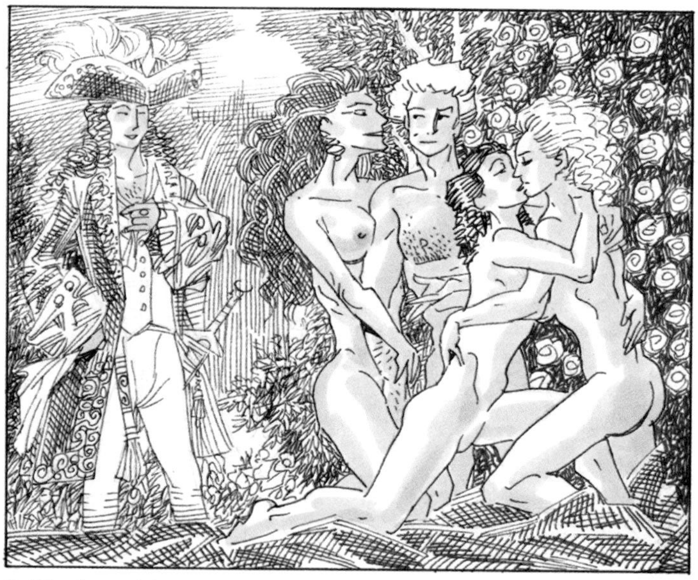

5. Having aided Percy Blakeney during France's revolution, come century's end I frequently accompanied him, Marguerite and Fanny on the trio's annual sojourns through erotic Europe, with our weeks spent in twilit Horselberg being most memorable.

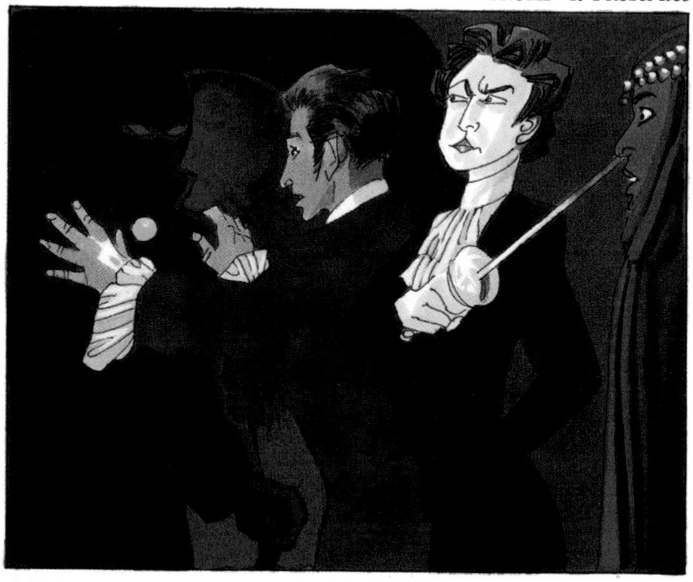

6. With the remarkably elderly Gulliver's demise in 1799, the league once more disintegrated. I spent much of the nineteenth century in France as companion to either superhuman aesthete Fortunio, or ambiguous Mademoiselle de Maupin.

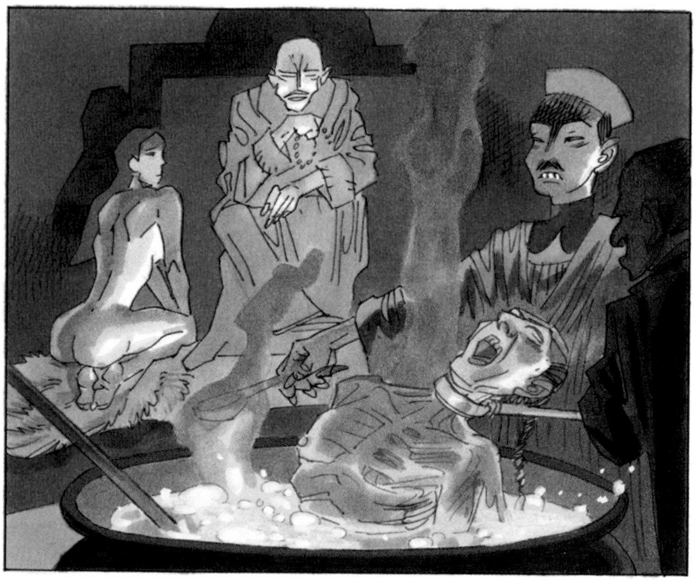

7. 1906 found me female, travelling in Tibet where, at the monastery So Sa Ling, I was captured by Bon sorcerers, who used me dreadfully, but didn't make me into ointment, as they did young men.

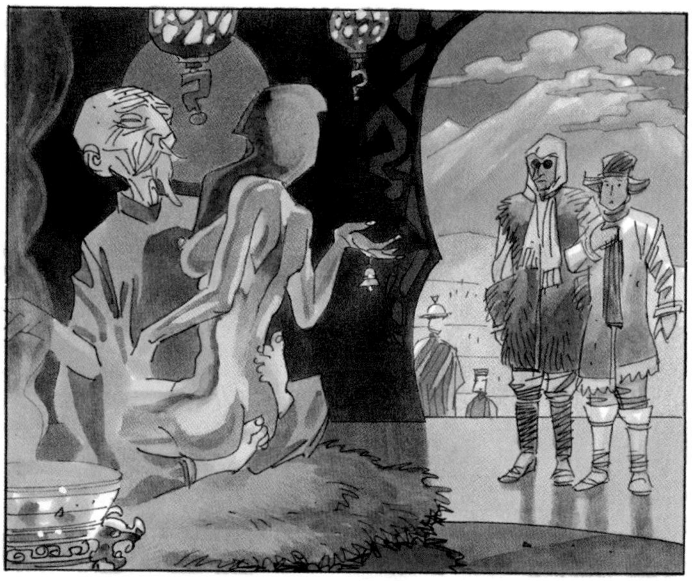

8. Escaping, I reached the azure Mount Karakal and dragon-blazoned Shangri-La, where I was learning yoga from a willing lama when interrupted by an English couple who were undertaking expeditions in the area.

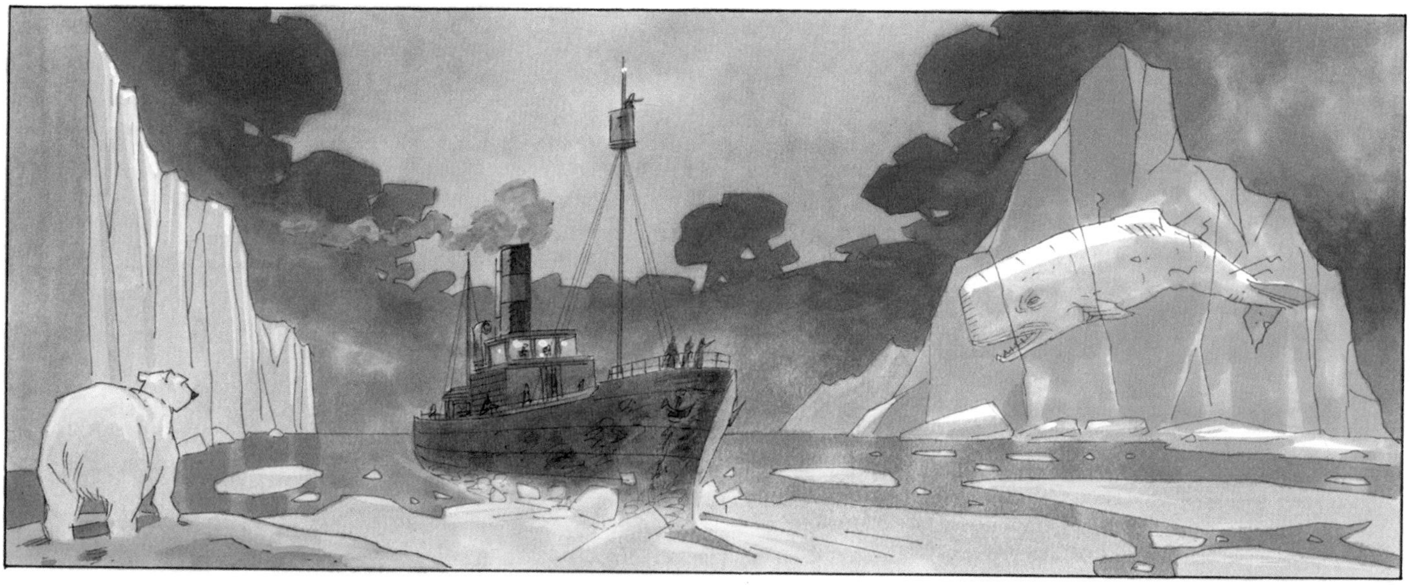

9. The pair, Allan and Wilhelmina, turned out to be agents of the English Crown, affiliated to the latest incarnation of the cabal previously led by Prospero and Gulliver. It transpired we had much in common, and they were the most delicious company as we returned to England via the North Pole, having many grand adventures on the way. I was finding this modern world most agreeably entertaining. *Concludes next week*

The Life of ORLANDO

Chapter Nine: I Conclude My Account

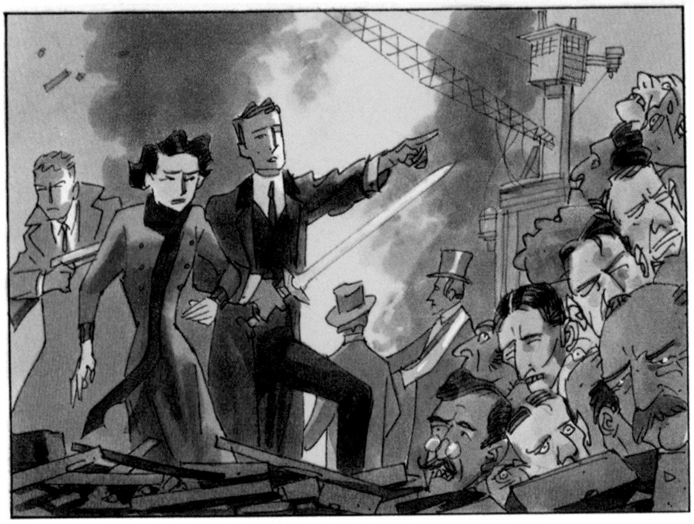

1. Ancient and of varying gender, I contributed enthusiastically to Wilhelmina's 20th century team. In 1910, male again, I strived alongside her, Allan, the thief Raffles and occultist Carnacki to avert disaster at King George's coronation.

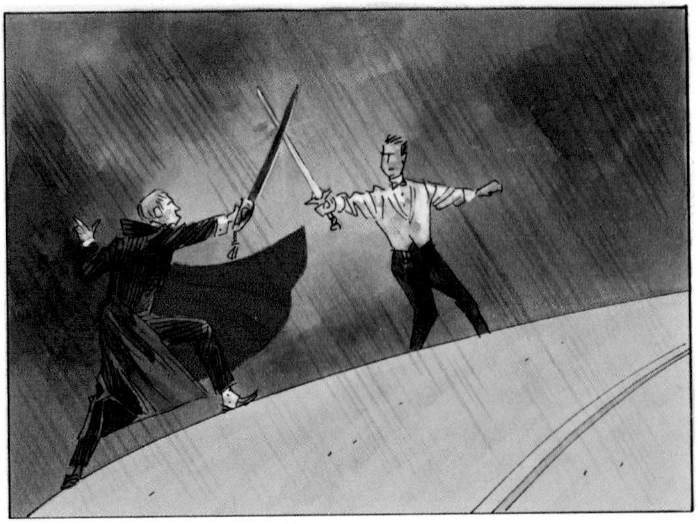

2. In 1913, assisting the team against French counterparts Les Hommes Mysterieux, I nearly died battling the albino, Zenith, in pounding rain atop the Paris Opera. Clearly, this new century was as dangerous as any other.

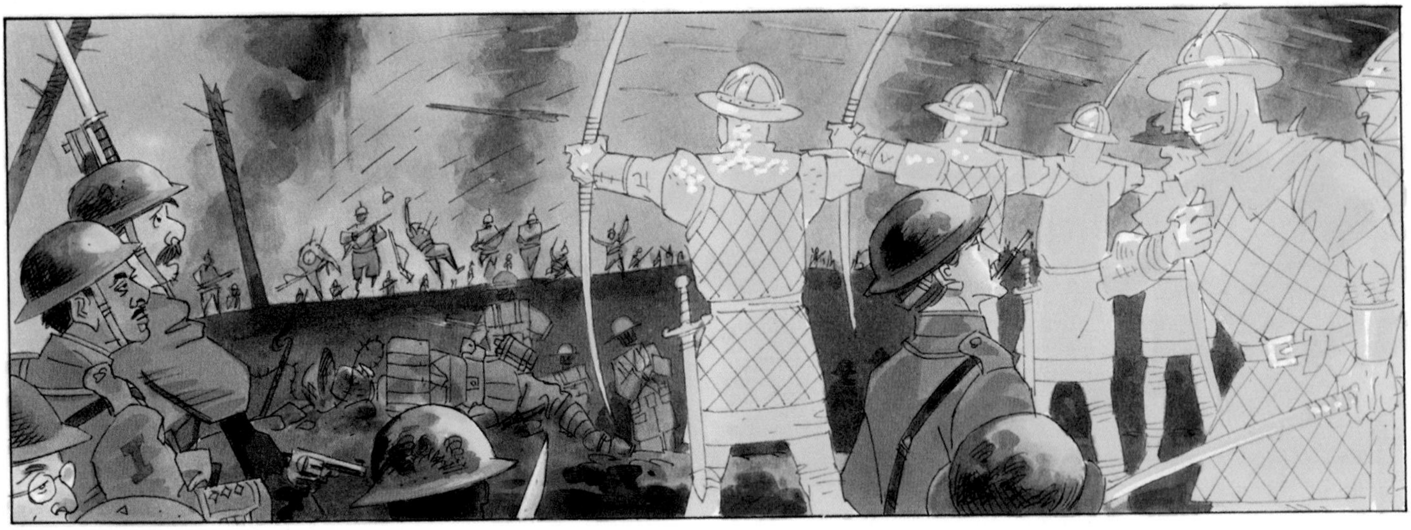

3. It was certainly as warlike. Having some military experience, I fought for Britain in World War One, as did my colleague, penitent bandit A. J. Raffles, who'd lose his life during the conflict. At the Battle of Mons, I was lucky enough to see Agincourt's phantom bowmen aiding the English. One ghost claimed to recognise me, though I don't think that I was even *at* Agincourt. Who knows? Perhaps I was.

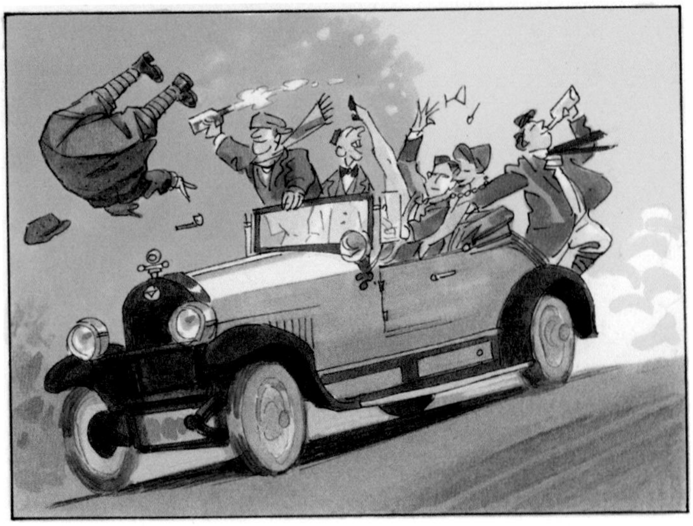

4. After the war, I'm afraid I spent the 1920s enjoying myself. I belonged to poor Agatha Runcible's set. We knew the Woosters, the Claytons, Jay and Daisy, absolutely everyone. It was all such smashing fun.

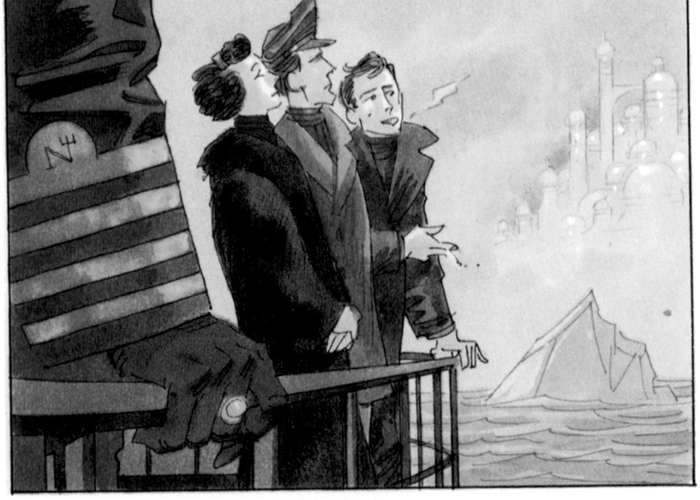

5. The 1930s, less so: throughout the decade one could feel stormclouds gathering. With Mina, Allan and other new friends, I revisited the Blazing World and the Polar wastes beyond, where we made some important allies.

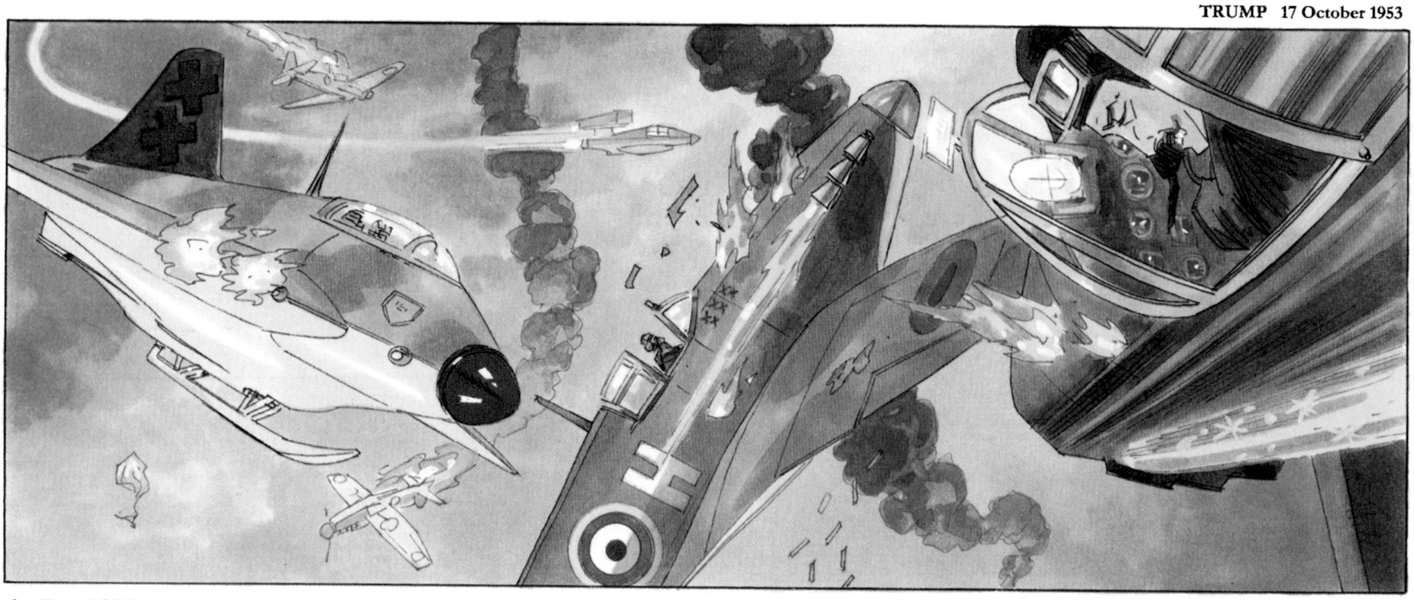

6. By 1939, of course, the dictator Adenoid Hynkel had dragged the world into a new and even more destructive war. Keen to keep abreast of changing times, I mastered aeronautics and enlisted in the Royal Air Force, flying with aces such as Bigglesworth, Hebblethwaite, and visiting yank G-8 (who seemed, frankly, bonkers). Shot down over France I escaped back to Blighty to find my comrades missing in action, their headquarters deserted.

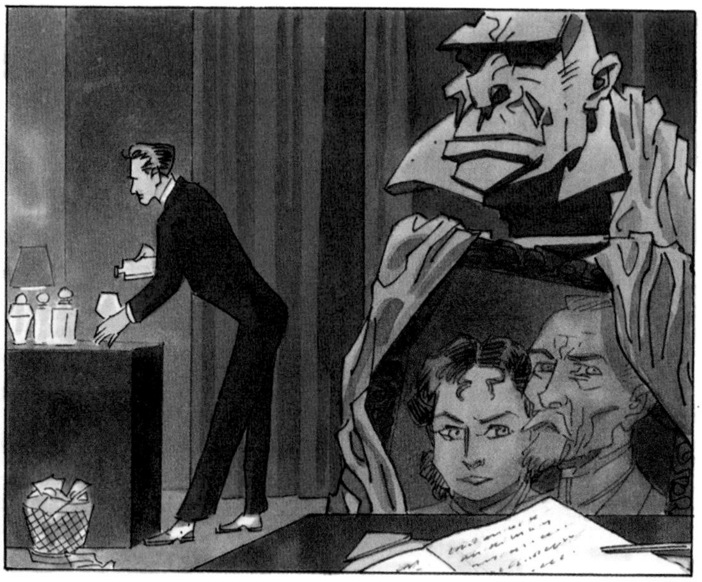

7. Now it is 1943. My tale is almost over, while outside the air-raid continues. I know that Allan and Mina are alive somewhere, and expect that I shall see them, sooner or later.

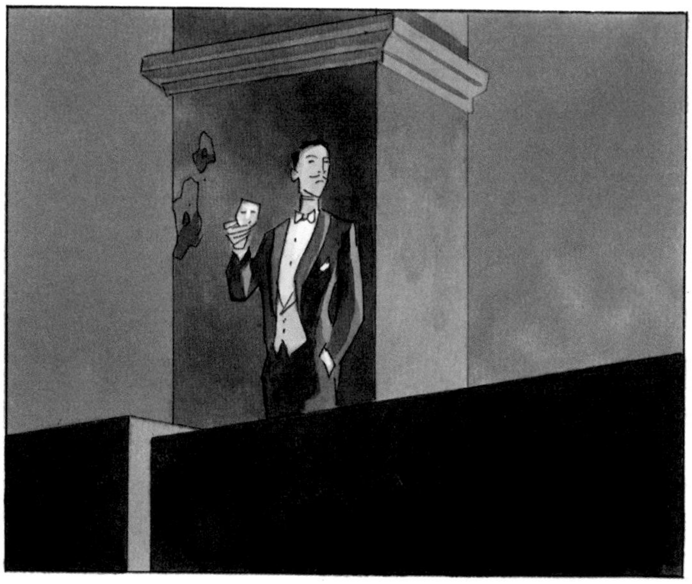

8. As for myself, I was three thousand two hundred and three years old last week, and I endure. I saw London founded, hewn with Trojan blades, and now see it flattened by German incendiary devices.

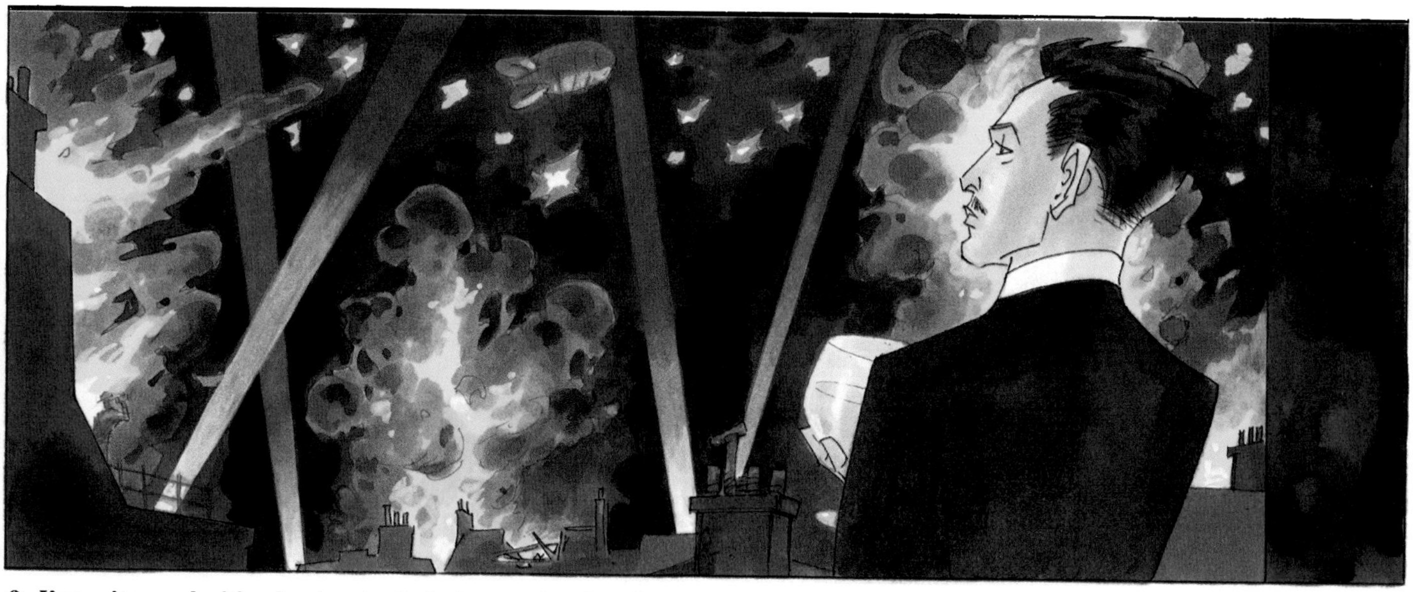

9. I've witnessed cities beaten to their knees, fought all our pointless wars, seen millions slaughtered, peerless cultures smudged by History's thumb, and, all things considered, wouldn't change a moment. I was Bio, I was Vita, and where human life went, there went I. It was a very great adventure, and I am proud to have been a man; to have been a woman. To have been Orlando. *- The End -*

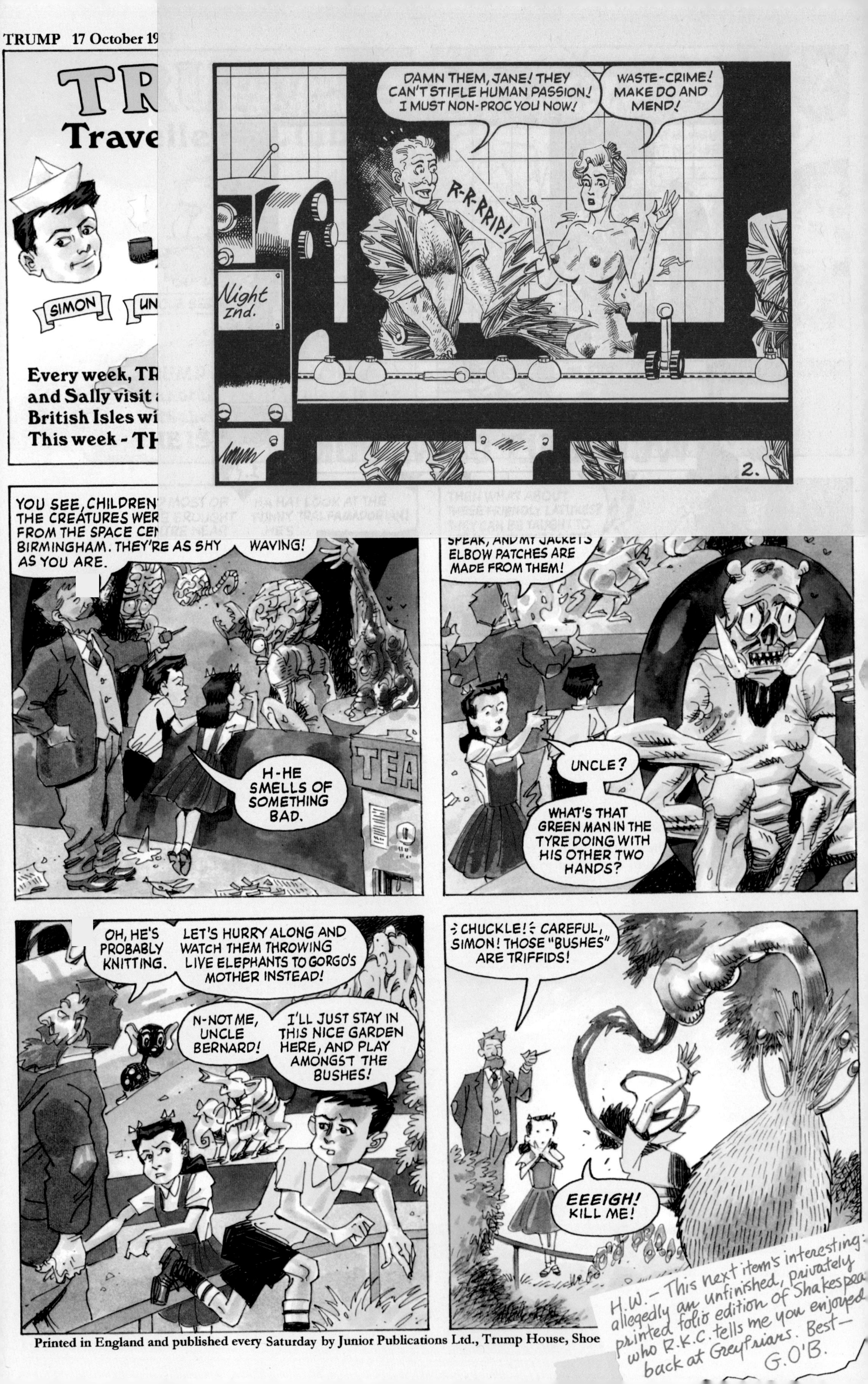
TRUMP 17 October 19
TR
Travel
SIMON
UN
Every week, TR
and Sally visit
British Isles wi
This week - TH
DAMN THEM, JANE! THEY CAN'T STIFLE HUMAN PASSION! I MUST NON-PROC YOU NOW!
WASTE-CRIME! MAKE DO AND MEND!
R-R-RRIP!
Night Ind.
2.
YOU SEE, CHILDREN, MOST OF THE CREATURES WERE BROUGHT FROM THE SPACE CENTRE NEAR BIRMINGHAM. THEY'RE AS SHY AS YOU ARE.
HA HA! LOOK AT THE FUNNY TRALFAMADORIAN! HE'S WAVING!
H-HE SMELLS OF SOMETHING BAD.
TEA
THEN WHAT ABOUT THESE FRIENDLY LATINES? THEY CAN BE TAUGHT TO SPEAK, AND MY JACKET'S ELBOW PATCHES ARE MADE FROM THEM!
UNCLE?
WHAT'S THAT GREEN MAN IN THE TYRE DOING WITH HIS OTHER TWO HANDS?
OH, HE'S PROBABLY KNITTING.
LET'S HURRY ALONG AND WATCH THEM THROWING LIVE ELEPHANTS TO GORGO'S MOTHER INSTEAD!
N-NOT ME, UNCLE BERNARD!
I'LL JUST STAY IN THIS NICE GARDEN HERE, AND PLAY AMONGST THE BUSHES!
CHUCKLE! CAREFUL, SIMON! THOSE "BUSHES" ARE TRIFFIDS!
EEEIGH! KILL ME!
Printed in England and published every Saturday by Junior Publications Ltd., Trump House, Shoe
H.W. - This next item's interesting: allegedly an unfinished, privately printed folio edition of Shakespea who R.K.C. tells me you enjoyed back at Greyfriars. Best - G.O'B.

The True Chronicle of
certain Mysterious Events
in and around the Courte of
our Noble QUEEN GLORIANA,
in a playe called:

FÆRIE'S
FORTUNES
FOUNDED

By William Shakespeare

AT LONDON
Printed by I. R. for *B. Bond* and are to be sold
by private subscription only, inquiries at
his offyce near *St. Austin's Gate*
1620

DRAMATIS PERSONÆ

PROSPERO, *Duke of Milan*
ORLANDO, *Squire to Prospero*
GLORIANA, *Queen of England*
SIR JOHN WILTON, *Servant to the Crowne*
SIR BASILDON BOND, *an Intelligencer*

MASTER SHYTTE
MASTER PYSSE
Gatekeepers

DOGROSE
GORSE
LOVE-LIES-BLEEDING
Færies

Færie's Fortunes Founded

Actus Primus, Scena Prima

The gates of Nonsuch Palace. Master Shytte and Master Pysse occupying separate gate-houses. Master Shytte enters from gate-house left.

Shytte.

Another morn in this hag-ridden land,
  Our right Queen Mary sickened to her crypt
And leaves enthroned a changeling in her stead.
Why does the very Sun himself not shy
In his ascent, from such iniquity?
Come, Master Pysse! Throw off your lively sheets!
Now let us be about our grudging round.
Make fast these gates at Nonsuch and besides
Keep safe she that deserves salvation least.

Enter Master Pysse from gate-house right.

Pysse. Insistent Shytte, again you waken me.
Pluck'd from such dreams as break my heart to quit.
Of time to come, when all the world's set right
And sweet young Jacobus the Scottish King
Is grown, brought to his just inheritance.
That are these wraiths and sorc'ries cast aside
With her alike, whom are we made to call
Our good Queen —

Shytte. Hold thy water, Pysse! Speak not
Her cog, lest like her kin she come when hailed.
Let us to work, such dang'rous chat put by.
Sufficient in our private thought that these
Opinions spilled delinquent out our mouths
Are truth, like all we speak, true as our names!

Pysse. Ah, noble names indeed, everywhere known.
Sentinels at the gates of Life itself.
'Tis said that all men, commoner and King,
Are come into this world 'twixt Pysse and Shytte.
But hold! I see two travellers bide near,
Mayhap the lords Her Majesty awaits.

Shytte. I mark them now, the both
near damn'd as she.
The elder is a Duke sailed from Milan.
One Prospero, an alchemist by trade
With not yet forty Summers 'neath his cap
And sure to catch the Queen's lascivious eye;
The other man, scarce more than boy, his squire.
Orlando called, that gossips would unpick,
Declare not man at all but rather dame
In manly guise, or thing of doubled sex.
A will-gill or a child of Herm - yet soft!
They tread too soon upon our whisperings.

Prospero and Orlando enter left.

Prospero. Good squire, behold the palace of None-Such.
Nor such as mortals shall e'er see again.
Where are we fetched from Italy to meet
Fair Gloriana, England's færie Queen.
But what is this? Can this drab pair ahead
Be their lords Bond and Wilton we were told
Should meet us here, and hence accompanye
Our joining with her gracious Majesty?

Orlando. Why, my lord Prospero, I will confess
I have heard much of England's poverty
Yet did not think to see her thus reduced,
Her lords with gunny-sack for ermine swap'd.
I shall inquire, and know the truth of it.
If these be the intelligencers we
Were told to seek, or else tares in our way.

to gatemen

Hail, fellows. We are come from far Milan
In search of two within your Queen's employ
As spies, and we would know if you are they.

Shytte. Do we spy? Aye, we spy, we watch, we see.
Have we not each these two balls in our heads?

Pysse. More than are in your britches, if the tales
That coster-men speak everywhere be true.

Orlando, *aside.* They jest with me, I shall give jibe for jibe.

to gatemen

Why, sirs, you make me testy with your talk
And test me sorely. Must I testify

As once did I in ancient Rome with hand
On heart, or other muscle made for love?
Though I be fair and orchidaceous, know
My *Orches* are in place, may orchestrate
A love-air sweet as any orchestra
Might play at the famed dances of your Queen,
Reknowned, 'tis said, for her great, splendid
balls.

Shytte. Your wit fair spins my head with all
its play!

Pysse. Yet have we cudgels that shall
spin your own!

Prospero. Orlando, hold thy wounding barbs.
'Tis plain
These are but gatemen, not the ones we seek.

to gatemen
Now, gentlemen, thy cudgels put aside
Or be advised Orlando here has blade
yet keener and more practised than his tongue.

*enter Sir John Wilton and
Sir Basildon Bond, right*

Bond. Noble Sir Jack, 'tis our Italic guests
That we must take before the strangeling
Queen.
Already is their Latin blood aflame
And set to quarrel with the lackards here.

Wilton. Cease, men of Lombardy, in thine
affray.
Sheathe thy stilletos and restrain thy boot.
I am Jack Wilton, this Basildon Bond,
Your escorts to our fledgling monarch's side.

Orlando. I am at fault, good gatemen. You are
not
The ones for whom I, erring, did you take.

Shytte. Ho, took us, did you? Are we taken
then?

Pysse. Why, hadst thou best inform Her
Majesty
Thou took both Pysse and Shytte at Nonesuch
gates.

Prospero. Put off these pratings! Good lords,
I am come
Through many seas this audience to find
And would bright Gloriana soonest see
If here in England I'm to have my notch.

Wilton. Well said, friend alchemist, with
leaden thought
Made wisdom's gold on thine alembic lips.
Come, bring your squire. Step with us through
these gates
To venture on her presence half-divine
And scrye there vasty empires' secret fates.
Let our talks be unknown, our words erase:
In Nonsuch Palace, none such did take place.

Curtain

Scena Secunda

*Gloriana's throne-room. The Queen sits, attended
by færies.*

Gloriana. My pretty devils, fold thy prism'd
wings.
Halt now thy flutt'ring galliard and draw near,
For spies and sorcerors would have my ear
To weave their schemes, whilst weave I better
things.

Dogrose. You play a higher, broader game than
they!

Gorse. The spots you've reckoned ere their
die are cast!

Gloriana. Fine webs of circumstance shall
hold them fast.
And though they wriggle shall I have my way
To write a hist'ry that I've ten times read —
Yet hush! Methinks to hear their falt'ring tread.

Enter Wilton, Bond, Prospero and Orlando, left

Bond. This scented atmosphere do I despise,
Thick with the reek of myrrh and færie musks.

Wilton. Say nothing. Here the very walls
have wits
And ears. E'en private thought be overlooked.

to Glorianna
Sweet Majesty, I come, thy prince of spies
With stout Basildon Bond, in your domain

And bring the alchemist, the Milanese,
Here with his squire, the both for you to meet.

Love-Lies-Bleeding. He sweats. Sour
diamonds mist upon his brow.

Dogrose. The other as milk-pudding heaves
and shakes.

Gloriana. Why, though their perspirations
sink fresh lakes,
The foreigners they bring would I quiz now.
Stand forward, alchemist. Stand forward,
squire.
It is proposed you should positions find
In my employe, the one with agile mind,
The other, agile blade to fit my hire.
Kindly Duke Prospero, of you 'tis said
That knowledge both of metals and of tides,
Of stars, and of math'matic art resides,
Orbits the heavens, in thy black-capp'd head.
Thus should it please me that you now remain
By London here, at Mortlake to the West.
In secret wait my call and my behest,
Which means my sly Lord Jack might next
explain.

Wilton. Gladly, Your Highness. Good Duke
Prospero,
May I suggest, referring to thy fame,
That here you wear another name, become
An altered personality, take guise
As one John Suttle, born in Wor'stershire,
And subtle both in name and nature be.
Then should thy veiled utility be twinned,
Both conj'ror to Her Radiant Majesty
And spy, a wand'ring alchemist abroad
Who might from the low countries make
report,
So serving my intelligencers' band.

Prospero. What band is this, of agents
clandestine?

Bond. It is an instrument that serves the
crown
Through stealth, its master my Lord Wilton
here:
Its 'M', for em's but double-U disguised.
We are by letters, else by numbers masked.

Prospero. Shall I, then, newly named, be
numbered thus?

Wilton.   *produces paper*
I have your own appointed symbol drawn,
See, with its dotted circles like to eyes
That glower beneath the straight line of a
brow.

Prospero. It seems like bosoms, or a brace of
noughts.
Two 'O's, within a seven bracketed.

Wilton. Then two 'O's and a seven is your
sign,
And to this mark are all your payments writ.

Prospero. They've called me Faust, for one
that I once knew,
Call me by numbers, Suttle, Prospero.
Caught at my aliases' delta now
Hang I as in a saddle-wire, a dee.

Orlando. What of I, and my part? I am unsure
If I'm to Arthur or else Martha be.

Bond. Stay at our beckon as a sword for hire
Lodged here in London, ours to fetch and send.
When not employed you may, for all I care,
Hack at a dangled Tartar's head for sport.

Gloriana. My good Sir Basildon, your words
offend.
You and my good Lord Wilton must go hence.
Leave me to salve my guests of thine offence
And to my duties as hostess attend.

Wilton. Your Majesty, forgive me my protest,
Dismiss'd with such irregularity —

Gorse. Go, or thy wits lose in our ludic maze!

Love-Lies-Bleeding. Go, or misplace recall of
thine own names!

Exeunt Wilton and Bond, right

Gloriana. We are alone. Jack Wilton fears my
games
More than the peeking pass-time that he plays.
Now, master alchemist and master squire,
Can I make my true purposes more plain,
A confidence spies' ears shall not retain,
Not England's scheme, but Fairyland's desire.
Bronz'd Duke, I see the future, so may plan
A league of champions, yours to convene.
Nor yet, but when I'm dead and 'neath the
green.

These earthly heroes, bridging Gods and man
A glorious roster that I now may sight:
The mariner, bedraggled and in debt,
Your spirits and your selves, not to forget
The courtesan, nor sweet deluded knight,
Nor pilgrim with his bundle knotted, furled,
That shall precede you to a blazing world!

Prospero. Most lovely Queen, I am confounded quite
To hear you talk, so young, of your demise.
When shall be acted, then, thy prophecies
Of this brave band? Please God it is not yet!

Dogrose. Horse-blinkered mortal, know ye not that Time
Is made in Færie's realm a single day?

Gorse. We're not yet born; our dusts long blown away,
All hours immortal in this spell sublime.

Gloriana. What Dogrose, Gorse, and Love-Lies-Bleeding sing
Is Færie truth: Time's but a painted screen
Whereon our shadows fatten then grow lean,
Reflections pale of the eternal thing.
Yet be assured that my time is not yet,
Nor 'til our sixteenth century be done
When shall a new King scorn our færie fun,
Shall bid men plough us under and forget.
But you, good Duke, have much to do ere then,
Shall live at Mortlake, study, take a wife,
Raise children, lead a fulsome earthly life
And then, bereaved, shirk from the world of men.
My foresight has you cloistered on an isle
With daughter, books and sprites of earth and air
Until such time as sailors, venturing there,
Should tell thee that I have been dead the while.
Then shall thou make for Albion to enlist
The paragons and powers I have foretold,
Your friends 'til the new century grow old,
When shalt thou disappear, as arctic mist.

Prospero. Pray hold! Fair Queen, I should not have my days
Set out before me as a butcher's roll.
May we, perhaps, not speak of sweeter things?
With such as thou beside me, bright and pale,
I would not all our talks be death or fate.

Gloriana. Thinkest me fair? Would I hear more of this,
Should not a young man's flattery despise,
Would see mine self there mirror'd in his eyes
As object fit to worship, woo, and kiss.

Prospero. Jew'ld Queen, how might I flatter such as thee
Whom Ocean called his Cynthia, his Moon?
Why art thou not that very silver'd orb

That off in far Cathay men style Chang-O.
Night's goddess, seen there when the disc is full,
And near her skirts a cunny, or else hare?

Gloriana. Why, should I like a cunny-hare to pet,
They are both soft and warm, and likewise quick.
How might I set its velvet ear a-prick
Or make its nose to twitch, so pink and wet?
Then should I have about me, by my troth,
That which is cunny and a-prick the both.

Orlando.   aside
She tells it as it were a novelty,
Yet should she truly be thus twice endow'd
Then would I sympathy with this queen share!

Prospero. Nacreous, opalescent majesty,
O how thy scents and atmospheres enchant!
Pray send me not to Mortlake, there to wed,
Have children, have another life and name
When sooner would I here with thee abide,
Here in thy bow'r, white rose without compare.

Orlando. Beware, young Duke, lest thou impert'nent be!
Art thou made by this Cynthia bewitched,
A moon-calf, struck whilst twin white crescents rise
Past the horizon of her bodice there?
Then have a care: though heady be her bloom
Her thorns, conceal'd, are sharp, shall stab the heart.
In my great span, since far-off Thebes have I
Some few queens known, and several been besides,
That would doom milling thousands with less heed
Than they might blue a lid or paint a lash.
Fear not! How dismal might thine exile be,
In pretty Mortlake with a comely wife?
Think of me there, languish'd by Bloomsb'ry Park,
Sat idle, slicing at the heads of Turks!

Prospero. Good fellow, boyhood friend, thou warn'st me right,
I am made lunatic by this moon's light.

to Gloriana
Glorious one, my foolish words forgive
And set me to thy bidding as thou would.

Gloriana. Go then, wise Prospero, and subtle be
At Mortlake, while thine young yet aged squire
Make off, at sep'rate lodgings to retire.
In both thy dreams, see that thou lovest me.

*exeunt Prospero and
Orlando, right*

Love-Lies-Bleeding. They are well gone, and take the reek of man.
You had them dazzl'd, blinded in your thrall.

Dogrose. At laſt they hardly knew themselves at all
And so may willingly act Færie's plan.

Gorse. How would thy mother, lushly-fingered Anne,
Or thy great-uncle Oberon rejoice
To know thy scheme; know that thy cunning choice
Gifts Færie's wish since hiſtory began?

Gloriana. Dear moths, draw in thine orbit to my flame,
For I am satisfied, would drowse and play
And count my acts sufficient to this day,
Or the advantage of my gem-tiled game.
Our kind, from other æthyrs, came before
Mankind, to ſtamp a foot upon this Earth.
Fourfold, eternal, ſtrange to death and birth,
Sprung up from angels or else fiends of yore,
We watch'd man born, we monſters, gods and sprites,
And fear'd what enmities there might arise.
Ourselves made deities to crowd Man's skies,
Or ghouls and devils to diſtress his nights,
We sought to make a bridge that spann'd the twain,
Spawn'd heroes, half-bred gods, in this employ;
Saw them go mad, then cull'd them all at Troy,
Vowing that we should not so err again.
This league of champions that I propose,
Though not convened whilſt am I in this world
Is our next try to have two realms knit, purled
Into one seamless drama without close.
Our Duke shall near two centuries survive,
Suttle at Mortlake, Prosp'ro on his Isle,
Shall found my league and keep with them a while,
And thence into the myſtery shall dive.
There is, paſt Britain's tip, like to a gate,
A blazing world, door to a diff'rent plane.
There Prosp'ro goes, nor shall his league remain,
But in Time follow to another ſtate,
'Til when the years have in their hundreds passed,
'Til other men else women lead my band
And in this Blazing World shall take their ſtand,
A bridge-head 'tween our realms secur'd at laſt.
Now sleep. There are dire days to come ere then,
Our bright kind scourged by new Kings and their men,
Burn'd out from woodland, driven off from fen,
And would I know Dream's moonlit towns again.

they sleep

Finis Actus Primus

The present publication is an unaltered facsimile, reproducing a previously undiscovered limited first folio edition from 1620 of what is alleged to be an uncompleted final play by Shakespeare, *Færie's Fortunes Founded,* said to have been commenced by the great biographical dramatist in 1616, its writing presumably curtailed later that same year, after only one act of two scenes, by Shakespeare's death at the age of fifty-two. Although the provenance and pedigree of the preceding fragment has been vigorously disputed, the current editors of this facsimile edition have elected to make room for a brief note in which the main points raised by the foregoing piece's critics and debunkers may be answered, it is hoped conclusively.

Several commentators have suggested that the two scenes which survive of *Færie's Fortunes Founded* are unlikely to be Shakespeare's work, if only on account of the unflattering references to Queen Gloriana, who had, as sceptics have quite rightly pointed out, been Shakespeare's patron, and at least on friendly terms with her most celebrated play-write. While the present editors have no wish to refute these well-established facts, they would point out that *Færie's Fortunes Founded,* being written in 1616, was obviously commissioned a considerable while after Gloriana's death in 1603, some twelve years into the reign of Gloriana's deeply Christian and deeply resentful nephew and successor, King Jacob the First.

If the uncompleted play under discussion had indeed been written at the King's request, it is perhaps not wholly unexpected, then, that Shakespeare may have felt compelled to include sentiments that were both hostile to the late Queen, and also to the idea of færie-kind in general. Let us recall that Jacob's animosity both to his aunt and to the færie breed she represented was both fierce and deadly. Barely had the new King claimed the throne on Gloriana's death than he released an edict branding færies and associated beings as 'Devils,' or as Jacob himself put it at the time in his book *Dæmonologie,* 'That kinde of devils conversing in the earth may be divided in four different kinds...The fourth is these kinde of spirites that are called vulgarlie the Fayrie.' (III,i)

Indeed, so great was Jacob's loathing of the fairy race that his reign saw the ruthlessly efficient purges of the species from the British Isles, with the destruction of their woodland habitats. By 1616, at the time of this play's writing, there were no more fairies to be found in England, and in Shakespeare's references to the Queen's fairy attendants as 'my pretty devils,' it may be that the author was attempting to play to his royal master's prejudices. However, it should be observed that most of this piece's anti-fairy sentiment is placed into the mouths of characters who are themselves either buffoonish, like the coarsely-named and almost certainly fictitious gatemen, or else devious and duplicitous, like the spymaster Wilton and his chief intelligencer, Bond. (While Sir John Francis Wilton, more commonly called Jack, was a young adventurer who'd risen to a prominent position in the court of Gloriana, whose existence can be verified, Sir Basildon Bond's name does not appear, at least in the official records of the period, and it may be that he, like the comic gatemen, was invented by the bard entirely for dramatic purposes.) Perhaps by attributing such cruel views of the Queen and her attendants to such obviously unsympathetic characters, Shakespeare hoped to make his own true feelings plain without offending the strict sensibilities of his royal patron, Jacob.

One other, smaller, bone of some contention that the critics have seen fit to worry over and hold up as proof that *Færie's Fortunes Founded* could not have been penned by Shakespeare, is the unobtrusive reference made by Prospero, during his musings on the many names by which he has been labelled, to 'a saddle-wire, a dee.' Such critics have declared the English usage of the word 'dee' to denote a d-shaped loop of wire by which means objects such as weapons or canteens may be hung from a saddle, does not commence until the early 18th century, more than a hundred years after Shakespeare's demise. To these learned pontificators we would only timidly observe that many of the words within the English language have been found, upon examination, to have their first printed usage in the works of Shakespeare. Might it not be that only the comparatively late discovery of *Færie's Fortunes Founded* has prevented the word 'dee' from having its rightful inclusion in the Swan of Stratford-Upon-Avon's almost prescient vocabulary?

There is no doubt that history will be the final judge of this work's authenticity, and with that firmly in our minds let us, then, in conclusion, ask the reader to place such controversies to one side as they read and hopefully enjoy what is at very least a fascinating and most entertaining curiosity in its own right.

Sincerely,

The Editors

H.W.—
The next piece is pretty filthy, but it pertains to the 18th century incarnation of these probably-mythical agents. I know how you and Bessy feel about this sort of muck, so I've left the pages uncut, to be opened at your discretion. Best—

G. O'B.

→

THE NEW ADVENTURES OF
FANNY HILL
Or, The Further Memoirs of a Woman of Pleasure
as recounted to Mr. John Cleland

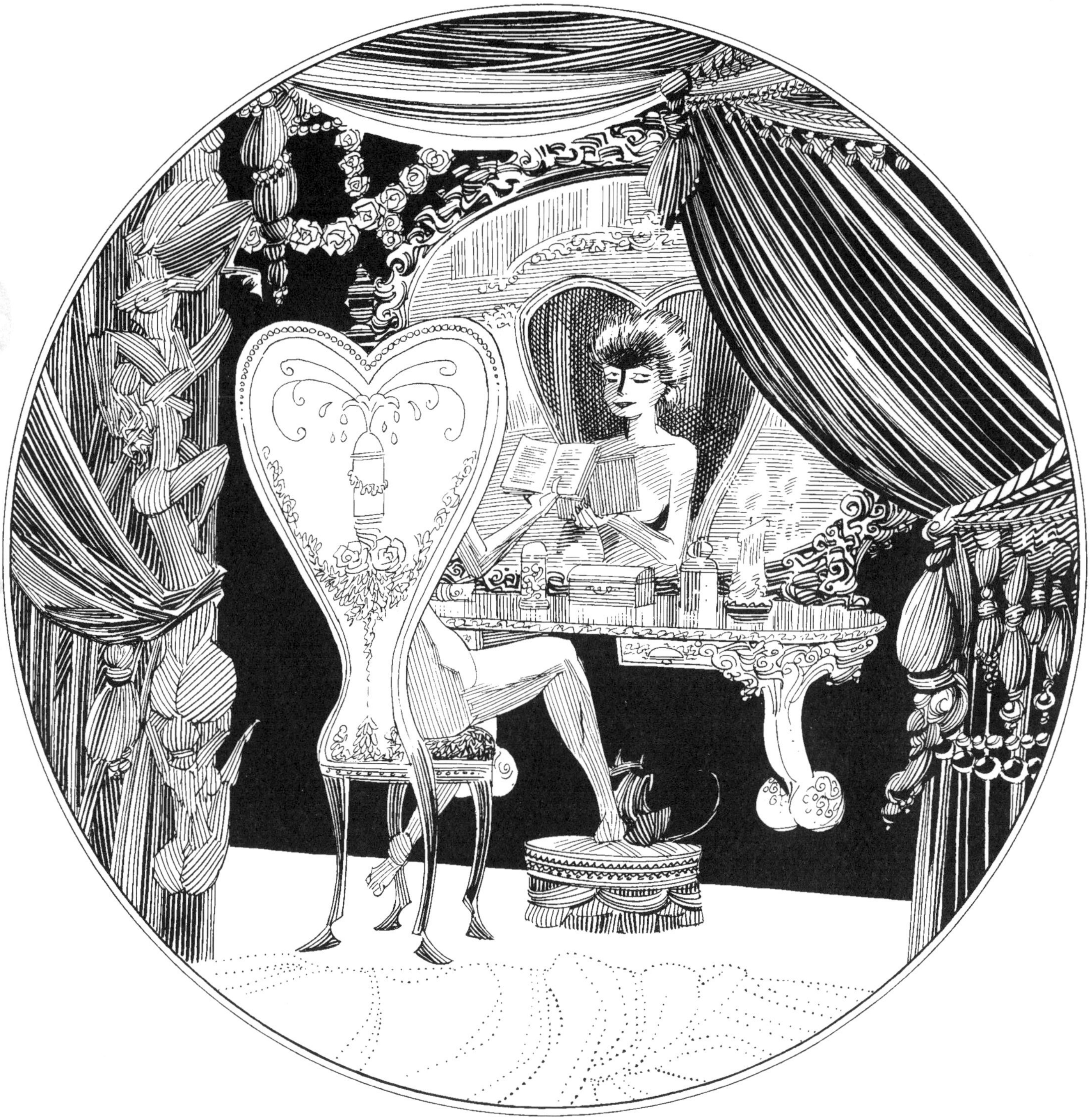

LONDON:
MCMXII

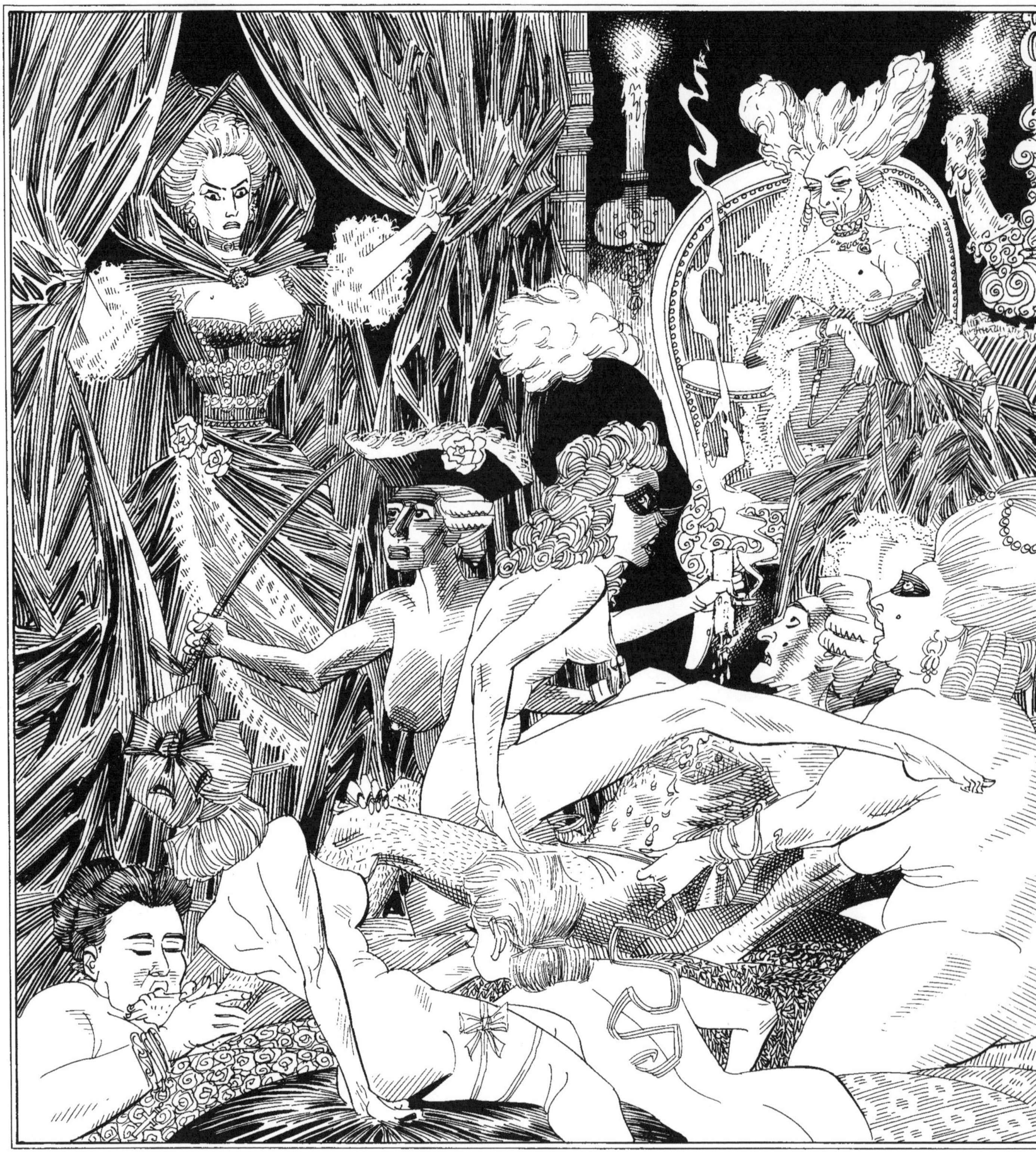

My Dearest Mr. Cleland,

You are surprised, no doubt, to hear from one whose exploits were the substance of a book you wrote some forty summers gone. Given the troubles heaped upon you following that publication, might I hope that said surprise is not unpleasant, at a correspondence unexpectedly renewed after so long? I am, you may be sure, still your own sweet, young Fanny, yet the worrisome idea occurs that you, dear Mr. Cleland, must be older now if, please God, you are yet alive. You surely have not been preserved in so remarkable a fashion as have I, by methods I shall presently explain. Kindly biographer, it is my hope that these lines find you well, and young enough, at least in some part, to respond as once you did to my adventures, frankly told. You may recall when last I wrote I had just married Charles and settled to a life of wifely virtue. This was not to be. Advised by friends I soon surprised Charles at a bawdy-house kept by the elderly, infamous Madame St. Clair. Cutting him off without a sou, I sold the home that had become a grave, now, to our love, and thought that I should like to travel and forget.

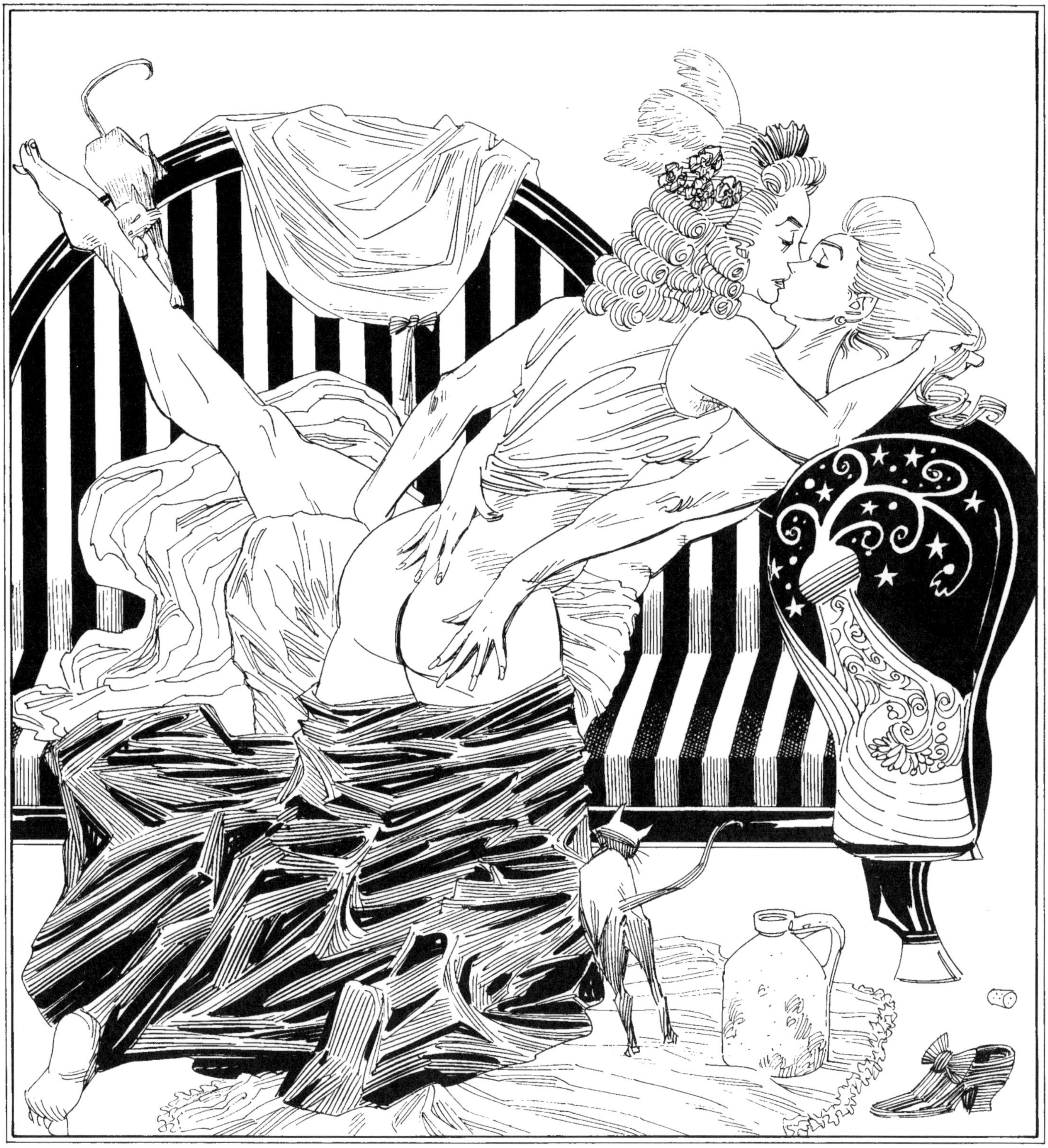

Do not think me hasty in my sudden urge to journey. Rather, I was powerfully sensitive to my uncommon situation: after the release of your biography, good Mr. Cleland, my most intimate affairs were seemingly made plain to all the world. In subsequence, I had received (as have you, I am sure) both smirking admiration and rebuke, in equal measure. Seeking guidance, yet with no one sharing my condition to whom I might turn, I was thus glad to learn that the notorious Mistress Flanders was returned, a wealthy widow, from her sorry transportation to Virginia. Visiting her London residence I found a handsome, generously-made wench, fifty-and-some years of age, her situation not unlike my own, happy to share the benefits of her experience. She bade me travel broadly and love freely, though advised that readers only love a wanton if she make pretence at penitence. "Discussing love, your warmest treasure," here she gestured, "is your euphemism. Whether writ or spoke, the hand glides smoothly to it, else it lingers, tart and wicked, on the lips, the tongue." Here were our conversation's thread, sweet Molly's hand below my petticoats and all our raiment lost, yet I took home from our encounter her advice, and fresh resolve to roam the globe.

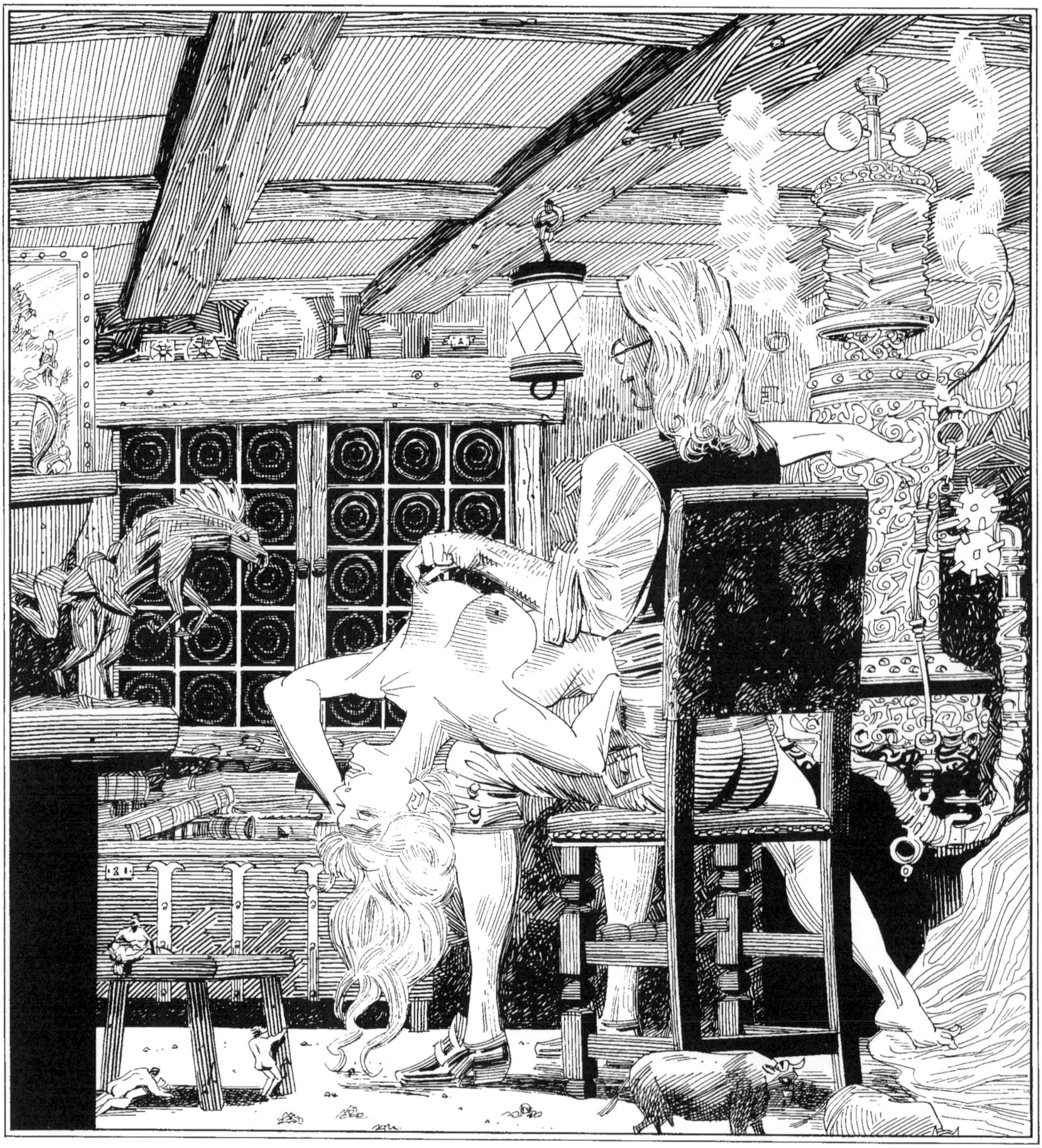

And so, in 1754, some six and twenty years of age, I set out for my foreign jaunt upon a clipper out of Bristol where, narrowly having missed the evening's tide, I was obliged to wait until the morning after, finding myself unexpectedly without accommodation. Fortunately, I fell into discourse with a former shipboard surgeon, one Lemuel Gulliver, who gallantly proposed I share his rooms above a nearby tavern, *The Admiral Benbow*. Though like Mistress Flanders he had twice my years, he made, like she, for stimulating company. He too had suffered scandals from dissemination of an over-candid memoir, but suggested that such bawdy tales might be more widely tolerated if there were a comic or fantastical approach to their recounting. We then passed the night with an agreeable discussion of my host's many adventures and the keepsakes that remained from them, such as the miniature-made garden of the Zipangese kind that he kept there as a window-box and habitat for tiny, bare homunculi; a dozen lewd and acrobatic natives he had smuggled out from distant Lilliput. He also demonstrated a device from science-crazed Laputa, to invigorate tired skin, that I found endlessly delightful. I sailed next day, thinking I should not meet my friend again.

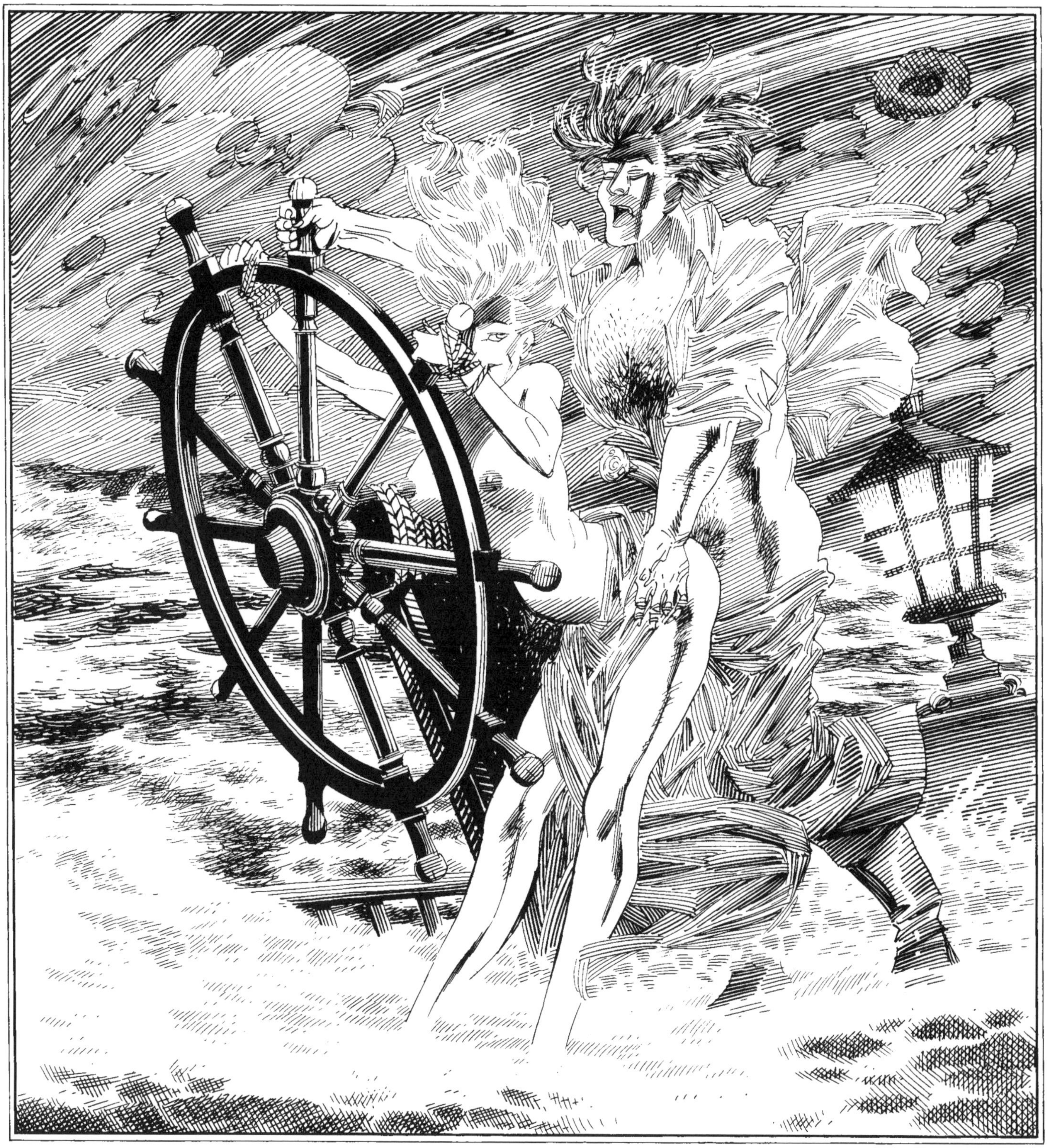

And now, my dear biographer, I must narrate one of my most surprising misadventures hereto. We were not far sailed from England when our ship fell foul of pirates, captained by one Clegg, whose youth belied his infamy. I dare not think what fate befell my fellow travellers, for the handlings I received were stern and vigorous. Taken aboard the buccaneer's ship *Imogene*, you may imagine that I was the subject of much ribald commentary and not a little solitary ardour in the rigging. This persisted until Captain Clegg himself elicited my name, and on the instant swore himself my most sincere admirer, having read my exploits in your own account, sweet Mr. Cleland, which I gathered had been something of a favourite with the *Imogene's* discerning crew. With my credentials thus established, the young brigand's attitude towards me was entirely changed, so that he was made more concerned for my well-being. During a fierce tempest, he insisted that I be lashed to the wheel for my own safety, sheltering my body with his own, close pressed. He even offered me a tour of the Malaccan Straits, suggesting that he take me up the southeast passage, although I declined, asking instead to be set down somewhere in Europe.

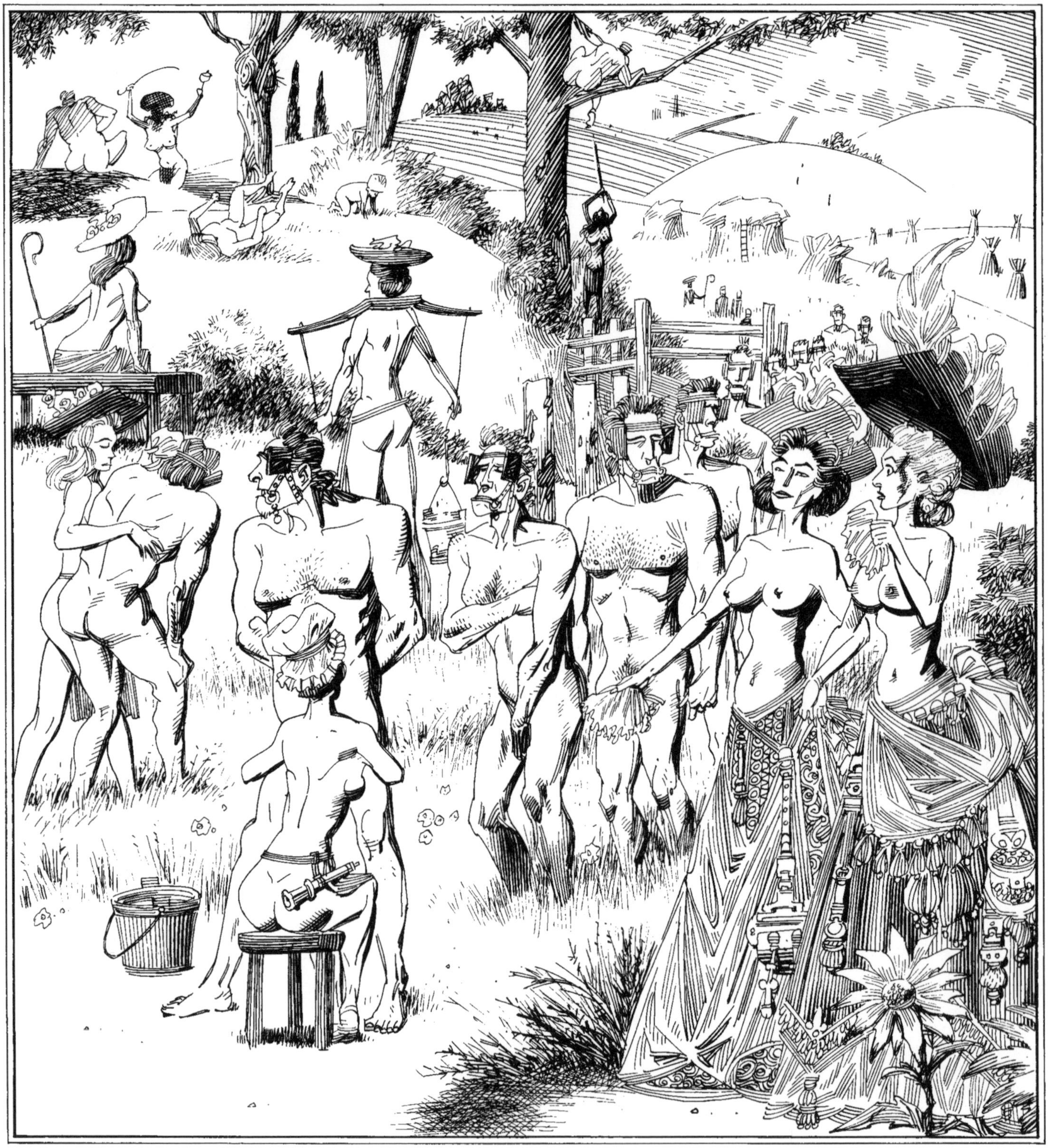

Thus I came eventually to be put ashore in Rotterdam, greatly surprised that I had not had my considerable fortune taken from me by my roughneck captors. As it was, the gallant Captain Clegg insisted I be paid a proper wage for what he called my services aboard the *Imogene*, and to this end had passed a hat amongst the crew for their donations. I thanked them sincerely, though it seemed to me I had not done a stroke. From Holland, then, I next made my way south by carriage into Germany, where near the border shared with France I came at last to Micromona, a peculiar country that is ruled by women and where men are kept only as slaves. Affecting to be angels plunged from Paradise, the Micromonan ladies claim to get themselves with child by rattling the branches of a certain tree brought there from Heaven, though in truth this is accomplished with the necessary substances delivered by means of a large cake-icing mechanism, or syringe. Indeed, my hostesses took me to see a novel type of dairy-farm whereat the vital raw ingredient concerned was humanely collected and then taken off for future usage. I remained in Micromona for perhaps a month, then travelled on.

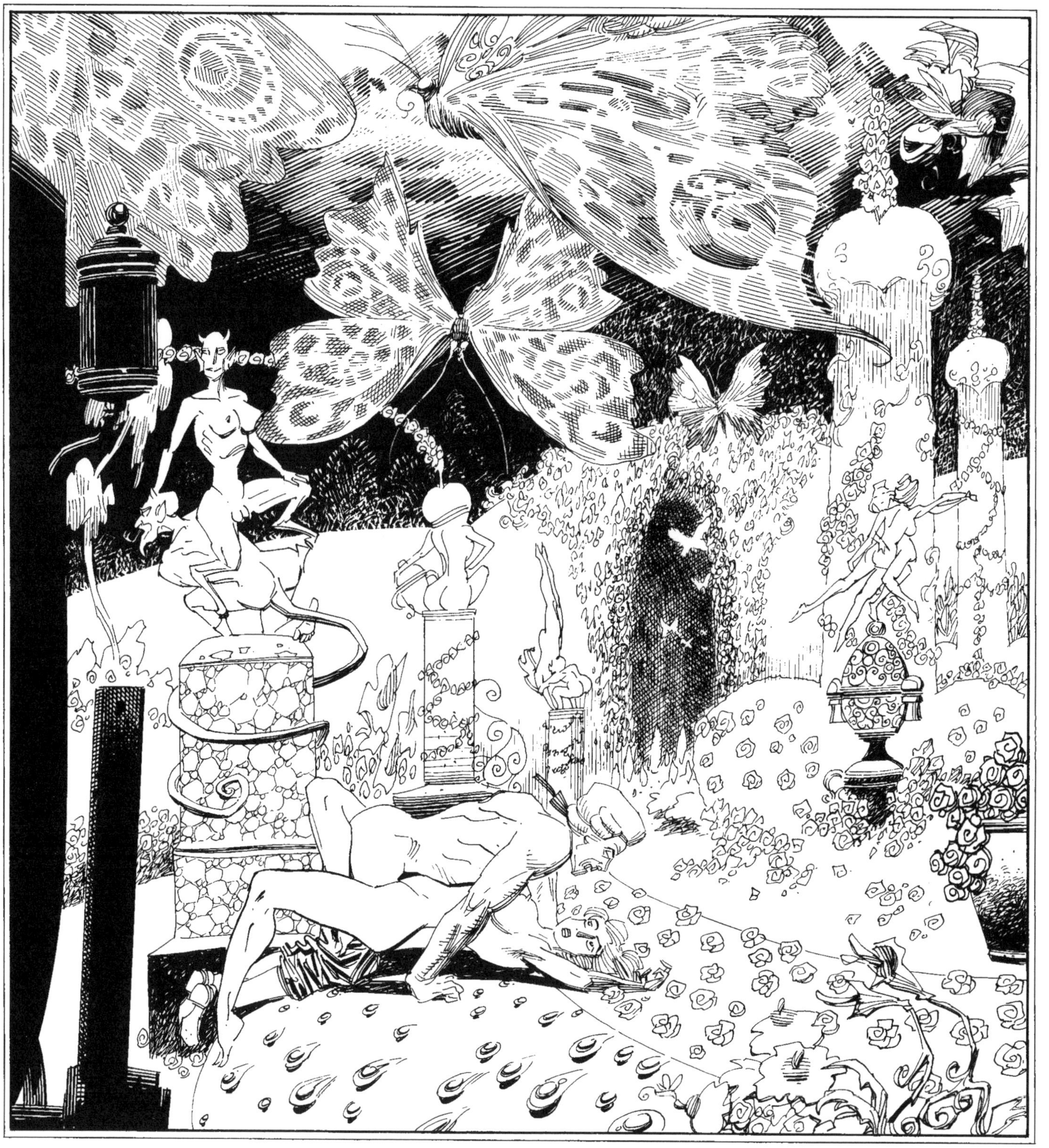

And so it was that I reached Horselberg, called sometimes Venusberg, beneath which mountain in a wanton, twilit sprawl exists the realm of amorous Queen Venus. In exquisitely suggestive ornamental gardens spread about the tunnel-mouth that let into this perfumed underworld itself, I paid my coachman, not in coin, though to my way of thinking very generously, and then ventured alone down that pellucid passageway under the hill, the very mound of Venus. Here there flapped nocturnal butterflies of a prodigious size, their vast sails stained with vivid arabesques richer than all the tapestries of the Orient. Having attained the cavern's furthest end, I came into the country proper and was greeted in a most surprising although not unwelcome fashion by the Queen herself, surrounded by her playful courtiers. Later, when we were by ourselves, Her Majesty revealed the means by which the huge and lovely tunnel-moths were fed, anointing our most sensate parts with fragrant treacle as we slumped together on a lush and velvet grassy slope. Soon we were each attended by some half-a-dozen of the gorgeous, fluttering things that cleaned us with long sable tongues, curled up like gentle whips, and lulled us to exhausted slumber with the soft petticoat whisper of their wings.

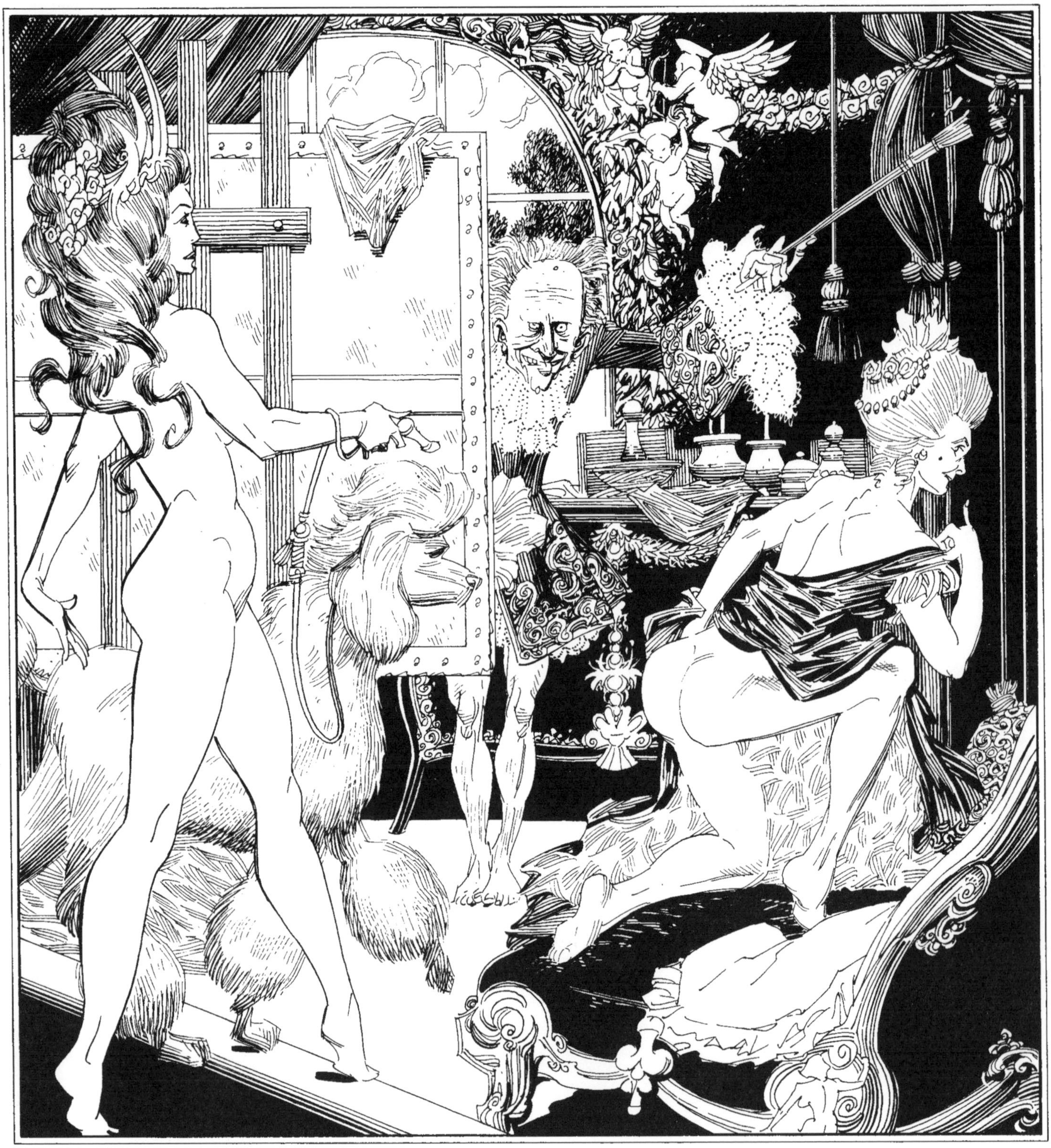

I would not have you think, kind Mr. Cleland, that my time there under Horselberg was in entirety consumed by the pursuit of sybaritic pleasures, for I had occasion also to acquaint myself with many lively and inventive works of literature, and was indeed myself allowed to make in some small means a contribution to the Arts. Residing in one wing of the extensive palace was an illustrator, a Marquis named Dorat, kept there at the Queen's behest as painter and official portraitist by Royal appointment. Taking something of a shine to me, the talented Marquis suggested I should pose for his next composition, which he told me was intended to imply that sacred union which exists between the various and innumerable living things in God's creation. Supine upon a decorative chaise-longue, I was to represent humanity, while standing for the kingdom of the beasts we had the Marquis' own firmly-built hunting dog, a puddle-hound (so called for their wet-looking coats) named Franz. Years afterwards, revisiting that land, I showed my dear friend Marguerite the illustration that resulted, although she, disdainful, did not recognise my likeness, whereon I thought better of confessing.

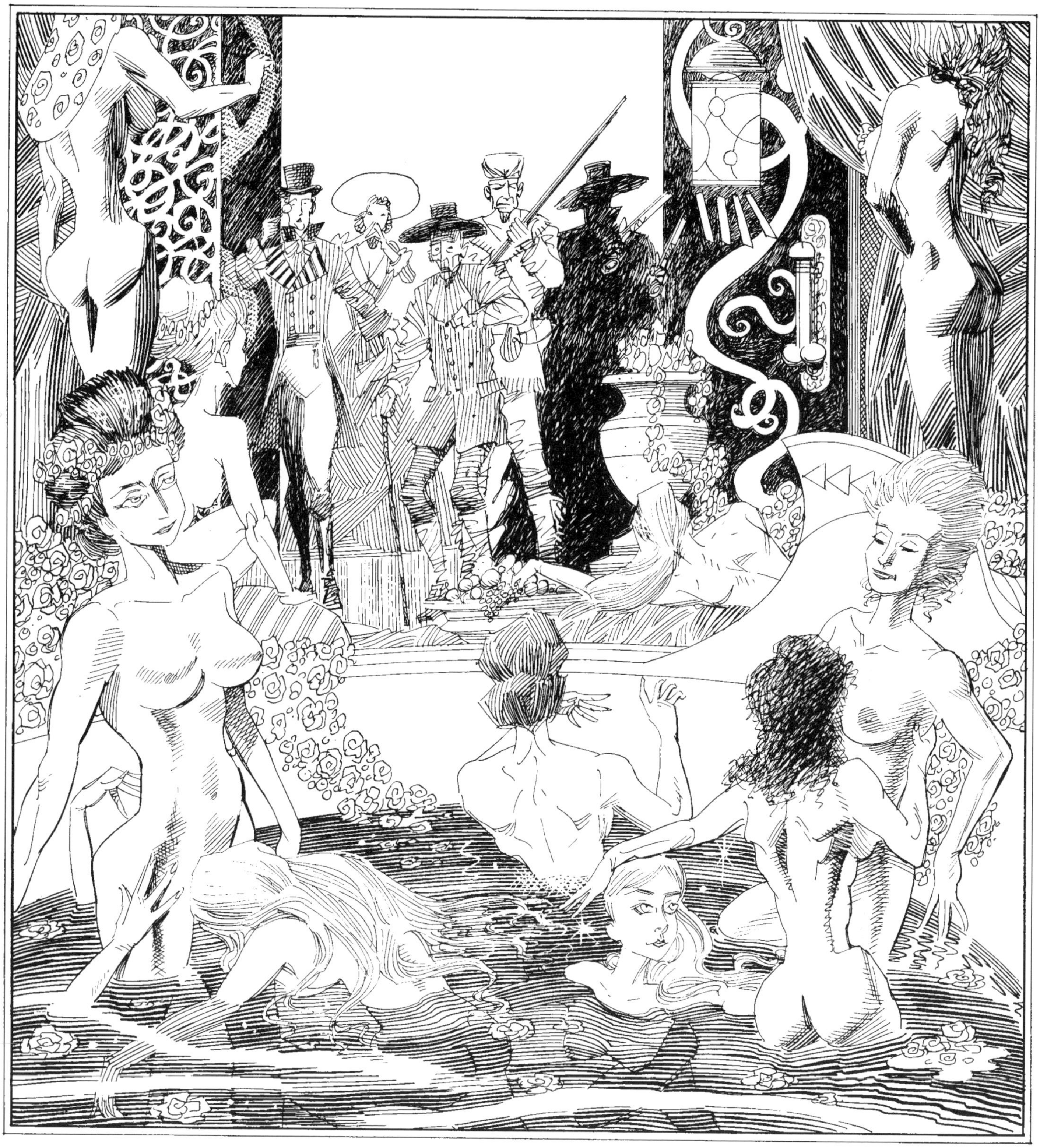

Time passed so oddly there beneath the mountain that it scarcely seemed to pass at all. For all I knew it was yet the late months of 1754, or early on in 1755 at worst, myself not yet quite twenty-seven years upon the world. One afternoon, the Queen and I reclined together in the lavender-oil scented waters of her marvellous bath-house, fashioned in what I construed to be an Ottoman or else Byzantine style, where we were suffering the quite delicious ministrations of the 'minnows' Venus kept there for this very purpose, although also for their decorative worth. These slipped and darted into each submarine cranny, nibbling where the dark weed drifts slow and luxuriant beneath the water, so that when the bath-house doors burst rudely open, interrupting us, it took both Venus and myself some several moments to become again composed. Recovered from our crises, we discovered our intruders to be an outlandish crew led by my former intimate acquaintance Mr. Gulliver, who, though it seemed to me but some few months since our encounter was now frail and in his dotage, ninety years or more in age. Apparently, the year was 1793, so when my new companions finally left Horselberg, I travelled with them.

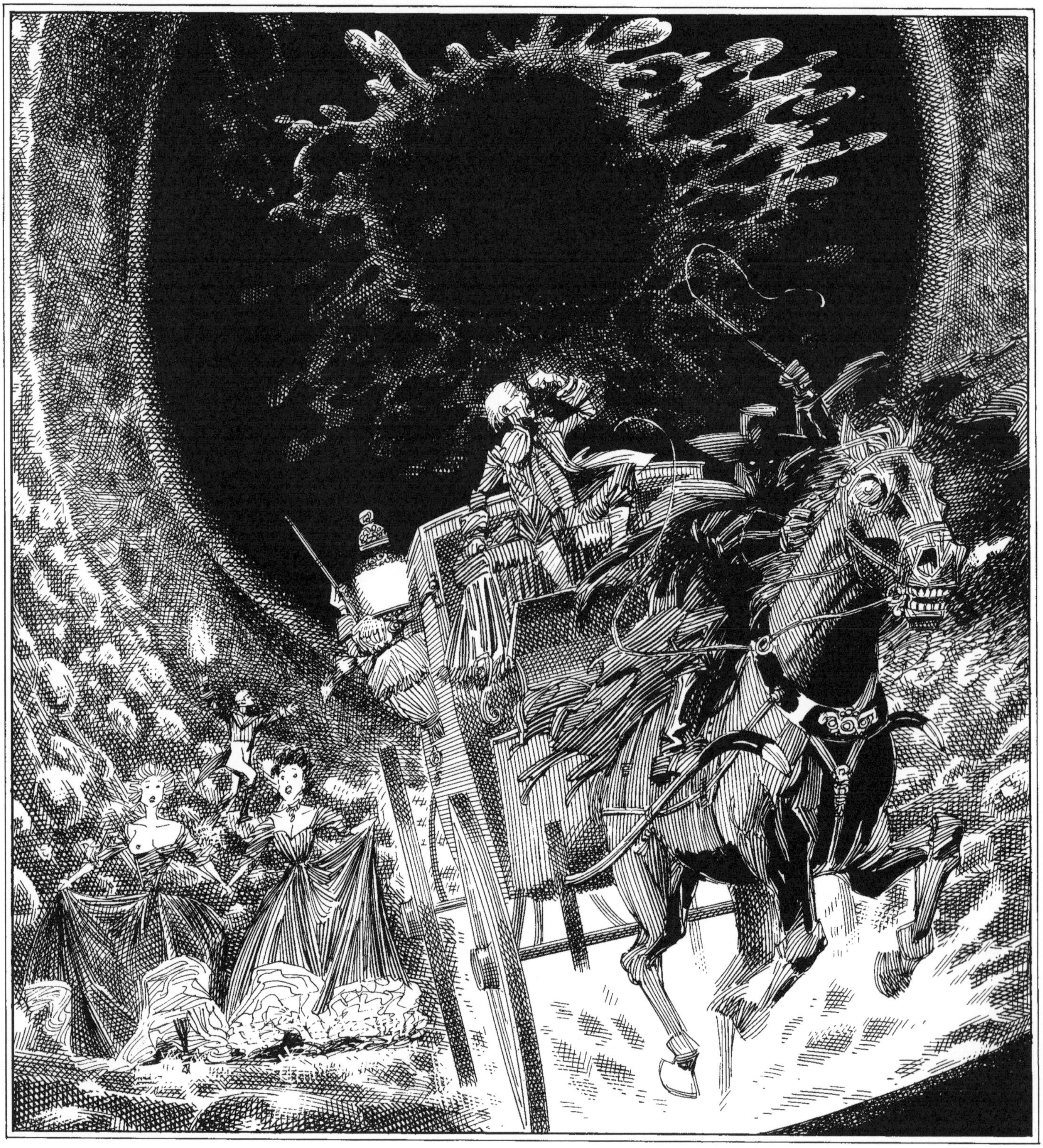

What an adventurous gang they were! Besides the now-elderly Gulliver, the group included a tatterdemalion smuggler who, beneath his mask, proved to be yet another old companion, namely Captain Clegg, himself aged to a silver-haired man of some five and sixty years. A huntsman from America, one Mr. Bumppo, was a younger man, but had a rather cocksure manner that I did not care for, and it was with the two youngest members of the fellowship, a very pretty English couple called the Blakeneys, Marguerite and Percy, that I found the deepest friendship. Our extraordinary band, I learned, were catspaws of the British Crown, and I had many startling exploits in that company. Upon the westerly American peninsula called Brobdingnag, inhabited by giants, we became embroiled in wars between Brobdingnagians and displaced colossi, descendants of the towering Pantagruel, come from Utopia in the southern seas. Once, whilst attempting to negotiate a truce in secret with a sympathetic giantess, her hostile spouse returned home unexpectedly, whereupon we were hid about her person. Horrifyingly, her husband chose this moment to insist on conjugal activity, so that we, with our coach and horse, were only spared when, evidently, he decided on some other method of ingress at the last instant.

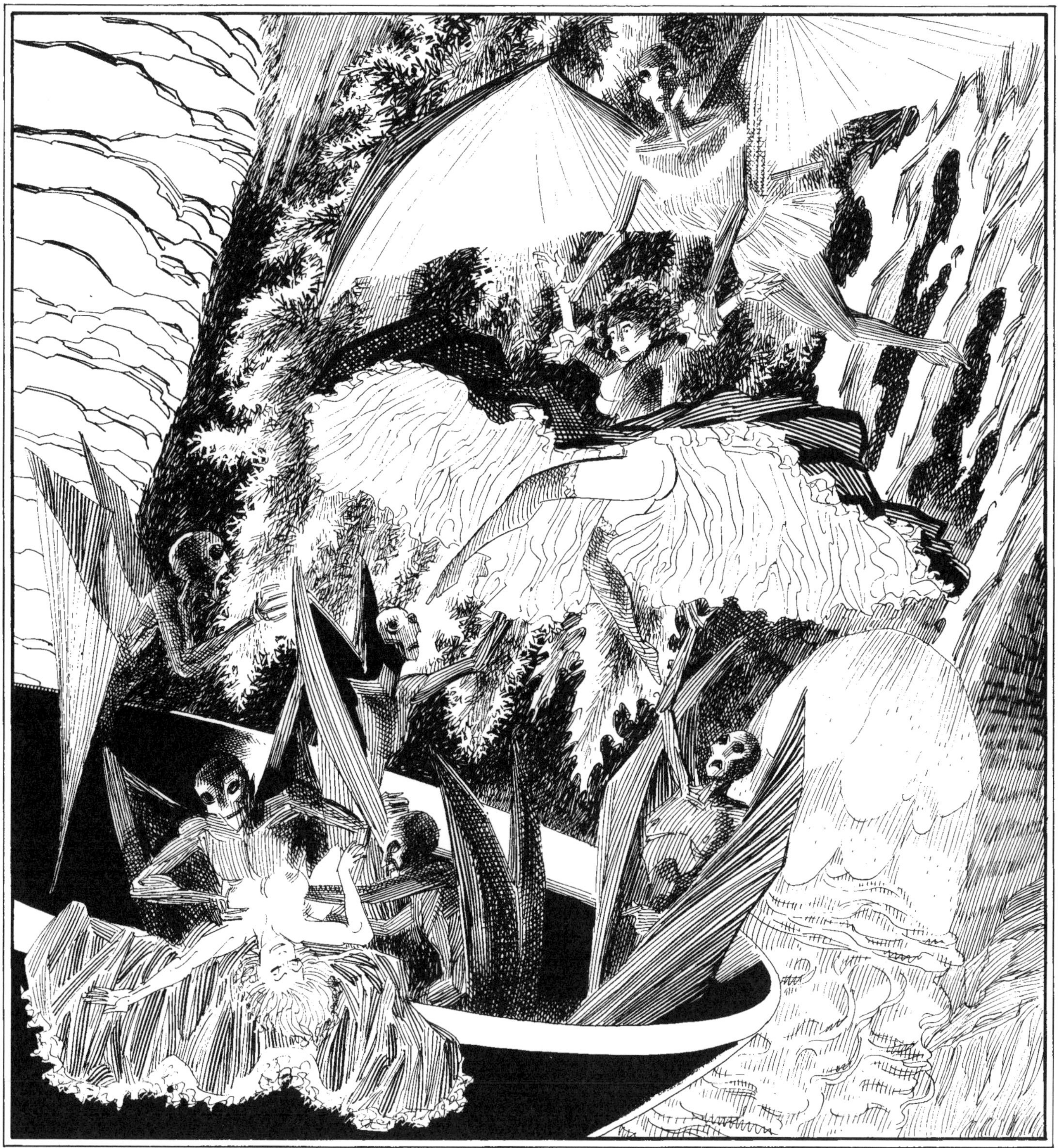

Our other outings were no less alarming nor intriguing, as when we investigated the extensive subterranean territories of the Earth in 1796. I was at this time, I suppose, a septuagenarian, although despite having commenced the normal processes of aging once again on leaving Venusberg, I was to all appearances a comely girl of not yet thirty. In our underground adventures we clashed with the legionnaires of Roman State 'neath northern England, and in monstrous vaulted caves below what we supposed to be the town of Newcastle or thereabouts, we first encountered the strange, stygian civilization of the Vril people or 'Vril-ya' as they called themselves. It was Marguerite and I who fostered an amicable relationship between our league and this remarkable winged breed, after the mutual misunderstandings and hostilities of our first confrontations. Snatched aloft and kidnapped by a female of the species, we were taken to a wide bowl of carved pumice raised atop a stalagmite, that served as nursery to her adolescent young, with Marguerite and I delivered up to these as morsels or confectionary treats. We quickly found the Vril to be a loving, noble folk, whose kisses had the power to thrill or heal, and learned why they are sometimes called 'the coming race.'

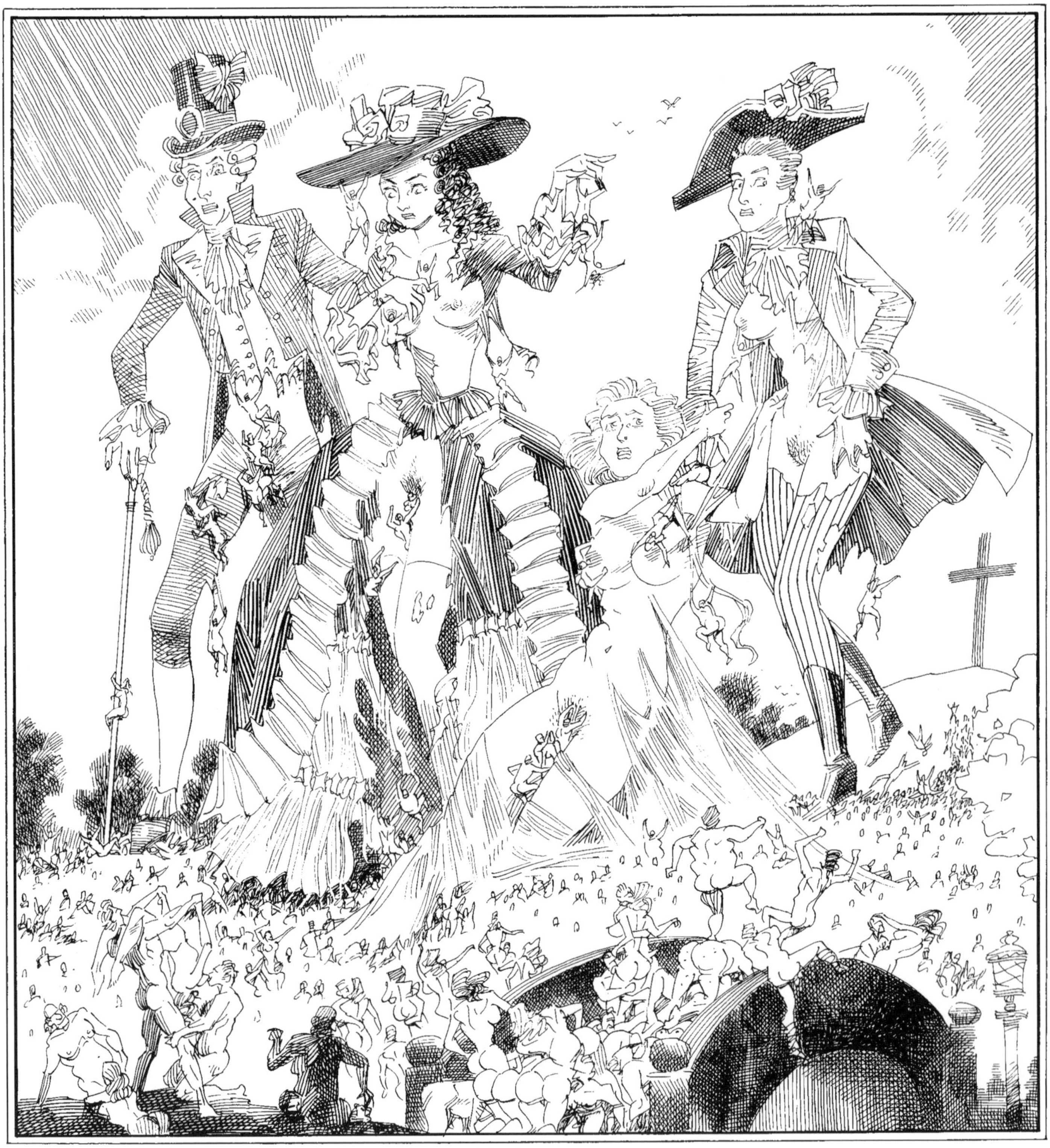

Many were our adventures of a like to this, although these ceased in 1799 upon the death of our beloved mentor, Lemuel Gulliver. He had, to all appearances, died in the arms (and bedchamber) of a sometime addition to our league, the changeable, immortal warrior Orlando, who was female at the time of Gulliver's demise. With Captain Clegg and Mr. Bumppo having quitted our ensemble sometime previously, it was left to Orlando, with the Blakeneys and myself, to see acted our leader's often and fondly expressed wish that he be buried on the isle of Lilliput, so that his grave, a shallow mound to us, should be a grassy hill where youthful Lilliputian lovers should have fine, gay picnics on the gentle slopes. Distressingly, the case of wine we'd brought with us to toast our comrade's passing fell instead into the tiny hands of Lilliput's native community, and was enough to make them wildly drunken in their thousands. A dreadful, seething orgy then broke out, in which it seemed that every member of their population, young or old, was feverishly involved, so that with clothing ripped or chewed to ribbons, it was only by the grace of Providence that we were able to crawl free and find our ship again.

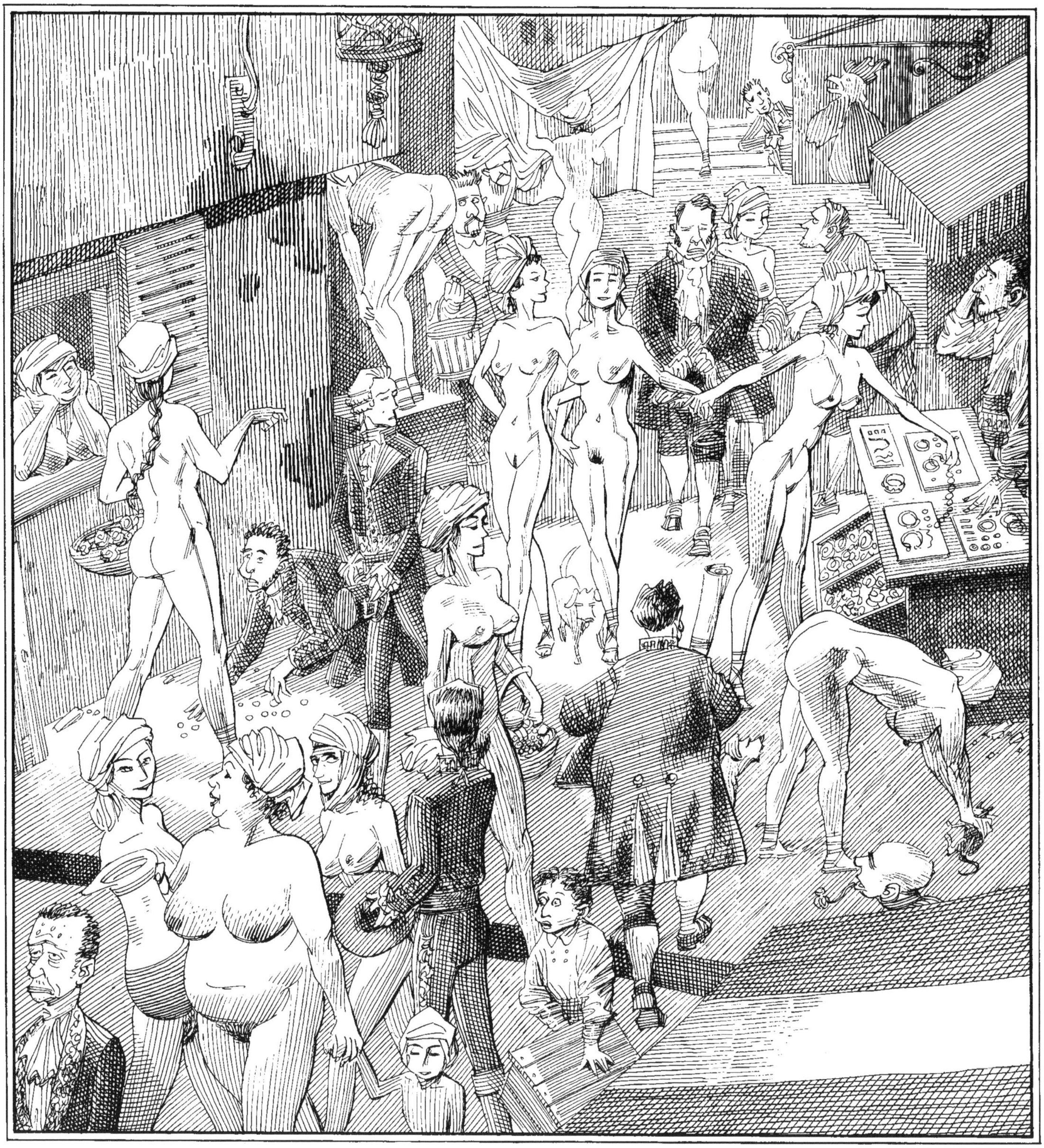

With wise and kindly Gulliver dead, it seemed that those of us remaining were not much inclined to risk our youthful health and beauty in pursuit of dangerous adventure, and preferred instead idle devotion to the pleasures of the senses. For some years, resting between exploits, Percy, Marguerite and I, sometimes accompanied by glamorous Orlando, had been holidaying at some of the European continent's most amatory resorts, including Horselberg, and it was on a tour of such agreeable locations that we now embarked, our services no longer, it would seem, required by our shadowy paymasters in England. One erotic paradise we often visited was the delightful kingdom of Tryphême upon the coast of the Mediterranean, close to the Balearic Isles. Here, in a society refreshingly made free of all shame and pretence, all actions which do not distress one's neighbours are allowed, and women are encouraged to go naked save for silver sandals and a yellow scarf upon their heads to shield them from the constant sunshine. Men, less pleasing to the eye, go dressed and have felt hats to spare them from the blaze of noon, although for reasons that are presently obscure to me they never wear these, but rather elect to carry them by hand from place to place.

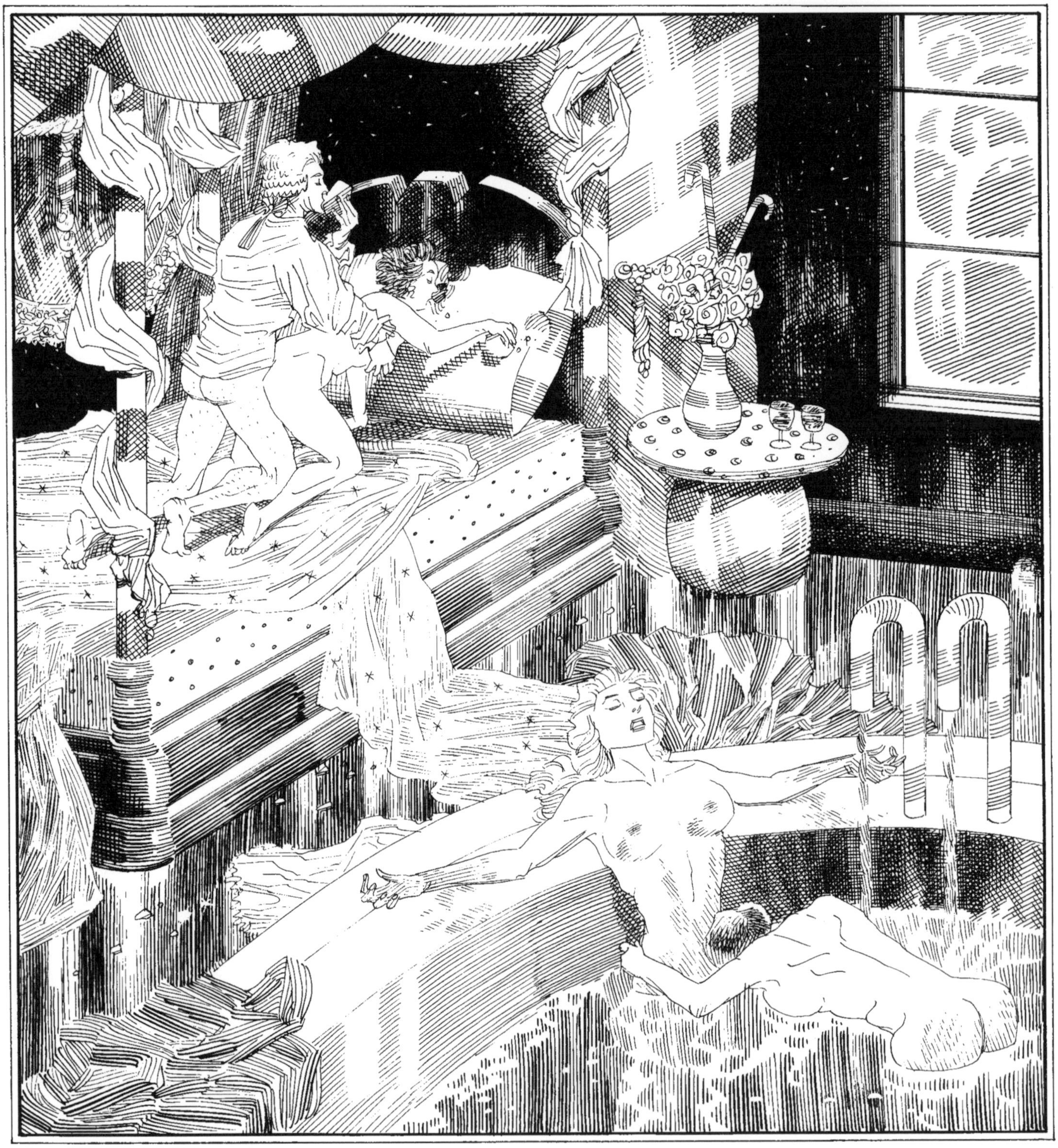

Another favourite destination was Cockaigne, often called also Cocaigne or Cuccagna, a small inland country at the edge of Germany that we were told could also sometimes be an island when the vast, wide lake surrounding it was not dried up. Here, all was dedicated to contentment, so that there were laws where anyone found working might be gaoled. The physical delights of love were not neglected, with the city's wondrously decorated palace library containing helpful charts of the venereal postures and positions, alongside such classic writings as *The Thirty-Two Gratifications*. But it was in pleasures culinary and gastronomic that Cockaigne excelled, with almost every building and its furnishings or fittings made from the most sweet and toothsome delicacies. The hotel where customarily we stayed was an enormous and elaborate moulded aspic that let in the light through walls of colourful and delicately-flavoured gelatine. Percy and Marguerite would roll and slide upon the sticky counterpane of icing spread across their gateaux bed, while in a sunken tub of hard-glazed golden honey-crystal I would frolic with Orlando in the warm and swirling cocoa-au-lait pouring from the peppermint-cane spigots. Thus we passed the years until perhaps 1802, when I decided to return alone to Venusberg.

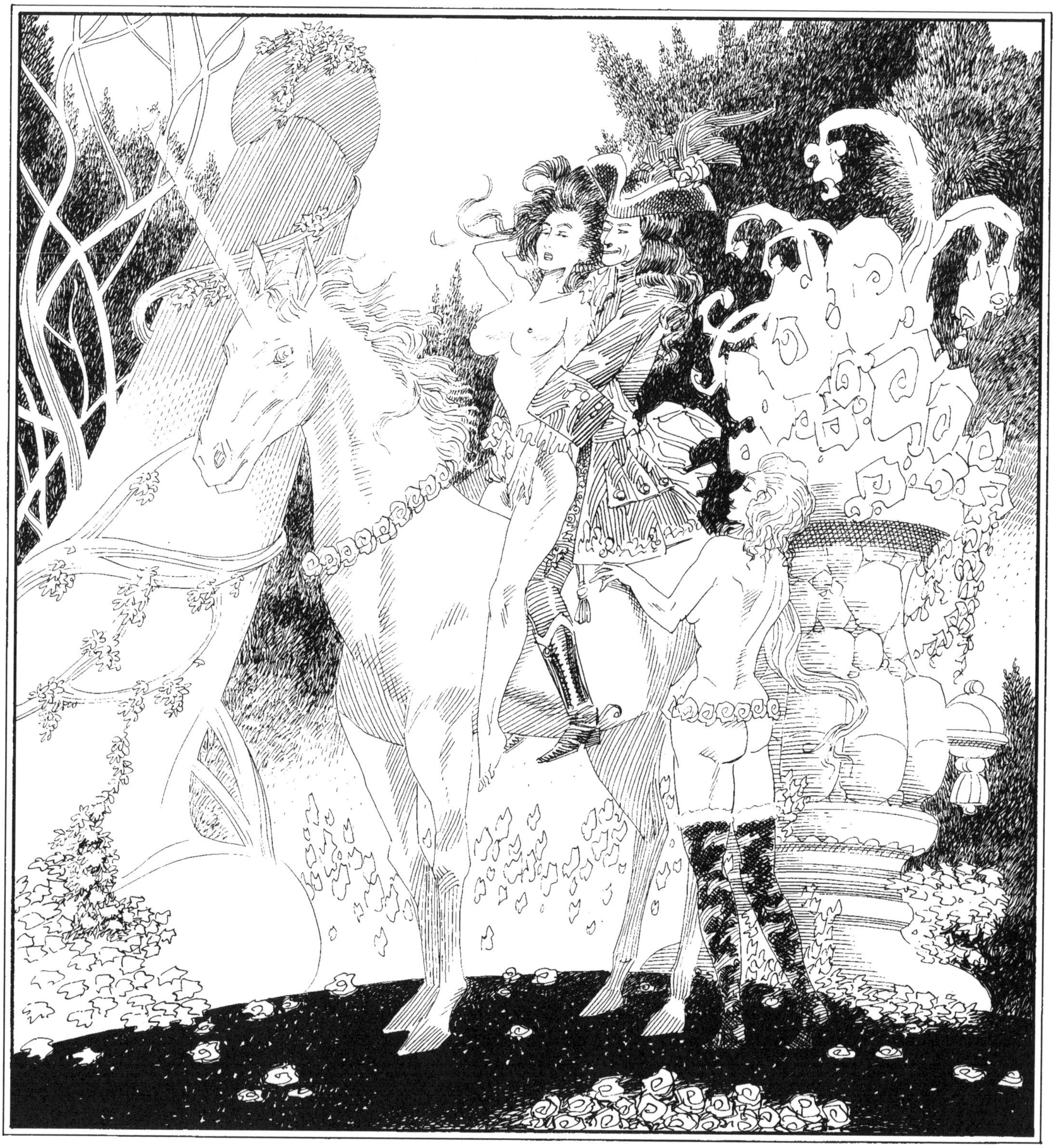

Do not infer from this, good Mr. Cleland, that I spurned my comrades, nor they me. Indeed, we parted as the very best of friends and all expect that we might see each other soon enough when next they venture in their journeying to Horselberg. I left my lovely Marguerite and Percy to enjoy (particularly Percy, I suspect) the newly-altered nature of Orlando, who was by this time become a man again, and went back a girl still little more than thirty years of age to that sublime town underneath the hill, where I knew I would not again grow old. In truth, time is so queer within this place that generous Queen Venus introduced me to her best-beloved, the chevalier Tannhauser, though I had seen with mine own eyes the sprouting traveller's staff some way from Horselberg said to commemorate the knight's death in the thirteenth century after Our Lord. Think kindly of me, Mr. Cleland, endlessly at sport and fun amidst the perfumed gardens of this glorious, time-forsook domain, and if these further memoirs should afford you but the slightest surge in your former affections for me, then be assured that I am pleased, and that moreover I remain your own, true

Fanny Hill

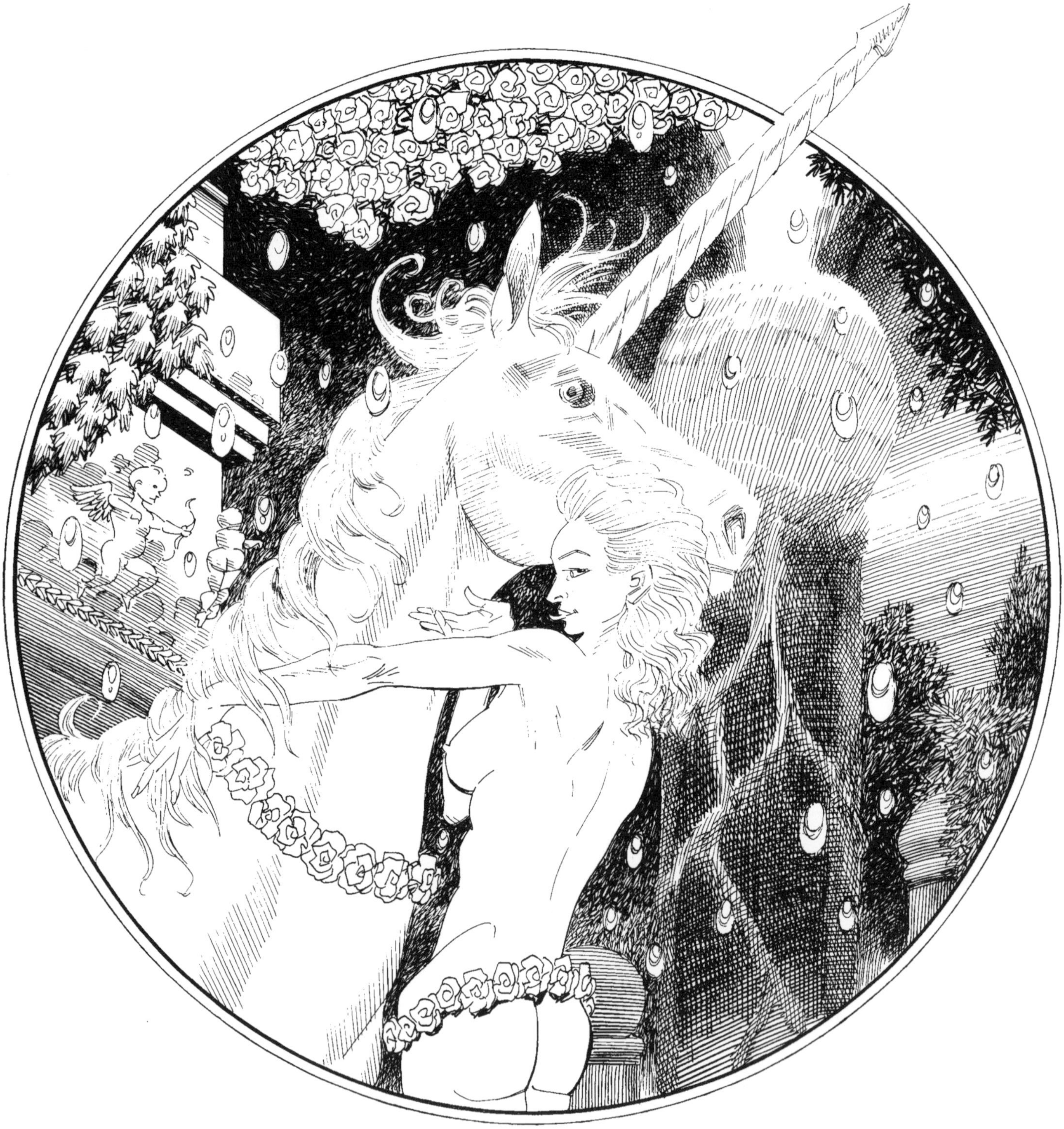

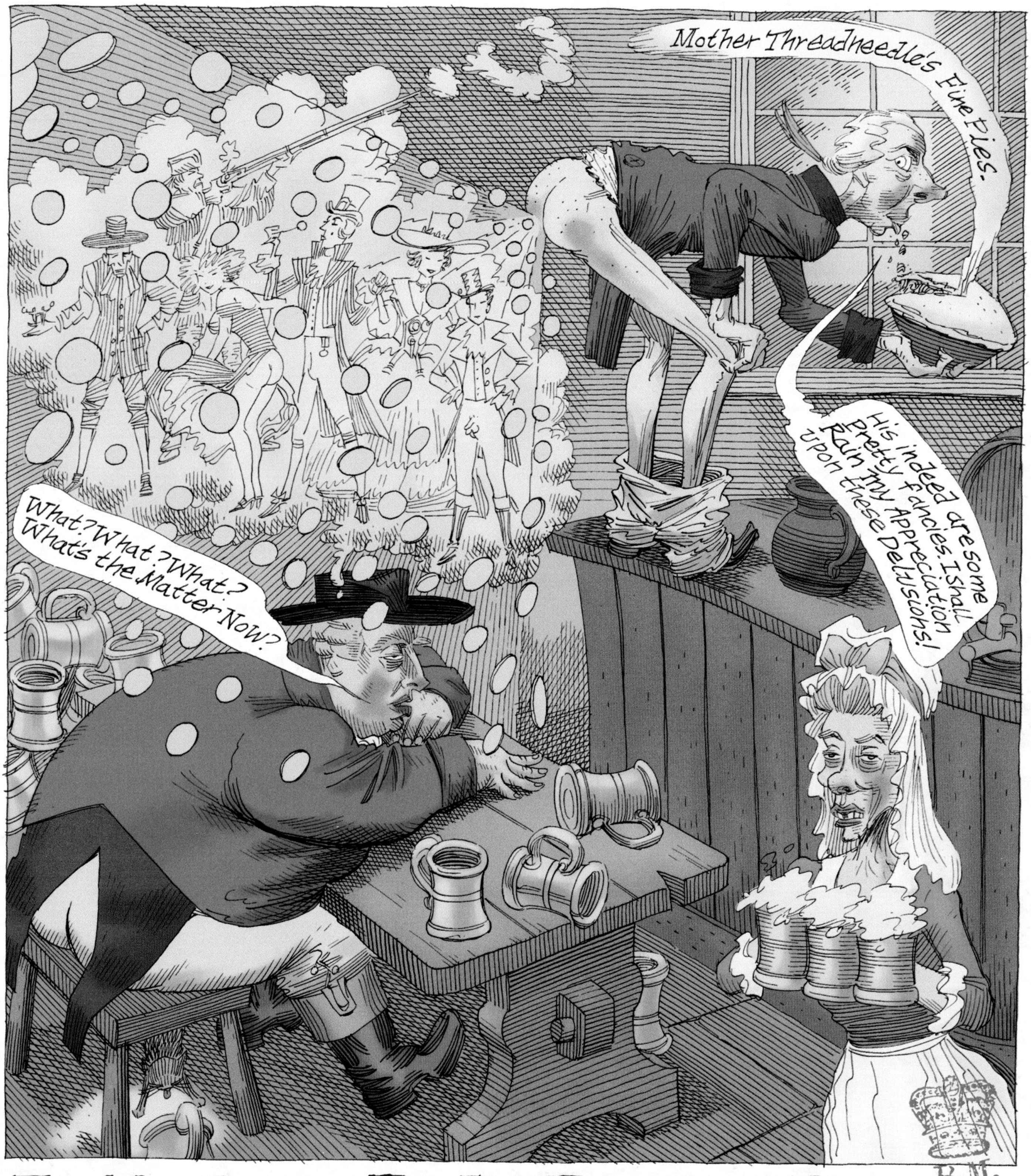
Mother Threadneedle's Fine Pies.
His indeed are some Pretty Fancies. I shall Rain my Appreciation upon these Delusions!
What? What? What? What's the Matter Now?
B.M.

The Most Popular Tall-Tale Teller in the Tavern.

Farmer George, in his cups, delights the Ale-House with his merrie nonsense, rewarded by Billy the Bursar, who showers the Great Land-Owner with a precious country-side commodity. Let us hope the honest rustic wakes to share with us more of his Gulli-vants, Fanny-tasies, and his Pimpern-eloquence!

In this 1794 cartoon by 18th Century master Humphreys, we see mentally-weak King George III, often called "Farmer George," as a tavern bore slumped half-insensible across a table, muttering his catch-phrase "What? What? What? What's the matter now?" Meanwhile, erupting from his ailing mind are the forms of fictional characters such as Gulliver and Fanny Hill, whom the deluded monarch believed to comprise a secret band protecting him from foreign assault. "Billy the Bursar," simultaneously eating one of "Mother Threadneedle's Fine Pies" (a reference to the Bank of England, in Threadneedle Street) while evacuating gold coins from his bowels, is George's Prime Minister William Pitt, then facing criticism for lavishing funds upon yet another of the King's ridiculous Royal indulgences.

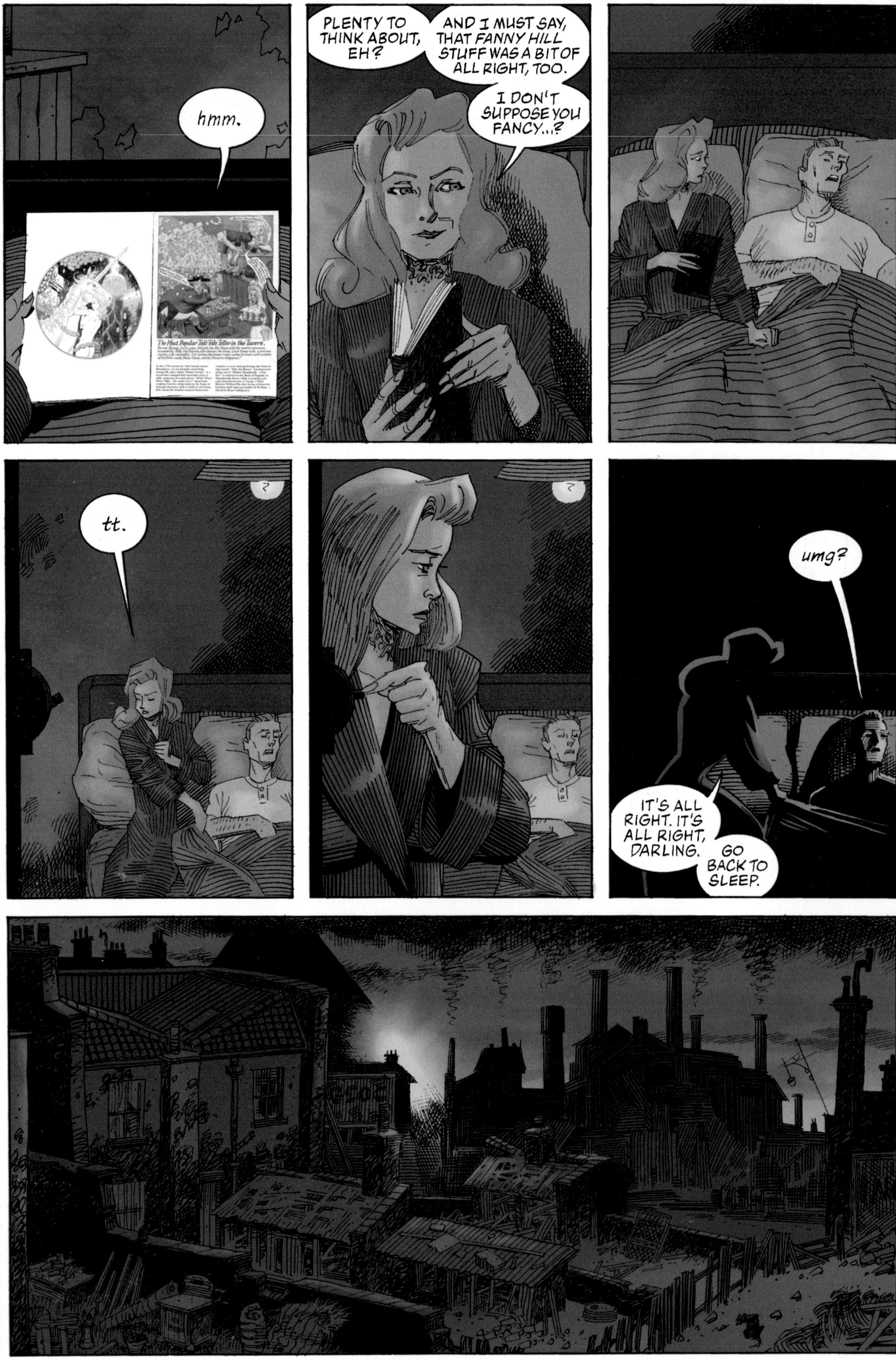
hmm.
The Most Popular Tall-Tale Teller in the Tavern.
PLENTY TO THINK ABOUT, EH?
AND I MUST SAY, THAT FANNY HILL STUFF WAS A BIT OF ALL RIGHT, TOO.
I DON'T SUPPOSE YOU FANCY...?
tt.
umg?
IT'S ALL RIGHT. IT'S ALL RIGHT, DARLING.
GO BACK TO SLEEP.

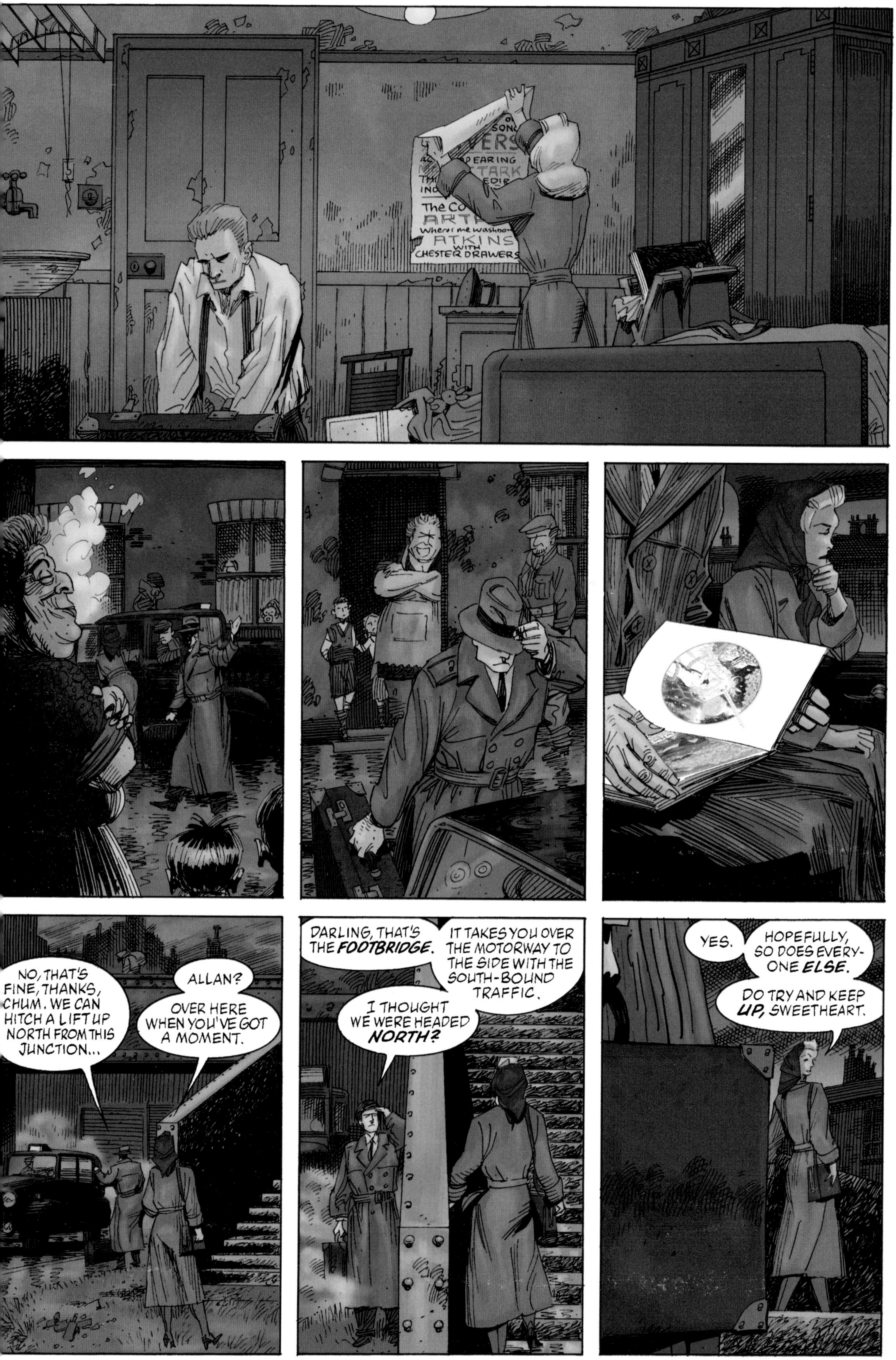
ATKINS
WITH
CHESTER DRAWERS
NO, THAT'S FINE, THANKS, CHUM. WE CAN HITCH A LIFT UP NORTH FROM THIS JUNCTION...
ALLAN?
OVER HERE WHEN YOU'VE GOT A MOMENT.
DARLING, THAT'S THE FOOTBRIDGE.
IT TAKES YOU OVER THE MOTORWAY TO THE SIDE WITH THE SOUTH-BOUND TRAFFIC.
I THOUGHT WE WERE HEADED NORTH?
YES.
HOPEFULLY, SO DOES EVERY-ONE ELSE.
DO TRY AND KEEP UP, SWEETHEART.

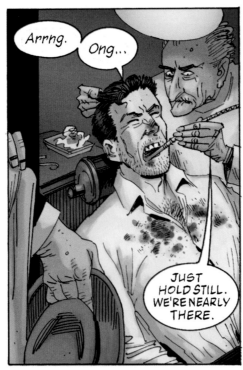

Arrng.

Ong...

JUST HOLD STILL. WE'RE NEARLY THERE.

Oh, Jimmy.

JIMMY, JIMMY, JIMMY.

THEY'VE MADE YOU LOOK A BIT OF A CUNT, HAVEN'T THEY, OLD MAN?

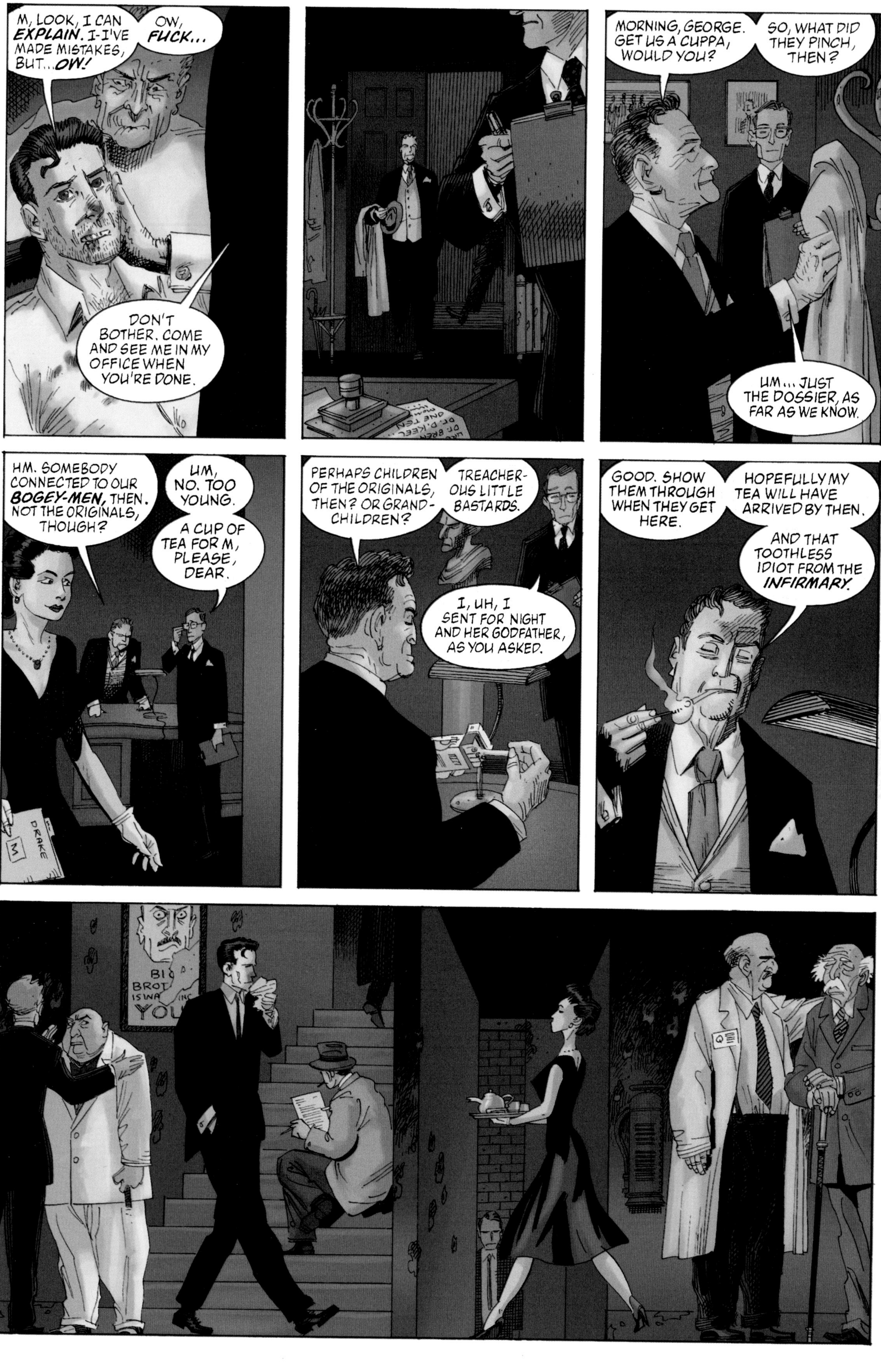
M, LOOK, I CAN EXPLAIN. I-I'VE MADE MISTAKES, BUT... OW!
OW, FUCK...
DON'T BOTHER. COME AND SEE ME IN MY OFFICE WHEN YOU'RE DONE.
MORNING, GEORGE. GET US A CUPPA, WOULD YOU?
SO, WHAT DID THEY PINCH, THEN?
UM... JUST THE DOSSIER, AS FAR AS WE KNOW.
HM. SOMEBODY CONNECTED TO OUR BOGEY-MEN, THEN. NOT THE ORIGINALS, THOUGH?
UM, NO. TOO YOUNG.
A CUP OF TEA FOR M, PLEASE, DEAR.
DRAKE
M
PERHAPS CHILDREN OF THE ORIGINALS, THEN? OR GRAND-CHILDREN?
TREACHER-OUS LITTLE BASTARDS.
I, UH, I SENT FOR NIGHT AND HER GODFATHER, AS YOU ASKED.
GOOD. SHOW THEM THROUGH WHEN THEY GET HERE.
HOPEFULLY MY TEA WILL HAVE ARRIVED BY THEN.
AND THAT TOOTHLESS IDIOT FROM THE INFIRMARY.

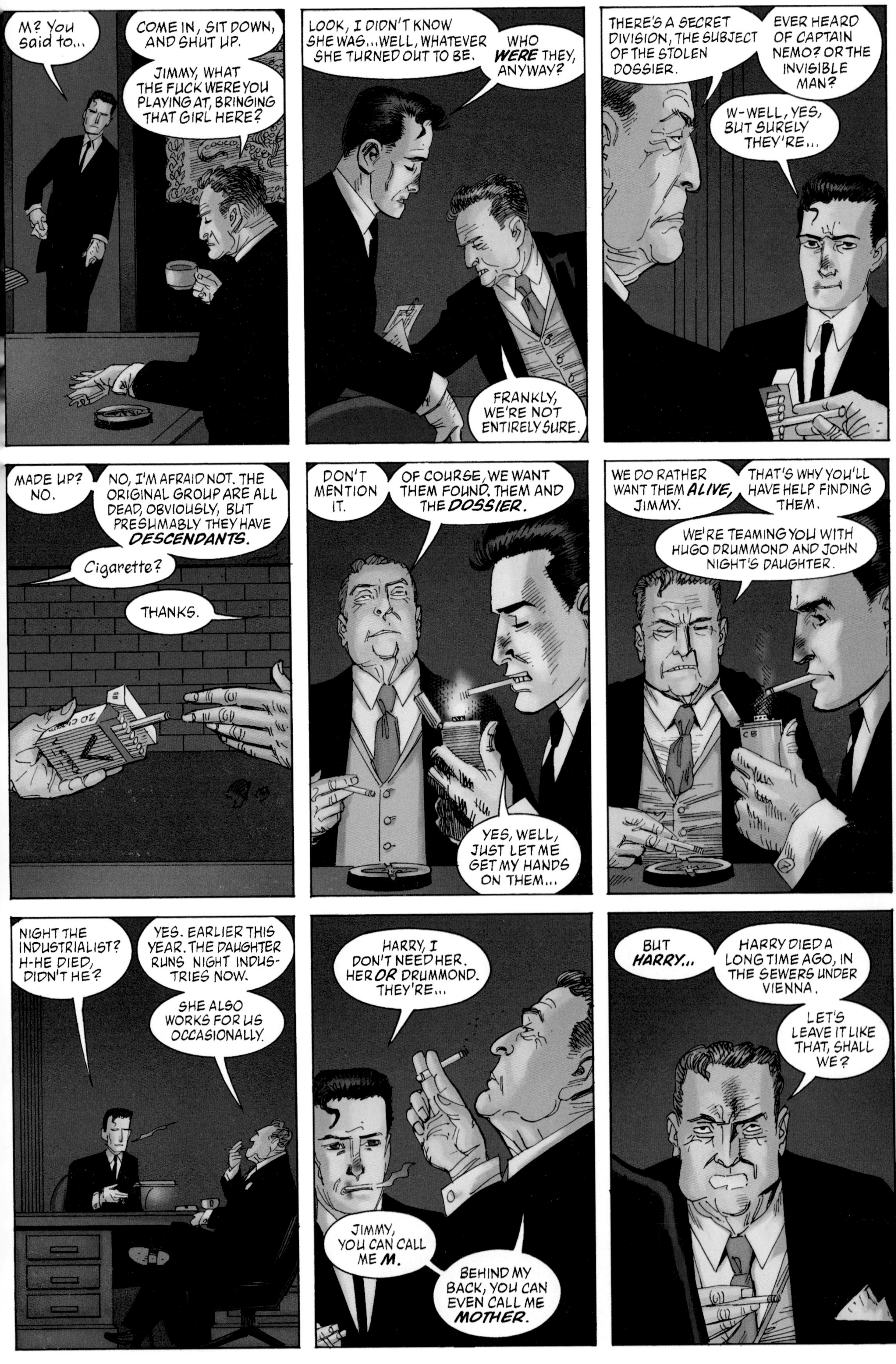
M? You said to...
COME IN, SIT DOWN, AND SHUT UP.
JIMMY, WHAT THE FUCK WERE YOU PLAYING AT, BRINGING THAT GIRL HERE?
LOOK, I DIDN'T KNOW SHE WAS...WELL, WHATEVER SHE TURNED OUT TO BE.
WHO WERE THEY, ANYWAY?
FRANKLY, WE'RE NOT ENTIRELY SURE.
THERE'S A SECRET DIVISION, THE SUBJECT OF THE STOLEN DOSSIER.
EVER HEARD OF CAPTAIN NEMO? OR THE INVISIBLE MAN?
W-WELL, YES, BUT SURELY THEY'RE...
MADE UP? NO.
NO, I'M AFRAID NOT. THE ORIGINAL GROUP ARE ALL DEAD, OBVIOUSLY, BUT PRESUMABLY THEY HAVE DESCENDANTS.
Cigarette?
THANKS.
DON'T MENTION IT.
OF COURSE, WE WANT THEM FOUND. THEM AND THE DOSSIER.
YES, WELL, JUST LET ME GET MY HANDS ON THEM...
WE DO RATHER WANT THEM ALIVE, JIMMY.
THAT'S WHY YOU'LL HAVE HELP FINDING THEM.
WE'RE TEAMING YOU WITH HUGO DRUMMOND AND JOHN NIGHT'S DAUGHTER.
NIGHT THE INDUSTRIALIST? H-HE DIED, DIDN'T HE?
YES. EARLIER THIS YEAR. THE DAUGHTER RUNS NIGHT INDUSTRIES NOW.
SHE ALSO WORKS FOR US OCCASIONALLY.
HARRY, I DON'T NEED HER. HER OR DRUMMOND. THEY'RE...
JIMMY, YOU CAN CALL ME M.
BEHIND MY BACK, YOU CAN EVEN CALL ME MOTHER.
BUT HARRY...
HARRY DIED A LONG TIME AGO, IN THE SEWERS UNDER VIENNA.
LET'S LEAVE IT LIKE THAT, SHALL WE?

SORRY, M. WON'T HAPPEN AGAIN.

BUT I MEAN, *DRUMMOND*. I THOUGHT HE'D *RETIRED*...

HE HAD. STILL, I KNEW HE'D WANT IN ON THIS.

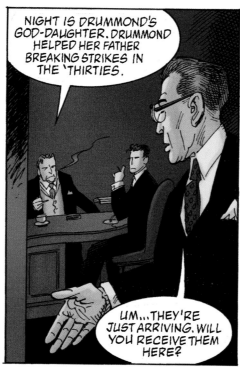

NIGHT IS DRUMMOND'S GOD-DAUGHTER. DRUMMOND HELPED HER FATHER BREAKING STRIKES IN THE 'THIRTIES.

UM...THEY'RE JUST ARRIVING. WILL YOU RECEIVE THEM HERE?

NO. LET'S GO AND GREET THEM.

AND JIMMY, NO MORE *OBJECTIONS*. NOT AFTER LAST NIGHT.

YOU CAN'T DO THIS...NOT TO ME...

JIMMY, YOU DID VERY WELL AGAINST OUR YELLOW PERIL FRIEND. WE'RE *TERRIBLY* GRATEFUL.

THAT'S WHY WE HAVEN'T... RETIRED YOU, OVER ALL THESE BATTERED *TARTS*.

BUT PLEASE, DON'T OVER-ESTIMATE YOUR OWN *IMPORTANCE*, EH?

I MEAN, LET'S FACE IT, JIMMY. YOU'RE NO SIDNEY REILLY.

YOU'RE JUST A BIT OF FUN.

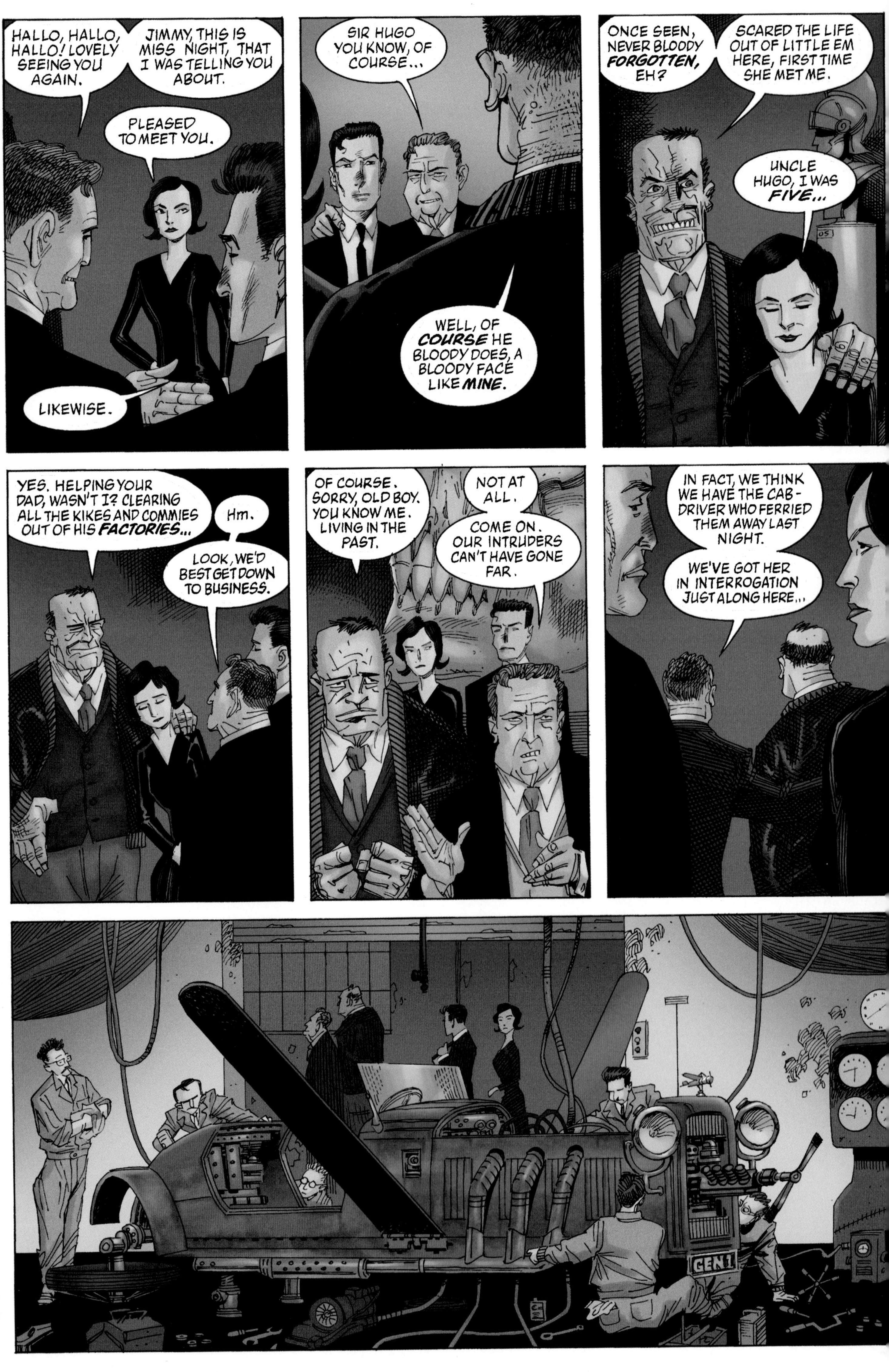
HALLO, HALLO, HALLO! LOVELY SEEING YOU AGAIN.
JIMMY, THIS IS MISS NIGHT, THAT I WAS TELLING YOU ABOUT.
PLEASED TO MEET YOU.
LIKEWISE.
SIR HUGO YOU KNOW, OF COURSE...
WELL, OF COURSE HE BLOODY DOES, A BLOODY FACE LIKE MINE.
ONCE SEEN, NEVER BLOODY FORGOTTEN, EH?
SCARED THE LIFE OUT OF LITTLE EM HERE, FIRST TIME SHE MET ME.
UNCLE HUGO, I WAS FIVE...
YES. HELPING YOUR DAD, WASN'T I? CLEARING ALL THE KIKES AND COMMIES OUT OF HIS FACTORIES...
Hm.
LOOK, WE'D BEST GET DOWN TO BUSINESS.
OF COURSE. SORRY, OLD BOY. YOU KNOW ME. LIVING IN THE PAST.
NOT AT ALL.
COME ON. OUR INTRUDERS CAN'T HAVE GONE FAR.
IN FACT, WE THINK WE HAVE THE CAB-DRIVER WHO FERRIED THEM AWAY LAST NIGHT.
WE'VE GOT HER IN INTERROGATION JUST ALONG HERE...
GEN 1

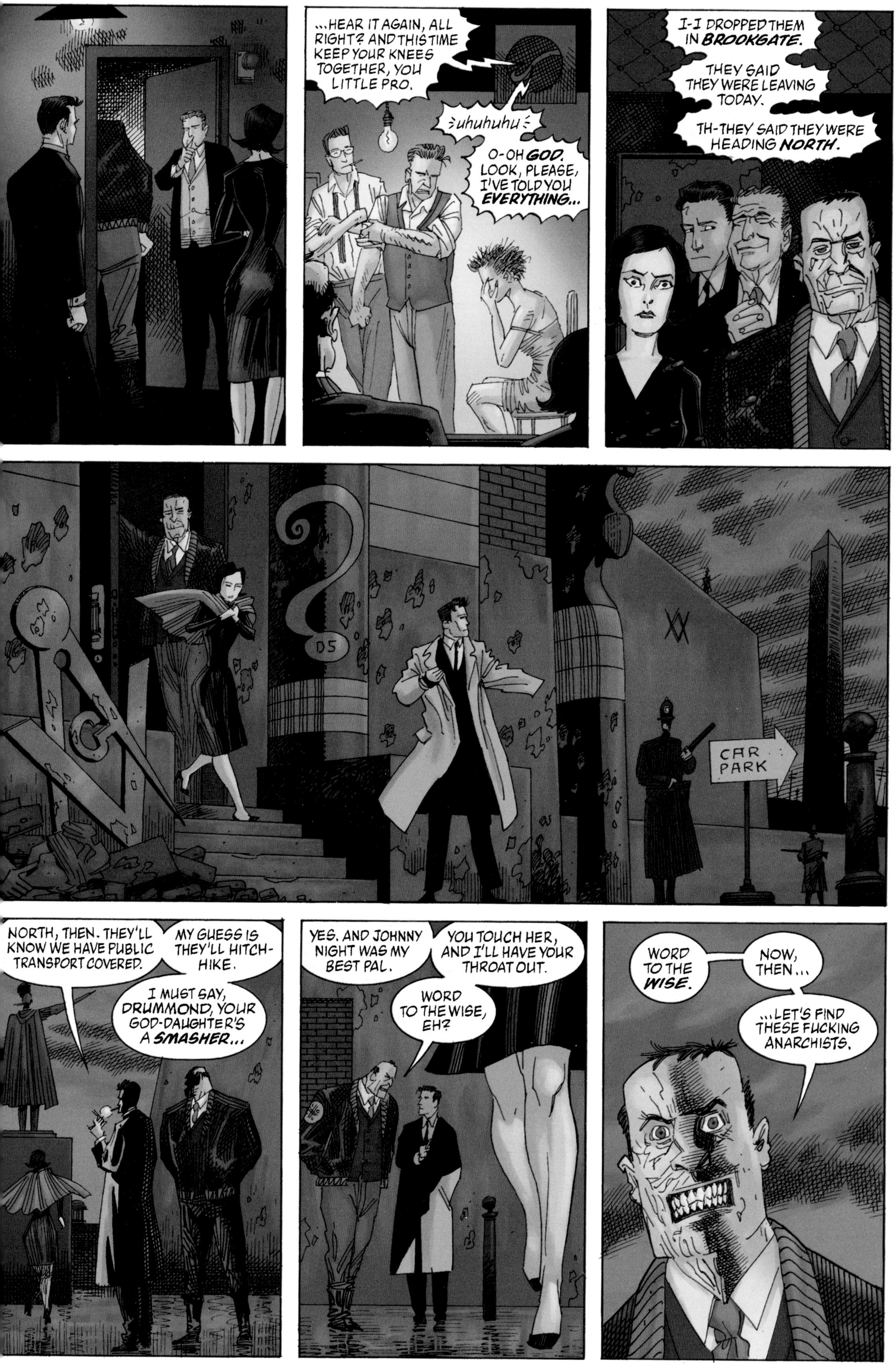
...HEAR IT AGAIN, ALL RIGHT? AND THIS TIME KEEP YOUR KNEES TOGETHER, YOU LITTLE PRO.
uhuhuhu
O-OH GOD. LOOK, PLEASE, I'VE TOLD YOU EVERYTHING...
I-I DROPPED THEM IN BROOKGATE.
THEY SAID THEY WERE LEAVING TODAY.
TH-THEY SAID THEY WERE HEADING NORTH.
D5
CAR PARK
NORTH, THEN. THEY'LL KNOW WE HAVE PUBLIC TRANSPORT COVERED.
MY GUESS IS THEY'LL HITCH-HIKE.
I MUST SAY, DRUMMOND, YOUR GOD-DAUGHTER'S A SMASHER...
YES. AND JOHNNY NIGHT WAS MY BEST PAL.
YOU TOUCH HER, AND I'LL HAVE YOUR THROAT OUT.
WORD TO THE WISE, EH?
WORD TO THE WISE.
NOW, THEN...
...LET'S FIND THESE FUCKING ANARCHISTS.

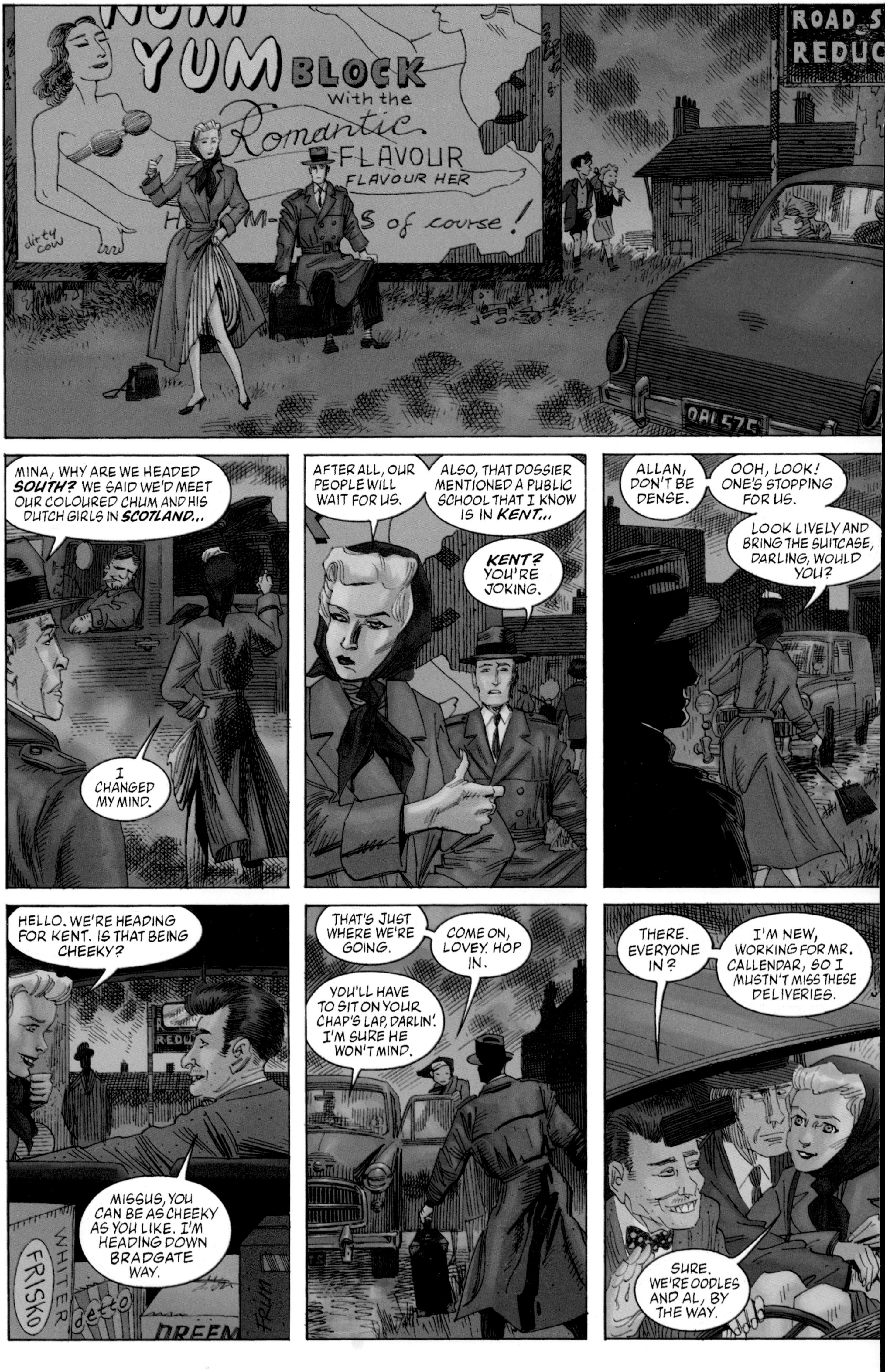

YUM BLOCK
with the
Romantic
FLAVOUR
FLAVOUR HER
S of course!
ditty cow
ROAD S
REDUC
MINA, WHY ARE WE HEADED SOUTH? WE SAID WE'D MEET OUR COLOURED CHUM AND HIS DUTCH GIRLS IN SCOTLAND...
I CHANGED MY MIND.
AFTER ALL, OUR PEOPLE WILL WAIT FOR US.
ALSO, THAT DOSSIER MENTIONED A PUBLIC SCHOOL THAT I KNOW IS IN KENT...
KENT? YOU'RE JOKING.
ALLAN, DON'T BE DENSE.
OOH, LOOK! ONE'S STOPPING FOR US.
LOOK LIVELY AND BRING THE SUITCASE, DARLING, WOULD YOU?
HELLO. WE'RE HEADING FOR KENT. IS THAT BEING CHEEKY?
MISSUS, YOU CAN BE AS CHEEKY AS YOU LIKE. I'M HEADING DOWN BRADGATE WAY.
FRISKO
WHITER
THAT'S JUST WHERE WE'RE GOING.
COME ON, LOVEY. HOP IN.
YOU'LL HAVE TO SIT ON YOUR CHAP'S LAP, DARLIN'. I'M SURE HE WON'T MIND.
THERE. EVERYONE IN?
I'M NEW, WORKING FOR MR. CALLENDAR, SO I MUSTN'T MISS THESE DELIVERIES.
SURE. WE'RE OODLES AND AL, BY THE WAY.

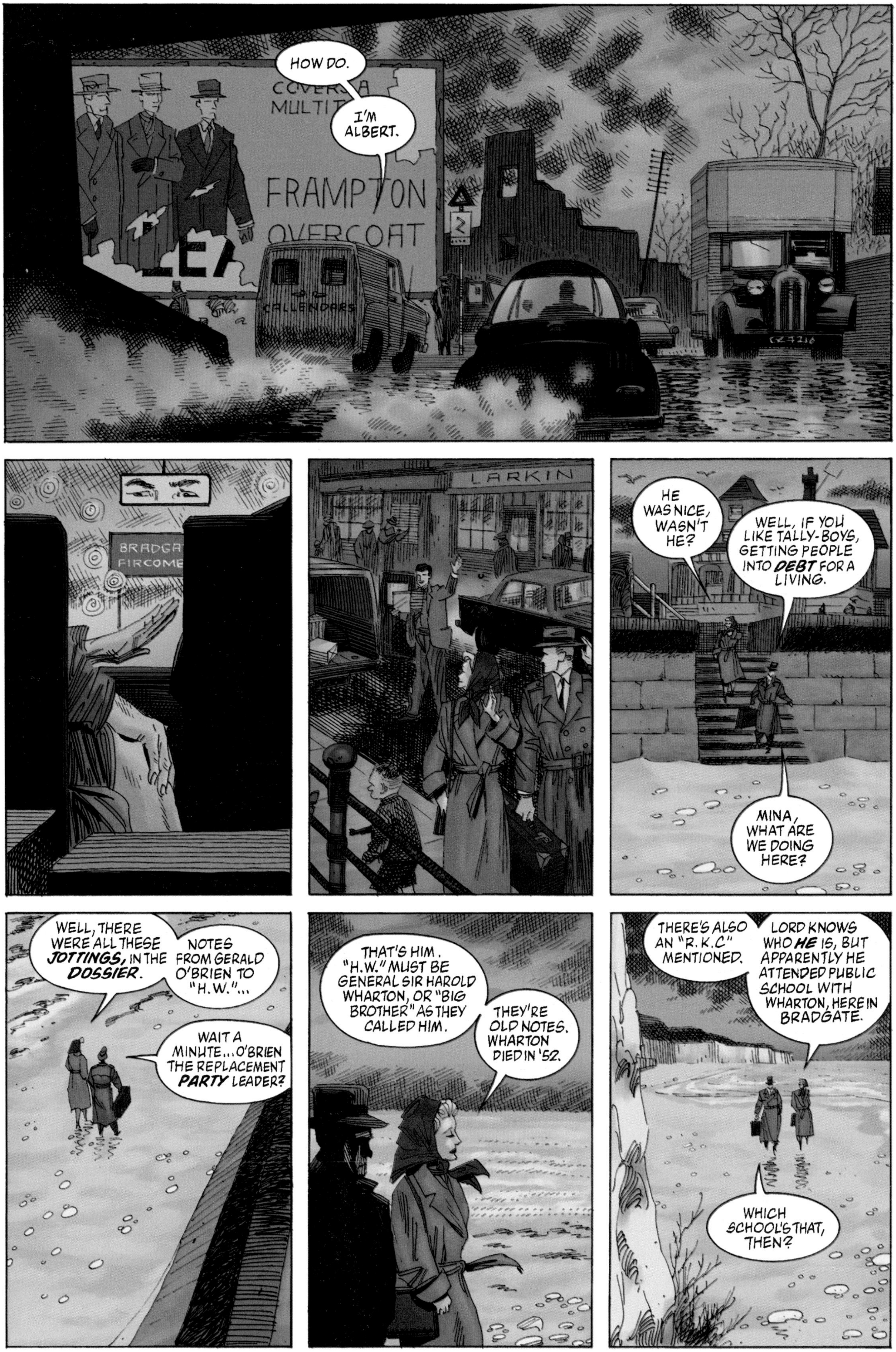
COVERS A
MULTIT
FRAMPTON
OVERCOAT
HOW DO.
I'M ALBERT.
CALLENDARS
LARKIN
BRADGAT
FIRCOMB
HE WAS NICE, WASN'T HE?
WELL, IF YOU LIKE TALLY-BOYS, GETTING PEOPLE INTO DEBT FOR A LIVING.
MINA, WHAT ARE WE DOING HERE?
WELL, THERE WERE ALL THESE JOTTINGS, IN THE DOSSIER.
NOTES FROM GERALD O'BRIEN TO "H.W."...
WAIT A MINUTE... O'BRIEN THE REPLACEMENT PARTY LEADER?
THAT'S HIM. "H.W." MUST BE GENERAL SIR HAROLD WHARTON, OR "BIG BROTHER" AS THEY CALLED HIM.
THEY'RE OLD NOTES. WHARTON DIED IN '52.
THERE'S ALSO AN "R.K.C" MENTIONED.
LORD KNOWS WHO HE IS, BUT APPARENTLY HE ATTENDED PUBLIC SCHOOL WITH WHARTON, HERE IN BRADGATE.
WHICH SCHOOL'S THAT, THEN?

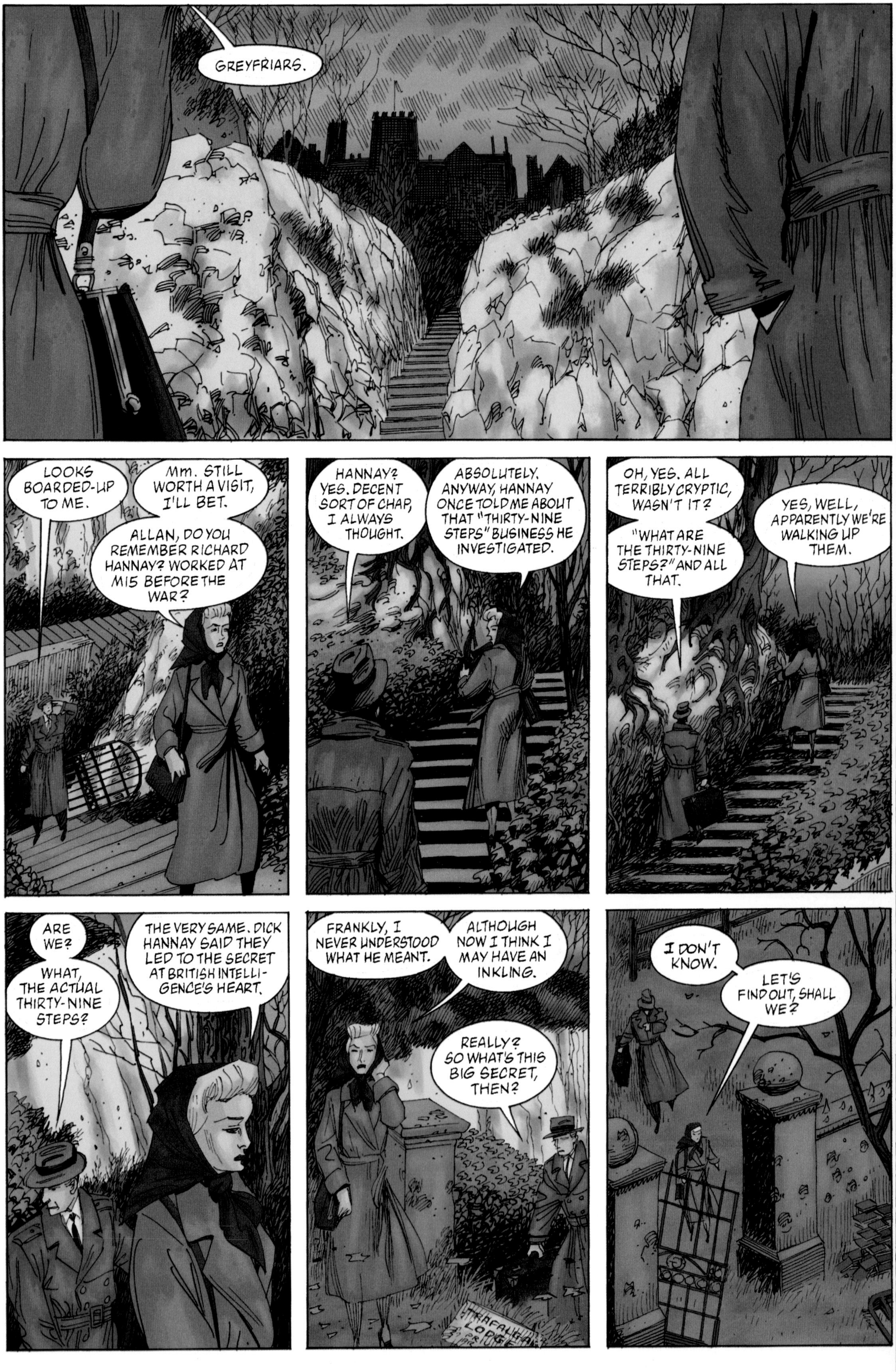
GREYFRIARS.
LOOKS BOARDED-UP TO ME.
Mm. STILL WORTH A VISIT, I'LL BET.
ALLAN, DO YOU REMEMBER RICHARD HANNAY? WORKED AT MI5 BEFORE THE WAR?
HANNAY? YES. DECENT SORT OF CHAP, I ALWAYS THOUGHT.
ABSOLUTELY. ANYWAY, HANNAY ONCE TOLD ME ABOUT THAT "THIRTY-NINE STEPS" BUSINESS HE INVESTIGATED.
OH, YES. ALL TERRIBLY CRYPTIC, WASN'T IT?
"WHAT ARE THE THIRTY-NINE STEPS?" AND ALL THAT.
YES, WELL, APPARENTLY WE'RE WALKING UP THEM.
ARE WE?
WHAT, THE ACTUAL THIRTY-NINE STEPS?
THE VERY SAME. DICK HANNAY SAID THEY LED TO THE SECRET AT BRITISH INTELLI-GENCE'S HEART.
FRANKLY, I NEVER UNDERSTOOD WHAT HE MEANT.
ALTHOUGH NOW I THINK I MAY HAVE AN INKLING.
REALLY? SO WHAT'S THIS BIG SECRET, THEN?
I DON'T KNOW.
LET'S FIND OUT, SHALL WE?

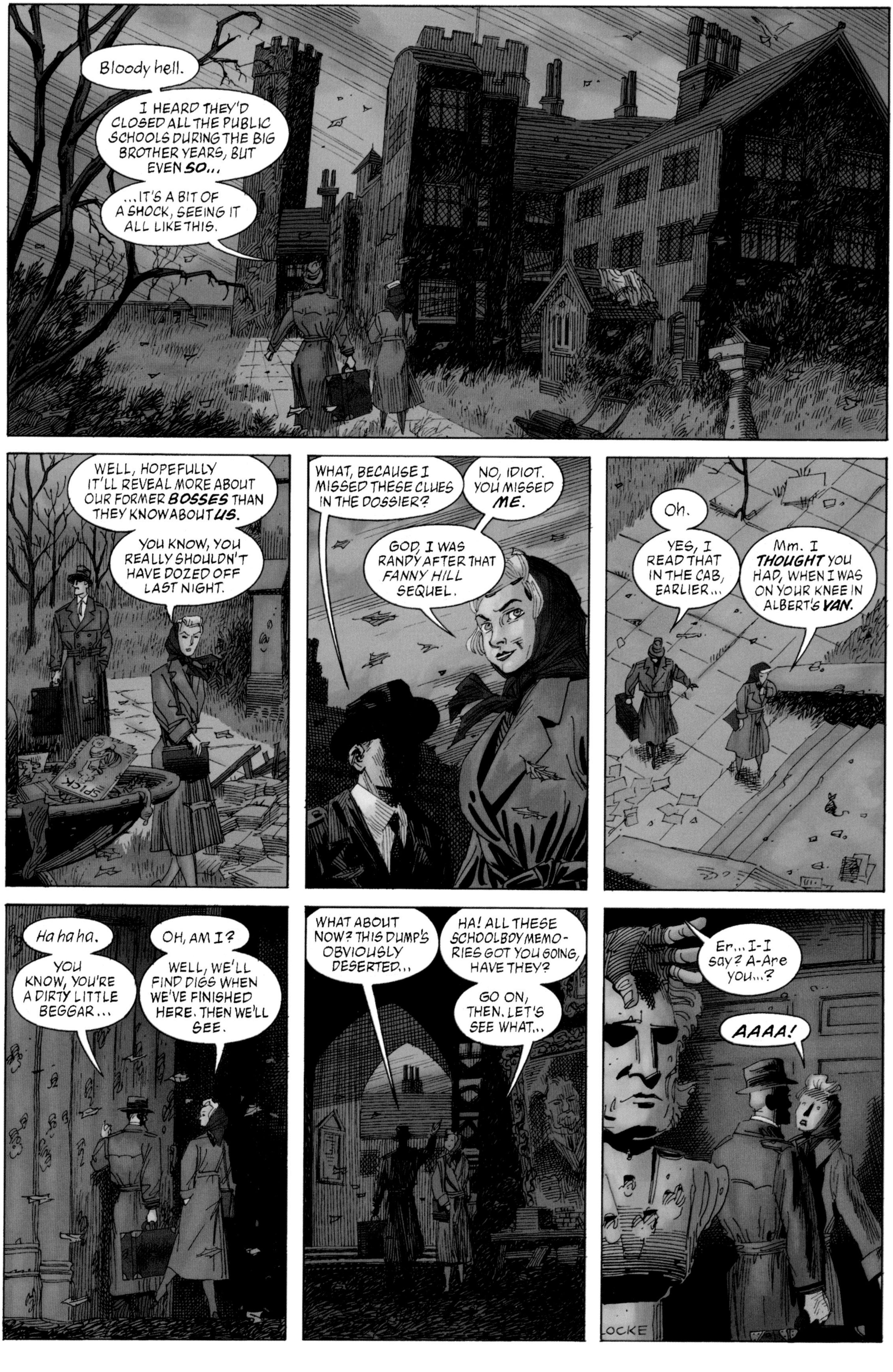
Bloody hell.
I HEARD THEY'D CLOSED ALL THE PUBLIC SCHOOLS DURING THE BIG BROTHER YEARS, BUT EVEN **SO...**
...IT'S A BIT OF A SHOCK, SEEING IT ALL LIKE THIS.
WELL, HOPEFULLY IT'LL REVEAL MORE ABOUT OUR FORMER **BOSSES** THAN THEY KNOW ABOUT **US**.
YOU KNOW, YOU REALLY SHOULDN'T HAVE DOZED OFF LAST NIGHT.
SPICK
WHAT, BECAUSE I MISSED THESE CLUES IN THE DOSSIER?
NO, IDIOT. YOU MISSED **ME**.
GOD, I WAS RANDY AFTER THAT *FANNY HILL* SEQUEL.
Oh.
YES, I READ THAT IN THE CAB, EARLIER...
Mm. I **THOUGHT** YOU HAD, WHEN I WAS ON YOUR KNEE IN ALBERT'S **VAN**.
Ha ha ha.
YOU KNOW, YOU'RE A DIRTY LITTLE BEGGAR...
OH, AM I?
WELL, WE'LL FIND DIGS WHEN WE'VE FINISHED HERE. THEN WE'LL SEE.
WHAT ABOUT NOW? THIS DUMP'S OBVIOUSLY DESERTED...
HA! ALL THESE SCHOOLBOY MEMO-RIES GOT YOU GOING, HAVE THEY?
GO ON, THEN. LET'S SEE WHAT...
Er... I-I say? A-Are you...?
AAAA!
LOCKE

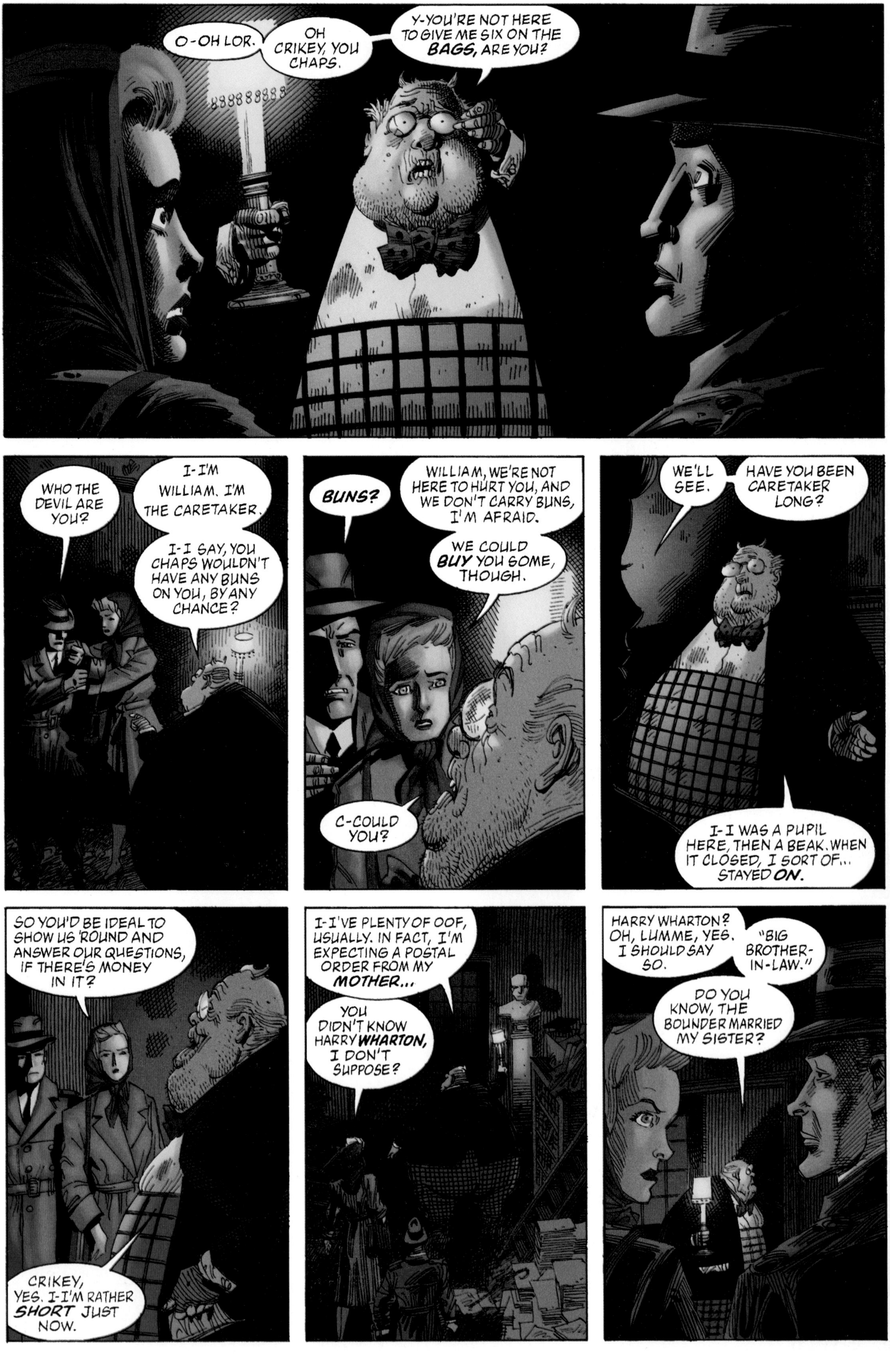

O-OH LOR.
OH CRIKEY, YOU CHAPS.
Y-YOU'RE NOT HERE TO GIVE ME SIX ON THE BAGS, ARE YOU?
WHO THE DEVIL ARE YOU?
I-I'M WILLIAM. I'M THE CARETAKER.
I-I SAY, YOU CHAPS WOULDN'T HAVE ANY BUNS ON YOU, BY ANY CHANCE?
BUNS?
WILLIAM, WE'RE NOT HERE TO HURT YOU, AND WE DON'T CARRY BUNS, I'M AFRAID.
WE COULD BUY YOU SOME, THOUGH.
C-COULD YOU?
WE'LL SEE.
HAVE YOU BEEN CARETAKER LONG?
I-I WAS A PUPIL HERE, THEN A BEAK. WHEN IT CLOSED, I SORT OF... STAYED ON.
SO YOU'D BE IDEAL TO SHOW US 'ROUND AND ANSWER OUR QUESTIONS, IF THERE'S MONEY IN IT?
CRIKEY, YES. I-I'M RATHER SHORT JUST NOW.
I-I'VE PLENTY OF OOF, USUALLY. IN FACT, I'M EXPECTING A POSTAL ORDER FROM MY MOTHER...
YOU DIDN'T KNOW HARRY WHARTON, I DON'T SUPPOSE?
HARRY WHARTON? OH, LUMME, YES. I SHOULD SAY SO.
"BIG BROTHER-IN-LAW."
DO YOU KNOW, THE BOUNDER MARRIED MY SISTER?

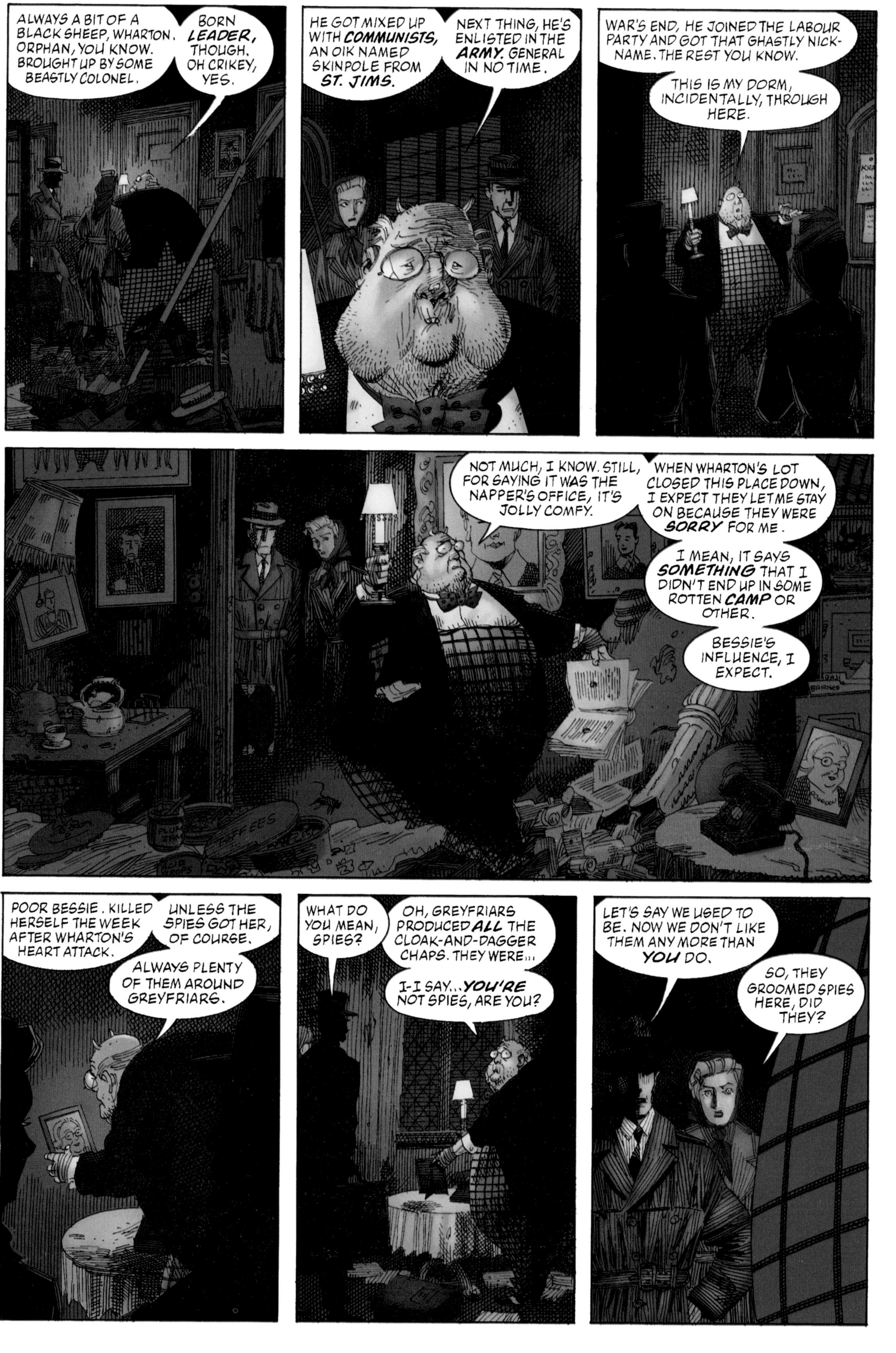

ALWAYS A BIT OF A BLACK SHEEP, WHARTON. ORPHAN, YOU KNOW. BROUGHT UP BY SOME BEASTLY COLONEL.
BORN LEADER, THOUGH. OH CRIKEY, YES.
HE GOT MIXED UP WITH COMMUNISTS, AN OIK NAMED SKINPOLE FROM ST. JIMS.
NEXT THING, HE'S ENLISTED IN THE ARMY. GENERAL IN NO TIME.
WAR'S END, HE JOINED THE LABOUR PARTY AND GOT THAT GHASTLY NICK-NAME. THE REST YOU KNOW.
THIS IS MY DORM, INCIDENTALLY, THROUGH HERE.
NOT MUCH, I KNOW. STILL, FOR SAYING IT WAS THE NAPPER'S OFFICE, IT'S JOLLY COMFY.
WHEN WHARTON'S LOT CLOSED THIS PLACE DOWN, I EXPECT THEY LET ME STAY ON BECAUSE THEY WERE SORRY FOR ME.
I MEAN, IT SAYS SOMETHING THAT I DIDN'T END UP IN SOME ROTTEN CAMP OR OTHER.
BESSIE'S INFLUENCE, I EXPECT.
POOR BESSIE. KILLED HERSELF THE WEEK AFTER WHARTON'S HEART ATTACK.
UNLESS THE SPIES GOT HER, OF COURSE.
ALWAYS PLENTY OF THEM AROUND GREYFRIARS.
WHAT DO YOU MEAN, SPIES?
OH, GREYFRIARS PRODUCED ALL THE CLOAK-AND-DAGGER CHAPS. THEY WERE...
I-I SAY... YOU'RE NOT SPIES, ARE YOU?
LET'S SAY WE USED TO BE. NOW WE DON'T LIKE THEM ANY MORE THAN YOU DO.
SO, THEY GROOMED SPIES HERE, DID THEY?

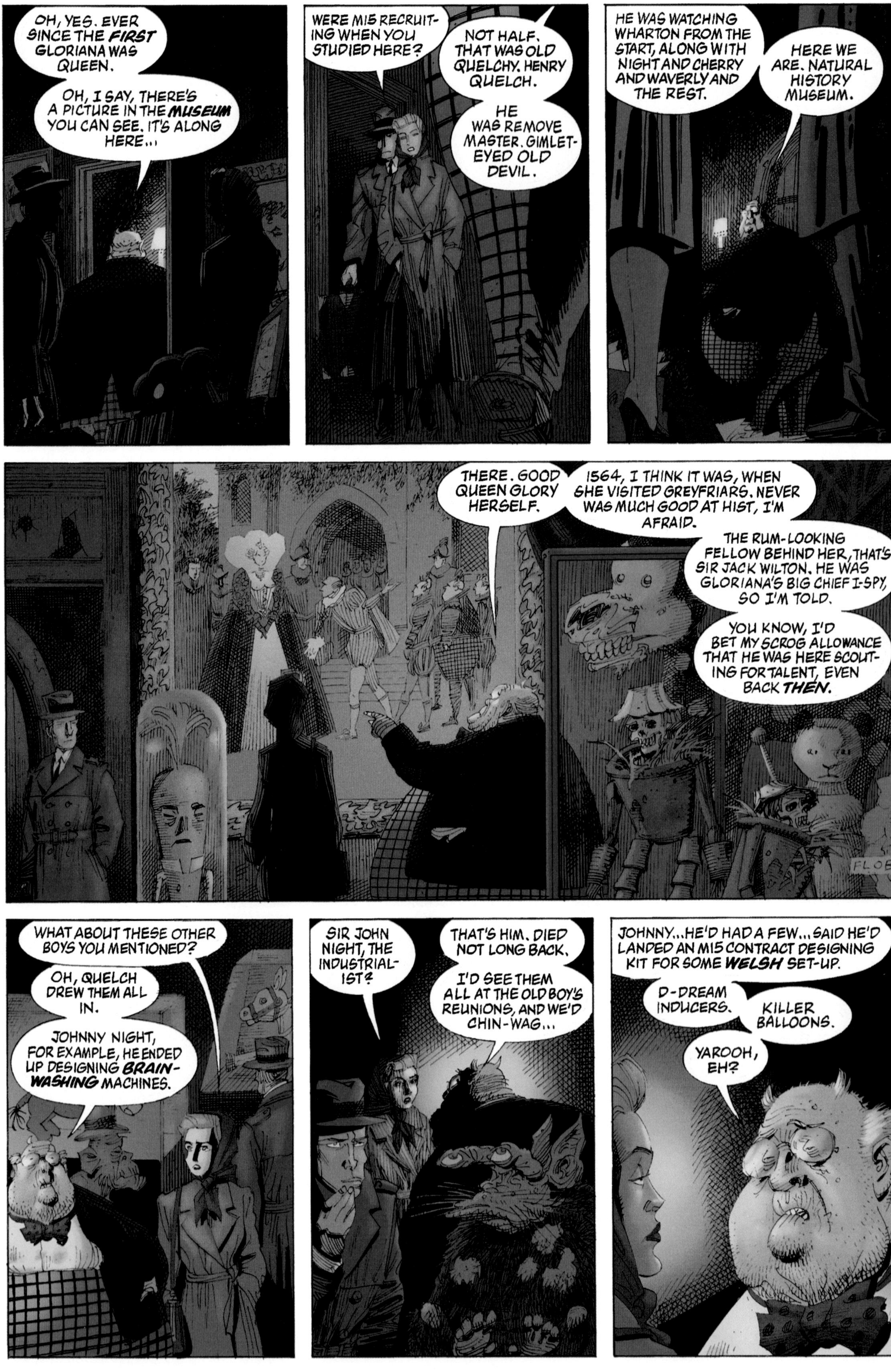
OH, YES. EVER SINCE THE FIRST GLORIANA WAS QUEEN.
OH, I SAY, THERE'S A PICTURE IN THE MUSEUM YOU CAN SEE. IT'S ALONG HERE...
WERE MI5 RECRUITING WHEN YOU STUDIED HERE?
NOT HALF. THAT WAS OLD QUELCHY. HENRY QUELCH.
HE WAS REMOVE MASTER. GIMLET-EYED OLD DEVIL.
HE WAS WATCHING WHARTON FROM THE START, ALONG WITH NIGHT AND CHERRY AND WAVERLY AND THE REST.
HERE WE ARE. NATURAL HISTORY MUSEUM.
THERE. GOOD QUEEN GLORY HERSELF.
1564, I THINK IT WAS, WHEN SHE VISITED GREYFRIARS. NEVER WAS MUCH GOOD AT HIST, I'M AFRAID.
THE RUM-LOOKING FELLOW BEHIND HER, THAT'S SIR JACK WILTON. HE WAS GLORIANA'S BIG CHIEF I-SPY, SO I'M TOLD.
YOU KNOW, I'D BET MY SCROG ALLOWANCE THAT HE WAS HERE SCOUTING FOR TALENT, EVEN BACK THEN.
FLOB
WHAT ABOUT THESE OTHER BOYS YOU MENTIONED?
OH, QUELCH DREW THEM ALL IN.
JOHNNY NIGHT, FOR EXAMPLE, HE ENDED UP DESIGNING BRAIN-WASHING MACHINES.
SIR JOHN NIGHT, THE INDUSTRIALIST?
THAT'S HIM. DIED NOT LONG BACK.
I'D SEE THEM ALL AT THE OLD BOY'S REUNIONS, AND WE'D CHIN-WAG...
JOHNNY...HE'D HAD A FEW...SAID HE'D LANDED AN MI5 CONTRACT DESIGNING KIT FOR SOME WELSH SET-UP.
D-DREAM INDUCERS.
KILLER BALLOONS.
YAROOH, EH?

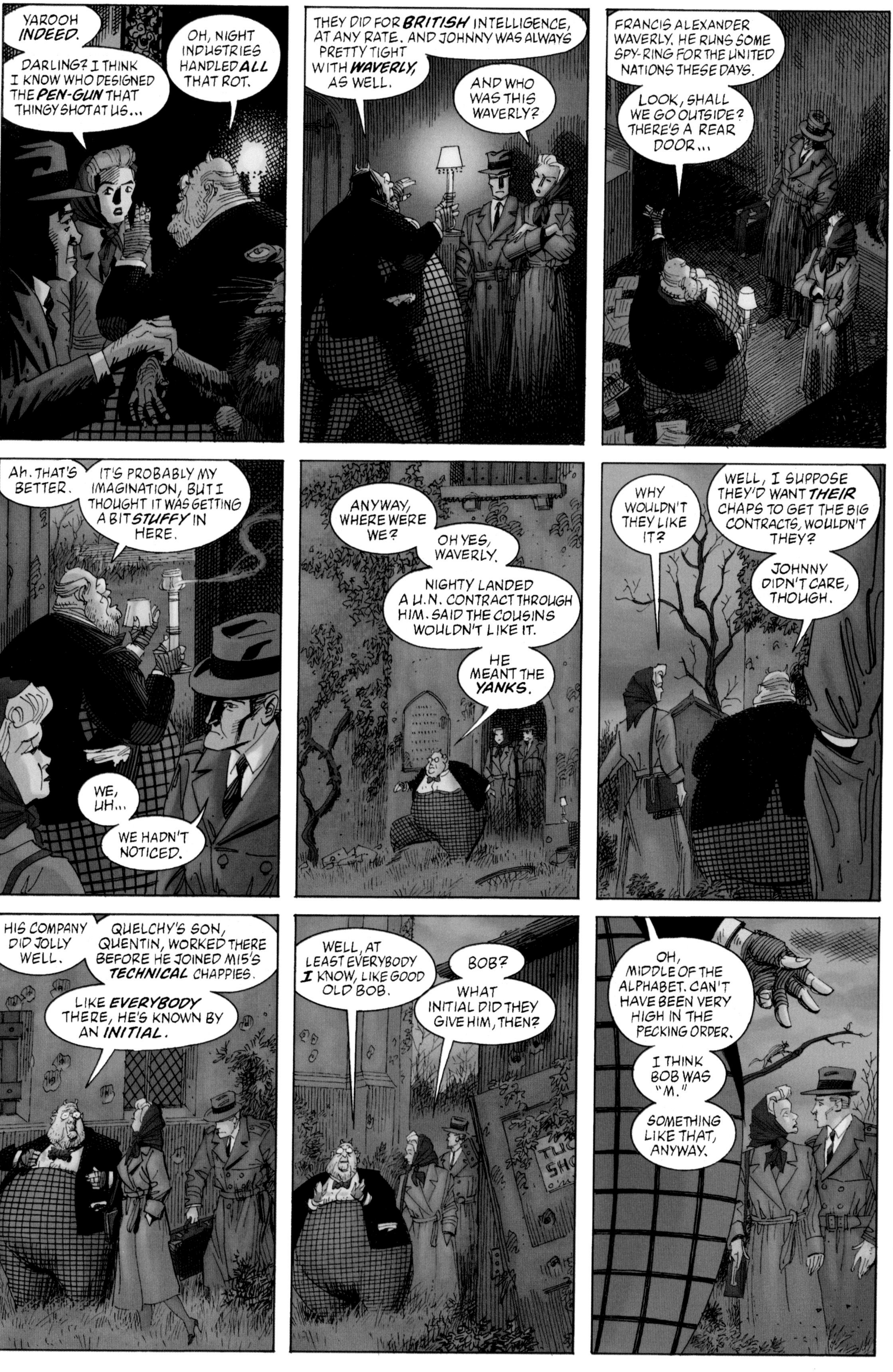
YAROOH INDEED.
DARLING? I THINK I KNOW WHO DESIGNED THE PEN-GUN THAT THINGY SHOT AT US...
OH, NIGHT INDUSTRIES HANDLED ALL THAT ROT.
THEY DID FOR BRITISH INTELLIGENCE, AT ANY RATE. AND JOHNNY WAS ALWAYS PRETTY TIGHT WITH WAVERLY, AS WELL.
AND WHO WAS THIS WAVERLY?
FRANCIS ALEXANDER WAVERLY. HE RUNS SOME SPY-RING FOR THE UNITED NATIONS THESE DAYS.
LOOK, SHALL WE GO OUTSIDE? THERE'S A REAR DOOR...
Ah. THAT'S BETTER.
IT'S PROBABLY MY IMAGINATION, BUT I THOUGHT IT WAS GETTING A BIT STUFFY IN HERE.
WE, UH...
WE HADN'T NOTICED.
ANYWAY, WHERE WERE WE?
OH YES, WAVERLY.
NIGHTY LANDED A U.N. CONTRACT THROUGH HIM. SAID THE COUSINS WOULDN'T LIKE IT.
HE MEANT THE YANKS.
WHY WOULDN'T THEY LIKE IT?
WELL, I SUPPOSE THEY'D WANT THEIR CHAPS TO GET THE BIG CONTRACTS, WOULDN'T THEY?
JOHNNY DIDN'T CARE, THOUGH.
HIS COMPANY DID JOLLY WELL.
QUELCHY'S SON, QUENTIN, WORKED THERE BEFORE HE JOINED MI5'S TECHNICAL CHAPPIES.
LIKE EVERYBODY THERE, HE'S KNOWN BY AN INITIAL.
WELL, AT LEAST EVERYBODY I KNOW, LIKE GOOD OLD BOB.
BOB?
WHAT INITIAL DID THEY GIVE HIM, THEN?
OH, MIDDLE OF THE ALPHABET. CAN'T HAVE BEEN VERY HIGH IN THE PECKING ORDER.
I THINK BOB WAS "M."
SOMETHING LIKE THAT, ANYWAY.

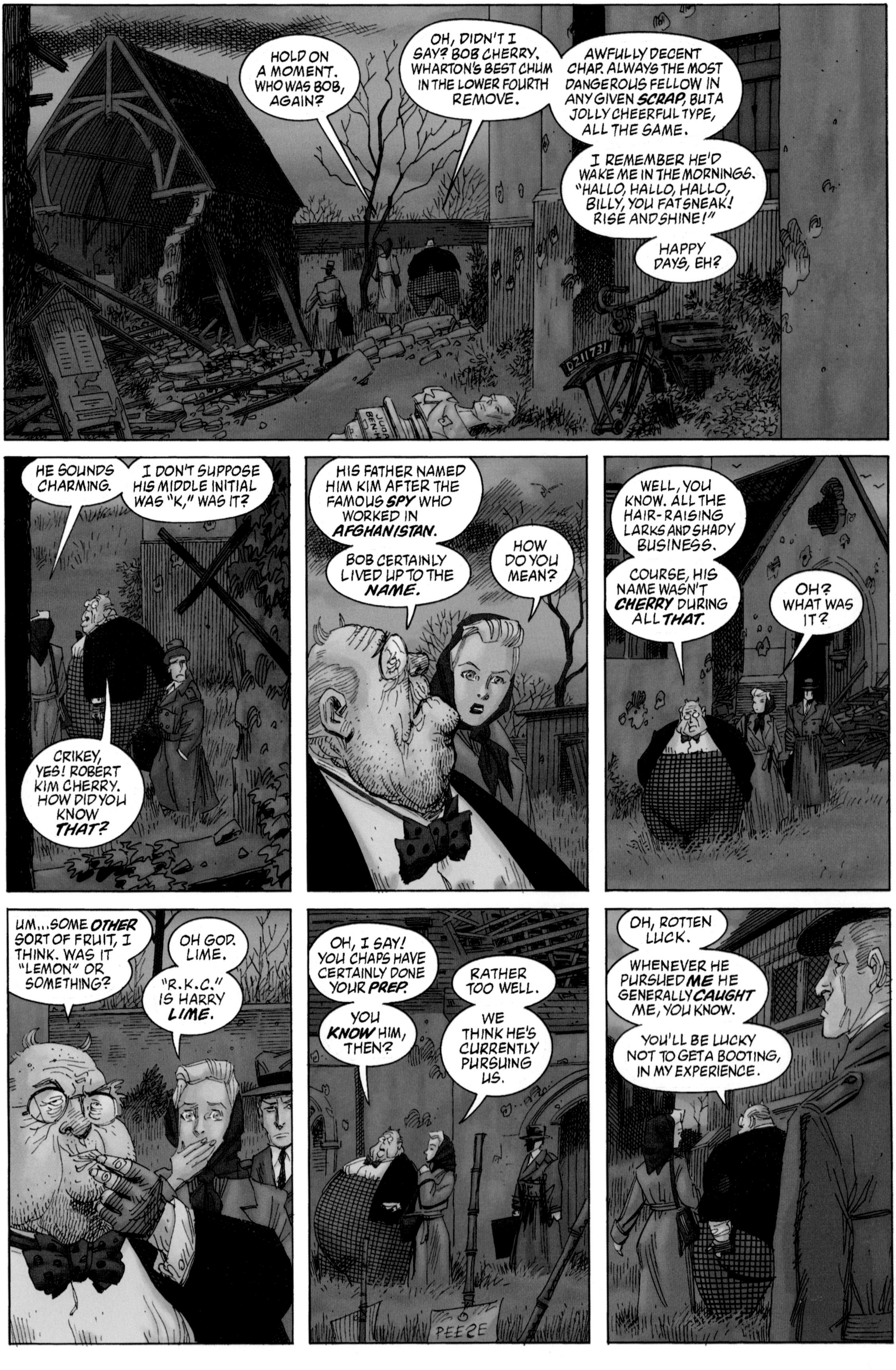
HOLD ON A MOMENT. WHO WAS BOB, AGAIN?
OH, DIDN'T I SAY? BOB CHERRY. WHARTON'S BEST CHUM IN THE LOWER FOURTH REMOVE.
AWFULLY DECENT CHAP. ALWAYS THE MOST DANGEROUS FELLOW IN ANY GIVEN SCRAP, BUT A JOLLY CHEERFUL TYPE, ALL THE SAME.
I REMEMBER HE'D WAKE ME IN THE MORNINGS. "HALLO, HALLO, HALLO, BILLY, YOU FAT SNEAK! RISE AND SHINE!"
HAPPY DAYS, EH?
DZ11731
HE SOUNDS CHARMING.
I DON'T SUPPOSE HIS MIDDLE INITIAL WAS "K," WAS IT?
CRIKEY, YES! ROBERT KIM CHERRY. HOW DID YOU KNOW THAT?
HIS FATHER NAMED HIM KIM AFTER THE FAMOUS SPY WHO WORKED IN AFGHANISTAN.
BOB CERTAINLY LIVED UP TO THE NAME.
HOW DO YOU MEAN?
WELL, YOU KNOW. ALL THE HAIR-RAISING LARKS AND SHADY BUSINESS.
COURSE, HIS NAME WASN'T CHERRY DURING ALL THAT.
OH? WHAT WAS IT?
UM...SOME OTHER SORT OF FRUIT, I THINK. WAS IT "LEMON" OR SOMETHING?
OH GOD. LIME.
"R.K.C." IS HARRY LIME.
OH, I SAY! YOU CHAPS HAVE CERTAINLY DONE YOUR PREP.
RATHER TOO WELL.
YOU KNOW HIM, THEN?
WE THINK HE'S CURRENTLY PURSUING US.
PEERE
OH, ROTTEN LUCK.
WHENEVER HE PURSUED ME HE GENERALLY CAUGHT ME, YOU KNOW.
YOU'LL BE LUCKY NOT TO GET A BOOTING, IN MY EXPERIENCE.

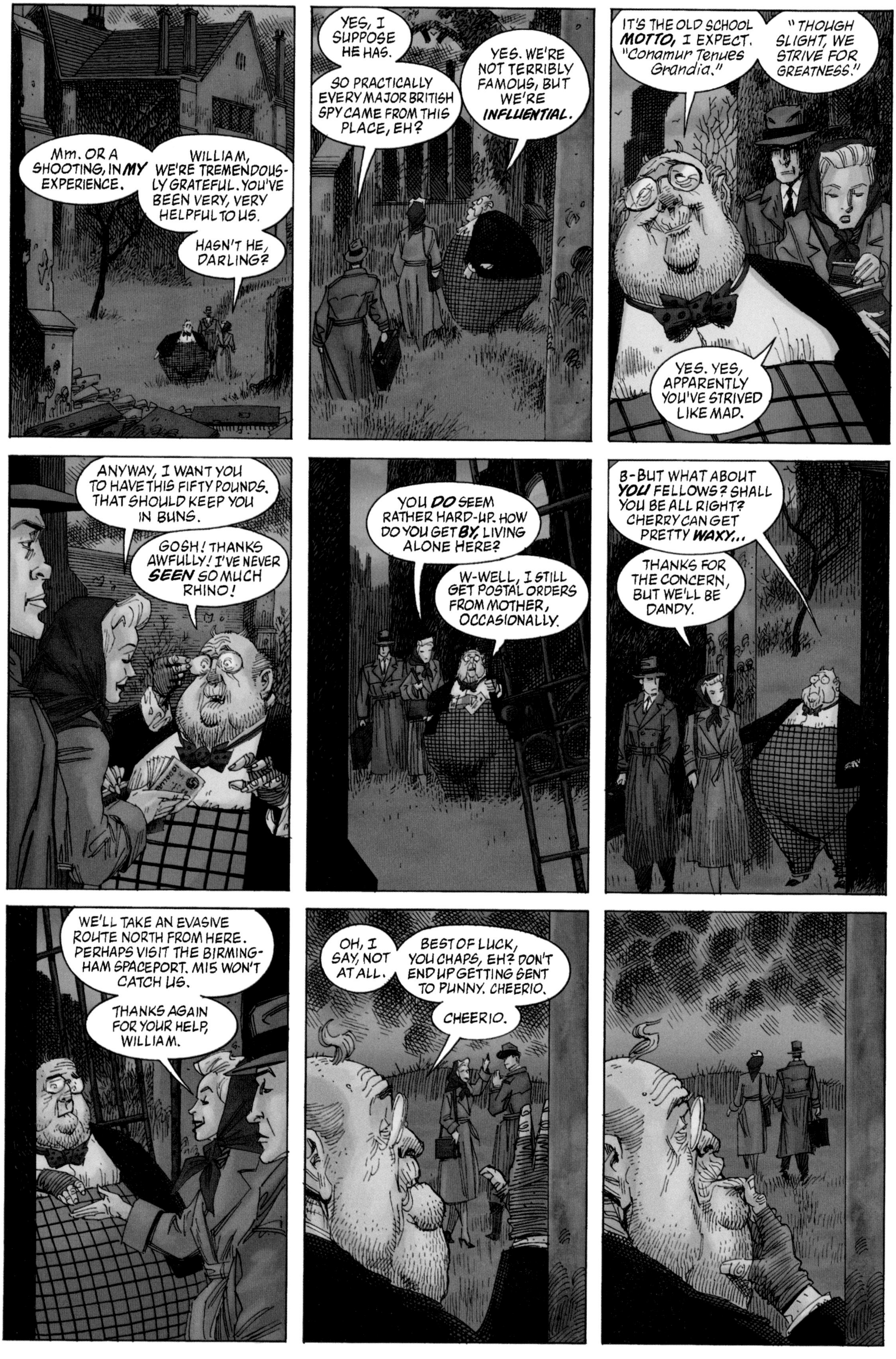
Mm. OR A SHOOTING, IN **MY** EXPERIENCE.
WILLIAM, WE'RE TREMENDOUSLY GRATEFUL. YOU'VE BEEN VERY, VERY HELPFUL TO US.
HASN'T HE, DARLING?
YES, I SUPPOSE HE HAS.
SO PRACTICALLY EVERY MAJOR BRITISH SPY CAME FROM THIS PLACE, EH?
YES. WE'RE NOT TERRIBLY FAMOUS, BUT WE'RE **INFLUENTIAL**.
IT'S THE OLD SCHOOL **MOTTO**, I EXPECT. "*Conamur Tenues Grandia*."
"THOUGH SLIGHT, WE STRIVE FOR GREATNESS."
YES. YES, APPARENTLY YOU'VE STRIVED LIKE MAD.
ANYWAY, I WANT YOU TO HAVE THIS FIFTY POUNDS. THAT SHOULD KEEP YOU IN BUNS.
GOSH! THANKS AWFULLY! I'VE NEVER **SEEN** SO MUCH RHINO!
YOU **DO** SEEM RATHER HARD-UP. HOW DO YOU GET **BY**, LIVING ALONE HERE?
W-WELL, I STILL GET POSTAL ORDERS FROM MOTHER, OCCASIONALLY.
B-BUT WHAT ABOUT **YOU** FELLOWS? SHALL YOU BE ALL RIGHT? CHERRY CAN GET PRETTY **WAXY**...
THANKS FOR THE CONCERN, BUT WE'LL BE DANDY.
WE'LL TAKE AN EVASIVE ROUTE NORTH FROM HERE. PERHAPS VISIT THE BIRMINGHAM SPACEPORT. MI5 WON'T CATCH US.
THANKS AGAIN FOR YOUR HELP, WILLIAM.
OH, I SAY, NOT AT ALL.
BEST OF LUCK, YOU CHAPS, EH? DON'T END UP GETTING SENT TO PUNNY. CHEERIO.
CHEERIO.

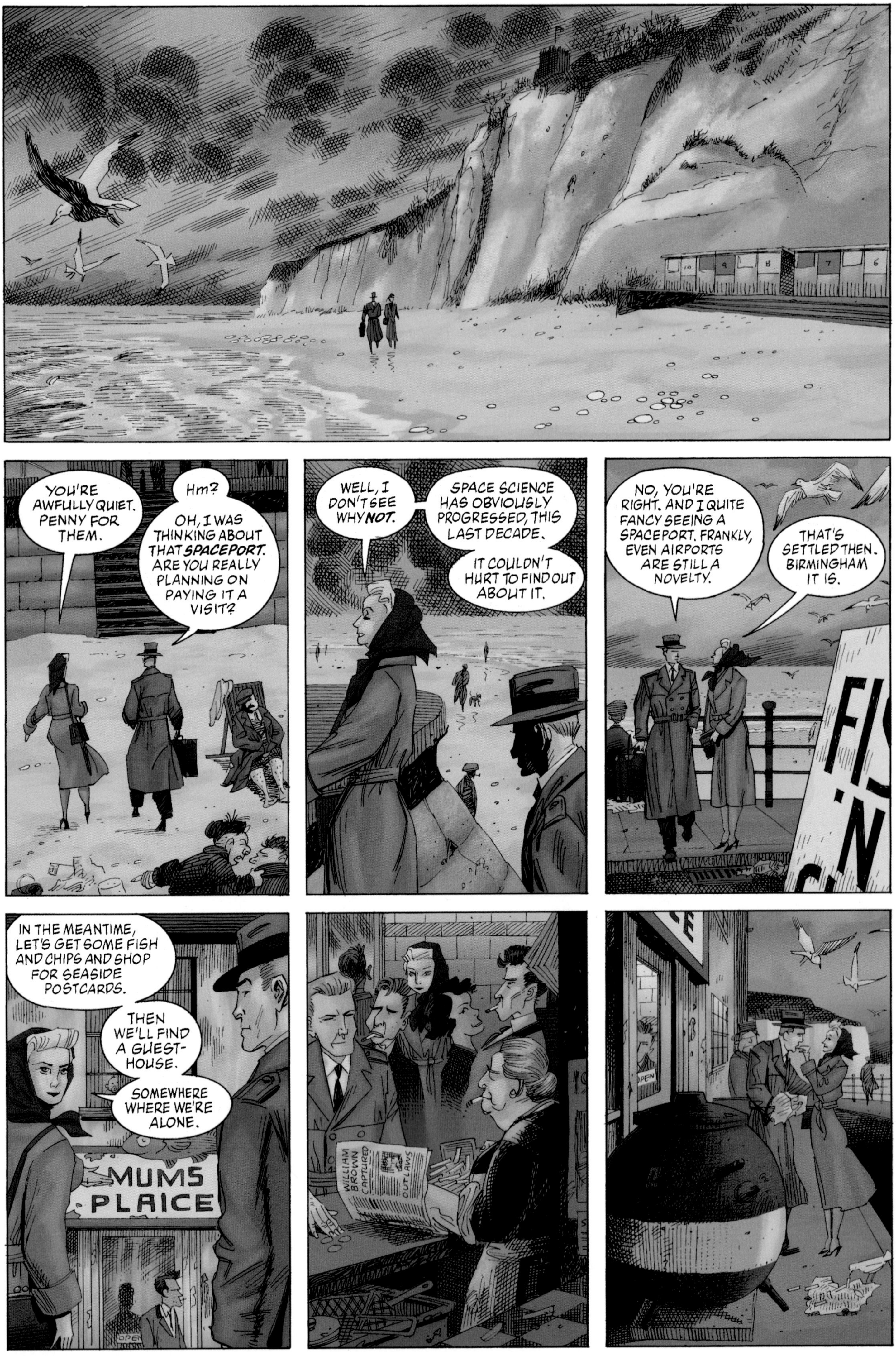
YOU'RE AWFULLY QUIET. PENNY FOR THEM.
Hm?
OH, I WAS THINKING ABOUT THAT **SPACEPORT.** ARE YOU REALLY PLANNING ON PAYING IT A VISIT?
WELL, I DON'T SEE WHY **NOT.**
SPACE SCIENCE HAS OBVIOUSLY PROGRESSED, THIS LAST DECADE.
IT COULDN'T HURT TO FIND OUT ABOUT IT.
NO, YOU'RE RIGHT. AND I QUITE FANCY SEEING A SPACEPORT. FRANKLY, EVEN AIRPORTS ARE STILL A NOVELTY.
THAT'S SETTLED THEN. BIRMINGHAM IT IS.
IN THE MEANTIME, LET'S GET SOME FISH AND CHIPS AND SHOP FOR SEASIDE POSTCARDS.
THEN WE'LL FIND A GUEST-HOUSE.
SOMEWHERE WHERE WE'RE ALONE.
MUMS PLAICE
OPEN
WILLIAM BROWN CAPTURED
OUTLAWS
OPEN

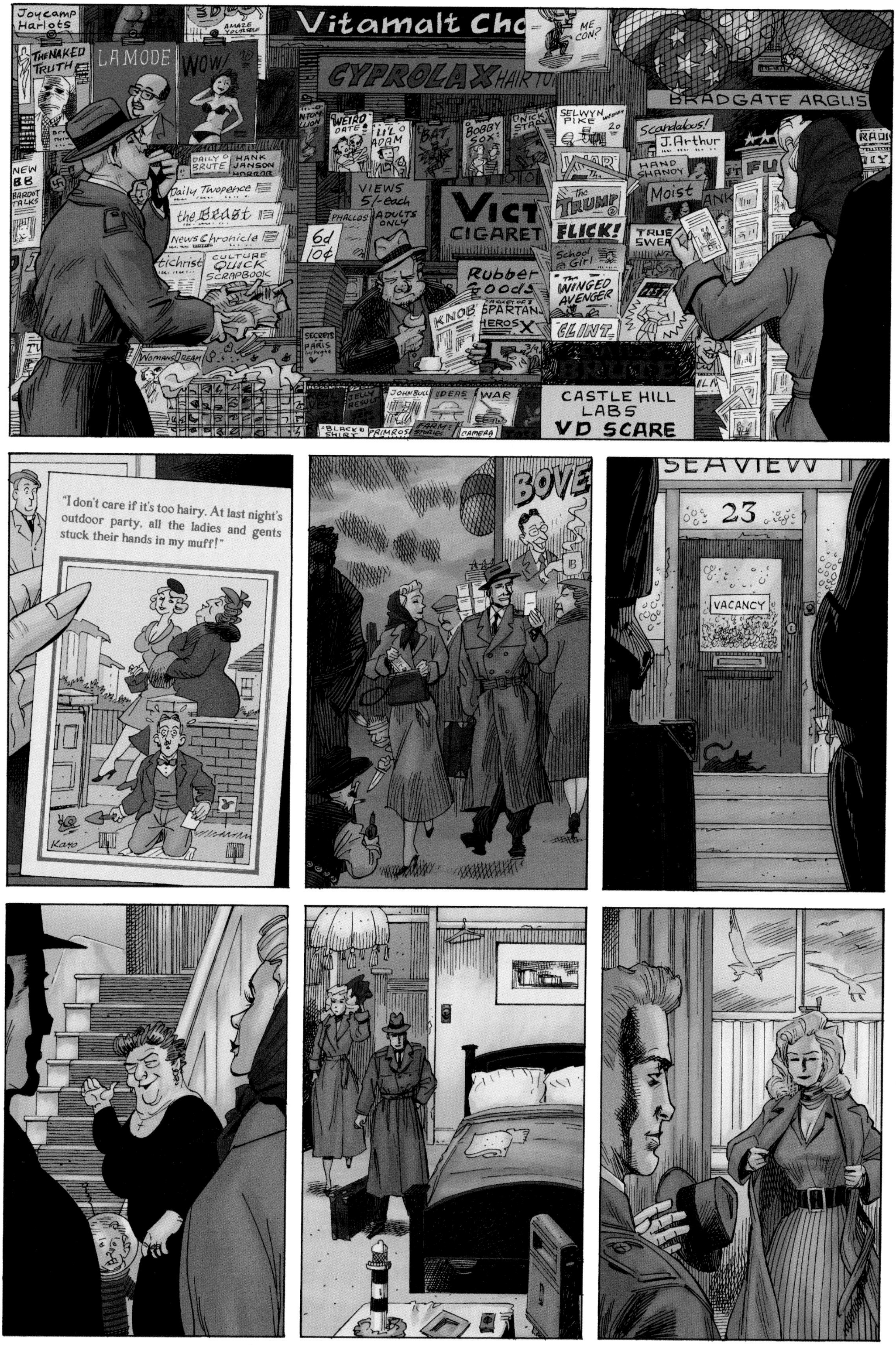

Joycamp Harlots
3D
AMAZE YOURSELF
THE NAKED TRUTH
LA MODE
WOW!
Vitamalt Cho
ME CON?
CYPROLAX HAIR TO
NEW BB BARDOT TALKS
DAILY BRUTE
HANK JANSON HORROR
Daily Twopence
the Beast
News Chronicle
tichrist
CULTURE QUICK SCRAPBOOK
WEIRD DATE
LI'L ADAM
BAT
BOBBY SOX
SELWYN PIKE WEEKLY 2d
BRADGATE ARGUS
Scandalous!
J. Arthur
HAND SHANDY
Moist
VIEWS 5/- each
PHALLOS
ADULTS ONLY
6d 10¢
Vict CIGARET
The TRUMP
FLICK!
TRUE SWEA
School Girl
Rubber Goods
PACKET OF 3 SPARTAN
HEROS X
KNOB
The WINGED AVENGER
CLINT
SECRETS OF PARIS
WOMANS DREAM
JOHN BULL
IDEAS
WAR
BLACK SHIRT
PRIMROSE
FARM STORIES
CAMERA
CASTLE HILL LABS VD SCARE
"I don't care if it's too hairy. At last night's outdoor party, all the ladies and gents stuck their hands in my muff!"
Karo
BOVE
B
SEAVIEW
23
VACANCY

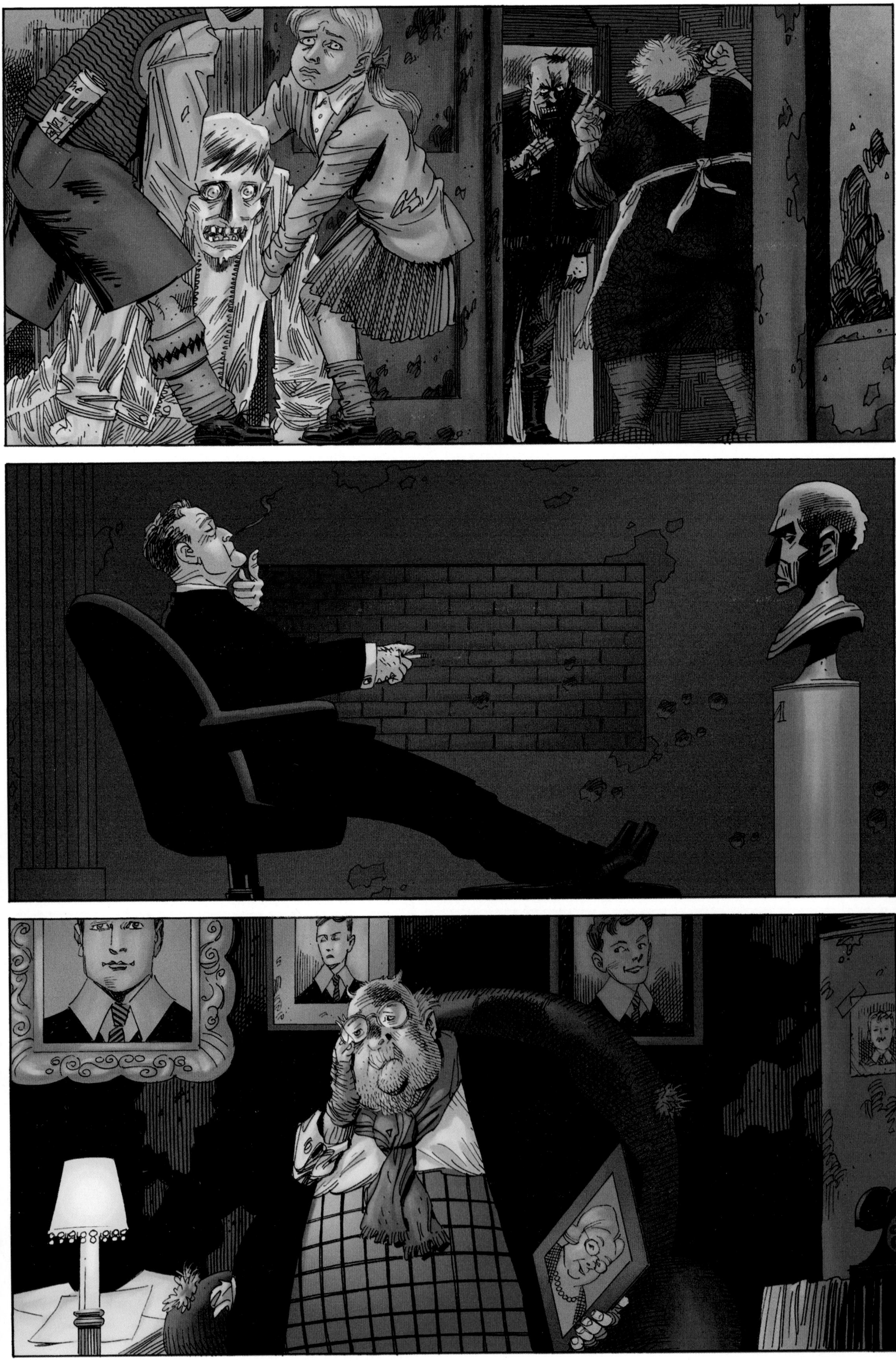

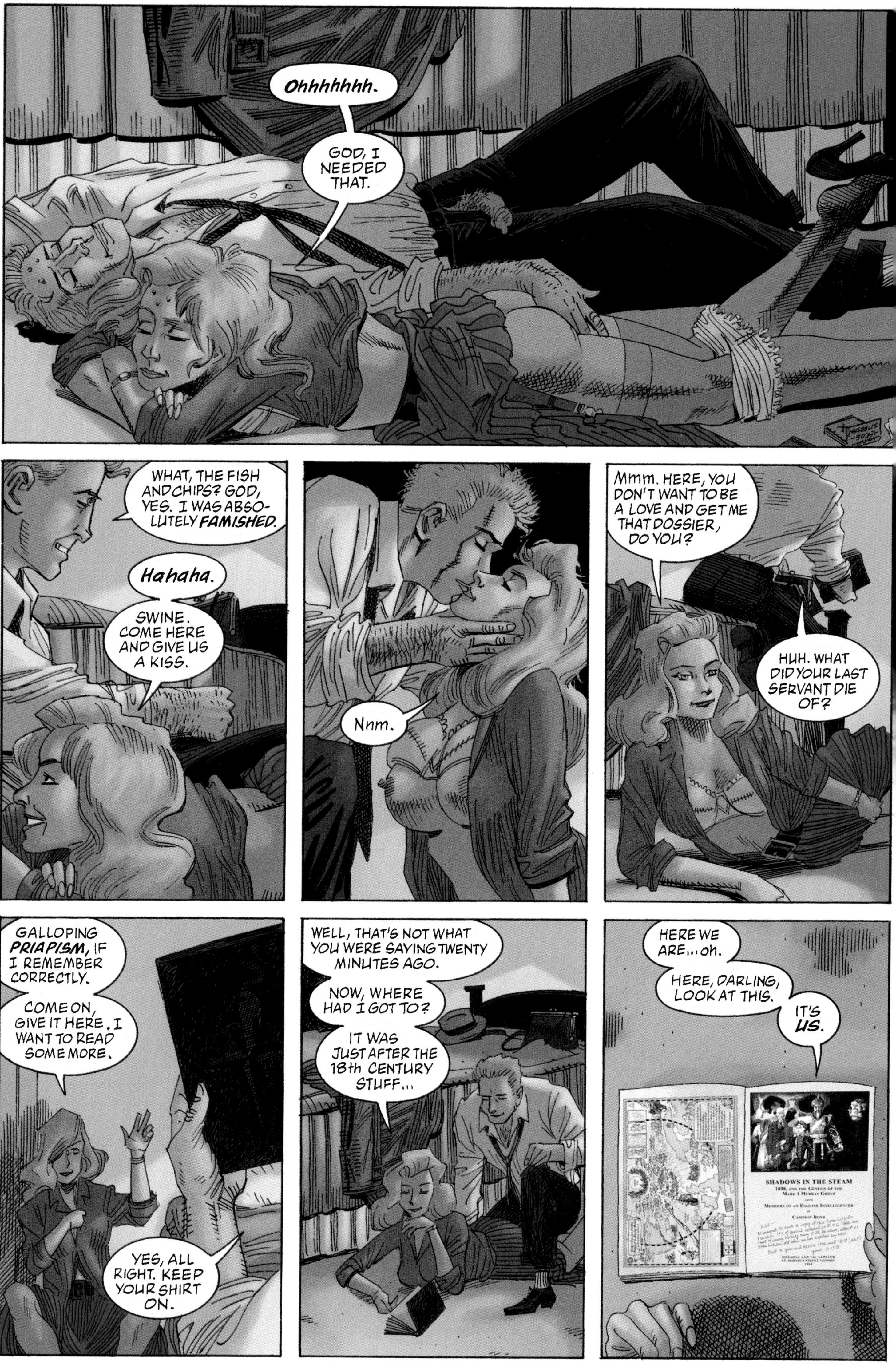
Ohhhhhhh.
GOD, I NEEDED THAT.
WHAT, THE FISH AND CHIPS? GOD, YES. I WAS ABSOLUTELY FAMISHED.
Hahaha.
SWINE. COME HERE AND GIVE US A KISS.
Nnm.
Mmm. HERE, YOU DON'T WANT TO BE A LOVE AND GET ME THAT DOSSIER, DO YOU?
HUH. WHAT DID YOUR LAST SERVANT DIE OF?
GALLOPING PRIAPISM, IF I REMEMBER CORRECTLY.
COME ON, GIVE IT HERE. I WANT TO READ SOME MORE.
YES, ALL RIGHT. KEEP YOUR SHIRT ON.
WELL, THAT'S NOT WHAT YOU WERE SAYING TWENTY MINUTES AGO.
NOW, WHERE HAD I GOT TO?
IT WAS JUST AFTER THE 18th CENTURY STUFF...
HERE WE ARE...oh.
HERE, DARLING, LOOK AT THIS.
IT'S US.
SHADOWS IN THE STEAM
1898, AND THE GENESIS OF THE MARK I MURRAY GROUP
FROM
MEMOIRS OF AN ENGLISH INTELLIGENCER
BY
CAMPION BOND
MEESONS AND CO. LIMITED
ST. MARTIN'S STREET, LONDON

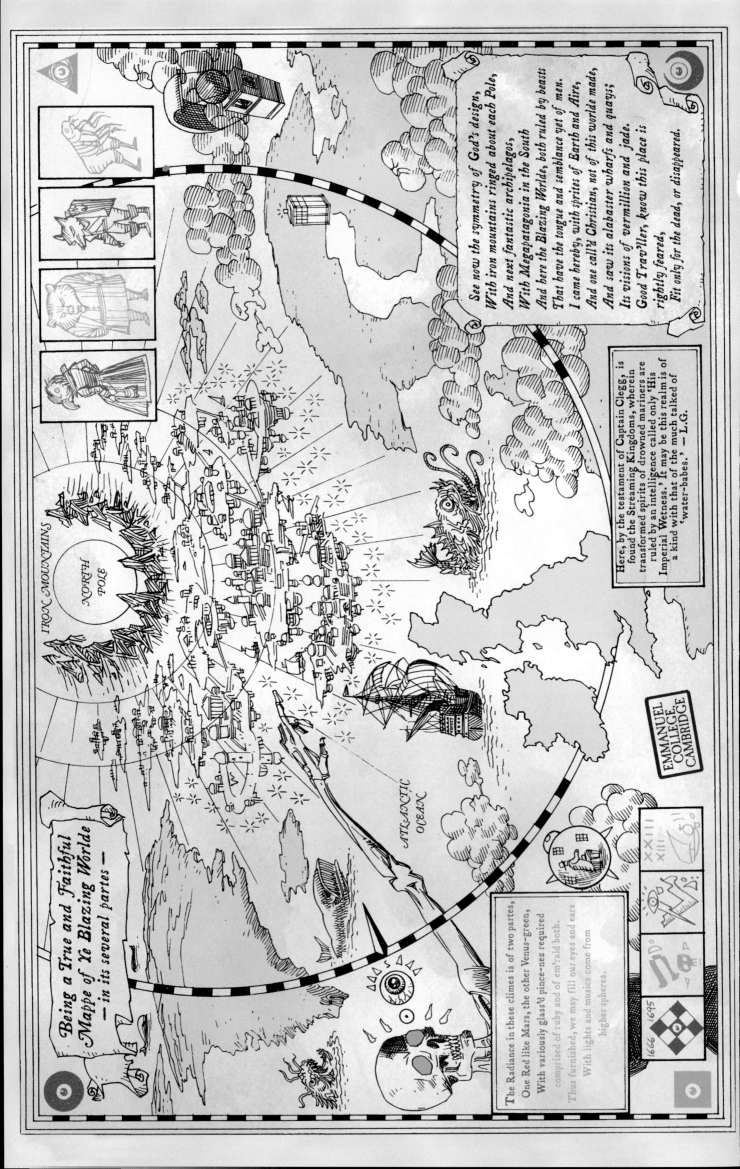

Being a True and Faithful
Mappe of Ye Blazing Worlde
— in its several partes —

IRON MOUNTAINS

HARMONIC POLE

ATLANTIC OCEAN

See now the symmetry of God's design,
With iron mountains ringed about each Pole,
And next fantastic archipelagos,
With Megapatagonia in the South
And here the Blazing Worlde, both ruled by beasts
That have the tongue and semblance yet of men.
I came hereby, with sprites of Earth and Aire,
And one call'd Christian, not of this worlde made,
And saw its alabaster wharfs and quays.
Its visions of vermillion and jade.
Good Trav'ller, know this place is
rightly feared,
Fit only for the dead, or disappeared.

Here, by the testament of Captain Clegg, is found the Streaming Kingdoms, wherein transformed spirits of drowned mariners are ruled by an intelligence called only 'His Imperial Wetness.' It may be this realm is of a kind with that of the much talked of 'water-babes.' — L.G.

EMMANUEL COLLEGE CAMBRIDGE

The Radiance in these climes is of two partes,
One Red like Mars, the other Venus-green,
With variously glass'd pince-nez required
comprised of ruby and of em'rald both.
Thus furnished, we may fill our eyes and ears
With lights and musics come from
higher spheres.

1666   1695

SHADOWS IN THE STEAM
1898, AND THE GENESIS OF THE
MARK I MURRAY GROUP

FROM

MEMOIRS OF AN ENGLISH INTELLIGENCER

BY

CAMPION BOND

H.W.—
Managed to save a copy of this from Litpol's furnaces. It's of special interest, as R.K.C. tells me that Murray herself may still be alive, albeit as some hideous old relic in her eighties by now.

Best to you and Bessie (the real "B.B.", eh?)

yours, G.O'B.

MEESONS AND CO. LIMITED
ST. MARTIN'S STREET, LONDON
1908

IT WAS DURING the late months of 1897 that I was required to visit the impressively (and also, to my way of thinking, startlingly) appointed offices of England's Military Intelligence command at Vauxhall Cross, where I was welcomed by the serving head of operations, universally acclaimed professor of mathematics, the esteemed James Moriarty, since deceased. A well-liked, lively-minded gentleman of middle years, he always had what seemed a merry twinkle in his eye, even whilst in discussions of great gravity or moment, and in this regard the instance of my visit would prove no exception. Sitting there across the generous expanse of his broad, handsome desk from me, he smiled and gestured most engagingly, his pale, delicate hands in almost constant motion as he outlined for me what he thought, with his chess-master's foresight, would be the unprecedented challenges to Great Britain's security during the twentieth century, which at that time seemed to be looming somewhat ominously, not so very far ahead.

The way that 'M' (as we referred to the professor) saw things, unknown and potentially apocalyptic dangers lurked within the breathtaking advances made by science itself, along with the appearance of a new and ruthless breed of man who would not hesitate to take advantage of such new discoveries despite, or even possibly because of, their alarming nature. As evidence of this new savage strain of science-brigand, Moriarty cited the example of the Hunnish "Luft-Piraten," Captain Mors, along with that of his French rival, the repulsive Monsieur Robur.

Yet it was not in the realm of the known sciences alone that the professor felt our hydra-headed threat was skulking. He believed, perhaps eccentrically, that Britain might prove subject to hostilities emerging from the area most commonly regarded as the haunted terrain of the supernatural. I must stress here that the professor, putting his more lately manifested megalomania for a moment to one side, was a fierce rationalist and firm materialist, intensely logical in all his ways. Thus he regarded the occurrence of peculiar phenomena not as an evidence of supernature, but, more properly, as evidence of nature incompletely comprehended.

Perhaps adhering to the ancient (and, if but considered for a moment, dangerously misguided) dictum that exhorts us to fight fire with fire, it was to this end that 'M' ventured his proposal, which suggested an assembly, in the manner of a team or squadron, of unusually gifted or experienced individuals working clandestinely for the Crown, by which means England might successfully repel and counter such incursions from the unknown as it seemed that the professor now daily anticipated. His idea was not, he put it to me, wholly without precedent, and indicated to me a stout pile of dusty folders that had up until that moment gone unnoticed, heaped upon a distant corner of Professor Moriarty's desk. Perusing these antique and badly faded documents, I learned that such a cabinet of human oddities was first convened by England's first head of intelligence, the legendary Sir Jack Wilton, early in the reign of England's so-called "fairy monarch" Gloriana in the sixteenth century. Further to this, it seemed that during the ill-starred reign of King George the Third the scheme was resurrected with a fresh ensemble of unlikely and outlandish characters to fill the vacancies left by the former members of the group, long since departed.

When I asked where we were to discover latter-day equivalents of the unusual personalities comprising these two earlier assemblages, 'M' merely smiled and gestured, calling my attention to a single folder, far less tattered and of clearly a more recent vintage than its fellows. Opening it to peer within I found it to contain a small selection of newspaper articles and brief appended notes, mostly pertaining to events that had occurred within the previous ten years or so. It gradually dawned upon me that these various reports concerned the actions of just five specific individuals.

One set of documents pertained to the purchase of heliotropes, imported from the remote nation of Bengodi by a student at the London University, while supplementing these receipts were newspaper accounts of an "invisible monstrosity" which, several commentators speculated, might have some connection to the probably-invented "horla" creature that the French claimed to have captured in the later 1880s. Other papers had circled obituaries: an explorer who had been reported killed in some lost kingdom far away in Africa; a fiendishly inventive Indian mutineer believed to have been drowned almost a quarter-century before; also, a medical practitioner from Edinburgh transplanted down to London and apparently become a suicide in 1886. Added to these were files relating to the recent scandalous divorce of a young lady music teacher by the name of Harker, clipped to which there were bewildering appended notes referring to unpleasant graveyard desecrations up in the vicinity of Highgate Cemetery, with decapitated corpses and the like in evidence.

It was to these last writings that Professor Moriarty now drew my attention. He explained to me the scarcely credible events in which our Mrs. Harker (who, reverting to her maiden name immediately after her divorce, now styled herself Miss Wilhelmina Murray) had become embroiled at the beginnings of the current year. As the professor saw things, this young woman had survived, both physically and mentally, an onslaught instigated by a prime mature male from a species of which we had hitherto refuted the existence. In addition, she possessed invaluable and almost certainly unique experience concerning the direct effect of so-called supernatural phenomena at first hand, and with her divorce had demonstrated, at least in the eyes of the professor, a determined spirit that he thought might qualify her as the head of his proposed team. I protested that, entirely to the contrary, her very gender had disqualified her from consideration as a seriously-regarded leader, at which the professor glanced with much significance towards a portrait of Her Majesty that hung adorning his far office wall. He stated his belief that wilful, self-directed men such as those he proposed should make up the remainder of this curious league would not feel the same territorial rivalry towards a woman as they would invariably feel, confronted by a male commander. Whilst at the time I will admit to a belief that the professor's theories were outlandish and unnecessarily progressive, I must equally concede that over time his insights proved to be correct in almost every measure.

Further to the matter of Miss Murray, he observed that after her alleged violation by a creature that was less than human and her subsequent divorce from the estate agent who'd previously been her husband, she would surely find herself in a precarious and vulnerable position, by virtue of her newly found pariah status as both ruined woman and a willing divorcee. Ostracised by polite society on these accounts, it seemed, then, a foregone conclusion that our music-teacher would quite shortly come to be in a condition of considerable monetary hardship, which, so the professor reasoned, might make her unusually susceptible to our proposal of a lucrative, albeit rather hazardous mode of employment. He suggested that I first recruit this woman (who had currently, by all accounts, found rented rooms in

Bermondsey), and next enlist her to locate and hire the other persons that 'M' wished to see included in his nightmarish ensemble.

Suffice it to say that by the following day I had made postal contact with our quarry, guardedly making ambiguous remarks as to the possibility of subsequent employ. Meeting with an enthusiastic, even slightly desperate response by a return of post, I had arranged to meet with her beside the lake there in St. James's Park. Arriving early for our assignation I was earnestly engaged in throwing breadcrumbs to the ducks when a polite cough by my shoulder gave me cause to turn.

The first thing to impress itself upon me was the slightness of her build, and her diminutive appearance, standing little more than five feet tall. It seemed to me that a strong wind might snap her in two at the waist, let alone the more vigorous and actively aggressive forces that Professor Moriarty had it in his labyrinthine mind for her to meet with. Next I noticed the tight-wound suggestion of repression and restraint she seemed to carry with her, an impression of some furious resentment that she kept withheld beneath her perfectly-composed exterior. As if to emphasise this, though the day was by no means a cold one, she wore tightly wrapped about her throat a long red scarf with which she toyed self-consciously throughout our interview, her eyes filled with darting suspicion and uncertainty, her lips pursed in what seemed a moue of almost constant disapproval or distaste.

Our discussions by the waterside, with trees made dark inverted masses of viridian reflected in the lake before us, were both brief and to the point. Though she seemed mistrustful of me from the start until the finish of our conversation, once I had remarked on the impressive sum her reimbursements would amount to, and assured her there should be no immorality in her employ, she readily agreed and asked me what should be her first assignment. I explained that my employer, Mr. 'M', would presently arrange for her to be transported in a British naval vessel to the waters west of South America. There she'd be put down in a boat and left to make her own way to the enigmatic Lincoln Island, where it was her task to enlist the reputedly-dead Indian Mutineer turned science-rogue that I had read of in Professor Moriarty's notes.

Amusingly, Miss Murray (as she constantly insisted she be called), believing herself to be both well read and shrewd, had seemingly assumed, from various pointed remarks she made, that 'M' was Mr. Mycroft Holmes, who would succeed Professor Moriarty as head of intelligence. I did not, it must be said, seek at the time to rectify her quite erroneous conclusions. Rather, I informed her that, anticipating her agreement to our princely offer, we had opened an account for her at Lloyd's, and had secreted in advance her first month's wage. This was upon the understanding that she would report to Government-maintained docks close to Wapping at her earliest convenience, where she would next commence her journey to the South Pacific.

All this was settled without disagreement, and some eight days later our absurdly tiny suffragettist music-teacher was en route for South America and, hopefully, for Lincoln Island with its brilliant, dangerous Sikh inhabitant. According to the naval officers accompanying Miss Murray on this first leg of her journey, she kept to her cabin for the trip's duration, studying the files pertaining to the Indian privateer that we'd provided, this despite some several invitations to dine at the captain's table, her refusal earning her the soubriquet of 'Iron Drawers' amongst the lower ranks. At length, when it had been decided that the ship was now but some short distance to the south-east of the island that was its objective, Murray was set down within a lifeboat that contained provisions more than adequate for the brief bout of rowing that would take her to the shores of Lincoln. Unexpectedly, however, Murray's craft had not gone more than ten lengths from our naval steamer when it was enveloped in a dense fog that had seemingly swelled up from nowhere. Some years later, we discovered that these permanent great banks of mist conceal the group of islands called the Riallaro Archipelago, but at the time of Miss Murray's adventure, lacking all such information, we were unprepared and thus lost contact with her scarcely moments after setting her adrift. An hour later violent storms arose and, fearing the worst, our ship set sail for Blighty, leaving our poor music-instructress for dead. The following entries, then, collated from Miss Murray's journal notes, are our sole record of what next transpired.

"It is now some few days since I was parted from the ship, and yet this is the first occasion I have had to make a full account within this journal. Briefly, then, I was set down within my rowboat on the ship's port side, at night, almost a week ago exactly from today. I was at the time experiencing some relief to find the waters nowhere near as rough as I had previously anticipated, and was to a small extent congratulating myself on how jolly brave and capable I had turned out to be, despite my wholesale lack of any previous experience with this kind of high jinks. It was at this point that the ship behind me, along with the waters that surrounded me and stars above, completely vanished, swallowed in an instant by a dense white fog that all but instantly reduced me to an abject and despicable example of the most utterly useless whimpering femininity, with no idea of which way she was headed or of where she was, save that she was most probably in the most awful trouble. This fact was confirmed, with what seemed an unnecessarily harsh emphasis, perhaps a half-hour later, when a wind began to rise that was attended by some of the largest waves that I have ever seen, let alone been adrift by night amongst.

"I am not wholly certain as to in quite what order the events that next transpired occurred, since I was, you may imagine, in a state of dreadful panic at the time. I was huddled, at some point, there at the bottom of my lifeboat, clinging to the waterproof trunk which contained all my provisions (with this journal in amongst them), unable to hear my own frantic screaming for the anvil waves that smashed and crashed about me. All at once, amidst my terror, I felt in my stomach a most frightful sense of bottomlessness that I knew must mean my fragile craft had been raised high aloft atop some towering wave, where it now hung for but a second before dropping through the air to land inverted in a churning foam of white and midnight green.

"I have a memory of being underwater with no clear sense of where 'up' might be, and feel I may have rather bashed my head upon my boat's disintegrating timbers, but at any rate it seems that I did not release my hold upon the trunk, which, being watertight, presumably at last bobbed to the surface, acting as a kind of buoy. It was to this I found myself still clinging when I woke, my cheek pressed in a reach of pale blonde sand spread between knuckles of obsidian rock, on what I hoped to be the shores of Lincoln Isle. It was first light, the eastern heavens now a nacreous grey as I climbed to my feet unsteadily and looked about me in the pre-dawn twilight. At my back the surf retreated, hissing, leaving tiny crabs of brilliant green stranded in sinks and pools amongst dark granite crags. Before me, the fine talcum of the beach rose at a gentle incline to its crest, a spinal ridge where tufts of maram-grass made a fine hatching, penned in jet against the lightening sky.

"The various layers of formal clothing I had been impractical enough to dress myself in were now soaked, and thus become intolerably heavy. Since the morning did not seem by any means a cold one, having dragged my trunk first further up the sands to safety from the frothing tidal edge, I next removed my garb down to my modest under-things and spread the sloughed-off coats and skirts like black and saturated banners on the rough-cut stony outcrops. It was my intention to eat first from my provisions, safe within the trunk, and possibly compose some plan of action whilst I waited for my garments to be dried by the soon-risen sun, but this was not to be. As I sat on a somewhat higher rocky perch, plucking my damp chemise away from goose-bumped skin and looking, I suppose, to all the world like some American advertisement for soap, I was surprised by what seemed like a great and silent tidal surge of men, shadowy forms that welled up of a sudden from the gloaming to engulf my lofty spar and wash me quite away upon a current of strong arms, my sopping crimson scarf trailed out behind me in the wake, cry stifled by a leathery hand that smelled of rope and tar across my mouth.

"When my assailants had delivered me once more to level ground I was set down, at which a low voice close beside my ear cautioned me three times not to scream again, this admonition not only enunciated in clear English, but likewise in German and in French. Having nodded in compliance, the firm grip across my mouth was next released and I was able thus to turn my head and take the measure of my captors stood about me there, their features being by the moment more discernible, both from the gradually improving light and from my eyes having become accustomed to the gloom. They were a motley, roughneck crew some five or six in number, and amidst even so small a sample it was evident that these men hailed from a variety of continents and likewise were the issue of some several different races. One, I think, was a Malay, another being a tall Negro with the elegant bone-structure and near-indigo complexion that I most associate with Africa's Ivory Coast. There was an older man that I assumed to be American whose voice had a New England twang about it, and a fellow similarly aged, dressed up in what appeared to be an ancient, threadbare uniform such as were common during the Sepoy Rebellion.

"The man who'd spoken and whose hand had gagged me was, as it turned out, a young and rather well-built Englishman whose name, I later learned, was Jack. This last stood barefoot there upon the glistening, tide-smoothed sands, nude to his waist so that between his shoulder-blades I could make out in broad tattoo an arrow that I took to be a mark of former penal servitude, perhaps implying him to be a transportee escaped whilst bound for New South Wales or some such ghastly destination. Having first established I was English, he proceeded to interrogate me as to both my name and to the nature of my business there on Lincoln Island, which at least confirmed to me, were confirmation needed, that I had indeed arrived at my intended destination.

"Thinking honesty to be upon consideration the best policy, I gave them my full name and told them that I had been paid to come here by British Intelligence in order to convey their highly generous offer to the personage whom I assumed was owner of this island, one Prince Dakkar, Indian nobleman turned technologic buccaneer.

"At this their narrow-eyed suspicion turned upon the instant into raucous, ridiculing laughter, and the tattooed man who was my chief interrogator struggled to contain his mirth as he assured me that he knew of no-one here who ever had been called by such a name, putting much stress on the two syllables of 'no-one' as he did so, to renewed amusement from his colleagues. He then asked me if this was the only name I had been given by the British agents who had sent me here. Had they not given me some other name, he asked, perhaps one more immediately recognisable, by which the Indian prince I sought was known? When my only reply was to shake my head in bewilderment, the company once more erupted with hilarity, and only the New Englander who looked to be the oldest of the crew seemed genuinely indignant upon my behalf. His features crumpled in a disapproving scowl, he muttered that he thought it shameful how these men of government would send a mere girl to approach one they dare not approach themselves, and, worse than this, did not even see fit to tell her the most common name of he she sought, no doubt for fear that she would flee in terror from their enterprise should she be so informed. My momentary displeasure at his calling me a 'mere girl' was immediately displaced by the deep, stomach-churning resonance, as from a gong of dire foreboding that rang through me. Had I been, so to speak, kept in the dark, upon a mission that already seemed to me quite hazardous enough, concerning its true dangers?

"I asked them, trying with some difficulty to subdue the tremor in my voice, who, then, it was, if not Prince Dakkar, that resided here? The tattooed individual merely shook his head, repeating the word 'no-one,' and commanded me to walk ahead of them as they escorted me to see their captain. I protested that I was not dressed, and could not leave my trunk and clothing here within the tide's reach unattended, at which the New Englander took off his trailing oilskin coat and let me wear it draped about my shoulders. He instructed the Malay to bring my sodden clothing, and the former Sepoy to retrieve my trunk, and thereupon they marched me up the shore's soft incline, headed for the isle's interior.

"We walked in silence for perhaps some twenty or so minutes and in all that time saw not another living soul, save for an incident near the beginning when we were scarcely past the beach's edge, about to venture into the low, cattle-cropped grass reaching off beyond: a kind of cottage built from bluish-white stones stood there at the sandbar's upper margin, and within the darkness of its wooden doorframe I could see a lovely Indian woman in a kind of turquoise skirt or wrapping, standing watching us. She was perhaps some thirty or so years of age, her smouldering umber beauty only partly hidden by the air of melancholy hung across her features like a veil. She stared across the sand and grass towards us from the shadows of her doorway, and the small child she held swaddled in her arms stared also, a pretty, dark-ringleted girl of but a few years old, who had the biggest, brownest and most knowing eyes that I have ever seen. I later learned that these two were the estranged wife and daughter of the man I had been sent to find, but at the time saw only the suspicion and resentment in the woman's gaze: the keen intelligence that glowed within the child's. My captors did not give me leave to ask about the pair, but with a gentle push propelled me on across flat scrubland, making for the

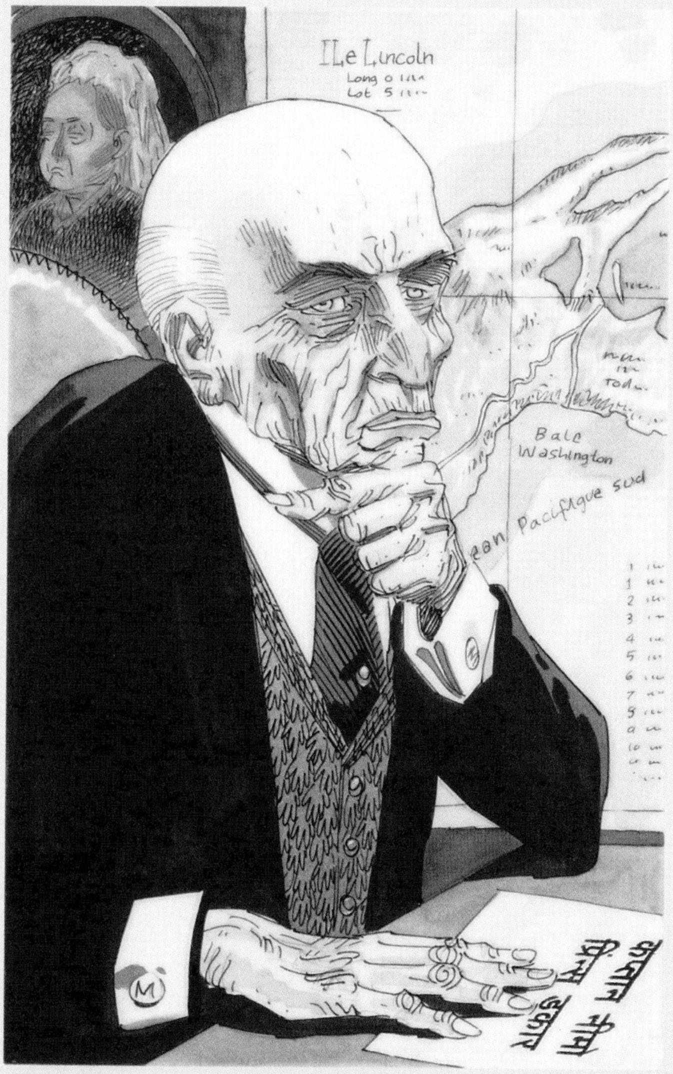
ILe Lincoln
Baie Washington
Pacifique sud

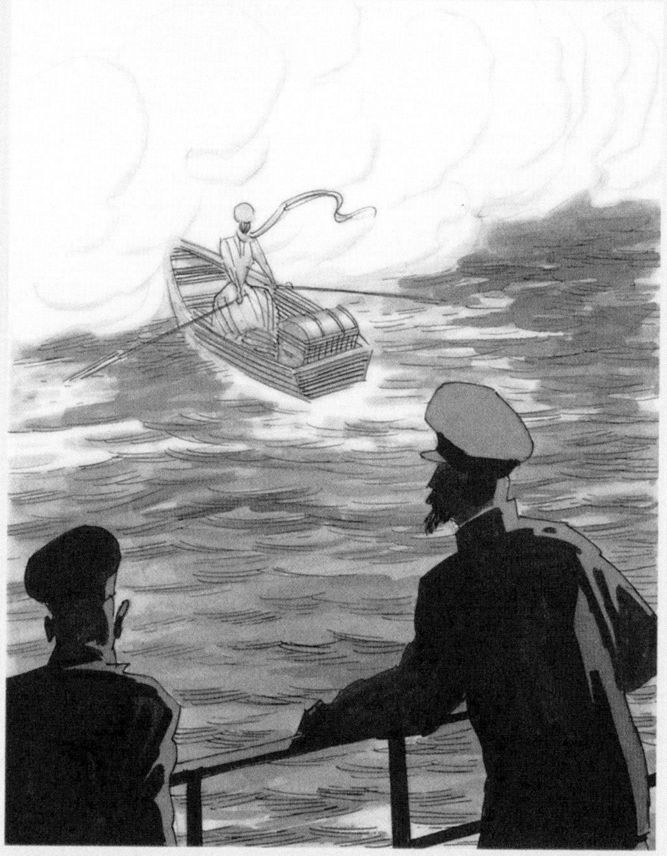

TOP LEFT: Professor James Moriarty, (or 'M'), officiating at Vauxhall Cross. TOP RIGHT: Captain Kettle watches Miss Murray commencing her adventure. BELOW: The rebuilt Nautilus, in dock on Lincoln Island.

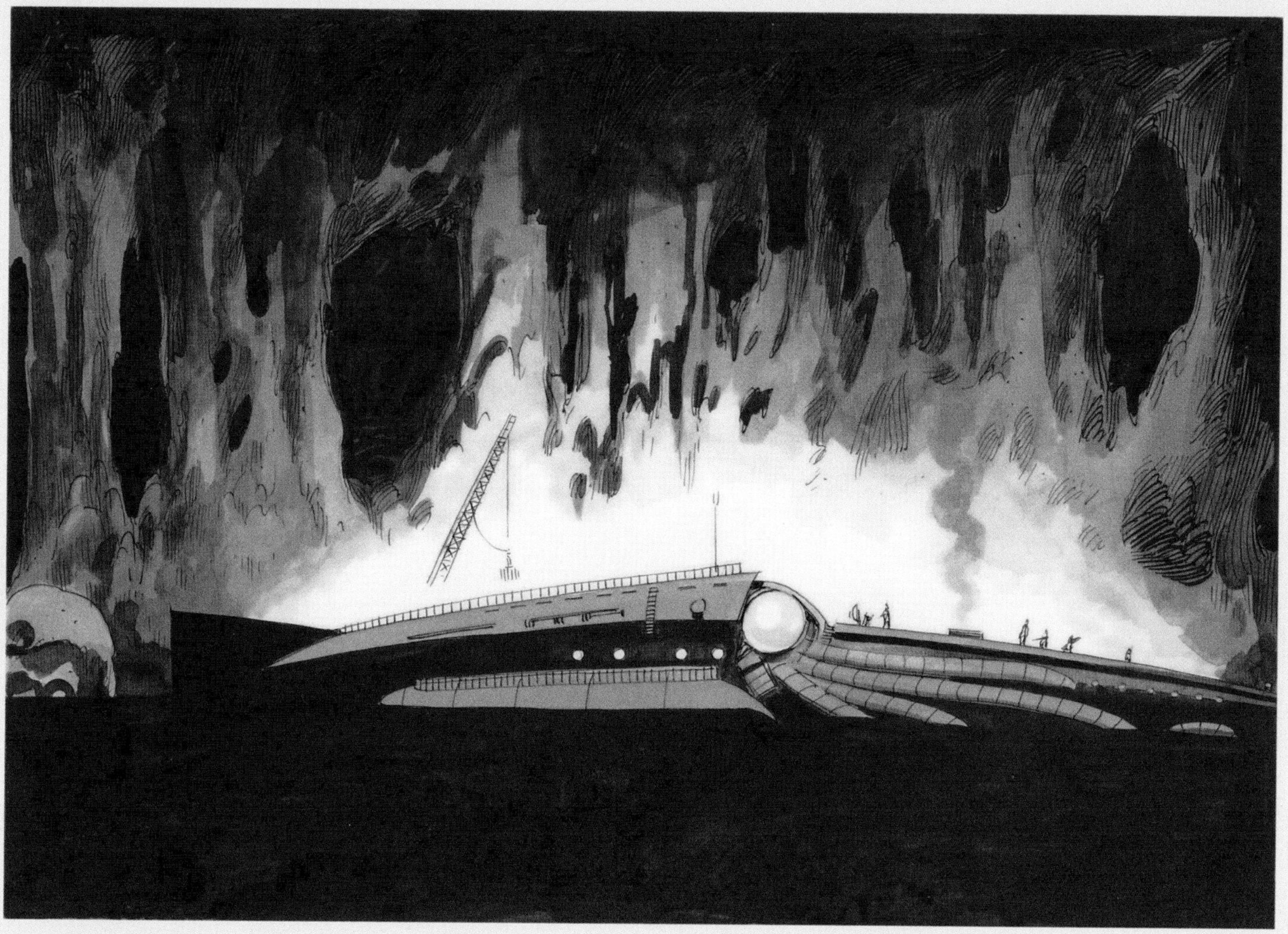

threads of wood-smoke twisting up from what I took to be a camp or colony upon the lower flank of purpled, supine hills that seemed the island's only landmark.

"The shanty-town, for so it proved to be when finally we reached it, was both more extensive and well-built than I'd anticipated, with its buildings rising up the hillside's gentle slope in ladder-accessed terraces, and graceful (although sturdy) walkways of bamboo and hawser strung between them. This novel settlement was also not by any means so mean or bleak as I'd imagined, with instead bright colour and outlandish decorations everywhere, both on its house-fronts and upon its population. These I estimated to be several dozen persons of almost as many nationalities, of which men comprised by far the greater part, although they numbered many women and some children in amongst their ranks besides. I noticed some men walking hand in hand, both with each other or with younger boys, and so concluded Lincoln Isle to be a province founded upon anarchistic principles, providing haven for the deviants…be they political or sexual by inclination…of the world and all its countries, in a type of libertine utopia, such as was exampled by Port Royal in the Caribbean and its many kindred pirate sanctuaries, during earlier centuries.

"At length, walked up a winding path towards the low hill's uppermost extremities, I was brought to a temple-like construction, all of stone, that seemed almost a sumptuous palace in compare with the by-no-means meagre structures spread below it upon the inferior slopes of this mauve tumulus. Wide gates of burnished brass opened upon the circle of a courtyard flagged with basalt, around which was statuary arranged depicting Hindu deities, plundered perhaps from many different sources. I waited under guard within this yard beneath the cold, accusing frowns of octopus-limbed and exotic gods while the New Englander ventured alone into the residence itself, after some moments reappearing to escort me in.

"I stepped into what seemed a dazzling, regal chamber hung with splendid tapestries, where at the centre, on a gilded throne whose back was an exquisitely embroidered peacock tail, sat a tall, turbaned figure of the most alarming and ferocious aspect, clad in a long coat of such elaborate finery that it appeared at least the jacket of an Admiral, with its epaulettes and decorative frogging, but in bottle green as rich and fraught with both enigma and romance as the jade ocean deep itself.

"My New Englander escort having now withdrawn I stood alone there in the silence of that opulent pavilion, beneath the hawklike and unblinking gaze of that disarming eminence. At last, unable to bear any more of the unbroken hush, I spoke, and asked him if he was Prince Dakkar. At this, I thought he almost smiled, but seeing that his eyes remained as cold and as indifferent, I concluded it to be some aberration of the light. When he replied it was in flawless English almost too precise in its enunciation, only faintly accented, his voice deep as the creak in salt-caked timbers. 'Perhaps I was once, but not now. Now I am no-one.' Here he paused for but a single beat and stared unnervingly into my eyes before he went on. 'I am Nemo.'

"The impact of his name upon me was not unlike that of a steam locomotive. I am sure that all the colour drained immediately from my face as finally I understood the constant harping upon 'no-one,' and the Latinate equivalent that was implied. The figure sitting here before me, his ring-heavy mocha-coloured fingers toying with his greying beard, was Captain Nemo. Nemo, the tall, imposing, dusky enemy of all western society, who'd waged a war of terror on the high seas and appalled the civilised world at his potent mix of the most up-to-date and modern science or engineering with a bloodily-expressed fanaticism that was all but medieval. Nemo, whose alarming likeness had appeared in newspapers and broadsheets all across the length and breadth of Europe, frightening children and their seniors alike till his reported death sometime during the middle eighteen seventies, a year or two before I had been even born. I can remember, as a baby playing near my mother's skirts, hearing my father and my grandfather debating as to whom had been the inspiration for more nightmares, Nemo or Napoleon, and now I stood before the man himself, become once more a trembling, stammering infant, scarcely able to believe that my employers had, quite knowingly, sent me unwitting to approach this England-hating monster in his den. Did they consider me so casually expendable that they would send me, careless, to my certain death? Or did they reason me to be equipped uniquely in surviving this encounter, having earlier this present year lived through the onslaught of a fabulous antagonist more dreadful even than the glowering Sikh?

"Clinging to this last notion and its implication that I was a valued agent in whom my superiors held the highest confidence, I started, hesitatingly, to outline the proposal which I had been sent to put before the captain. Realising that essentially this was an offer of employment from a nation and a government that Captain Nemo famously despised, I thought to take on a more diplomatic tone and couch the bald entreaty in terms more respectful (if not actually obsequious) to this evidently proud and isolated self-determined man. I told him that I came to Lincoln Island as the emissary of a British Empire that had lately come to understand the grievous error of their enmity towards the captain, that now realized it was his genius alone that could assist them in their hour of need and so enlisted me to venture here and beg him, on my bended knees if necessary, to enlist with them and to accept their reparations, namely a full pardon and a handsome reimbursement, along with the promise of adventures extraordinary, here on the coming twentieth century's brink.

"This last assurance was my own invention, tendered somewhat desperately as I noticed from the way the captain's brow had clouded that the British Empire's purse or pardon interested him not even slightly. Hoping that I'd judged his personality correctly, which is to say as one with overweening pride as its main principle, I dropped my gaze here to the floor and made apology for having ventured childish imprecations to adventure when I should have understood that such suggestions were, by virtue of the captain's venerable age, entirely inappropriate. I said that I was sorry to have thus intruded upon his retirement here and offered to remove myself forthwith if only there might be a simple rowboat found for me, my own having been smashed to driftwood by the recent squall. When these words met with no response save silence and that same unwavering gaze, I hung my head and turned towards the chamber's tile-rimmed door that I had entered by, making as if to walk away and thinking that my ploy had failed, when suddenly, behind me, Nemo spoke.

"He told me that, to him, the Empire's offers of forgiveness and of money were both deathly insults which, were he but of a different humour, would ensure that my remains were being feasted on by fish before the sun had set that day. However, he went on, he had been pining lately for the exploits that were his in former times, with only a disastrous circumnavigation of Antarctica attempted three years previously to relieve the cosseted monotony of his listless retreat here upon Lincoln Isle. He told me to go with his crew, who waited outside in the courtyard still, and that they would find quarters for me where I might rest overnight while he gave my proposal due consideration. He also made sardonic note of my attire, with oilskin coat worn over only underwear, suggesting I might try the local woman's wrap, which he referred to as, I think, a 'sa-ree,' until my own clothing could be laundered properly and then returned to me. I thanked him for his generosity and did as he'd suggested, though I will confess I passed a nearly sleepless night there at the pirate stronghold, much of it spent in a vain attempt to wrap my borrowed tangerine-and-emerald skirts correctly.

"The next morning, having had my own attire replaced outside my cabin's door just when I finally appeared to have my 'sa-ree' mastered, I was breakfasted alone upon a kedgeree of wood-smoked fish and rice, then taken by the arrow-tattooed man to meet the captain in a kind of cove there on the island's north-most shore, from which deep, dripping caves bored down into the rocky earth and buried waterways below. Attended by some thirty members of the Indian science-pirate's crew, who carried torches and, I thought, seemed almost bursting with a school-boyish excitement they could scarce conceal, we went into these caverns and down winding passageways made slippery by moss or algae, coming finally upon a massive, yawning vault whose ceiling, high above, the flickering radiance of the crewmen's fire-brands did not touch. Contained within this stygian and echoing expanse there was a night-black subterranean lake, perhaps a furlong wide, while there upon its waters floated an enormity so utterly unprecedented that even the tide-weathered mariners surrounding me, familiar with this spectacle, seemed breath-taken to see it now.

"There on the lake's jet mirror was the Nautilus, the captain's legendary submersible device, though not, I was assured, the same craft that had terrorized our planet's waterways in Nemo's heyday, this having been sunken some decades before, replaced by the remarkable machine that, in its underground dock, hung suspended there before us now. This latest vessel seemed more like some new, unearthly creature than it did a mere insensate mechanism, or perhaps it was instead two undersea leviathans, a kraken and a whale, locked in an embrace that was mortal or else amorous. Taken along a swaying gangway and aboard, the captain thought to tell me that he had decided to accept my offer, and that we were bound for England. He also, in a matter-of-fact way, informed me that if this should prove to be some English ruse I would immediately be put to death and all of Britain's coastal installations would be levelled by bombardment. I was then escorted to a pleasantly-appointed cabin in the submarine's unusually-embellished innards, where I found my watertight trunk and therefore this journal waiting for me. We put out to sea an hour ago, and I am presently still sat within my bunkroom, making these extensive entries and anticipating my return to England, along with the many pointed questions I shall have for the superiors who sent me, unprepared, upon so perilous a quest."

So ended Murray's narrative, and I must with regret report that when we met next upon her return to these shores she indeed regaled me bitterly with her presumptuous questions and hysterically-delivered accusations, which, attributing her outburst to some female difficulty or perhaps an inflammation of the womb, I generously ignored. She'd come ashore alone to make report upon her jaunt, while the suspicious Captain Nemo and his fascinating craft remained submerged at some unknown location, waiting cautiously to see what happened next. So it was that I did not see the captain in the flesh until the next occasion when I met Miss Murray, being some weeks later at the then still-uncompleted channel causeway, jutting proudly and preposterously out from Dover and into the iron-grey waters of the English Channel.

I explained her next assignment to her, the retrieval of another superannuated and presumed-dead legend, and endured the sniping and superior tone that had, it seemed, become her custom to use whilst addressing me, along with her naive, misguided speculations as to the identity of 'M,' our ultimate employer. Walking down with her across the boards and ladders to the ocean's edge, I was perhaps taken somewhat aback to notice that a frightful churning had commenced there in the ferrous waters not so very far beneath us, as if some great unruly serpent of the depths were surfacing amidst the boiling froth and spume. It was, of course, the captain's monstrous underwater battleship, which, though I had by then seen it described in Murray's notes, I was by no means quite prepared for in its awesome actuality. A metal gangplank was extended for Miss Murray to repair aboard, and once she'd done so there was a brief, chilling moment when another, larger figure next appeared there at the aperture by which she'd entered, staring out directly at me from beneath the dark briar-hedges of his brows with eyes full of a wintry, sere contempt that I remember with a shudder to this day. This, then, was Nemo, the most deadly and notorious scientific villain that the nineteenth century had spawned. He briefly held my gaze, then with a sneer slammed shut the hatchway, thus allowing his unfathomable engine to once more submerge. In only a few moments every trace of it was gone and I was left to stare in stupefaction at the circling, screaming gulls and foam-laced breakers that remained.

As it eventually transpired, Miss Murray and the captain were amongst the least alarming presences that came to be included in Professor Moriarty's league of curiosities, and I must question now, as then, his wisdom in assembling an entourage of such unbalanced, dangerous individuals. It seems to me the British Empire has always encountered difficulty in distinguishing between its heroes and its monsters, and if the professor had not some ten years ago been taken to his lonely, stratospheric grave, I cannot help but feel that he himself might, albeit reluctantly, concur with my assessment. My own ruinous association with the team, extending although tenuously to the present day, has been to the great detriment of my career and is, I have concluded, the main factor which contributes to my current desk job in the files department, that I shall discuss in detail and at length in my next chapter.

For now, let it suffice to say that one should never suffer to command a host of nightmares, lest they shrug your yoke and turn upon you in your sleep. The coming years, I hope, will not be blighted by such rude awakenings, but, as ever, we shall see.

MOBILIS IN MOBILE

TRANSLATION: MOBILE WITHIN A MOBILE ELEMENT

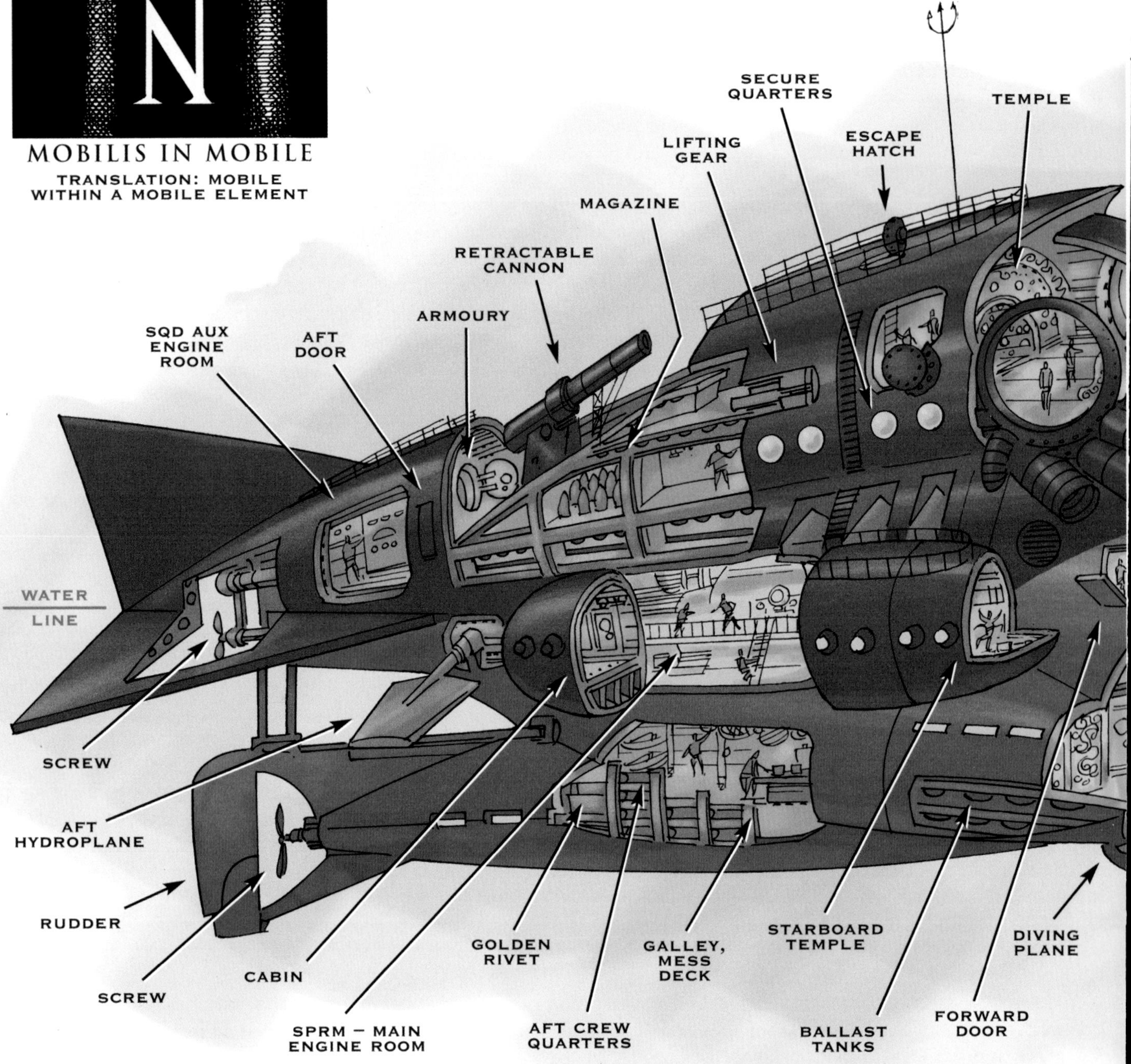

SECURE QUARTERS
TEMPLE
LIFTING GEAR
ESCAPE HATCH
MAGAZINE
RETRACTABLE CANNON
ARMOURY
SQD AUX ENGINE ROOM
AFT DOOR
WATER LINE
SCREW
AFT HYDROPLANE
RUDDER
SCREW
CABIN
SPRM – MAIN ENGINE ROOM
GOLDEN RIVET
AFT CREW QUARTERS
GALLEY, MESS DECK
STARBOARD TEMPLE
BALLAST TANKS
FORWARD DOOR
DIVING PLANE

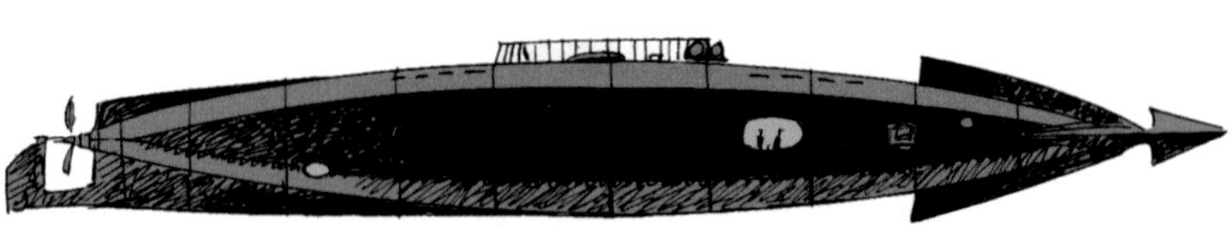

NAUTILUS I, 1865

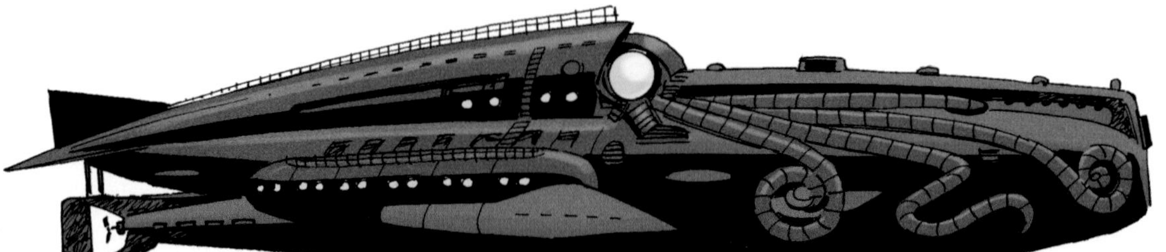

NAUTILUS II, 1878

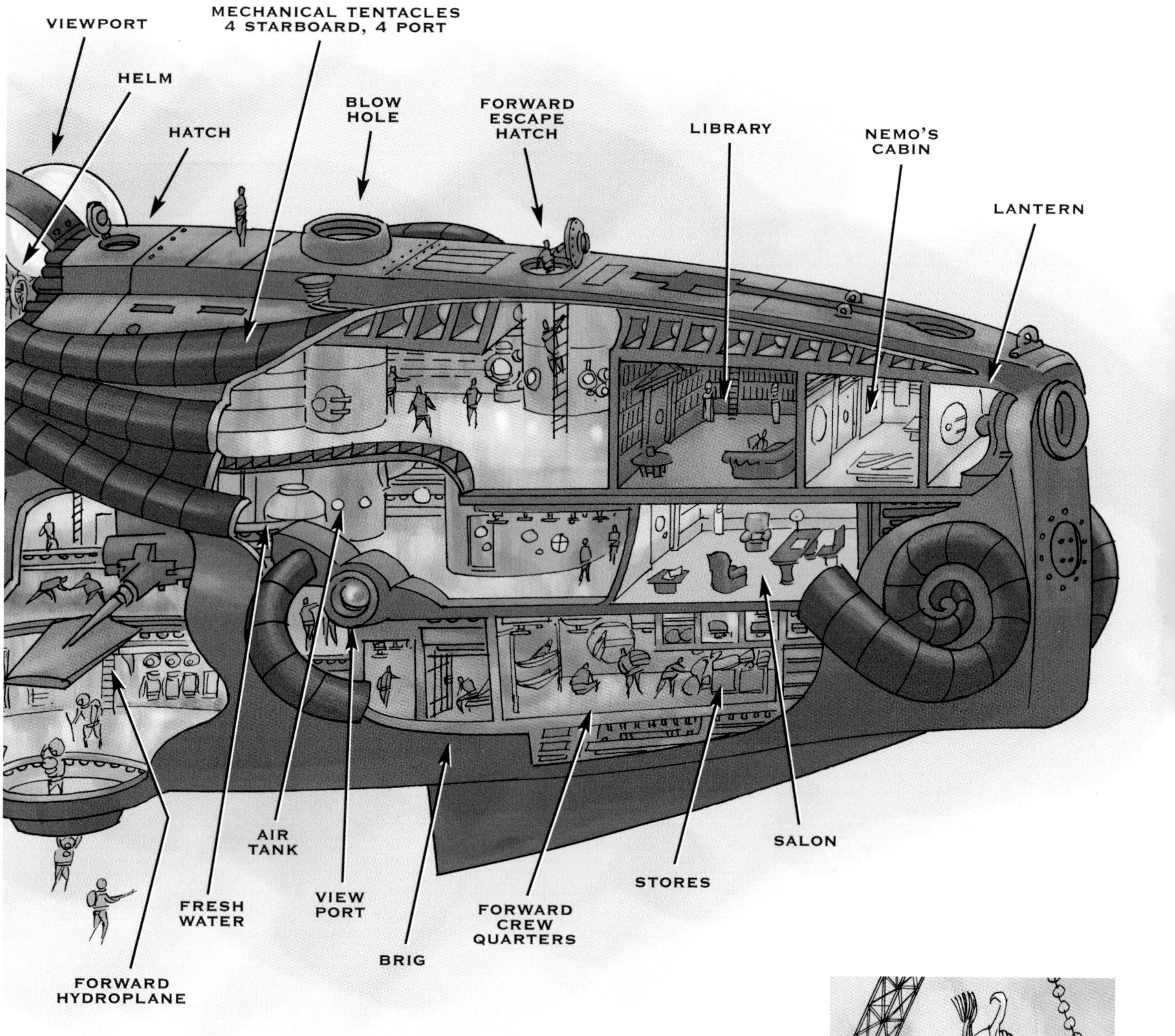
VIEWPORT
MECHANICAL TENTACLES
4 STARBOARD, 4 PORT
HELM
HATCH
BLOW
HOLE
FORWARD
ESCAPE
HATCH
LIBRARY
NEMO'S
CABIN
LANTERN
AIR
TANK
FRESH
WATER
VIEW
PORT
BRIG
FORWARD
CREW
QUARTERS
STORES
SALON
FORWARD
HYDROPLANE

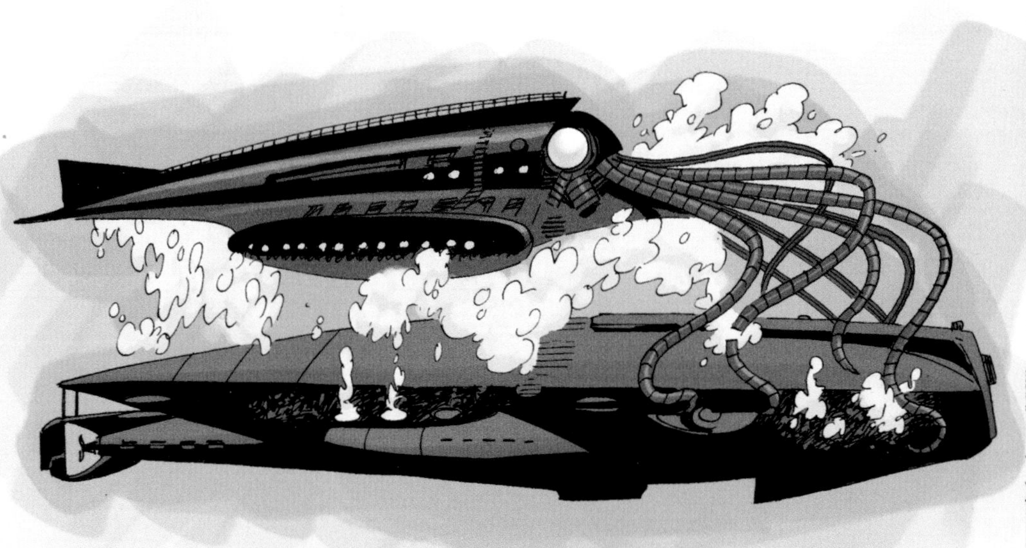

NAUTILUS II
SEPARATING KRAKEN SECTION
FROM WHALE HULL

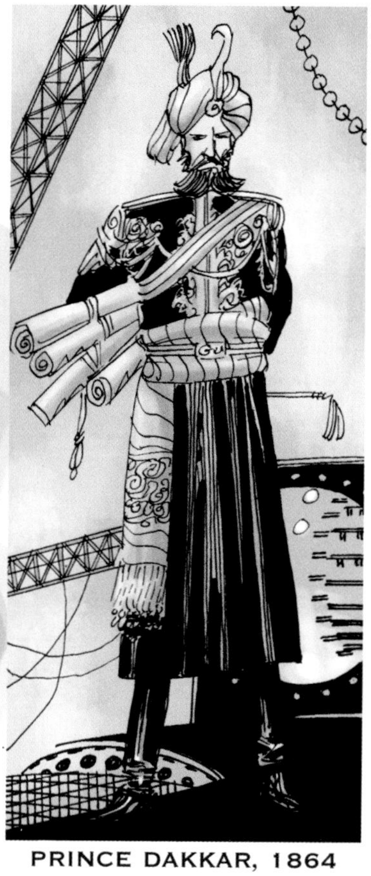

PRINCE DAKKAR, 1864

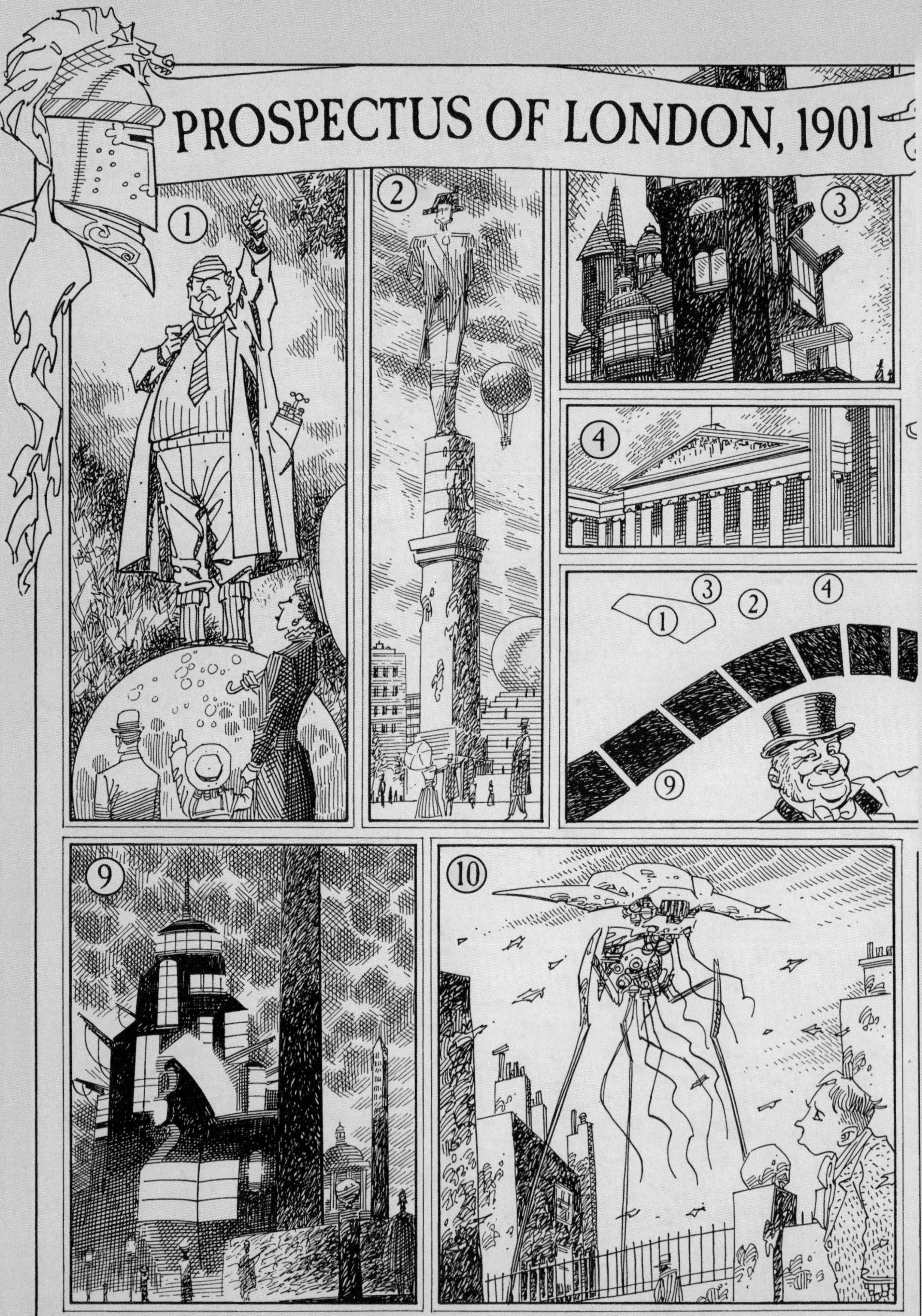

PROSPECTUS OF LONDON, 1901
1
2
3
4
3
2
4
1
9
9
10

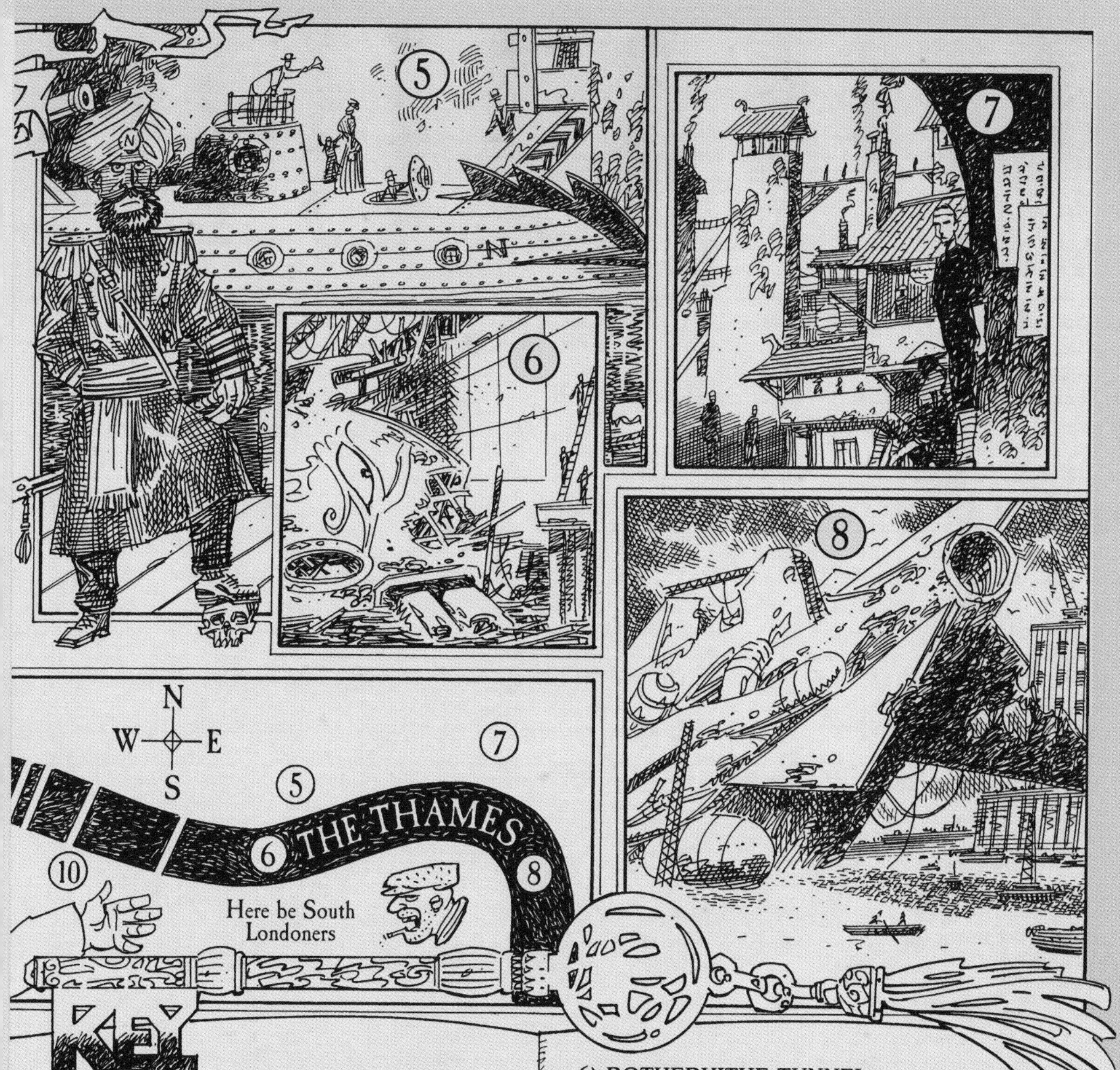
5
6
7
8
N
W
E
S
THE THAMES
10
Here be South Londoners
KEY

1) THE CAVOR MONUMENT

Erected in St. James Park, London's most recent statue commemorates the late eccentric visionary Selwyn Cavor, driving force behind 1901's lunar expedition and the subsequent annexation of the moon as part of the British Empire.

2) HORNBLOWER'S COLUMN

Although rendered almost unrecognisable by pigeon-droppings, the statue of Napoleonic naval hero Horatio Hornblower atop its tall column in Trafalgar Square remains one of the capital's best-known and best loved landmarks.

3) THE DIOGENES CLUB

Though increasingly seen as an anachronism in our new century, this staid and exclusive gentlemen's club is still popular, with a surprising number of Prime Ministers and cabinet members frequently popping in for a chat.

4) THE BRITISH MUSEUM

This institution incited controversy during 1900 when newspapers spread rumours of a secret 'locked wing' housing fantastical exhibits and tended by equally improbable caretakers. Denials were issued, although requests to investigate the wing were refused.

5) WAPPING DOCKS

Formerly a harbour for Captain Nemo's *Nautilus,* an inaccurate floating plywood replica of the science-pirate's submersible boat has been assembled, with a blackface actor impersonating the Captain, greatly boosting the East End's tourist trade.

6) ROTHERHITHE TUNNEL

Intended to replace Rotherhithe Bridge, destroyed during 1898, work on the tunnel has been impeded by the discovery of airship wreckage of Oriental design, and a distressing number of drowned workers or crewmen, all Chinese.

7) LIMEHOUSE

Apparently the principal target of 1898's aerial bombardment, this district has recovered swiftly, with looters and opportunists strangely absent. Inhabitants attribute their neighbourhood's good fortune to a local philanthropist, a doctor who protects the area.

8) PROFESSOR MORIARTY'S AIRSHIP

Since plummeting into the Thames near Limehouse Reach in 1898, the late Professor James Moriarty's airship has proven intractable, despite frequent salvage attempts. Its conversion into an 18th century-style 'prison hulk' is currently being considered.

9) FREEMASONS HALL, VAUXHALL

While architecturally an acquired taste, this riverside landmark is an undoubted benefit to the community, as the worthy fraternity within are believed to occupy themselves mainly with organising charitable jumble-sales and similar altruistic activities.

10) INVASION MEMORIAL PARK

At London Bridge's southern end, this small memorial garden contains a monument to the military dead of 1898's invasion. A Martian tripod has been rebuilt into a children's play area, albeit one shunned by children.

THE MURRAY GROUP, CORRESPONDENCE, 1899-1913

Following the successfully-routed Martian invasion of August, 1898, the group formed by Wilhelmina Murray earlier that year was almost completely defunct. With Hawley Griffin and Henry Jekyll both dead and Captain Nemo having resigned from the unit, Miss Murray apparently felt that there was little point in continuing as team leader to a team which no longer existed. Being in addition emotionally exhausted after the events of the previous few years, she elected to retreat for some time from the world into the pleasant confines of the matriarchal ladies' commune Coradine in the northwest of Scotland. Mr Allan Quatermain, the only other member still remaining out of the initial group, stayed in London, living at the team's former headquarters in the British Museum's private wing and keeping a low profile since he was at this time still believed to be dead by the general public.

This state of affairs prevailed until the Summer months of 1899 when Murray, who had been in correspondence with her older colleague, was prevailed upon to let him visit her in Coradine, whereat he forwarded to her the proposition that she should return to her employment with the Crown, who had a foreign jaunt in mind for both of them. Perhaps becoming bored with the unending calm of Coradine, Murray accepted and in August she embarked along with Quatermain for the United States, there to investigate unsettling reports concerning the New England town of Arkham, Massachusetts. Returning during the September of that same year after some unpleasant exploits, Murray and her elderly companion next commenced investigations into the communitarian Phalanstery movement, then but recently established in the western English county Avondale.

The couple were involved in undercover operations at the Avondale Phalanstery for almost a year, and did not venture overseas again until mid-August, 1900, when the pair set out for Africa on an assignment that required them to find and test the immortality-bestowing waters of a pool or fountain said to be located somewhere in the British Protectorate of Uganda. It proved to be a hoax, possessing no life-giving properties at all, and also proved to be the final quest of Allan Quatermain, the venerable explorer dying in the lost last of Zuvendis during the first months of 1901. Seemingly not fazed by her bereavement, Wilhelmina Murray next took up with the explorer's long lost son, also named Allan, whom they'd met in the Zuvendian capital, Milosis. She returned to England with her new companion in July of that same year, where the pair became embroiled in various domestic issues that would occupy them until February of 1906. 1901 saw a visit to the incarcerated lunatic Dr Eric Bellman at an asylum in Oxford, while between 1902 and 1903, Miss Murray and the junior Quatermain were on Ireland's west coast. 1904 and 1905 entailed travels within England, including a visit to the recently-resurfaced brother of Mycroft Holmes at his home in Fulworth. At last, in March, 1906, the couple were dispatched to Russia on a diplomatic mission, strengthening ties in preparation for the Anglo-Russian Convention, forged the same year, that was to govern Tibet, Persia and Afghanistan.

Their travels took in most of Asia, and it was in Tibet that they met an individual of uncertain gender who purported to be the selfsame Orlando who has been referred to in the annals of this team throughout its various incarnations since at least the sixteenth century. Travelling home to Britain with this person by way of the Arctic territories, they reached these shores during April in 1907, where the trio would remain for quite some time. This was to be the genesis of what has been referred to as the second Murray team. In various adventures over those next years, Quatermain, Murray and the individual who professed to be Orlando gathered other members to their group, including the reformed thief Anthony John Raffles and the then-fashionable "psychic sleuth," Thomas Carnacki. It was this ensemble who responded to Carnacki's premonition of a catastrophic foreign-instigated raid on London coinciding with the Royal Coronation of His Majesty King George VI in 1910. During these escapades the fellowship encountered a dockside hotel worker and sometime prostitute named Diver, of whom we know very little save that she apparently became a regular associate of Murray's second team during the first two or three decades of our current century.

In 1912 this resurrected team was active in the north of England, journeying to France the following year for an encounter with French counterparts "Les Hommes Mysterieux" in natural caverns underneath the Paris Opera in 1913. With Europe on the brink of war, the group's preferred means of communication, namely picture postcards, would become impractical, forcing its members to relay their messages by other means. However, in the fifteen years that until then had passed since the inception of the Murray team, British Intelligence amassed a sizeable collection of such postcards, with a representative selection here included on the following pages. We feel that these are documents of some importance in that they, however sketchily, fill in some of the gaps among the team between the conclusion of their most famed early adventures with the ending of the Mars invasion in late 1898, and their later exploits after the Great War. As such, the ephemera presented overleaf can only aid our fuller understanding of this semi-legendary assembly, and, increasingly, the worrisome phenomenon they have become.

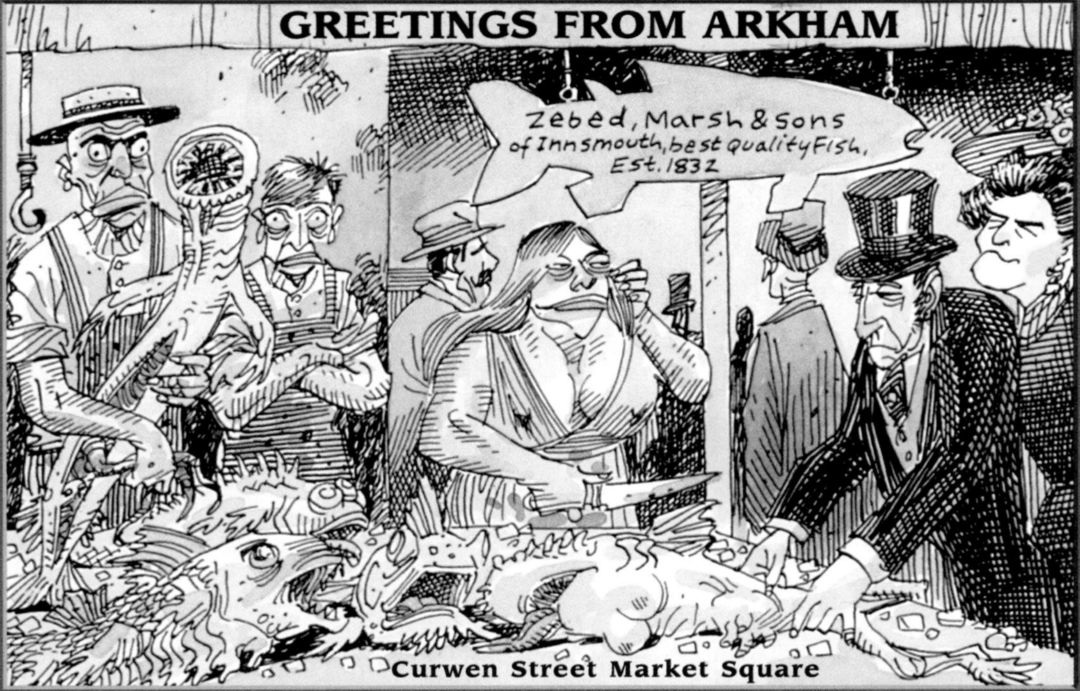
GREETINGS FROM ARKHAM
Zebed, Marsh & Sons of Innsmouth, best quality Fish, Est. 1832
Curwen Street Market Square

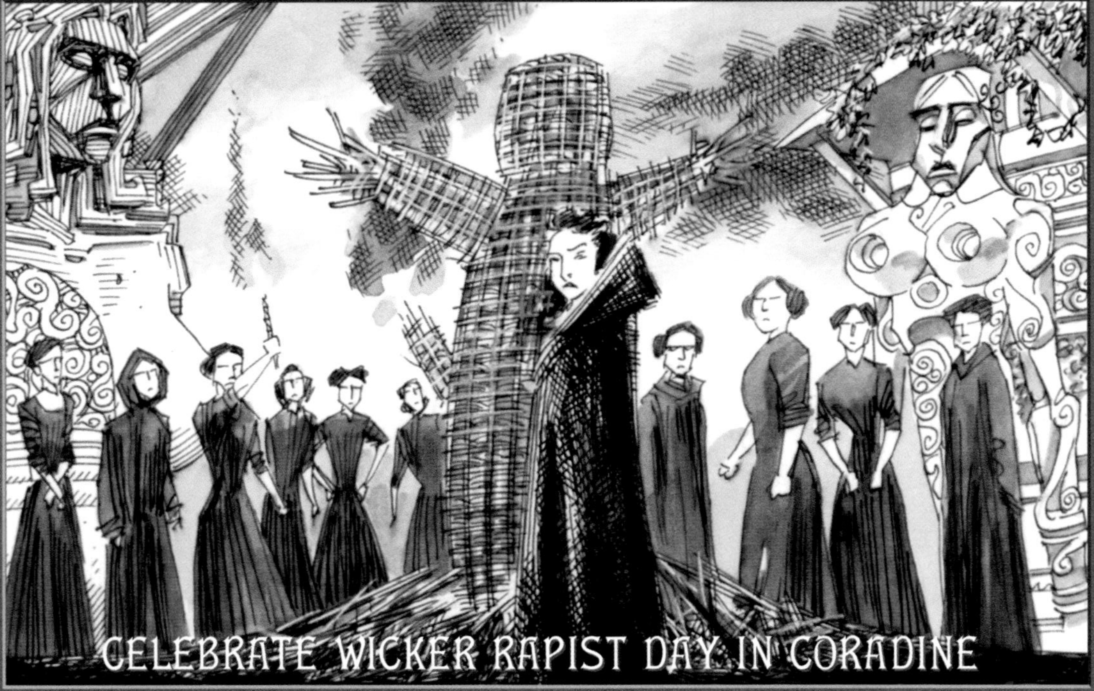
CELEBRATE WICKER RAPIST DAY IN CORADINE

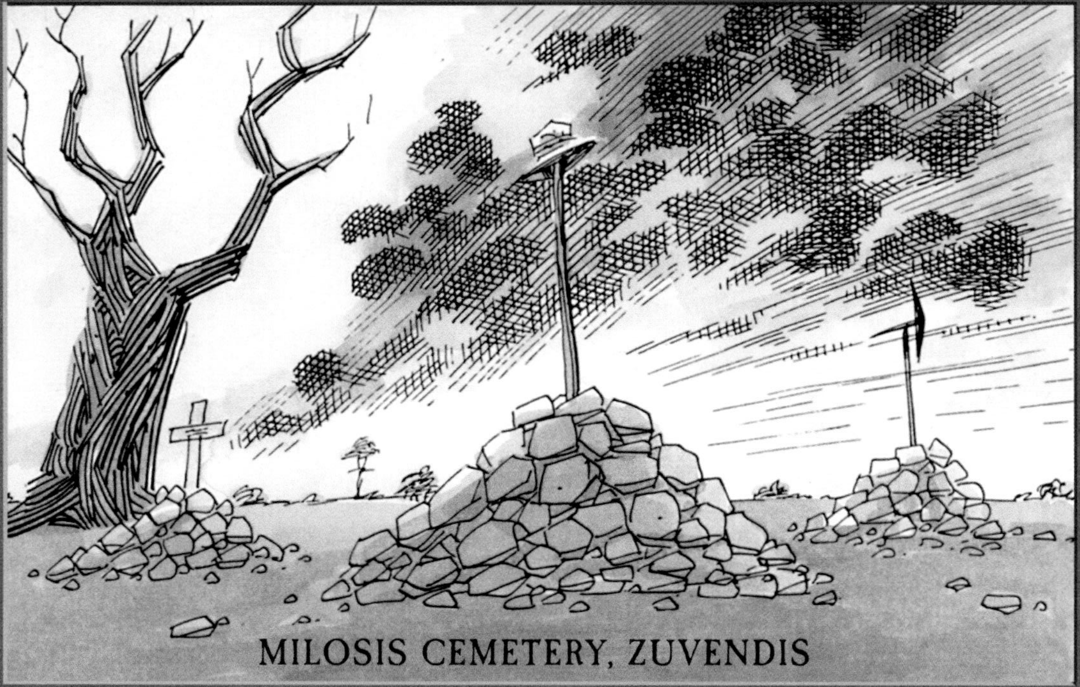
MILOSIS CEMETERY, ZUVENDIS

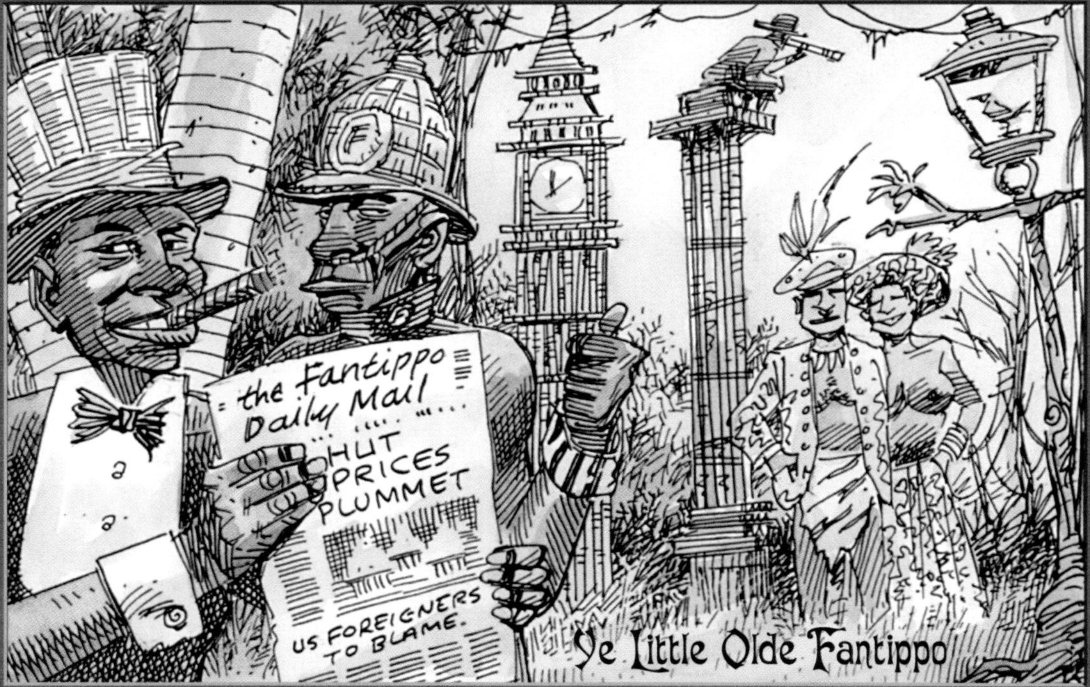
the Fantippo Daily Mail
HUT PRICES PLUMMET
US FOREIGNERS TO BLAME.
Ye Little Olde Fantippo

POST CARD

CORADINE 7.45 PM JULY 7 1899 SCOTLAND

My Dearest Allan,
Of course you may visit me in Coradine, you silly thing. The ladies reserve their contempt for local men, so you're quite safe. I hope you have news of fresh work, as I fear I'm getting rather fed up of women. Do write soon.
Yours affectionately,
Mina

To

Mr A. Q.
c/o Private Wing
British Museum
Bloomsbury
London W1

POST CARD

LORIMER E. BRACKETT
ARKHAM, MASS.

MESSAGE | ADDRESS

BOSTON, MASS. SEPT 8 5 PM 1899

Bond-

Coming home immediately. Met one R. Carter who took us to a ruin near Dunwich - beastly business. Mina almost abducted by something ghastly, and now very feverish. If you or Holmes had any idea this might happen, I'll horsewhip you to within an inch of your lives.

Quatermain

Campion Bond
c/o Freemason's Hall
Vauxhall Cross,
London SE11
Great Britain

FOREIGN POST CARD

FOR COUNTRIES INCLUDED IN THE POSTAL UNION.

FANTIPPO 3:30 PM DEC 27 1900 AFRICA

Dear Bond,
We've crossed most of Africa looking for Ayesha's city, and have found directions to it here in Fantippo. I think we could get there in a fortnight, with weather permitting. Must admit, am greatly enjoying my return to Africa. Have never felt better.

Yours,
Quatermain

C. Bond
c/o Freemason's Hall
Vauxhall Cross
London SE11
Great Britain

POST CARD.

DIS FEB 3 1901

Dear Mr Bond,
I have dreadful news. Uganda's "pool of life" didn't work, and poor Mr Quatermain has died here in Zuvendis, although I've met a young, long-lost son of his, which is some consolation. Please excuse the jerky handwriting as I am currently racked with grief.
Yours sincerely, Wilhelmina Murray

Mr Campion Bond
c/o Freemason's Hall
Vauxhall Cross
London SE11
Great Britain

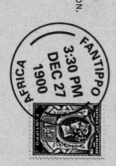

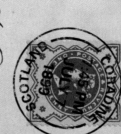

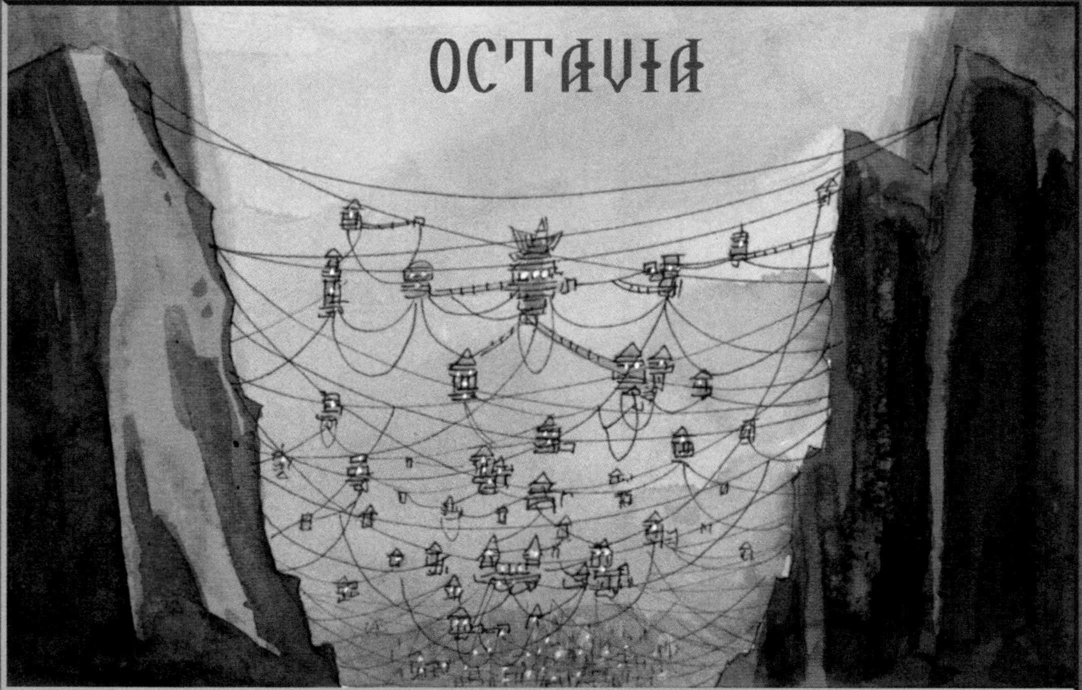
OCTAVIA

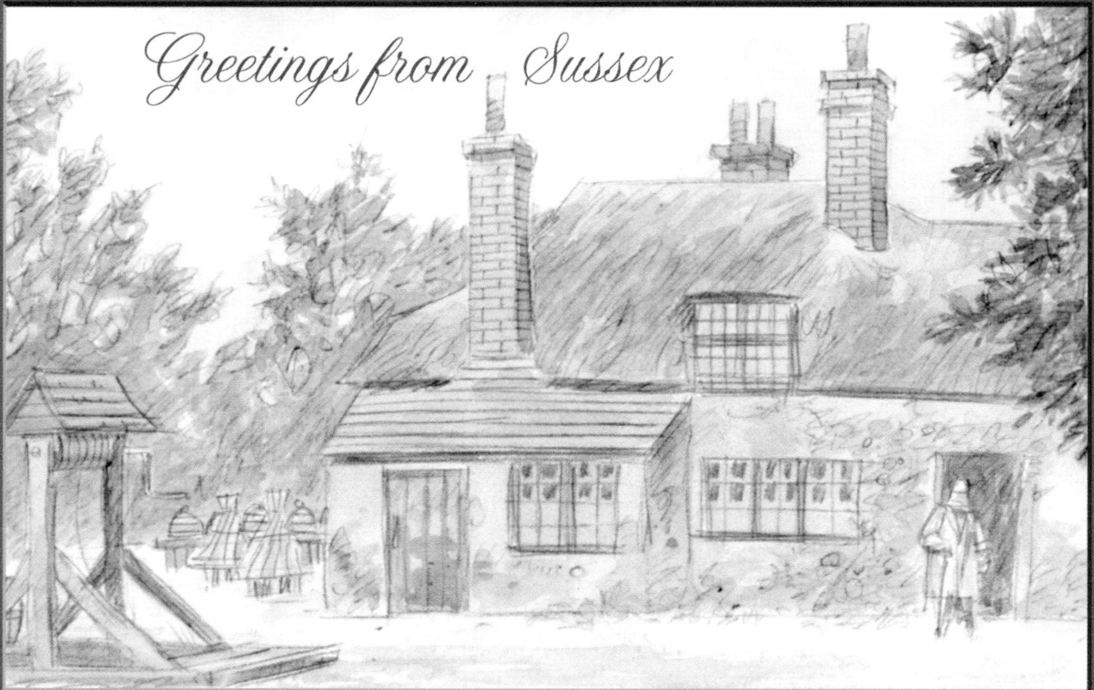
Greetings from Sussex

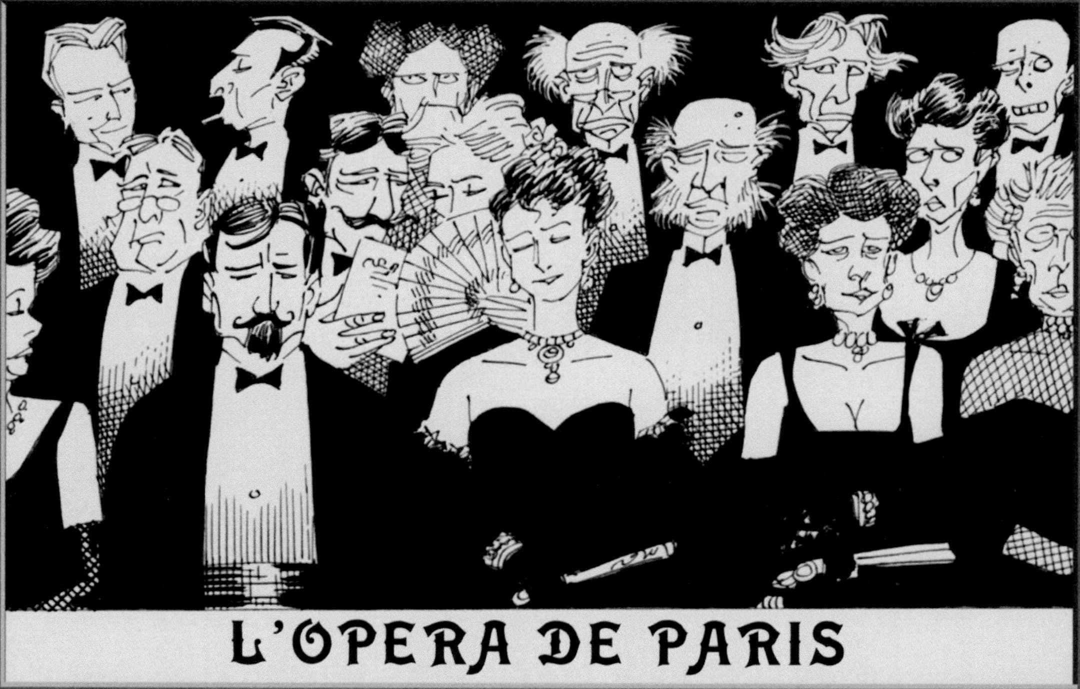
L'OPERA DE PARIS

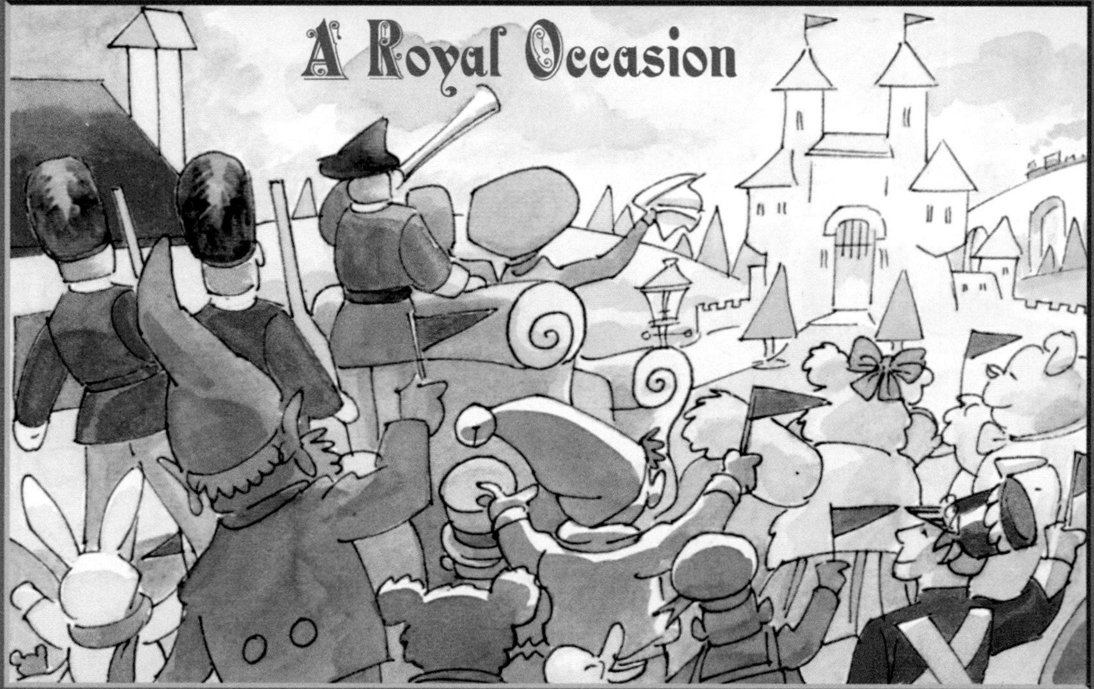
A Royal Occasion

POST CARD

My Darling,

Sussex is dreadful, but I've met the gentleman I came here to visit. Yes, it's really him. He assured me his bee, and I'm sure I gave the impression of being an awe-struck schoolgirl. I'm hanging on every word. Will be home soon.

With all my love,

Mina

To

Mr C. Q. R.
c/o Private Wing
British Museum
Bloomsbury
London N1

Postmark: FULWORTH SUSSEX, 11 AM MAY 12 1904

Dear Mr Bond,

I'm uncertain if you will actually receive this, but our hosts tell me their postal service is very good. We're all three in good health and are currently guests of Toylands Queen. Will explain when we arrive home in perhaps a week.

Yours most sincerely,

Wilhelmina Murray

Mr Campion Bond
c/o Freemasons Hall
Vauxhall Cross
London SE11
Great Britain

Postmark: TOYTOWN POST, MARCH 10th 1907 — 1 KISS TOY TOWN POST

ОТКРЫТОЕ ПИСЬМО

ИНОГОРОДНОЕ.

Мѣсто для адреса.

Shangri-La Sept. 5th, 1906

Bond - Purchased this card in Octavia, but am posting it from a Tibetan lamasery, where we've just met a fascinating young woman who claims to be Orlando, both Prospero and Gulliver's associate. We expect to be returned to Moscow with her by year's end. Please advise.

Yours,

Quatermain Jr.

C. Bond
Freemason's Hall
Vauxhall Cross
London SE11
Great
Britain

Grands Magasins
DE LA
VILLE DE SAINT-DENIS
Nouveautés

Faub.g St Denis et Rue de Paradis - PARIS.

Dear Tom,

Well, it's over, though in truth they very nearly finished us. Fantomas was a horror, and the albino almost as bad. Whether the European war you foretold has been averted or not, we shall see. We'll all be home presently, my dear friend.

Yours faithfully,

Orlando

Mr Thomas Carnacki
c/o Private Wing
British Museum
Bloomsbury
London W1
Great Britain

Postmark: PARIS 1913, BOSQUE

THE SINCEREST FORM OF FLATTERY: Les Hommes Mysterieux and others, 1909 – 1924

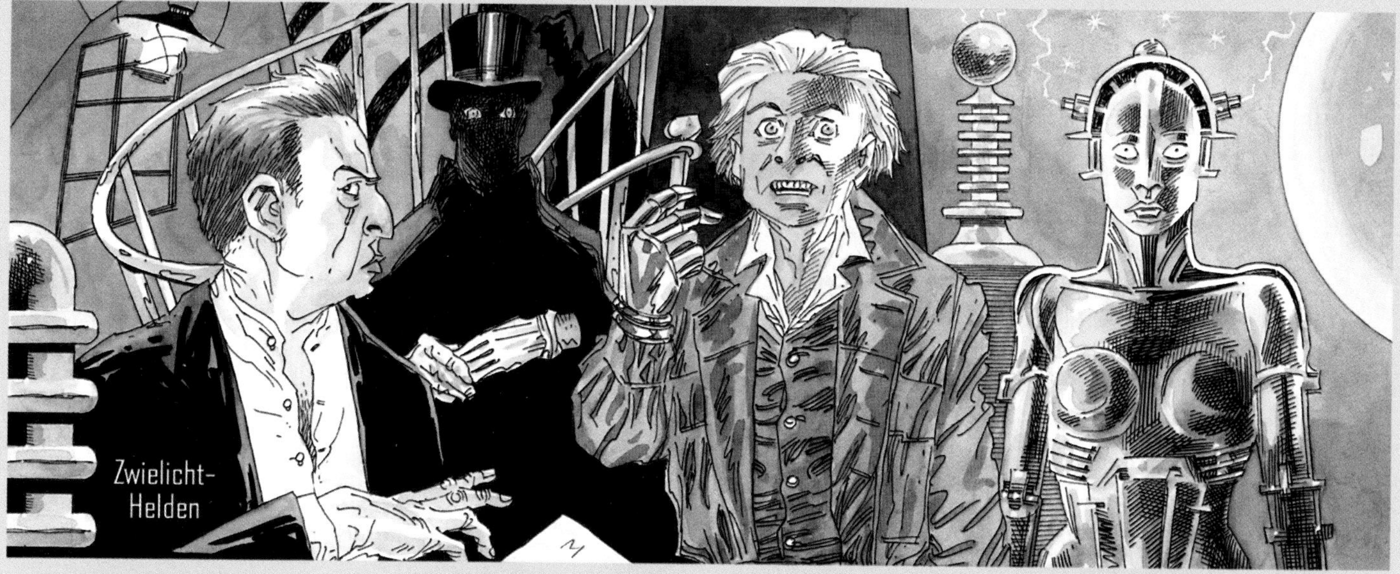
Zwielicht-
Helden

Since the formation of the first Murray group in 1898, which involved the supposedly dead Captain Nemo, a figure well known to the French, in the retrieval of Dr. Henry Jekyll/Mr. Edward Hyde from a Paris address, it may be supposed that the French authorities have been in some measure aware of the existence of a team of extraordinary individuals, convened by the British Crown for purposes of espionage, sabotage and security. While information received by British Intelligence suggests that the French may have been discussing the formation of a similar ensemble from as early as 1901, there is no evidence showing that this was accomplished until mid-1911, when an increasingly desperate French government decided to grant amnesty to several personages who had until then been seen as enemies of mankind. France had initially been scornful of England's reliance on such mentally aberrant personalities as Griffin, Hyde and Nemo, but it would seem that in the attempt to form a unit of their own, they had reluctantly reached the selfsame conclusion, namely that in this area of employment, fiends are both more plentiful and more effective than are heroes.

It is now believed that "The Mysterious Men," as they were known informally, were first convened as a response to unconfirmed reports of a German conspiracy intended to bring war to Europe. Germany, it later transpired, had assembled its own clandestine group of unusual individuals by as early as 1909, and it is indeed possible that this Teutonic group played some part in the sinister activities that plagued the coronation of King George VI in 1910. The German group, based in the newly constructed Berlin Metropolis, included deviants as bad as or else worse than any in the French or English versions. The criminal mastermind Mabuse seems to have done most of the thinking for the team, aided by a mesmerist named Caligari, with other members, if reports are to be believed, including a mesmerised assassin and an unlikely sounding female automaton and her creator, one Dr. Rotwang. Learning something of this group's activities, the French at last decided on their policy of amnesty, and set about constructing their own league of monsters and peculiarities.

Their first recruit was also the group's senior member, megalomaniac and innovatory aeronaut Jean Robur, France's so-called "Master of the World." Initially inspired by the exploits of Captain Nemo, if reports are to be believed, Robur elected to become a science buccaneer in the element of air rather than that of water, and as a member of the fledgling French team proved invaluable, especially in providing much of the team's weaponry and transportation. It may be that it was Robur who suggested the ingenious criminal mastermind Arsene Lupin as a prospective member of the formative ensemble, since the aeronaut had on occasion, in his private correspondence, voiced his personal admiration for the so called "gentleman thief." At the time however, Military Intelligence suspected that the French planned an assault upon their English counterparts, and that they had included Lupin as way to cancel out any advantages afforded to the British by the fact that British born "gentleman thief" Anthony Raffles was a member of Miss Murray's second group.

The three other members that comprised the French team were more problematical, in that at least Lupin and Robur seemed to cleave to some strict moral code, however idiosyncratic and outlandish their behaviour may have appeared to be. Their three teammates, on the other hand, cannot be said to have shown the first vestige of morality in any of their doings, and in fact do not appear to be entirely human in the normal definition of that term. The international arch-villain Monsieur Zenith, for example, was a pure albino who used drugs that overcame the weaknesses of his condition and indeed allowed him physical abilities beyond the ordinary. Even this chalk-white near-superhuman, though, seems like the very model of humanity when we compare him to his teammate, the unnerving Nyctalope. This creature, more some new, sophisticated breed of animal than man, had beating in his breast a manmade heart superior to the human model. He could breathe with equal ease in both our normal atmosphere and also underwater, and his eyes were such that the most stygian, impenetrable darkness seemed to him as brightly lit as if in the full glare of noon. The Nyctalope's monstrosity was confined, for the most part, to his physical abilities and his appearance, for in terms of sheer inner monstrosity one struggles to imagine any mind or heart more genuinely alien than those belonging to the final member of this Gallic team, the horror Fantomas.

Even at this extremely early juncture of his long career, the archfiend Fantomas already had the blood of scores of innocents upon his hands, about which fact he scarcely seemed aware, much less concerned. It also seems he was precocious in the guarding of his true identity, in that those few early acquaintances of Fantomas who lived to tell the tale could not between them give an accurate description of the man. Robur describes the archfiend as "a masked man of unusual proportions in that he was not high-built but rather seemed broad-set and dense, fostering an impression of tremendous mass," whilst Wilhelmina Murray gave her own impression of a figure that was "quite preposterously tall and thin, at least some seven feet in height. Other than that I have a memory of some kind of black mask, I have no other recollection of its face at all, which seemed to me a dark, miasmal blur." Her colleague A. J. Raffles even ventured the suggestion that, at least in his perception, something in the voice and movements of this quite demonic being seemed to indicate that Fantomas might be a woman. All, however, were agreed that the most noticeable aspect of the archfiend's presence was the sense of unrelenting dread that he engendered. Even the usually composed Miss Murray stated that she'd "never been as scared as when it had me cornered underneath the Paris Opera. Fantomas, I think, had me more frightened than I'd been of my Romanian Count, who, it seemed to me, at least had once been human and known human passions. Fantomas, in contrast, was a thing; had always been a thing." Whatever the true nature of this most dangerous individual, his presence in the ranks of the French team was undeniably just cause for alarm.

Not until almost a decade later did British Intelligence manage to piece together what had in all likelihood been the true order of events concerning the encounter between these "Mysterious Men" and Murray's team. It seems events were first precipitated by the Germans, Doctors Caligari and Mabuse, who were then working on behalf of Germany, at least ostensibly, whilst secretly pursuing personal agendas whereby each might profit from the war they hoped to bring to Europe. When they learned that the French had at least some faint inkling what was going on and were preparing their own team of misfits as a counter measure, Caligari and Mabuse decided to retaliate with subterfuge. Using a potent mixture of Dr. Mabuse's wiles and Caligari's mesmerism, they contrived to lead astray the English and the French intelligence communities alike with the dissemination of false information, so that each believed the other's team of extraordinary agents to be plotting against their opposite numbers on the channel's far side. In this way, embroiling both the French and English teams in conflict, Germany was free to further its ambitions without fear of foreign interference...or at least to further the ambitions of Doctors Mabuse, Rotwang and Caligari with their shadowy associates, the noxious group referred to by the Kaiser as "mein Zwielicht-Helden."

Complicating matters further for the second Murray unit, during 1912 the "ghost hunter" Carnacki had encounters with some form of spirit that allowed him brief, fragmentary visions of the future. These included glimpses of his colleagues battling their French counterparts in Paris and terrifying vistas of a Europe caught up in the horrors of the First World War. Whilst both these portents would prove accurate, with hindsight we can see that our mistake was to assume that the two visions were connected in some direct, causal way. If the young Quatermain or Murray had been present they might not have been so quick to leap to these conclusions, but as it transpired the pair were off globe-trotting on their own during that year, having first visited the tomb of Launcelot up in Northumberland and then set out for Europe, passing through the nosferatu-haunted peaks of the Carpathians to holiday upon the coast of the Black Sea, near to the kingdom of Evarchia. Thus it was that only the supposed "Orlando" and his friends Anthony Raffles and Thomas Carnacki were in residence at the ensemble's British Museum hideaway when first the threads of this apparent intrigue came to light. The premonitions granted to Carnacki were soon supplemented by the artful propaganda of the Kaiser's "Twilight Heroes," leading our intelligence appraisers to suppose that France was planning to provoke a world war through the agency of their crude copy of the Murray team. Consequently, Wilhelmina Murray and the junior Quatermain were called back from their idyll in the closing months of 1912, and by the February of the following year the whole team, save for Carnacki who was by then feverishly ill, embarked for France intent upon confronting their French imitators.

The disastrous opening skirmish in this confrontation took place on the 23rd of February, 1913, when the four-strong Murray group attempted a balloon-assault upon the airship of Jean Robur, possibly with the intent of recreating the same tactics they'd successfully employed in 1898 to board and incapacitate the airship of the late Professor Moriarty. Jean Robur, however, was no first-time aeronaut as the Professor had been, nor was his craft powered by Cavorite, which Robur had dismissed as "unscientific." In addition, Murray's second team consisted of four relatively ordinary human individuals, lacking the weaponry of Captain Nemo, the ferocious strength of Edward Hyde or the unique abilities of Hawley Griffin. By that time convinced by the misinformation campaign waged by Germany, believing England to be the aggressor in this action, Robur simply shot them down before they came within a half-mile of his craft. Crash-landed in the wilds of rural France, having against all odds escaped their swift, flaming descent with only minor injuries, the quartet opted to attempt their next approach by stealth and to this end next made their way to Paris. There, in rented rooms not far from the Rue Morgue where they had first encountered Edward Hyde some fifteen years before, they planned their next moves while at the same time investigating the Parisian underworld, with A. J. Raffles trying to track down and thus outwit his rival master-thief, Arsene Lupin.

The Murray team were not aware that Lupin had been set as bait by his superiors in crime, the demon Fantomas and deadly, pallid Monsieur Zenith. In this manner were the team lured to the Paris Opera on the night of March 14th, 1913, when the establishment was crowded by its patrons. Finding no trace of the French team, Quatermain and Murray argued over where best to commence their search, the argument apparently concluding with Miss Murray storming off in frosty silence to pursue some female intuition of her own and leaving her three male companions to debate amongst themselves the merits of a search inside the Opera house against those of a sortie to the building's rooftops. Finally, Orlando and young Quatermain elected to explore the upper reaches of the Opera's exterior while A. J. Raffles with his burglar's expertise slipped into the crowd-packed interior to see if he could spot Arsene Lupin amidst the throng. Failing to do so, he checked out the building thoroughly and, with a knack for finding secret doors and panels, soon discovered hidden stairs that led down from the Opera's basement area, seemingly into the earth.

Meanwhile, Wilhelmina Murray had decided to investigate a rumour that she'd lately come across in her extensive readings, this pertaining to vast natural caves existing underneath the Opera building, where some thirty or so years before the monstrously disfigured madman Erik had resided while he carried out his terror campaign as the Opera's so-called "Phantom." Having read of this intriguing subterranean space just two years earlier in a book written about the crimes, Miss Murray found her way down into it through a surrounding tunnel system underlying most of Paris. Here she was confronted by the frightful quartet of Lupin, Robur, the Nyctalope and Fantomas, along with the belated realisation that she'd walked into a carefully-sprung trap.

At the same time, above the Opera house, Orlando had been set upon by Monsieur Zenith, there on the precarious rooftops where a pounding rain had just commenced to fall. Despite the fact that his claims to have fought at Troy and Salisbury Plain are clearly bogus, the ambiguously-sexed Orlando is undoubtedly a fighter of considerable experience, yet found himself hard-pressed by the albino's onslaught. When his pale and gloating foe spoke of a bomb concealed beneath the Opera house, Orlando was just able to relay this news to Quatermain, watching the combat helplessly from balconies below, unable to assist Orlando in the struggle against Zenith. Quatermain burst instead into the Opera's main hall and announced the presence of a bomb beneath the building, trying to find A. J. Raffles in the subsequent stampede and panic, but without success.

Beneath the opera house, Miss Murray had been hunted down by the inhuman Nyctalope, who was untroubled by the darkness in which Murray stumbled blindly. Rising from the underground stream that the frightened woman splashed through in the hope of baffling her pursuer's more-than-human sense of smell, the Nyctalope dragged Murray underneath the surface where he breathed with ease while she, quite understandably, had greater difficulty. When Miss Murray managed to break free he followed her back to the surface to resume his murder attempt, at which juncture A. J. Raffles, who had by then fortunately happened on the scene, shot the amphibious abomination in the chest. (Since it would seem the Nyctalope survived this shooting, we can but surmise that Raffles' bullet failed to penetrate the creature's artificial heart, his wounded form perhaps retrieved by Robur and Lupin, who similarly seem to have survived the Opera's subsequent near devastation.)

Trying to escape from the dark, subterranean caverns, Raffles and Miss Murray had a hair-raising encounter with the terrifying Fantomas, which was ended when the villain uttered, in unaccented plain English, the two chilling words "I win," just as he detonated the explosives hidden elsewhere in the Phantom's former lair. Up above, despite the younger Quatermain's attempts to clear the building, some two hundred people were killed or else injured in the blast, which saw one side of the afflicted building subside into empty space beneath the Opera house. Up on the roof, the battle between Zenith and Orlando was concluded indecisively by the collapsing building, with Orlando barely managing to leap to safety as the stonework underneath his feet gave way. Both he and Quatermain helped dig bodies from the Opera's rubble, but unable to find either Raffles or Miss Murray amongst the survivors, feared the worst. Not until some days later were they reunited with the pair, who had escaped the conflagration through the sub-Parisian tunnel system by which Murray had been able to locate the cavern in the first place. Quatermain at first chose not to credit the pair's tale of having been diverted for three days within a subterranean Graveyard of Unwritten Books or an underground land lit up by luminous balloons, suspecting that it had instead been some romantic interlude between the couple that was the true cause of their delay. Feelings in the group being thus strained, to say the least, all were returned to London and their museum headquarters, hoping that they at least had somehow managed to avert the world war glimpsed in their friend Tom Carnacki's supernatural visions. We assume that in their victory the French were likewise hopeful that the plot to wreck the peace of Europe was thus over with, allowing Germany's nefarious "Twilight Heroes" to pursue this goal uninterrupted.

In the First World War that followed the next year, both Murray's team and their French counterparts were to lose members, with Jean Robur's airship shot down at the battle of the Somme and A. J. Raffles giving up his life on the front line at Ypres. "Les Hommes Mysterieux" would seem to have disbanded shortly after the conclusion of the war, with Military Intelligence failing to receive fresh information on the unit since that time. There is some evidence that Kaiser Wilhelm's "Zweilicht-Helden" were, in one form or another, operating as late as the early 1930s, but failing confirmation of such rumours we conclude that Murray's team were the sole group of extraordinary operatives extant upon the Earth by the onset of World War II, after which time the Murray group itself broke contact with the British Government and fell into obscurity.

This summary contains all of the useful information that's available on foreign versions of Miss Murray's league. If, however, further detail or clarification is required then do not hesitate to get in touch through the regular channels.

Long Live Big Brother.

Les Hommes
Mysterieux

H.W.—This is all we have on what they were up to in the 1930s. Incidentally, are you still free for dinner at the Ingsoc Eat-Hall, the former Savoy, on the 27th? R.K.C. thinks we have things to discuss regarding administration plans for 1953.

Best G.O.B.

WHAT HO, GODS
of the ABYSS By
The Rt. Hon. Bertram Wooster

Friendship can be a rather sticky wicket now and then, as when one's anxious to assure one's chums that one does not regard them as a hideous embarrassment, when actually one rather does. Old hands amongst you will have no doubt guessed ahead that the source of my discomfort was that same Augustus, he of the Fink-Nottles, whom I've previously lamented in these pages. The occasion was a dinner thrown by my Aunt Dahlia at her Brinkley Court dive, off in Worcestershire, and I was trying to pay attention to the conversation of my Aunt and her unusually Bohemian guests, while at the same time shooting furtive peeks at Gussie, seated at the table's end.

He sat there with spoon poised between his dish and mouth, which hung even more slackly open than was usual, staring at the piece of cutlery as if he didn't have the first idea what he was looking at. Fearing he'd shove it in his eye, I gave a complicated cough in Morse code as a distress signal, which worked after a fashion in that Jeeves glided as if on casters to my side, though it turned out he hadn't cottoned on to my Morse code and feared instead that I was going to choke to death.

"I'm all right," I gasped out *sotto voce* as Jeeves brutally compressed my sternum in a harsh remedial manoeuvre of his own device, "It's Gussie. Look at him, for heaven's sake! He wiped his lips on a bread roll a moment back, and now he's trying to eat his napkin. Go and see if he's all right, Jeeves, there's a good chap, otherwise that beastly business with the copper cylinders will all come out in front of Auntie and your friends from the museum, and then we should have a right to-do."

It strikes me that there maybe some of you out there who do not count yourselves amongst the various ne'er-do-wells and publicans who've hung upon my lips for previous yarns and thus won't have the faintest what I'm on about. Perhaps I should go back and start from the beginning, as they used to make me do if I should be caught cheating on cross-country runs at dear old Malvern House, when I was younger. I suppose this current business all kicked off when I received an invitation from my Aunt to spend the summer helping her with some odd jobs at Brinkley Court. I should point out that we are not discussing my regrettable Aunt Agatha who uses battery-acid as a gargle and shaves with a lathe, but rather my Aunt Dahlia, an altogether more agreeable and lively proposition, who insisted that she did not mind at all if I should bring along my erstwhile pal, the aforesaid Gussie Fink-Nottle, to assist me and provide companionship whilst I was at my arduous labours.

"Yes, by all means bring Drink-Bottle with you. The estate's a jungle at the moment, and if both of you young oafs get eaten by wild swine while clearing it, I'm certain that society will be doubly grateful," were her exact words, as I recall them.

Anyway, with Jeeves in tow, Gussie and I decamped for Worcestershire and Brinkley Court, where we discovered to our horror that Aunt Dahlia had not exaggerated in the slightest when comparing the estate's grounds to an Amazonian forest. Frankly, if you ask me, she'd been rather modest. The gazebo and the tennis court were both entirely lost from view beneath an overgrowth that pressed against the lofty windows of the drawing room, blocking the light, and making matters worse it looked like there were nasty foreign weeds amongst the tangled mass, including one variety with thick and sticky petals that looked just like tongues, if tongues were eighteen inches long and violet, and another that was lit up brighter than my wristwatch after it got dark.

"Honestly, aged relative," I sputtered at my aunt when I confronted her, "you can't expect me and poor Gussie to trim that Sargasso for you. Where's that groundskeeper you hired a year or two ago, that Yankee chap from Massachusetts or Pocahontas or wherever he was from? Peabody, wasn't it? Or has he joined some new groundskeepers union and come out on strike? It really is too bad."

Aunt Dahlia gave me one of her affectionate sneers in reply. "Oh, shut your vacuous trap, you work-shy lout. Poor Mr. Peabody has been wretchedly ill this last six months. The poor man can't even come out of his groundskeeper's shed since his condition took a sharp turn for the worse. He sleeps in there at night between the sacks of fertiliser, I expect, and don't you dare suggest that I get rid of him. That man has been a font of knowledge when it comes to folk traditions from rural America, which I believe that I may write a piece on for *Milady's Boudoir*."

This was a weekly periodical, intended for the sensitively reared, of which my Aunt was the proprietor. I looked her in the eye and said "Tish-tosh," which I am not afraid to state that I intended as a cut. I informed her that I had not realised rural folk traditions were now such great shakes, and that I next supposed she would keep hens and take up Morris dancing, although I confess I didn't put it quite as smartly at the time and when I turned indignantly upon my heel to go and have a word with this Peabody fellow I collided violently with Gussie who was standing right behind me, grinning pointlessly like an unreasonably happy cod, out of politeness. Leaving Gussie there to beam uncomprehendingly through Auntie's well-intentioned mortal insults, I stormed proudly out past a bored looking Jeeves into the grounds, only to find myself instantly lost amongst the towering, vaguely leprous foliage. Only by some wonder did I find my way, within approximately half an hour, to the groundskeeper's lodge that was perhaps two hundred yards away from my Aunt Dahlia's front door.

I burst in, in high dudgeon, and prepared to give this idler Peabody a fair piece of my mind, of which I have a good few pieces left to spare, despite what everyone who knows me cares to say upon the topic.

"Now look here," I raged, "this simply isn't on. The place is overrun with all this fancy rot that you've imported, and the smell in here would choke a horse. Are you by some chance keeping iguanas without my Aunt's knowledge?"

It was awfully dark within the spacious hut (a symptom of Peabody's illness, as I later learned, had made him sensitive to light), but I could just about make the poor fellow out as he sat motionless in what appeared to be a cast-off and dilapidated armchair on the room's far side, shrouded by gloom. The moment that he spoke it was quite evident that his complaint had also left him with the most intolerable sore throat, so that I was reminded by his rasping buzz of a badly-concluded boyhood episode in which I had attempted to collect fifteen live wasps inside a cocoa tin.

"I apologise for the unpleasant odour," he began, "but it is caused by my condition, which I think today maybe a little better. As for the unusual weeds you mention, be assured that our great benefactors from beyond the abyss find it a most comfortable habitat, and that its blossoms shall with certainty attract the Shambler in Darkness."

I supposed he meant Aunt Dahlia, who sometimes keeps odd hours and has a tricky hip, and I must say that hearing him explain things in a plain, straightforward manner like that made the whole thing seem entirely reasonable. In fact, the fellow had such a persuasive, deucedly engaging way about him that I pulled a sack of fertiliser up to perch on and sat down to listen to him chin-wag for an hour or more. He was a marvellous old character, with all the colourful and slightly baffling turns of phrase you tend to get from an American. He told me about friends of his who came from Yuggoth, which I would imagine is some town in Massachusetts, or perhaps an outpost like Rhode Island since he specified it was "beyond the rim." He made it sound a jolly interesting place, at any rate, and even offered me a trip there with, as he said, my intelligence contained in an appropriate vessel. I imagine *The Queen Mary* was the vessel that he had in mind, and I'll admit to being flattered by the way he'd noticed my intelligence on such a short acquaintance, since it is a quality that far too many people seem to overlook.

He rattled on like this for absolutely ages, telling me about all these retired chaps that he knew, "old ones" as he referred to them, who'd apparently been overseas or somewhere, but were anxious to return here "when the stars were right." I believe he mentioned an endearing rogue called something like "Cool Lulu," which to my ears sounded like it might be a Red Indian name, who seemed to lead a leisurely, agreeable old life, sleeping and dreaming at a place called Riley, possibly a reservation of some kind. Peabody also mentioned some old goat who had misspent his youth so badly that he had a thousand young, which to me sounded like impressive going in anybody's book. There were odd morsels of homespun philosophy amidst all this, much of it far too brainy for the likes of me, especially the bits about the three-lobed burning eye and how the screaming tentacles of retribution would surely sweep the human pestilence from off the Earth, but by and large he made what I expect was quite a lot of sense.

When finally I had to tear myself away, the dear old thing asked me my name so that he could arrange my trip to Yuggoth, Massachusetts, safe in "an appropriate vessel." Here he nodded to some dusty copper cylinders on a high shelf that I'd assumed contained weed killing preparations or the like. I didn't have the foggiest idea what he was on about, so nodded knowingly in lieu of a reply. I must confess that I was starting to regret having seemed so enthusiastic when he'd made the invitation earlier of a trip to the United States, and I'm ashamed to say that when he asked my name I said it was Fink-Nottle, but that he should call me Gussie.

It was almost midnight when Jeeves managed to locate me by my faint, despairing cries, hopelessly lost amidst the partly phosphorescent vegetation. I recounted to him much of what the groundskeeper had told me and his usually unruffled brow creased with a frown of concern, notably when I was going on about the Indian chief or whatever he was, this Great Cool Lulu who spends all his time asleep at Riley. Jeeves appeared to recognise the name from somewhere, and suggested he might get in contact with a remote cousin of his, on the Silversmith side of his family, who worked as deputy curator for the British Museum, which, Jeeves fancied, had employees of some kind who were ideally suited to investigate extraordinary matters such as those he seemed to think were currently unfolding at my Aunt's estate. I told him that as usual he was making far too much of things that in all likelihood would turn out to be wholly innocent, and then retired to bed, knowing that Gussie and myself should be up early the next morning, to begin the Herculean labours that Aunt Dahlia had made the chief condition of our stay.

I tossed and turned all night, racked with a strong yet inexplicable conviction that my room's geometry was somehow faulty, even though if I'm entirely honest I'm not sure exactly which one's algebra and which one's geometry. If I'm wrong and geometry's the one with all the letters, then I mean that my room's algebra was wrong. Whichever one it was I hardly slept a wink and so was less than chirpy when at first light my Aunt Dahlia instructed Gussie and myself to clear an area that was equivalent in its dimensions to the misplaced tennis court. Asked why, she told us that she had invited friends to visit for an outdoor soiree, folklore enthusiasts like herself, who would be driving down that evening from homes in nearby Wales or from the town of Goatswood, close to Brichester, for the occasion. Why my aunt required so large a patch of weed-free ground on which to hold her barn-dance or whatever she intended I had no idea, and as a general rule of practice I've found with my aunts it's usually better not to ask.

By noon, when we paused briefly for some roast beef sandwiches and barley-water, Gussie and I had done a first-rate job, if I say so myself, with half the space we were to mow and to make tidy done already. Hacking through an undergrowth of vivid yellow creeper that to all appearances was quietly suppurating, Gussie gave us both a scare when he discovered a dead animal, considerably dead mind you, amongst the jaundiced shrubbery. It was, we estimated, three or four feet long and roughly barrel shaped, its head resembling an elaborately ugly starfish and some ghastly tattered things that jutted from what we assumed to be its torso, these resembling fins or wings but fearfully decomposed, so that the whole monstrosity ponged to high heaven and our eyes were watering as we discussed what it might be. I guessed, perhaps a little feebly, at a cow that had been through a combine harvester, while Gussie thought it might be some deceptively flesh-like rare sprout or cabbage like Vegetable Lamb of Tartary, though neither of our explanations seemed entirely likely and at last we simply buried it and got on with our hoeing.

As we neared our work's conclusion at the first approach of dusk we found ourselves not far from the groundskeeper's lodge, from which there intermittently came bursts of the metallic insect buzzing that I'd heard the previous night, which I assumed must be poor Mr. Peabody clearing his throat. Gussie inquired as to the nature of my conversation with the sick New Englander the previous night, seeming quite captivated when I mentioned the groundskeeper's offer of a holiday in Yuggoth, Massachusetts, and particularly when I told him of the frozen methane mining that I'd been assured was the community's main industry, which to Gussie's way of thinking made it all sound rather swaggering and adventurous, a little like the Klondike. We resumed our work, finishing before dark when Auntie's guests arrived, and a peculiar lot they were. I was so fagged out from the struggles of the day and my entirely sleepless night before that I elected to retire directly to my room, though Gussie thought he might stay up a while and have a poke around to see if he could find Aunt Dahlia's liquor cabinet. I wished him luck and went to bed, where scarcely had my head made contact with the pillow than I fell into a deep and dreamless snooze.

It must have been soon after midnight when I was awakened by the simultaneous agencies of vile subhuman chanting from the garden and a grim-faced Jeeves shaking me doggedly by the lapels of my pyjamas. While I made a vain attempt to chisel open gummed-up and reluctant eyes, Jeeves told me that the experts from the British Museum had arrived and were downstairs now trying to decide what they should do about my aunt, who, it appeared, had taken a severe turn for the worse. I was halfway through asking my manservant what he was suggesting with his last remark when the repulsive moaning from outside began again, this time with my Aunt Dahlia's voice distinctly audible above the guttural slur of her associates. To my bewilderment her wild entreaties seemed to be directed at the Great Cool Lulu, Mr. Peabody's elderly Indian friend, who I had until then assumed was still in Riley and enjoying his lie-in. Jeeves handed me my dressing gown and ushered me downstairs, still half asleep, where in the drawing room were gathered the quartet of individuals that my startlingly well-connected servant's cousin had alerted to the fishy goings-on at Brinkley Court.

They were a dashing crew, I must say, even if they did appear to have a girl in charge of them, a pretty little thing called Min, with steely eyes and a thick muffler around her neck despite it being then the stifling height of summer. With her was a wiry gentleman around her age, whom she called Allan, and another person, called Orlando Something, who despite his deep voice and deportment looked to me the very spit of Gussie's fatuous fiancée, the appalling Madeline Bassett of the limpid eyes and weeping-spasms. Rounding out the foursome was an older man who introduced himself as Tom Carnacki, and who seemed to be regarded by the others as rather an expert on the sort of business going on within my aunt's estate, whatever that might be. He asked me a barrage of questions, most of them concerning my quite innocent and genial chat with Mr. Peabody on the preceding evening.

When he'd finished, he and his companions gave each other shifty looks of great significance before the filly in the scarf fixed me with her somewhat disdainful gaze and started to address me.

"Mr. Wooster, we believe your aunt and her companions to be in thrall to a force not unlike mesmerism, a force directed, it is likely, by whatever kind of entity is posing currently as Mr. Peabody. Far from teaching them about the rustic folklore of America, I fear he has inducted them into an occult brotherhood, and that these dismal wailings from outside are rather loathsome incantations to the cult's foul deities. We would, with your permission, interrupt their ceremony before its intended purpose is achieved. We shall, of course, endeavour to prevent harm from occurring to your aunt or to her visitors. May we have your assent in this?"

I nodded eagerly although I hadn't understood one word in four of what she'd said. She had such an old-fashioned air about her for a mere slip of a thing and such a stuffy turn of phrase that I was terrified she might explain it all again if I failed to agree. This seemed to do the trick, and she with her three male companions marched outside to see what on earth my Aunt Dahlia was playing at, after admonishing both Jeeves and I to stay within the house since she could not give guarantee as to our sanity or safety if we ventured out of doors. No sooner had we heard the front door slam behind them than I wondered, with a sort of miserable presentiment of doom, why Gussie hadn't been alerted by the uproar and come trotting downstairs to enquire what all the fuss was over. Alarm mounting in my voice I turned, as I so often seem to do on these occasions, to the maddeningly competent and level headed Jeeves.

"I say, Jeeves, I've just had a nasty notion pop into my noodle. You don't for a minute think that even someone as devoid of gorm as Gussie would go blundering out alone into a hoodoo ceremony, do you? Tell me that you looked in on his room and that he's drunk himself into insensibility, Jeeves, there's a sport."

Jeeves seemed to close his eyes in weariness or possibly refusal to accept the likely circumstances that we were entangled in. After some moments, when he opened them and spoke he almost sounded thoroughly fed up with me and Gussie both, though I expect it was the tiredness that gave this impression. "Sir, I am reluctant to point out what we both know to be the truth, which is that young Fink-Nottle has all the survival instincts of an accident-prone lemming. I indeed made bold enough to look into his room, but he was nowhere to be seen. I fear he will be almost certainly involved in whatever manner of unpleasantness is going on outside, and furthermore I fear it is incumbent on us to assist him."

This was just the sort of thing I'd feared that Jeeves might say, but I reluctantly agreed to follow him outside into the mayhem and cacophony, in which we passed unnoticed. As we came upon the clearing where my Auntie and her guests were holding what she'd called an outdoor soiree, Jeeves gasped out an oath that I have never heard him or, now that I think about it, anyone else use before. He warned me that I should not look, but all his warnings came too late as I beheld a vision more nightmarish yet than any that I'd hoped to see in this world or beyond.

My aunt and all her pals were twitching and convulsing on the clipped grass, foaming at their mouths and jabbering in tongues, with not a stitch of clothing on between the lot of them. I'd feared that Morris dancing might result from all this folk tradition lark, but naturism really was the limit. So transfixed was I by all the unexpected, vigorously thrashing flesh that I did not immediately register the shrieking and inhuman form that reared above the scene with bloodworm tendrils writhing at the centre of its starfish face, from which the torn and paper like visage of Mr. Peabody still dangled, flapping mournfully. The foursome from the Museum were in combat with the brute, the girlish-looking chap Orlando hacking gamely at it with a large and terribly impressive sword while simultaneously Mr.

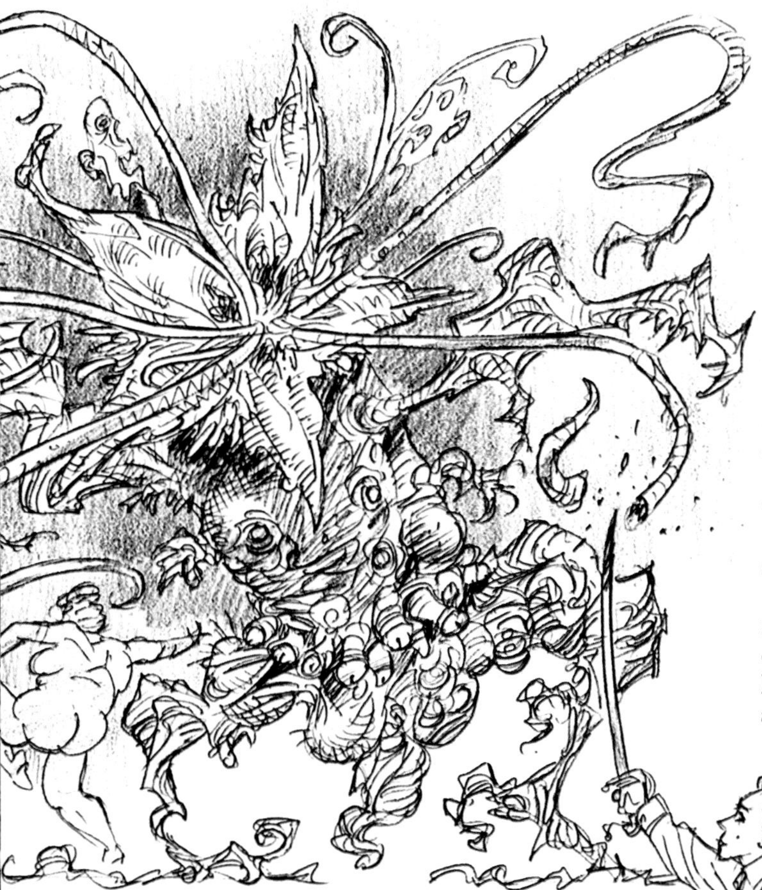

Carnacki bellowed out what might have been some form of ritual banishing. The other two, most sensibly in my opinion, simply shot at it with matched revolvers. While I gawped at all this, Jeeves had noticed that poor Gussie did not seem to be amongst the writhing nudists, and suggested we might find him in the groundskeeper's now evidently empty hut.

As usual, Jeeves was bang on target. There in the pitch black sat Gussie with an object resting on the table next to him which I at first assumed to be half of a coconut then realised with a startled yelp was actually the top of Gussie's head. My manservant drew in his breath, then sighed and spoke.

"I feared as much, sir. If what I have heard of these abominable creatures is correct, Mr. Fink-Nottle's most essential self is at this moment being carried to the place called Yuggoth that they mentioned, possibly some other planet or dimension, in the confines of a copper cylinder. Put simply, sir, I fear they have removed his brain and left him here like a boiled egg that's had its top sliced off."

"Oh bother, have they really? Do you know, I thought that I was feeling muzzy."

Gussie sat up slowly in the armchair, lifting one hand gingerly to feel around inside his open and demonstrably deserted cranium. His goldfish eyes gazed up imploringly towards my manservant. "I say, you couldn't fix my lid back so that it wouldn't show, Jeeves, could you? If Miss Bassett saw me like this I should never hear an end to it."

Wearing a look of incredulity that bordered on the insolent, and muttering about a tube of glue he thought that he might have, Jeeves led the pair of us back to the house past what survived of Auntie's soiree. The remains of what I cannot help but think of still as Mr. Peabody were being wound in oilcloth and transported to a rear compartment of the motor car in which the foursome had arrived by the man Allan and the indeterminate Orlando, whilst Carnacki and the woman wrapped my dazed Aunt Dahlia and her accomplices in blankets as they led them gently back indoors. It was quite evident that Auntie didn't have the first clue what had happened, yet possessed enough innate good breeding to invite her rescuers to dinner on the evening following, which brings me back to where I started this unfortunate account, with Gussie spooning pea soup into his breast pocket while I hoped no-one would notice.

As it happened, no-one did, not even Miss M. Bassett after she and Gussie were eventually reunited. As Jeeves pointed out when we'd successfully concluded that nerve-wracking meal, the young Fink-Nottle had devoured his napkin on at least five previous occasions, and at least this time had spared the napkin ring.

"Gosh, Jeeves. Do you suppose that this new Gussie might be an improvement?"

"Sir, I find it difficult to picture how it could conceivably be otherwise."

Down at the table's end, Gus rapped upon his forehead with one knuckle, opening and closing his delighted-looking mouth to modulate the ringing, hollow sound it made. I beamed at Jeeves and he allowed himself a faint smile in reply.

It was all going to be tickety-boo, in the most meaningful interpretation of that phrase.

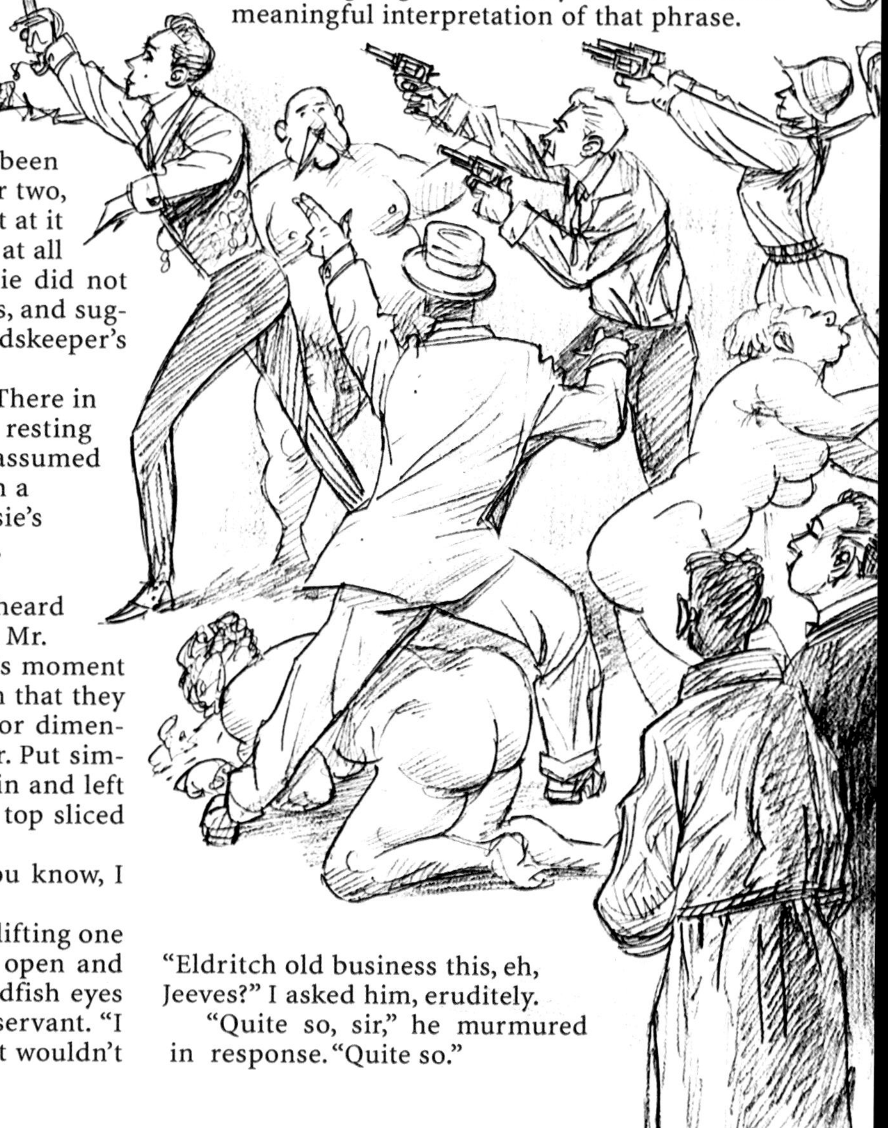

"Eldritch old business this, eh, Jeeves?" I asked him, eruditely.

"Quite so, sir," he murmured in response. "Quite so."

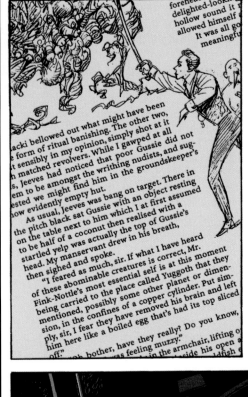

acki bellowed out what might have been
e form of ritual banishing. The other two,
t sensibly in my opinion, simply shot at it
n matched revolvers. While I gawped at all
s, Jeeves had noticed that poor Gussie did not
em to be amongst the writhing nudists, and sug-
ested we might find him in the groundskeeper's
how evidently empty hut.

As usual, Jeeves was bang on target. There in
the pitch black sat Gussie with an object resting
on the table next to him which I at first assumed
to be half of a coconut then realised with a
startled yelp was actually the top of Gussie's
head. My manservant drew in his breath,
then sighed and spoke.

"I feared as much, sir. If what I have heard
of these abominable creatures is correct, Mr.
Fink-Nottle's most essential self is at this moment
being carried to the place called Yuggoth that they
mentioned, possibly some other planet or dimension, in the confines of a copper cylinder. Put simply, sir, I fear they have removed his brain and left
him here like a boiled egg that's had its top sliced
off."

oh bother, have they really? Do you know,
was feeling muzzy."
in the armchair, lifting o
eside his open
dfish e

forehea
delighted-look
hollow sound it
allowed himself
It was all go
meaningful

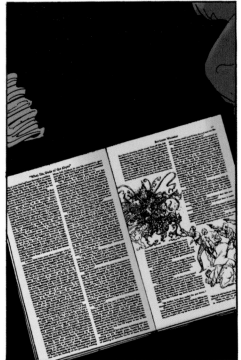

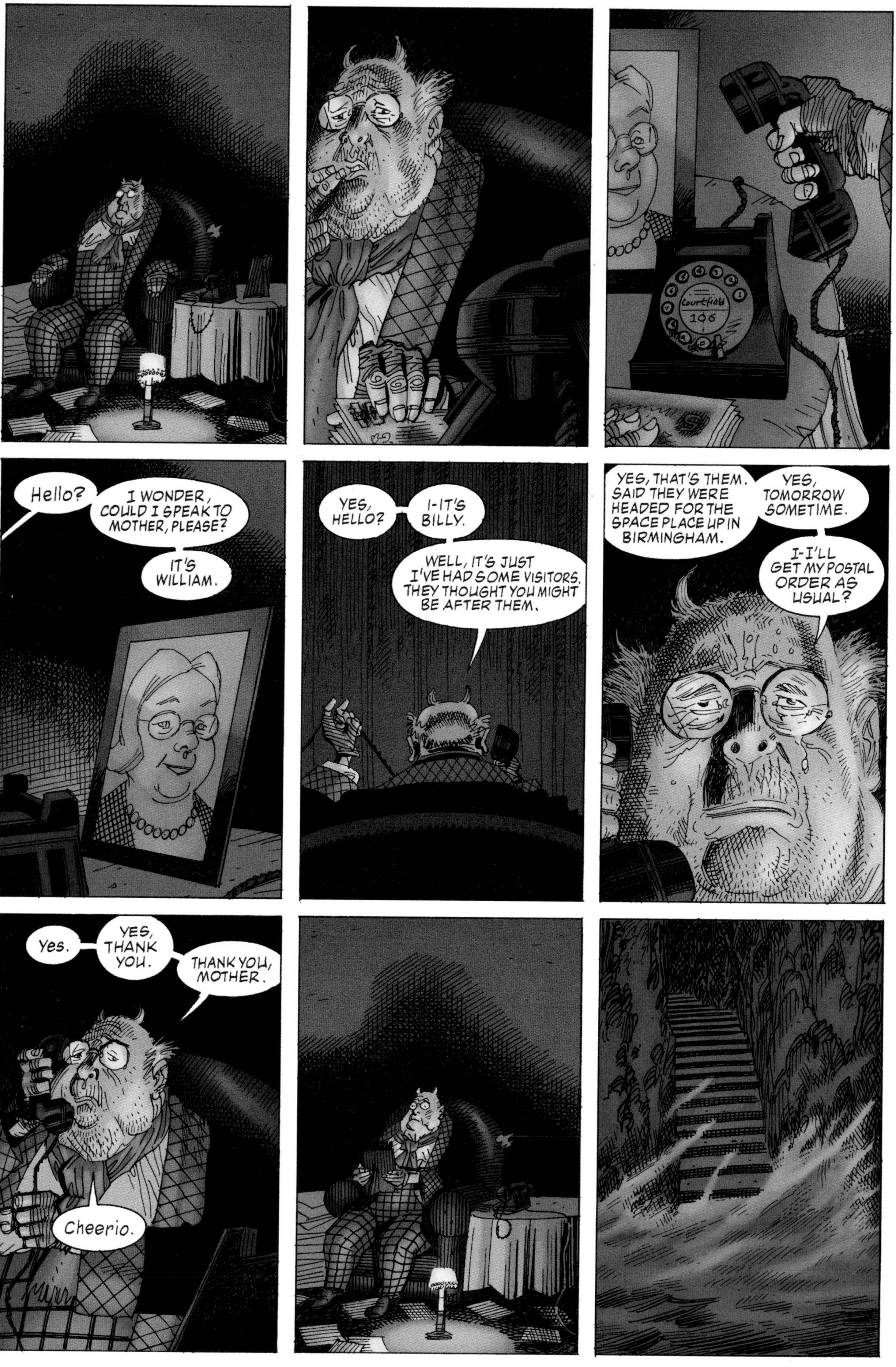
Courtfield
106
Hello?
I WONDER, COULD I SPEAK TO MOTHER, PLEASE?
IT'S WILLIAM.
YES, HELLO?
I-IT'S BILLY.
WELL, IT'S JUST I'VE HAD SOME VISITORS. THEY THOUGHT YOU MIGHT BE AFTER THEM.
YES, THAT'S THEM. SAID THEY WERE HEADED FOR THE SPACE PLACE UP IN BIRMINGHAM.
YES, TOMORROW SOMETIME.
I-I'LL GET MY POSTAL ORDER AS USUAL?
Yes.
YES, THANK YOU.
THANK YOU, MOTHER.
Cheerio.

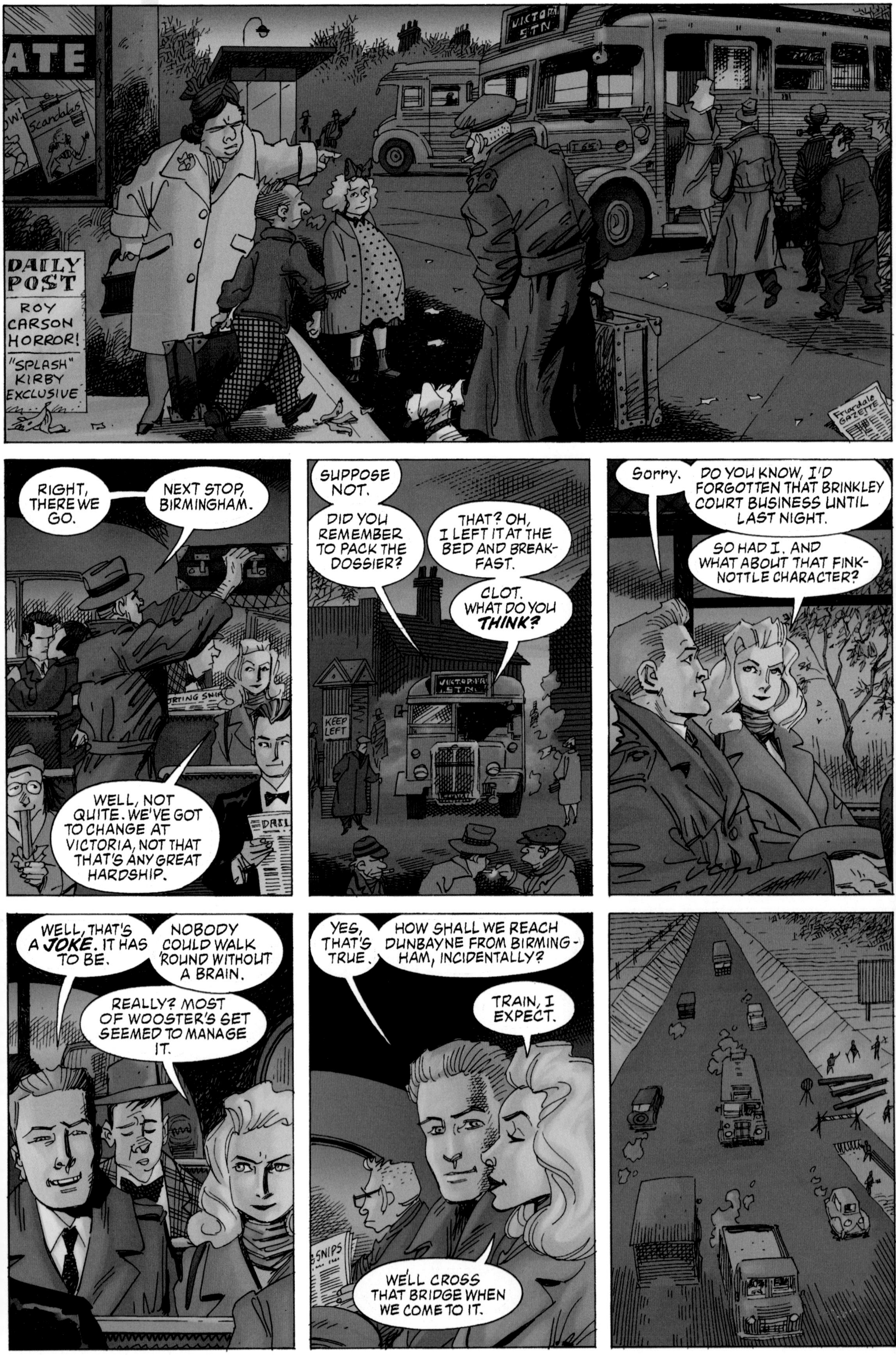
ATE
Scandalus
DAILY POST
ROY CARSON HORROR!
"SPLASH" KIRBY EXCLUSIVE
VICTORIA STN
Friardale GAZETTE
RIGHT, THERE WE GO.
NEXT STOP, BIRMINGHAM.
WELL, NOT QUITE. WE'VE GOT TO CHANGE AT VICTORIA, NOT THAT THAT'S ANY GREAT HARDSHIP.
SUPPOSE NOT.
DID YOU REMEMBER TO PACK THE DOSSIER?
THAT? OH, I LEFT IT AT THE BED AND BREAKFAST.
CLOT. WHAT DO YOU THINK?
KEEP LEFT
VICTORIA STN
Sorry.
DO YOU KNOW, I'D FORGOTTEN THAT BRINKLEY COURT BUSINESS UNTIL LAST NIGHT.
SO HAD I. AND WHAT ABOUT THAT FINK-NOTTLE CHARACTER?
WELL, THAT'S A JOKE. IT HAS TO BE.
NOBODY COULD WALK 'ROUND WITHOUT A BRAIN.
REALLY? MOST OF WOOSTER'S SET SEEMED TO MANAGE IT.
YES, THAT'S TRUE.
HOW SHALL WE REACH DUNBAYNE FROM BIRMINGHAM, INCIDENTALLY?
TRAIN, I EXPECT.
WE'LL CROSS THAT BRIDGE WHEN WE COME TO IT.

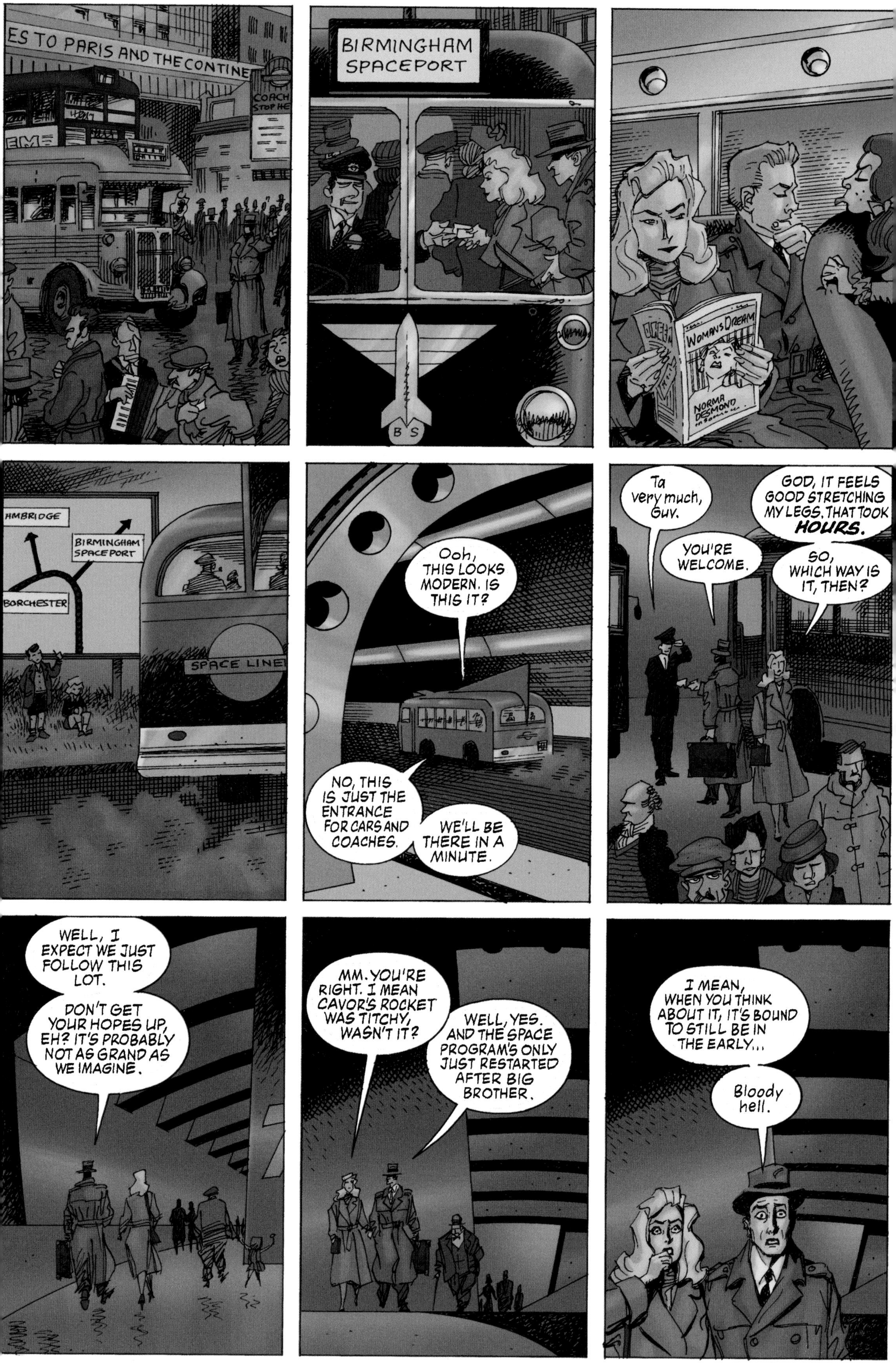
ES TO PARIS AND THE CONTINE
COACH STOP HE
BIRMINGHAM SPACEPORT
B S
WOMAN'S DREAM
NORMA DESMOND
HMBRIDGE
BIRMINGHAM SPACE PORT
BORCHESTER
SPACE LINE
Ooh, THIS LOOKS MODERN. IS THIS IT?
NO, THIS IS JUST THE ENTRANCE FOR CARS AND COACHES.
WE'LL BE THERE IN A MINUTE.
Ta very much, Guv.
YOU'RE WELCOME.
GOD, IT FEELS GOOD STRETCHING MY LEGS. THAT TOOK HOURS.
SO, WHICH WAY IS IT, THEN?
WELL, I EXPECT WE JUST FOLLOW THIS LOT.
DON'T GET YOUR HOPES UP, EH? IT'S PROBABLY NOT AS GRAND AS WE IMAGINE.
MM. YOU'RE RIGHT. I MEAN CAVOR'S ROCKET WAS TITCHY, WASN'T IT?
WELL, YES. AND THE SPACE PROGRAM'S ONLY JUST RESTARTED AFTER BIG BROTHER.
I MEAN, WHEN YOU THINK ABOUT IT, IT'S BOUND TO STILL BE IN THE EARLY...
Bloody hell.

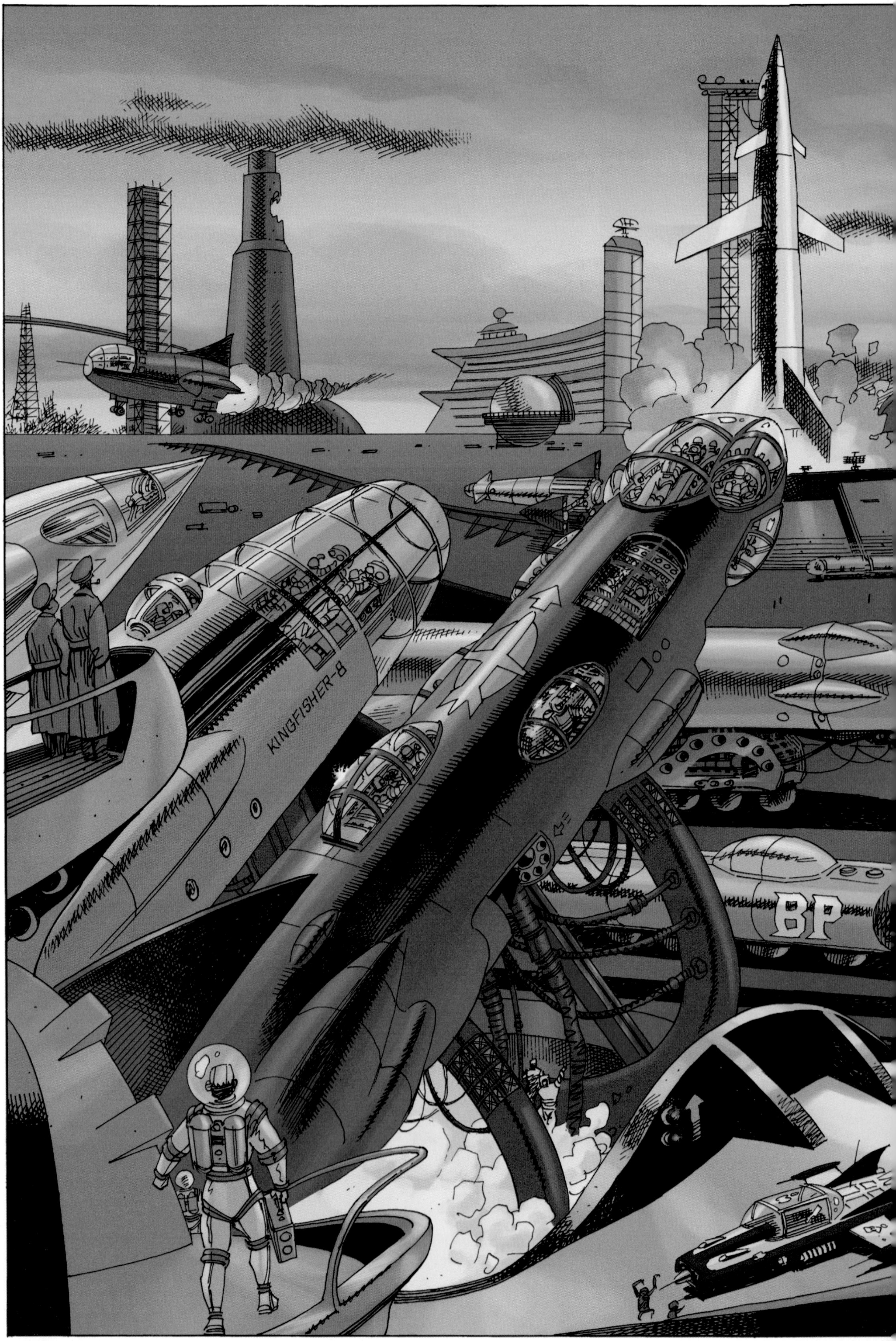

KINGFISHER-8
BP

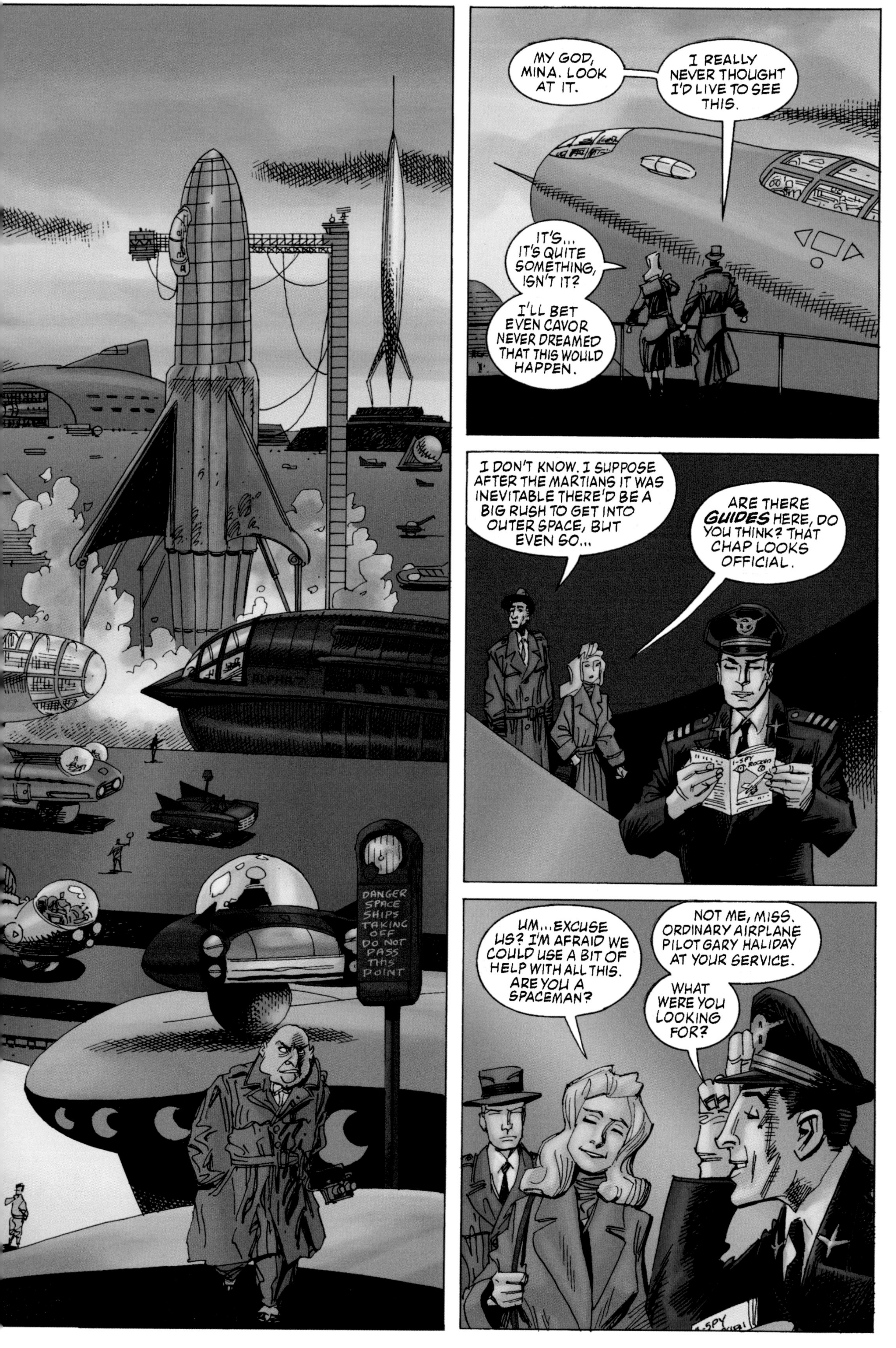
DANGER SPACE SHIPS TAKING OFF DO NOT PASS THIS POINT
MY GOD, MINA. LOOK AT IT.
I REALLY NEVER THOUGHT I'D LIVE TO SEE THIS.
IT'S... IT'S QUITE SOMETHING, ISN'T IT?
I'LL BET EVEN CAVOR NEVER DREAMED THAT THIS WOULD HAPPEN.
I DON'T KNOW. I SUPPOSE AFTER THE MARTIANS IT WAS INEVITABLE THERE'D BE A BIG RUSH TO GET INTO OUTER SPACE, BUT EVEN SO...
ARE THERE **GUIDES** HERE, DO YOU THINK? THAT CHAP LOOKS OFFICIAL.
UM... EXCUSE US? I'M AFRAID WE COULD USE A BIT OF HELP WITH ALL THIS. ARE YOU A SPACEMAN?
NOT ME, MISS. ORDINARY AIRPLANE PILOT GARY HALIDAY AT YOUR SERVICE.
WHAT WERE YOU LOOKING FOR?

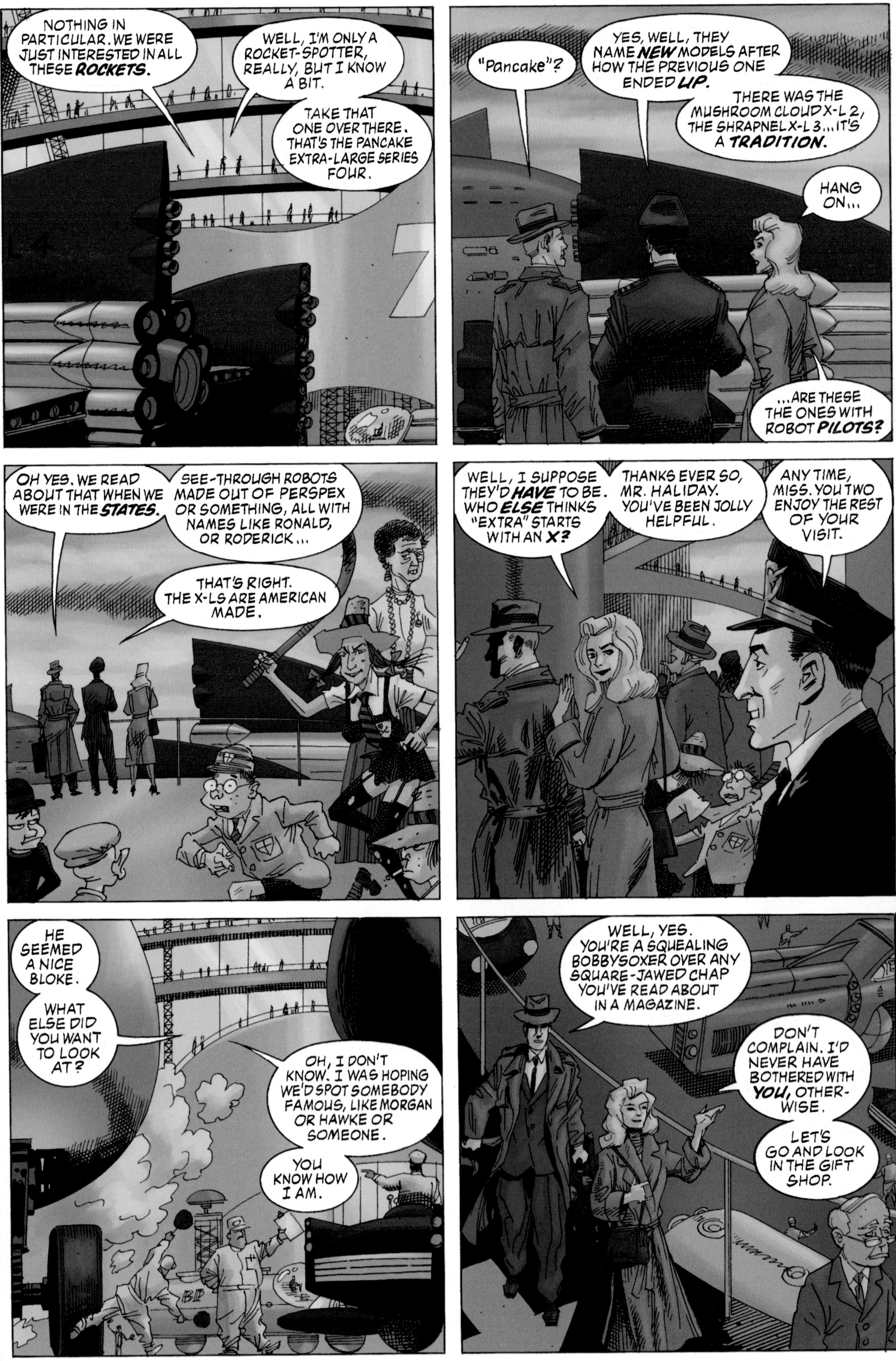
NOTHING IN PARTICULAR. WE WERE JUST INTERESTED IN ALL THESE ROCKETS.
WELL, I'M ONLY A ROCKET-SPOTTER, REALLY, BUT I KNOW A BIT.
TAKE THAT ONE OVER THERE. THAT'S THE PANCAKE EXTRA-LARGE SERIES FOUR.
"Pancake"?
YES, WELL, THEY NAME NEW MODELS AFTER HOW THE PREVIOUS ONE ENDED UP.
THERE WAS THE MUSHROOM CLOUD X-L 2, THE SHRAPNEL X-L 3... IT'S A TRADITION.
HANG ON...
...ARE THESE THE ONES WITH ROBOT PILOTS?
OH YES. WE READ ABOUT THAT WHEN WE WERE IN THE STATES.
SEE-THROUGH ROBOTS MADE OUT OF PERSPEX OR SOMETHING, ALL WITH NAMES LIKE RONALD, OR RODERICK...
THAT'S RIGHT. THE X-LS ARE AMERICAN MADE.
WELL, I SUPPOSE THEY'D HAVE TO BE. WHO ELSE THINKS "EXTRA" STARTS WITH AN X?
THANKS EVER SO, MR. HALIDAY. YOU'VE BEEN JOLLY HELPFUL.
ANY TIME, MISS. YOU TWO ENJOY THE REST OF YOUR VISIT.
HE SEEMED A NICE BLOKE.
WHAT ELSE DID YOU WANT TO LOOK AT?
OH, I DON'T KNOW. I WAS HOPING WE'D SPOT SOMEBODY FAMOUS, LIKE MORGAN OR HAWKE OR SOMEONE.
YOU KNOW HOW I AM.
WELL, YES. YOU'RE A SQUEALING BOBBYSOXER OVER ANY SQUARE-JAWED CHAP YOU'VE READ ABOUT IN A MAGAZINE.
DON'T COMPLAIN. I'D NEVER HAVE BOTHERED WITH YOU, OTHER-WISE.
LET'S GO AND LOOK IN THE GIFT SHOP.

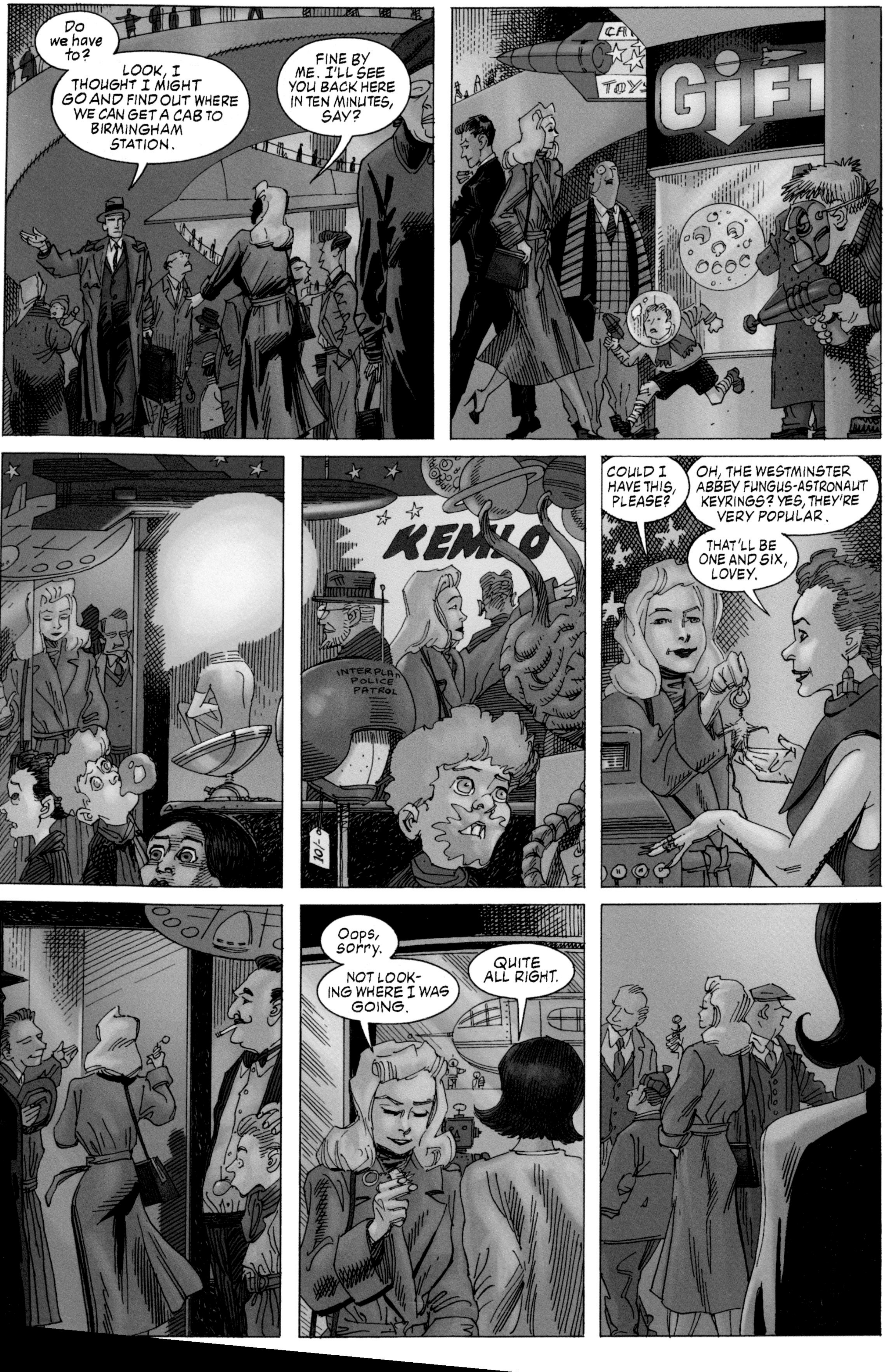
Do we have to?
LOOK, I THOUGHT I MIGHT GO AND FIND OUT WHERE WE CAN GET A CAB TO BIRMINGHAM STATION.
FINE BY ME. I'LL SEE YOU BACK HERE IN TEN MINUTES, SAY?
TOYS
GIFT
KEMLO
INTERPLAN POLICE PATROL
10/-
COULD I HAVE THIS, PLEASE?
OH, THE WESTMINSTER ABBEY FUNGUS-ASTRONAUT KEYRINGS? YES, THEY'RE VERY POPULAR.
THAT'LL BE ONE AND SIX, LOVEY.
Oops, sorry.
NOT LOOKING WHERE I WAS GOING.
QUITE ALL RIGHT.

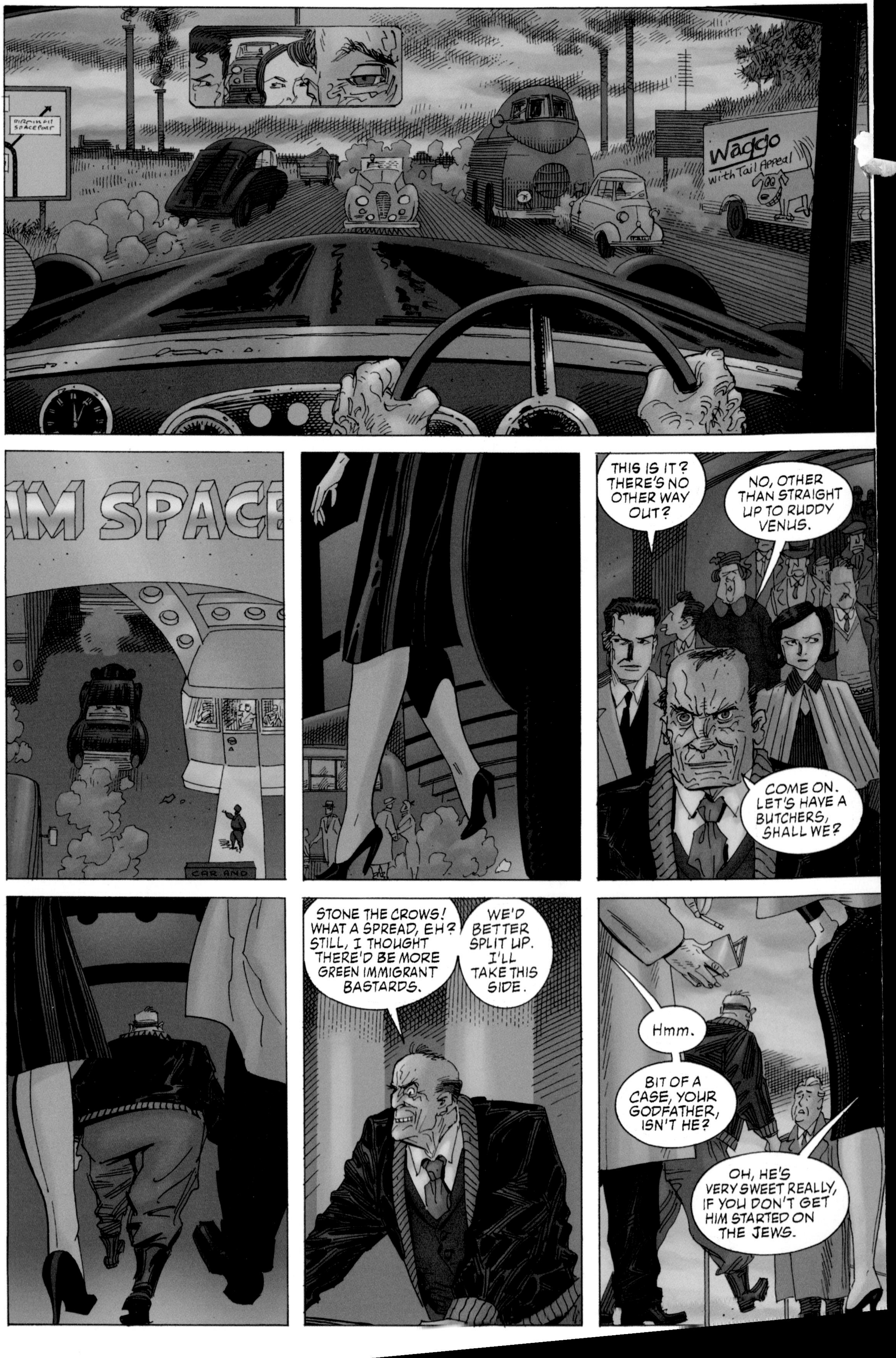
Waggo
with Tail Appeal
AM SPACE
CAR AND
THIS IS IT? THERE'S NO OTHER WAY OUT?
NO, OTHER THAN STRAIGHT UP TO RUDDY VENUS.
COME ON. LET'S HAVE A BUTCHERS, SHALL WE?
STONE THE CROWS! WHAT A SPREAD, EH? STILL, I THOUGHT THERE'D BE MORE GREEN IMMIGRANT BASTARDS.
WE'D BETTER SPLIT UP. I'LL TAKE THIS SIDE.
Hmm.
BIT OF A CASE, YOUR GODFATHER, ISN'T HE?
OH, HE'S VERY SWEET REALLY, IF YOU DON'T GET HIM STARTED ON THE JEWS.

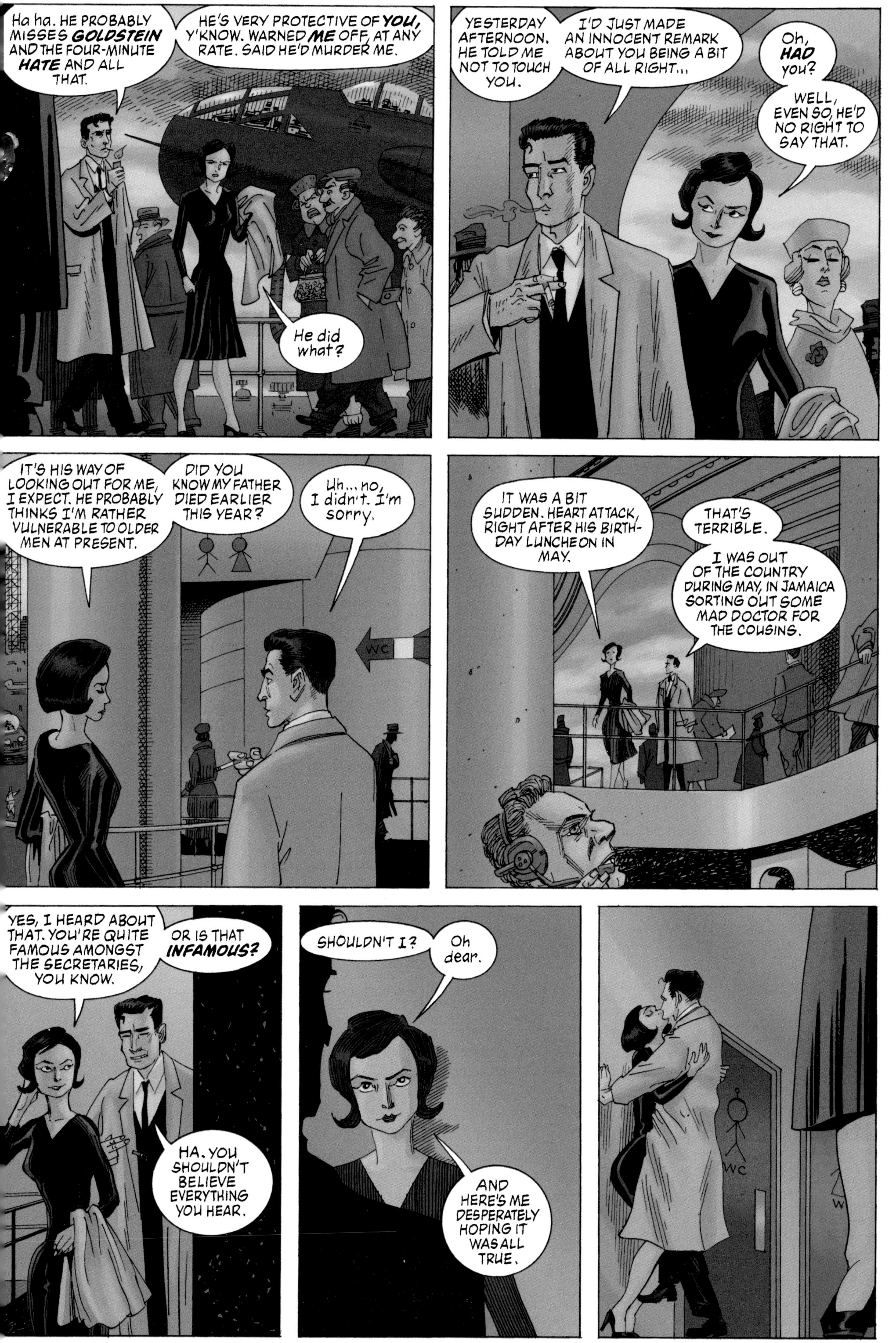

Ha ha. HE PROBABLY MISSES GOLDSTEIN AND THE FOUR-MINUTE HATE AND ALL THAT.
HE'S VERY PROTECTIVE OF YOU, Y'KNOW. WARNED ME OFF, AT ANY RATE. SAID HE'D MURDER ME.
He did what?
YESTERDAY AFTERNOON. HE TOLD ME NOT TO TOUCH YOU.
I'D JUST MADE AN INNOCENT REMARK ABOUT YOU BEING A BIT OF ALL RIGHT...
Oh, HAD you?
WELL, EVEN SO, HE'D NO RIGHT TO SAY THAT.
IT'S HIS WAY OF LOOKING OUT FOR ME, I EXPECT. HE PROBABLY THINKS I'M RATHER VULNERABLE TO OLDER MEN AT PRESENT.
DID YOU KNOW MY FATHER DIED EARLIER THIS YEAR?
Uh... no, I didn't. I'm sorry.
WC
IT WAS A BIT SUDDEN. HEART ATTACK, RIGHT AFTER HIS BIRTHDAY LUNCHEON IN MAY.
THAT'S TERRIBLE.
I WAS OUT OF THE COUNTRY DURING MAY, IN JAMAICA SORTING OUT SOME MAD DOCTOR FOR THE COUSINS.
YES, I HEARD ABOUT THAT. YOU'RE QUITE FAMOUS AMONGST THE SECRETARIES, YOU KNOW.
OR IS THAT INFAMOUS?
HA. YOU SHOULDN'T BELIEVE EVERYTHING YOU HEAR.
SHOULDN'T I?
Oh dear.
AND HERE'S ME DESPERATELY HOPING IT WAS ALL TRUE.
WC

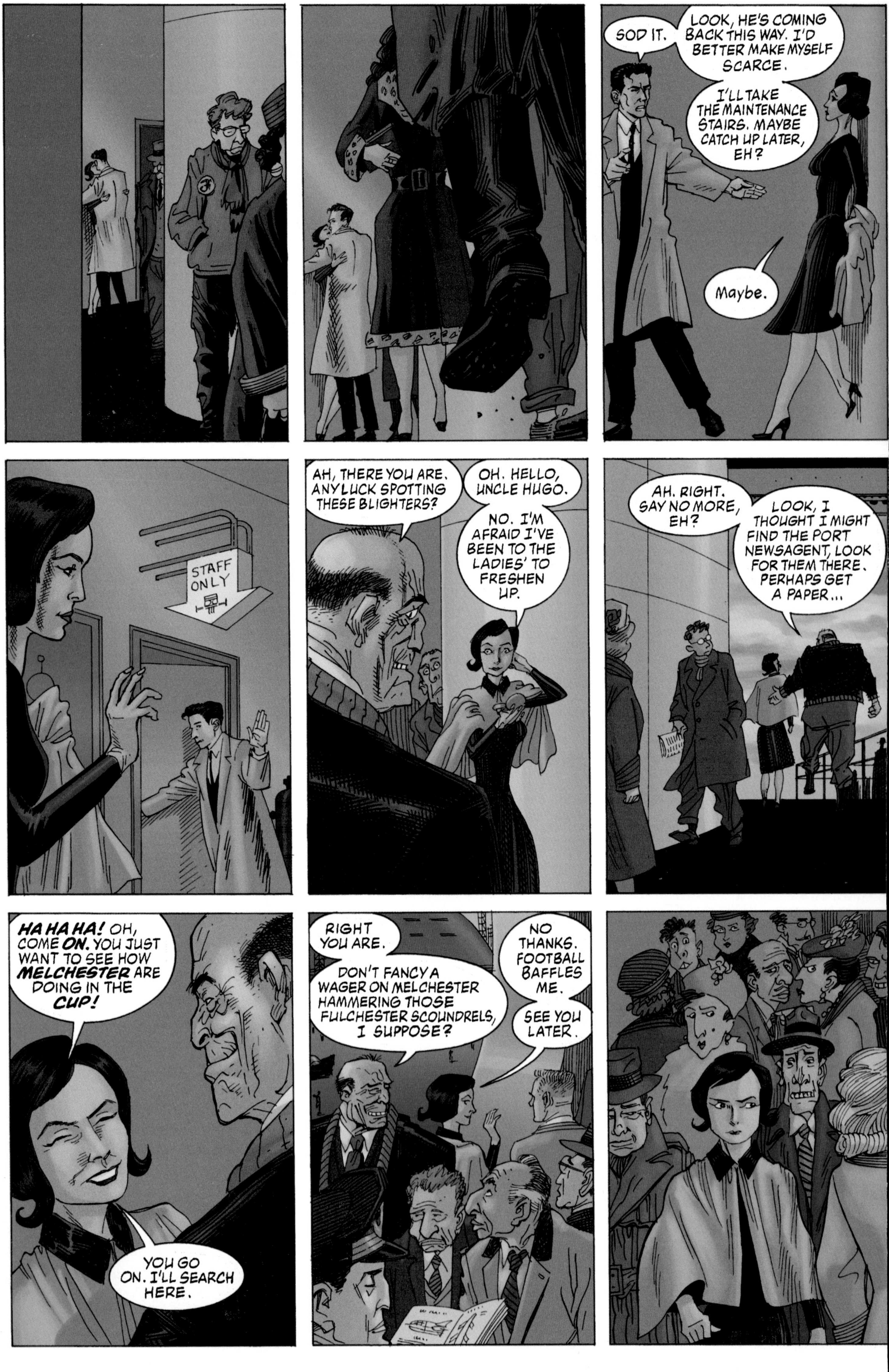

SOD IT.
LOOK, HE'S COMING BACK THIS WAY. I'D BETTER MAKE MYSELF SCARCE.
I'LL TAKE THE MAINTENANCE STAIRS. MAYBE CATCH UP LATER, EH?
Maybe.
STAFF ONLY
AH, THERE YOU ARE. ANY LUCK SPOTTING THESE BLIGHTERS?
OH. HELLO, UNCLE HUGO.
NO. I'M AFRAID I'VE BEEN TO THE LADIES' TO FRESHEN UP.
AH. RIGHT. SAY NO MORE, EH?
LOOK, I THOUGHT I MIGHT FIND THE PORT NEWSAGENT, LOOK FOR THEM THERE. PERHAPS GET A PAPER...
HA HA HA! OH, COME ON. YOU JUST WANT TO SEE HOW MELCHESTER ARE DOING IN THE CUP!
YOU GO ON. I'LL SEARCH HERE.
RIGHT YOU ARE.
DON'T FANCY A WAGER ON MELCHESTER HAMMERING THOSE FULCHESTER SCOUNDRELS, I SUPPOSE?
NO THANKS. FOOTBALL BAFFLES ME.
SEE YOU LATER.

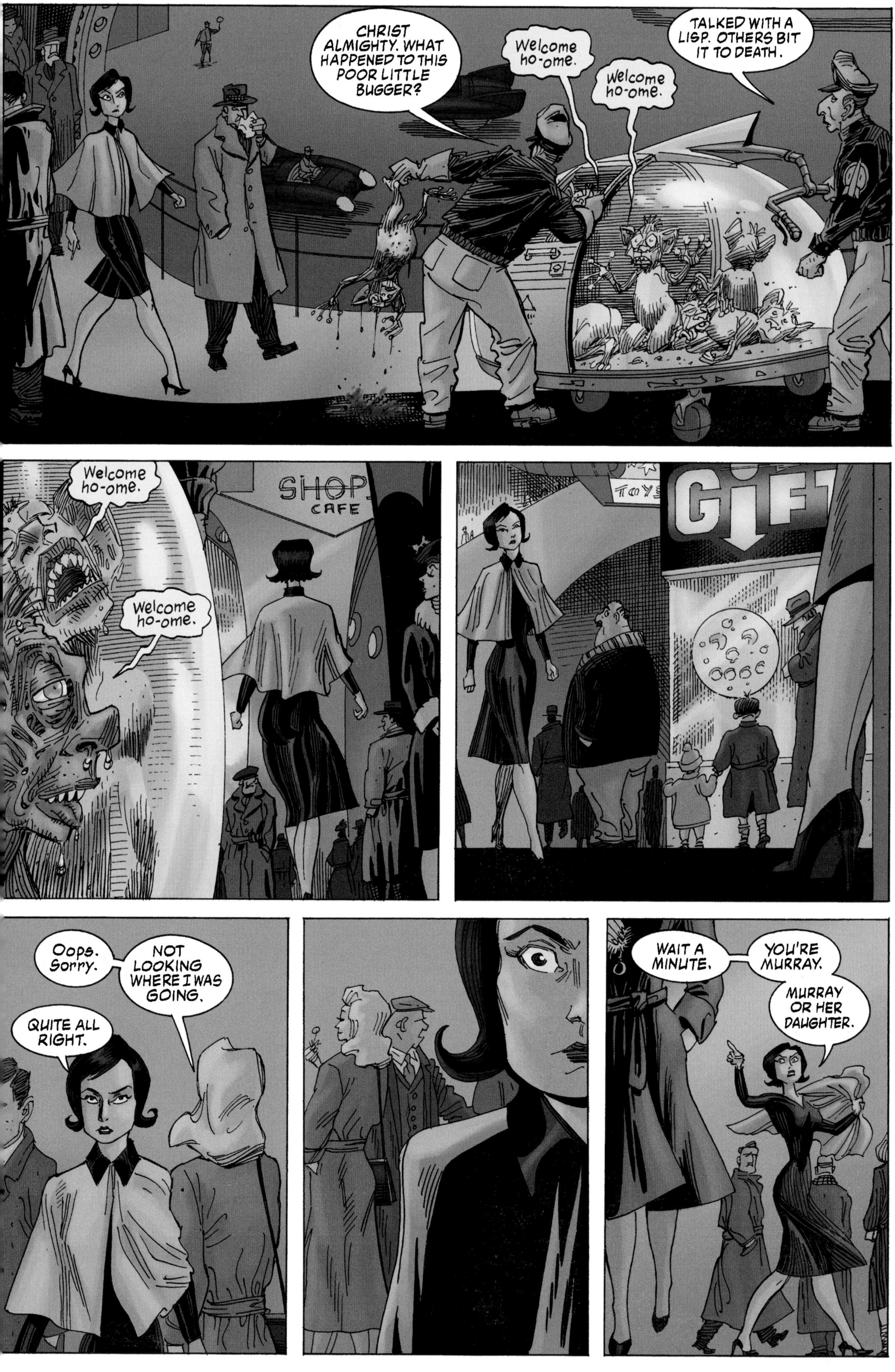
CHRIST ALMIGHTY. WHAT HAPPENED TO THIS POOR LITTLE BUGGER?
Welcome ho-ome.
Welcome ho-ome.
TALKED WITH A LISP. OTHERS BIT IT TO DEATH.
Welcome ho-ome.
Welcome ho-ome.
SHOP
CAFE
GIFT
Oops. Sorry.
NOT LOOKING WHERE I WAS GOING.
QUITE ALL RIGHT.
WAIT A MINUTE.
YOU'RE MURRAY.
MURRAY OR HER DAUGHTER.

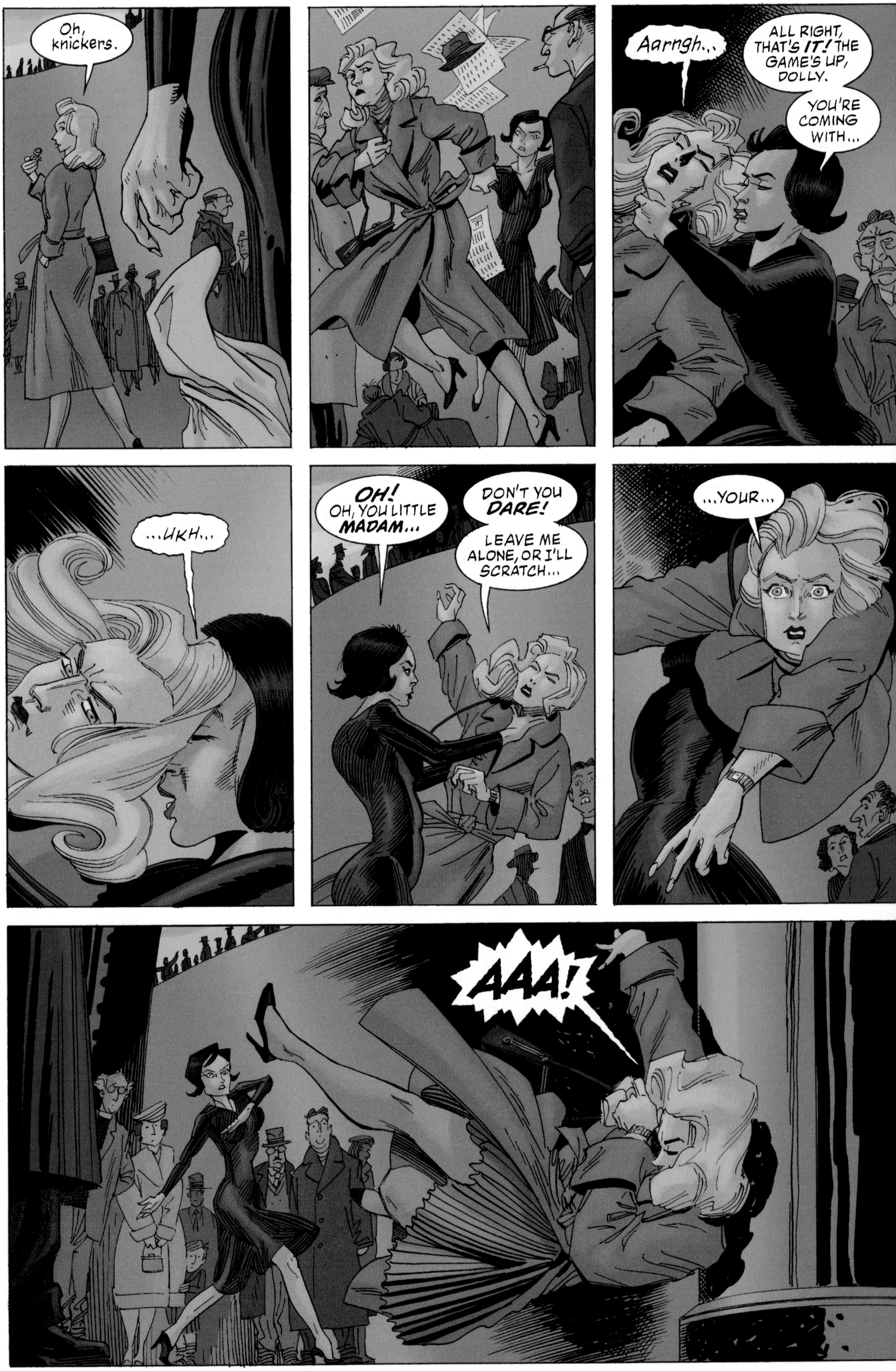
Oh, knickers.
Aarngh...
ALL RIGHT, THAT'S IT! THE GAME'S UP, DOLLY.
YOU'RE COMING WITH...
...UKH...
OH! OH, YOU LITTLE MADAM...
DON'T YOU DARE!
LEAVE ME ALONE, OR I'LL SCRATCH...
...YOUR...
AAA!

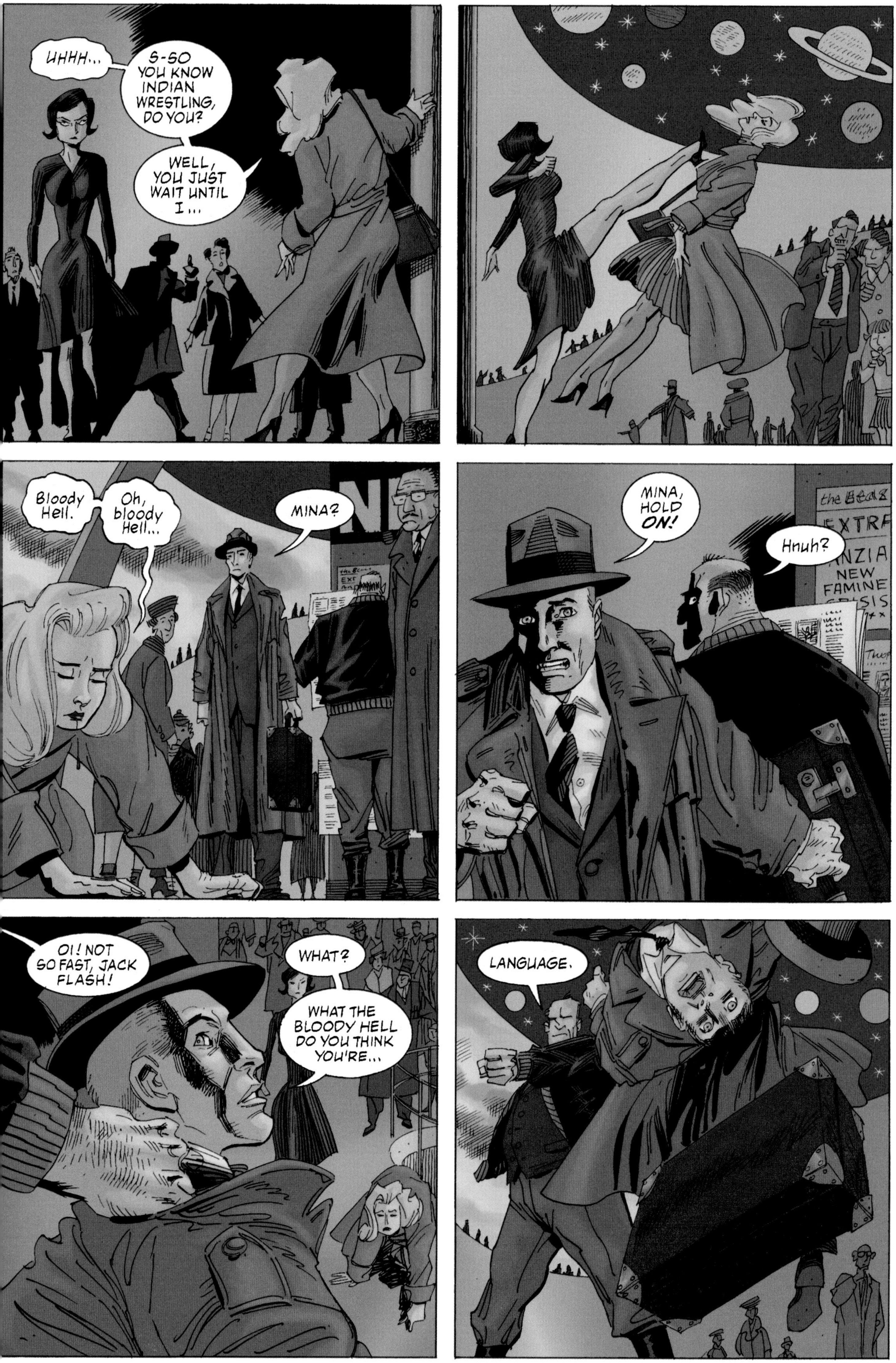
UHHH...
S-SO YOU KNOW INDIAN WRESTLING, DO YOU?
WELL, YOU JUST WAIT UNTIL I...
Bloody Hell.
Oh, bloody Hell...
MINA?
MINA, HOLD ON!
Hnuh?
NEW FAMINE
OI! NOT SO FAST, JACK FLASH!
WHAT?
WHAT THE BLOODY HELL DO YOU THINK YOU'RE...
LANGUAGE.

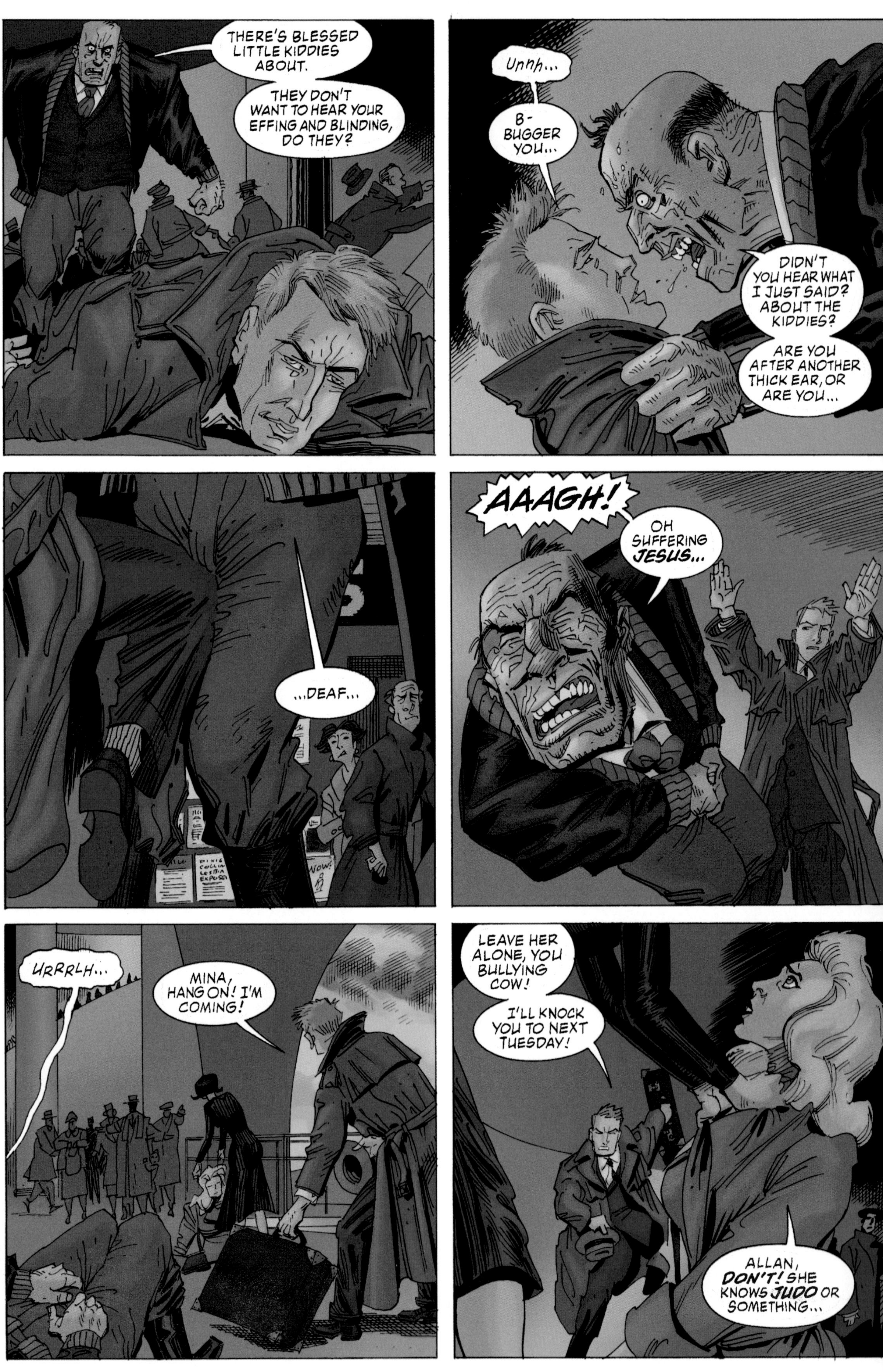
THERE'S BLESSED LITTLE KIDDIES ABOUT.
THEY DON'T WANT TO HEAR YOUR EFFING AND BLINDING, DO THEY?
Unnh...
B-BUGGER YOU...
DIDN'T YOU HEAR WHAT I JUST SAID? ABOUT THE KIDDIES?
ARE YOU AFTER ANOTHER THICK EAR, OR ARE YOU...
...DEAF...
AAAGH!
OH SUFFERING JESUS...
URRRLH...
MINA, HANG ON! I'M COMING!
LEAVE HER ALONE, YOU BULLYING COW!
I'LL KNOCK YOU TO NEXT TUESDAY!
ALLAN, DON'T! SHE KNOWS JUDO OR SOMETHING...

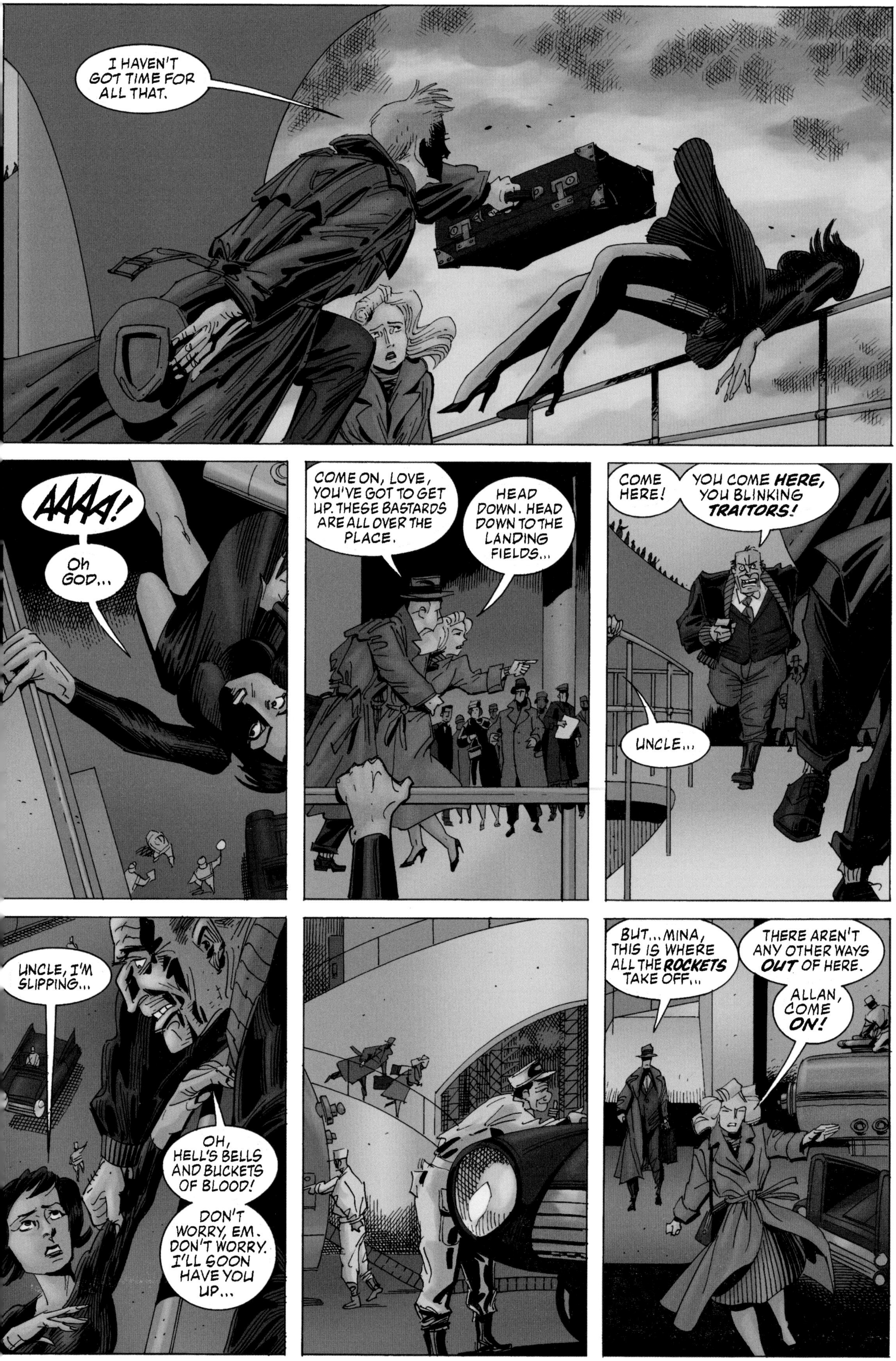
I HAVEN'T GOT TIME FOR ALL THAT.
AAAA!
Oh GOD...
COME ON, LOVE, YOU'VE GOT TO GET UP. THESE BASTARDS ARE ALL OVER THE PLACE.
HEAD DOWN. HEAD DOWN TO THE LANDING FIELDS...
COME HERE!
YOU COME **HERE,** YOU BLINKING ***TRAITORS!***
UNCLE...
UNCLE, I'M SLIPPING...
OH, HELL'S BELLS AND BUCKETS OF BLOOD!
DON'T WORRY, EM. DON'T WORRY. I'LL SOON HAVE YOU UP...
BUT... MINA, THIS IS WHERE ALL THE ***ROCKETS*** TAKE OFF...
THERE AREN'T ANY OTHER WAYS ***OUT*** OF HERE.
ALLAN, COME ***ON!***

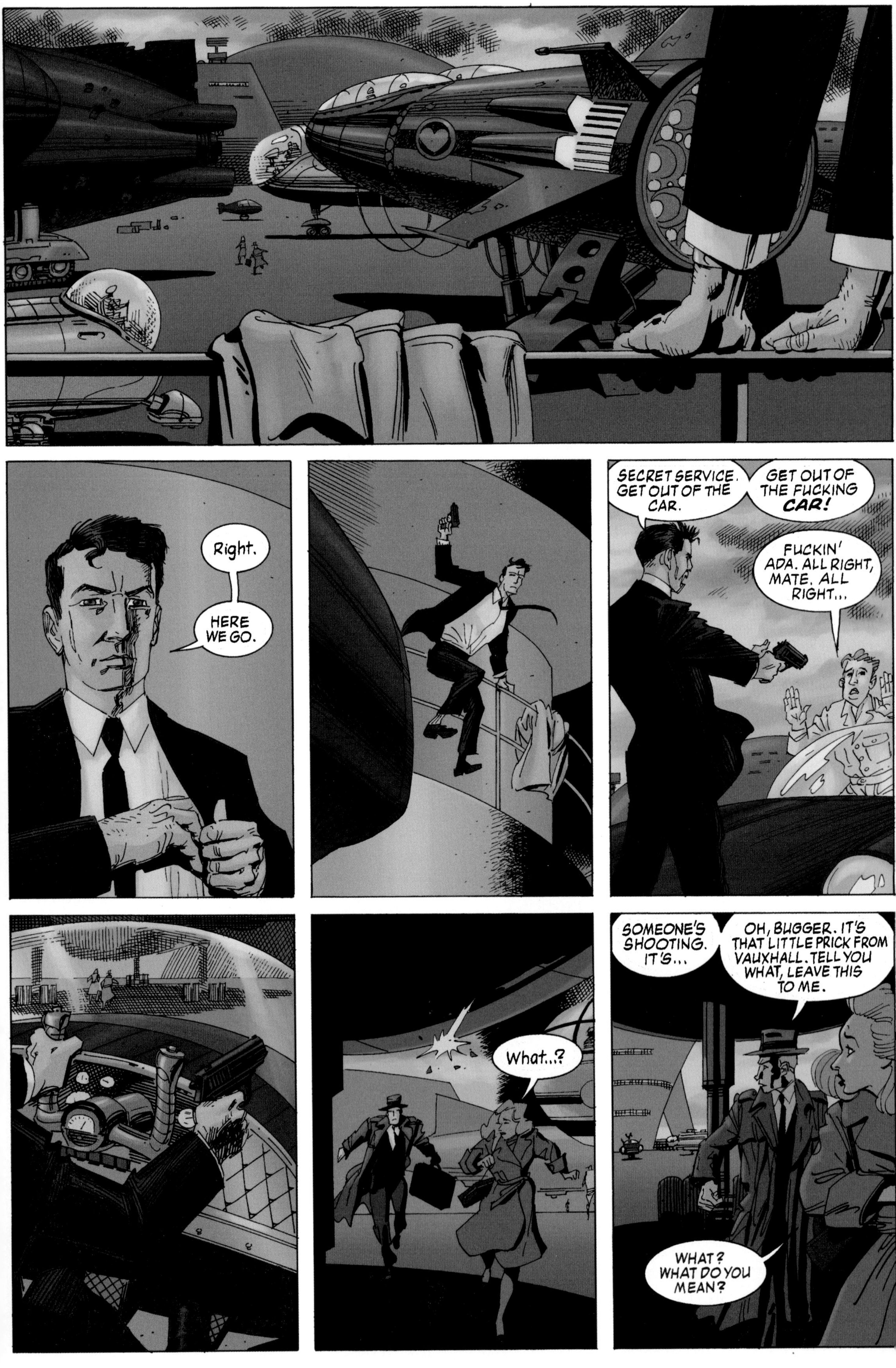
Right.
HERE WE GO.
SECRET SERVICE. GET OUT OF THE CAR.
GET OUT OF THE FUCKING CAR!
FUCKIN' ADA. ALL RIGHT, MATE. ALL RIGHT...
What..?
SOMEONE'S SHOOTING. IT'S...
OH, BUGGER. IT'S THAT LITTLE PRICK FROM VAUXHALL. TELL YOU WHAT, LEAVE THIS TO ME.
WHAT? WHAT DO YOU MEAN?

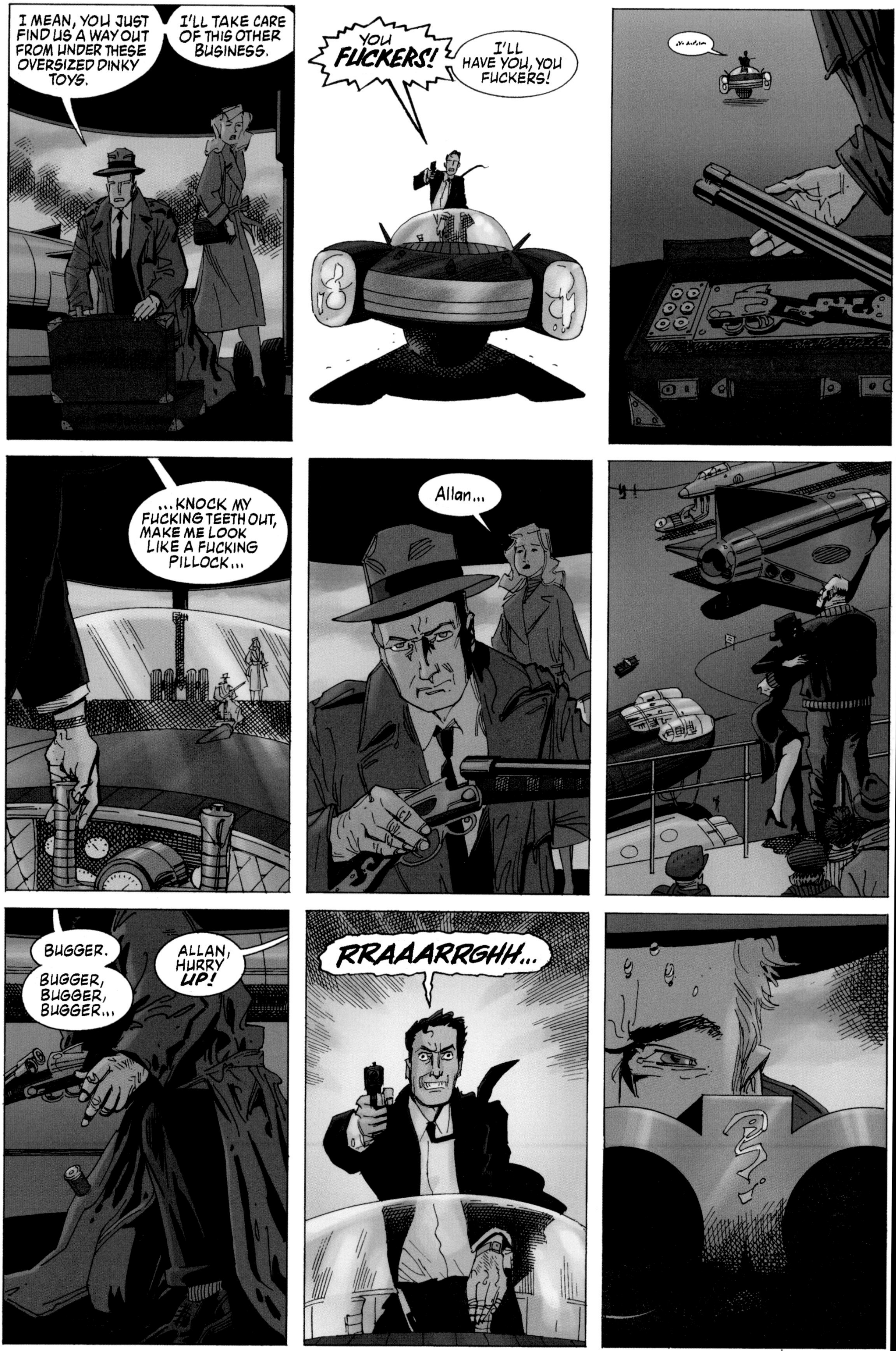
I MEAN, YOU JUST FIND US A WAY OUT FROM UNDER THESE OVERSIZED DINKY TOYS.
I'LL TAKE CARE OF THIS OTHER BUSINESS.
YOU FUCKERS!
I'LL HAVE YOU, YOU FUCKERS!
...KNOCK MY FUCKING TEETH OUT, MAKE ME LOOK LIKE A FUCKING PILLOCK...
Allan...
BUGGER.
BUGGER, BUGGER, BUGGER...
ALLAN, HURRY UP!
RRAAARRGHH...

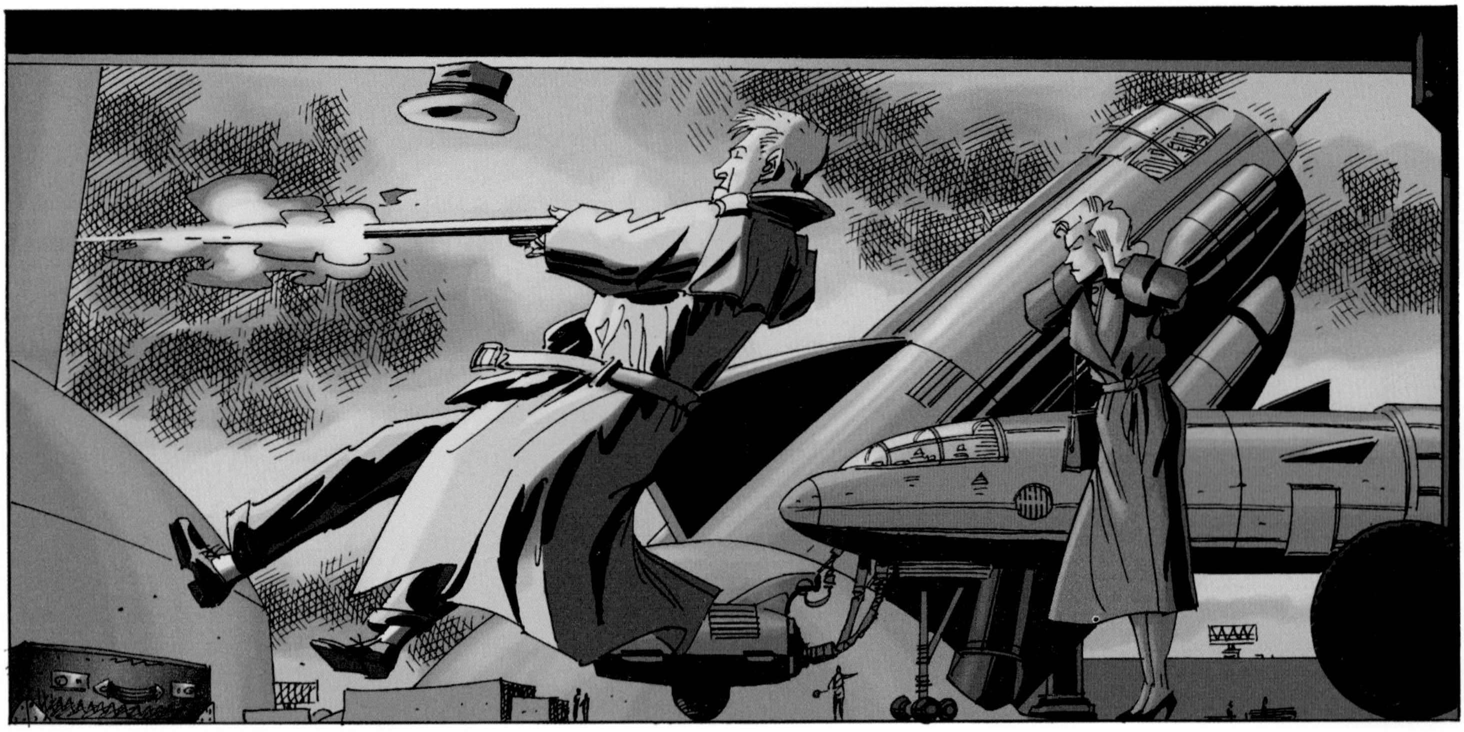

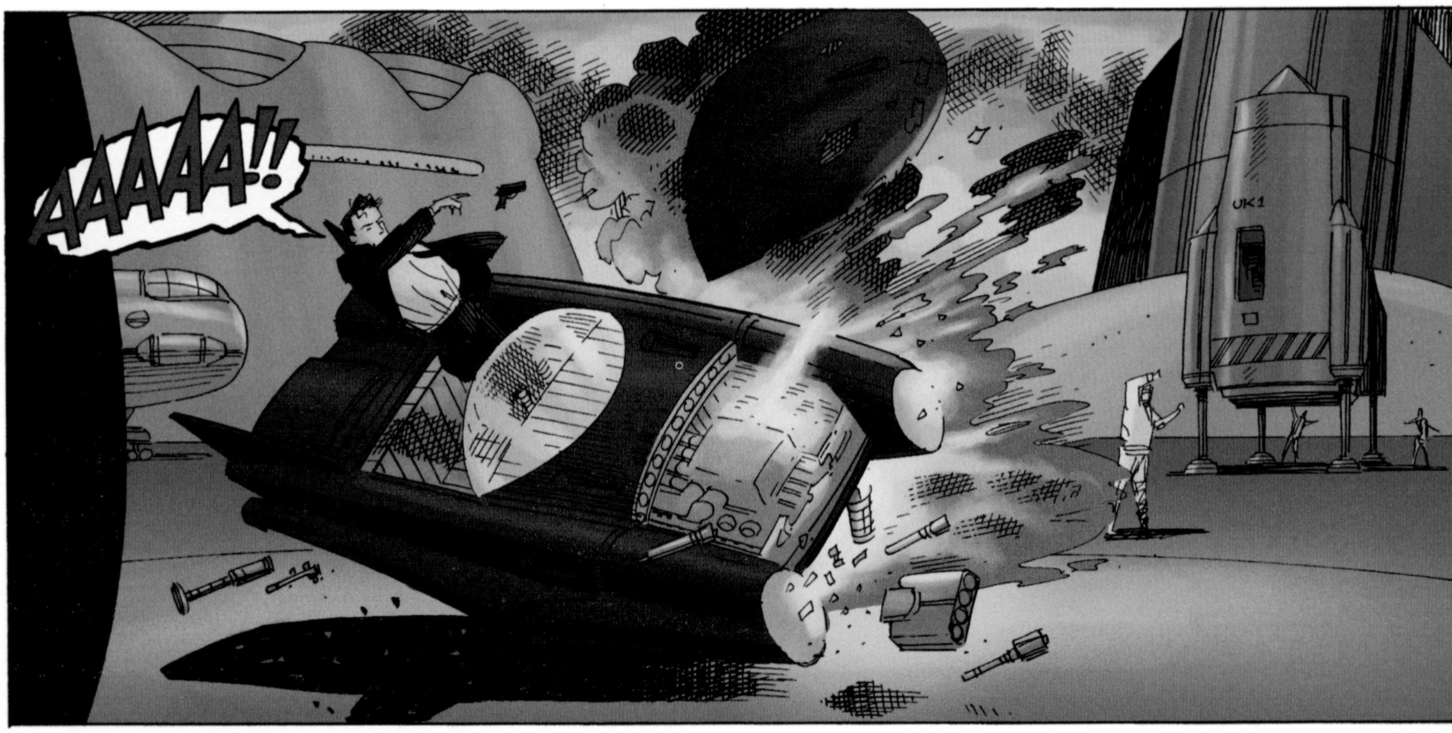
AAAAA!!
UK1

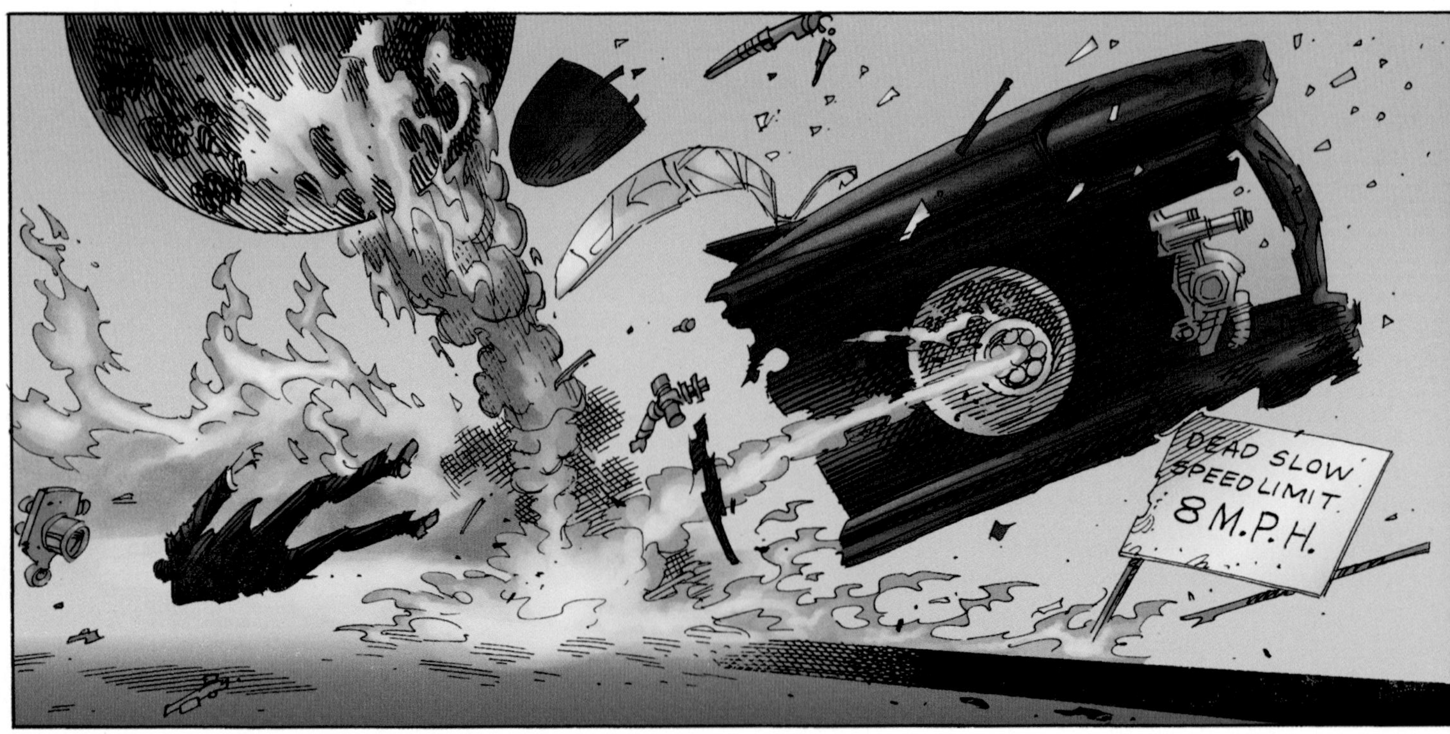
DEAD SLOW
SPEED LIMIT
8 M.P.H.

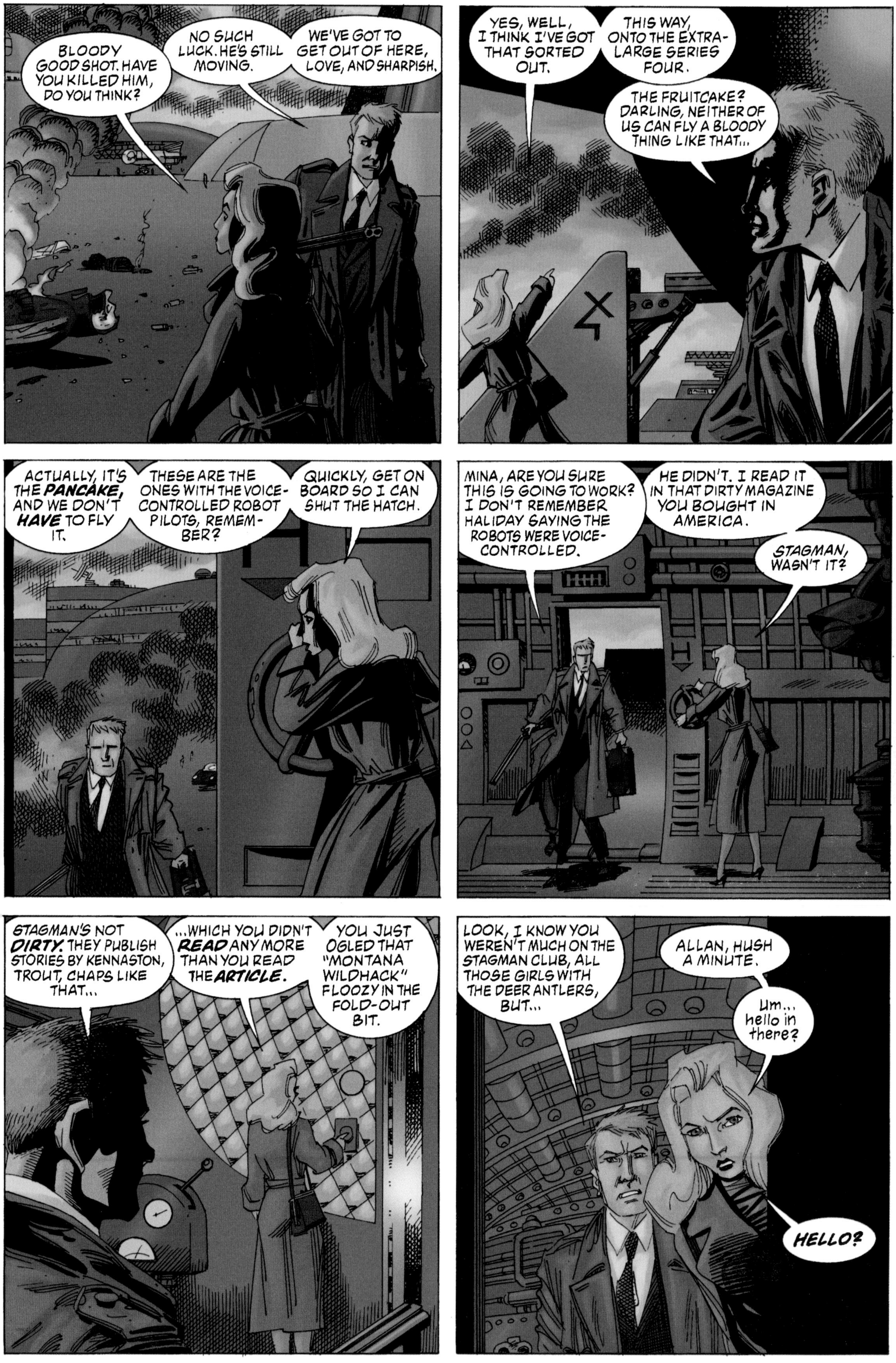
BLOODY GOOD SHOT. HAVE YOU KILLED HIM, DO YOU THINK?
NO SUCH LUCK. HE'S STILL MOVING.
WE'VE GOT TO GET OUT OF HERE, LOVE, AND SHARPISH.
YES, WELL, I THINK I'VE GOT THAT SORTED OUT.
THIS WAY, ONTO THE EXTRA-LARGE SERIES FOUR.
THE FRUITCAKE? DARLING, NEITHER OF US CAN FLY A BLOODY THING LIKE THAT...
ACTUALLY, IT'S THE PANCAKE, AND WE DON'T HAVE TO FLY IT.
THESE ARE THE ONES WITH THE VOICE-CONTROLLED ROBOT PILOTS, REMEMBER?
QUICKLY, GET ON BOARD SO I CAN SHUT THE HATCH.
MINA, ARE YOU SURE THIS IS GOING TO WORK? I DON'T REMEMBER HALIDAY SAYING THE ROBOTS WERE VOICE-CONTROLLED.
HE DIDN'T. I READ IT IN THAT DIRTY MAGAZINE YOU BOUGHT IN AMERICA.
STAGMAN, WASN'T IT?
STAGMAN'S NOT DIRTY. THEY PUBLISH STORIES BY KENNASTON, TROUT, CHAPS LIKE THAT...
...WHICH YOU DIDN'T READ ANY MORE THAN YOU READ THE ARTICLE.
YOU JUST OGLED THAT "MONTANA WILDHACK" FLOOZY IN THE FOLD-OUT BIT.
LOOK, I KNOW YOU WEREN'T MUCH ON THE STAGMAN CLUB, ALL THOSE GIRLS WITH THE DEER ANTLERS, BUT...
ALLAN, HUSH A MINUTE.
Um... hello in there?
HELLO?

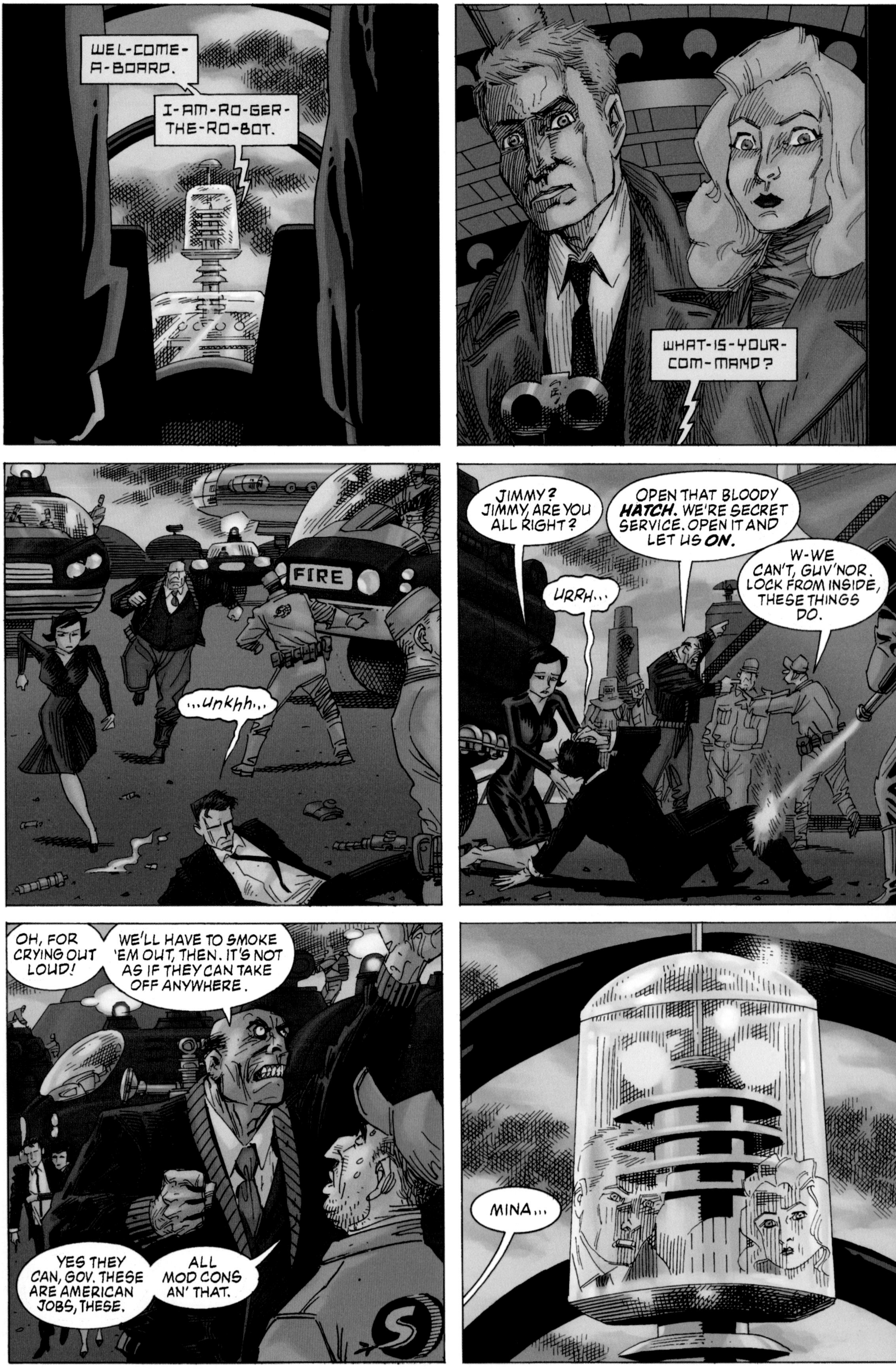
WEL-COME-A-BOARD.
I-AM-RO-GER-THE-RO-BOT.
WHAT-IS-YOUR-COM-MAND?
FIRE
...unkhh...
JIMMY? JIMMY, ARE YOU ALL RIGHT?
URRH...
OPEN THAT BLOODY **HATCH**. WE'RE SECRET SERVICE. OPEN IT AND LET US **ON**.
W-WE CAN'T, GUV'NOR. LOCK FROM INSIDE, THESE THINGS DO.
OH, FOR CRYING OUT LOUD!
WE'LL HAVE TO SMOKE 'EM OUT, THEN. IT'S NOT AS IF THEY CAN TAKE OFF ANYWHERE.
YES THEY CAN, GOV. THESE ARE AMERICAN JOBS, THESE.
ALL MOD CONS AN' THAT.
MINA...

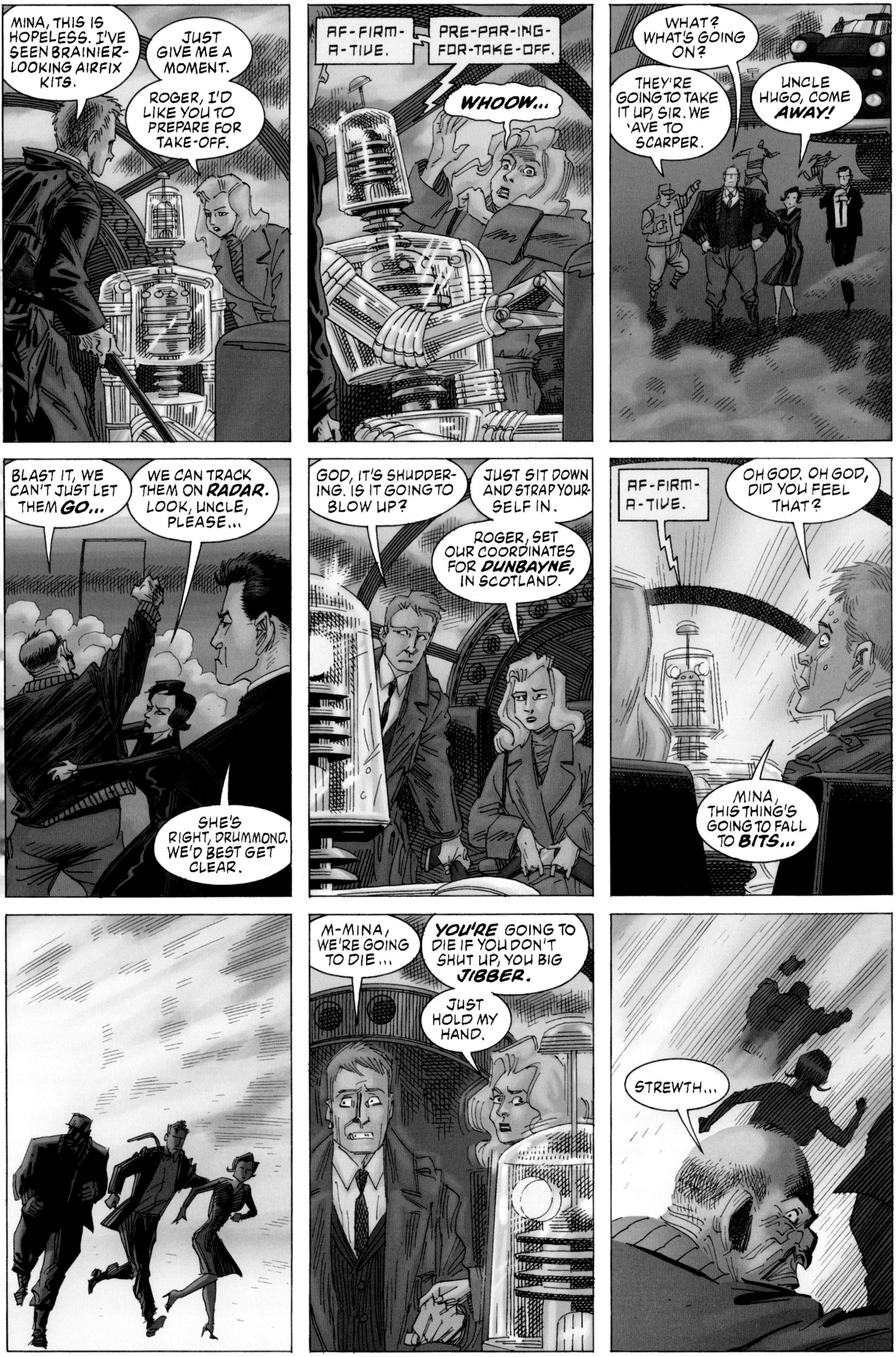
MINA, THIS IS HOPELESS. I'VE SEEN BRAINIER-LOOKING AIRFIX KITS.
JUST GIVE ME A MOMENT.
ROGER, I'D LIKE YOU TO PREPARE FOR TAKE-OFF.
AF-FIRM-A-TIVE.
PRE-PAR-ING-FOR-TAKE-OFF.
WHOOW...
WHAT? WHAT'S GOING ON?
THEY'RE GOING TO TAKE IT UP, SIR. WE 'AVE TO SCARPER.
UNCLE HUGO, COME AWAY!
BLAST IT, WE CAN'T JUST LET THEM GO...
WE CAN TRACK THEM ON RADAR. LOOK, UNCLE, PLEASE...
SHE'S RIGHT, DRUMMOND. WE'D BEST GET CLEAR.
GOD, IT'S SHUDDER-ING. IS IT GOING TO BLOW UP?
JUST SIT DOWN AND STRAP YOUR-SELF IN.
ROGER, SET OUR COORDINATES FOR DUNBAYNE, IN SCOTLAND.
AF-FIRM-A-TIVE.
OH GOD, OH GOD, DID YOU FEEL THAT?
MINA, THIS THING'S GOING TO FALL TO BITS...
M-MINA, WE'RE GOING TO DIE...
YOU'RE GOING TO DIE IF YOU DON'T SHUT UP, YOU BIG JIBBER.
JUST HOLD MY HAND.
STREWTH...

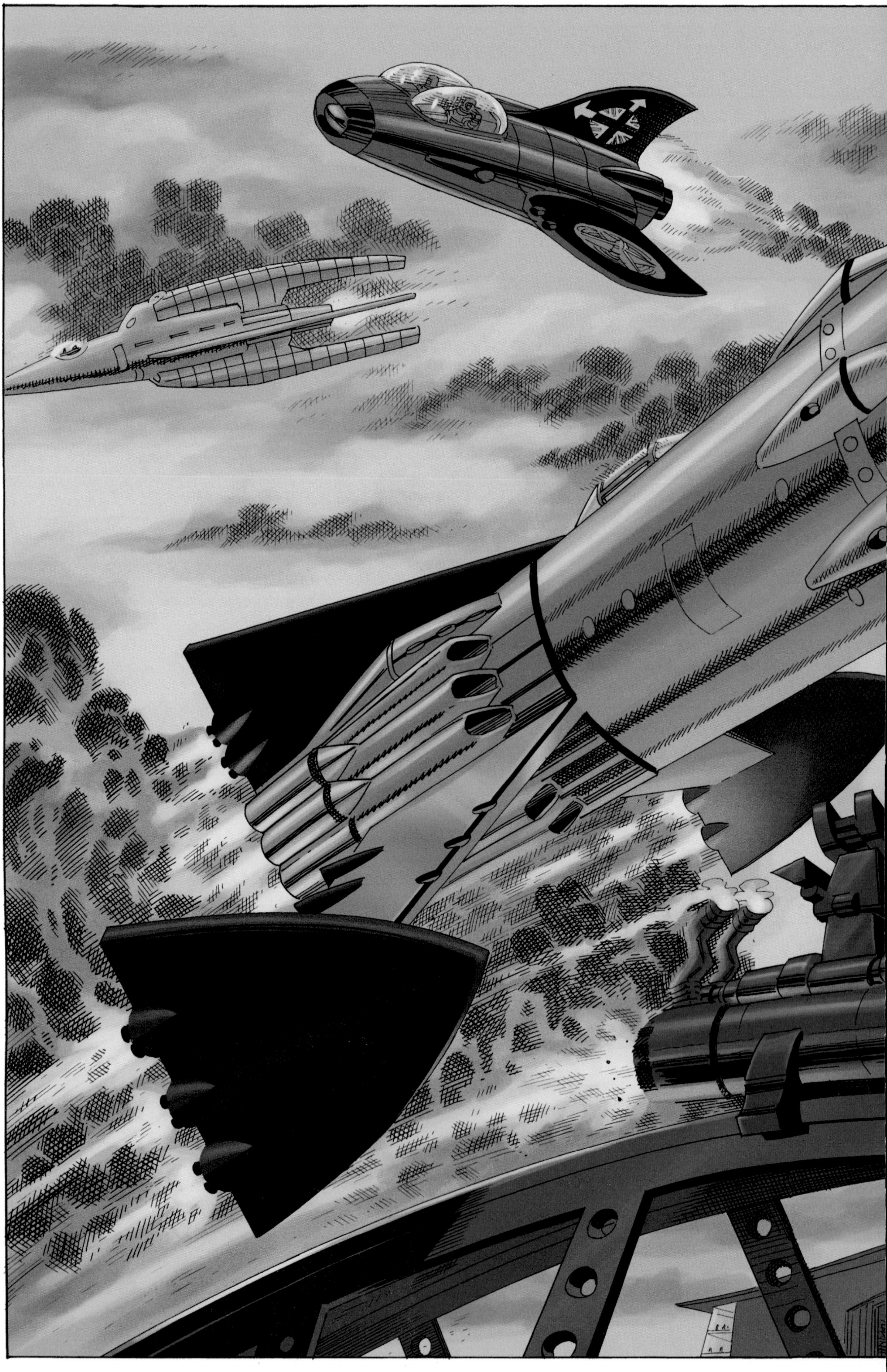

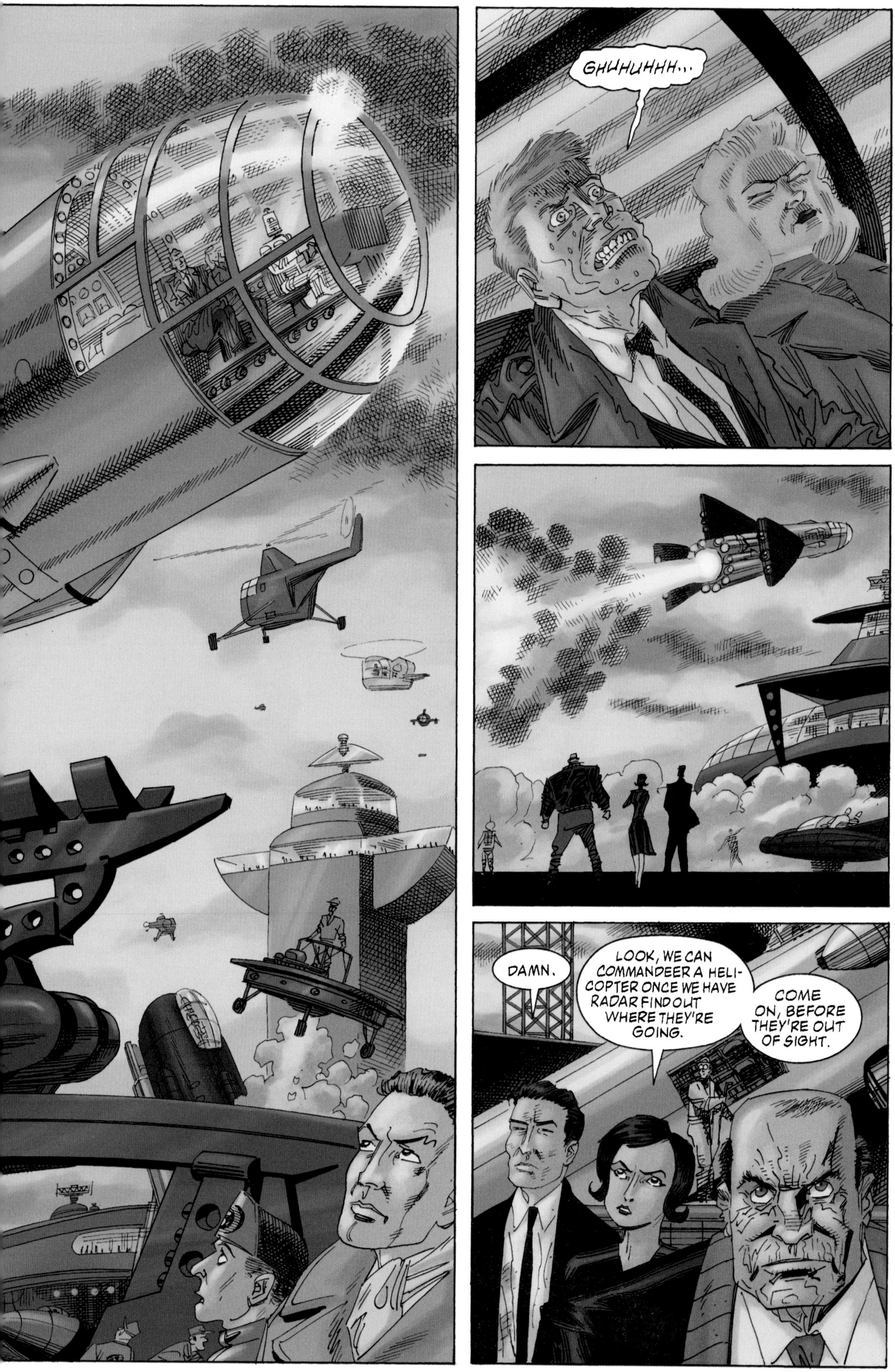

GHUHUHHH...
DAMN.
LOOK, WE CAN COMMANDEER A HELICOPTER ONCE WE HAVE RADAR FIND OUT WHERE THEY'RE GOING.
COME ON, BEFORE THEY'RE OUT OF SIGHT.

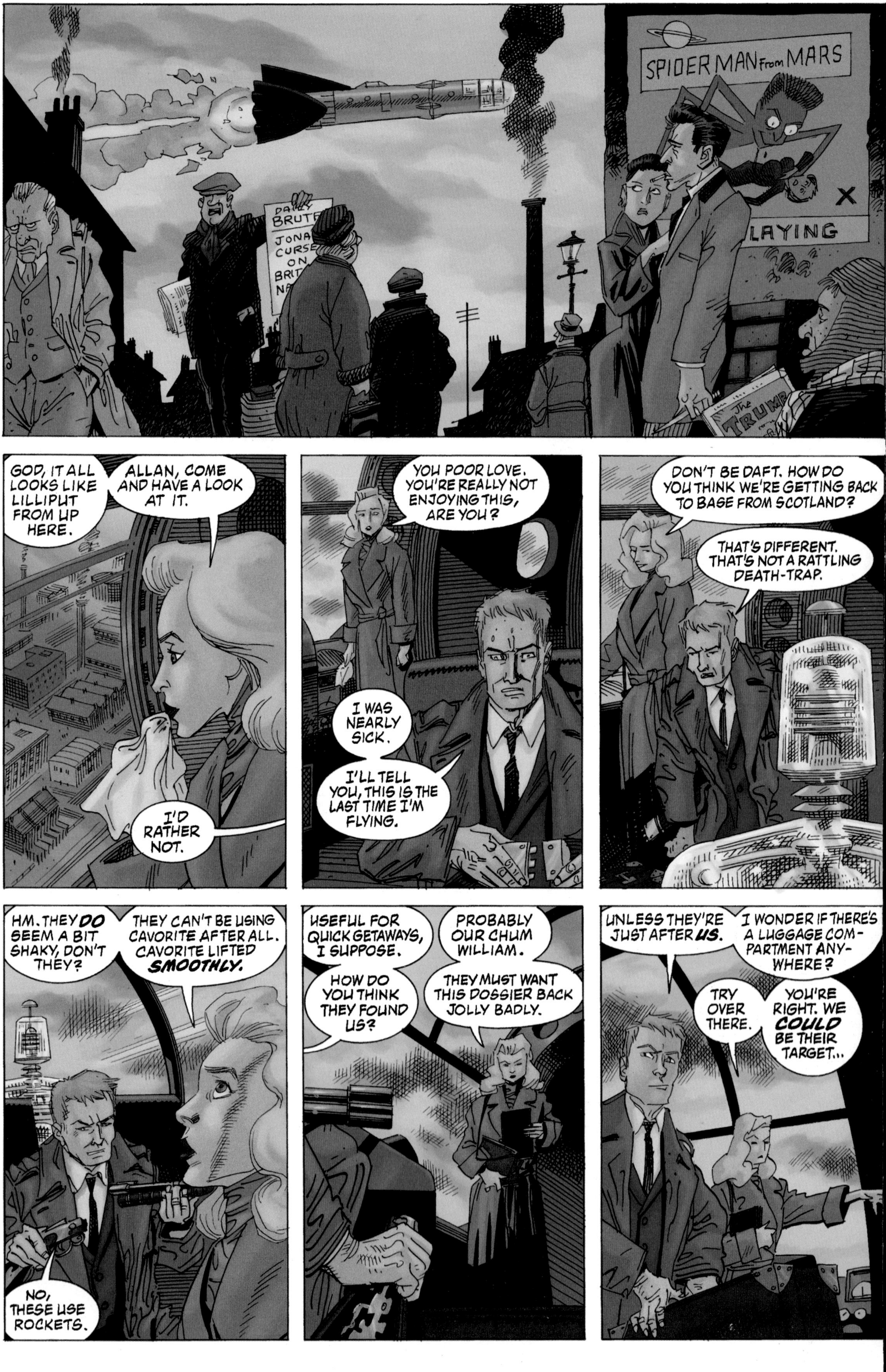

SPIDER MAN From MARS
GOD, IT ALL LOOKS LIKE LILLIPUT FROM UP HERE.
ALLAN, COME AND HAVE A LOOK AT IT.
I'D RATHER NOT.
YOU POOR LOVE. YOU'RE REALLY NOT ENJOYING THIS, ARE YOU?
I WAS NEARLY SICK.
I'LL TELL YOU, THIS IS THE LAST TIME I'M FLYING.
DON'T BE DAFT. HOW DO YOU THINK WE'RE GETTING BACK TO BASE FROM SCOTLAND?
THAT'S DIFFERENT. THAT'S NOT A RATTLING DEATH-TRAP.
HM. THEY *DO* SEEM A BIT SHAKY, DON'T THEY?
THEY CAN'T BE USING CAVORITE AFTER ALL. CAVORITE LIFTED ***SMOOTHLY.***
NO, THESE USE ROCKETS.
USEFUL FOR QUICK GETAWAYS, I SUPPOSE.
HOW DO YOU THINK THEY FOUND US?
PROBABLY OUR CHUM WILLIAM.
THEY MUST WANT THIS DOSSIER BACK JOLLY BADLY.
UNLESS THEY'RE JUST AFTER ***US.***
I WONDER IF THERE'S A LUGGAGE COMPARTMENT ANYWHERE?
TRY OVER THERE.
YOU'RE RIGHT. WE ***COULD*** BE THEIR TARGET...

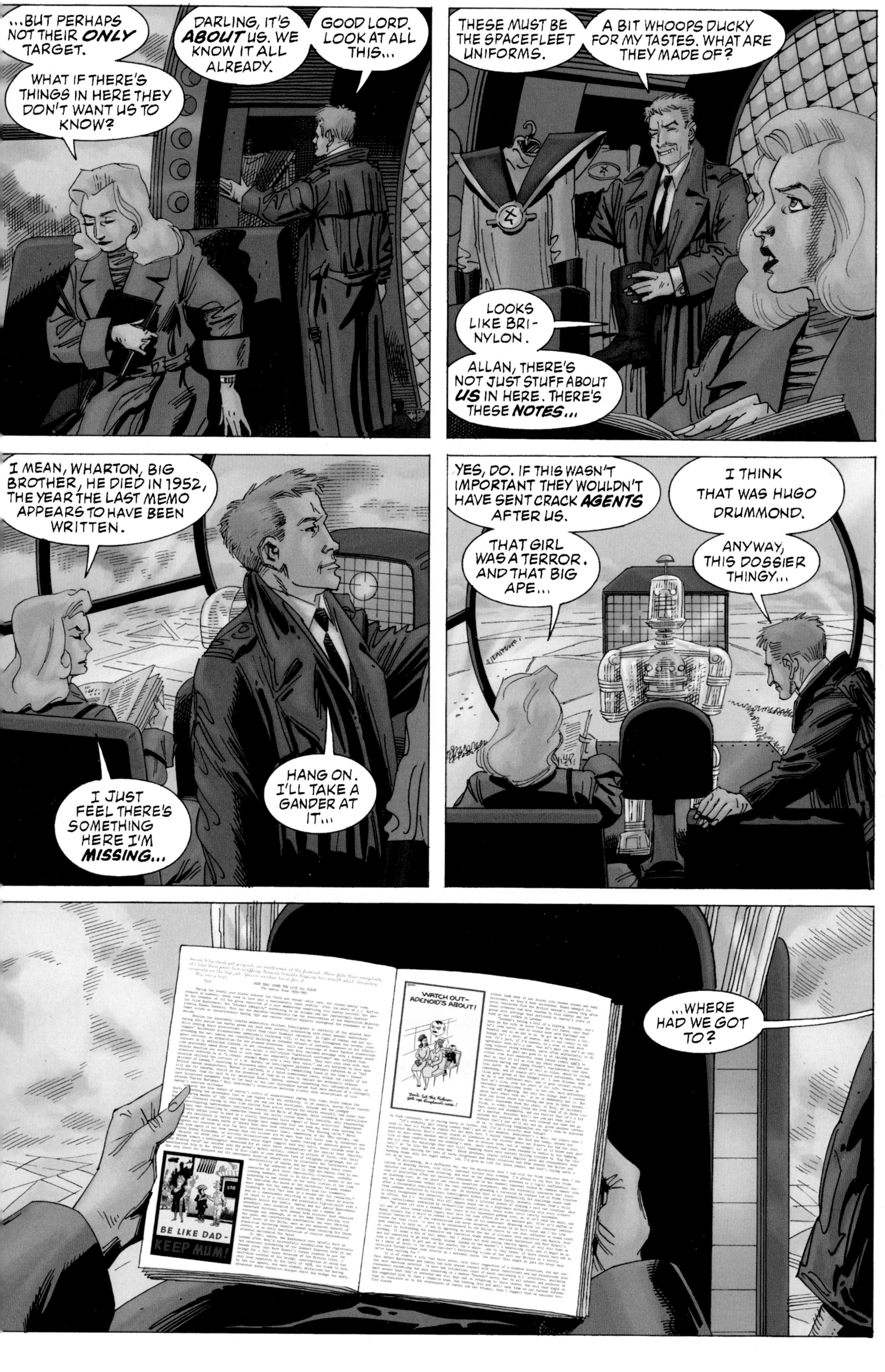

...BUT PERHAPS NOT THEIR *ONLY* TARGET.
WHAT IF THERE'S THINGS IN HERE THEY DON'T WANT US TO KNOW?
DARLING, IT'S *ABOUT* US. WE KNOW IT ALL ALREADY.
GOOD LORD. LOOK AT ALL THIS...
THESE MUST BE THE SPACEFLEET UNIFORMS.
A BIT WHOOPS DUCKY FOR MY TASTES. WHAT ARE THEY MADE OF?
LOOKS LIKE BRI-NYLON.
ALLAN, THERE'S NOT JUST STUFF ABOUT *US* IN HERE. THERE'S THESE *NOTES*...
I MEAN, WHARTON, BIG BROTHER, HE DIED IN 1952, THE YEAR THE LAST MEMO APPEARS TO HAVE BEEN WRITTEN.
I JUST FEEL THERE'S SOMETHING HERE I'M *MISSING*...
HANG ON. I'LL TAKE A GANDER AT IT...
YES, DO. IF THIS WASN'T IMPORTANT THEY WOULDN'T HAVE SENT CRACK *AGENTS* AFTER US.
THAT GIRL WAS A TERROR. AND THAT BIG APE...
I THINK THAT WAS HUGO DRUMMOND.
ANYWAY, THIS DOSSIER THINGY...
WATCH OUT— ADENOID'S ABOUT!
BE LIKE DAD— KEEP MUM!
...WHERE HAD WE GOT TO?

Here's Wharton's pet project, as mentioned at the funeral. More fate than morphate, eh? And then poor bun-scoffing Bessie's trouble keeping her mouth shut. Anyway, congrats on the top job. You've worked hard for it.

My very best,

Bob

WHEN THEY SOUND THE LAST ALL CLEAR
The Murray Team 1939-1945

During the twenty year hiatus between the first and second World Wars, the second Murray team, reduced in numbers, would seem to have kept a considerably lower profile. After the death of A.J. Raffles in the trenches of WWI the group consisted of a core membership comprising Miss Murray herself, the junior Allan Quatermain, the "eternal ambiguity" professing to be Orlando and the increasingly haunted-seeming Thomas Carnacki. This was the ensemble responsible for the intervention at the bedevilled Brinkley Court estate in Worcestershire during 1930 and various similar exploits throughout the remainder of the decade.

Despite the apparently limited membership, Military Intelligence is currently of the opinion that during this period the Murray group may have been covertly associating with other unusual individuals while keeping these associations a secret from their Vauxhall employers. In light of Murray and her colleagues' deliberate disappearance immediately following WWII, it may be that throughout the several years preceding the war, Murray was stealthily building an extended network of contacts, unknown to the intelligence services, as preparation for her planned desertion. While our knowledge of these further clandestine liaisons is by definition limited, we are reasonably sure that they included meetings with a former wharf-side prostitute named Diver and, at one point, a self-styled "surrealist sportsman" who suffered from chronic dwarfism and whose first or last name was apparently Engelbrecht. They were also seen with what witnesses referred to as "a stocky, unkempt Negro with a very deep voice," and are believed to have upon occasion utilised the services of a Mr. Norton, an intelligence gatherer sometimes referred to as "the prisoner of London." According to discarded notes in Murray's handwriting found at the team's former British Museum headquarters, Norton is confined, in a third dimensional sense, within the limits of the city and its suburbs, whilst in the dimension of time he is able to explore the metropolis without restriction, from its past to its uncertain future. Indeed, perhaps supporting this outlandish claim, we have discovered documents from as far back as the late Glorianian period that make mention of a strangely attired "Master Nortonne," this individual's description matching closely with descriptions of Miss Murray's sometime colleague.

Whatever the true extent of Murray's circle of acquaintances during this time, there remain few facts concerning her adventures that we can regard with any certainty. As an example, Murray filed reports for the Spring months of 1937 claiming that she and her two associates, Orlando and the younger Quatermain (Carnacki having by this time retired from active service for health reasons), had spent that period investigating subterranean territories beneath the North of England, while according to surveillance sources they were travelling by submarine towards the Arctic circle when they vanished, only reappearing roughly three months later to hand in a clearly fabricated false report of their activities. Department analysts who specialise in Murray and her doings have suggested that her team may have been looking for the fabled group of islands north of Orkney that have been referred to as "The Blazing World." Naval Intelligence has searched in vain for this location several times, commencing in the 18th century, and time and time again it has been proven that the islands are no more than tall tales spun by windswept and inebriated Orkney fishermen, or possibly hallucinations caused by sudden venting of undersea gasses in the area. Despite the utter lack of any evidence which might suggest that they exist, these islands seem to have become almost a pathological obsession for at least three incarnations of the special team. Possibly "The Blazing World" has entered into the group's mythic history, almost an article of faith, with their unauthorised trip to the Arctic seen in this light as some debased form of religious pilgrimage, but at the very least the incident and its subsequent cover-up should serve to illustrate the furtiveness and unreliability of Murray and her team during these years.

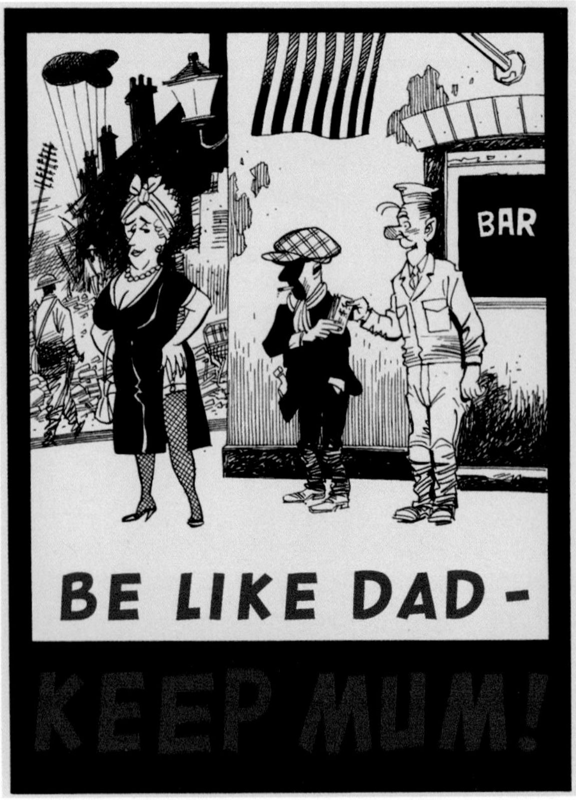
BAR
BE LIKE DAD -
KEEP MUM!

At the outbreak of war in 1939 the Murray team by now consisted of just three impressively vivacious, youthful seeming members, which is to Miss Murray's credit as she was according to our records in her early sixties at the time. The charlatan who posed as the historical Orlando seemed more eager for the coming conflict than his teammates, claiming to have "not been in a decent war for centuries," and as a consequence enlisting in the RAF, where he proved at least to be a skilled and creditable fighter-pilot with a genuine thirst for battle. Murray and the junior Quatermain, meanwhile, were occupied in carrying out a number of important missions, both abroad with missions that entailed espionage and sabotage, or on the home front dealing with the spies and racketeering opportunists who were thriving under cover of the Blitz, such as the apparent dynasty of black-clad burrowing bandits intent upon stealing the Crown Jewels, or an early manifestation of elusive international criminal mastermind The Voice.

In 1941, Murray and Quatermain were briefly back in London after they'd successfully accomplished the regrettable but necessary dynamiting of the Channel Causeway when it had become clear that Herr Hynkel's forces planned to use the bridge for a full scale invasion of the British Isles. A half-mile section of the bridge, construction of which had only been completed by the April of 1908, was blown to bits by the two agents, who were roundly criticised for having detonated their explosive charges while the bridge was empty

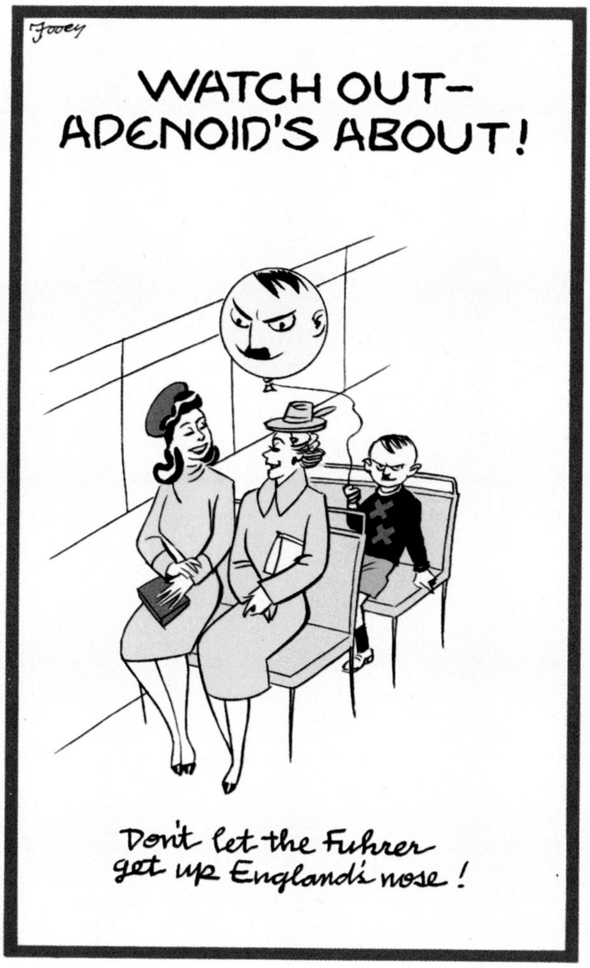
Fovey
WATCH OUT–
ADENOID'S ABOUT!
Don't let the Fuhrer
get up England's nose!

rather than when it was choked with German troops and tank divisions, as they'd been instructed. Found amongst the notes retrieved from the British Museum's locked wing after those premises had been vacated by Miss Murray and her group were jottings that pertained to Murray's state of mind on her return to London:

"London's taking a hell of a kicking. Orlando, who's back in the city on leave from the air force, says that he's seen worse, and we should have seen Carthage and Pompeii and so on and so on. He got on my nerves a bit, though he's a dear, of course, and it was lovely to see him. It's just, if I'm honest, he's ever so much more agreeable when he's a her. When he's male you can't go very long without being reminded, quite often unpleasantly in my experience, of just how good he is at killing people, either with that wonderful sword (which simply <u>can't</u> be what he says it is) or with any other weapon that man has invented during our young friend's considerable span upon this Earth. He can shoot as well as Allan, which is saying something, and of course he's mastered aeroplanes, which Allan goes green at the thought of. I love Orlando, both of us do in our different ways, and it goes without saying that he's also, over the years of his life, become an extremely accomplished lover. So has she, most definitely. 'F---ing and Fighting, the only two things that I learned which have stuck with me,' as he so memorably put it. But then you think about him hewing men down in their dozens, in their thousands down the years, at Troy, at Salisbury Plain, in every bloody field men ever read of in their history books and shuddered, and you realise that he's a bit of a monster. Possibly that's how you get when you've watched the utopias and the wars without end come and go. Perhaps that's how we'll all end up, given another century or so. As shuffling troglodytes who can't even be bothered to form sentences, or as raving barmy as Ayesha. God, I'm in a cheerful mood tonight.

"It's probably just seeing London that's got me all maudlin. Everywhere's a mess, the places that I used to know all blown to rubble for the most part. I walked through the East End today, around the architect Nicholas Dyer's creepy church at Limehouse in the streets where our Chinese foe had his lair, back in what seems another world entirely. How we dressed then, how we thought, all of it blown away just like so much confetti when the wedding's done. Whole streets had been reduced to rubble by the bombing, and all over the buildings that were still standing there were posters telling everyone to 'dig for victory,' or 'be like Dad and keep mum.' These precious, stupid little English jokes and catchphrases when they've been pulling the bits of their neighbours and their relatives out from beneath the bricks and burning beams only the night before. God, I'd give my life for these people, and that's saying quite a lot in my case.

"As disturbing, in a different way, was the discussion that I had with the Prime Minister when I was called to Downing Street, with Allan, somewhat earlier this evening. I'm afraid to say that the Prime Minister had obviously been drinking, and what we had imagined was intended as a highly confidential session of debriefing after our explosive escapades out on the channel causeway seemed to somehow wander into an alarming rant. He saw plots and secret societies everywhere, and was especially concerned that there may be rogue factions within MI5 who were currently grooming a successor to replace him as Prime Minister after a favourable conclusion to the war. He believed that in all probability the challenge would come from someone installed by Military Intelligence within the Labour Party, probably someone from a solid military background and intensely charismatic with a splendid chance of winning a post war election. Once in office, the P.M. believed, this MI5 puppet would see in a nightmare dictatorship with every citizen under surveillance, patrolled by Gestapo-like secret police, their every civil liberty suspended.

"He broke off with a haunted look there in his bloodshot gundog eyes, as if he'd said too much, and lit one of those caber-sized cigars that have the same effect on me as mustard gas. After he'd puffed in moody silence for a while he seemed to gather some of his composure. Brushing aside his sinister conspiratorial fantasies as if the conversation had never occurred, he moved on to tell Allan and I the true reason for this visit. We were to be despatched to the United States to see what influence we could exert upon America to help us, if not by agreeing to enter the war in alliance with ourselves and Russia, then at least by forbidding the repulsive and lucrative trade between American businesses and Herr Hynkel's Germany. It seems a bit of tall order, but I should not mind seeing America again, if only this time we are not compelled to go near bloody Arkham. London at the moment's a depressing ruin, and it might do us both a bit of good to get out of the country for a while...and to stay there, if there should turn out to be a shred of truth in the Prime Minister's distressing vision of the post war Britain as a beastly Socialist forced-labour camp erected on a national scale. Who knows? This might be just the break that we've been waiting for."

It is of course a pity that these notes, with their suggestion of a planned desertion, did not surface before Quatermain and Murray had both broken contact with their supervisors and had disappeared into the vast American interior. We have had intimations since of their continuing U.S. activities, including characters resembling the pair occurring in a modern "beatnik" novel, but to all intents and purposes we must assume that they've defected and will thus not be returning to these shores. Our best hope might be the suggested plan to form a stand-in team, but barring this and until such time as any further information is available as to the whereabouts of Murray and her friends, then I suggest that we consider this file closed.

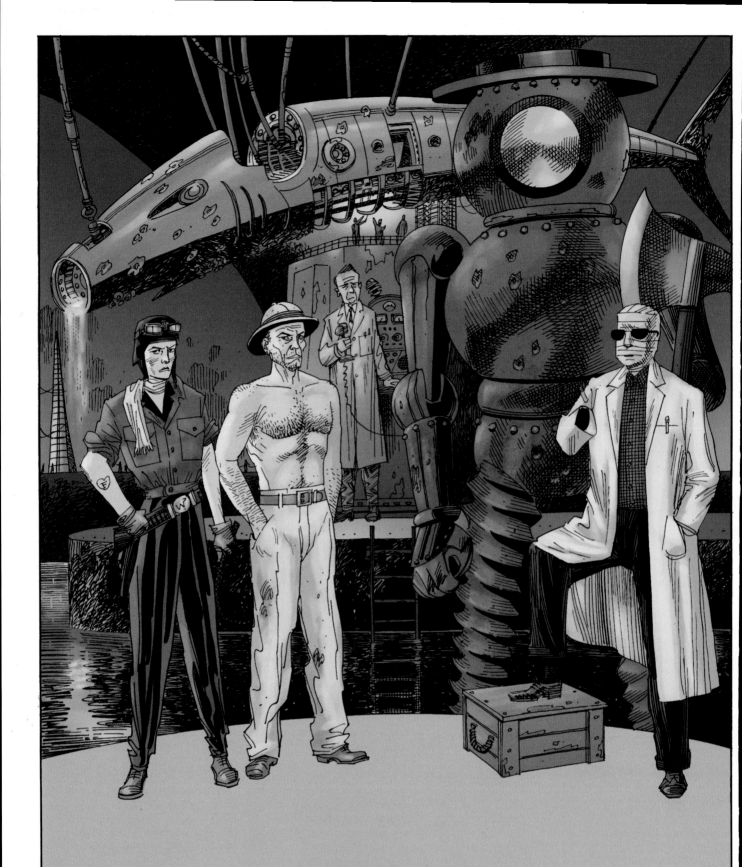

THE WARRALSON TEAM, 1946-1947

When by 1946 it was apparent that Miss Murray and her colleagues had deserted our employ by going missing in America, MI5 elected to replace the group with surrogates in an attempt to recreate the impact of the 1898 ensemble, widely held to be the most dynamic incarnation of the team. To this end they enlisted the distinguished Women's Air Force Captain, Miss Joan Warralson as team leader, evidently seeking a replacement for the capable Miss Murray. Lacking Captain Nemo and his *Nautilus,* the engineer and icthyologist Professor James Grey was recruited in his stead, while standing in for Allan Quatermain was William Samson Junior, the son of an Intelligence employee, who'd already proved his mettle in Afghanistan. One Dr Peter Bradey, who'd duplicated the experiments of Hawley Griffin, became a second (and distinctly second rate) Invisible Man, and rounding out the team in lieu of Mr Hyde was a somewhat dilapidated 1930s prototype robotic man of military origin and known as the Iron Warrior. Fraught with tensions from the outset (Miss Warralson's previously unsuspected tribadism and Mr Samson's attempts to recreate the Murray/Quatermain relationship with her being just one example), the new group was disbanded after just one unsuccessful sortie against a pairing of pirate-slaver James Soames and Italian master-criminal Count Zero.

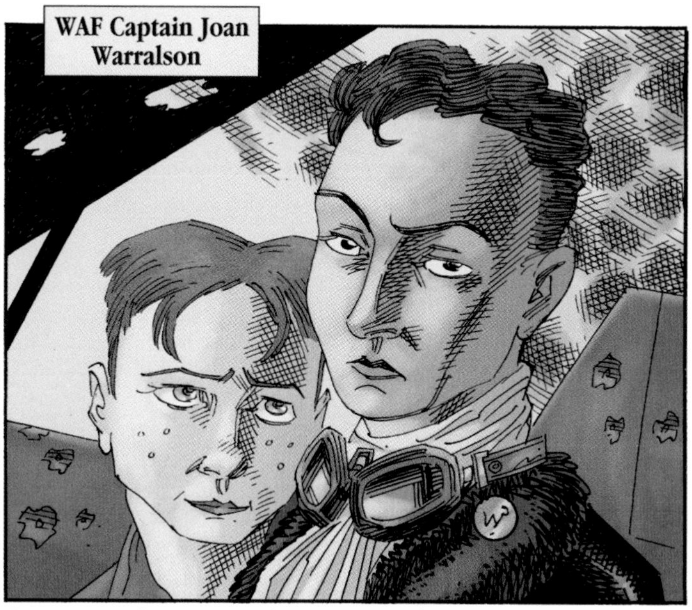
WAF Captain Joan Warralson

Captain Warralson was used by the War Office as a female role model to attract girl recruits during WW1. Not entirely 'as other women,' she has resided since then with her companion 'Frecks,' apparently an old school chum.

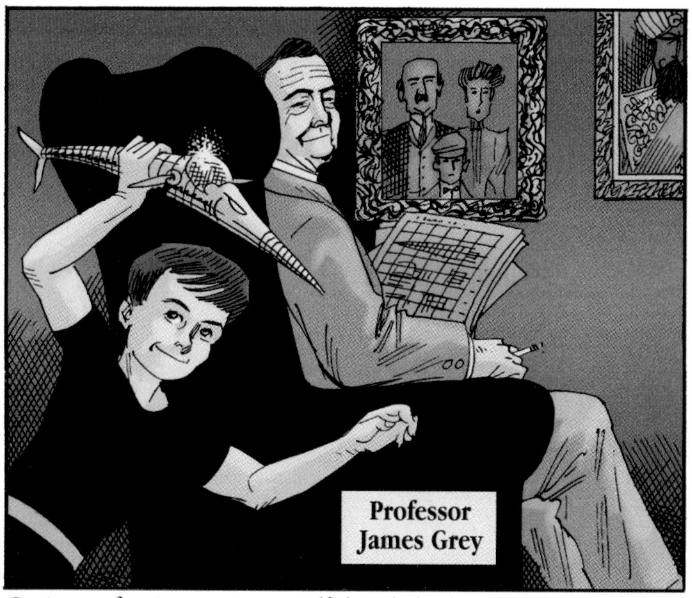
Professor James Grey

Designer of an impressive swordfish-styled submarine, Professor Grey claimed to have been inspired while travelling, during boyhood, upon the original *Nautilus,* which apparently rescued him from the attack which killed his parents during the 1898 Martian Invasion.

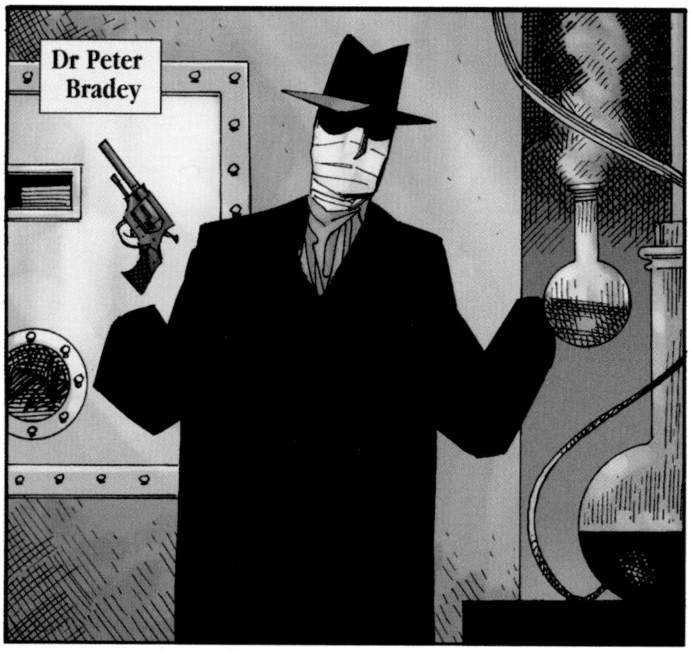
Dr Peter Bradey

Recreating Hawley Griffin's original experiment from discovered notebooks, Dr Bradey successfully achieved invisibility, but was less impressive as an operative due to his compulsive chain-smoking and coughing fits, which, upon numerous occasions, gave him away.

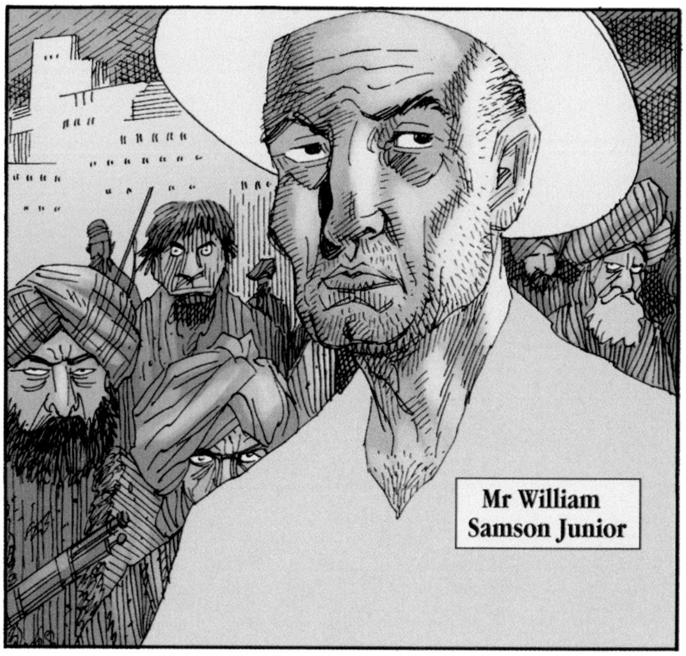
Mr William Samson Junior

After many notable exploits in Afghanistan alongside his deadly cricket-bat wielding colleague Chung, the younger Mr Samson resigned from the substitute team when his advances towards Captain Warralson were predictably rebuffed, and returned to Kabul.

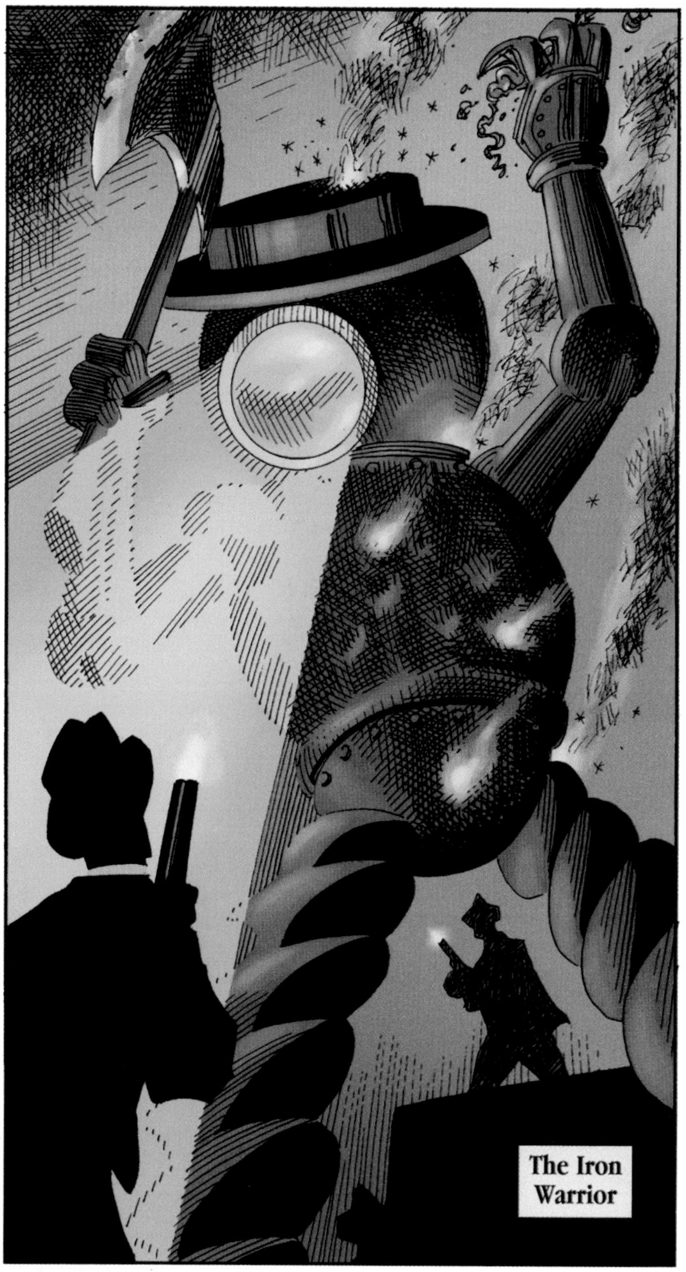
The Iron Warrior

A faintly desperate attempt to lend the new team Edward Hyde's ferocious power, this 1930s military automaton with its oversized chopper was dangerous even when switched off. The abortive Soames/Zero battle concluded with the Iron Warrior's accidental explosion.

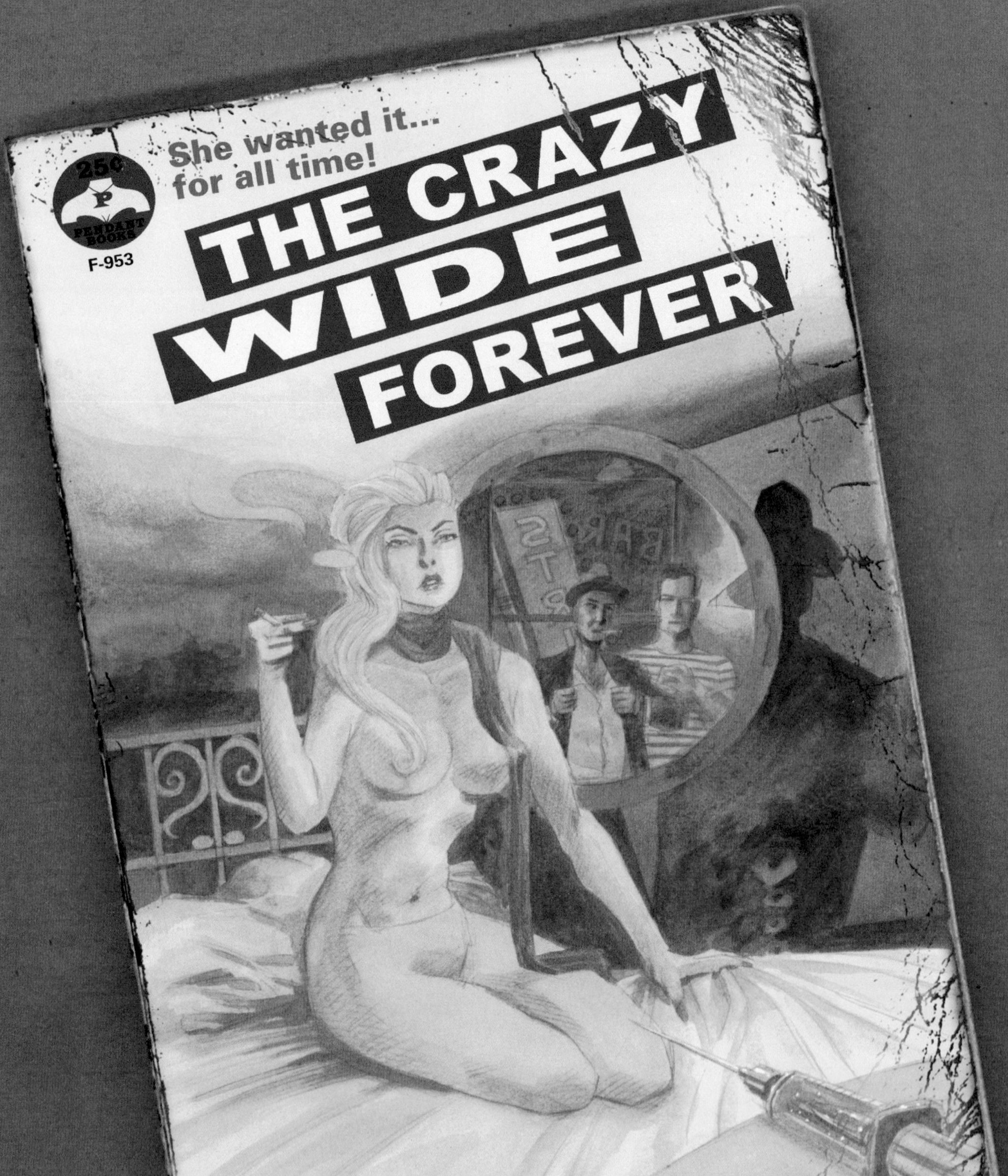
She wanted it...
for all time!
25¢
P
PENDANT BOOKS
F-953
THE CRAZY
WIDE
FOREVER
SAL
PARADYSE
Complete and
Unabridged

1 Burped out of a beanery one more warm molecule jigged in a loud gas of sailors an whalers an failers ole fellers an cellarboys all a big comforting Buddha fart sneaked out and leaked to the street seeping down Vanness Avenue pungent and not yet diffused in confetti stars exploding weddingcake neon and dimestore night angels who wipe down their counters in sad little ovals glass track bird-eye black through the morgue dust & so forth & so forth into the blue wonder of evening with side-walk unrabbled unspooled like a typewriter ribbon got dropped bunchin up inta hillup an trough an the roll an the coast of it tempting the feet to a hot trot gavotte where the shoe come down chik on the typewalk chachik chik there's metalpress letters vowel horseshoes nailed onto the soles stamp-ing accident prose on the asphalt with every step every bum-stumble footslap tataptap you roll up an over each brow with a peek from the peak at the road rumpled onward to Fisherman's Wharf an the bay an the burn o' burlesque bulbs an bars in a glimmery mirrer o' brine what a night what a sight what a sigh what a kick in the eye that's Satori to you son an on down you run from illuminate state from the height from the light the true view and descend into Maya again to the valley an dammed if you don't fergit all what you knew on the brink in the sleep of the deeps badoobeep badoobeep where the hunchback horizons crowd in black as crow soot as creosote crouchin like criminals then crawled up over the crest creeps that powder blue Dodge with its lamps bright white dynamite fine in the damp in the wheezin ole dogfog an rolls in to graze up the curb right ahead and stops dead with a shudder right down to the chrome an it's almost some sweet heartbroke waitress et out in sum mattress-jazz moth-sweat motel room when gray railroad dawn tried to peep through the blind from outside with one hand in its baggy tramp pants an the Dodge kills its beams an a back door uncracks like a ladybug's jacket with one corner flakin its paint on the scrape o' the street where dumb dinosaur ants struggle hopeless in tar pit trap spilt soda scum an unfoldin out frum sum rear seat in a fresh hatched flamingo of movie star nylon she come with a double bass swivel an sway a drum jumble of heels on the street there in front of you blockin the way in her second skin skirt feet apart in a capital A and her body commences the alphabet of a whole language right there buddy right there not three feet away in this cornerbound crease of the phosphorous Universe with all its cheerleaders cracker crumbs moonlight an cheese an volcanoes an switchblades an sweepstakes an Irishmen sleeping through trolleycar stops an made new evry immanent immigrant instant the fresh breath of Now Tathagata Now everything Now an yr eyes flutter up zigzag swoop over hipswell an pelvis an strut an jut bugs to a flashlight her face candlewhite Sunday ice cream its flame curlin out on the wind fudge sauce auburn an likewise the scarf in a twist at her throat tussled also an there in th' bottle green glass of her eyes I first see the Forever wide crazy and bottomless em'rald Pacific with conches an corals in columns of weed color light an th' centuries shoalin all solemn like turtle in mystical hieroglyph shells through the full fathom five of her stare's Saratoga you fall in an don't take a breath till you drag yrself drippin back out agin back on dry land an she calls you the name that your own Sainted mother bestowed calls you Sal calls you Paradyse tells you she's Minnie but never mooched ner kicked a gong an the Dodge runs its engine an seen through the wipe o' the wind-screen her man sittin quiet at the wheel with his eyes same as hers full o' years what he shouldn't of owned so they say to get inna the car but yr still in the heavenly swill of the alkahole where alla this is adventure in newspulp cologne Captain Easy boots Lone Ranger mask and why not and why not throw yrself careless out on the dice diamond bosom of chance with the rattling stop signs holes shot in the carcass of dark bleeding fire an if in this world we can't trust midnight caprice then what can we trust answer me that you get in an it pulls away into the mystery into yr luck an yr puff an yr life -

2 O little did we know but Dr. Sachs was settin fer us even then an comin through the night air soup of cotton candy snatch an motor oil in paranoiac radio transmissions relayed back n forth on cockroach aerial conducted by electrolytic sweat o' bad Ed Dunkel rollin lushes at the depot an the guilty traitor spoff o'married cops collectin payments offa wrung out gals what work the docks - Ole Dr. Sachs slips wi' the ease o' breeze roun' Chinatown in alley steam firecracker strings o' light an golden flags or lazy drums his mand'rin hypodermic fingernails on mustard mess an mottled mica in the restless fidget of a diner 4AM with outside pale light in the east an all the few first birds the virtuosos warbling silver frills to flounce an bounce off an ionosphere all hunkered down aginst the cold afore o' sunrise heavy with the lonely radio ham voices o' retired storekeepers schoolteachers stump preachers drunk in Delaware in Denver wireless whales what wail their woes across the deep salt ether squeal an pop an static crackle flak an Dr. Sachs stirs alla that into his schnapps an snaps it back lips smack the whole great sparklin dark burns like a warehouse in his throat on its way down damn if he don't know everthin ole Dr. Sachs gets it fum taxi hacks clairvoyant strippers pinkface laundry girls in hot cross ponytails gattlin' Chinese fum out the backroom ole queens wisprin over cocktails stuff what blind bums mumble in their sleep an evryone's his snitch his stoolie nothin gets by Dr. Sachs not even words spelt out from alphabet block accident by harmless babbies dribblin in their bibs their cribs he reads it all reads the whole town five minits top t' bottom like some big stone Mayan sports page stubs his gage an goes an flows he's opium tar it skitters on hot foil he's printers ink what pools and pours in gutter subway ditch n drain he slides across the rooftops sizzles in the wires an aerials an dawgs awl whine n teaheads git the fear n Dr. Sachs flaps black above the chimney stacks sad sacks the railroad tracks what run like suicide into the weeds he feeds on needs an greeds bleeds into telegraph transmissions scrambles messages to random voodoo poetry he is the scrawld phone number what makes lovers fight and I will tell you this of infamy he is Mahatma in the Mission district's tinders he makes winos dream that there's no cigarette alight between their fingers uz they slobber down to sleep he leaps fum little children's wardrobes he's the blues the news the bruise round momma's eye the East Saint Louis Toodle-oo comin fum somewhere in a shut down barber shop with dead hair like n autumn onna checkered floor he is the Boss of Shame his voice a gila monster lisp all stept-on leaves an creak o hangin tree an muttrin wind through potters field an some say as his tailored suit's got pictures painted on all over like a carny hoardin men with gator faces Fiji mermaid in a pickle jar a map of Egypt an the martyrdom o blessed Cath'rin there on one lapel Jack Dempsey on the other Borgia popes all roun his hatband Lusitania sinkin on his fine silk tie his breath is smoke n aniseed an on his white Italian shoes is spats of iridescent rattlesnake n cufflinks made fum smoldrin meteorites n chews a toothpick nail fum the true cross an Dr. Sachs swells up n swallers all th' fire escape n washin line n silhouetted tenement n lonesome attic lamp through threadbare curtains n he fills the quilted moonless sky tobacco stain eyes blottin out the Milky Way an poses like some Sat'day fiend fum RKO fee fie foe fum drummin acrost almighty heaven an by gum there's nothin an nobody he can't reach what with them spidercrabs them peril-yeller claws in evry mortal heart n through the clouds right now right now he's squintin down fer us an our blue Dodge an smiles n shows his marble teeth with names an dates all chiselled on an sure enough his phlegm is green ball lightnin when he spits -

3   Back in the wild ride crankin winder down to flip a butt a tiny red hot acrobat it somersaults away towards the smearin streakin road below an gone an sinkin back in an ass-plastrin' bake o Summer leatherette I'm prop'ly innerduced t' Minnie n her boyfriend English Al who's drivin face all dashlit green n Halloween knows all about me me n Dean flat broke n sacred drivin down between the big black sheets o sputnik spangled space above Highway beneath us with that white line stitchin 'long its hem unpicked an ravelled out t' destiny n Minnie sez how everythin's a vital mission n they're in *The Thin Man* English Al an she they're Willum Powell n Myrna Loy spinnin about th globe in diner cars n great cruise liner Queens n limousines avertin villainies n rightin ruin an ya buy it all the whole thousand n one Arabian nights t' hear her delicate best Sunday china voice with all its tinkling silverware an what a tale boys what a tale she tells above the motor's satisfied tin pusscat purr of lo an ho an long ago in London Town a-drown in deep deerstalker fog an how a mad perfesser an a wily oriental demon come ta blows with airboats spoffin flame down on sum grum Victoriolan slum beedum beedeebeedeebeedum n both t' grief they cum n sum say as their seed is feudin yit in grandsons far across the cold Atlantic settled in Amerikee where has the devilish chinee an offspring sprung son of a son o that inhuman Fu man Dr. Sachs by name a roamer come by choo choo train down Frisco way they say a fishhook finger sunk in evry pie in evry goosebump thigh in evry last gasp sigh n blackened spoon n goon n meat rack smudge muff magazoon the purest pizen e'er distilled swilled through the town's drain veins n straind brains Dr. Sachs by name an here's the rub bub his ole grandad's foe no reglar Joe but the Napoleon o crime n craft this mad perfesser Moriarty his own grandson his own line all unbeknown aint no one else but Dean machine oil mean Dean Moriarty unsuspectin spielin wheelin dealin words in quickfire spit through pill dry lip

th' monkey wrench flip an be Jaysus hip the very soul o Hip itself wuz in the direst danger dum dum dum an that's how English Al an Minnie put it down for me an axed did Dean been seen or where o where he be an in th' thrall o this appall recall a date not too late right tonight a time a place a rant n rhyme at the Spaghetti Fact'ry in among the nod n bleu French fume cats mumblin masterpieces t' their scrappy armpit beards n Dean hd flipped his wrench an said that he'd be there you understand maybe git sum student o litrachure back inna sack n Al he looks to Min n spin the Dodge aroun n uptown bound an ax the way to this event then take off so the burnd up rubber smell like some Ceylon plantation all ablaze all bats n lemurs bustin from its foliage n spark n so into th' vasty danks o dark we skwheel an thru th' movin glass n gen'ral worn-out quality o streetlite San Francisco looks th' cover fum a painted pulp with colors lurid faded deep sincere rose petal maiden aunt pinks a graverobber blue all run together in th' rear view n we go t' rip th' Torquemada corset offa treason -

4   Now he is the very devil Dr. Sachs an wurse he is the champ o' hell ousts Faust whups Krupp makes Nero zero he's Mephrisco Bayzeebub incarnate Lucifornia Satandreas Asmode o Day deeoodah gla boo zoo bah zo zee zah dirty Pennecost his name in asslick pussyluppin tongues o fuck n fire n he don't make no pact not wi' juss any two bit purgatory punkass pup o' pah pah pah pah pandemonium not Dr. Sachs he deal with top hat hoo hah Haiti cemeterrians shoot craps wit' jackalheads in Memphis alleyway clinches hiz biz wit' titan ole boy Greek godpappy baby eaters neat 'z pie slicks in a fix onna four horse apocalix got that great twat o' Revelations turnin' tricks n sells out alla man an babykind to pinkbrain gumball Martians cum fum outta space n places west o' there where Great Cthula does the hula hula n ole Yoggy Soggy rools n drools n creeps croon n th' chaoz crawls n Dr. Sachs got contacts contracts compacts dun in blud in jiz in cat tears n Death Valley rain writ out in smoke fum opium n rum n nun-cum n th' sweet sweet sweat o Dizzy's brow in puke in pus in piss on parchmint n papyrus King Tut catgut Cat'lic priestskin on the dried fried hide o Rin Tin Tin does Dr. Sachs n calls his markers in cuz boy tonight's th' night th' snakebite prizefite Mardi Gras o' mayhem murk n moanin' Macbeth merder comma monstruss masterplans an crapped out captured cornered careless inna cunt hair crosshairs o' this crimminent catastrophe none other than unclean machine-oil Dean who broke hearts fixed exhausts charm wealthy widders fum the trees juss takin' off his shirt n talk rings round th' mighty dawn at Big Sur n at Berkley with Bull Hubbard sleepin' innercent as babies inna backseat unna dark dilutin' down inta lagoon blue n laburnum ore Dean Moriarty who right now right on the burnin' hot Zen billspike o' this moment is all busted mussed concussed n trussed up inna cellar subterraneous n secret unner th' Spaghetti Fact'ry one wall wet n glistnin' gray like toad tongue in yer stannard yeller flyshit light you understand n Dr. Sachs strut down n up n forth n back black whacko cackle thretnin' knuckle crack his shadder flung up tall 'z Plastic Man behine him n in one claw hand a big ole nitemare outhouse needle fulla calibrated serum look like locust syrup glass gleam ting in lightbulb swing n drippin at the tip plip plip which Dr. Sachs explain accordin t' sum ole Republic serial script in hiz flophouse fire matchbook whisper how this is some Aztec virus junk what's stewed n stilled fum foot long cennipedes n boiled up maniac spines n jimson weed iguana glands blood 'v a screamin schizophrenic syphilitic saint n such how juss one jot o this hot junglerot shot up th' mainline whatcha got is right away alla these Quetzacoatl vampire dybbuk ghouls an ziggurat-hat gore-drunk gods on welfare homin' in like whinin thousan-year ole junkie warhead missuls on that exac' jaggid narco frequency what's now within yer brainstream n yer bloodstem alla them death jaguars n corn-bloodiers n parrotsnakes cum pourin downa waveband slap inside yer head they got 'emselves new handles better threads more suited t' our peasant present time n sticky pastel polyester clime with these Great Old Uns known more lately 'z th' Nova Mob pug-ugly spirits real fun guys fum Yuggoth dun up wid a lick o' paint ain't nothin wrong widdat so Narlyhooly haunter o' th' dark what done fer poor young Bobby Blake now calls hisself as th' Sublim'nal Kid jumps in an out TV commercials so's ya barely see holds signs up say fuck granma an drink pepsi an bow down afore th' Red Chinese an shoot yerself right after this next beer n he ain't but the half of it you take ol' Hastur what they call Unnameable now new improved regrooved answers to Mr. Bradley/Mr. Martin two ole waspy fruits in one suit like when ya fergit ta wind th' camera on double explosure ain't it now n these n all their polterghostly pals r simmrin in the cringe o' th' syringe juss waitin' fer ter git banged inna old Dean Moriarty's veins n brains change alla wirin' round change alla grammer on his pill pop non stop yammer make him nothin' 'cept a smallpox jukebox rattlin toxic tunes Frankenstein propaganda ravin' railin' glos-solollygagger spoutin word disease Cthulhu fhtargle gargle R'Lyeh n bop virus festrin inna ears o' all what listen openin' channels so Sublim'nal crim'nals Mr. Bradley/Mr. Martin n Hamburger Mary alla rest o these primordial yeggs n cosmic dregs n anti matter bums n beggars can seep in yer scooped out skull lay eggs ad jingle caviar control bugs slaver ants is what they are got wiretaps on yer daydreams sex schemes holy blazin visions in their dogditch convict searchlight beams n all yoomanity'll soon be pressin levers in its ratbox gittin monkeyshocks 'z soon 'z Dr. Sachs gits dun with his expository rant whacks that big hypodoomic spike in Dean then shoves him babblin onna stage to rage n roar infect the whole Spaghetti Fact'ry crowd wid sick new language finger-snappin approbation even 'z th' Nova Mob come thrashin down like psychic tapeworm hook itself onna third eye pineal gland the neck hairs stand n juss like that they's in they win n infernal eternal subjuga-tion c'n begin n Dr. Sachs tracks this way n then that his boot heels clackin onna flags he brags he promises alla this awful an stupendous stuff ta Missus Moriarty's bound-up n befuddled boy all sprawled agin the wall afore him in that fact'ry cella fulla ole I-talian migrant worker ghosts what died fum wheat n semolina lung granson o his granpappy's gratest gaslight grudge n Dean looks up n shrugs as best he can wit' alla rope n' dope n' lack o hope but never unnerestimate nobuddy whut gut Master Criminul genes n rag ass jeans like Dean's born onna road wit Burma Shave his birth-sign born in back 'v a junkyard jalopy judderin through Salt Lake City all that preachin n polygamy juss percolatin in down hiz umbilical n never did stop talkin ever since talkin thru creampuff cake n sprayin flakes in Hector's cafeteria thru tetanus tapwater toothpaste suds in Spanish Harlem talk thru cow manure n snow in Colorado n now Denver cannot sleep fer its lost heroes Dean juss smugs shrugs up ut Dr. Sachs an right away starts in wid all his piston injin perfect prattle prose "Yes yes I am of course aware o all these matters you describe an have in fact give them my full considera-tion but it seems t me there's one thing you're fergettin in all this n what it is is Schopenhauer what said how God is th' creator o the Universe you unnerstand but in th' imminent sense rather thun th' transitive that's right so in my comprehension o these facts I must conclude how you n me n that syringe n these spaghetti splinners onna floor n the almighty state o California herself yes yes that's right all busted inna being just this second now with all our mem'ries o Grandfeudin' Fathers milk duds dodos Mayan gods n such all come inta existence th' same time n I can't help but think how all this unnermines yer supposition o sum family vendetta immemorial when there weren't nuthin here but nuthin one half second back you unnerstand n all this spinnin world plainly th' vain dance o illusion which puts me in mind o certin episodes what I may not have previously bin forthcomin over these concernin incidents an' items from my disaffected youth like this one Puerto Rican kid knew how to blow smoke out the corners of his eyes n suck his own dick back there up in Booneville reformatory..." Dean runs on an on that way he had back then like evry conversation wuz juss end-less white line road he'd gotta burn up on his way t' th' celestial Monet smudge o th' horizun n ole Dr. Sachs sags flags collapses back t' sit on flour bags n ole pasta sacks jaw slack his wicked works hung wiltin fum his wizened wizzerd lizzerd fingertips cain't git a wurd in edgewise an muss wait like evvabody else fer Dean t' lose hiz steam what he's got more uv 'n a reverse Chinese laundry what takes clothes in clean n sends 'm back near black wi' bullshit so the mental institution monolog slogs on whilst up above out in the clammy satin glove o San Francisco night there's foetus lightnin kickin in th' stretched-thin belly o the sky an trouble backed up out th' drains n sewers like a mess o poor rejected baby alligaters all grew up n hungry fer revenge like all of us n the blue Dodge roars on non stop thru storm an slap an puddle slop like Continental Op on rum run bloody pulp n thun-der n the dark split n th' world undone -

5   Now me an Min an English Al wuz pals in swerve n veer careen screen idol style n while this vileness wuz unfolded we wuz wailin up the wide wet way wit' water droplets wobblin up the glass juss like ice skaters lost their nerve an teeterin' back towardsa safety o th' rinkscreen's edge an there's no time ta lose Al's ridin a short fuse o bad news got them minutes left ta save th' planet blues hunched in abuv th' wheel he's lookin grim Jim an the baldin' rear tyre squeals the way he feels he's tense n juss about t' jump the corral fence o common sense n right then Min starts in ter hum sum

dum n humdrum number cum fum offa radio sum croony moonyjoony freshman matin' call what y' recall fum Summer afore last *Immortal Love* 'r sum such nuisance nunsince bland n canned out 'v Amerkin Bandstand Land n right away Al's big knot shoulder muscle slacks relaxes n he settles back there inna driver's chair cranks downa window lets th' wind slick back hiz hair an dam if he ain't joinin in t' sing along wit' Min both grinnin now like Dr. Sachs ain't gonna doom damn an destructify Dean Moriarty n the hole world both right after these commercials n when I'm impertinent enuff t' mention all this smoochy stuff Min sez how while back she n Al wuz in New York where Hyman Solomon fuck sea-heart sailors inna washroom ut th' Port Authority scream "feed me I'm a Jew" at Rabbis n sing holy holy holy Willyum Blake almighty in th' beat up negro dawn n Min an Al back then sit talkin all one night wid wud-be Hoagy Carmichael song ritin' genwine genie-ass up in sum old cold water tenement next thing ya know they're lissnin onna radio show by late nite firelite glow n Lo it's their life story bin stole whole n stuck inside a song immortal love immortal love immortal lop op op op op op pom an when I heard that an I sore the smile what sparked between um then I knew anew thut it wuz true what I'd first seen thur in hur eyes th' crazy wide forever n then English Al he hits the brakes n takes th' blue Dodge halfway uppa curb out front o th' Spaghetti Fact'ry n we're spillin out inta the shuv un shout makin the scene eyes out fer Dean who's nowhere t' be seen n so we go low shumblin' downa cellar stair an there right there he is in sideshow Major Domo full flow go man go n Dr. Sachs juss settin dazed crazed n amazed wit dat soul-poison icepick hypodermic tricklin fum its pointy prick there clickin tickin fore n aft atween hiz fingertips n wam bam straight up English Al's Tom Mix Bill Boyd Floyd Patterson dun up in wun he guns hisself acrost th' cellar's fungal floor n scraps n slaps n smacks Sachs who snaps back on th' attack both 'v um wrasslin in spaghetti dust while Min steps in cuts Dean loose wit a switchblade hatpin alla time him keepin up his furthermores n heretofores n yesyesyes that's right that's right that way he had you unnerstand n alla sudden strugglin' unner English Al ole Dr. Sachs cracks n by accident he jacks all dat cake froster fulla fearful fluid fantoms smack right inna hiz own groin his bulgin' eggwhite stare flaps back n Dr. Sachs start slappin mat n foamin fum the thighs n in hiz eyes surprise to realize how all them Mayan monster boys gonna be teemin streamin inna forebrain backbrain wuss thun Night Train spout their virus gibb'rish out his mouth n wid a wild old-fangled strangled cry he bust fum out the celler up the stair hell bent intent on pukin out his pois'nous purple parlance on the patrons o this poetry affair but Min's prepared an out her bag she grab a neat no-nunsense needle uv hur own turns out as Novocain is what it is havin anticipated as these mental maladies o bygone Yucatan get spread fum head t' head in word o' mouth n Min wades in jumps up on Sachs's back n hikes that spike right ouch aw jesus thru his chalky cheek an inta gum n off the scrabblin babblin Doc gets flung as desp'rit on he run invade stage n get set t' rage all o th' uncaged Nova mugwumps 'v ar modern age down onna audience all hushed n reverent n hip but soon uz he tries makin wit' da lip all th' inflection an infection plain refuse t' cum struck dum jaw numb lung bum n stunglin nung mung gung bung n the Mayan mind mob mill confused inside o him n cain't git out n Dr. Sachs that hero bold gon bad juss stand there globberin n slobberin arms thrashin flashin lites n snarlin' rarebit faces meltin in n outta place aroun' him Mr. Bradley/Mr. Martin got three eyes two mouths two noses optical illusion flarin up n gone Sublim'nal Kid inna periph'ral flicker holds up button readin I Like Ike then disappear fasser un fasser in a spittin sputtin an spectac'lar pinwheel Djinn-spin "Everybody down" scream Min an SPOO! ole Dr. Sachs he blew explodes so goo n grue blue glue cerebrospinal spew flew all about th' view leave nuttin' 'cept fer yeller smoke a ringin prehistoric curse n smell kinda like burnin tooth enamel anna whole Spaghetti Fact'ry crowd stand still n stund n speechliss sev'ral seconds 'fore the silence lapses inna claps n finger snaps roars uv applause n nun what don't agree that Dr. Sachs man that cat is real gone n San Francisco life goes gloriously uproariously on n me n Dean n English Al n Min head out inta th' parkin lot t' kick a stick o tea aroun hardly a sound th' rain let up evvawhere wet n fresh n better yet the cushion clouds unpicked n threadbare stuffd wit stars soon evvabody gigglin like kids Min grin with lazy lapid lids lets Dean blow slinky serpent smoke between hr lustruss lappin lips n evry flag o fate n blazin houri o th' Interstate was shimm'rin in a Bodhisattva bedsheet Borealis shook out like a blessin over Golden Gate over the gone world wit' its Vaudeville villains n Paramount paragons its stockyard sunsets fruit crate labels hubcaps children n goodnight n goodnight n goodnight -

DIRECTOR'S SUMMARY Updated 7.9.'56 FYEO G. O'Brien

My dear Gerry,
Here's the most recent summary of verifiable facts (few) and wild rumours (many) that concern the Murray team, although I realise that at the present moment you have far more pressing matters on your plate. I hate to say this, but I really think that Wharton's great political experiment, the Ingsoc years, has rather run its course and had its chips. And while you know I've always had the greatest confidence in you...look how I looked after your interests when the problem with H.W. came up...I must say that your attempt to raise the party's flagging fortunes by re labelling it "New Ingsoc," although well intentioned, is most probably a tactic doomed to failure. I know that you had little choice but to concede to the Conservatives' demands that they be reinstated as official opposition party, especially with those documents concerning government irregularities and illegalities falling into Tory hands like that, and with that step once taken then I understand that furthermore agreeing to demands for an election became something of an inevitability, but I'm afraid to say I really don't see any way that you can win. While obviously in my official capacity as head of Military Intelligence I remain impartial and look forward to working alongside your successor, on a personal level may I say that I have always thought of you as a dear pal and will regret that I could not have done more to avert these difficulties.

Incidentally, I've heard the odd disquieting bit of gossip around Miniluv in Vauxhall that some junior party members, possibly those ghastly oiks at Minitru, are trying to convince you that somehow either myself or my department had a hand in engineering this whole dismal business, even going so far as to claim that MI5 had been responsible for the release of the aforementioned incriminating documents to the Conservatives. Gerry, I'd like to think you know me well enough to realise that I'm not that sort of chap, the sort who'd treat you as a chum while plotting your demise. Wharton, of course, was the exception, and I know that both of us were in agreement in that instance over how it should be handled. So come on, let's not have any more muckraking, accusations or absurd suspicions coming in between us, eh? I'm your most loyal colleague, Gerry. You know that, and I'd advise you to be careful about letting people put about wild stories to the contrary. I say this as a friend who has your own interests at heart.

Returning to the subject of this summary, as I suppose we should, there really has been very little fresh material of late concerning whatever is left of Murray and her squadron of odd fish. As you know, Murray and the younger Quatermain were sent out to America in 1941 in order to persuade the USA that it should cut industrial ties with the Third Reich and join the war on England's side. Unfortunately, the then Prime Minister had by that time been made aware of certain elements within British Intelligence, myself presumably included, who intended with war's end to engineer election victory for an ex military "Strongman" candidate of suitable charisma who'd remodel England along lines which we'd suggested. The Prime Minister, regrettably, hinted as much to Murray just before he sent her and her boyfriend to America, and we believe that this accounts for Quatermain and Murray's failure to return to Britain with the war's conclusion: having had advance word of what was intended for the country, we presume that they elected to go absent without leave in the United States rather than come home to the rigours of BB's regime, to which they clearly felt considerable antipathy. Adding to this the oft expressed resentment of Miss Murray for the machinations of British Intelligence, we believe that Murray and such few associates as she has left should now be classified as hostile.

You will note that there are photographs attached to this report, purportedly of Quatermain and Murray in America, taken on various occasions during the last decade, but we are reluctant to conclude with certainty that the young couple in the pictures are our duo of misplaced adventurers. For one thing, it is difficult to square the age of the depicted couple with that of our former agents. When Miss Murray brought the younger Quatermain back home from Africa to England with her following the unexpected death of Allan senior, his father, in 1901, both she and her young paramour were in their early twenties. This suggests that both must, if they are indeed alive, be currently in their late seventies. Our inference is that at some point over the last forty or so years Murray and Quatermain have somehow found the time to raise a family in secret and have substituted both a son and daughter without letting us become aware of this, or else have by some other means produced a pair of lookalikes as substitutes. I will admit that neither of these explanations are entirely satisfying, but must serve until such time as further facts become apparent.

Whomever the individuals that we have identified as Quatermain and Murray may turn out in actuality to be we do, as indicated previously, have various reports of their activities in the United States across the last ten years. Scant references within the opening chapters of the here appended copy of The Crazy Wide Forever by S. Paradyse suggest that during the last year or two the couple (or a pair strikingly like them) were in San Francisco mixing with bohemians and criminals, while elsewhere in this same text it's implied that our rogue agents were the inspiration for a gramophone recording of the current U.S. type, which similarly is included elsewhere in this dossier but fails to offer any clues to Murray and her partner's whereabouts, being a rather fanciful, insipid and romantic song of little consequence such as Americans are, one supposes, presently in favour of.

According to our source, the duo seem to have laid low while in the U.S. for the most part keeping to small towns dotted about the country such as Maybury or Riverdale and making only infrequent excursions into metropolitan environments like Central City, Gotham, San Francisco, or New York. Perhaps predictably there are reports of Quatermain and Murray seeking out examples of the latest transatlantic novelties and fads, arranging meetings with contemporary recording artists and, on at least one occasion, socialising with the lower echelons of that most startling and deplorable of post war U.S. trends, the "mystery man" or costumed vigilante set. In New York it's alleged that they encountered the supposed goddess of love called Venus and through her met several minor representatives of this unusual sub group such as Gotham's by then elderly Crimson Avenger, film star Linda Turner's close associate the Black Cat, mental marvel Brain Boy and a thirteen-year-old orphan said to draw fantastic powers and abilities from an adjoining extra spatial region or dimension ruled by technologically advanced fly people. Make of this what you will, although the current MI5 position on these U.S. "supermen" is that they are, in every likelihood, a showy and elaborate propaganda exercise of the by now familiar American variety, most probably intended to scare off and put the wind up the Chinese and Soviets, with their reputed supernatural powers supplied by film effect technicians drafted in from Hollywood.

One incident stands out, from the pair's brief unwelcome stay in Maybury, North Carolina, only sketchily recorded in the Maybury press and elsewhere going unreported, this being the couple's unsought intervention into local politics and issues of a sensitive and racial nature. Seemingly, a Negro man from out of town had been held in the Maybury jail on morals charges, including an accusation of procuring, with his two white skinned female accomplices who were apparently twin sisters from the Netherlands. The Negro, possibly suffering from birth deformities, was at the time described as being little more than five feet tall but of enormous bulk and weight with a skin colouring recorded as "matt black" since it apparently was textured in a manner that did not permit even expected normal highlights and reflections. More intriguingly, his two reportedly extremely highly sexed female companions each had a full complement of what were said to be "unusually lifelike and well engineered prosthetic limbs," suggesting they were both multiple amputees of some description, possibly fleeing with their black protector from a touring carnival or freak show such as are still evident in many areas of the West, although bewilderingly the Negro is also implied to be "an aviator" of some kind. Indeed, it seems that once Murray and Quatermain (if that is truly who they were) had freed this fellow and his harem from imprisonment by means of a highly destructive jailbreak, the quintet made their escape in what according to one sheriff's deputy's account was "exactly like one of them there hot air balloons, 'ceptin it weren't." Whatever we may make of this, it stands as the most detailed record of the couple's doings in America.

The only other member of the team still living during wartime in the 1940s was of course the sex change charlatan Orlando, who indeed had thoroughly distinguished his or herself in the conflict with an eventful stint spent in the R.A.F. Orlando seemingly came back to London several times on leave during the early 'forties, but would appear to have slipped silently from view sometime in 1944, as expertly and thoroughly as his former companions. He or she has not been seen or otherwise reported since, although there was a frankly stupid rumour that for a brief period the self styled legendary adventurer evaded notice by the novel means of having been against his or her will transformed into an animal by sorcery.

I think that's pretty much it for the Murray group, and as I mentioned at the outset of this piece, I'm sure you have more pressing matters on your mind at present though before I close there was a bit of unrelated business that I thought I should bring up concerning both my own and poor old H.W's old school chum Johnny Night. As you're aware, Night Industries are helping us tremendously with the unusual equipment they're providing for our projects at Port Merion and elsewhere, and even Sir John's teen age daughter Ema looks extremely promising as a department agent in the future. You may also know that yet another former Greyfriars chap, Al Waverly, is currently constructing an intelligence department under the auspices of the United Nations, and that to everyone's surprise Night Industries received the contract for equipping this new outfit. It appears that the Americans are hopping mad about all this, having expected one of their big companies to get the juicy contract. One of their Central Intelligence lot, F. Gordon Leiter, has made clear that he suspects some English public school old boy conspiracy is swindling Uncle Sam out of his just rewards. Heaven forbid and all that, but I really feel we've made the cousins awfully shirty over this one and should keep an eye out for U.S. retaliation. The most obvious way, of course, would be to sabotage Night Industries or even get at Night somehow. With this in mind we have him under careful watch and also closely monitor Americans arriving in this country, so I can't see any way that they could pull it off without us knowing. So basically problem solved, I think.

Anyway. I believe that's everything. My best to you and Julia, and I'm sure however these elections go you'll be as right as rain in no time. Chin up, eh?

I remain, of course, yours most sincerely,   Robert Cherry

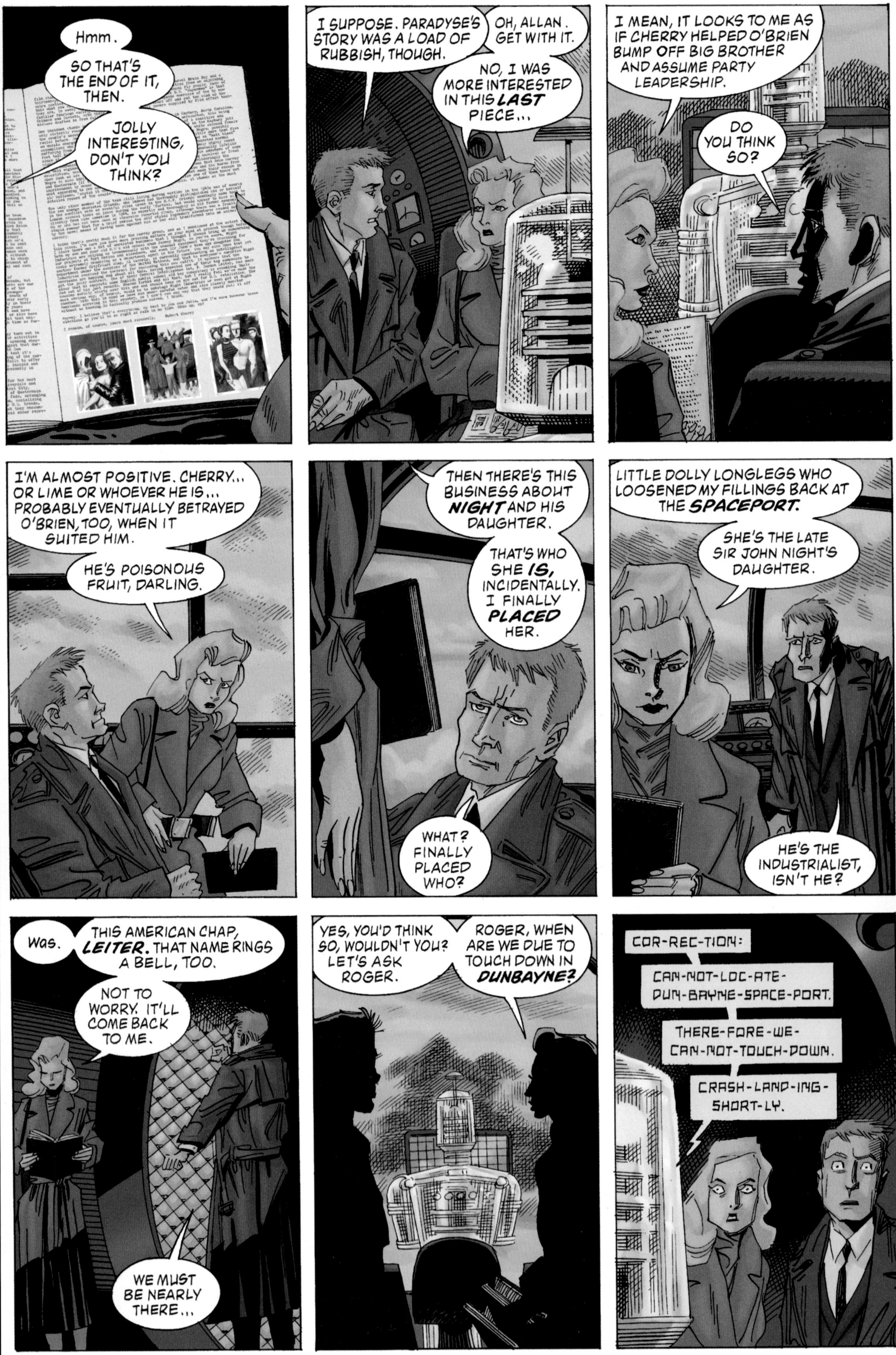
Hmm.
SO THAT'S THE END OF IT, THEN.
JOLLY INTERESTING, DON'T YOU THINK?
I SUPPOSE. PARADYSE'S STORY WAS A LOAD OF RUBBISH, THOUGH.
OH, ALLAN. GET WITH IT.
NO, I WAS MORE INTERESTED IN THIS LAST PIECE...
I MEAN, IT LOOKS TO ME AS IF CHERRY HELPED O'BRIEN BUMP OFF BIG BROTHER AND ASSUME PARTY LEADERSHIP.
DO YOU THINK SO?
I'M ALMOST POSITIVE. CHERRY... OR LIME OR WHOEVER HE IS... PROBABLY EVENTUALLY BETRAYED O'BRIEN, TOO, WHEN IT SUITED HIM.
HE'S POISONOUS FRUIT, DARLING.
THEN THERE'S THIS BUSINESS ABOUT NIGHT AND HIS DAUGHTER.
THAT'S WHO SHE IS, INCIDENTALLY. I FINALLY PLACED HER.
WHAT? FINALLY PLACED WHO?
LITTLE DOLLY LONGLEGS WHO LOOSENED MY FILLINGS BACK AT THE SPACEPORT.
SHE'S THE LATE SIR JOHN NIGHT'S DAUGHTER.
HE'S THE INDUSTRIALIST, ISN'T HE?
Was.
THIS AMERICAN CHAP, LEITER. THAT NAME RINGS A BELL, TOO.
NOT TO WORRY. IT'LL COME BACK TO ME.
WE MUST BE NEARLY THERE...
YES, YOU'D THINK SO, WOULDN'T YOU? LET'S ASK ROGER.
ROGER, WHEN ARE WE DUE TO TOUCH DOWN IN DUNBAYNE?
COR-REC-TION:
CAN-NOT-LOC-ATE-DUN-BAYNE-SPACE-PORT.
THERE-FORE-WE-CAN-NOT-TOUCH-DOWN.
CRASH-LAND-ING-SHORT-LY.

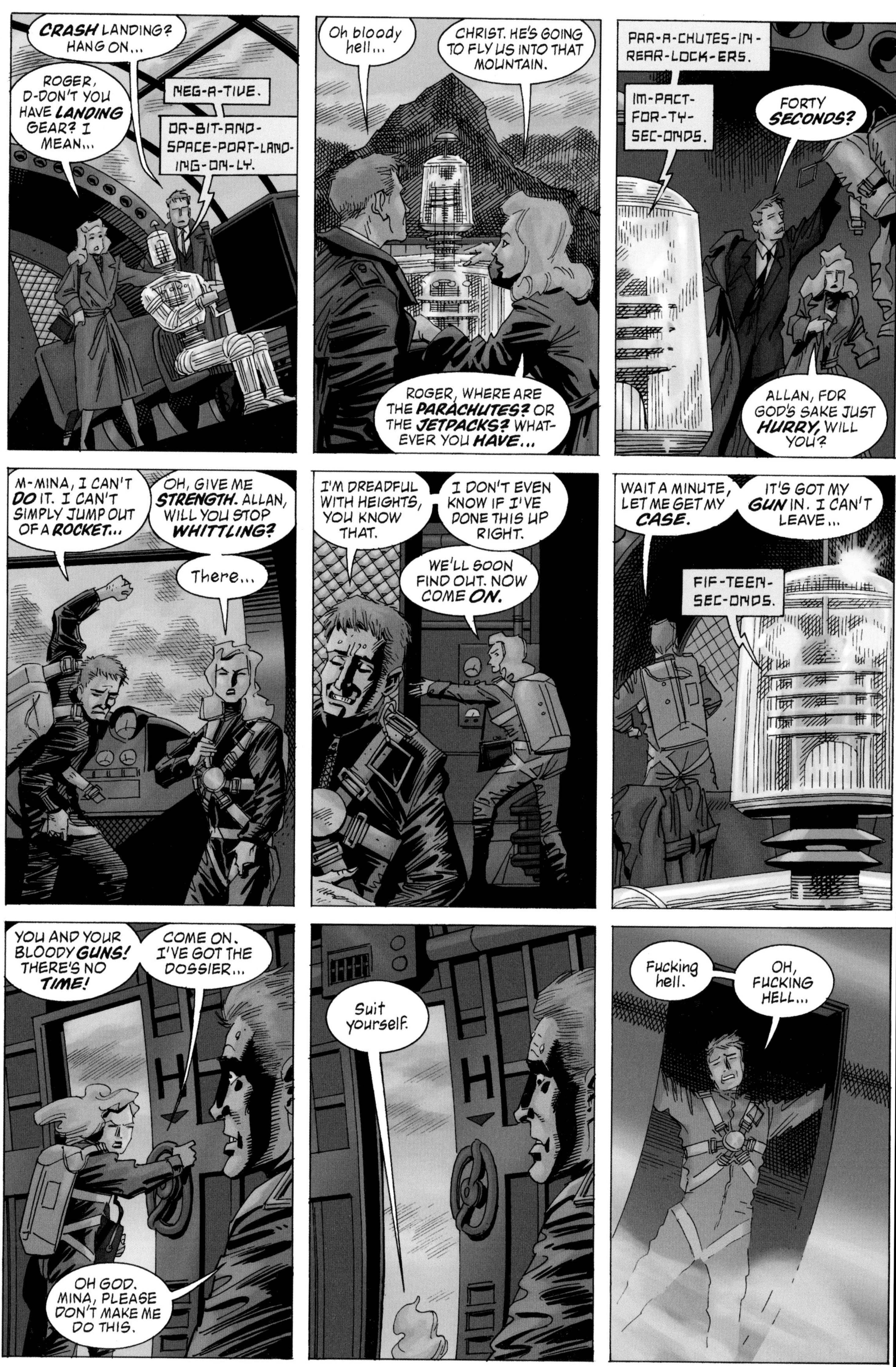

CRASH LANDING? HANG ON...
ROGER, D-DON'T YOU HAVE LANDING GEAR? I MEAN...
NEG-A-TIVE.
OR-BIT-AND-SPACE-PORT-LAND-ING-ON-LY.
Oh bloody hell...
CHRIST. HE'S GOING TO FLY US INTO THAT MOUNTAIN.
ROGER, WHERE ARE THE PARACHUTES? OR THE JETPACKS? WHATEVER YOU HAVE...
PAR-A-CHUTES-IN-REAR-LOCK-ERS.
IM-PACT-FOR-TY-SEC-ONDS.
FORTY SECONDS?
ALLAN, FOR GOD'S SAKE JUST HURRY, WILL YOU?
M-MINA, I CAN'T DO IT. I CAN'T SIMPLY JUMP OUT OF A ROCKET...
OH, GIVE ME STRENGTH. ALLAN, WILL YOU STOP WHITTLING?
There...
I'M DREADFUL WITH HEIGHTS, YOU KNOW THAT.
I DON'T EVEN KNOW IF I'VE DONE THIS UP RIGHT.
WE'LL SOON FIND OUT. NOW COME ON.
WAIT A MINUTE, LET ME GET MY CASE.
IT'S GOT MY GUN IN. I CAN'T LEAVE...
FIF-TEEN-SEC-ONDS.
YOU AND YOUR BLOODY GUNS! THERE'S NO TIME!
COME ON. I'VE GOT THE DOSSIER...
OH GOD. MINA, PLEASE DON'T MAKE ME DO THIS.
Suit yourself.
Fucking hell.
OH, FUCKING HELL...

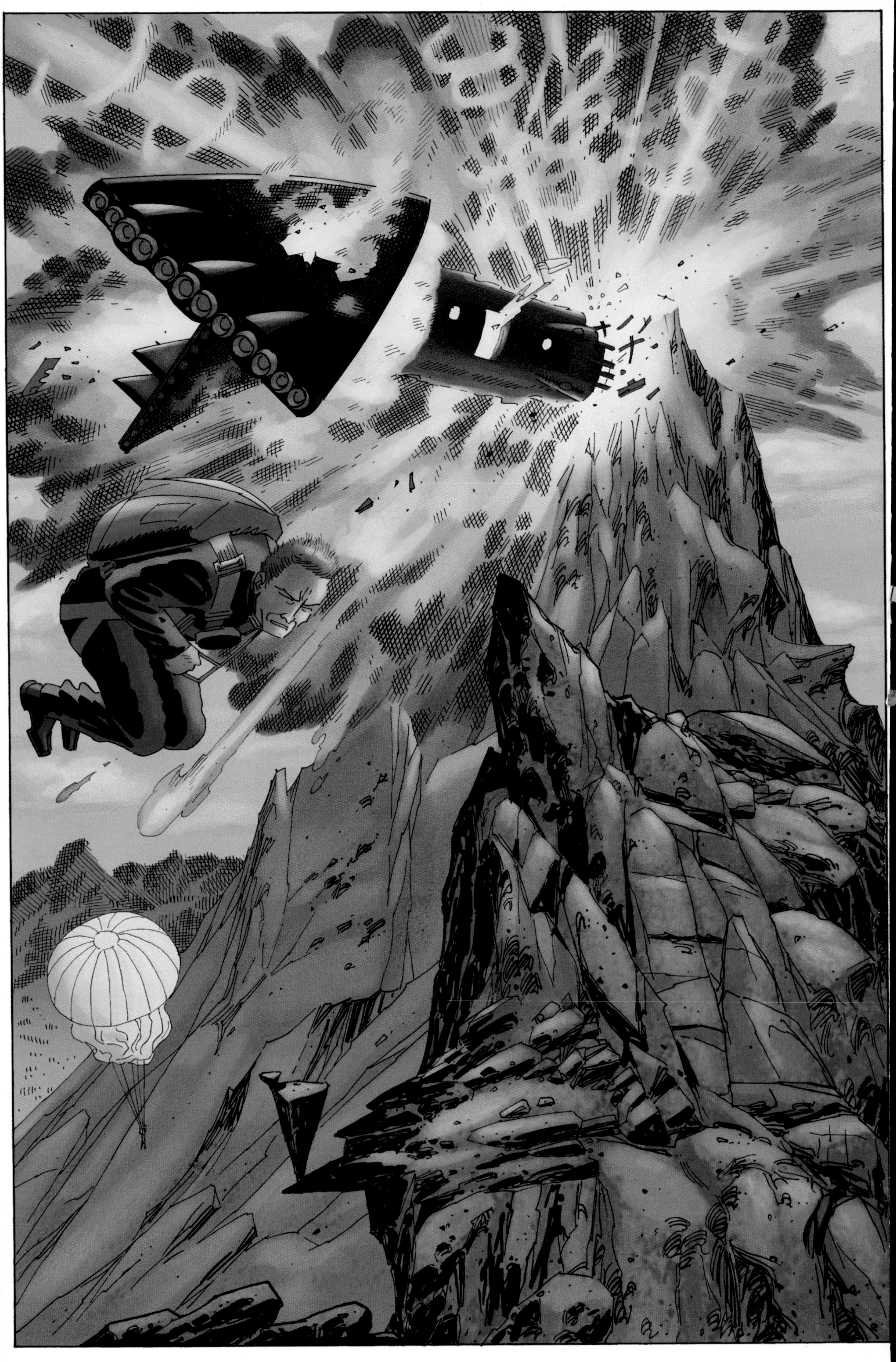

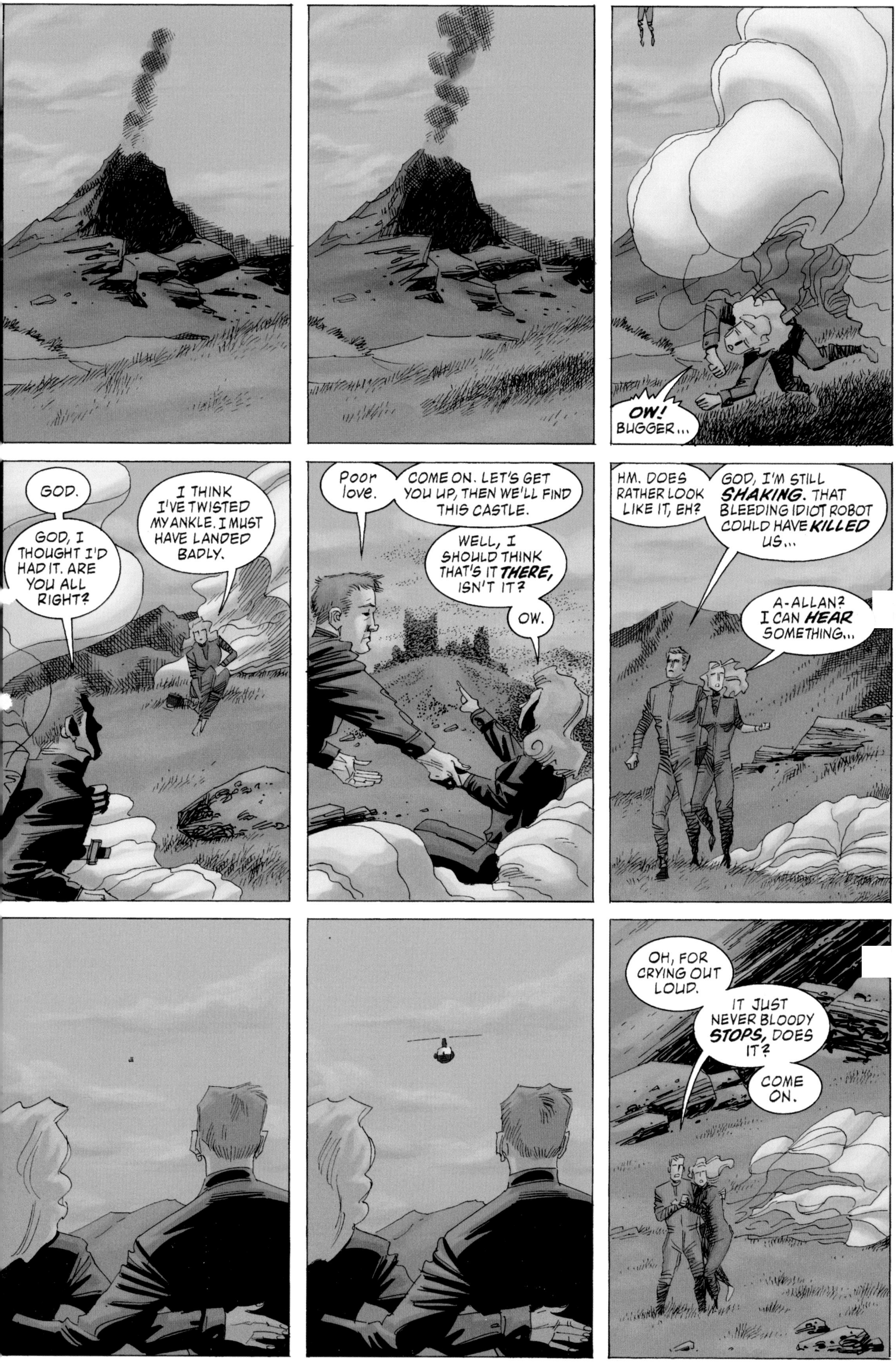
OW! BUGGER...
GOD.
GOD, I THOUGHT I'D HAD IT. ARE YOU ALL RIGHT?
I THINK I'VE TWISTED MY ANKLE. I MUST HAVE LANDED BADLY.
Poor love.
COME ON. LET'S GET YOU UP, THEN WE'LL FIND THIS CASTLE.
WELL, I SHOULD THINK THAT'S IT THERE, ISN'T IT?
OW.
HM. DOES RATHER LOOK LIKE IT, EH?
GOD, I'M STILL SHAKING. THAT BLEEDING IDIOT ROBOT COULD HAVE KILLED US...
A-ALLAN? I CAN HEAR SOMETHING...
OH, FOR CRYING OUT LOUD.
IT JUST NEVER BLOODY STOPS, DOES IT?
COME ON.

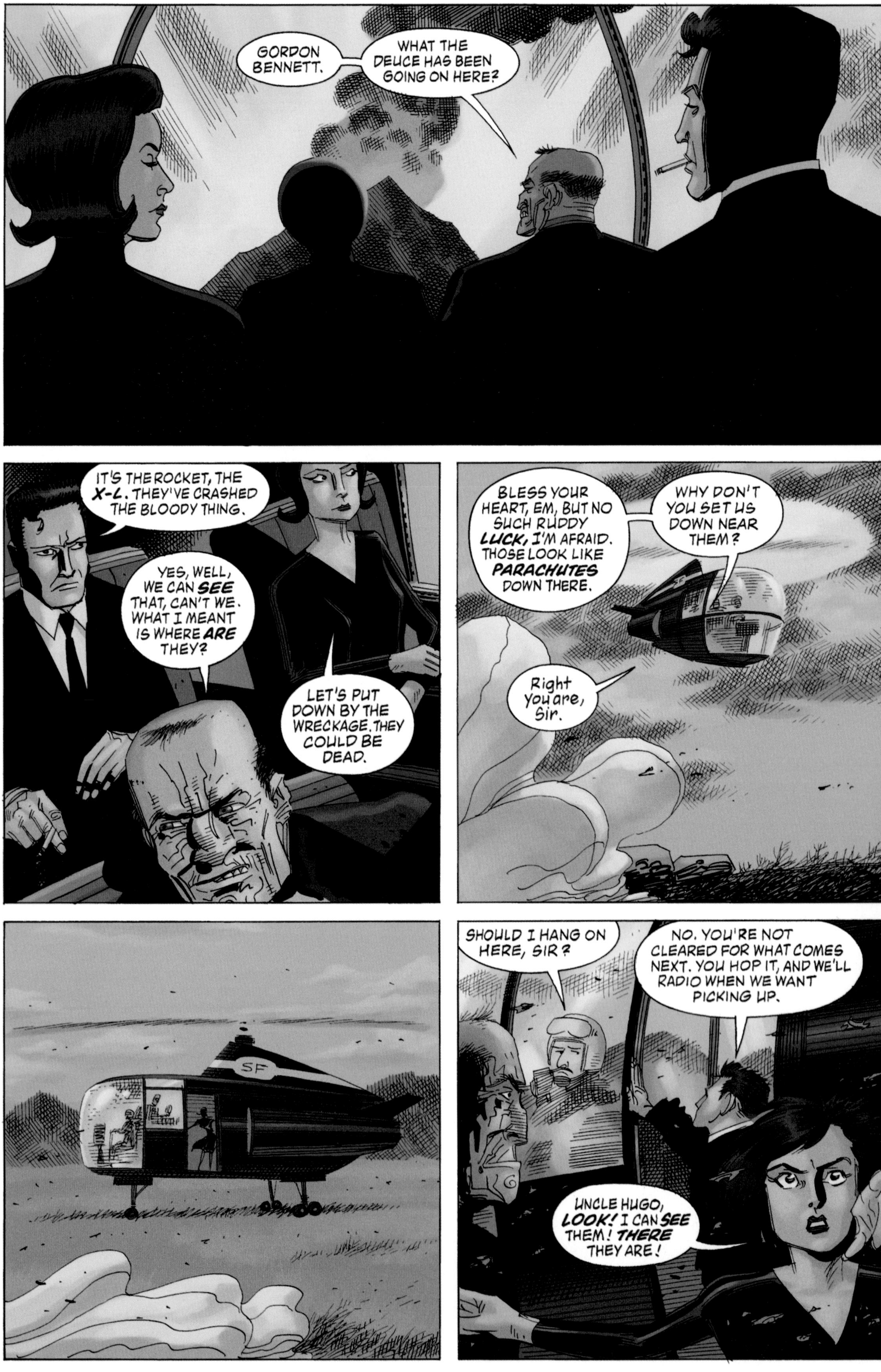
GORDON BENNETT.
WHAT THE DEUCE HAS BEEN GOING ON HERE?
IT'S THE ROCKET, THE X-L. THEY'VE CRASHED THE BLOODY THING.
YES, WELL, WE CAN SEE THAT, CAN'T WE. WHAT I MEANT IS WHERE ARE THEY?
LET'S PUT DOWN BY THE WRECKAGE. THEY COULD BE DEAD.
BLESS YOUR HEART, EM, BUT NO SUCH RUDDY LUCK, I'M AFRAID. THOSE LOOK LIKE PARACHUTES DOWN THERE.
WHY DON'T YOU SET US DOWN NEAR THEM?
Right you are, Sir.
SF
SHOULD I HANG ON HERE, SIR?
NO. YOU'RE NOT CLEARED FOR WHAT COMES NEXT. YOU HOP IT, AND WE'LL RADIO WHEN WE WANT PICKING UP.
UNCLE HUGO, LOOK! I CAN SEE THEM! THERE THEY ARE!

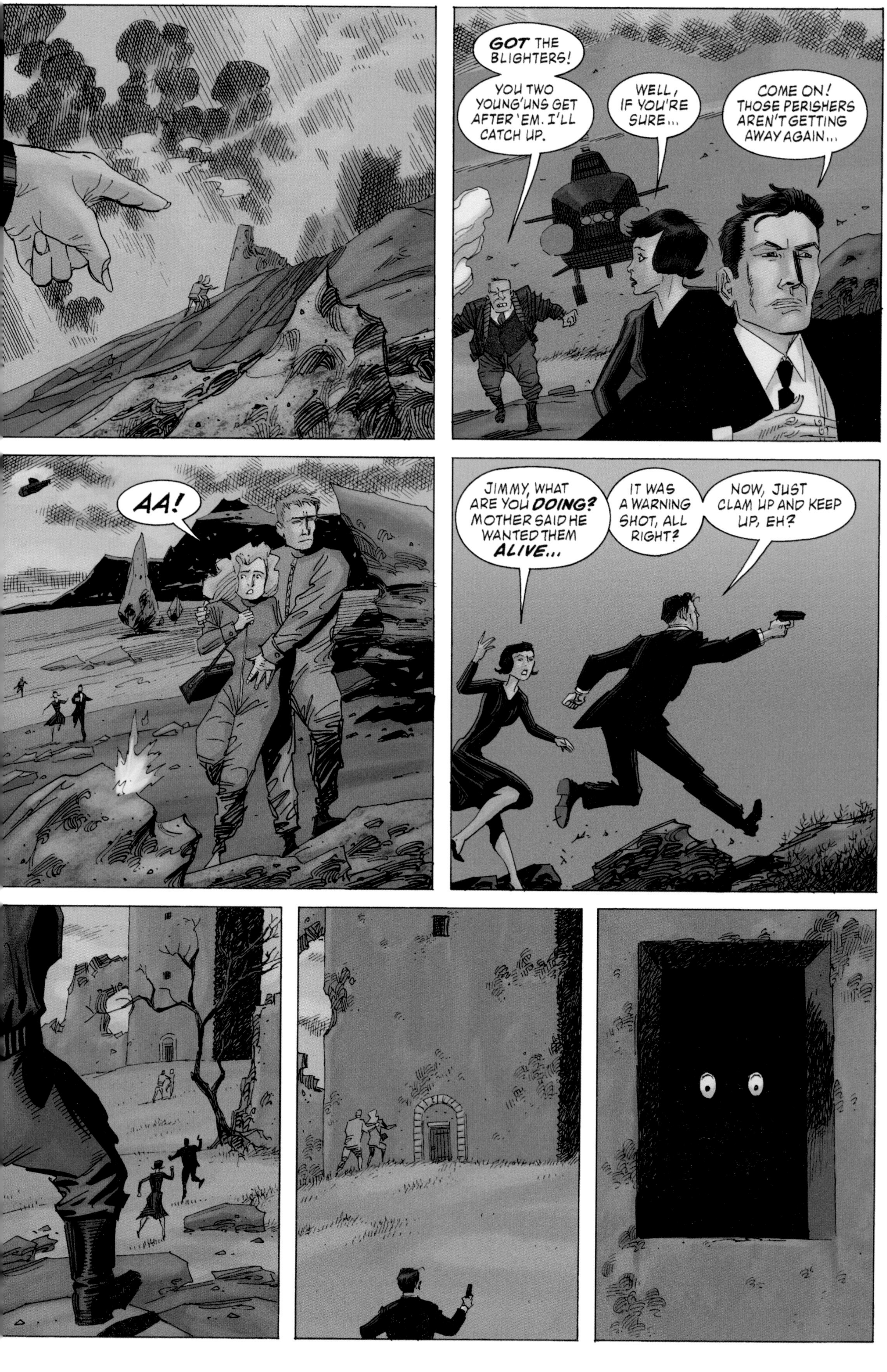
GOT THE BLIGHTERS!
YOU TWO YOUNG'UNS GET AFTER 'EM. I'LL CATCH UP.
WELL, IF YOU'RE SURE...
COME ON! THOSE PERISHERS AREN'T GETTING AWAY AGAIN...
AA!
JIMMY, WHAT ARE YOU DOING? MOTHER SAID HE WANTED THEM ALIVE...
IT WAS A WARNING SHOT, ALL RIGHT?
NOW, JUST CLAM UP AND KEEP UP, EH?

BLOOD-FUDGE AND BLUDGEON AND PRICKS OF THE PARAGONS. THEY COME WITH A GUNPOWDER GUST AT THEIR HOOVES!

FOREMATE AND AFTMATE, CEASE YER SALLYMAPPIN' AND MAKE FIT THE ROSE OF NOWHERE FER ITS ROARING TANTARA!

WIJ ZULLEN HET DADELIJK VOOR U DOEN, ONZE DAPPERE HELD. WIJ ZIJN VERZOT OP U.

WAAR GAAT U HEEN, TROTSE KAMPIOEN DER LIEFDE?

I FARE TO SPARE OUR PIE-FELLOWS, BY MY THUMP! NOW, LOOK LAMPY...

...ERE I SHOUT AWAY THE SURE AND SHIVERY STARS!

HIJ HEEFT EEN SLECHT HUMEUR. LATEN WIJ ONS MAAR AANKLEDEN.

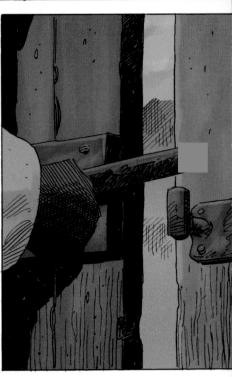

Oh God. Oh God, they're going to get us...

WE'RE ALMOST THERE. WE'RE...

...almost...

Wh-WHAT THE BLOODY HELL IS THAT?

GOOD GOD...

ALLAN, GET DOWN!

GET DOWN AND COVER YOUR EARS! HE'S GOING TO YELL...

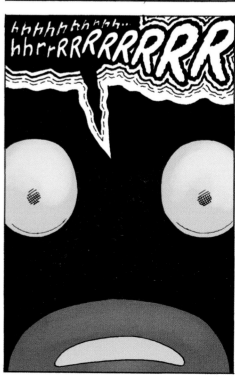
hhhhhhhhh... hhrrRRRRRRRRR

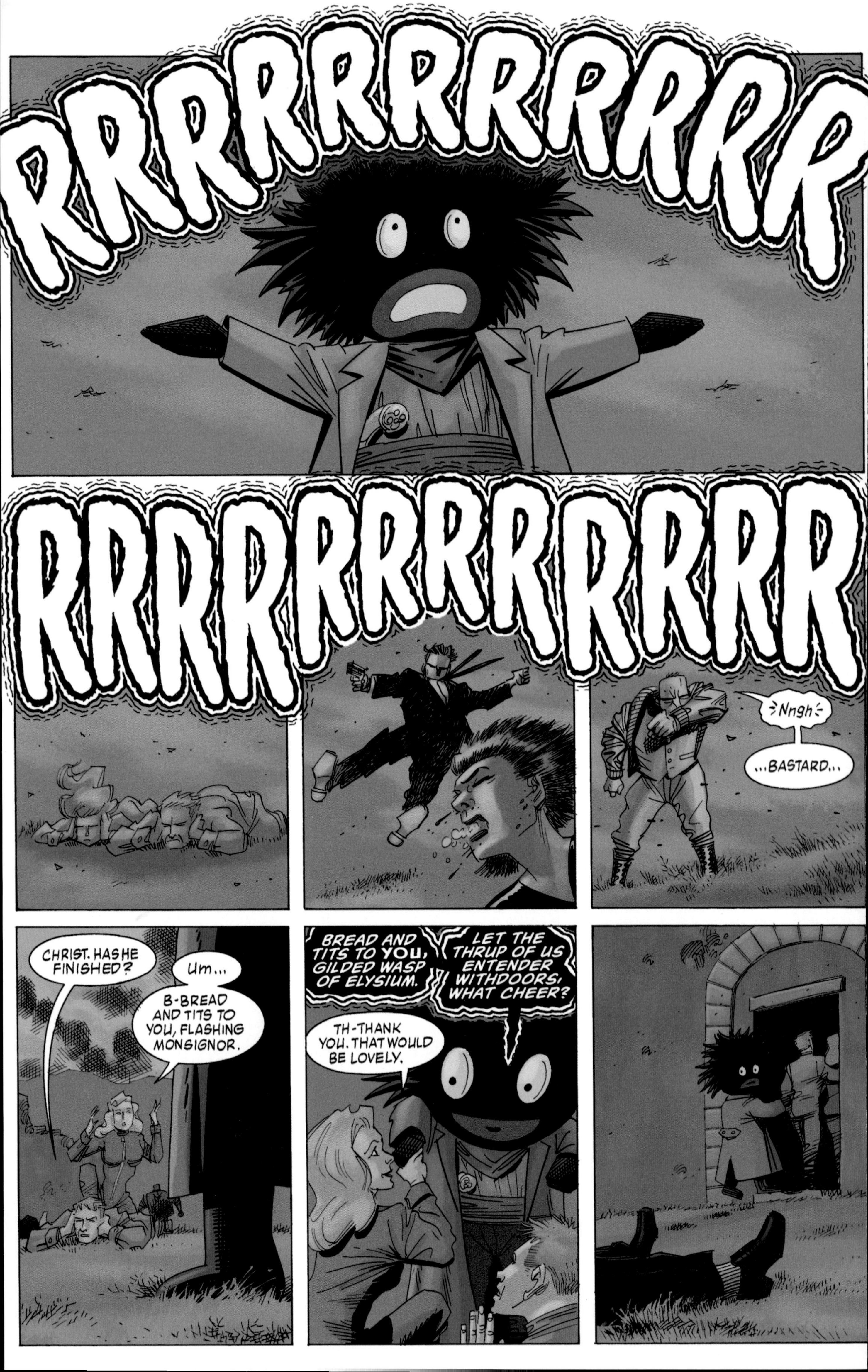
RRRRRRRRRRRRR
RRRRRRRRRRRRR
Nngh
...BASTARD...
CHRIST. HAS HE FINISHED?
Um...
B-BREAD AND TITS TO YOU, FLASHING MONSIGNOR.
BREAD AND TITS TO YOU, GILDED WASP OF ELYSIUM.
LET THE THRUP OF US ENTENDER WITHDOORS; WHAT CHEER?
TH-THANK YOU. THAT WOULD BE LOVELY.

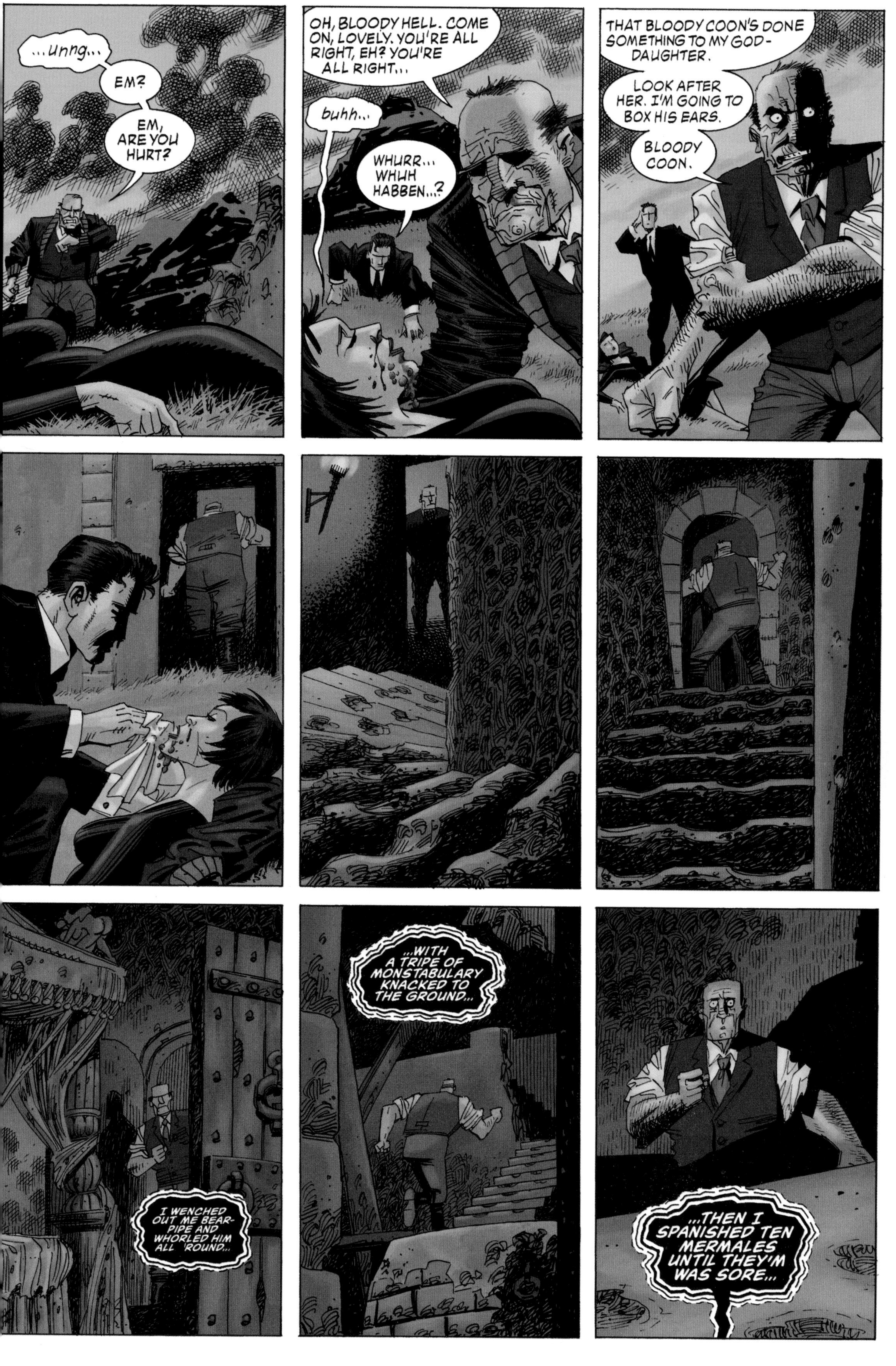
...unng...
EM?
EM, ARE YOU HURT?
OH, BLOODY HELL. COME ON, LOVELY. YOU'RE ALL RIGHT, EH? YOU'RE ALL RIGHT...
buhh...
WHURR... WHUH HABBEN...?
THAT BLOODY COON'S DONE SOMETHING TO MY GOD-DAUGHTER.
LOOK AFTER HER. I'M GOING TO BOX HIS EARS.
BLOODY COON.
I WENCHED OUT ME BEAR-PIPE AND WHORLED HIM ALL 'ROUND...
...WITH A TRIPE OF MONSTABULARY KNACKED TO THE GROUND...
...THEN I SPANISHED TEN MERMALES UNTIL THEY'M WAS SORE...

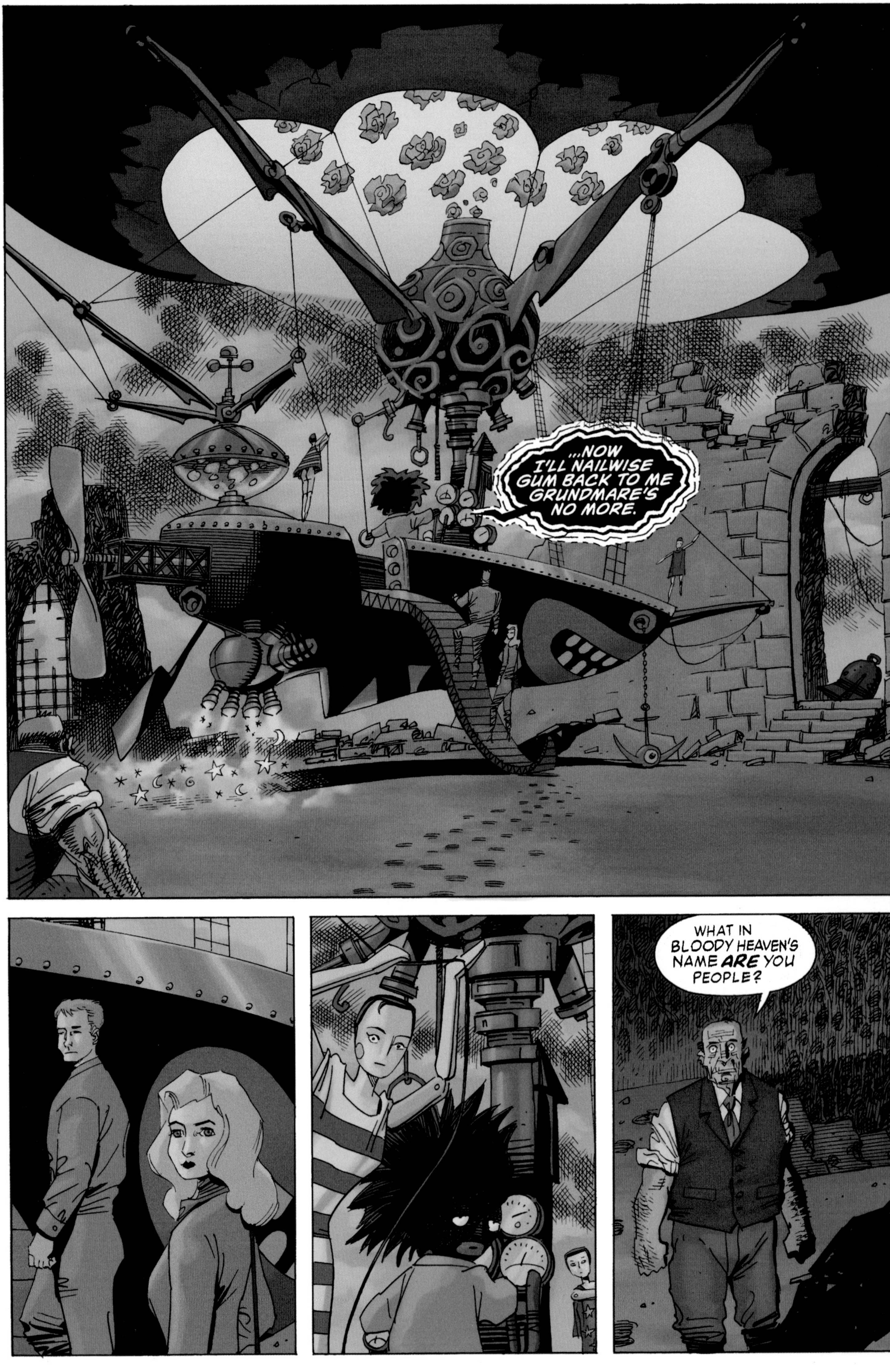
...NOW I'LL NAILWISE GUM BACK TO ME GRUNDMARE'S NO MORE.
WHAT IN BLOODY HEAVEN'S NAME **ARE** YOU PEOPLE?

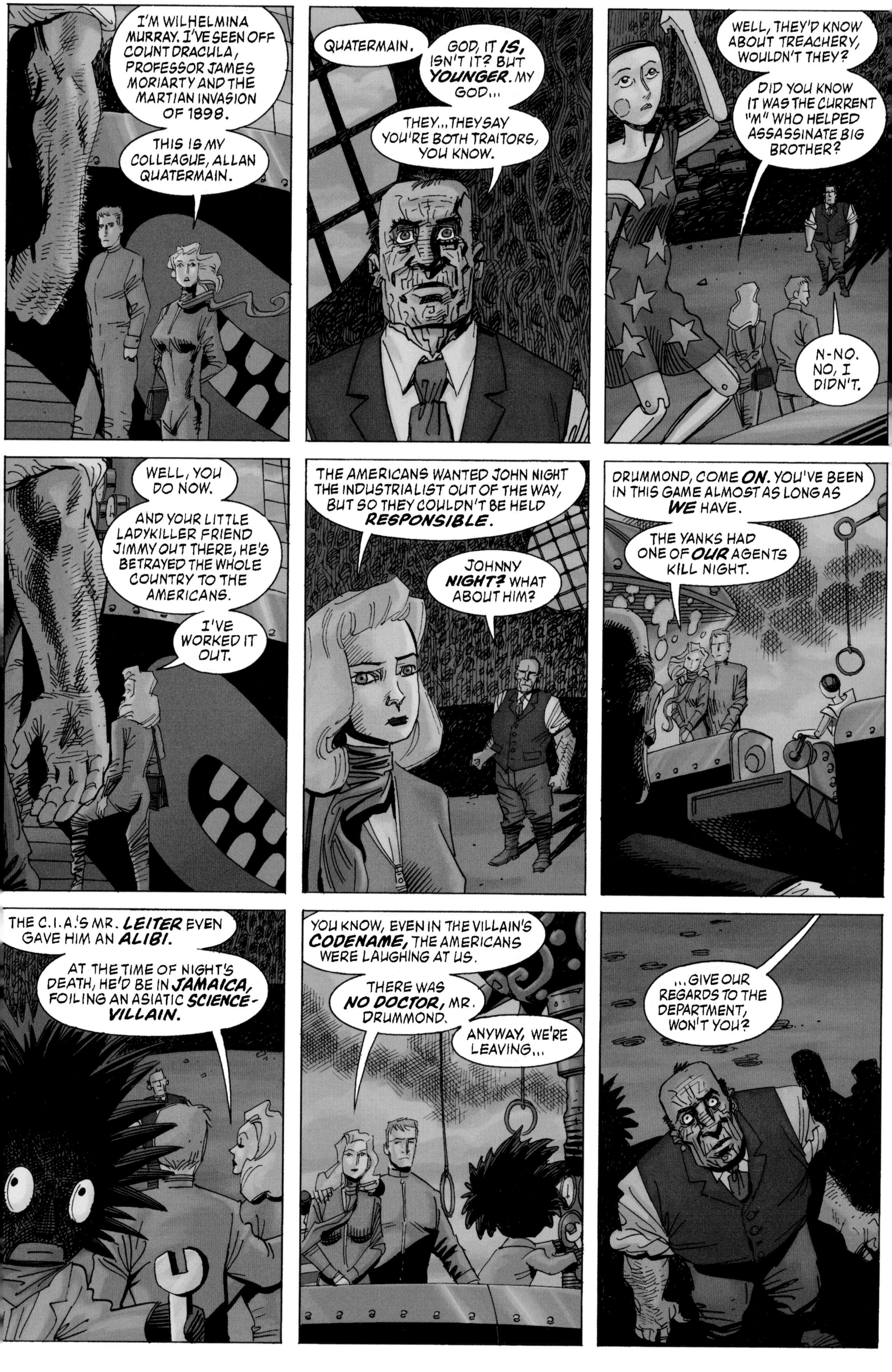

I'M WILHELMINA MURRAY. I'VE SEEN OFF COUNT DRACULA, PROFESSOR JAMES MORIARTY AND THE MARTIAN INVASION OF 1898.
THIS IS MY COLLEAGUE, ALLAN QUATERMAIN.
QUATERMAIN.
GOD, IT IS, ISN'T IT? BUT YOUNGER. MY GOD...
THEY... THEY SAY YOU'RE BOTH TRAITORS, YOU KNOW.
WELL, THEY'D KNOW ABOUT TREACHERY, WOULDN'T THEY?
DID YOU KNOW IT WAS THE CURRENT "M" WHO HELPED ASSASSINATE BIG BROTHER?
N-NO. NO, I DIDN'T.
WELL, YOU DO NOW.
AND YOUR LITTLE LADYKILLER FRIEND JIMMY OUT THERE, HE'S BETRAYED THE WHOLE COUNTRY TO THE AMERICANS.
I'VE WORKED IT OUT.
THE AMERICANS WANTED JOHN NIGHT THE INDUSTRIALIST OUT OF THE WAY, BUT SO THEY COULDN'T BE HELD RESPONSIBLE.
JOHNNY NIGHT? WHAT ABOUT HIM?
DRUMMOND, COME ON. YOU'VE BEEN IN THIS GAME ALMOST AS LONG AS WE HAVE.
THE YANKS HAD ONE OF OUR AGENTS KILL NIGHT.
THE C.I.A.'S MR. LEITER EVEN GAVE HIM AN ALIBI.
AT THE TIME OF NIGHT'S DEATH, HE'D BE IN JAMAICA, FOILING AN ASIATIC SCIENCE-VILLAIN.
YOU KNOW, EVEN IN THE VILLAIN'S CODENAME, THE AMERICANS WERE LAUGHING AT US.
THERE WAS NO DOCTOR, MR. DRUMMOND.
ANYWAY, WE'RE LEAVING...
...GIVE OUR REGARDS TO THE DEPARTMENT, WON'T YOU?

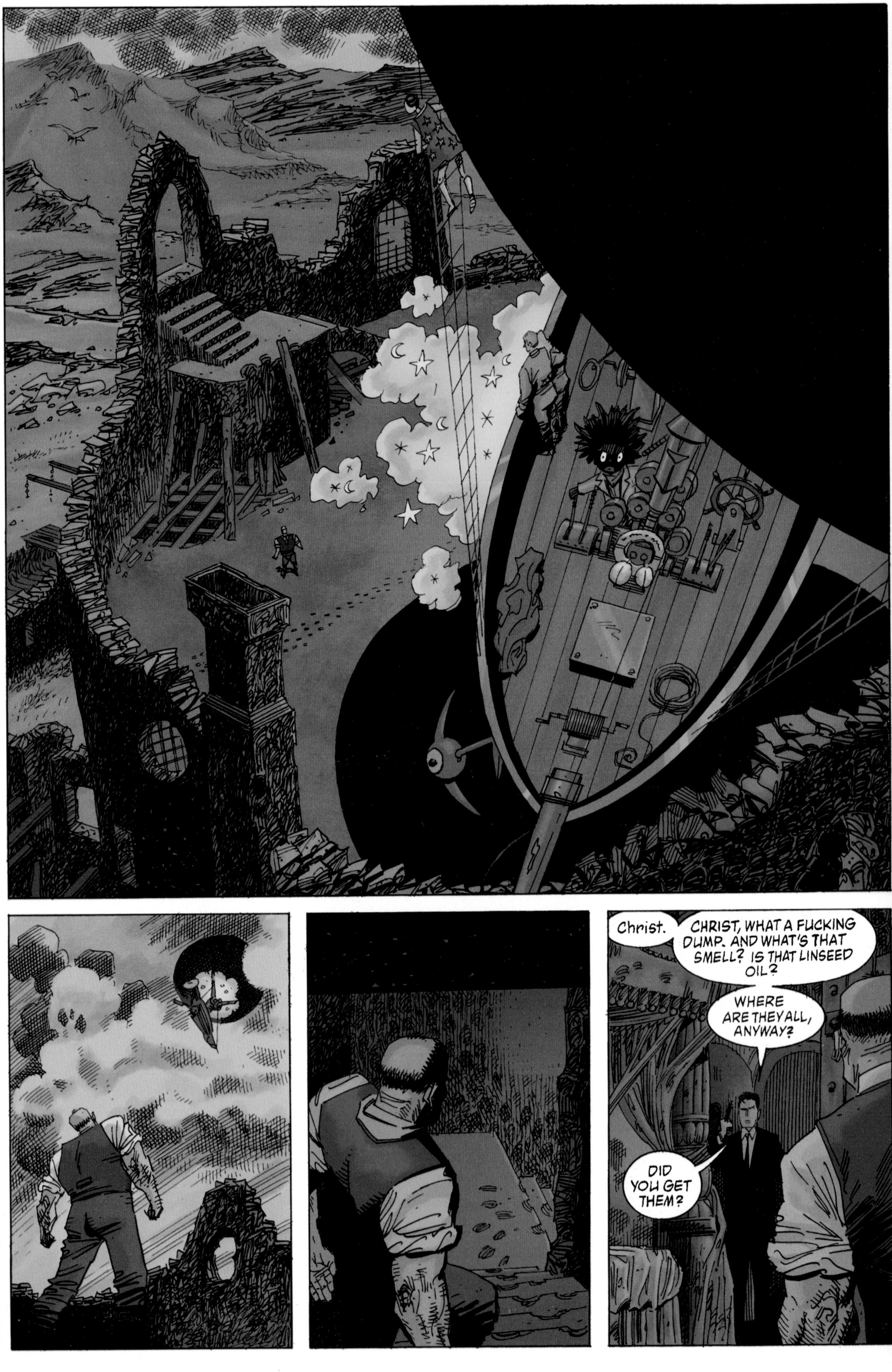
Christ.
CHRIST, WHAT A FUCKING DUMP. AND WHAT'S THAT SMELL? IS THAT LINSEED OIL?
WHERE ARE THEY ALL, ANYWAY?
DID YOU GET THEM?

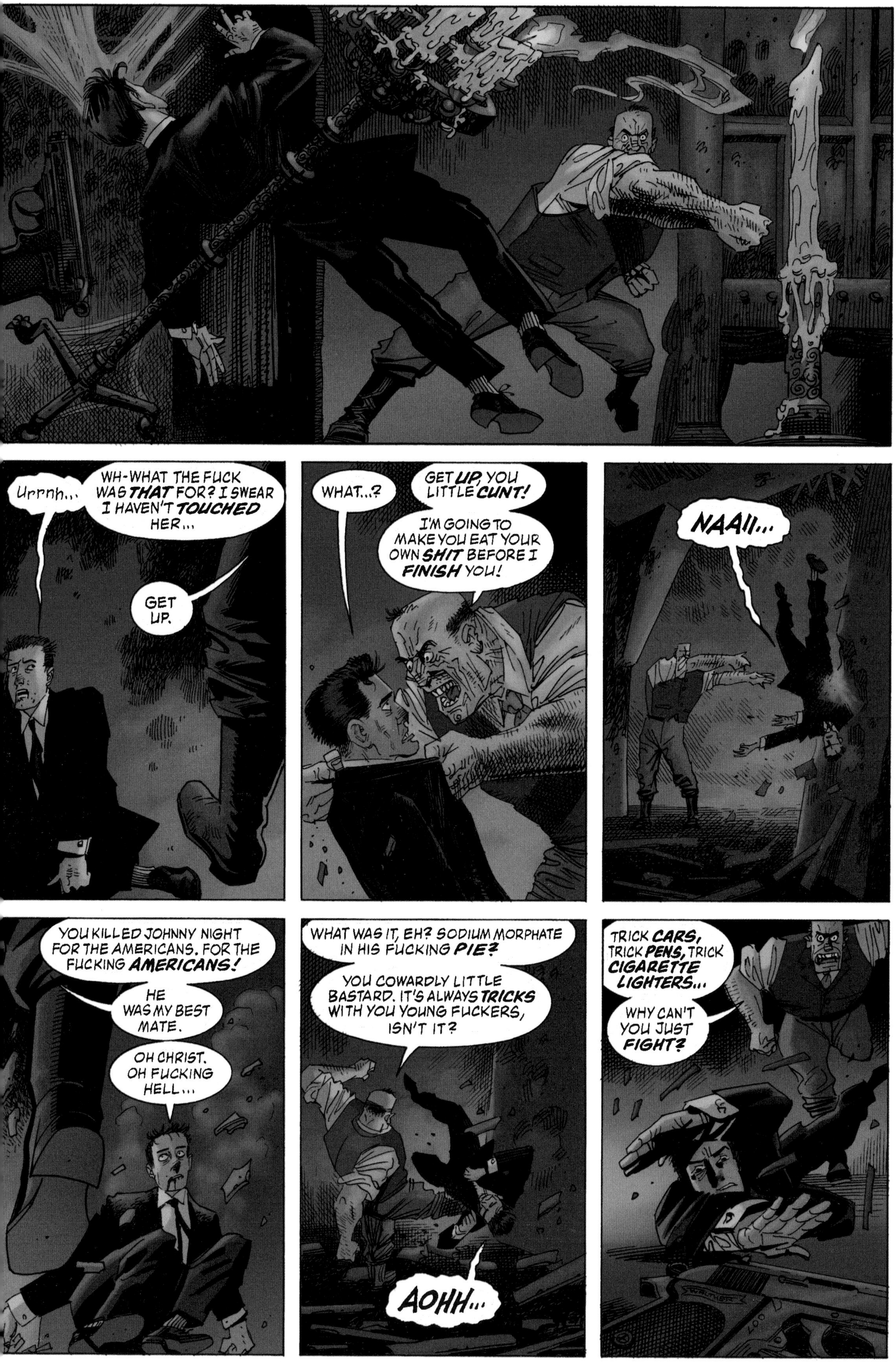
Urrnh...
WH-WHAT THE FUCK WAS THAT FOR? I SWEAR I HAVEN'T TOUCHED HER...
GET UP.
WHAT...?
GET UP, YOU LITTLE CUNT!
I'M GOING TO MAKE YOU EAT YOUR OWN SHIT BEFORE I FINISH YOU!
NAAII...
YOU KILLED JOHNNY NIGHT FOR THE AMERICANS. FOR THE FUCKING AMERICANS!
HE WAS MY BEST MATE.
OH CHRIST. OH FUCKING HELL...
WHAT WAS IT, EH? SODIUM MORPHATE IN HIS FUCKING PIE?
YOU COWARDLY LITTLE BASTARD. IT'S ALWAYS TRICKS WITH YOU YOUNG FUCKERS, ISN'T IT?
AOHH...
TRICK CARS, TRICK PENS, TRICK CIGARETTE LIGHTERS...
WHY CAN'T YOU JUST FIGHT?

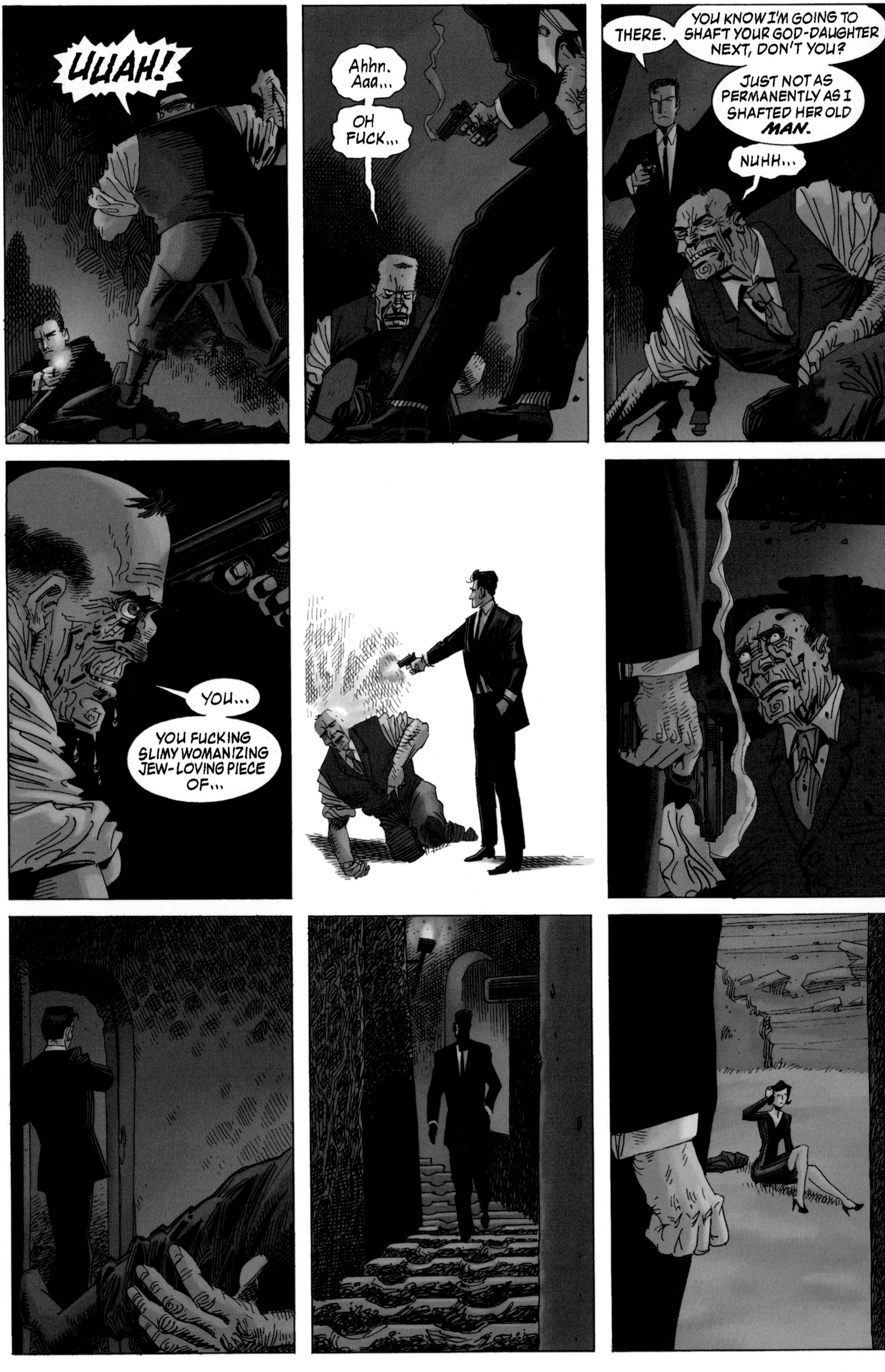
UUAH!
Ahhn. Aaa...
OH FUCK...
THERE.
YOU KNOW I'M GOING TO SHAFT YOUR GOD-DAUGHTER NEXT, DON'T YOU?
JUST NOT AS PERMANENTLY AS I SHAFTED HER OLD MAN.
NUHH...
YOU...
YOU FUCKING SLIMY WOMANIZING JEW-LOVING PIECE OF...

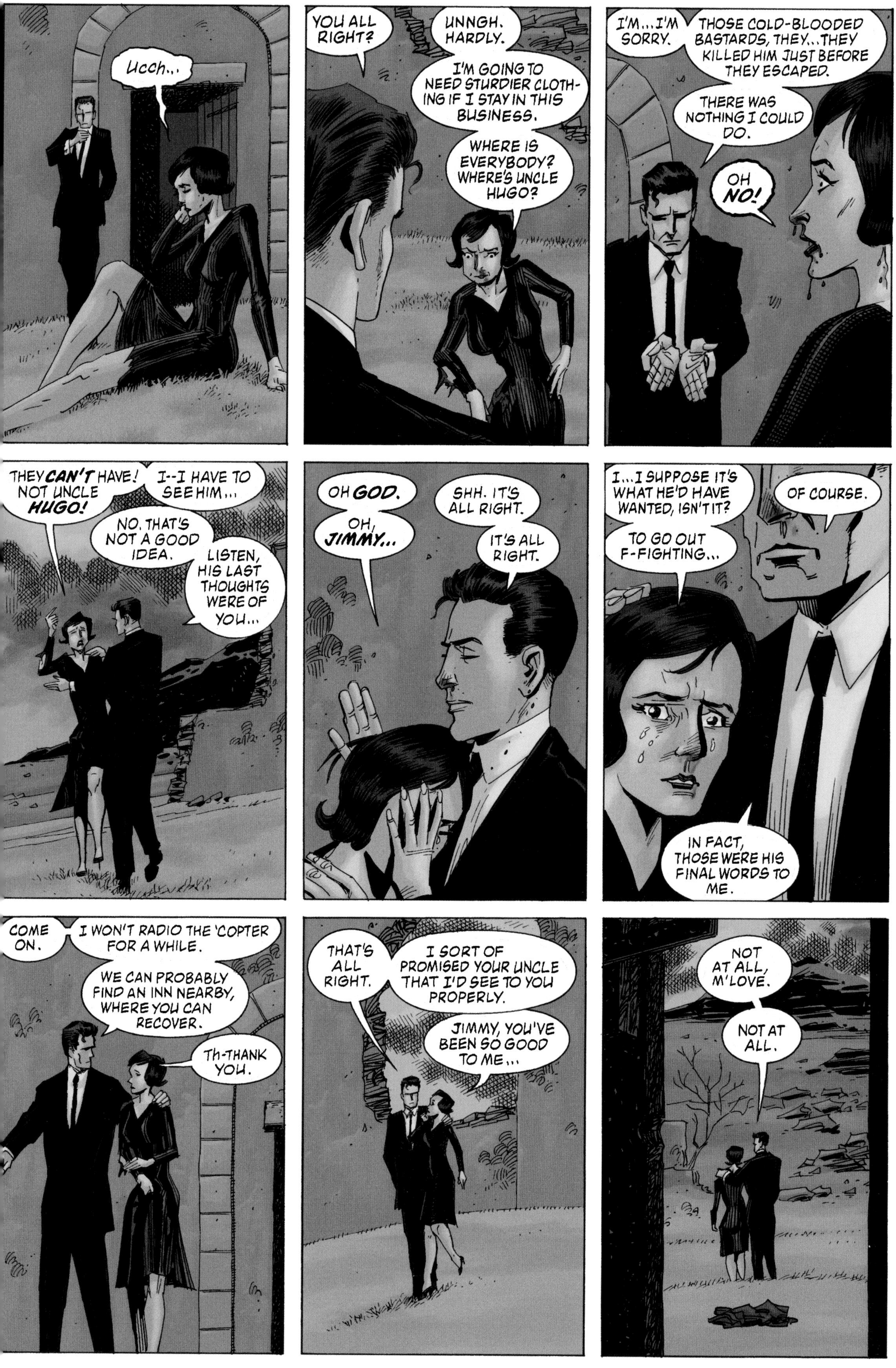
Ucch...
YOU ALL RIGHT?
UNNGH. HARDLY.
I'M GOING TO NEED STURDIER CLOTHING IF I STAY IN THIS BUSINESS.
WHERE IS EVERYBODY? WHERE'S UNCLE HUGO?
I'M...I'M SORRY.
THOSE COLD-BLOODED BASTARDS, THEY...THEY KILLED HIM JUST BEFORE THEY ESCAPED.
THERE WAS NOTHING I COULD DO.
OH NO!
THEY CAN'T HAVE! NOT UNCLE HUGO!
I--I HAVE TO SEE HIM...
NO. THAT'S NOT A GOOD IDEA.
LISTEN, HIS LAST THOUGHTS WERE OF YOU...
OH GOD.
OH, JIMMY...
SHH. IT'S ALL RIGHT.
IT'S ALL RIGHT.
I...I SUPPOSE IT'S WHAT HE'D HAVE WANTED, ISN'T IT?
TO GO OUT F-FIGHTING...
OF COURSE.
IN FACT, THOSE WERE HIS FINAL WORDS TO ME.
COME ON.
I WON'T RADIO THE 'COPTER FOR A WHILE.
WE CAN PROBABLY FIND AN INN NEARBY, WHERE YOU CAN RECOVER.
Th-THANK YOU.
THAT'S ALL RIGHT.
I SORT OF PROMISED YOUR UNCLE THAT I'D SEE TO YOU PROPERLY.
JIMMY, YOU'VE BEEN SO GOOD TO ME...
NOT AT ALL, M'LOVE.
NOT AT ALL.

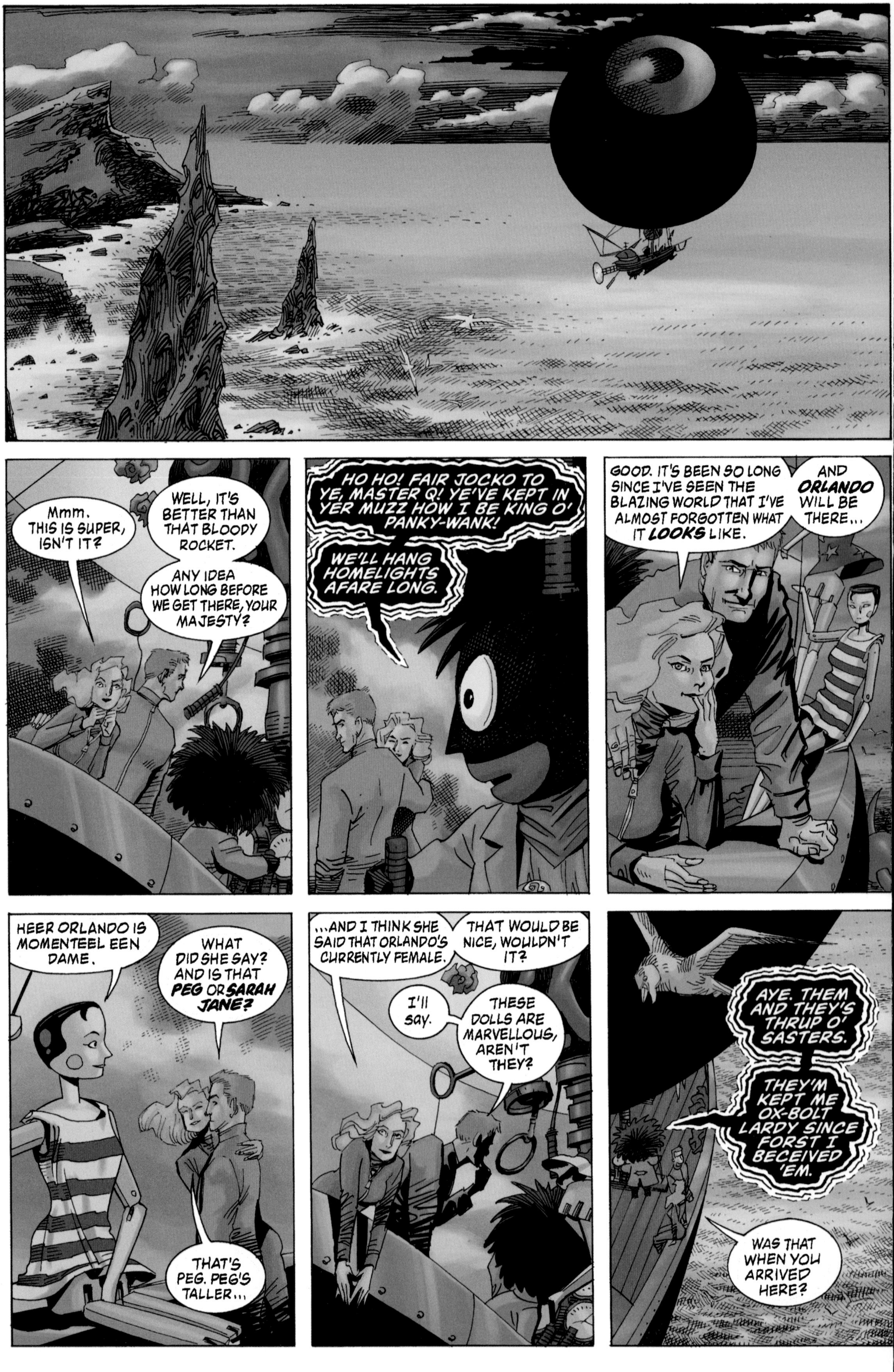
Mmm. THIS IS SUPER, ISN'T IT?
WELL, IT'S BETTER THAN THAT BLOODY ROCKET.
ANY IDEA HOW LONG BEFORE WE GET THERE, YOUR MAJESTY?
HO HO! FAIR JOCKO TO YE, MASTER Q! YE'VE KEPT IN YER MUZZ HOW I BE KING O' PANKY-WANK!
WE'LL HANG HOMELIGHTS AFARE LONG.
GOOD. IT'S BEEN SO LONG SINCE I'VE SEEN THE BLAZING WORLD THAT I'VE ALMOST FORGOTTEN WHAT IT LOOKS LIKE.
AND ORLANDO WILL BE THERE...
HEER ORLANDO IS MOMENTEEL EEN DAME.
WHAT DID SHE SAY? AND IS THAT PEG OR SARAH JANE?
THAT'S PEG. PEG'S TALLER...
...AND I THINK SHE SAID THAT ORLANDO'S CURRENTLY FEMALE.
THAT WOULD BE NICE, WOULDN'T IT?
I'll say.
THESE DOLLS ARE MARVELLOUS, AREN'T THEY?
AYE. THEM AND THEY'S THRUP O' SASTERS.
THEY'M KEPT ME OX-BOLT LARDY SINCE FORST I BECEIVED 'EM.
WAS THAT WHEN YOU ARRIVED HERE?

YARSE. FORST HITHERED FRO ME DARKLY-SUBSTANCED HOME-WHIRL LUNDERED I IN TOY-LEND.

Ah. SO QUEEN *OLYMPIA* PRESENTED YOU WITH THE DOLLS?

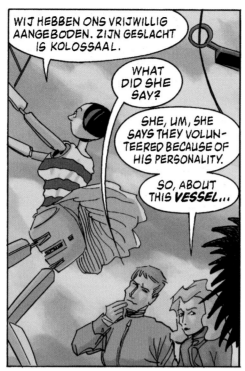

WIJ HEBBEN ONS VRIJWILLIG AANGEBODEN. ZIJN GESLACHT IS KOLOSSAAL.

WHAT DID SHE SAY?

SHE, UM, SHE SAYS THEY VOLUNTEERED BECAUSE OF HIS PERSONALITY.

SO, ABOUT THIS *VESSEL*....

I MEAN, ARE THESE THINGS *COMMON* IN YOUR BLACK-MATERIAL COSMOS?

THESE CRAFTS THAT SAIL BETWEEN DIMENSIONS?

CUMMUN? WHY, BLISS YER SLAP, NO.

BELTED "THE ROSE O' NOWHERE" ALL ON ME JINGLE, DID I.

TUTHER GALLEY-WAGS SID AS IT'D NAILWISE BE DUNNED.

WHAT SQUINT, SAREY JANE?

IK DENK DAT DIE GROTE WOLK DAAR DE WEG NAAR HUIS IS.

IS THAT VERRIBLE?

WELL, IN THAT STAMP I'D BEST PAW OUT THE QUIZGOGS.

WHAT DID SHE SAY? ARE WE NEARLY THERE?

AYE-SO. THROUGH THE BIG CLODDER AHEAVE O' WE.

THUNCE WE SHALL REQUEER OUR BLINK WEAR.

OF COURSE.

MY. THAT *IS* A BIG CLOUD. AND VERY *TWINKLY,* TOO.

DO YOU NEED ANY HELP WITH THOSE, DARLING?

NO, NO, I'M FINE.

THERE. WHAT ABOUT THE *DOLLS*? WILL THEY BE ABLE TO SEE?

OH, DON'T YOU'M FRIZZLE ABOUT THEY. THEY'M MOCKINICAL.

YOU'M JUST PEER OFFLY...

THARBLO.

HUFF YER OVVER IN A, YOU'M TICK SENNED SUCH A PLUMIOUS SPARKTACLE?

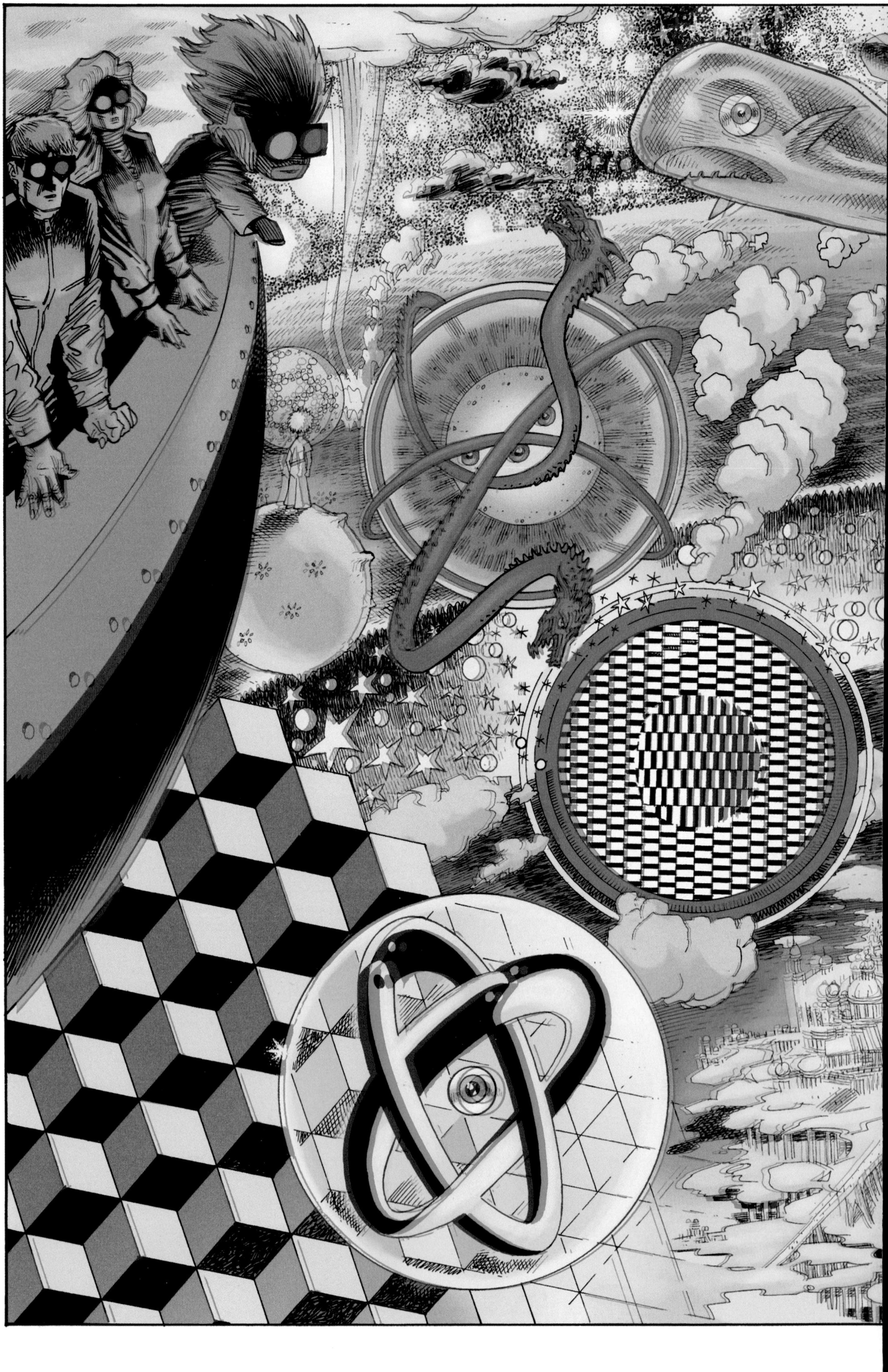

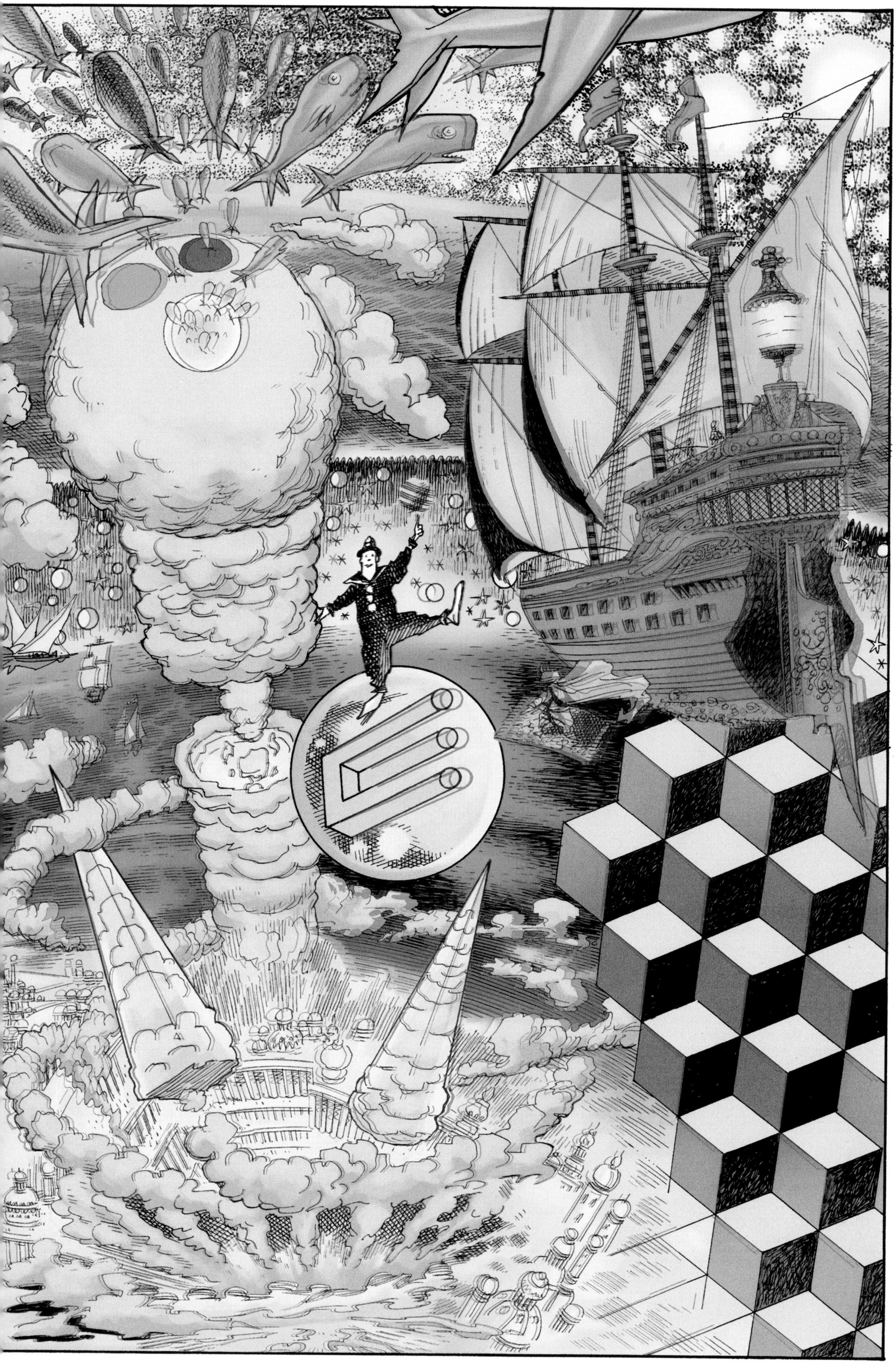

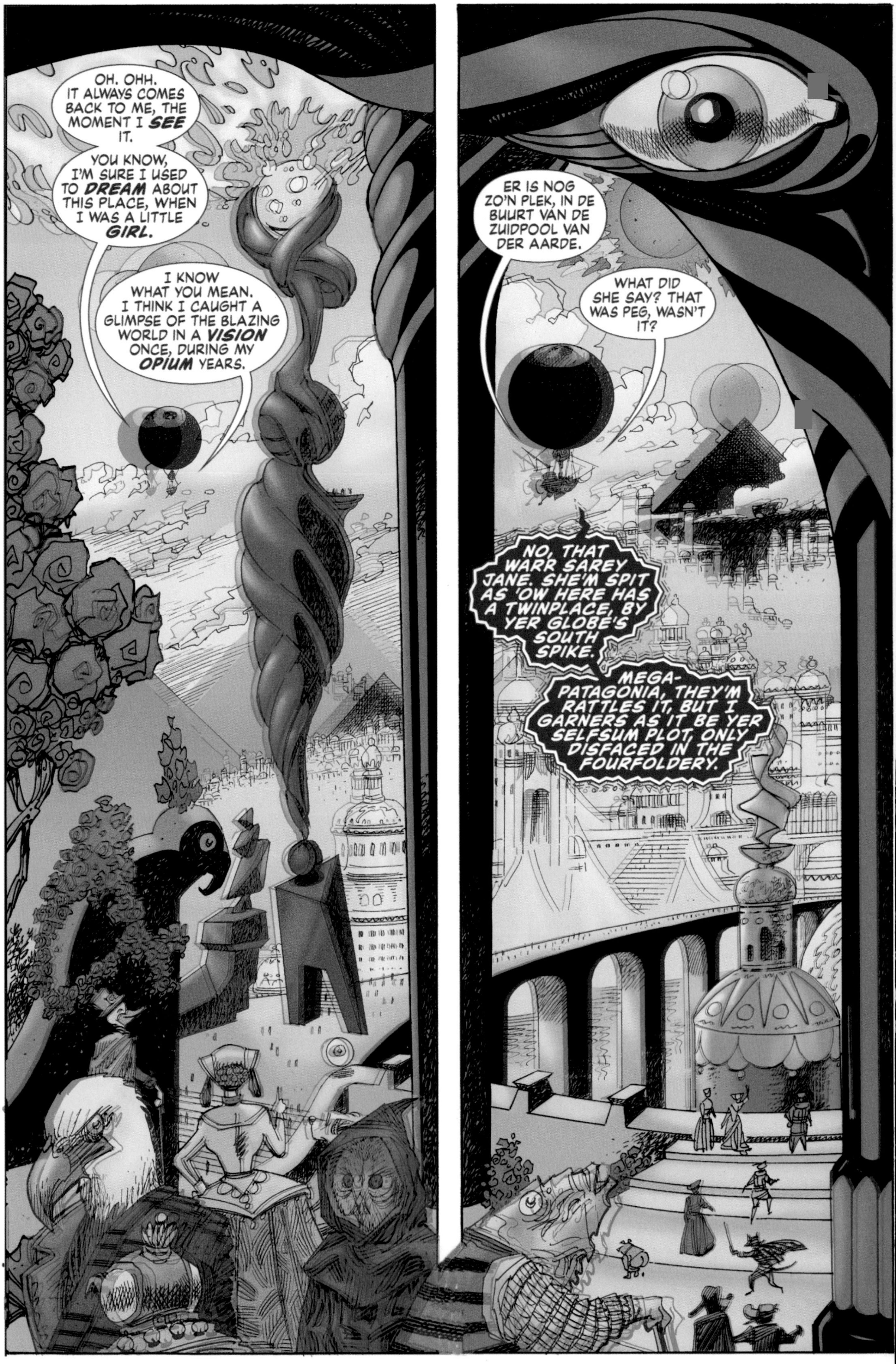
OH. OHH. IT ALWAYS COMES BACK TO ME, THE MOMENT I SEE IT.
YOU KNOW, I'M SURE I USED TO DREAM ABOUT THIS PLACE, WHEN I WAS A LITTLE GIRL.
I KNOW WHAT YOU MEAN. I THINK I CAUGHT A GLIMPSE OF THE BLAZING WORLD IN A VISION ONCE, DURING MY OPIUM YEARS.
ER IS NOG ZO'N PLEK, IN DE BUURT VAN DE ZUIDPOOL VAN DER AARDE.
WHAT DID SHE SAY? THAT WAS PEG, WASN'T IT?
NO, THAT WARR SAREY JANE. SHE'M SPIT AS 'OW HERE HAS A TWINPLACE, BY YER GLOBE'S SOUTH SPIKE.
MEGA-PATAGONIA, THEY'M RATTLES IT, BUT I GARNERS AS IT BE YER SELFSUM PLOT, ONLY DISFACED IN THE FOURFOLDERY.

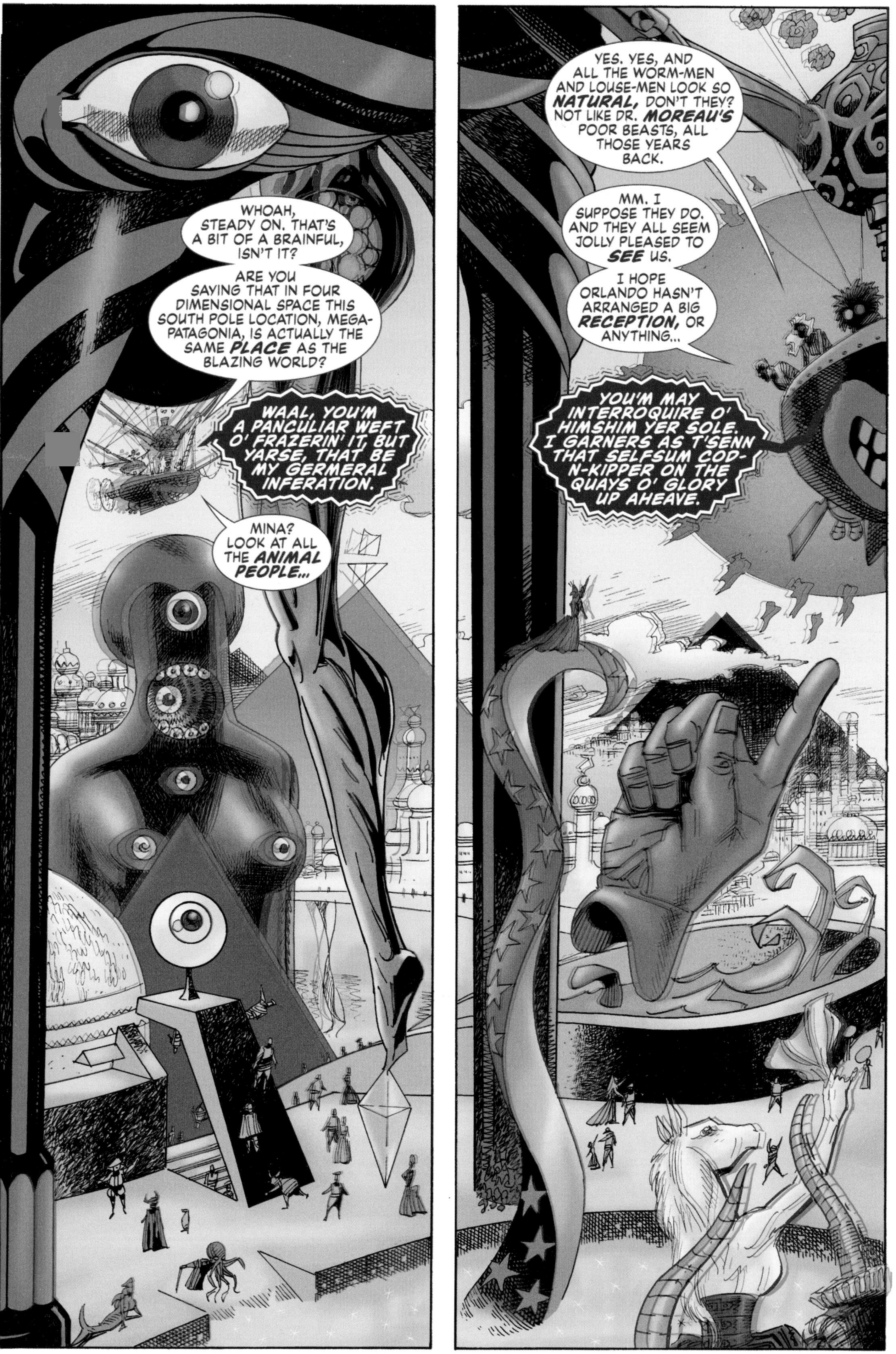
WHOAH, STEADY ON. THAT'S A BIT OF A BRAINFUL, ISN'T IT?
ARE YOU SAYING THAT IN FOUR DIMENSIONAL SPACE THIS SOUTH POLE LOCATION, MEGA-PATAGONIA, IS ACTUALLY THE SAME PLACE AS THE BLAZING WORLD?
WAAL, YOU'M A PANCULIAR WEFT O' FRAZERIN' IT, BUT YARSE, THAT BE MY GERMERAL INFERATION.
MINA? LOOK AT ALL THE ANIMAL PEOPLE...
YES. YES, AND ALL THE WORM-MEN AND LOUSE-MEN LOOK SO NATURAL, DON'T THEY? NOT LIKE DR. MOREAU'S POOR BEASTS, ALL THOSE YEARS BACK.
MM. I SUPPOSE THEY DO. AND THEY ALL SEEM JOLLY PLEASED TO SEE US.
I HOPE ORLANDO HASN'T ARRANGED A BIG RECEPTION, OR ANYTHING...
YOU'M MAY INTERROQUIRE O' HIMSHIM YER SOLE. I GARNERS AS T'SENN THAT SELFSUM COD-N-KIPPER ON THE QUAYS O' GLORY UP AHEAVE.

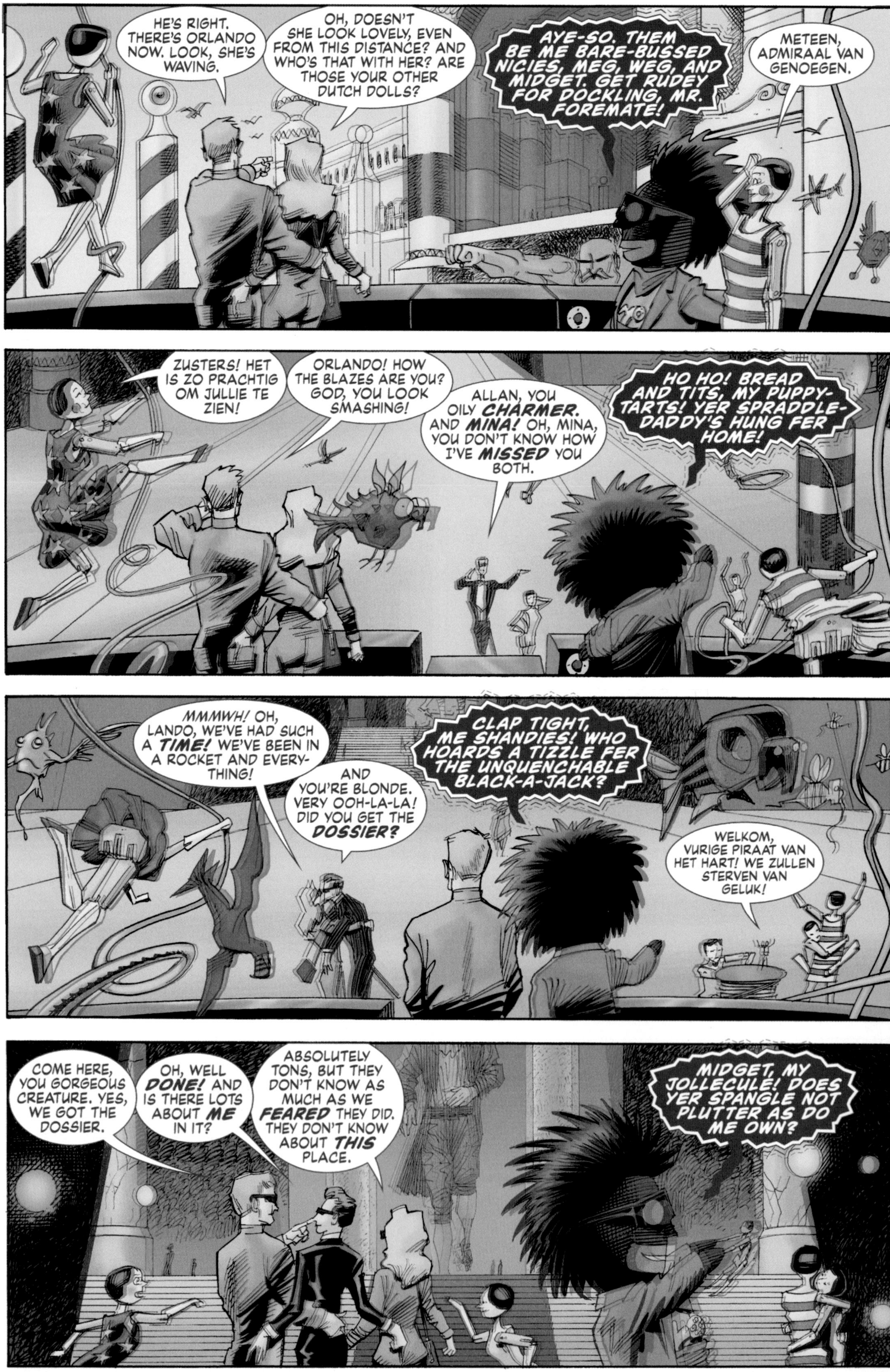
HE'S RIGHT. THERE'S ORLANDO NOW. LOOK, SHE'S WAVING.
OH, DOESN'T SHE LOOK LOVELY, EVEN FROM THIS DISTANCE? AND WHO'S THAT WITH HER? ARE THOSE YOUR OTHER DUTCH DOLLS?
AYE-SO. THEM BE ME BARE-BUSSED NICIES, MEG, WEG, AND MIDGET. GET RUDEY FOR DOCKLING, MR. FOREMATE!
METEEN, ADMIRAAL VAN GENOEGEN.
ZUSTERS! HET IS ZO PRACHTIG OM JULLIE TE ZIEN!
ORLANDO! HOW THE BLAZES ARE YOU? GOD, YOU LOOK SMASHING!
ALLAN, YOU OILY CHARMER. AND MINA! OH, MINA, YOU DON'T KNOW HOW I'VE MISSED YOU BOTH.
HO HO! BREAD AND TITS, MY PUPPY-TARTS! YER SPRADDLE-DADDY'S HUNG FER HOME!
MMMWH! OH, LANDO, WE'VE HAD SUCH A TIME! WE'VE BEEN IN A ROCKET AND EVERY-THING!
AND YOU'RE BLONDE. VERY OOH-LA-LA! DID YOU GET THE DOSSIER?
CLAP TIGHT, ME SHANDIES! WHO HOARDS A TIZZLE FER THE UNQUENCHABLE BLACK-A-JACK?
WELKOM, VURIGE PIRAAT VAN HET HART! WE ZULLEN STERVEN VAN GELUK!
COME HERE, YOU GORGEOUS CREATURE. YES, WE GOT THE DOSSIER.
OH, WELL DONE! AND IS THERE LOTS ABOUT ME IN IT?
ABSOLUTELY TONS, BUT THEY DON'T KNOW AS MUCH AS WE FEARED THEY DID. THEY DON'T KNOW ABOUT THIS PLACE.
MIDGET, MY JOLLECULE! DOES YER SPANGLE NOT PLUTTER AS DO ME OWN?

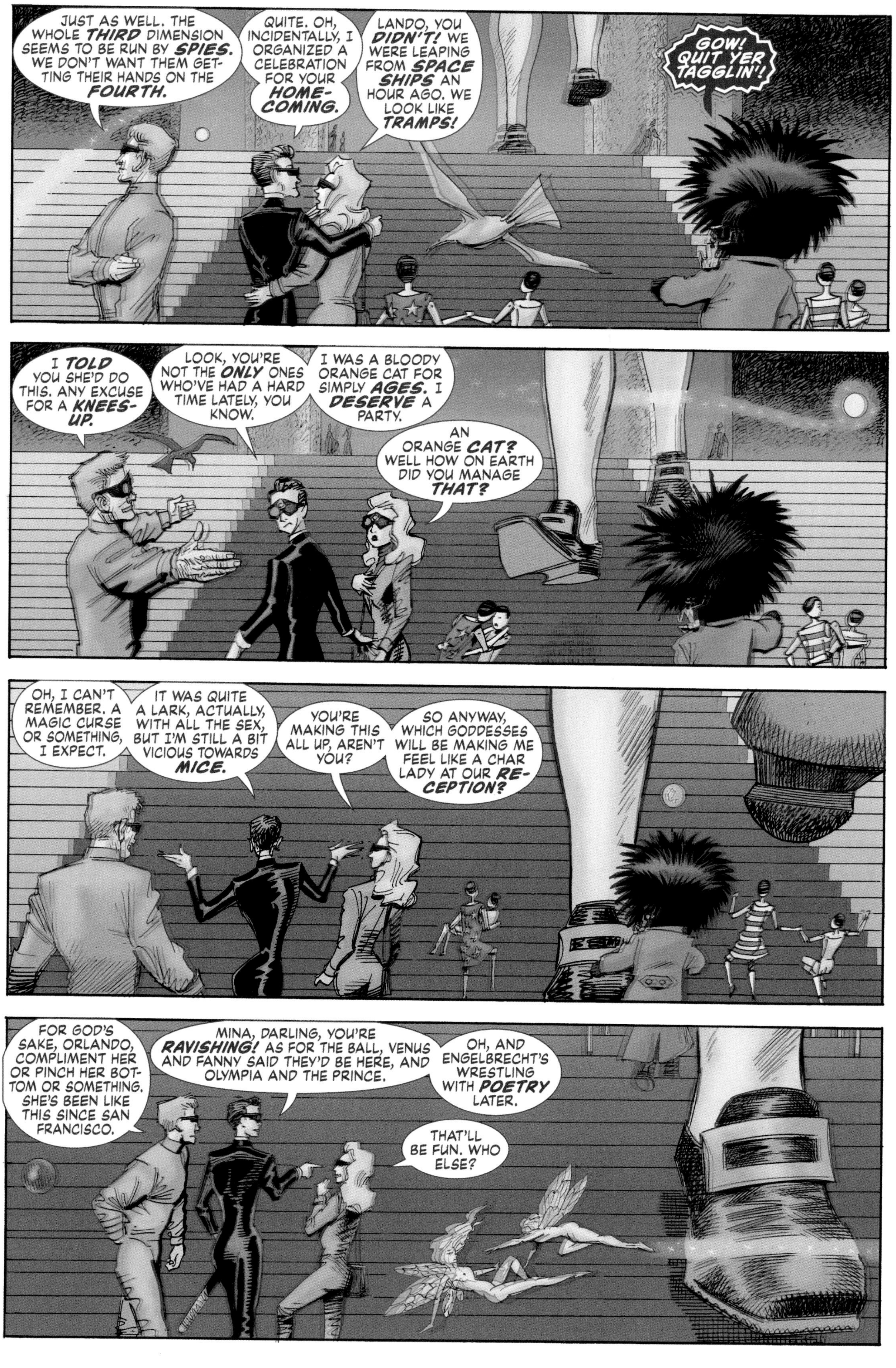
JUST AS WELL. THE WHOLE THIRD DIMENSION SEEMS TO BE RUN BY SPIES. WE DON'T WANT THEM GETTING THEIR HANDS ON THE FOURTH.
QUITE. OH, INCIDENTALLY, I ORGANIZED A CELEBRATION FOR YOUR HOMECOMING.
LANDO, YOU DIDN'T! WE WERE LEAPING FROM SPACE SHIPS AN HOUR AGO. WE LOOK LIKE TRAMPS!
GOW! QUIT YER TAGGLIN'!
I TOLD YOU SHE'D DO THIS. ANY EXCUSE FOR A KNEES-UP.
LOOK, YOU'RE NOT THE ONLY ONES WHO'VE HAD A HARD TIME LATELY, YOU KNOW.
I WAS A BLOODY ORANGE CAT FOR SIMPLY AGES. I DESERVE A PARTY.
AN ORANGE CAT? WELL HOW ON EARTH DID YOU MANAGE THAT?
OH, I CAN'T REMEMBER. A MAGIC CURSE OR SOMETHING, I EXPECT.
IT WAS QUITE A LARK, ACTUALLY, WITH ALL THE SEX, BUT I'M STILL A BIT VICIOUS TOWARDS MICE.
YOU'RE MAKING THIS ALL UP, AREN'T YOU?
SO ANYWAY, WHICH GODDESSES WILL BE MAKING ME FEEL LIKE A CHAR LADY AT OUR RECEPTION?
FOR GOD'S SAKE, ORLANDO, COMPLIMENT HER OR PINCH HER BOTTOM OR SOMETHING. SHE'S BEEN LIKE THIS SINCE SAN FRANCISCO.
MINA, DARLING, YOU'RE RAVISHING! AS FOR THE BALL, VENUS AND FANNY SAID THEY'D BE HERE, AND OLYMPIA AND THE PRINCE.
OH, AND ENGELBRECHT'S WRESTLING WITH POETRY LATER.
THAT'LL BE FUN. WHO ELSE?

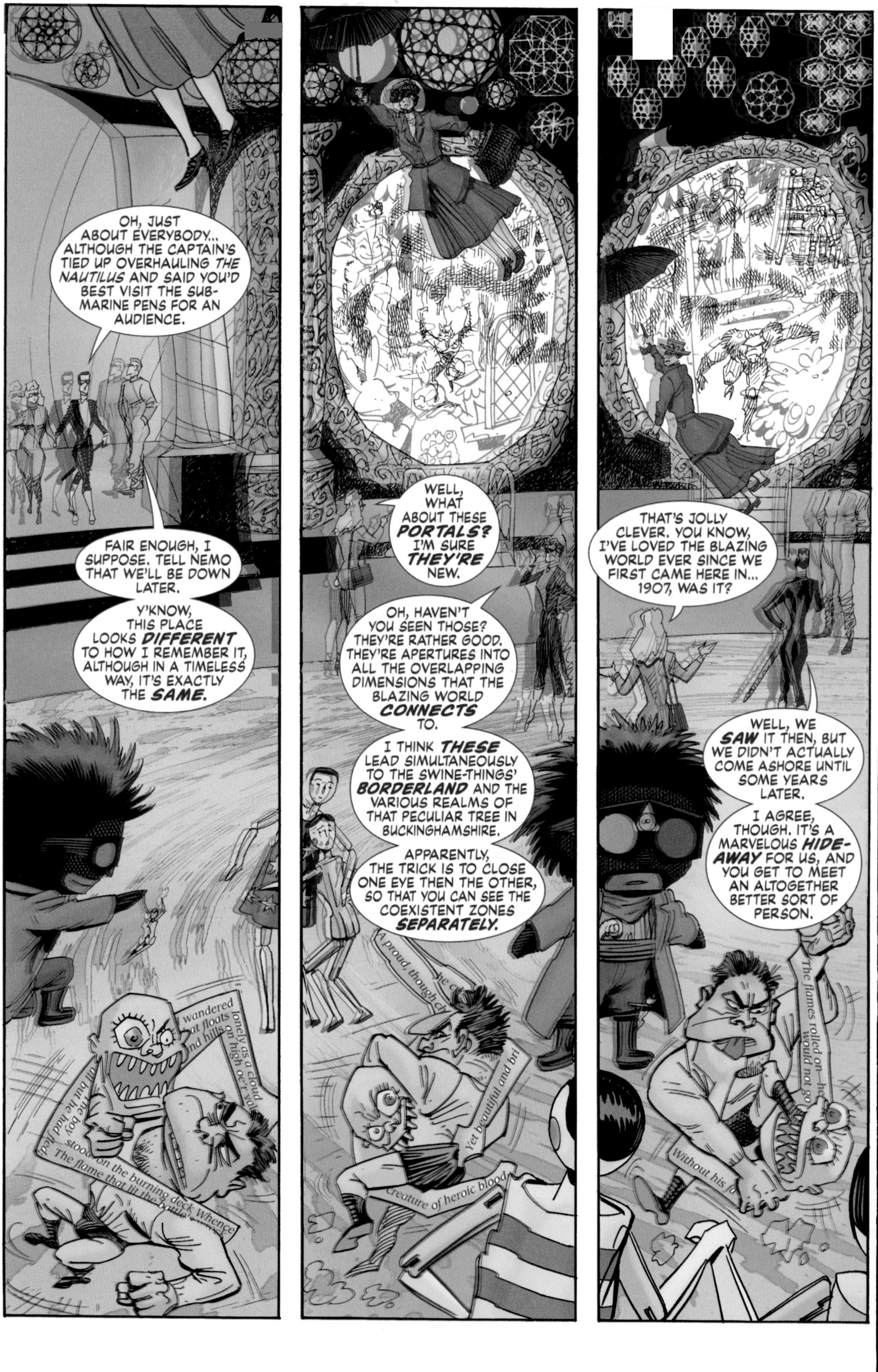
OH, JUST ABOUT EVERYBODY... ALTHOUGH THE CAPTAIN'S TIED UP OVERHAULING THE NAUTILUS AND SAID YOU'D BEST VISIT THE SUB-MARINE PENS FOR AN AUDIENCE.
FAIR ENOUGH, I SUPPOSE. TELL NEMO THAT WE'LL BE DOWN LATER.
Y'KNOW, THIS PLACE LOOKS DIFFERENT TO HOW I REMEMBER IT, ALTHOUGH IN A TIMELESS WAY, IT'S EXACTLY THE SAME.
WELL, WHAT ABOUT THESE PORTALS? I'M SURE THEY'RE NEW.
OH, HAVEN'T YOU SEEN THOSE? THEY'RE RATHER GOOD. THEY'RE APERTURES INTO ALL THE OVERLAPPING DIMENSIONS THAT THE BLAZING WORLD CONNECTS TO.
I THINK THESE LEAD SIMULTANEOUSLY TO THE SWINE-THINGS' BORDERLAND AND THE VARIOUS REALMS OF THAT PECULIAR TREE IN BUCKINGHAMSHIRE.
APPARENTLY, THE TRICK IS TO CLOSE ONE EYE THEN THE OTHER, SO THAT YOU CAN SEE THE COEXISTENT ZONES SEPARATELY.
THAT'S JOLLY CLEVER. YOU KNOW, I'VE LOVED THE BLAZING WORLD EVER SINCE WE FIRST CAME HERE IN... 1907, WAS IT?
WELL, WE SAW IT THEN, BUT WE DIDN'T ACTUALLY COME ASHORE UNTIL SOME YEARS LATER.
I AGREE, THOUGH. IT'S A MARVELOUS HIDE-AWAY FOR US, AND YOU GET TO MEET AN ALTOGETHER BETTER SORT OF PERSON.

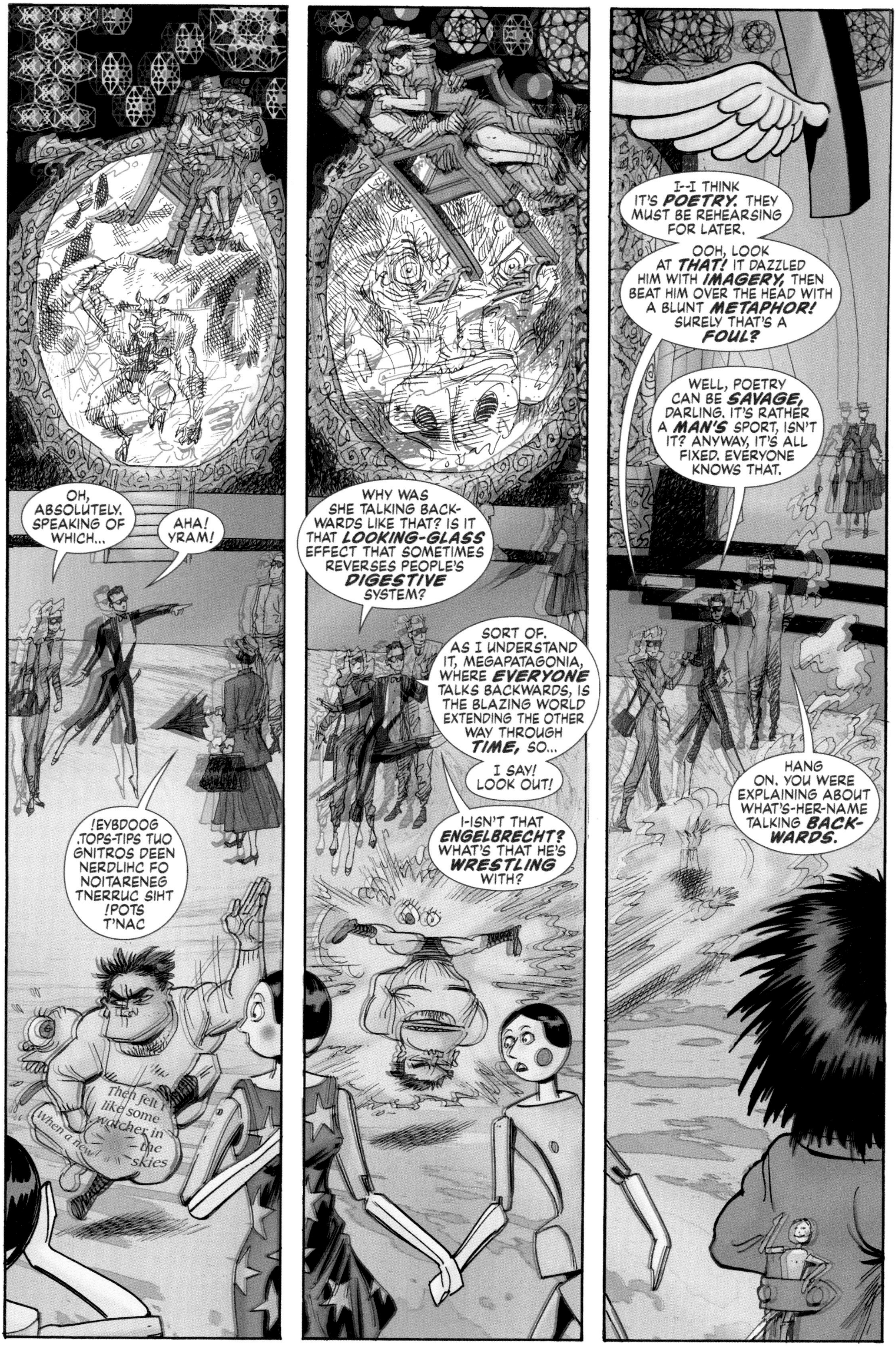
OH, ABSOLUTELY. SPEAKING OF WHICH...
AHA! YRAM!
!EYBDOOG .TOPS-TIPS TUO GNITROS DEEN NERDLIHC FO NOITARENEG TNERRUC SIHT !POTS T'NAC
Then felt I like some watcher in the skies When a new
WHY WAS SHE TALKING BACKWARDS LIKE THAT? IS IT THAT LOOKING-GLASS EFFECT THAT SOMETIMES REVERSES PEOPLE'S DIGESTIVE SYSTEM?
SORT OF. AS I UNDERSTAND IT, MEGAPATAGONIA, WHERE EVERYONE TALKS BACKWARDS, IS THE BLAZING WORLD EXTENDING THE OTHER WAY THROUGH TIME, SO...
I SAY! LOOK OUT!
I-ISN'T THAT ENGELBRECHT? WHAT'S THAT HE'S WRESTLING WITH?
I--I THINK IT'S POETRY. THEY MUST BE REHEARSING FOR LATER.
OOH, LOOK AT THAT! IT DAZZLED HIM WITH IMAGERY, THEN BEAT HIM OVER THE HEAD WITH A BLUNT METAPHOR! SURELY THAT'S A FOUL?
WELL, POETRY CAN BE SAVAGE, DARLING. IT'S RATHER A MAN'S SPORT, ISN'T IT? ANYWAY, IT'S ALL FIXED. EVERYONE KNOWS THAT.
HANG ON. YOU WERE EXPLAINING ABOUT WHAT'S-HER-NAME TALKING BACKWARDS.

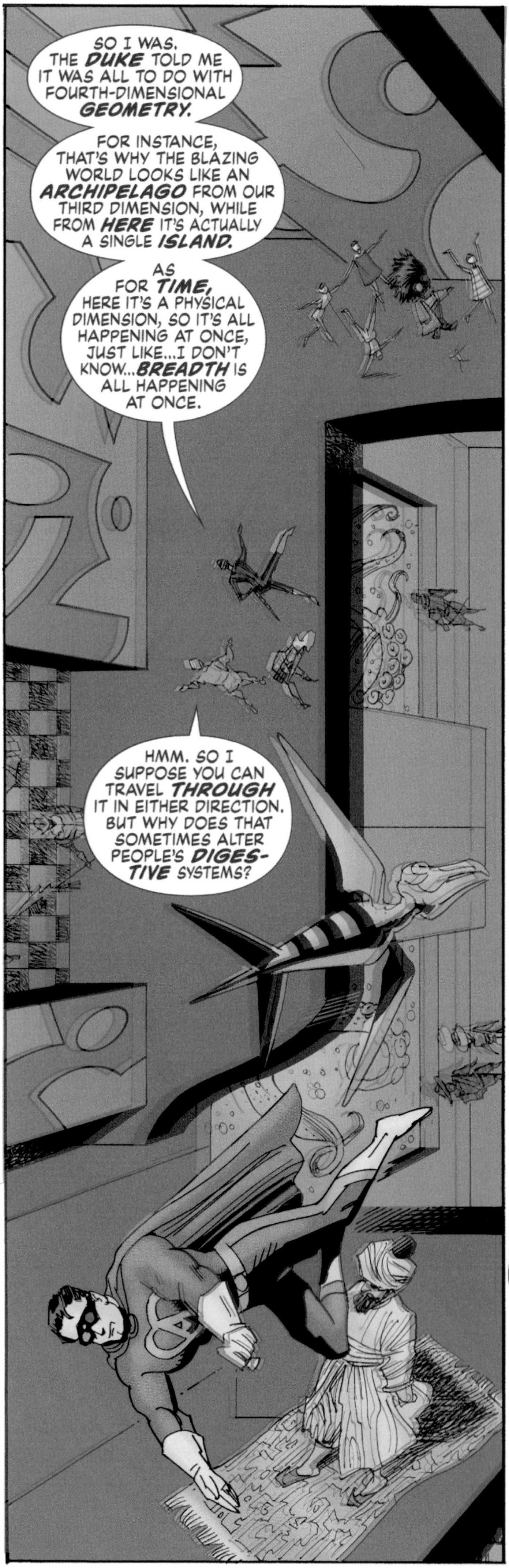
SO I WAS. THE DUKE TOLD ME IT WAS ALL TO DO WITH FOURTH-DIMENSIONAL GEOMETRY.
FOR INSTANCE, THAT'S WHY THE BLAZING WORLD LOOKS LIKE AN ARCHIPELAGO FROM OUR THIRD DIMENSION, WHILE FROM HERE IT'S ACTUALLY A SINGLE ISLAND.
AS FOR TIME, HERE IT'S A PHYSICAL DIMENSION, SO IT'S ALL HAPPENING AT ONCE, JUST LIKE...I DON'T KNOW...BREADTH IS ALL HAPPENING AT ONCE.
HMM. SO I SUPPOSE YOU CAN TRAVEL THROUGH IT IN EITHER DIRECTION. BUT WHY DOES THAT SOMETIMES ALTER PEOPLE'S DIGESTIVE SYSTEMS?

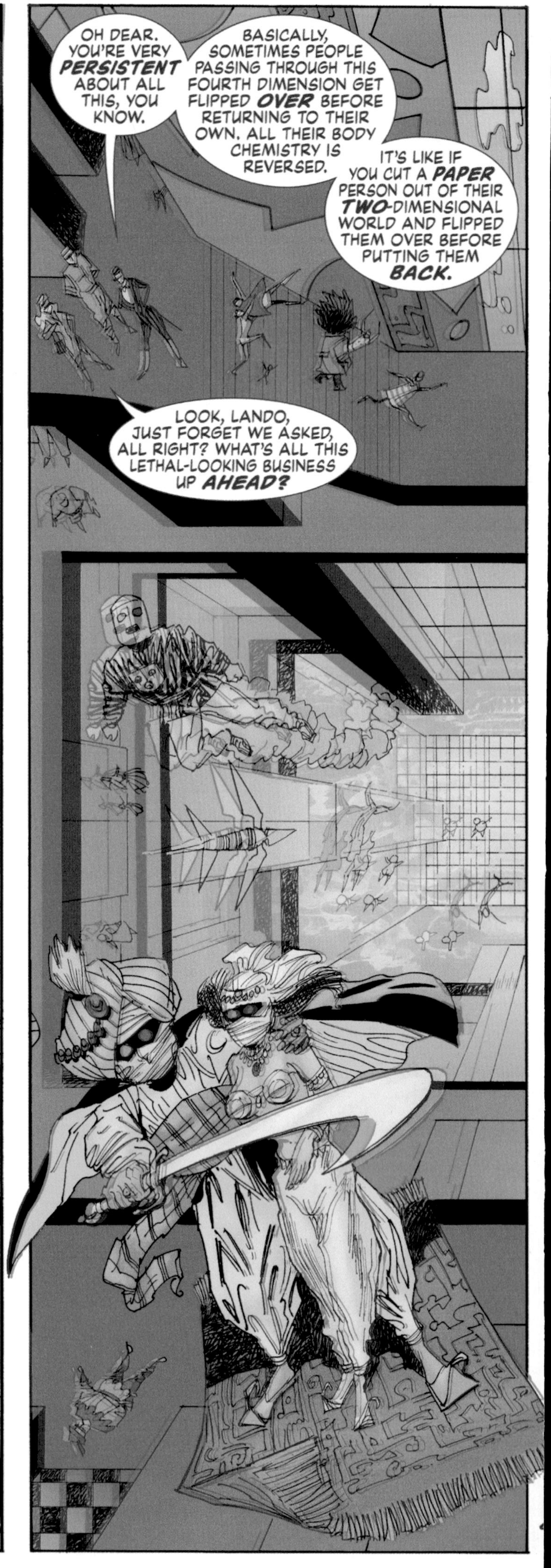
OH DEAR. YOU'RE VERY PERSISTENT ABOUT ALL THIS, YOU KNOW.
BASICALLY, SOMETIMES PEOPLE PASSING THROUGH THIS FOURTH DIMENSION GET FLIPPED OVER BEFORE RETURNING TO THEIR OWN. ALL THEIR BODY CHEMISTRY IS REVERSED.
IT'S LIKE IF YOU CUT A PAPER PERSON OUT OF THEIR TWO-DIMENSIONAL WORLD AND FLIPPED THEM OVER BEFORE PUTTING THEM BACK.
LOOK, LANDO, JUST FORGET WE ASKED, ALL RIGHT? WHAT'S ALL THIS LETHAL-LOOKING BUSINESS UP AHEAD?

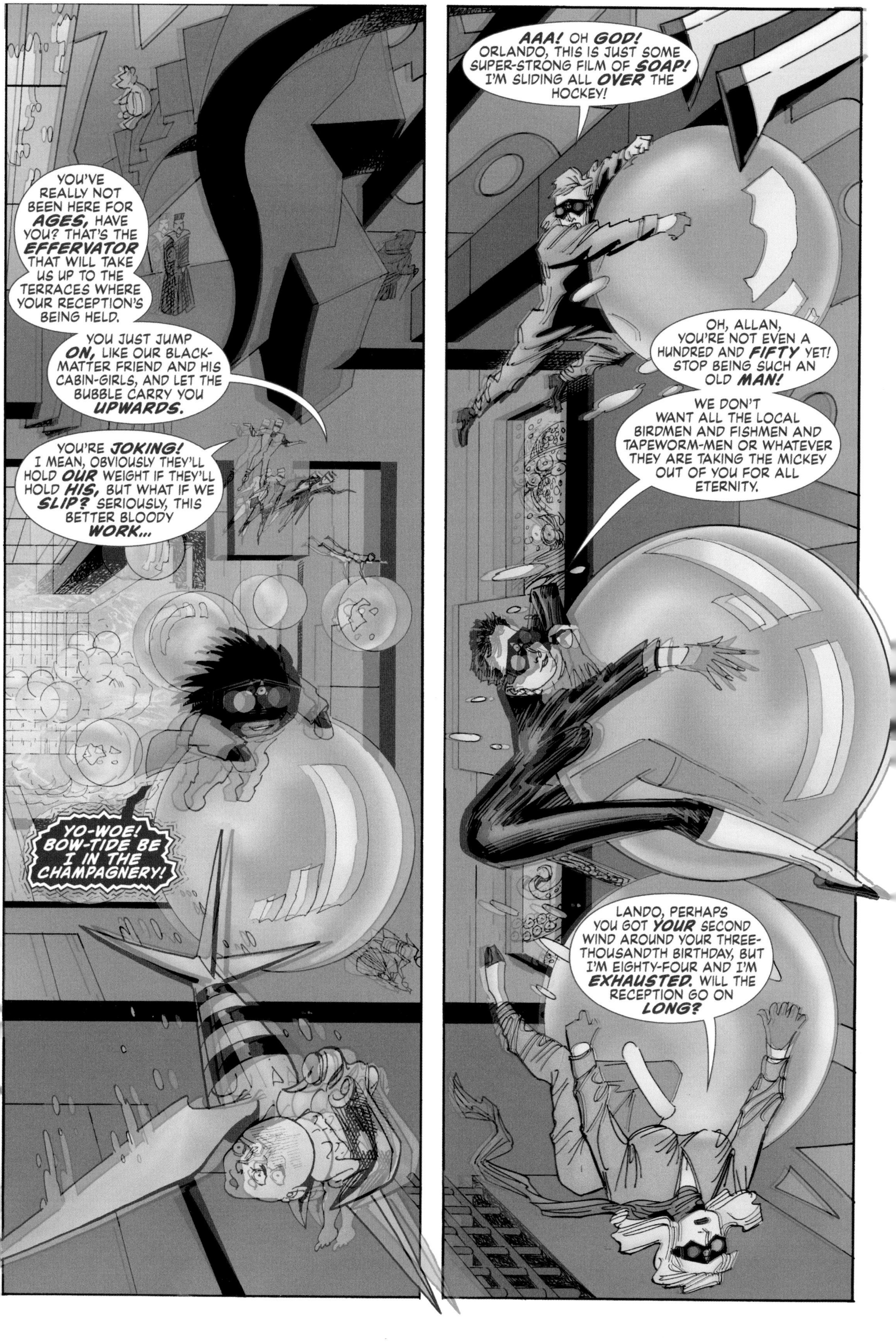

YOU'VE REALLY NOT BEEN HERE FOR AGES, HAVE YOU? THAT'S THE EFFERVATOR THAT WILL TAKE US UP TO THE TERRACES WHERE YOUR RECEPTION'S BEING HELD.
YOU JUST JUMP ON, LIKE OUR BLACK-MATTER FRIEND AND HIS CABIN-GIRLS, AND LET THE BUBBLE CARRY YOU UPWARDS.
YOU'RE JOKING! I MEAN, OBVIOUSLY THEY'LL HOLD OUR WEIGHT IF THEY'LL HOLD HIS, BUT WHAT IF WE SLIP? SERIOUSLY, THIS BETTER BLOODY WORK...
YO-WOE! BOW-TIDE BE I IN THE CHAMPAGNERY!
AAA! OH GOD! ORLANDO, THIS IS JUST SOME SUPER-STRONG FILM OF SOAP! I'M SLIDING ALL OVER THE HOCKEY!
OH, ALLAN, YOU'RE NOT EVEN A HUNDRED AND FIFTY YET! STOP BEING SUCH AN OLD MAN!
WE DON'T WANT ALL THE LOCAL BIRDMEN AND FISHMEN AND TAPEWORM-MEN OR WHATEVER THEY ARE TAKING THE MICKEY OUT OF YOU FOR ALL ETERNITY.
LANDO, PERHAPS YOU GOT YOUR SECOND WIND AROUND YOUR THREE-THOUSANDTH BIRTHDAY, BUT I'M EIGHTY-FOUR AND I'M EXHAUSTED. WILL THE RECEPTION GO ON LONG?

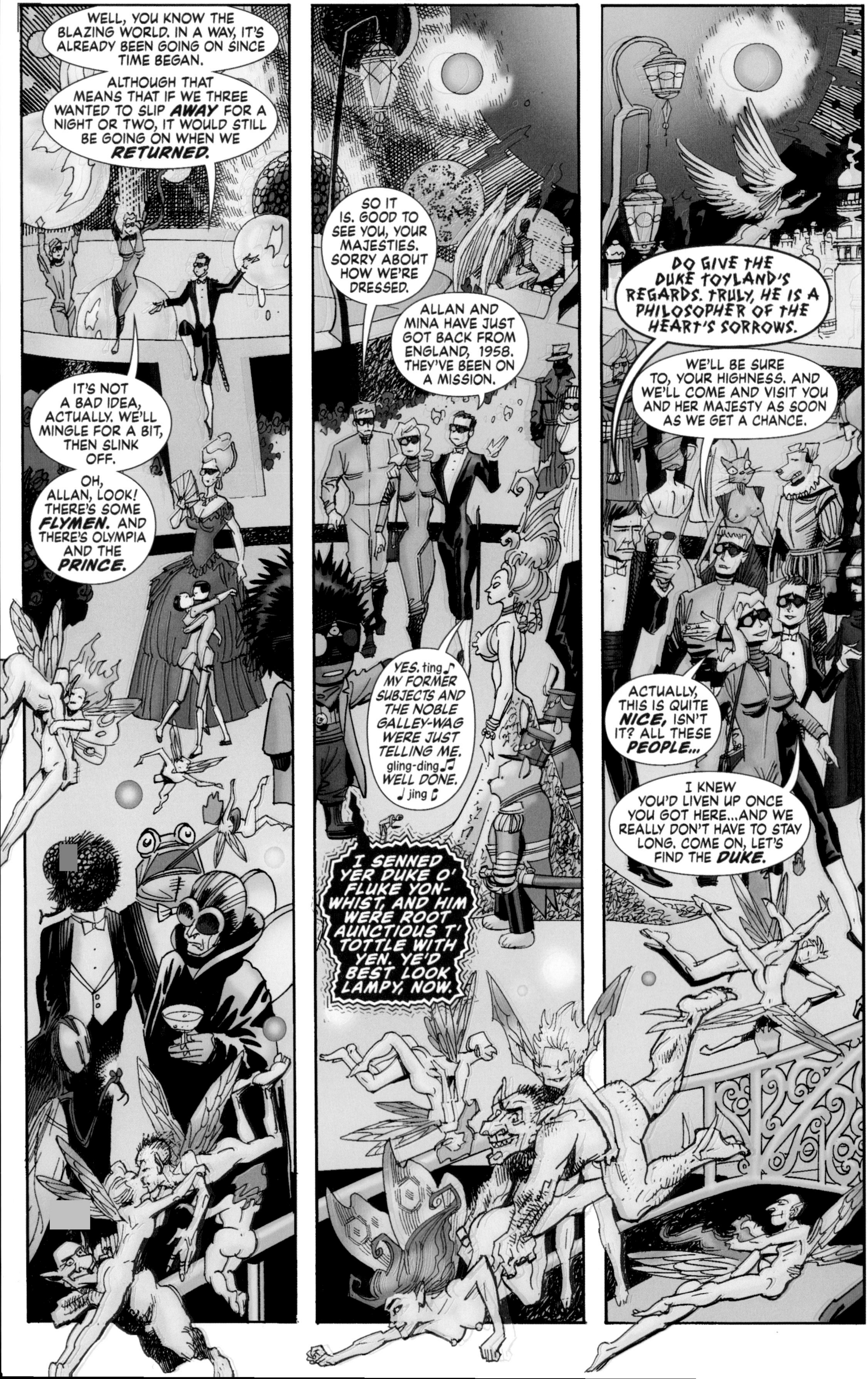
WELL, YOU KNOW THE BLAZING WORLD. IN A WAY, IT'S ALREADY BEEN GOING ON SINCE TIME BEGAN.
ALTHOUGH THAT MEANS THAT IF WE THREE WANTED TO SLIP AWAY FOR A NIGHT OR TWO, IT WOULD STILL BE GOING ON WHEN WE RETURNED.
IT'S NOT A BAD IDEA, ACTUALLY. WE'LL MINGLE FOR A BIT, THEN SLINK OFF.
OH, ALLAN, LOOK! THERE'S SOME FLYMEN. AND THERE'S OLYMPIA AND THE PRINCE.
SO IT IS. GOOD TO SEE YOU, YOUR MAJESTIES. SORRY ABOUT HOW WE'RE DRESSED.
ALLAN AND MINA HAVE JUST GOT BACK FROM ENGLAND, 1958. THEY'VE BEEN ON A MISSION.
YES. ting MY FORMER SUBJECTS AND THE NOBLE GALLEY-WAG WERE JUST TELLING ME. gling-ding WELL DONE. jing
I SENNED YER DUKE O' FLUKE YON-WHIST, AND HIM WERE ROOT AUNCTIOUS T' TOTTLE WITH YEN. YE'D BEST LOOK LAMPY, NOW.
DO GIVE THE DUKE TOYLAND'S REGARDS. TRULY, HE IS A PHILOSOPHER OF THE HEART'S SORROWS.
WE'LL BE SURE TO, YOUR HIGHNESS. AND WE'LL COME AND VISIT YOU AND HER MAJESTY AS SOON AS WE GET A CHANCE.
ACTUALLY, THIS IS QUITE NICE, ISN'T IT? ALL THESE PEOPLE...
I KNEW YOU'D LIVEN UP ONCE YOU GOT HERE...AND WE REALLY DON'T HAVE TO STAY LONG. COME ON, LET'S FIND THE DUKE.

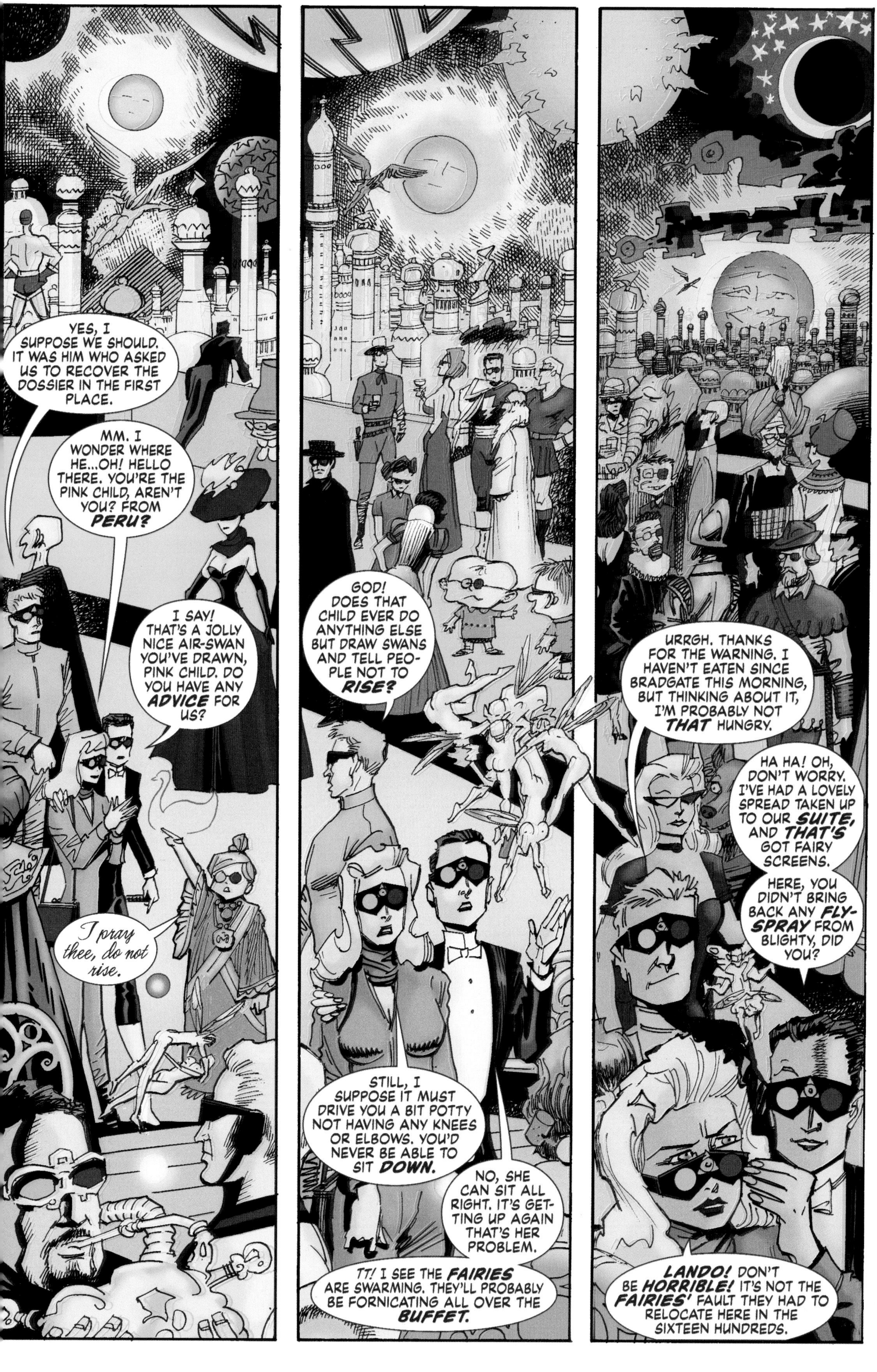
YES, I SUPPOSE WE SHOULD. IT WAS HIM WHO ASKED US TO RECOVER THE DOSSIER IN THE FIRST PLACE.
MM. I WONDER WHERE HE...OH! HELLO THERE. YOU'RE THE PINK CHILD, AREN'T YOU? FROM PERU?
I SAY! THAT'S A JOLLY NICE AIR-SWAN YOU'VE DRAWN, PINK CHILD. DO YOU HAVE ANY ADVICE FOR US?
I pray thee, do not rise.
GOD! DOES THAT CHILD EVER DO ANYTHING ELSE BUT DRAW SWANS AND TELL PEOPLE NOT TO RISE?
STILL, I SUPPOSE IT MUST DRIVE YOU A BIT POTTY NOT HAVING ANY KNEES OR ELBOWS. YOU'D NEVER BE ABLE TO SIT DOWN.
NO, SHE CAN SIT ALL RIGHT. IT'S GETTING UP AGAIN THAT'S HER PROBLEM.
TT! I SEE THE FAIRIES ARE SWARMING. THEY'LL PROBABLY BE FORNICATING ALL OVER THE BUFFET.
URRGH. THANKS FOR THE WARNING. I HAVEN'T EATEN SINCE BRADGATE THIS MORNING, BUT THINKING ABOUT IT, I'M PROBABLY NOT THAT HUNGRY.
HA HA! OH, DON'T WORRY. I'VE HAD A LOVELY SPREAD TAKEN UP TO OUR SUITE, AND THAT'S GOT FAIRY SCREENS.
HERE, YOU DIDN'T BRING BACK ANY FLY-SPRAY FROM BLIGHTY, DID YOU?
LANDO! DON'T BE HORRIBLE! IT'S NOT THE FAIRIES' FAULT THEY HAD TO RELOCATE HERE IN THE SIXTEEN HUNDREDS.

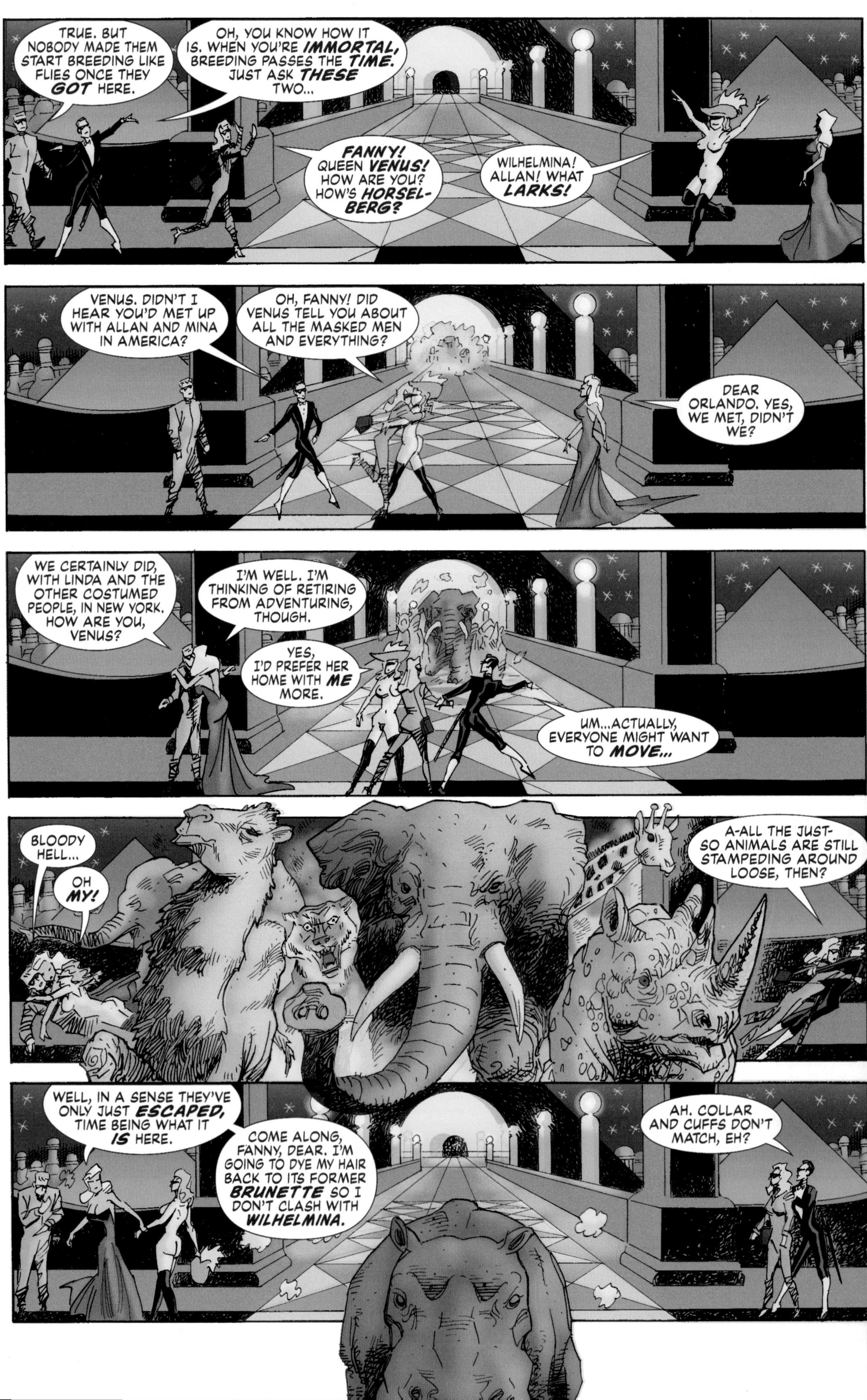
TRUE. BUT NOBODY MADE THEM START BREEDING LIKE FLIES ONCE THEY GOT HERE.
OH, YOU KNOW HOW IT IS. WHEN YOU'RE IMMORTAL, BREEDING PASSES THE TIME. JUST ASK THESE TWO...
FANNY! QUEEN VENUS! HOW ARE YOU? HOW'S HORSELBERG?
WILHELMINA! ALLAN! WHAT LARKS!
VENUS. DIDN'T I HEAR YOU'D MET UP WITH ALLAN AND MINA IN AMERICA?
OH, FANNY! DID VENUS TELL YOU ABOUT ALL THE MASKED MEN AND EVERYTHING?
DEAR ORLANDO. YES, WE MET, DIDN'T WE?
WE CERTAINLY DID, WITH LINDA AND THE OTHER COSTUMED PEOPLE, IN NEW YORK. HOW ARE YOU, VENUS?
I'M WELL. I'M THINKING OF RETIRING FROM ADVENTURING, THOUGH.
YES, I'D PREFER HER HOME WITH ME MORE.
UM...ACTUALLY, EVERYONE MIGHT WANT TO MOVE...
BLOODY HELL...
OH MY!
A-ALL THE JUST-SO ANIMALS ARE STILL STAMPEDING AROUND LOOSE, THEN?
WELL, IN A SENSE THEY'VE ONLY JUST ESCAPED, TIME BEING WHAT IT IS HERE.
COME ALONG, FANNY, DEAR. I'M GOING TO DYE MY HAIR BACK TO ITS FORMER BRUNETTE SO I DON'T CLASH WITH WILHELMINA.
AH. COLLAR AND CUFFS DON'T MATCH, EH?

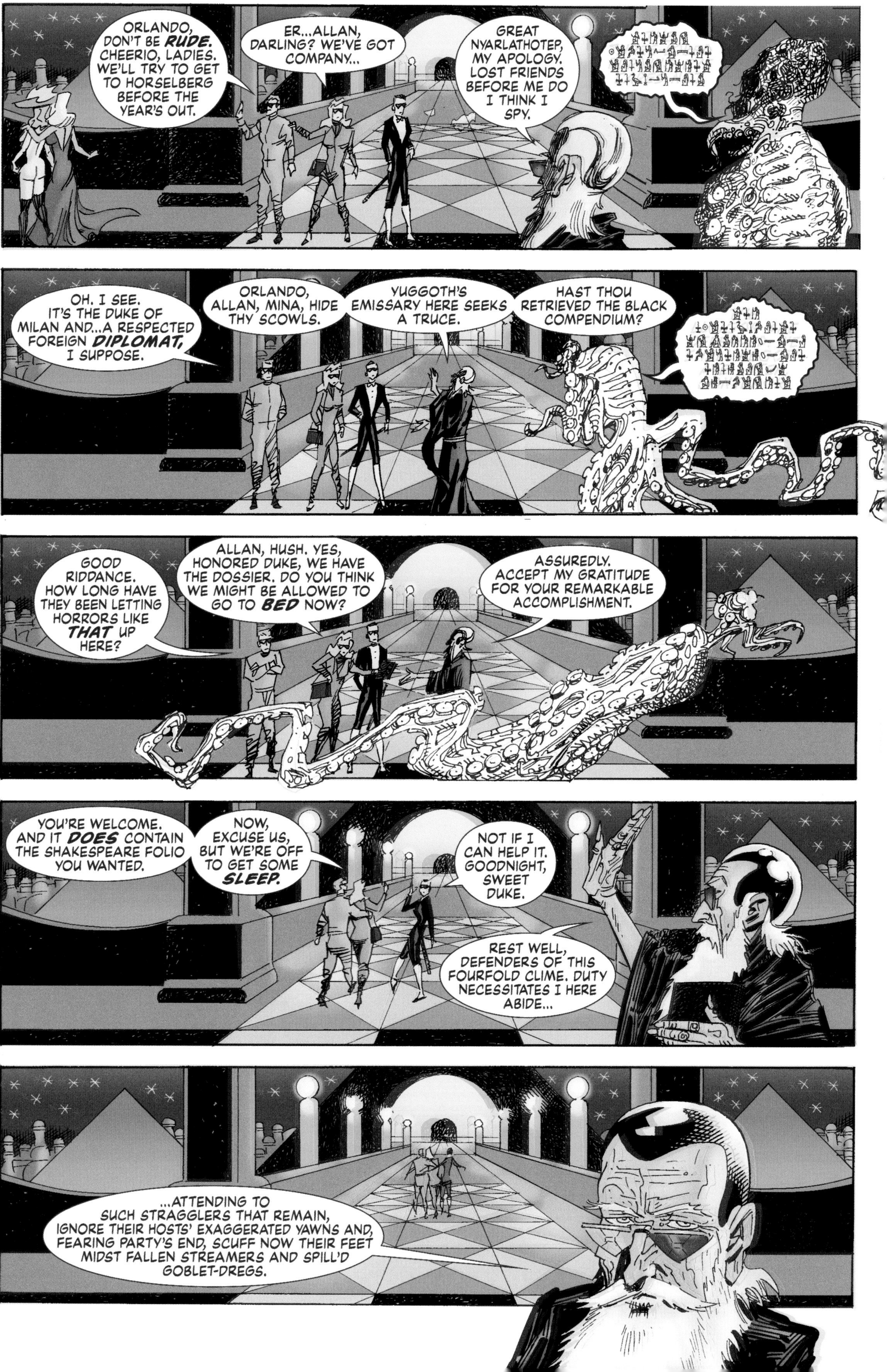
ORLANDO, DON'T BE RUDE. CHEERIO, LADIES. WE'LL TRY TO GET TO HORSELBERG BEFORE THE YEAR'S OUT.
ER...ALLAN, DARLING? WE'VE GOT COMPANY...
GREAT NYARLATHOTEP, MY APOLOGY. LOST FRIENDS BEFORE ME DO I THINK I SPY.
OH. I SEE. IT'S THE DUKE OF MILAN AND...A RESPECTED FOREIGN DIPLOMAT, I SUPPOSE.
ORLANDO, ALLAN, MINA, HIDE THY SCOWLS.
YUGGOTH'S EMISSARY HERE SEEKS A TRUCE.
HAST THOU RETRIEVED THE BLACK COMPENDIUM?
GOOD RIDDANCE. HOW LONG HAVE THEY BEEN LETTING HORRORS LIKE THAT UP HERE?
ALLAN, HUSH. YES, HONORED DUKE, WE HAVE THE DOSSIER. DO YOU THINK WE MIGHT BE ALLOWED TO GO TO BED NOW?
ASSUREDLY. ACCEPT MY GRATITUDE FOR YOUR REMARKABLE ACCOMPLISHMENT.
YOU'RE WELCOME. AND IT DOES CONTAIN THE SHAKESPEARE FOLIO YOU WANTED.
NOW, EXCUSE US, BUT WE'RE OFF TO GET SOME SLEEP.
NOT IF I CAN HELP IT. GOODNIGHT, SWEET DUKE.
REST WELL, DEFENDERS OF THIS FOURFOLD CLIME. DUTY NECESSITATES I HERE ABIDE...
...ATTENDING TO SUCH STRAGGLERS THAT REMAIN, IGNORE THEIR HOSTS' EXAGGERATED YAWNS AND, FEARING PARTY'S END, SCUFF NOW THEIR FEET MIDST FALLEN STREAMERS AND SPILL'D GOBLET-DREGS.

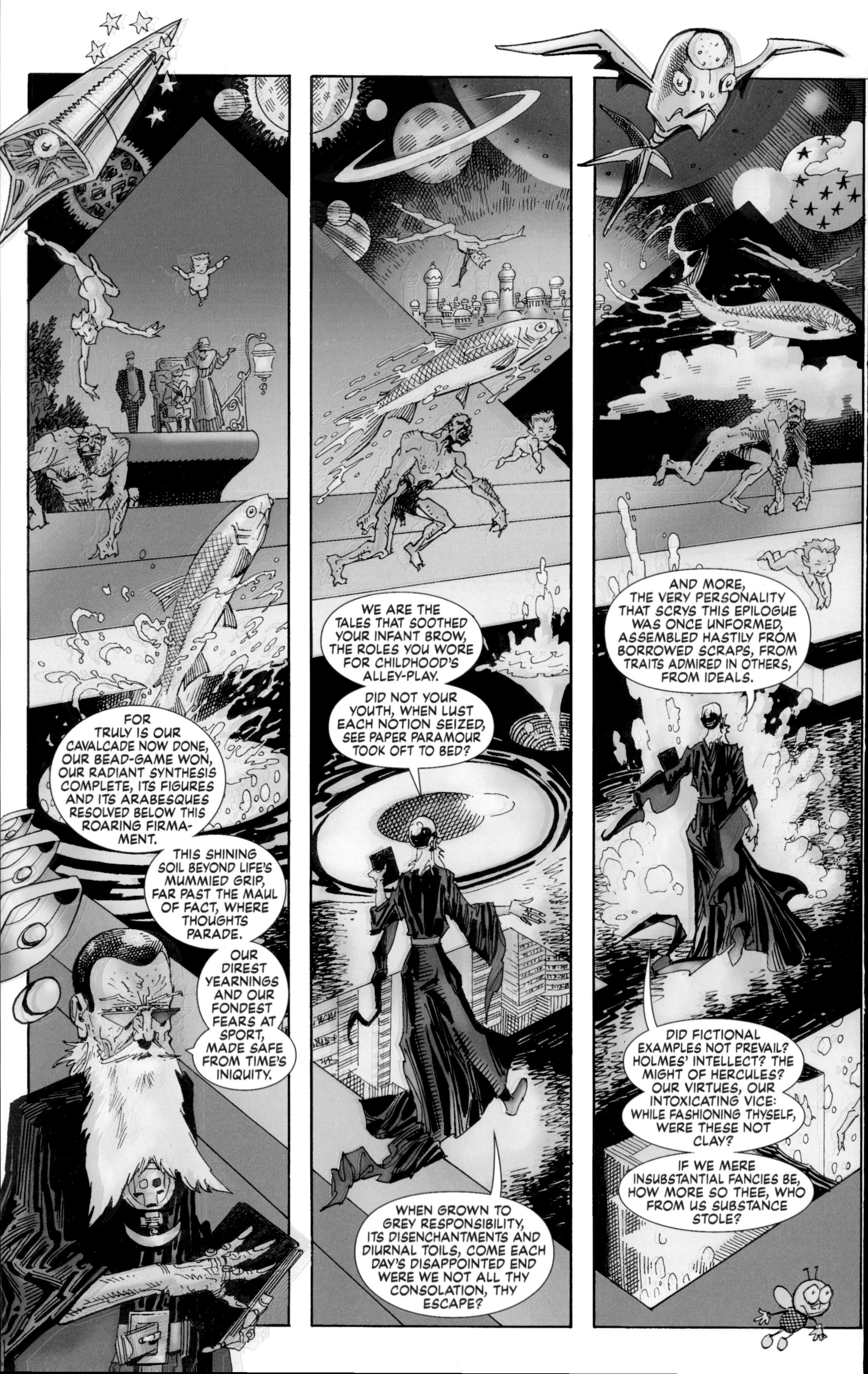
FOR TRULY IS OUR CAVALCADE NOW DONE, OUR BEAD-GAME WON, OUR RADIANT SYNTHESIS COMPLETE, ITS FIGURES AND ITS ARABESQUES RESOLVED BELOW THIS ROARING FIRMA-MENT.
THIS SHINING SOIL BEYOND LIFE'S MUMMIED GRIP, FAR PAST THE MAUL OF FACT, WHERE THOUGHTS PARADE.
OUR DIREST YEARNINGS AND OUR FONDEST FEARS AT SPORT, MADE SAFE FROM TIME'S INIQUITY.
WE ARE THE TALES THAT SOOTHED YOUR INFANT BROW, THE ROLES YOU WORE FOR CHILDHOOD'S ALLEY-PLAY.
DID NOT YOUR YOUTH, WHEN LUST EACH NOTION SEIZED, SEE PAPER PARAMOUR TOOK OFT TO BED?
WHEN GROWN TO GREY RESPONSIBILITY, ITS DISENCHANTMENTS AND DIURNAL TOILS, COME EACH DAY'S DISAPPOINTED END WERE WE NOT ALL THY CONSOLATION, THY ESCAPE?
AND MORE, THE VERY PERSONALITY THAT SCRYS THIS EPILOGUE WAS ONCE UNFORMED, ASSEMBLED HASTILY FROM BORROWED SCRAPS, FROM TRAITS ADMIRED IN OTHERS, FROM IDEALS.
DID FICTIONAL EXAMPLES NOT PREVAIL? HOLMES' INTELLECT? THE MIGHT OF HERCULES? OUR VIRTUES, OUR INTOXICATING VICE: WHILE FASHIONING THYSELF, WERE THESE NOT CLAY?
IF WE MERE INSUBSTANTIAL FANCIES BE, HOW MORE SO THEE, WHO FROM US SUBSTANCE STOLE?

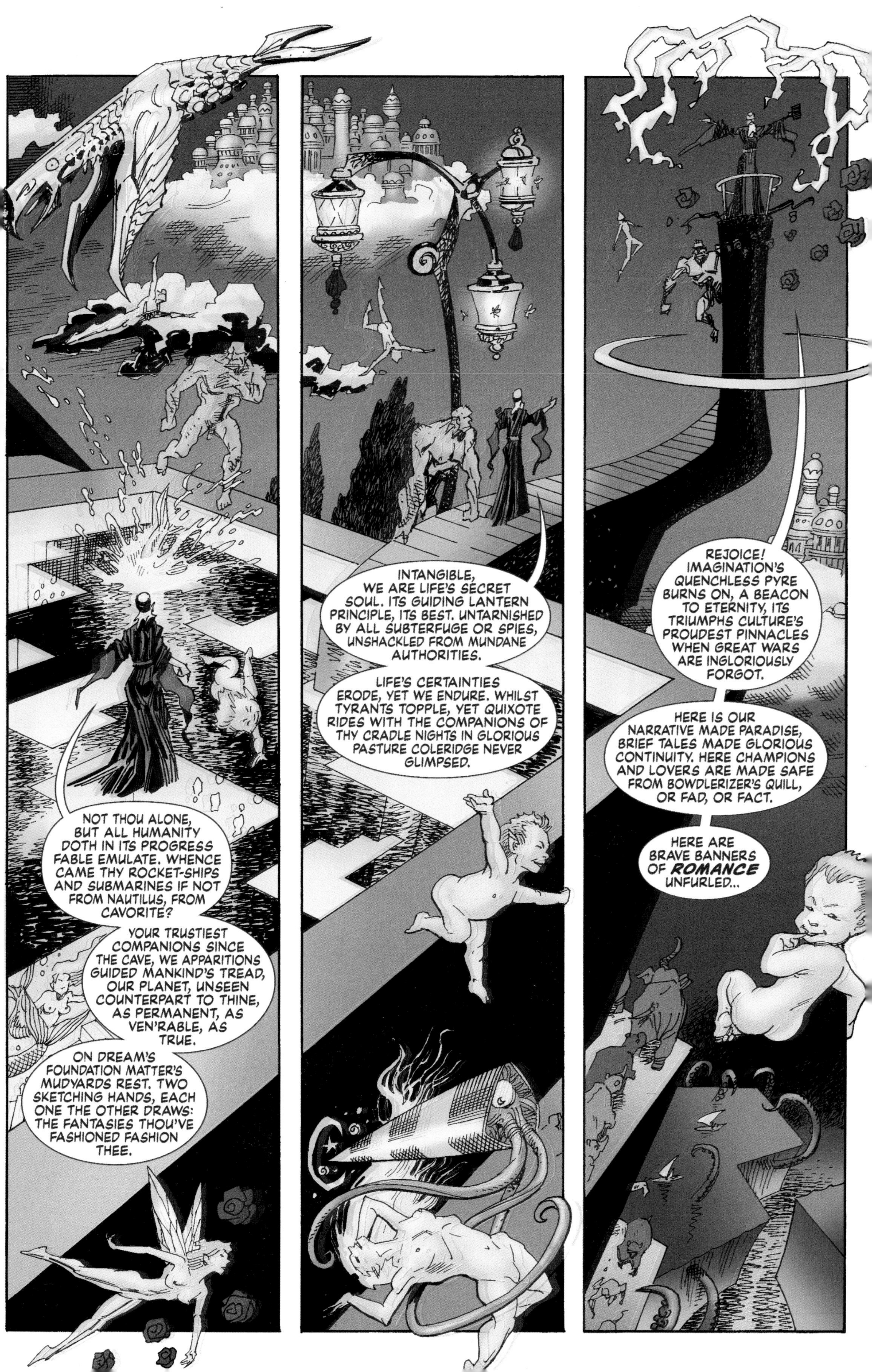

NOT THOU ALONE, BUT ALL HUMANITY DOTH IN ITS PROGRESS FABLE EMULATE. WHENCE CAME THY ROCKET-SHIPS AND SUBMARINES IF NOT FROM NAUTILUS, FROM CAVORITE?
YOUR TRUSTIEST COMPANIONS SINCE THE CAVE, WE APPARITIONS GUIDED MANKIND'S TREAD, OUR PLANET, UNSEEN COUNTERPART TO THINE, AS PERMANENT, AS VEN'RABLE, AS TRUE.
ON DREAM'S FOUNDATION MATTER'S MUDYARDS REST. TWO SKETCHING HANDS, EACH ONE THE OTHER DRAWS: THE FANTASIES THOU'VE FASHIONED FASHION THEE.
INTANGIBLE, WE ARE LIFE'S SECRET SOUL. ITS GUIDING LANTERN PRINCIPLE, ITS BEST. UNTARNISHED BY ALL SUBTERFUGE OR SPIES, UNSHACKLED FROM MUNDANE AUTHORITIES.
LIFE'S CERTAINTIES ERODE, YET WE ENDURE. WHILST TYRANTS TOPPLE, YET QUIXOTE RIDES WITH THE COMPANIONS OF THY CRADLE NIGHTS IN GLORIOUS PASTURE COLERIDGE NEVER GLIMPSED.
REJOICE! IMAGINATION'S QUENCHLESS PYRE BURNS ON, A BEACON TO ETERNITY, ITS TRIUMPHS CULTURE'S PROUDEST PINNACLES WHEN GREAT WARS ARE INGLORIOUSLY FORGOT.
HERE IS OUR NARRATIVE MADE PARADISE, BRIEF TALES MADE GLORIOUS CONTINUITY. HERE CHAMPIONS AND LOVERS ARE MADE SAFE FROM BOWDLERIZER'S QUILL, OR FAD, OR FACT.
HERE ARE BRAVE BANNERS OF ROMANCE UNFURLED...

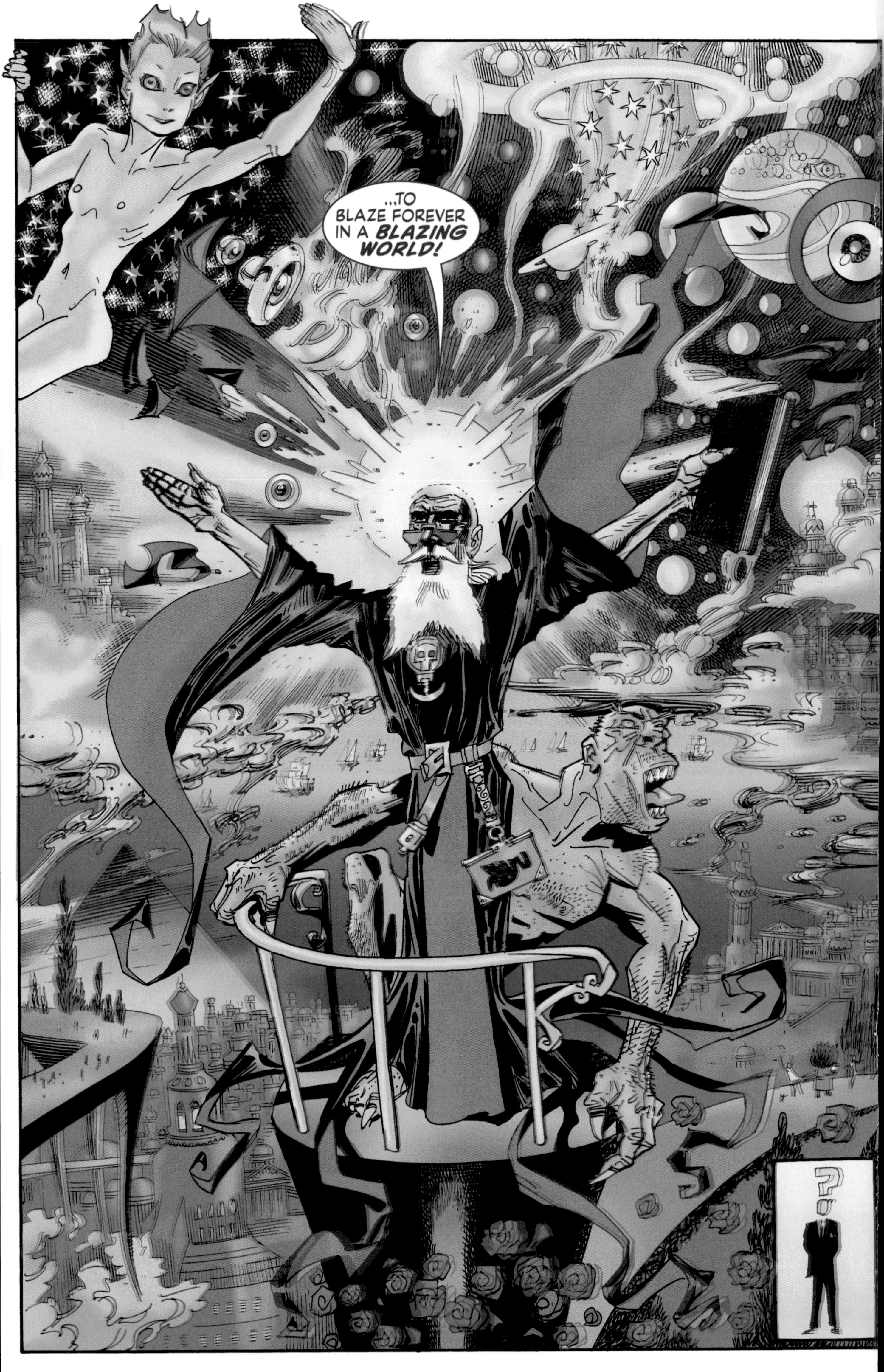
...TO BLAZE FOREVER IN A BLAZING WORLD!

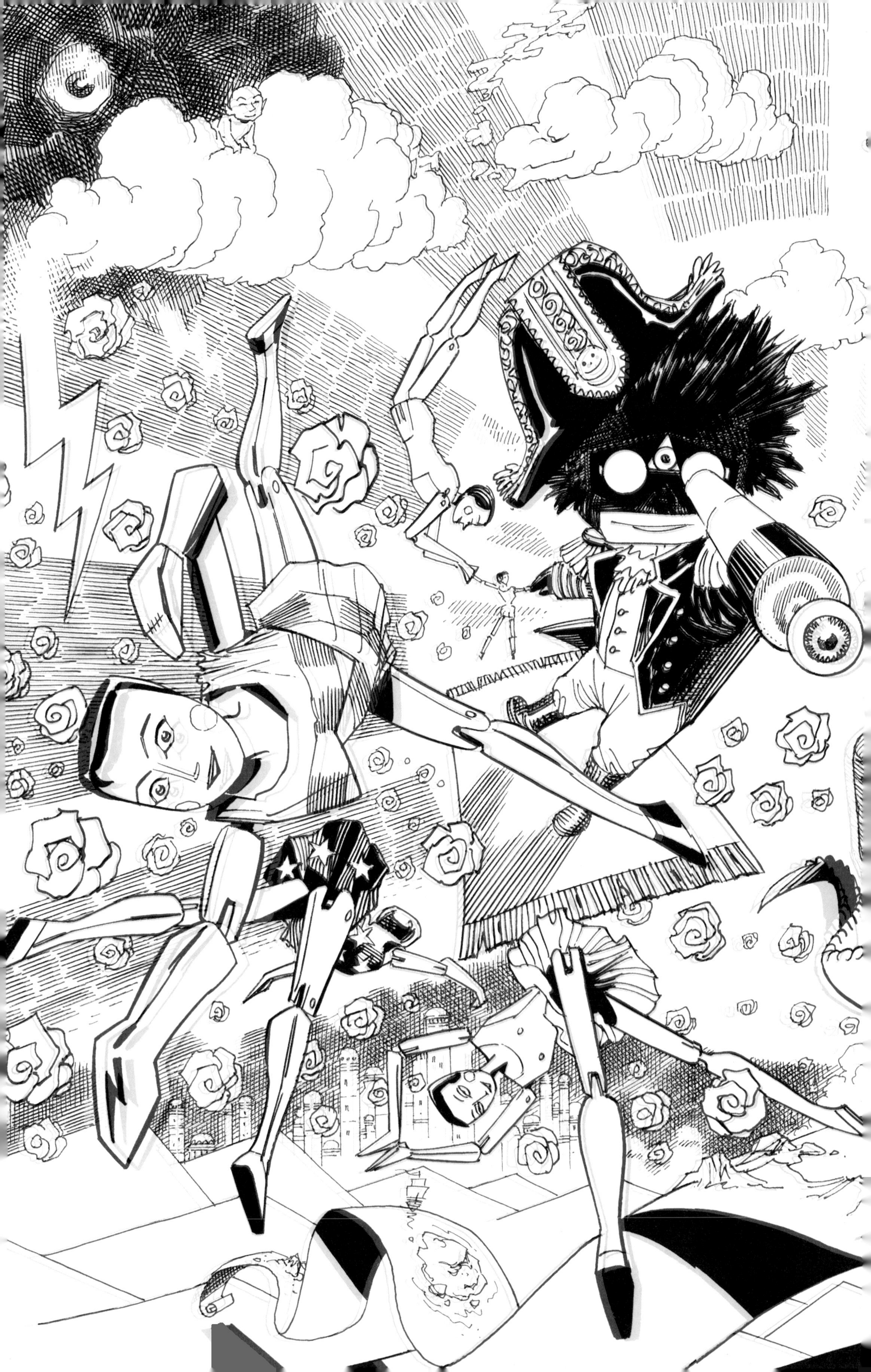